GUIDE TO THE NATIONAL WILDLIFE REFUGES

GUIDE TO THE NATIONAL
WILDLIFE REFUGES
REVISED AND EXPANDED

*Recommended by the National Audubon Society
and the National Wildlife Federation*

LAURA AND WILLIAM RILEY

COLLIER BOOKS

MACMILLAN PUBLISHING COMPANY

NEW YORK

MAXWELL MACMILLAN CANADA

TORONTO

MAXWELL MACMILLAN INTERNATIONAL

NEW YORK   OXFORD   SINGAPORE   SYDNEY

Collier Books
Macmillan Publishing Company
866 Third Avenue
New York, NY 10022

Maxwell Macmillan Canada, Inc.
1200 Eglinton Avenue East
Suite 200
Don Mills, Ontario M3C 3N1

Macmillan Publishing Company is part of the Maxwell Communication Group of Companies.

Library of Congress Cataloging-in-Publication Data
Riley, Laura.
Guide to the national wildlife refuges / Laura and William Riley.
—Rev. and expanded, 1st Collier Books ed.
p.   cm.
Includes index.
ISBN 0-02-063660-1
1. Wildlife refuges—United States—Guidebooks.   2. National parks
and reserves—United States—Guidebooks.   I. Riley, William, 1931–
II. Title.
QH76.R54   1993
333.95'0973—dc20   92-15459
CIP

Macmillan books are available at special discounts for bulk purchases for sales promotions, premiums, fund-raising, or educational use. For details, contact:

Special Sales Director
Macmillan Publishing Company
866 Third Avenue
New York, NY 10022

First Collier Books Edition 1993
10 9 8 7 6 5 4 3 2 1
Printed in the United States of America

Acknowledgments

For their enthusiastic cooperation we greatly thank Director John Turner and his staff at the U.S. Fish and Wildlife Service, Department of the Interior, in Washington. Nancy Marx was particularly helpful.

The wellspring of this book is the accumulated experience, knowledge and insight of more than 200 highly competent refuge managers and their staffs, whose names appear at the end. They provided comprehensive background material, answered detailed questionnaires and talked at length with us, providing a wealth of information available in no other way. They also read and checked every entry, providing helpful corrections, amplifications and improvements. We could not overstate our debt to them. This book stands on their shoulders.

We also thank Sandi D'Andrea, Johanna Van Davelaar and Allegra Klein, who were indispensably involved in every logistical aspect of the project; and John DeMarrais, who with a superb naturalist's eye read the manuscript and made invaluable suggestions.

Any errors that remain are our responsibility and we earnestly solicit corrections from readers for possible future editions.

Laura and William Riley
PITTSTOWN, NEW JERSEY
JULY, 1992

Contents

New York

Pennsylvania

New Jersey

Delaware

West Virginia

Maryland

Virginia

THE SOUTHEAST STATES..93

North Carolina

South Carolina

Georgia

Florida

Puerto Rico

Minnesota

Wisconsin

Michigan

Illinois

Indiana

Ohio

Arkansas

Tennessee (and Kentucky)

Mississippi

Alabama

Louisiana

North Dakota

South Dakota

Nebraska

Iowa

Kansas

Missouri

Arizona

New Mexico

Texas

Oklahoma

Idaho

Montana

Wyoming

Nevada

Utah

Colorado

The National Wildlife Refuges

The national wildlife refuges of the United States are unmatched by those of any other country in the world in the geographic span they cover, the diversity of habitat they provide, and the variety and number of wild creatures they harbor.

Most of our endangered species would not survive now except for these protected places. Other species almost certainly would have become endangered but for this protection.

Huge brown bears weighing a half ton, the largest land carnivores in the world, roam Alaskan refuges, fishing where millions of salmon fight their way up rushing streams and rivers. Brilliant painted buntings nest on coastal Georgia and South Carolina islands. Bald eagles congregate by the hundreds in sanctuaries in the lower 48 states as well as Alaska.

Millions of waterfowl darken the sky as in a bygone age when they visit Tule Lake in California's Klamath Basin. Millions of shorebirds gather in spring in Bowerman Basin at Grays Harbor (a subrefuge of Nisqually) on the coast of Washington, and on the East Coast at Cape May in New Jersey, essential stopovers to rest and store up fat reserves en route to Arctic breeding grounds.

The howl of the red wolf is once again heard in the wild at Alligator River. Florida panthers have their own refuge where it is hoped their small numbers will increase. Primeval alligators, once endangered, bellow through the night in Louisiana, Georgia, and Florida marshes, one of many endangered species brought back from the edge of extinction at refuges.

More than 475 of these remarkable places exist, at least one in every state. They cover 91 million acres and protect substantially every kind of wild animal native to the continent. It is an extraordinary list—more than 220 species of mammals, more than 600 of birds, 250 reptiles and amphibians, over 200 species of fish and uncounted numbers of plants, from wild orchids to unique palm trees.

Most refuges are open to the public for various wildlife-oriented activities. Prime among these is nature observation, but they range also through photography, hiking, backpacking, fishing. Hunting is included at many, mainly regarded these days as a management tool to keep wildlife populations in balance. To decide deer may proliferate freely, for example, can mean eliminating the woods understory where towhees might nest. But at some refuges hunting remains a central activity, albeit controversial, following state regulations, often on land that became a refuge on condition these traditional activities be allowed to continue. This can interfere with wildlife observation (sometimes it's best to inquire ahead in fall, especially at southern and western refuges). Some refuges also are closed, partly closed, or closed seasonally to protect sensitive wildlife nesting or other vulnerable situations.

This book tells where these refuges are, how to get there, what to see and do, where to stay or camp nearby, best times to visit, any special equipment needed, and how to get more information. It contains more than 200 maps to help in quickly locating the refuge. The information is based on many hundreds of hours of interviews as well as personal observation by the authors at more than 180 staffed refuges and many that are unstaffed. Every fact has been double-checked by refuge personnel reviewing a draft entry provided after the interviews.

Many refuges were established for special purposes, as was the first, tiny Pelican Island in Florida, created by President Theodore Roosevelt in 1903 to protect nesting birds from human marauders. Later came Wichita Mountains in Oklahoma and National Bison Range in Montana to protect the American bison, once the most numerous land mammal in the world, which had been all but exterminated. Kofa in Arizona and Desert in Nevada harbor desert bighorn sheep. Sheldon Antelope in Nevada and Hart Mountain in Oregon were set aside for the pronghorn antelope.

The majestic trumpeter swan, largest waterfowl in the world, was brought back from the brink of extinction in the 48 states at Red Rock Lakes in Montana—and even persons with only a passing interest in wildlife know of the whooping crane and the stand against its extinction at Aransas Refuge on the Texas Gulf Coast.

Other refuges provide habitat for creatures that while not officially endangered have felt pressure from onrushing civilization, such as National Elk in Wyoming, Kodiak for the Alaskan brown bear, Kenai in Alaska and Agassiz in Minnesota for the moose.

Many are aimed at providing special refuge for birds while they are breeding, migrating, and wintering. These include great nesting bird sanctuaries in the north-central "prairie pothole" region, and others strategically located along the various flyways for migratory and wintering protection.

Cape May in New Jersey, a new refuge, is the first to focus on neotropical songbirds, many of whose populations have dropped dangerously low.

But most refuges set aside for a particular species and purpose evolve quickly into general refuges for every kind of wildlife that can appropriately be sheltered in that environment—the prairie potholes, for example, have shrubby areas that serve not only waterfowl but also passerines and small mammals. Grasslands where pronghorns graze also offer nest habitat for longspurs, grouse, and prairie chickens.

Each refuge is unique, with an ecological composition of plant and animal inhabitants different from any other. Refuges as close together as Iroquois and Montezuma in upstate New York show quite different migration patterns due to their different habitat. Dramatically different are Brigantine/Forsythe, the great coastal New Jersey refuge with large numbers of migrating waterfowl and raptors, and the same state's Great Swamp Refuge, inland and just a short distance from New York City, with its deer and beautiful wood ducks.

Many refuges are in or close to metropolitan areas such as Tinicum (John Heinz) (designated a "Center" but managed as a refuge) in Philadelphia, Mason Neck near Washington, D.C., Nisqually on Puget Sound in the Seattle-Tacoma-Olympia metropolis, Bayou Sauvage in New Orleans, and San Francisco Bay Refuge. These offer sanctuary not only to wild creatures but to their human neighbors, who can go there to escape urban clamor as well as to encounter wildlife in natural settings.

Many refuges were restored from places that had been all but destroyed by deplorable land use—fire, drainage, erosion, destructive logging practices. They are lessons in how such land can be brought back to beauty and productivity. Of many of these, outstanding are Seney in Michigan's Upper Peninsula, Moosehorn in northeast Maine, and Piedmont in Georgia.

Even their names are evocative: Mingo... Mattamuskeet... Iroquois... Montezuma... Loxahatchee. Sabine and Lacassine and Catahoula; Kootenai and Malheur and Shiawassee—names of wild places, of explorers and Indian tribes. Laguna Atascosa, Cabeza Prieta, Bosque del Apache—the list goes on (much more appropriate for these great natural places than the names of human benefactors, however worthy).

Many offer chances to experience the country as it was when early explorers saw it, when the whole continent was a wilderness. Great Dismal Swamp in Virginia is like this; Okefenokee on the Georgia-Florida line; the great river bottom refuge, White River, in Arkansas. And there are many in the West, like Charles M. Russell in Montana, little changed since Lewis and Clark came through in their Missouri River exploration in the early 1800s.

Not all species of birds and mammals are commonly present every place, of course, but most can be seen by a careful, quiet, persistent observer at one or another of the refuges. Larger mammals, generally most affected by human disturbance and diminishing habitat, are warier, but they include black bears, wolves, wolverines, lynx, bobcats, mountain lions, ocelots, jaguarundis and coyotes, and a wide range of herbivores, including elk, caribou, mountain goats, musk-oxen, and mule, blacktailed, and white-tailed deer, plus the water-dwelling mammals—northern and California sea otters, river otters, manatees, walruses, and a half-dozen kinds of seals.

Of the smaller mammals, beavers and muskrats are present in large numbers, as are opossums, raccoons, skunks, gray and red fox, weasels, marmots, ground and flying squirrels, badgers, martens, fishers, rabbits, hares, and many others.

Of the more than 600 bird species on the refuges, many are of special interest to birders. Some in this category that occur commonly at various refuges are listed following the introductions to geographic regions.

Waterfowl include great numbers of geese: several races of Canadas, snows in both color phases, white-fronted, Ross', barnacled, and emperor; among the ducks, mallards, black and mottled, gadwalls, pintails, canvasbacks, green-, blue-winged, and cinnamon teal, wigeons, shovelers, common and Barrow's goldeneyes, buffle-heads, old squaws, ruddies, harlequins, and multihued wood ducks, called the most beautiful duck in the world.

Refuges these days are far from being the "duck farms" they were once regarded. Graceful whistling, trumpeter, and tundra swans are among the water-oriented birds. There are also white and brown pelicans; lovely long-legged wading birds—six kinds of herons, four of egrets, four ibises, and the breath-taking roseate spoonbills; and shorebirds and pelagic sea birds by the many millions—plovers, sandpipers, gulls, terns, shearwaters, puffins.

Both bald and golden eagles soar over many refuges, and there are four species of kite, including the endangered Everglade kite; swift prairie and peregrine falcons, Cooper's, rough-legged, and ferruginous hawks, ospreys, and many other raptors, including commonly eleven kinds of owls. There are eleven kinds of hummingbirds, also prairie chickens, pheasants, more than a dozen woodpeckers, and a tremendous number of small songbirds—warblers, buntings, too many to list here but described in detail throughout the book. Most refuges have lists showing relative abundance by seasons, and many are among the country's best birding spots, showing highest counts in the nation in the annual Audubon Society Christmas Bird Count.

One way to understand the value and importance of these refuges is to contemplate what would happen should they cease to exist. The loss can hardly be imagined. Literally millions of wild creatures—most of those just described—would shortly go out of existence or be under desperate pressure, because—except for some of our semi-domesticated lawn and garden birds and mammals—most wild creatures require wild land, both to support the unpolluted food chains of which they are a part and to provide needed places where they can rest and reproduce. There is less and less of it every day.

There are several ways to use this book effectively. If you wish to learn quickly what is in a particular region, turn to the introduction to that region for summaries of refuges there and a map showing their general location. If you want to know about a particular refuge, find it in the Table of Contents. To determine where a certain wild creature can be found, look it up in the index.

IN VISITING THE REFUGE there are dos and don'ts that will help make your time there productive and enjoyable.

• Visit early and late—not midday, when most birds and other wildlife are least active. Best is close to dawn and dusk; worst, between 11 a.m. and 3 p.m. Use the midday for a nap (as many creatures do) or picnic lunch. This is worth any inconvenience—dawn in December at Bosque del Apache becomes a magical place with thousands of snow geese and sandhill cranes coming awake, stretching and gathering to fly to feeding grounds. Dusk at "Ding" Darling on Sanibel in April can bring long lines of sunset-lit roseate spoonbills coming in to roost. At coastal refuges, low or incoming tide is best as it draws birds to feed.

• Spend time on the walking trails. Many refuges have excellent auto-tour routes where much wildlife can be seen (and often they are more readily observed from a car, which serves as a good blind). But try the trails, too, to feel the wildness of the place. Walk quietly. Stop from time to time and just look around, without talking. It takes awhile for wildlife to forget you're there and resume their activities. Visit, then talk later. You'll see more.

• Don't expect manicured grounds. Refuges are not parks. Most wild creatures require cover as well as food and water, and these necessities usually mean marsh and woods and lots of "edge" where different habitats come together.

• Try to acquire an understanding of what you are looking at. Why does this habitat attract these particular creatures? If they are not residents, where did they come from and where are they going? At what stage of "succession" is the habitat? No natural place is static—brush becomes woodlands and then climax forest. Ponds become marshes and then dry land. What geological forces shaped the refuge? Use the refuge leaflets to help in understanding. Your trip will be far more interesting.

• If coming from a distance, write or call the refuge office ahead, and stop by in any case. Usually the staff can tell you what's been seen lately and suggest best ways to see the refuge. Inquire before coming to see a certain kind of wildlife to be sure it is there—things change; maybe it's late this year. Remember that words like "common" and "abundant" involve certain assumptions: "common" eagles are not as numerous as "common" starlings, and any wildlife observation requires a patient, quiet viewer. Refuges are not zoos.

• Take insect repellent (not always needed but one can be miserable without it); binoculars and if possible a spotting scope; field guides such as Peterson's, the Audubon Guide, or the Golden Book of Birds, and others on fields of special interest; proper clothing in layers of sweaters, jackets, and so on to allow for temperature changes; boots if hiking off-trail; hat, sunglasses, sun lotion. In sparsely populated or remote areas, be sure your gas tank is full, take a canteen and some food, at least a modest first-aid kit, a compass, and be sure you have a jack and a good spare tire.

• STAY IN THE CAR where specified on auto-tour routes. You will see more and so will those behind you. Obey refuge signs. "Closed" means what it says, usually for good reason—the road may be unsafe, or pass near a nesting colony where disturbance may be harmful. If in doubt, ask at the refuge office. Permission to enter will sometimes be granted if no harm will be done to visitors or wildlife.

• PHOTOGRAPHERS especially should stay back and obey the rules. When they don't they make it hard for other photographers, other visitors, and the wildlife, and give photographers generally a bad name.

• If you see something of special interest, tell the staff about it. Many refuges keep logs of interesting sightings available to all visitors.

• Write or call ahead for motel reservations, especially at peak travel times.

• If in doubt, clarify refuge hours. Most refuge offices are open weekdays, most refuges dawn to dusk—but some are open 24 hours, and some take a weekday off to give the wildlife a rest from visitors. Most are closed on federal holidays but visitor centers may be manned by volunteers. Some charge entrance fees.

• A good idea for wildlife viewing is to stop and look back every so often. Both mammals and birds often freeze or duck back as visitors pass, then resume activity soon thereafter. Remember, wild creatures that are easy to see seldom survive long.

• Human activity on refuges must be consistent with wildlife welfare. Stay out of nesting areas; don't pick or remove plants; leave artifacts—tepee rings, pony express stations—as you find them.

Many refuges now have facilities for handicapped visitors, and can with prior arrangement give tours and film and slide shows for groups, especially from schools. Many refuges, working with teachers, have become outdoor classrooms.

Some refuges also administer wetland easements and waterfowl production areas, unstaffed, maintained largely for habitat, with varied wildlife, where visits can be arranged.

A wildlife corridor is a wonderful new concept in refuges. Land is being acquired to link refuges—islands of habitat—advantageous for four-footed wildlife that cannot fly from place to place. This is being done from Santa Ana along the Rio Grande River in south Texas, for 200 miles along the Sacramento River in California, and in areas reaching out from the Okefenokee Swamp.

Every refuge visit is different. Each person sees something slightly altered from the person who preceded or follows; and if a visitor comes again and again, he or she sees a slightly different thing each time. This is the essence of a natural situation. It can cause disappointment—or, more frequently, elation. It is one of the sources of fascination to those who come to love and enjoy refuges and come repeatedly, never knowing what they will see—but observing and understanding more each time. It is part of the dynamic nature of the natural state and wildness itself not to be predictable.

Because of space limitations we have not dealt at length with the history of the refuge movement, its current problems and issues, nor the interesting developments in refuge management practices. Some things, though, should be said.

"Seldom a day passes when a wildlife refuge somewhere in the country is not threatened by forces that would turn out the wildlife," George Laycock pointed out in his excellent book, *The Sign of the Flying Goose*. Sometimes the threat is to use a refuge for a bombing range, sometimes for a highway, an amusement park, sometimes as a water-skiing lake. The hazards are constant, and not always turned back. Each requires a mobilization of effort by those who love wild places to save the day.

Many refuges have been adopted by citizens' groups who organize as "friends of the refuge" to act as volunteers in almost every capacity where helpful work can be done—bird-banding, manning visitor centers, and many other tasks—and to stave off such infringements. They can act as community advocates for refuges in controversies over land use and water rights. Many local National Audubon Society chapters have "adopted" refuges. Other good work has been done by the National Wildlife Refuge Association, the National Wildlife Federation, Defenders of Wildlife, the Sierra Club, the Wilderness Society, The Nature Conservancy, and local conservation groups. Some visitors volunteer their efforts individually. All this has helped greatly.

To those seriously interested in refuge administrative practice and policy issues a good place to start is by reading *The United States Fish and Wildlife Service*, a book by Nathaniel P. Reed and Dennis Drabelle, which outlines the background and history of the refuges and many of the policy issues that continue to be debated. "Refuges 2003" is a series of public hearings and reports held under the auspices of the service that offers citizens a direct opportunity to affect the future of the refuges. And the nongovernmental organizations mentioned above offer specific opportunities to help the refuges throughout the country.

There is more than one reason to have wildlife refuges, going beyond benefit to the animals. They are also for us. "Preservation of wildlife and of wildlife habitat," Rachel Carson noted, "means also preservation of basic resources of earth . . . which men as well as animals must have in order to live."

The Northeast and
Mid-Atlantic States

Some of the refuges of the Northeast and mid-Atlantic states are within or on the edge of great metropolitan areas—Boston, New York, Philadelphia, and Washington. Others are in places as wild and unpeopled as any in the country.

A visitor to the *Great Dismal Swamp* in Virginia or *Monomoy* in Massachusetts, an island that extends eight miles out into Nantucket Sound, can feel as if no one has ever been there before him. But even at *Tinicum*, surrounded by superhighways, oil storage tanks, and crowded housing within a mile of Philadelphia's International Airport, one can sometimes get the same sense watching white-tailed deer browsing, a red fox chasing meadow voles, and short-eared owls hunting low over the fields in late afternoon.

Parker River and *Great Meadows*, too, near Boston, *Great Swamp* in New Jersey near New York City, and *Mason Neck* near Washington, D.C., offer humans not only a contact with wildlife and wild places but an escape from urban pressures that is rare and precious.

MAINE

The noted naturalist *Rachel Carson* is remembered with a necklace of refuges protecting nine fragile estuarine marshes and a tidal pool extending 45 miles along the southern Maine coast from Kittery to Cape Elizabeth.

Moosehorn is as rich in wildlife as any U.S. refuge. Black bears forage on blueberries in August. Warblers come through in May. Beavers have built homes in all the waterways. Porcupines shuffle along through fallen leaves. But undoubted star of this northeasternmost refuge is the woodcock, so inconspicuous it can be unobserved a few feet away—until it launches into its courtship flight, as spectacular as any in the world of nature.

Some of the largest and most diverse seabird nesting colonies on the East Coast are at *Petit Manan*, a relatively new refuge made up of islands and an almost-island just north of Mount Desert and Acadia National Park. Birds there include razor-billed auks, black guillemots, Atlantic puffins, Leach's storm petrels, and Arctic, common, and (endangered) roseate terns.

Sunkhaze Meadows is a wild and wonderful place not far from Bangor, another relatively new refuge with most of the wild creatures that may have inhabited it when the first settlers came—moose, bears, otters, fishers, fox, beavers, coyotes, deer, mink, and bobcats.

VERMONT

Marshes of *Missisquoi* are rich with wild rice and other nourishing plants that support hundreds of young waterfowl in spring and many thousands that migrate in fall through this refuge just south of the Canadian border and just east of Lake Champlain on the delta of the Missisquoi River. Beavers build dome-shaped houses 20 feet across and 10 feet high of whitened barkless limbs, readily visible along the waterways.

MASSACHUSETTS

Parts of *Great Meadows's* 3,000 acres of marsh, riverbank, and upland with ruffed grouse and otters are little changed from when Henry Thoreau visited and wrote in his journals about plant and animal observations there—despite problems connected with its being 15 miles from the center of Boston (poor water quality, heavy public use).

Thoreau called *Monomoy* "a place where a man may stand and put all America behind him." It also is one of the most significant locales in eastern North America for migrating shore- and water birds—a fragile and beautiful paradise just off the "elbow" of Cape Cod. Extending eight miles south into Nantucket Sound, surrounded by treacherous waters, shifting sandbars, and strong currents—a visit here can be the experience of a lifetime.

Parker River can have some of the most unusual bird sightings in the country, indeed the world—Ross' gull, ivory gull, black swan and others. The reason is its location, a barrier island just north of Boston where birds migrating by or blown off course can come down to a welcoming habitat. The bird list tops 300 species, including delicate warblers that may stay all winter, offshore eiders, scoters, occasionally gannets, great cormorants, and others.

RHODE ISLAND

Several relatively small and diverse refuges in Rhode Island include salt pond, peninsula, island, salt meadow, and riverine habitats, all administered by *Ninigret* with headquarters in Charlestown. *Trustom Pond's* 641 acres includes the state's last undeveloped coastal pond, with otters, muskrats, coyotes, gray and red fox, and some 300 species of birds.

NEW YORK

Where the last glacier left behind a huge lake, *Iroquois* refuge now offers a wonderful wildlife diversity including 700 nesting pairs of great blue herons. Hundreds of hooded mergansers compete with dazzling wood ducks for suitable nest quarters, resulting sometimes in mixed flocks. Over 500 wildflower species have been tabulated.

The *Long Island* complex is a half-dozen small refuges offering quiet human surcease from urban stress as well as, on a total of 6,000 acres, room for all the 50 habitats found in New York State and many of its endangered and threatened species as well. (Unfortunately these refuges have been plagued with incompatible use and other problems, casting doubt on whether they can properly perform their function.)

Montezuma got its name because it reminded someone of a marsh he saw in Mexico. Its 6,300 acres are still impressive, with nesting bald eagles and ospreys, over 100,000 waterfowl, and a wide variety of shorebirds coming through in spring and fall migration.

PENNSYLVANIA

Erie, located just south of the lake that bears its name, is a relatively small (8,516-acre) refuge with an interestingly diverse wild population. Beavers and their workings are readily visible and deer are everywhere. Most years there are several fox dens. An unusually beautiful succession of wildflowers blooms from April through June and huge old sugar maples blaze with color in fall.

Tinicum-Heinz (recently renamed for Senator John Heinz, a great friend of wildlife and the environment who was killed in an air crash) shows the extraordinary tenacity and vitality of wild creatures if given a bit of suitable habitat. Short-eared owls, fox, and many others are here within the shadow of planes taking off from Philadelphia's International Airport.

NEW JERSEY

Brigantine/Forsythe on the New Jersey coast (still known affectionately as "Brig" despite its recent name change) is a birder's refuge, outstanding for waterfowl, shorebirds, wading birds, and raptors. There can be superb warbler migrations in May. But something interesting is here year-round for the naturalist, including a good chance to see otters playing and red fox hunting, both at the northwest corner of the wildlife drive.

Cape May is a new refuge and first to take as a major concern neotropical migrants—songbirds under pressure because of destruction of tropical forests and fragmentation of northern woodlands. This locale is famous for its May peaks of these colorful small birds. It is equally known for its amazing shorebird concentrations in spring, and for its fall raptor migration. On one October day here an observer might see over 100 peregrine falcons, 200 ospreys, 150 northern harriers, and 7,000 American kestrels.

Great Swamp, which almost became a jetport, supports a wonderful wildlife diversity on 7,000-plus acres almost within sight of New York City. Deer are plentiful, so much so that a managed hunt to reduce their numbers has occasioned much controversy. Raccoon, fox, mink, and even occasional otter tracks are seen along the waterways. Several years ago a black bear was sighted. The bird list contains more than 200 species, and the refuge has a notable nesting population of colorful wood ducks that produce more than 2,500 ducklings every year.

DELAWARE

Visitors come from all over the East in late fall to see up to 75,000 greater snow geese arrive to spend the winter at *Bombay Hook,* on the south edge of Delaware Bay, from nesting grounds in the high Arctic tundra. When here they can cover the marsh and water like a blanket of snow. Shorebirds can be equally spectacular in May, when tens of thousands of red knots, ruddy turnstones, semipalmated sandpipers, and black-bellied plovers come to feast on billions of horseshoe crab eggs laid on tidal shores by these ancient crustaceans.

Prime Hook, just down the road from Bombay Hook, shares many of its attractions—tens of thousands of snow geese in fall and similar numbers of shorebirds in May (almost three-fourths under water, it can best be seen by canoe).

WEST VIRGINIA

Ohio River Islands (headquartered in Parkersburg) is more than a dozen islands stretching along the Ohio River from Manchester, Ohio, to Shippingport, Pennsylvania. Deer are here, as well as beaver and nesting blue herons. Songbirds use these islands as a migration corridor in spring. Eventually they may include islands over 362 miles of the Ohio River, but at present the refuge is so new that many visitor facilities are still in the planning stage.

MARYLAND

Blackwater, one of six staffed Eastern Shore refuges, is the center of the largest nesting concentration of southern bald eagles on the East Coast north of Florida, with a half-dozen nests and 60 or so individuals year-round. It also is an outstanding fall waterfowl refuge. Among its interesting mammals are sika deer (actually elk), a small Asiatic species that was released on James Island in Chesapeake Bay early in the century, swam here, and prospered.

Just across the bay from Annapolis is *Eastern Neck,* a 2,286-acre island refuge, originally a waterfowl haven but with other interesting inhabitants as well, including large resident populations of zebra butterflies and thousands of monarchs in migration.

VIRGINIA

Back Bay, just south of the Norfolk–Virginia Beach metropolitan area, is 4,600 acres of fragile dunes, shrub community, upland woods and bay straddling a narrow peninsula between the Atlantic Ocean and the bay for which it is named. It is best known for waterfowl and sea- and shorebirds, but mammals include gray fox, feral hogs wild for generations, mink, otter, and weasels.

Chincoteague, fronting on the Atlantic Ocean halfway down Virginia's Eastern Shore, is one of the nation's outstanding refuges. Visitors readily see sika and white-tailed deer as well as the famous wild ponies said to be descended from a Spanish herd shipwrecked in the 1500s. The endangered silvery Delmarva fox squirrel is here and an extraordinary 300 species on the refuge bird list. Chincoteague's main problem may be its popularity—between 1.3 and 1.5 million visits a year, with some visitor uses putting pressure on the resident wildlife.

Eastern Shore of Virginia is the southernmost of the Delmarva Peninsula refuges, extending to islands along the route of the Norfolk Bridge & Tunnel and spanning the wide entrance from the Atlantic into Chesapeake Bay. Its strategic location makes it a geographic funnel for birds migrating south along the Eastern Seaboard, and sometimes millions of raptors, songbirds, and waterfowl may stop and "stage" here, waiting for favorable north winds to assist them in making the watery crossing.

Great Dismal Swamp was a "glorious paradise" abundant with wildlife, according to George Washington, who owned part of it and surveyed it in 1793. It still is, in part because of the generosity of two companies—Union Camp and Weyerhaeuser—and effective action by The Nature Conservancy. Several hundred black bears are here, as well as bobcats, mink, white-tailed deer, gray fox, and otters. Ninety-seven species of birds, including golden prothonotary warblers, flame-crested pileated woodpeckers, and gorgeous multicolored wood ducks, nest on these 107,000 acres that are among the wildest and most interesting in the country.

Mason Neck, jutting out on a peninsula in the Potomac River just 18 miles from Washington, D.C., was founded in 1969 as one of the first national wildlife refuges set aside under the Endangered Species Act, and the first for the bald eagle. The results have been heartening. The refuge wintering population is 30 to 40 eagles, with 10 to 20 around in summer and regular nesting activity.

To get to *Presquile* one must cross Turkey Island Creek by refuge-operated cable ferry or private boat. On the other side one steps ashore into a jewel of the refuge system—1,329 acres once "almost an island," now an island in fact. Several of our most stunning birds are here in abundance—golden prothonotary warblers, eastern bluebirds, vivid-plumaged wood ducks. There are eagles, wild turkeys, red fox, and white-tailed deer, and sometimes otter, all in a self-contained wildlife oasis.

Following are birds of special interest found commonly at Northeast and Mid-Atlantic refuges at seasons indicated:

S: SPRING   s: SUMMER   F: FALL   W: WINTER

Red-throated Loon: Monomoy SF, Parker River F

Horned Grebe: Chincoteague SFW, Eastern Neck F, Petit Manan SFW, Mason Neck SF, Parker River SFW

Red-necked Grebe: Petit Manan SFW

Northern Gannet: Back Bay SFW, Monomoy SF

Brown Pelican: Back Bay SsF, Chincoteague S

Great Cormorant: Moosehorn W

Least Bittern: Great Swamp S

Tricolored Heron: Chincoteague sF

Glossy Ibis: Back Bay SsF, Brigantine Ss

Tundra Swan: Back Bay W, Blackwater FW, Chincoteague SFW, Eastern Neck SFW, Iroquois S

Brant: Brigantine SFW, Chincoteague SFW, Eastern Shore W, Monomoy SFW

Common Eider: Monomoy SFW, Parker River SW, Petit Manan SsFW

Oldsquaw: Chincoteague SW, Eastern Neck SFW, Long Island SFW, Monomoy SFW, Moosehorn SW, Parker River SW, Petit Manan SFW

Black Scoter: Chincoteague SFW, Eastern Shore W, Monomoy SFW, Moosehorn F, Parker River SF, Petit Manan S

Surf Scoter: Back Bay W, Chincoteague SFW, Eastern Shore SFW, Monomoy SFW, Moosehorn F, Parker River F, Petit Manan S

White-winged Scoter: Back Bay W, Chincotgeague SFW, Monomoy SFW, Petit Manan S

Bald Eagle: Blackwater SsFW, Eastern Neck SF

Rough-legged Hawk: Blackwater W, Montezuma W, Parker River W

Peregrine Falcon: Eastern Shore F, Petit Manan F

Clapper Rail: Brigantine SsF, Chincoteague SsF, Eastern Shore SsF

King Rail: Back Bay SsFW, Blackwater SsF, Easern Neck SsFW

Virginia Rail: Back Bay SsF, Blackwater SF, Eastern Neck SsF, Great Swamp SsF, Missisquoi sF, Montezuma SsF

Piping Plover: Monomoy Ss

American Oystercatcher: Chincoteague SsFW

Whimbrel: Chincoteague Ss, Monomoy SF

Hudsonian Godwit: Monomoy S
Pectoral Sandpiper: Monomoy F, Montezuma SsF
Stilt Sandpiper: Chincoteague sF
Black-legged Kittiwake: Monomoy SFW
Black Skimmer: Brigantine SsF, Chincoteague sF, Back Bay SsF
Black Guillemot: Petit Manan SsF
Prothonotary Warbler: Great Dismal Swamp SsF
Hooded Warbler: Great Dismal Swamp SsF
Olive-sided Flycatcher: Missisquoi s
Common Redpoll: Petit Manan W
Grasshopper Sparrow: Presquile SsF
Sharp-tailed Sparrow: Bombay Hook SsF, Brigantine SsF, Monomoy Ss, Parker River
   SsF
Seaside Sparrow: Bombay Hook SsF, Brigantine SsF

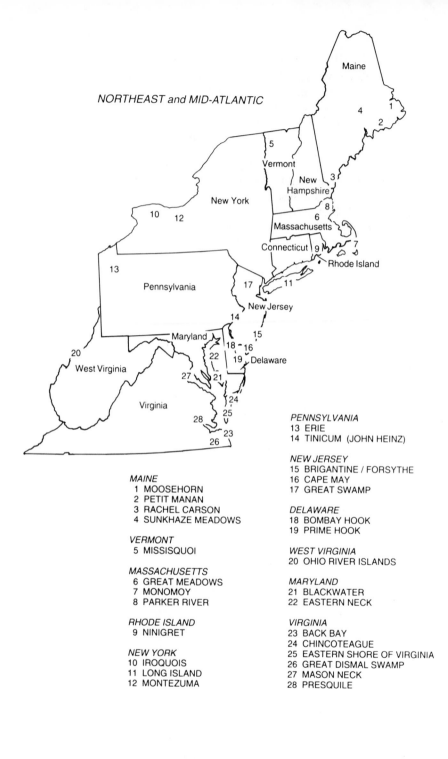

NORTHEAST and MID-ATLANTIC

Maine

Vermont

New Hampshire

New York

Massachusetts

Connecticut

Rhode Island

Pennsylvania

New Jersey

Maryland

West Virginia

Delaware

Virginia

MAINE
1 MOOSEHORN
2 PETIT MANAN
3 RACHEL CARSON
4 SUNKHAZE MEADOWS

VERMONT
5 MISSISQUOI

MASSACHUSETTS
6 GREAT MEADOWS
7 MONOMOY
8 PARKER RIVER

RHODE ISLAND
9 NINIGRET

NEW YORK
10 IROQUOIS
11 LONG ISLAND
12 MONTEZUMA

PENNSYLVANIA
13 ERIE
14 TINICUM (JOHN HEINZ)

NEW JERSEY
15 BRIGANTINE / FORSYTHE
16 CAPE MAY
17 GREAT SWAMP

DELAWARE
18 BOMBAY HOOK
19 PRIME HOOK

WEST VIRGINIA
20 OHIO RIVER ISLANDS

MARYLAND
21 BLACKWATER
22 EASTERN NECK

VIRGINIA
23 BACK BAY
24 CHINCOTEAGUE
25 EASTERN SHORE OF VIRGINIA
26 GREAT DISMAL SWAMP
27 MASON NECK
28 PRESQUILE

MOOSEHORN
★

Bangor •

MOOSEHORN (Maine)

No refuge is richer in wildlife than Moosehorn. Black bears forage in every blueberry field in August and through old apple orchards in October. Beaver workings—and often the beavers themselves—are visible around all the more than 50 lakes, marshes, and flowages. That quiet shuffling through the dry leaves, and that semi-shapeless object in a tree notch, is quite likely a porcupine. ("They have their good points," locals say, "but then they have their bad points, too.")

In mid-May the woods are filled with tremendous flights of bright warblers of every species found in the northeastern United States, including 21 that nest here—bay-breasted, mourning, chestnut-sided, magnolia, Wilson's, blackburnian, and many others.

Still the undoubted star of this 22,745-acre refuge of marshes, streams, woods, and rocky shoreline—nearly every kind of habitat found in the state of Maine—is the woodcock, a small brown bird so inconspicuous in its natural surroundings that it can sit a few feet away without being observed.

Yet each spring the woodcock performs one of the most spectacular mating displays in the world of nature. Visitors can watch while males stake out territories in clearings and then in their unique and wonderful way try to attract females to them. It is a stunning sight as the male, triggered by a specific intensity of light, soars hundreds of feet in the air, circles—outlining the area he has marked for his own—and finally reaches a peak from which he plummets like a bullet straight to earth, wings whistling as the air rips through his feathers, leveling out only a few feet off the ground.

He may repeat this dazzling performance several times any dawn or dusk between April 1 and May 20 while his intended presumably watches from the edge of the future nest site and listens to his twittering entreaty. Visitors can find out from refuge personnel where best to see them.

Moosehorn was established for the study and protection of the woodcock in 1937 and now has over 100 courting males, sometimes more than 2,000 birds by the time they prepare for fall migration. Research crews walk the woods from April to September to band and observe them, and interested visitors are welcome to go along; arrange a few days in advance.

Much has been learned about making habitat favor the woodcock—information that is shared with other refuges—and many other creatures feel welcome here, too. Over 200 bird and 39 mammal species have been seen on the two tracts of this northeasternmost U.S. refuge, which includes some 7,300 designated wilderness acres.

On the Cobscook Bay side, where tides may reach 28 feet—highest in the United States outside of Alaska—are harbor seals; in the upland and wooded areas are moose, deer, bobcats, otters, red foxes, coyotes, minks—even an occasional fisher.

Ospreys and eagles commonly swoop down for fish on both coastal and inland waters.

Here all year are gray jays, loons, boreal chickadees, evening grosbeaks, black-backed woodpeckers, spruce and ruffed grouse, and great horned, barred, and saw-whet owls; common or abundant except in winter are great blue herons, American bitterns, black, ring-necked, and wood ducks, hooded mergansers, snipe, northern harriers, whip-poor-wills, nighthawks, kingfishers, and bobolinks.

How to get there: From Bangor take Route 9 East about 90 miles to Baring, then Route 1 South about four miles to the Charlotte Road; turn right and go about three miles to refuge office.

Open: Office open 7:30–4 weekdays; roads and trails open for hiking dawn to dusk daily; cross-country skiing and snowshoeing 24 hours a day.

What to see: Woodcock, especially nuptial flights; warblers; osprey; eagles; waterfowl; good variety of songbirds and mammals, including bears and moose. Fall colors peak about October 1.

What to do: 60 miles of roads and trails. Blueberrying in August. Cross-country skiing and snowshoeing in winter.

Where to stay: Motels—several in Calais and Baring. Campgrounds—at Cobscook State Park, adjacent to Edmunds refuge unit.

Weather: On the cool side spring and fall, often severe in winter.

What to take and wear: Insect repellent a must May-August (some people opt for headnets during peak of black fly season). Waterproof footgear a good idea. Sweaters and windbreakers spring and fall. Warmest outerclothing November-March.

Points of interest nearby: Campobello International Park (Franklin Delano Roosevelt Home) 15 miles east; Machias Seal Island, puffin nesting site administered jointly by U.S. and Canadian authorities, 30 miles south, offshore; St. Croix Island National Park, Calais, 14 miles south.

For more information: Moosehorn National Wildlife Refuge, P.O. Box 1077, Calais, Maine 04619. Phone: (207) 454-3521.

Moosehorn also administers Carlton Pond, a 1,068-acre waterfowl production area six miles south of Detroit, Maine, on Route 220 between Routes I-95 and 202. Waterfowl are concentrated and highly visible; however, a boat or canoe is required for access.

Ellsworth

PETIT MANAN

PETIT MANAN (Maine)

Petit Manan is a refuge of islands and an almost-island that host thousands of sea and freshwater waterfowl as well as some of our rarest birds, spectacularly at nesting and migration times but to some extent most of the year.

The 3,335 acres of blueberry and hay fields, fresh and saltwater marsh, peatlands and spruce woods that make up Petit Manan Point are connected to the mainland by the slenderest of necks and are surrounded at any time of the year by up to 5,000 sea ducks. As many as 15,000 eider are bobbing in the sparkling waters around Petit Manan Island just offshore in August and September during their molt.

Endangered peregrine falcons course the uplands and edges in the spring and fall, as do eagles year-round (a half-dozen pairs nest within five miles of the refuge).

Migrating shorebirds drop down on the marshes and shore in July and August with large numbers of yellowlegs, dowitchers, turnstones, and semipalmated and black-bellied plover. There are rare-to-occasional glimpses of golden and piping plovers, Hudsonian godwits, and purple and Baird's sandpipers. Whimbrels stop over, sometimes a dozen or so at a time, in the blueberry fields.

Fall migration and to a lesser extent spring bring hawks in large numbers following the coastline—northern harriers, merlins, kestrels, and sharpshins as well as goshawks, which also nest on the refuge, and occasional roughlegs. Thousands of black ducks and others stop over in the freshwater marshes. Warblers make a good appearance in the spring; blackburnians, bay-breasted, magnolias, and others nest.

A unique aspect of Petit Manan is its seabird nesting colonies, some of the largest and most productive on the East Coast, of razorbills, black guillemots, Atlantic puffins, Leach's storm-petrels, laughing gulls, and Arctic, common, and endangered roseate terns. Some are on Petit Manan Refuge proper, which is made up of Petit Manan Point and the three nearby islands of Petit Manan, Nash, and Bois Bubert (the latter two partly in private hands); others are on Franklin Island, Cross Island, and Seal Island National Wildlife refuges, which also are administered by Petit Manan.

All are off-limits during the nesting season except by special permit; but anyone wishing a transcendent experience should apply a few days ahead to accompany refuge personnel to Petit Manan Island during June or July. Such a visitor will pass along a boardwalk completely surrounded by thousands of nesting terns, guillemots, eider ducks, and laughing gulls in a wilderness habitat so remote in feeling that no other world seems to exist except that of sea and sky, island and birds.

Among the refuge units, Petit Manan Point is the only one reachable by land—others require a boat—and has notable habitat range for plants as well as wildlife. Botanists come to observe and study such Arctic types as oysterleaf and roseroot and ericaceous sheep laurel.

Two trails (and an access road that serves also as a trail) go out from or near the parking lot. Birch Trail winds through woods and upland where there are spruce grouse, deer, and boreal chickadees. The Shore Trail passes through heathy areas to a rocky shore where harbor seals loaf in summer and where, from November to March, there are oldsquaw, goldeneyes, buffleheads, and sometimes white-winged scoters.

In nonnesting seasons all the islands are beautiful places to picnic and perhaps photograph (except Seal Island, a former artillery range always off-limits because of possible unexploded ordnance). Cross Island has an eagle nest and other eagles like to hang around. But they are sensitive to disturbance; don't get too near.

How to get there: From Route 1 in the town of Steuben take Pigeon Hill Road about 5 miles. It ends in the refuge parking lot and information kiosk. Refuge office is on Main Street in Milbridge.

Open: Refuge open daylight hours. Office hours irregular; best call ahead for appointment.

Best times to visit: August-September for moderate weather, fewer insects.

What to see: Nesting bird colonies; diverse wilderness-type habitat.

What to do: Walking trails (somewhat rugged; only for those in fairly good shape). Cross-country skiing in winter.

What to take and wear: Sturdy waterproof footgear; windbreaker and warm clothing most of the year. Insect repellent in summer.

Where to stay: Motel, bed-and-breakfast in both Milbridge and Cherryfield; private campground on Route 1 in Steuben.

Places of interest nearby: Acadia National Park (Schoodic section) 15 miles southwest.

For more information: Petit Manan National Wildlife Refuge, P.O. Box 279, Milbridge, Maine 04658. Phone (207) 546-2124.

Portland

RACHEL CARSON

RACHEL CARSON (Maine)

Rachel Carson is a chain of refuges that protect nine fragile estuarine marshes and a tidal pool extending 45 miles along the southern Maine coast from Kittery to Cape Elizabeth. The ducks and shorebirds that find rest and food there provide fitting recognition of the writer-environmentalist who so eloquently described the wonders of the sea and its life (and the "Silent Spring" dangers of pesticides).

These salt marshes surrounded by upland growth and hushed stands of 75-foot white pines are quiet oases alongside busy commercial areas and well-traveled highways. Although open to the public they are almost entirely in a wild state except for a mile-long self-guided trail at headquarters near Wells. Visitors must expect to get out of their cars and explore for themselves (public roads run alongside or through sections of most units).

Mallards, black ducks, and endangered piping plovers nest. Snowy egrets and great blue herons scout the water's edges. Buffleheads, goldeneyes, and red-breasted mergansers are in the marshes in winter, while common eider, oldsquaw, and scoters are offshore. Yellowlegs, whimbrels, and ruddy turnstones come through. Brown creepers and red- and white-breasted nuthatches raise broods in the wooded uplands. Barred owls call at night. Pink lady's slippers and trillium bloom in spring. Deer browse and, though seldom seen, otter and coyotes are here.

Some of the best birding is at Biddeford Pool, one of Maine's top birding spots for migratory shorebirds, at the mouth of the Saco River—a pristine 300-acre pool that drains and refloods each tide to support a complete ecosystem of small sea creatures. Rachel Carson would have enjoyed it as much as do the black ducks and mergansers that spend spring, fall, and winter here.

How to get there: From Portland airport go south on I-95 to Exit 2 (Wells), then Route 109 south to Route 1, north to Route 9 east and follow it .7 miles to refuge office.

Open: Daylight hours. Office 7:30–4 weekdays.

What to see: Pristine estuarine environment in midst of urban sprawl.

What to do: Nature observation; self-guided trail, wheelchair accessible.

Where to stay: Motels—in Wells, crowded in summer. Campgrounds—several in Wells area.

What to take and wear: Warm clothing—breeze off water can be cool even in summer.

Points of interest nearby: Scarborough Marsh State Wildlife Area with Audubon nature center, 20 miles north; Wells National Estuarine Research Reserve headquartered in historic farmstead, 8-mile trail system, adjacent on south.

For more information: Rachel Carson National Wildlife Refuge, R.D. 2, Box 751, Wells, Maine 04090. Phone: (207) 646-9226.

Rachel Carson also administers *Pond Island,* a rocky 10-acre island with nesting eider. Closed during nesting, and dangerous riptides make access difficult anytime.

SUNKHAZE
MEADOWS
★
Bangor •

SUNKHAZE MEADOWS (Maine)

Sunkhaze Meadows is a wild and wonderful place with moose, bears, otters, fishers, foxes, beavers, coyotes, deer, minks, bobcats—about all the wild creatures that may have inhabited it when white settlers came.

That's because it has been almost undisturbed—9,337 acres of bog peatland bisected diagonally by the Sunkhaze stream and further divided by a number of tributaries into lush wet meadows, woods, and upland.

A canoe trip through this clear cold-running stream—with portages over beaver dams, perhaps stopping to watch a moose drink or a flock of warblers moving through in spring—can be a transcendent experience.

This is such a new refuge that most visitor access to it is still in the planning stage. But miles of old logging roads are available for hiking and for snowshoes and cross-country skiing in winter (no snowmobiles except for a small corner of the refuge where an organized trail passes).

The area was considered for peat mining in the early 1980s but controversy arose, partly over destruction of the second largest peatland in Maine. The Nature Conservancy intervened and the Fish and Wildlife Service acquired it for a refuge in 1988.

The University of Maine has used it as a biological research area, and plans call for a continued emphasis on use by school and environmental groups as an outdoor classroom and research center. (One study with immediate usefulness calls for employment of beavers in doing what beavers do best—moving them about to places where their dams can create new water impoundments attractive to waterfowl.)

There is certainly much to study here.

The showy lady's slipper blooms in cedar swamp areas and possibly the rare calypso fairy slipper.

Peregrine falcons hunt over the open shrub heath. Bald eagles, numerous along the nearby Penobscot River, soar overhead. Uncommon in Maine but observed here are the long-eared owl, sedge wren, willow flycatcher, and Cooper's hawk. It is the only inland breeding place for the sharp-tailed sparrow.

Hooded mergansers nest along with blue-winged teal and wood, black, and ring-necked ducks. Goldeneyes stop by in migration.

Ruffed grouse are everywhere, drumming on logs in the spring, and woodcock are common.

Small rodents such as voles and meadow mice abound, supporting the large bird and mammal predator populations; and there are reptiles and salamanders rare elsewhere. Brook trout breed in large numbers in Sunkhaze stream, as do pickerel.

Fall colors of the alders, birch, and red maples can be dazzling from mid-September through October.

How to get there: From Bangor airport take I-95 north to Exit 51, then Stillwater Avenue east across second bridge to Route 2, north on it a short distance to County Road, east on it about four miles to refuge boundary signs. Watch then for openings to old logging roads for hiking.

Open: Sunrise to sunset daily.

Best times to visit: Late summer and early fall (spring-summer insects fierce, stream frozen mid-December–March).

What to see: Ruffed grouse; ducks; broad wildlife spectrum.

What to do: Canoeing; hiking on old logging roads; wildlife observation.

Where to stay: Motels—many in Bangor area. Campgrounds—15 miles south off I-95.

Weather: Can be cool September through May.

What to take and wear: Waterproof footgear, long sleeves and pants. Insect repellent.

Points of interest nearby: Acadia National Park, 65 miles southeast. Petit Manan National Wildlife Refuge, 50 miles southeast. Baxter State Park, 100 miles north. Moosehorn National Wildlife Refuge, 100 miles east.

For more information: Sunkhaze Meadows National Wildlife Refuge, 1033 S. Main Street, Old Town, Maine 04468. Phone: (207) 827-6138.

★ MISSISQUOI

Burlington

MISSISQUOI (Vermont)

This 5,839-acre refuge covers most of the Missisquoi River's bird's-foot delta, well-named for its shape but also the imprints left by tens of thousands of waterfowl and others that stop to nest or migrate through this welcoming tract on the northeastern shore of Lake Champlain.

The marshes, rich with wild rice, arrowhead, bulrush, and other nourishing plants, support hundreds of young goldeneyes, wood ducks, and hooded mergansers in spring and summer and up to 25,000 waterfowl of various kinds in fall. The area is a key stopover in the Atlantic Flyway, the northernmost inland link in a chain of refuges at strategic points through the eastern United States.

Other creatures naturally find it attractive, too. A morning walk along the nature trail may be punctuated by curious beaver slapping their tails on the stream surface to tell other beaver that you're coming. Then they all disappear in the direction of their dome-shaped house, 20 feet across and 10 feet high, built of whitened, barkless tree limbs.

Hummingbirds sip from orange jewelweed. Yellowthroat and yellow warblers, which nest here, abound in the shrubby understory—peak warbler migration is in May. Flame-crested pileated woodpeckers, our largest species of woodpecker and year-round residents, have drilled a dozen rectangular nest holes in a single giant dead elm.

The first few minutes along the walk may start a half-dozen woodcock, their wings whistling as they explode upward.

Vermont's largest great blue heron breeding colony is on Shad Island in the river delta, and the cacophony is audible over much of the refuge when these tall beautiful wading birds are attending the shrieks of their insistent young, perhaps 300 pairs of adults and 1,000 young a season. They are best seen from a canoe, and even then from a distance as the island is off-limits during nesting.

The whole refuge is, in fact, best seen in all but winter from a canoe. A visitor can slip quietly into a backwater and come upon a brood of downy goldeneyes feeding with a parent (they sometimes babysit for one another and assume responsibility for as many as 30 chicks per parent). Secretive ovenbirds and waterthrushes may be hopping about, a muskrat may swim alongside, and rafts of 200 to 2,000 ducks otherwise obscured by vegetation may become visible to the waterborne visitor.

Bitterns, gallinules, and black terns nest, along with meadowlarks, marsh wrens, rose-breasted grosbeaks, red-tailed hawks, and barred owls; kingfishers and a colony of bank swallows burrow into the riverbank.

Foragers can help themselves to delicious wild blueberries. And fishing is excellent—walleyed pike in the Missisquoi River in early May are famous, plus small- and large-mouthed bass, northern pike, and an occasional muskie. Ice fishing is popular in winter.

In fact, some prefer the refuge as winter closes in. Scoters and occasional eiders and oldsquaws are here and now and then a snowy owl. Mammals may be more easily seen then—deer, otters, red foxes, and coyotes—their tracks visible in the snow.

How to get there: From Burlington, Vermont, take I-89 to Swanton exit, then west on Highway 78 through Swanton Village and two miles to the refuge.

Open: Daylight hours (walking trails may be closed seasonally due to flooding—check with refuge headquarters). Office open weekdays 8–4:30.

Best times to visit: Late summer and early fall; May for warblers.

What to see: Waterfowl, especially in migration, and wood ducks, ring-necks, and hooded mergansers in breeding plumage; marsh hawks; great blue herons, sometimes coyotes and foxes.

What to do: Fishing; canoeing (inquire at office about canoe rentals nearby, or bring own canoe). Conducted group tours can be arranged.

Where to stay: Motels—several in Swanton and St. Albans (10 miles). Campgrounds— state campground 16 miles away; three private campgrounds within two miles of the refuge.

Weather: Can be 25 below in winter. Lake Champlain waters can be rough.

What to take and wear: Waterproof footgear in spring; a windbreaker, at least, in spring and fall; insect repellent May-October.

Points of interest nearby: Lake Champlain Islands, excellent birding opportunities. Mud Creek Wildlife Management Area, five miles west on Highway 78. Victory Bog on U.S. 2, 15 miles east of St. Johnsbury. Fall colors glorious throughout Vermont. Good skiing facilities within an hour of refuge.

For more information: Missisquoi National Wildlife Refuge, P.O. Box 163, Swanton, Vermont 05488. Phone: (802) 868-4781.

GREAT MEADOWS ★
Boston

GREAT MEADOWS (Massachusetts)

Great Meadows is 15 miles from the center of Boston, within an hour's drive of more than five million persons—but the visitor watching a gorgeous ring-necked pheasant or eight species of warblers from a single vantage point would never guess it.

Ospreys hover and plunge for fish regularly in summer and bald eagles scout for prey occasionally year-round on this wildlife oasis of more than 3,000 acres of marsh, riverbank, and upland that is probably little changed from the times naturalist Henry Thoreau visited and wrote in his journals about plants and animals he observed here.

Ruffed grouse drum for mates in spring and a half-dozen kinds of waterfowl parade downy broods of young, including teals, black ducks, mallards, gadwalls, and wood ducks—in a good year the refuge produces as many as 400 young of this beautiful species, encouraged by nest boxes provided.

Great blue herons and four species of rails are here, including the shy yellow, and Virginia and sora rails nest. So do warbling, yellow-throated, and red-eyed vireos, rose-breasted grosbeaks, chestnut-sided, yellow, and black-and-white warblers (the refuge is a mecca for birders during warbler migration), and black-crowned night herons have a small rookery.

A red-winged blackbird colony, whose males flash scarlet epaulettes to proclaim territories in the spring, has been probed as intensively as any in the world by local science groups. (One study showed that contrary to previous belief showy males are not necessarily most successful. While they were showing off many females mated in the marsh grass with males that were not displaying at all.)

Great Meadows is popular in winter for showshoeing and cross-country skiing and for winter birds such as juncos, tree sparrows, and occasional evening grosbeaks, pine siskins, redpolls, and barred owls. The quiet visitor might even spot a mischievous otter tearing into a domed muskrat house, or a mink or red fox streaking after a rodent.

The refuge is in two units. Nearby lies Thoreau's Walden Pond, worth a sentimental pilgrimage though its natural ambience is marred by a public bathing beach on the east end. Still, the water is as crystalline as when Thoreau peered into it looking for a shadowy pickerel, and a 30-minute walk to the site of Thoreau's cabin passes through woods in which the main sound is still that of chickadees, nuthatches, and squirrels.

How to get there: From Boston take I-90 west to Exit 13. Go east on Route 10 to Route 27, north on 27 into Sudbury center. At first traffic light in Sudbury turn right onto Concord Road, follow and bear right onto Lincoln Road for 1.5 miles to Weir Hill Road on the left. Follow signs to refuge.

Open: Daylight hours all year. Visitor center/headquarters 8-4 weekdays. (Parking limited to 35 cars so come early at peak times.)

Best times to visit: Spring and fall during migration and early nesting (though river flooding can prevent full use for several weeks in spring).

What to see: Spring warbler migrations, broods of young ducks, variety of song and wading birds, some mammals.

What do do: Three walking trails (can be closed during spring flooding). Canoeing. Snowshoeing and cross-country skiing in winter.

Where to stay: Motels—in nearby Concord and Sudbury. Campgrounds—Minuteman Campground, 10 miles west in Littleton.

Weather: Few extremes, mostly pleasant.

What to take and wear: Waterproof footgear during spring floods. Insect repellent.

Points of interest nearby: Minute Man National Historical Park, adjacent, where the embattled farmers stood to start the Revolutionary War; Thoreau's Walden Pond (see text).

For more information: Great Meadows National Wildlife Refuge, Weir Hill Road, Sudbury, Massachusetts 01776. Phone: (508) 443-4661.

Also administered by Great Meadows are several satellite refuges:

John Hay National Wildlife Refuge—163 acres near Newbury, New Hampshire, with a number of historic buildings, is planned as a combined center for study of natural as well as cultural history. Admission has been by permit only.

Massasoit National Wildlife Refuge—184 acres in Plymouth County, Massachusetts, established for preservation of the endangered Plymouth red-bellied turtle. No public access.

Monomoy National Wildlife Refuge—see later entry.

Nantucket National Wildlife Refuge—40 acres of beaches, dunes, and upland providing important habitat for sea, shore, and upland birds, overseen by the Nantucket Trustees of Reservations. Access by permit only.

Noman's Land Island National Wildlife Refuge—a 620-acre island off Martha's Vineyard, co-owned by the Defense Department and the U.S. Fish and Wildlife Service, which has been used as a strafing and bombing range. No public access.

Oxbow National Wildlife Refuge—711 acres of habitat surrounding river oxbows in all stages of succession located near Fort Devens in Harvard, Massachusetts. Black and wood ducks have nested, also great blue herons and several raptor species. A variety of mammals including otters, minks, beavers, coyotes, white-tailed deer, red and gray foxes, and, rarely, fishers. Trails exist but visitor facilities largely undeveloped.

Wapack National Wildlife Refuge—1,672 acres of timbered uplands on North Pack Monadnock Mountain near Greenfield, New Hampshire. A popular hawk migration area, also nest habitat for tree sparrows, winter wrens, Swainson's thrush, and magnolia warblers. Permanent residents include ruffed grouse, deer, minks, foxes, bobcats, and snowshoe hares. Only access to the interior is a three-mile segment of the Wapack Trail, which can be rugged and steep in spots, and, climbing 1,000 feet, noticeably cooler at the top. But views and fall color can be spectacular.

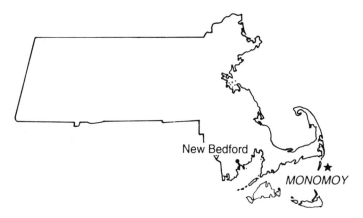

New Bedford

MONOMOY

MONOMOY (Massachusetts)

The naturalist Henry Thoreau sought "a place where a man may stand and put all America behind him."

This is it.

It is also no doubt partly why Monomoy—now two islands with official wilderness status, separated from the mainland since a 1958 hurricane—is one of the most significant wildlife areas in eastern North America.

Extending for eight miles off the "elbow" of Cape Cod, it can be host to a half-million birds, mostly with a water orientation, some nesting, some staging for migration, some wintering offshore—some seldom if ever seen elsewhere.

In September it may have up to 80 percent of the world population of endangered roseate terns—up to 9,000 of them—feasting on sand eels to replenish body reserves before migrating to South America.

Common shorebirds such as black-bellied plovers, red knots, and spotted sandpipers can be everywhere—along with such specialties as the lesser golden plover, Baird's and buff-breasted sandpipers, and marbled godwits.

One can see up to 60 Hudsonian godwits, a species never glimpsed by the much-traveled Audubon, plus an occasional red-necked phalarope and such rarities as a ruff or Eurasian curlew.

If the Eskimo curlew still exists, many feel that Monomoy is where it most likely will turn up some fall.

Common eider populations can peak at 85,000 birds in mid-December, with occasional massed flocks of up to a half-million birds flying over offshore ocean swells.

In summer nesting birds include terns, oystercatchers, endangered piping plovers, black-crowned night herons, and a colony that has contained up to 20,000 herring and black-backed gull nests.

Ducks nest, too—gadwalls, teals, blacks, shovelers, pintails, wigeon, and ruddies—as well as short-eared owls and northern harriers.

Common or abundant at various times of the year are gannets, great cormorants, oldsquaws, scoters, kittiwakes, goldeneyes, red-throated and common loons, and, all year, horned larks.

More than 1,000 harbor seals winter, along with some gray seals; in recent years gray seal pups have been born.

It is a naturalist's paradise.

But it is a fragile paradise. Disturbance can seriously impact feeding and nesting birds—even destroy a whole colony. So it may be just as well that access is not easy, and this 2,750 acres of insular refuge—once a Viking haven, then where the explorer Champlain landed after he broke a rudder—is surrounded by treacherous waters, shifting sandbars, and strong currents to confound even an expert mariner.

The best way to go is with a boatman who knows the waters intimately. Consult refuge headquarters; or contact the Cape Cod Museum of Natural History [telephone (508) 896-3867] or the Massachusetts Audubon Society [telephone (508) 349-2615], both of which arrange tours.

Boats approaching the island should take extreme care to watch for and obey refuge "closed area" signs, which protect sensitive areas.

It is well worth the trouble if one can make the trip safely to this rare and wonderful place.

How to get there: From Boston take I-93 to route 3 south to Route 6, east to Route 137, east to Route 28 into Chatham center. Once there ask for directions to the Morris Island headquarters.

Open: Daylight hours all year. Office hours irregular—best call ahead (but informational brochures always available outside office).

Best times to visit: All year rewarding.

What to see: Shore, marsh, and sea birds, sometimes in large numbers. Also plant life—roses, heaths, orchids. Deer in the uplands. Historic lighthouse.

What to do: Bird observation. Trail near mainland headquarters.

Where to stay: Motels—many in nearby Chatham. Campgrounds—Nickerson State Park, 10 miles north of Chatham (can be crowded in summer and is first come, first served).

Weather: Often misty and cool—sometimes dense fog.

What to take and wear: A windbreaker is always a good idea, and warmer clothing is needed in all but summer. Sun protection for bright days; insect repellent a MUST: deer are present, along with deer ticks and the attendant risk of Lyme disease. Tuck pants legs into socks or boots if hiking away from beach.

Points of interest nearby: Cape Cod National Seashore.

For more information: Monomoy National Wildlife Refuge, Morris Island, Chatham, Massachusetts 02633, phone (508) 945-0594, or Great Meadows National Wildlife Refuge, Weir Hill Road, Sudbury, Massachusetts 01776, phone (508) 443-4661. For trip information see Cape Cod Museum of Natural History or Massachusetts Audubon Society, in text above.

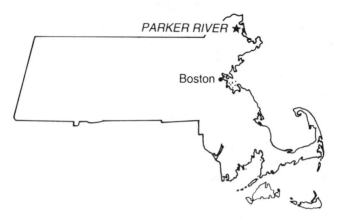

PARKER RIVER (Massachusetts)

The Parker River area is noted for some of the most unusual bird sightings in the country, indeed the world. Ross' gull, one of the world's most rarely seen birds, normally found in Siberia or Alaska and almost never south of the Arctic Circle, was spotted off adjacent Newburyport and attracted worldwide attention and tens of thousands of visitors.

Other rarities have been an ivory gull, black swan (native to Australia), little egret, garganey (a European teal), spotted redshank, and others.

The reason: Parker River is a bird magnet—a barrier island in the Atlantic Ocean where birds passing in migration or blown off course are offered 4,662 acres of diverse and welcoming habitat—coastal shore and dunes, salt marsh, fresh to brackish wetlands and upland growth with dense cover and lushly fruited thickets.

This is why Parker River's bird list tops 300 species—and those that come tend to stay longer than they might otherwise. Delicate warblers (yellow-rumped, pine, prairie) may be feeding all winter on its bayberries while offshore eiders, scoters, oldsquaws, and goldeneyes swim in the icy waters occasionally accompanied by gannets and great cormorants, dovekies, razorbills, and thick-billed murres.

Braving frigid temperatures on the shores and uplands may be a half-dozen snowy owls plus Iceland and glaucous gulls, snow buntings and lapland longspurs, redpolls, purple sandpipers, seaside sparrows and red and white-winged crossbills, and coursing over all these, rough-legged hawks, northern harriers, and occasional peregrine falcons.

There is no season when an interested birder would not find a visit here worthwhile.

Lacy-plumaged snowy egrets journey here in summer. A prime view in early

August is 200 to 300 of them roosting in refuge impoundments, feeding and preening as the sunset, brilliant in the flat coastal terrain, turns their white feathers to rose-crimson.

Shorebirds are on their southerly trek then, peaking in September with hundreds almost covering the shallow marsh ponds (called "pannes")—more than two dozen species, including Hudsonian and marbled godwits, ruffs and stilt, white-rumped and pectoral sandpipers.

Tree swallows gather in flocks of up to 10,000, sometimes covering entire trees with their twittering congregations, taking off suddenly like a great swirling cloud.

Canada geese and a half-dozen ducks nest—blacks, mallards, blue-winged teals, and gadwalls—and in the fall are joined by others until there are up to 5,000 geese—with some snows—and 15,000 ducks. Similar-sized groupings come back through in the spring but they don't linger unless planning to settle down.

Then, six courting mallard drakes may be seen pursuing a single female, pulling tailfeathers from rivals and engaging in aerial acrobatics. (Despite appearances, most are already paired when they arrive, females returning to their home areas to nest while males usually take up a new residence if they have chosen a mate from another area.)

Warblers come through in early May, their numbers varying from year to year but in wide variety—almost every species common in the eastern United States has been seen at Parker River.

Threatened piping plovers scrape out shallow nests on the beach, which is then closed off to human intrusion from April to August.

White-tailed deer are here, as are beavers, otters, and usually several red fox dens—the young, less cautious than their parents, can sometimes be seen mousing on the trails—and for the sharp-eyed, the well-named spadefoot toad, which can burrow ten feet in the ground; this is its northernmost known appearance (or disappearance).

The six-mile ocean beach is open to swimming and picnicking—though the water is so cold that few go in even on warmest days (swim at your own risk; there is a dangerous undertow and no lifeguards).

Plum Island is one of few natural barrier beach-dune complexes with its special life forms left in the northeastern United States, and its popularity and fragile habitat have led to rules limiting use to 360 cars. So best arrive early, even in winter.

How to get there: From Boston follow Route 1 north to I-95; take Newburyport exit to Route 113 east. Follow refuge signs from Route 113.

Open: One-half hour before sunrise to one-half hour after sunset except when closed due to bad weather/road conditions or by 360-car limit. (Entrance fee.)

Best times to visit: Spring and fall.

What to see: Waterfowl groups, migrating shorebirds and tree swallows, occasional rarities (like Ross' gull), peregrine falcons, and ocean sunfish (weighing several hundred pounds, their sharklike fins startling bathers). Several snowy owls on refuge salt marsh along with dovekies and guillemots on winter beach.

What to do: Wildlife viewing from road through refuge, also self-guided nature trails (stay on boardwalk and paths to avoid ticks with possible Lyme disease); observation towers and blind available for photography. Handicapped/wheelchair-accessible boardwalks available at parking lot no. 1; observation deck at beach edge.

Where to stay: Motels—nearest and best are at Amesbury and Ipswich; if necessary try Salisbury, a resort area. Campgrounds—Salisbury Beach State Reservation at nearby Salisbury.

Weather: Cool spring and fall; bitterly cold in winter.

What to take and wear: Windbreaker useful almost anytime. Insect repellent essential in summer. In winter, heavy insulated clothing and boots.

Points of interest nearby: Newburyport, historic clippership port; Crane Nature Reservation, tip of Argilla Road, Ipswich; Maudslay State Park, 12 miles west; Sandy Point State Reservation, adjacent to refuge on south.

For more information: Parker River National Wildlife Refuge, Northern Boulevard, Plum Island, Newburyport, Massachusetts 01950. Phone: (508) 465-5753.

Parker River also administers a satellite refuge, *Thacher Island,* Massachusetts—a rocky 22-acre island off Rockport with nesting gulls. Visits must be arranged through Thacher Island Association, Rockport, Massachusetts.

NINIGRET (Rhode Island and Connecticut)

Ninigret administers a collection of Rhode Island refuges and two in Connecticut that are gems of the national wildlife refuge system. Beautiful and interesting species range from harlequin ducks and yellow-breasted chats to peregrine falcons, foxes, and otters. Ocean views are spectacular. One unit is a former naval base with remnants of runways. Several show that—with proper management—size and previous use of habitat do not necessarily preclude success as a wildlife refuge.

Except for those located offshore, the units generally are within easy driving distance of one another and open from dawn to dusk daily, though some are closed or partly closed April to September to protect nesting of sensitive species. Information follows; detailed information on all can be obtained from Ninigret National Wildlife Refuge, Box 307, Route 1A, Shoreline Plaza, Charlestown, Rhode Island 02813 (office open 8–4:30 weekdays). Phone: (401) 364-9124.

They are:

Ninigret—Thousands of waterfowl come to 1,700-acre Ninigret Pond in fall and many stay the winter because this largest salt pond in Rhode Island with its connection to the ocean stays open year-round. Canvasbacks, buffleheads, red-breasted and common mergansers, and common goldeneyes are all here in good numbers.

Ninigret's brambles are the only known nesting area in Rhode Island for the yellow-breasted chat. Monarch butterflies cluster on trees and shrubs in late September and hawk migration goes on through early October. At peak times sharpshins may be zooming along 20 feet high every three minutes or so. Short-eared owls hunt the salt marsh and dunes. Woodcocks perform nuptial flights, up to 45 at a time, at dusk from March into June. These are particularly visible, along with deer, fox, and coyotes, along the former runways, which date from Ninigret's previous stint as a naval air station and now serve as good mile-long observation paths.

Block Island—These 46 acres of beaches and rolling dunes on part of a former lighthouse station are a place for unusual sightings, especially when a fall storm forces migrants down, sometimes off course. Any of Rhode Island's 325 bird species are possible here, some in unusual gatherings—brown creepers, lark and vesper sparrows, three peregrine falcons in view simultaneously, the full warbler range including prothonotaries and orange-crowns, plus such rarities for the area as a western kingbird. Vegetation is low and open so birds are easy to see.

Winter brings flocks of snow buntings to the dunes; offshore are common and red-throated loons, oldsquaws, harlequin ducks, eiders, scoters, and harbor seals.

Herring and great black-backed gulls nest in the spring (but view from a distance; these strong birds aggressively defend their domestic arrangements). Herons and egrets have a nest colony.

Stay on the paths to protect beach vegetation and also avoid contact with deer ticks.

Pettaquamscutt Cove—Riverine with some upland, salt marsh, and wintering black duck habitat. Land is still being acquired and visitor facilities are largely in the planning stage.

Sachuest Point—Harlequin ducks with their strikingly variegated plumage are a rare spectacular of the bird world, a common sight here from October to mid-April. Sometimes 85 or so will come up on the rocks to ride out a storm, attracting visitors from all over New England to this jagged peninsula jutting out into the Atlantic Ocean where there are marvelous panoramic views.

At least 234 bird species have been recorded on this 242-acre former naval communications station. Huge flocks of 10,000 or more tree swallows appear in September to fatten up on bayberries, along with songbirds of a dozen other species. Merlins, Cooper's, and sharp-shinned hawks and kestrels come through along with flyover flocks of herons and glossy ibis. Late fall brings flocks of black ducks, buffleheads, and red-breasted mergansers along with oldsquaws, loons, all the scoters, and usually a few rare Barrow's among the common goldeneyes. Snowy owls come during winter population peaks of rodents—sometimes three at one time—along with short-eared owls and rough-legged hawks, lapland longspurs, snow buntings, and purple sandpipers along the shore. Red foxes frequently pursue small rodents along the trails—so do weasel and mink—and harbor seals sometimes haul out on the rocks. Passerines start back in March—song sparrows can seem to be in every bush—and shorebirds of a half-dozen species peak here in their northward progress in May. Excellent coastal trails make it easy to see all this.

Salt Meadow—Three miles of self-guided walking trails wind through tidal marsh, woodlands, and open fields on this 187-acre tract near Westbrook, Connecticut, which serves as an important nesting, roosting, feeding, and wintering area for migratory birds as well as many species of waterfowl and shore, wading, and songbirds. A beautiful old stone house dates from 1750 and there is a cabin said to have been built for and used by Eleanor Roosevelt from trees felled in a hurricane. Bluebirds have responded eagerly to a nest box program, as have ospreys to a nest platform in the marsh. Flying squirrels occupy cavities in some of the old trees.

Stewart B. McKinney—Four separate tracts are included along the Connecticut coast—three islands and a six-acre barrier peninsula, Milford Point, which shelters adjacent salt marshes and nesting least terns and piping plovers. Milford Point has a short trail and observation platform. Falkner has nesting common and roseate terns, Chimon nesting glossy ibis, herons, and egrets. These three units are closed April 1 to August 31 to protect nesters. Sheffield Island, partly privately owned with diverse birdlife, is open year-round to boats.

Trustom Pond—This 641-acre refuge surrounds Rhode Island's last undeveloped coastal pond. Its tremendous diversity of habitat attracts some 300 bird species, ranging from endangered piping plovers and woodcock performing acrobatic mating flights to quail, nesting great horned owls, and sometimes snowy owls in winter. Bobolinks and meadowlarks nest in the fields in May. Northern harriers course the lowlands all year, and short-eared owls and rough-legged hawks in fall and winter. Peregrine falcons and merlins go through in migration. Hundreds of waterfowl rest and feed seasonally on the pond and offshore—blacks, greater scaups, goldeneyes, teals, canvasbacks, and gadwalls. White-tailed deer are around the trails at dawn and dusk and there are otters, muskrats, coyotes, and red and gray foxes. Some of the least visible birds of all—endangered piping plovers—attracted national press visibility when they decided to nest on secluded Moonstone Beach, which nude bathers had claimed for their own. But it is on refuge land, and courts ruled that the tiny plovers' nesting privacy takes precedence from April to mid-September— thus benefiting least and common terns, who like it as well.

IROQUOIS (New York)

After the last glacier receded, a huge lake covered what is now Iroquois National Wildlife Refuge. Seneca Indians later settled its higher places; then early settlers tried to drain it all for logging and farming. Luckily that proved too costly.

Now its 10,818 acres of woods and swamps, pastures and wet meadows support a great diversity of year-round wildlife which includes a colony of 700 nesting pairs of great blue herons as well as nesting eagles and deer, and resident foxes and beavers.

Springtime unofficially begins when up to 75,000 Canada geese and 24 species of ducks arrive and create bumper-to-bumper traffic as local residents come to witness the heartening event.

Many of the birds fly farther north but hundreds stay to nest. By May the refuge is awash in downy broods of goslings as well as the offspring of up to ten species of ducks—pintails, shovelers, gadwalls, wigeons, blacks, and especially mallards, blue-winged teals, and wood ducks.

Five hundred nest boxes produce up to 2,500 young of this most dazzling duck species every year, as well as a few hundred handsome hooded mergansers that share the nest boxes. (The two species compete for nest cavities, sometimes laying their eggs in such a disorganized way that mergansers end up with wood duck young and vice versa. One female may find herself trying to incubate 40 eggs of mixed parentage, more than she can handle judging by her distracted behavior after they hatch.)

Birdwatchers flock to Swallow Hollow trail in mid-May for migrating warblers— cerulean, Wilson's, blackpoll, black-and-white, magnolia, chestnut-sided, bay-breasted, and others. Warbling vireos are common, Philadelphia and yellow-throated available for the patient spotter.

Later on, prothonotary warblers find nest holes in flooded timber. Both blue-winged and golden-winged can be seen, along with hybrid Brewster's warblers that occur where these two species' ranges overlap.

Red-headed and pileated woodpeckers hammer out holes in Oak Orchard Creek and adjoining areas that are a National Natural Landmark, a climax virgin forest where hemlocks have trunks four feet in diameter, beeches up to six feet.

Sparrows, including vesper, Henslow's, and grasshopper, may share a single field with several hundred bobolinks.

There are also nesting great horned and barred owls, wood thrushes and rose-breasted grosbeaks, red-tailed and red-shouldered hawks, and woodcock, which put on dramatic courtship flights at dawn and dusk through May.

Grasslands can be pink, white, and gold with wildflowers—over 500 species were tabulated in a recent count—and red, white, and pink trilliums may be seen on hiking trails in spring.

Cauyga Pool overlook is a good place to see floating nests of pied-billed grebes in June, and much else, including common moorhens and the graceful black terns, a threatened species. Canoeists may come across beaver and muskrats, which are regarded as performing useful services here. Beaver dams shore up brood and nest areas for marsh and water birds, thus protecting them in dry times; muskrats clear out cattails, creating nesting openings.

The waterfowl throngs are repeated in fall as they go south for the winter with their young of the year. In the dead of winter snow buntings are here, with redpolls, evening grosbeaks, sometimes hundreds of horned larks, and occasionally a snowy owl.

How to get there: From Buffalo take New York Thruway to Pembroke Exit, then north on Highway 77 to Alabama, New York, then Highway 63 north to Casey Road and headquarters sign.

Open: Daylight hours year-round. Office open 7:30–4 weekdays, open weekends during spring and fall migration.

Best times to visit: Spring and fall for migrants, spring flowers; summer for nesting birds, fawns, waterfowl broods.

What to see: Waterfowl, nesting eagles, warblers, wildflowers.

What to do: Three hiking trails; roads crisscross refuge for viewing from cars; canoeing; cross-country skiing and snowshoeing trails in winter; photography (blinds are available overlooking waterfowl areas; can be reserved ahead).

Where to stay: Motels—in Batavia, 15 miles southeast, and Medina, seven miles north. Campgrounds—in Akron, 15 miles west; Darien, 20 miles south; also Letchworth State Park, 45 miles southeast.

Weather: Winters cold but usually without heavy snow cover.

What to take and wear: Heavy winter clothing; waterproof footgear spring and fall; insect repellent in summer.

Points of interest nearby: Bergan Swamp, 28 miles east—fascinating botanical area, 10,000 acres maintained privately, with dwarf trees, many orchids, including the white lady's slipper, and bog turtle. Letchworth State Park (see campgrounds) has spectacular scenic gorge and waterfalls, fine early October foliage colors. Also Tonawanda and Oak Orchard Wildlife Management Areas adjoining refuge.

For more information: Iroquois National Wildlife Refuge, Box 517, Casey Road, Alabama, New York 14003. Phone: (716) 948-5445.

New York City

LONG ISLAND

LONG ISLAND REFUGE COMPLEX
(New York)

More than a half-dozen national wildlife refuges dot Long Island, harboring creatures ranging from tiny golden-winged warblers to beautiful wood ducks to red foxes, peregrine falcons, and bald eagles.

Their area is small but significant both to the creatures on them and the 12 million people who live within driving distance, for they offer some of the last wild habitat remaining in this densely developed urban area.

On their 6,000-plus acres occur many of the endangered or threatened species in New York and all of the 50 habitat types in the state. Three of the tracts are completely protected; the rest are open to the public and administered from an office at Wertheim Refuge where maps and other information are available. They are:

Amagansett—36 acres of prime bog, dune, and beach habitat near the end of Long Island accommodating Ipswich sparrows, peregrine falcons, and other raptors. This is one of the few remaining undeveloped barrier beaches on Long Island. Public access is limited to the ocean beach between high tide line and the base of the dunes—but good sightings are often available from Atlantic Avenue, especially during migration.

Morton—Chickadees may alight on the shoulders, head, or hand to greet the visitor to this lovely 187-acre peninsular refuge that also has deer, opossums, raccoons, red foxes, and in the spring courting wood cocks that flutter skyward at dusk and dive to a spectacular finish on the ground to attract mates. Orchard orioles and redstarts nest, and artists come to paint and sketch the spectacular views along the bluffs and white sand beach. This former estate was the site of introduction in this area of Bartlett pears, apples, mulberry trees (for silkworm culture), shorthorn cattle, and merino sheep. Now it has nesting ospreys and, common seasonally, double-crested cormorants, green herons, black ducks, red-breasted mergansers, quail, and a variety of shorebirds and passerines. Endangered piping plovers nest and least and roseate terns feed. There is a self-guided trail. The chickadees formed their friendly habits at the encouragement of a former resident and, with handouts from visitors, have continued to make friends ever since.

Oyster Bay—95 percent of this 3,117-acre refuge is tidal bay bottom near the town of Oyster Bay, where sometimes huge rafts of migratory waterfowl (10,000–25,000 scaup) stop in the fall and shore and wading birds in spring. Peregrine falcons whiz by in migration. Bald eagles are around all winter feeding on fish. Limited to viewing from public roads and several public access points, and by boat.

Target Rock—Songbirds abound on this 80-acre former estate named after a huge boulder reputedly used for target practice in the Revolutionary War. Formal gardens now naturalized blaze in spring with hundreds of prize azaleas and rhododendrons. A self-guided trail follows along the shore of Huntington Bay and through woods and thickets where flocks of American redstarts and magnolia warblers sometimes appear, along with yellow and yellowthroat warblers, mockingbirds, catbirds, towhees, cardinals, doves, and kingbirds. It passes alongside a raccoon den tree and near at least one fox den. A fox litter was produced recently within 30 feet of the nature trail, to the delight of photographers. Hundreds of canvasbacks, buffleheads, and, to a lesser extent, eiders appear offshore in fall and winter. Bank swallows occupy a colony on Lloyd's Neck.

An awesome sight here as at Morton refuge sometimes is a school of 200 or 250 bluefish in an attack and killing frenzy, racing up and down offshore, feeding voraciously on smaller fish and driving them up on the beach, where they die by the thousands.

Wertheim—This 2,400-acre refuge on both sides of the Carmans River protects one of the last undeveloped estuaries on Long Island. It is accessible only by canoe but rentals are available nearby, and a trip in spring can be a magical experience, with fluffy young broods of black and wood ducks and Canada goslings, nesting songbirds, bitterns and great blue herons fishing around the edges, red-tailed hawks and ospreys soaring overhead, and deer and fox occasionally coming to peer out at the water's edge. Brown trout, restocked several years ago, now are returning to spawn. And fall finds waterfowl and raptors on the migratory trip south.

Three other refuges with no present public access are *Conscience Point*—60 acres of meadows, woodlands, and brackish marsh near North Sea, Long Island, with deer and migratory waterfowl, planned for environmental studies; *Lido Beach,* 22 acres frequented by wading birds on a barrier island off southwest Long Island; and *Seatuck*, 183 acres with deer, also good resting and nesting areas for least terns and waterfowl as well as songbirds. Operated as a research station.

Information and directions for all the Long Island refuges are available from the Wertheim office.

How to get there: From New York take the Long Island Expressway to Exit 68, then south on the William Floyd Parkway to the fourth traffic light, right or west there on the Montauk Highway to the second traffic light, left there on Smith Road .25 miles to refuge entrance on right.

Open: Refuge areas dawn to dusk; office 8–4:30 weekdays.

Best times to visit: Spring for songbirds, warblers; fall for migratory waterfowl.

What to see: Wide spectrum of passerines, waterfowl, wading birds, raptors.

What to do: Canoeing (rentals available nearby); self-guided trails on some tracts.

What to take and wear: Insect repellent, especially during tick season. Protect against ticks that might carry Lyme disease by tucking pants legs into socks, and wear light-colored clothing so they can be seen.

Where to stay: Motels—at Hauppauge and Medford, 10 miles west, and Riverhead, 20 miles east. Campgrounds—at Wading River, 15 miles north; South Haven County Park; and Greenport, 40 miles east (near Morton).

Points of interest nearby: Fire Island National Seashore, six miles south; Jamaica Bay (part of Gateway National Recreation Area—outstanding bird sanctuary adjacent to JFK International Airport on Long Island's south shore at its western tip).

For more information: Long Island National Wildlife Refuge Complex, P.O. Box 21, Shirley, New York 11967. Phone: (516) 286-0485.

MONTEZUMA (New York)

Ducks and geese numbering in the tens of thousands call stridently to one another as they fly out to the fields and back again to the marsh against a rosy dawn or sunset. It is a heart-stopping spectacular that occurs every day of the spring and fall at this 6,432-acre marsh and upland refuge in north-central New York State.

But there is much else here, too: nesting bald eagles and ospreys; a heronry of more than 120 courting pairs of tall, graceful great blue herons; impressive shorebird migrations; white-tailed deer and warblers throughout the woods.

A look at the map tells why Montezuma entertains some of the greatest concentrations of ducks and geese in the eastern United States—tens of thousands at a time. They follow a watery pathway from their Canadian nesting grounds near James Bay along the St. Lawrence and the Finger Lakes to here.

Their visit is enhanced by recent land-use changes. Larger and larger mechanical corn pickers needed large farm fields so hedgerows were removed. Larger fields made the birds feel more secure—plus the less efficient mechanical picker-heads on combines left behind up to six bushels of grain per acre. The birds quickly realized their improved situation and stayed to enjoy the bounty. Winters here tend to leave fields windswept of fluffy, lake-effect snow so food is available throughout the cold months.

Hence there occurs a pileup of waterfowl, which can add up to peaks in the fall of 150,000 ducks—some of the greatest concentrations anywhere of blacks—and more than 50,000 geese, with many now staying the winter, enjoying the open water or nearby Cayuga Lake. In the spring 100,000 geese, both Canada and snow, may be here, as well as large but dispersed numbers of ducks—seasonal variants because Montezuma is also a staging area where many gather to await the retreat of winter before flying farther north to nest.

Bald eagles have begun nesting again at Montezuma for the first time in more than a quarter century (and at many other places, too) because of a program started here in the 1970s. Young eaglets were brought from precarious wild situations and "hacked out"—raised and released in a way intended to help them live successfully in the wild and "imprint" on this area.

The program was so successful that it has been started elsewhere. Twenty-seven eaglets were "hacked out" here, and the first adult eagle that returned here to nest was a bird "hacked out" in the program.

The nest is in a remote situation but plans call for locating a camera through which television monitors in the visitor center can show the eagles going through their courtship, incubation, and entire nest cycle without disturbance to these still-rare birds.

Ospreys have nested successfully on a platform within easy view of the visitor center deck, another rare sight this far inland, especially since the osprey is threatened in New York State.

And more than 150 pairs of great blue herons court, build nests, incubate, and raise their young in a colony within easy view of an observation tower. After fledging there are sometimes several hundred of these tall slender birds fishing in the shallows and highly visible for photographers and others along the auto tour route.

Shorebirds stop off in impressive numbers in April and May and later in August and September to feed at the 200-acre May's Point Pool, where waters are drawn down to accommodate them on wet mudflats. There may be hundreds of short-billed dowitchers, lesser yellowlegs, and a dozen or so species of plovers and sandpipers.

Most of Montezuma, except for small areas of upland woods and fields, is marsh and swamp. It was not always so. A great wetland area historically stretched twelve miles northward from Cayuga Lake. Early French explorers told of waterfowl so numerous they blackened the sky. It all but disappeared after construction of the New York State Barge Canal in 1911. But droughts of the 1930s and their disastrous effects on waterfowl aroused interest in restoring such areas, and Montezuma Refuge was established in 1937. The name followed that given to the original vast marsh in 1806 by Dr. Peter Clarke after he visited Mexico City.

Mallards, wood ducks, and blue-winged teals nest commonly, along with others that sometimes nest and sometimes move through to other areas—northern pintail, gadwall, American wigeon, northern shoveler, redhead, merganser, and canvasback ducks.

Black-crowned night herons have a colony out of sight in the cattails but they fan out to be seen easily around the dikes. In the uplands in good numbers are nesting veeries, warbling and red-eyed vireos, and cerulean warblers, redstarts, and screech and great horned owls.

Spotted fawns show up in early summer about the same time armadas of downy ducklings and goslings begin bobbing along behind their parents on all the waterways.

Muskrats do their part in refuge maintenance, building domelike houses and keeping cattail areas open and so more readily available for food and cover by water birds.

Carp, some several feet long, mob dam structures by the thousands in spring spawning and later during lower water to seek oxygen, or so it's believed (interesting to see, but their presence in such great numbers is not welcome because their bottom-feeding habits increase water turbidity and temperature, both detrimental to aquatic plants and invertebrates on which young waterfowl feed).

How to get there: From Syracuse take I-90 west to Exit 41, then Route 414 south to Route 318 (at light); then left (east) on 318 until it dead-ends into Route 5/20 (about five miles), then left (east) on 5/20 one mile to refuge entrance (turns are marked by NYS "Trailblazer" signs).

Open: Daily year-round. Office open 7:30–4 weekdays; Visitor Center Tuesday 10–3, weekends 9–5.

Best times to visit: Spring and fall for migrants; shorebirds starting mid-August. Late spring for nesters.

What to see: Large numbers of migrating waterfowl; nesting waterfowl families; ospreys, possibly bald eagles; great blue herons; deer.

What to do: A five-mile self-guided auto tour route and miles of hiking trails that double as snowshoe and cross-country skiing trails in winter; visitor center; photography—good opportunities along auto tour route (visitors are urged to stay in their cars; it causes less disturbance).

Where to stay: Motels—several on Route 5/20 west in Seneca Falls (five miles) and east in Auburn (10 miles). Campgrounds—at Cayuga Lake State Park, Route 89, six miles south near Seneca Falls; also at other state parks in area (complete list available from state park division in Albany).

Weather: Influenced by proximity to Lake Ontario—often cloudy, winters can be quite cold and windy but otherwise few temperature extremes. Snow usually not heavy and trails are kept open to observation tower.

What to take and wear: Spotting scope can be handy.

Points of interest nearby: State parks (see campgrounds above) with impressive limestone formations; Howland's Island Management Area 12 miles northeast, beautiful with diverse birdlife; Cornell University Laboratory of Ornithology with raptor studies and birdwatching in Sapsucker Woods, 40 miles south (in Ithaca); various vineyards and lakes in Finger Lakes area.

For more information: Montezuma National Wildlife Refuge, 3395 Routes 5/20 East, Seneca Falls, New York 13148-9778. Phone: (315) 568-5987.

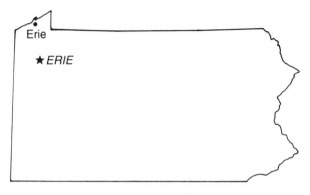

Erie

★ ERIE

ERIE (Pennsylvania)

A rich diversity of both flora and fauna characterizes this 8,516-acre refuge, located in Pennsylvania's northwestern corner.

Beavers building lodges and dams create ponds frequented by waterfowl and other water birds and do not seem to mind being observed dawn and dusk by the careful, quiet visitor. Deer are everywhere in the woods and fields winter and summer and can be seen with their dappled fawns starting in May.

A pair of eagles has been nesting in recent years in the top of a white pine. A nest-box program provides homes which are happily accepted by hundreds of beautiful wood ducks and bluebirds, whose offspring fledge and can be seen about with their parents starting in early summer.

And there is a succession of spring beauties, dwarf ginseng, trout lilies, wood anemones, trilliums, and other wildflowers blooming from April through June.

Erie is divided into two separate units, each supporting a distinct ecological population. The Seneca division is a hemlock swamp that has had little human management. Portions are designated as permanent natural areas. There are stands of huge old sugar maples. Through this division go a series of beaver flowages. Five species of wild orchids and numbers of ferns—cinnamon, hay-scented, sensitive, Christmas, and royal, among others—grow along a wandering stream. Hooded and mourning warblers nest among clumps of blackberry canes that have grown up in old logged-over areas.

The Sugar Lake division has additional ponds and uplands. Waterfowl can be seen in spring and fall migration, peaking in mid-April and late October, and great blue herons from the several small colonies on the refuge fish from the edges and bring their young families. Canada geese, whose resident population swells from 700 to 1,000 in the spring, parade and swim by with their downy young bobbing along after them.

Ruby-throated hummingbirds nest in wood patches on both divisions and their display can be seen by a delighted birder. The male flies up and then swings down in an arc close to earth and up again, almost as if on a pendulum, enhancing the display of his glittering crimson and green plumage, squawking to draw the female's attention to his performance. (This display is easier to see than the tiny nests constructed of spider webs and bits of lichen.)

Barred and great horned owls are common and can occasionally be spotted in daytime on shadowed tree branches. Screech owls take up residence in wood duck houses and often peer out in late afternoon.

Bobolinks, scarlet tanagers, and indigo buntings are common nesters, as are black-billed cuckoos, killdeer, ruffed grouse, red-eyed and warbling vireos, and blue-winged and black-throated green warblers. There are some wild turkeys, too, and the knowledgeable birder might spot a Henslow's sparrow. Red-tailed hawks are always around and frequently such other raptors as northern harriers and Cooper's, sharp-shinned, red-shouldered, and broad-winged hawks, which also nest. Short-eared owls hunt the fields spring and fall.

Most years there are several fox dens where young pups venture out early and late to play. Ask staff at the refuge office.

Two walking trails double as snowshoe and ski trails in winter. Sometimes a sparkling dry snow falls while the sun shines, and a hardy naturalist could be rewarded with such rare cold-season specialties as crossbills, pine grosbeaks, and occasional snow buntings.

How to get there: From Franklin take Route 8 north to Route 322; west on 322 about 14 miles to Route 173; north on 173 to Route 27; east on 27 to McFadden Road (dirt); north there to Route 198; west on 198 to refuge headquarters.

Open: Sunrise to sunset daily; office 8–4:30 weekdays.

Best times to visit: Spring and fall.

What to see: Deer; beavers; eagles; great blue herons; red-tailed hawks; waterfowl.

What to do: Nature trails, both auto and hiking; in winter, cross-country skiing; photography (blind available).

Where to stay: Motels—in Meadville, 10 miles west, and Titusville, 16 miles east. Campgrounds—six miles west toward Meadville, with swimming and recreational facilities.

Weather: Cold winters, sometimes with alternate freeze-thaw, drifting and blowing snow; also damp spells in April and August. Check with refuge office staff on road and trail conditions.

What to take and wear: Wet-weather gear, especially footwear, in spring.

Points of interest nearby: Allegheny National Forest, 40 miles east; Oil Creek State Park, 16 miles east; also Titusville, 16 miles east, site of first producing oil well in the United States, with museum and nearby Pithole, old oil boomtown.

For more information: Erie National Wildlife Refuge, R.D. 1, Wood Duck Lane, Guys Mills, Pennsylvania 16327. Phone: (814) 789-3585.

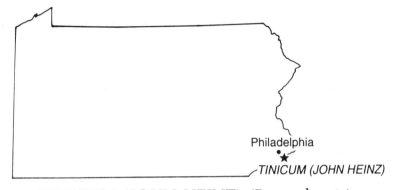

TINICUM (JOHN HEINZ) (Pennsylvania)

Wild rice grows and green-backed herons nest, short-eared owls hunt and white-tailed deer browse on this refuge surrounded by super-highways, oil storage tanks, and dense housing development all located within a mile of Philadelphia's International airport.

It is a near-miracle that it became a refuge at all. Donated originally in the 1950s by the Gulf Oil Company to the city of Philadelphia and maintained as a public park, it became in effect the largest city-owned wildlife refuge in the United States (then 145 acres, expected eventually to be 1,250 acres). But urban financial problems and development changes threatened its continuation.

Then citizens' groups rallied to its suport and in 1972 Congress authorized its transfer to the Fish and Wildlife Service.

Its designation as a national wildlife environmental center reflects its function in educational work with schools and nature groups. Hundreds of teachers have grad-uated from its environmental education workshops and brought their students back later.

And ducks, Canada geese, Carolina wrens, and mockingbirds find inviting shrubs and wetland where once were sidewalks, spoil dumps, and landfill (the wetlands recharge underground aquifers as well and so cleanse water supplies for surrounding areas).

Brilliant indigo buntings are common nesters as are northern orioles, warbling and white-eyed vireos, marsh wrens, and ring-necked pheasants, whose raucous cackling at all seasons almost drowns out the jetliners overhead.

Male woodcocks fly up in dramatic courtship display at field edges at dusk in mid-March.

Warblers of two dozen species go through in May—parulas, blackburnians, bay-breasted, Cape May—and yellowthroats and sometimes redstarts stay to raise families.

Hundreds of tree swallows as well as colorful wood ducks return to refuge nest boxes while egrets and herons decide on a new place for their heronry each year (away from a watchful pair of great horned owls).

Tiny fearless saw-whet owls sometimes stand their ground within arm's length of a visitor, perching where trolleys once ran.

Shorebirds migrate through in August—ruffs and Hudsonian godwits as well as thousands of more usual types—and hawks a little later, kettles of broadwings, and the occasional eagle. The mothlike flight of the northern harrier is over the marsh all year.

Red foxes pursue meadow voles. Endangered red-bellied turtles bask on logs. Bitterns stand like statues in the reeds.

All this—the existence of tens of thousands of wild creatures—because concerned citizens cared and acted.

How to get there: From Philadelphia International Airport take Route 291 east, left on Island Avenue, left at next light on Bartram Avenue and follow signs.

Open: Daylight hours all year. Office 8–4 weekdays.

Best times to visit: Spring and fall.

What to see: Excellent variety of birds.

What to do: Eight miles of trails; boardwalk; observation platform; photo blinds. Spring evening walk for night-calling frogs, owls.

Where to stay: Motels—many near airport. Campgrounds—closest are in New Jersey Pine Barrens, 25 miles east.

Weather: Winters can be windy and cold.

What to take and wear: Waterproof footgear on trails during wet springtimes.

Points of interest nearby: Many Philadelphia historical sites; Tyler Arboretum and Ridely Creek State Park, 10 miles northwest; New Jersey Pine Barrens, 25 miles east.

For more information: Tinicum (John Heinz) National Wildlife Refuge, Suite 104, Scott Plaza 2, Philadelphia, Pennsylvania 19113. Phone: (215) 521-0662.

Tinicum also administers *Supawna Meadows,* a tidal marsh and waterfowl nesting area three miles northwest of Salem, New Jersey, closed except for historic lighthouse tours and by special permission for birding.

BRIGANTINE/
FORSYTHE

Atlantic City

BRIGANTINE/FORSYTHE (New Jersey)

These thirty-six thousand acres of coastal marsh are a birder's dream. Probably there is no place—certainly no place on the Northeast and mid-Atlantic coast—where birders can find such large numbers, variety, and the occasional rarity. And what is here is unusually accessible, from a wildlife drive on top of a dike that divides salt marsh from freshwater impoundments.

October can bring a peak of more than 150,000 waterfowl of two dozen or so species, which may linger into midwinter depending on freeze-up in the coastal bays.

None are more spectacular than the snow geese, which can seem to fill the air with their cries. Thousands fly in at a height of less than 50 feet against a crimson sunset, returning from feeding in the marshes to spend the night in the pools. Their white bodies nearly cover the water.

More than 80,000 brant may come in—20 percent of the Atlantic population of this small dark goose that leads such a precarious existence, nesting in a small area north of the Arctic Circle. Their diet is so limited they nearly became extinct during an eelgrass blight in the 1930s. (Luckily eelgrass does well here now.)

Ducks will include pintails, gadwalls, American wigeons, blue- and green-winged teals, shovelers, and ruddy and black ducks, which also nest here. Among all these one may find a rare Eurasian wigeon, a ruff, or a Ross' or barnacled goose.

Endangered peregrine falcons are around most of the year. Two pairs that nest on the refuge usually bring off several youngsters each from nesting towers constructed for the peregrine, and others appear to hunt, sometimes thrilling a lucky observer with a lightning stoop on a migrating duck or a threatening dive on a marsh harrier invading its territory. Fierce great horned owls sometimes prey on the peregrines at night.

Beautiful tall wading birds can be found almost anywhere along the water's edge—great blues most of the year and little blue herons, snowy and great egrets, tricolored and black-crowned night herons, and, less obviously, American bitterns from April to October. In May and June glossy ibises are everywhere—hundreds of them, offering an unusual opportunity to see this retiring, darkly iridescent species.

The clattering call of the clapper rail is commonly heard even when the bird itself is too shy to be seen. Ospreys are here from March to November and an occasional bald eagle comes by in winter.

Warblers and songbirds make an appearance around upland walking trails about the same time horseshoe crabs show up on the beach to mate and lay their eggs. This coincides with the full moon and the highest tides of May—a phenomenon that attracts ruddy turnstones, dunlins, and other shorebirds by the thousands to fatten up on the eggs for their continuing journey northward to nesting grounds.

Sharp-tailed, seaside, and some grasshopper sparrows stay to nest, as do Forster's, least, and gull-billed terns. Canada geese bring downy broods to pose for photographers on the dikes.

The wetland habitat does not support a large mammal population but some— raccoons, skunks, weasels, muskrats, foxes (both red and gray), and otters—dwell here. One of the best ways to see otters playing—which is what they mostly do— as well as red foxes hunting is to wait and watch early at the northwest corner of the wildlife drive.

The beautiful rare Pine Barrens tree frog, bright green with plum body stripes, lives on a bog recently added to the refuge.

The refuge includes 6,000 acres of wilderness with such nowadays-rare features as several thousand acres of pristine salt marsh (accessible by small boat only), offering fascinating views of estuaries and salt marsh; and the undeveloped coastal barrier beaches of Holgate Unit and Little Beach Island, New Jersey's only offshore island not accessible by road. Here one finds plants rare elsewhere—state-endangered sea purslanes, sea beach sandworts, and literally millions of endangered seaside plantains; also the threatened piping plover as well as colonies of black skimmers and least terns. To protect them both the Holgate Unit and Little Beach Island are closed to public use during nesting, and the fragile dune area is closed all year.

The Barnegat Unit, more than 14,000 acres of salt marsh habitat, is accessible by boat or by viewing from several adjacent roads; otherwise it has no public use facilities.

How to get there: From Absecon, take Route 9 north about 4.5 miles to Great Creek Road in Oceanville. Turn right there to refuge office. (The Intracoastal Waterway bisects the refuge and boat landings are nearby.)

Open: Sunrise to sunset. Office 8–4 weekdays, volunteers available for information on busy fall and spring weekends. Entrance fee.

Best times to visit: Spring and fall.

What to see: Great numbers and variety of bird species.

What to do: Two self-guided walking trails; eight-mile wildlife drive surrounded by salt marsh with great diversity of birds from both fresh and salt estuary habitat in view simultaneously; observation towers; limited small boat launch facility at Scott's Landing.

Where to stay: Motels—on Route 9 and 30, around Absecon. Campgrounds—at Wharton State Forest and Bass River State Forest, adjacent to refuge on north.

Weather: Variable all year—come prepared for possibility of change. Winter ice can close wildlife drive—best call ahead.

What to take and wear: Insect repellent in summer. Sturdy waterproof footgear a good idea on the trails. A warm jacket November through March.

Points of interest nearby: Wharton State Forest (see campgrounds)—part of interesting Pine Barrens. Cape May Bird Observatory. Stone Harbor near Cape May worth a visit for its fascinating heronry, located right in the center of town.

For more information: Brigantine/Forsythe National Wildlife Refuge, P.O. Box 72, Oceanville, New Jersey 08231. Phone: (609) 652-1665.

CAPE MAY ⭑ 🦀 Atlantic City

CAPE MAY (New Jersey)

Millions of shorebirds, tens of thousands of raptors, and many thousands of warblers and other songbirds (including sometimes up to 100,000 tree swallows) stop down at this New Jersey coastal refuge, which is so new that visitor facilities are still in the formative stage.

The northward migration of shorebirds fattening up here en route to breeding grounds is one of nature's most impressive phenomena. Huge numbers of the little birds—including up to 200,000 red knots (80 percent of the Western Hemisphere population), 10,000 short-billed dowitchers, and half of the Atlantic sanderlings and North American ruddy turnstones—visit the Delaware Bay shore just as horseshoe crabs come ashore in spring to mate and lay eggs above the high-tide line as they have for perhaps 500 million years. Then one can hardly see the sandy beach for the constantly moving carpet of horseshoe crabs and birds. In some areas as many as 100,000 crabs nest in each kilometer.

The little birds rush greedily to gobble up the eggs—enough to increase body fat by 40–50 percent to ensure nesting in the far north, but not enough to endanger the next generation of horseshoe crabs.

Cape May is the first national wildlife refuge taking as a major objective the welfare of warblers and songbirds whose populations have been jeopardized by the destruction of the neotropical forests where the birds winter and the fragmentation of northern forests where they nest. Some 100 species of songbirds, including many threatened or declining, use the refuge, primarily its woodlands, as either a migratory stopover or nesting spot.

The Cape May area sees the greatest concentrations of raptors in the U.S. in fall migration. Hesitant to cross large stretches of open water, they use the bayshore upland edge as a migration corridor. An observer at Cape May Point on an exceptional day might see over 100 peregrine falcons, 200 ospreys, 150 northern harriers, and 7,000 American kestrels all in one October day. Through an entire season over 40,000 sharp-shinned hawks pass over the peninsula. Owls winter in the woodlands. Woodcocks concentrate in moist thickets in fall migration and perform courtship flights in spring.

River otters, white-tailed deer, endangered tiger salamanders, and Pine Barrens tree frogs are found here, as well as endangered plants like the lovely swamp pink, and large areas of undisturbed Atlantic white cedar, towering bog-associated trees that can have canopies 20 yards across.

The importance of this refuge is undeniable: without it—if housing and commerical development were allowed to take over these areas on which so many species have relied for food and rest on their long ancestral migration routes (as well as for nesting)—many would no longer be able to survive at all.

Public use has been in the planning stage. For further information contact Cape May National Wildlife Refuge, c/o Brigantine/Forsythe National Wildlife Refuge, P.O. Box 72, Oceanville, New Jersey 08231. Phone: (609) 652-1665.

GREAT SWAMP (New Jersey)

❋

The Great Swamp, where beautiful wood ducks, white-tailed deer, foxes, owls, and a profusion of warblers find homes almost within sight of New York City, was bought from the Delaware Indians in 1708 for a collection of blankets, kettles, whiskey, and 30 English pounds.

It was repurchased in 1960 for more than one million dollars by some 6,000 private citizens and 462 organizations so it could become a national wildlife refuge instead of a proposed metropolitan jetport.

Now it covers some 7,000-plus acres of wooded swamps, freshwater marshes, bogs, and uplands that support a wonderful diversity of wildlife.

Wood ducks, often described as our most beautiful waterfowl, produce more than 2,500 ducklings every year in nest boxes and natural cavities. They are easily seen in the pothole ponds along Pleasant Plains road where refuge headquarters is located, as well as from observation and photography blinds on the trails and impoundments.

So are white-tailed deer, especially at early morning and dusk. Muskrats build winter lodges in the fall and contend among the males for mates in the spring. Raccoon, fox, mink, and occasional otter tracks are seen along the waterways. Several years ago a black bear was sighted.

Bluebirds used to be rare here. Now, with 120 nest boxes producing families, they are a common sight.

Spring warbler migration brings birders from around the state. Twenty-nine species may be spotted coming through, and the prothonotary, blue-winged, chestnut-sided, and several others nest.

The bird list includes more than 220 species. Common or abundant are green-backed and great blue herons (which nest in good numbers), woodcock (their spring courtship flights visible from old refuge headquarters), kestrels, killdeer, Virginia and sora rails, and barred and great horned owls, which can be seen along the auto tour route. American bitterns are usually around.

Canada geese nest and parade their young, as do mallards and black ducks, the latter hard to see.

Small birds seasonally common or abundant include hermit, Swainson's, and wood thrushes, rose-breasted grosbeaks, scarlet tanagers, kingfishers, marsh wrens, willow and great crested flycatchers, and downy and hairy woodpeckers. Pileated wood-peckers nest occasionally, as do Acadian and least flycatchers.

Visitors can see much of this rich variety from the auto drive and hiking trails, especially those into the wilderness area that makes up about half of the refuge and was the first tract so designated in the national wildlife refuge system.

Though the refuge is surrounded by development, it is possible to get lost in this wild place full of bogs and great oaks and beeches with trunks up to four feet in diameter. The rare blue-spotted salamander and bog turtle live here, along with a fascinating array of botanical species—ferns and mosses, wild lilies and orchids, and, in the upland portions, gentians, primroses, marigolds, and spring beauties. The refuge has excellent lists of all these, plus the various mammal, reptile, fish, and amphibian residents. (Access is limited to the 90 cars that can fit into the parking areas so plan to go early, especially in fine weather.)

The refuge is on the edge of a raptor migration path along the Kittatinny Mountains and gets interesting drop-ins during the fall of northern harriers, occasionally a goshawk, peregrine falcon, or rough-legged hawk, and kettles of Cooper's and sharp-shinned hawks overhead. Red-tails and kestrels are around most of the year.

The New Jersey Audubon Society often schedules environmental awareness field trips under permit from the refuge, including evening frog and owl walks in the spring.

Idyllic as it seems, the Great Swamp is now almost completely surrounded by housing and other development and is increasingly troubled by encroachment from civilization. Located at the bottom of a 55-square-mile watershed, it receives storm water runoff. As the watershed becomes more developed, flooding in the Great Swamp becomes more frequent and severe. This runoff often carries pollutants and sediments. Sometimes the county road through the swamp is bumper-to-bumper, not with refuge visitors but commuters who speed when they can. One hazardous waste superfund site has been found, and there is another potential one—and other problems too numerous to mention here. The Great Swamp has been listed as one of our ten most endangered refuges by The Wilderness Society.

How to get there: From New York City take the Lincoln Tunnel to New Jersey Turnpike, then Exit 14 to I-78 West to I-287 North. Take Exit 26 at Basking Ridge onto North Maple Avenue, left at light on Madisonville Road, which becomes Lee's Hill Road. Continue on it, turn right on Long Hill Road, right on White Bridge Road, right on Pleasant Plains Road to headquarters.

Open: Wilderness observation and wilderness areas, dawn to dusk. Pleasant Plains Road, 8 a.m. to dusk. Headquarters 8–4:30 weekdays, and Sundays spring and fall (call ahead for hours).

Best times to visit: Mid-March to May for spring plumage, migrations, more visible behavior patterns; September to mid-November, fall colors and migrations.

What to do: Boardwalk, eight miles of marked hiking trails, 1.5-mile auto tour route (please stay in car to avoid wildlife disturbance), observation platforms and blinds for photography and watching, most of these wheelchair accessible.

Where to stay: Motels—in Bernardsville, three miles northwest; Morris Plains, 10 miles north; Somerville, 20 miles west. Campgrounds—Mahlon Dickinson Reservation, 35 miles north.

Weather: March-April and August can be wet.

What to take and wear: Waterproof footgear for off-boardwalk hiking, especially in wilderness area (compass handy there, too). Insect repellent all year, especially for ticks, which can appear even on warm winter days (and may carry Lyme disease).

Points of interest nearby: New Jersey Audubon Scherman Wildlife Sanctuary, four miles northwest; Morristown National Historical Park (Revolutionary War encampment) three miles north; Somerset County Environmental Center, office one mile west; Morris County Outdoor Education Center, office five miles northeast.

For more information: Great Swamp National Wildlife Refuge, R.D. 1, Box 152, Basking Ridge, New Jersey 07920. Phone: (201) 425-1222.

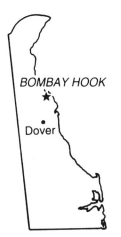

BOMBAY HOOK
★
Dover

BOMBAY HOOK (Delaware)

W hen the greater snow geese arrive at Bombay Hook from their nesting grounds in the high Arctic tundra, the sight is so overwhelming it has been likened to a waterfowl equivalent of the wildebeest hordes on Africa's Serengeti Plain.

Up to 75,000 of the glistening white birds, more than at any other refuge, gather to spend the fall and most of them the winter as well on these 15,122 acres of tidal marsh, fields, and water impoundments. They can seem to cover the water like a blanket of snow; when they rise all at once their high nasal calls and the whirring of their black-tipped wings fill the air and the effect is unforgettable.

The Canada geese present a different and no less wondrous sight as wave after wave of them, some 30,000 starting in early October, come into the marsh at dusk, their V-flight patterns and honking seeming to be everywhere overhead. Then, as if by signal, they will "whiffle" their wings and drop like falling leaves over the waving grass and simply disappear from view. The tall Spartina alterniflora appears exactly as it did before the geese came into view. It is like a fascinating optical trick.

This goes on until dark, when not even the marsh can be seen—and sometimes long afterward, for the geese here, as in some other places, have learned under hunting pressure to feed at night by moonlight. (They have also learned, it is reliably said, how to tell the exact hour when a field is opened to hunting; when a blind is safe to approach; and what is prudent height when flying a hazardous area. No one who has watched Canada geese long underestimates their intelligence.)

Ducks are abundant here, too, for while their numbers have dropped nationwide the habitat here has become more welcoming through the management of wetlands

65

and resulting increase in wild food plants. There are up to 30,000 pintails, green-winged teals, wigeons, shovelers, blacks, gadwalls, wood ducks, and blue-winged teals, many of which nest here also.

But waterfowl are not the only species here. Shorebird migrations can be spectacular spring and fall but especially in May. Then millions of horseshoe crabs (renowned for their blue blood and ancient lineage) crawl up on the tidal shores to lay their eggs, which the birds devour to fatten up for their further migration north. There may be tens of thousands of red knots, ruddy turnstones, semi-palmated sandpipers, and black-bellied plovers. They are best seen at half tide from a boat—preferably a shallow-draft jonboat. But the dikes also make a good vantage point, especially during the fall stopover when one may see, for example, a flock of 250 avocets (the late summer and fall shorebird migration here is as good as anywhere in the East).

Bald eagles nest successfully in most years and are often visible soaring or fishing around tidal flats.

Notable among the small birds are usually nesting prothonotary warblers, orchard orioles, grasshopper sparrows, and Louisiana waterthrush, and commonly nesting scarlet tanagers, blue grosbeaks, sharp-tailed and seaside sparrows, and Kentucky warblers. Common among larger varieties are nesting black-necked stilts, barred owls, pheasants, and bobwhite quail.

Diamondback terrapins, once close to extinction but now regular visitors, dig holes and deposit their eggs in July, often right alongside the dikes.

White-tailed deer appear with fawns in June, and there are foxes, muskrats, beavers, and a few otters to be seen by the careful observer.

How to get there: From Dover take Route 13 north to Route 42, then east to Leipsic and north on Route 9 to refuge sign (about two miles), then east on Route 85 to refuge.

Open: Sunrise to sunset. Refuge office 7:30–4; Visitor Center 7:30–4:30 Tuesday-Friday, 9–5 weekends spring and fall. Entrance fee.

Best times to visit: All year interesting—summer less comfortable, with biting insects. Peak waterfowl concentrations October-November.

What to see: Waterfowl and shorebirds can be spectacular; otherwise good general variety.

What to do: 12-mile auto-tour route; hiking trails; observation towers; visitor center; Allee House (handsome restored old farmhouse, open on weekend afternoons).

Where to stay: Motels—at Dover, 10 miles south. Campgrounds—Killens Pond State Park, 20 miles south; also Blackbird State Forest, 20 miles north.

Weather: Midwinter subject to brief snowy periods when roads may become impassable.

What to take and wear: Insect repellent (a must in summer).

Points of interest nearby: Two state wildlife management areas border the refuge, Woodland Beach to the north and Little Creek to the south. Prime Hook National Wildlife Refuge, 44 miles south. Island Field archeological dig, a substantial Indian excavation, open to visitors, 20 miles south. John Dickinson mansion, historic home, 14 miles south.

For more information: Bombay Hook National Wildlife Refuge, R.D. 1, Box 147, Smyrna, Delaware 19977. Phone: (302) 653-9345. Visitor Center phone: (302) 653-6872.

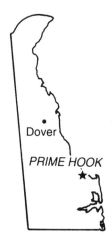

Dover

PRIME HOOK

PRIME HOOK (Delaware)

The best way to see this refuge on the eastern shore of Delaware is by canoe—about 70 percent of its 8,818 acres is either marsh or open water.

But there are foot trails, too, and roads from which visitors can catch glimpses of some of the spectacular natural occurrences at Prime Hook, when huge numbers of snow geese congregate in fall and shorebirds in spring sometimes cover the beach like a moving carpet.

The great white geese that nest in the high Arctic tundra start arriving in October and sometimes peak at 60,000 by the end of the year, literally covering the water impoundments. With them may be up to 27,000 ducks that have settled in by November—and 5,000 Canada geese, somewhat less than formerly since many of this species have chosen to winter farther north in recent years.

The spring spectacular coincides with the new moon in late May or early June, when the highest tides of the year occur and horseshoe crabs crawl up on shore in tremendous numbers to mate and lay their eggs where they will not wash away before hatching. They lay literally millions of eggs, enough to ensure survival of their species as well as that of tens of thousands of shorebirds—dunlins, red knots, sanderlings, ruddy turnstones, and small peeps that arrive at the same time to eat their share. Theirs is an urgent need also. Without this protein feast they might not be able to complete long migration flights to nest in the far north.

Others also arrive with nesting in mind, and many stay. Prothonotary warblers are abundant along Prime Hook Creek. Ducks go through courtship rituals of wing-fluttering and head-bobbing. These are blue-winged teals, gadwalls, mallards, and blacks; wood ducks have their choice of 300 nest boxes.

Chuck-will's-widows are here. And there are nesting black-necked stilts, scarlet tanagers, red- and white-eyed vireos, marsh wrens, yellow-billed cuckoos, sharp-tailed and seaside sparrows, northern harriers, both barred and great horned owls, and ruby-throated hummingbirds.

Canoe trails wind some 15 miles through woods and wetlands along which otters, muskrats (there are several thousand muskrat houses), bitterns, and great blue and green herons flourish, along with flowering mallows, water lilies, sweet pepperbushes, highbush blueberries, and the rare seaside alders. Pitcher plants glorify moist spots. It is a thoroughly delightful trip.

The upland trails offer sights to the quiet visitor of deer, red and gray foxes, pheasant and quail, and the rare Delmarva fox squirrel; and some visitors enjoy winter, when it's easier to see a playful otter leaping out of a breathing hole to slide and frolic on the ice, and a walk on the beach can provide offshore views of scoters, eiders, and oldsquaws.

How to get there: From Rehoboth follow Route 1 north about 12 miles, then east on Route 16 to first blacktop to the left; follow this and signs to refuge office.

Open: Dawn to dusk. Office open 7:30–4 weekdays.

Best times to visit: Spring and fall.

What to see: Prothonotary warblers; songbirds; shorebirds; waterfowl; occasional otters, deer, foxes.

What to do: Three foot trails, also good viewing from several public roads; canoeing by permission (canoe rentals at junction of Routes 1 and 5 on western edge of refuge); photography (blinds on reservation on first-come basis according to demand).

Where to stay: Motels—several on Route 1 south of refuge. Campgrounds—Cape Henlopen State Park, nine miles south, April-November; several private grounds about nine miles south and southwest.

Weather: Summers hot and humid.

What to take and wear: Waterproof footgear for hiking; insect repellent in summer.

Points of interest nearby: Cape Henlopen State Park (see *Where to stay*)—good birding, especially shorebirds after strong easterly winds; Lewes Beach, good for family outings; Delaware Seashore State Park from Rehoboth to Bethany, beautiful dune area; Bombay Hook National Wildlife Refuge, 40 miles northeast.

For more information: Prime Hook National Wildlife Refuge, R.D. 3, Box 195, Milton, Delaware 19968. Phone: (302) 684-8419.

OHIO RIVER
ISLANDS

Parkersburg

OHIO RIVER ISLANDS (West Virginia)

A new and diverse refuge has been established on this chain of more than a dozen islands that stretch for more than 300 miles along the Ohio River, from Manchester, Ohio, to Shippingport, Pennsylvania. Once surveyed by George Washington, they were on a major east-west route used by pioneers, and Native Americans camped on them.

Some still contain virgin sycamore and silver maple woods. Songbirds use them as a migration corridor in spring. Deer and beavers find quiet homes on them along with minks, muskrats, opossums, wood ducks and other waterfowl, and dozens of rare plants. In the waters around them are 55 fish species, many of which spawn, and the endangered pink mucket mussel. One nesting colony has 70 pairs of great blue herons. Spotted sandpipers and large flocks of semipalmated plovers visit the shores.

Without protection these remarkable islands had been losing wildlife and habitat, and some had disappeared entirely due to erosion from dredging and other abusive uses.

Ohio River Islands eventually may include all or a portion of 38 islands stretching over 362 water miles, along with nearby embayments and wetlands along riverbanks. For now, visitor facilities such as trails are still in the planning stage. For the latest information contact Ohio River Islands National Wildlife Refuge, P.O. Box 1811, Parkersburg, West Virginia 26102. Phone: (304) 420-7586.

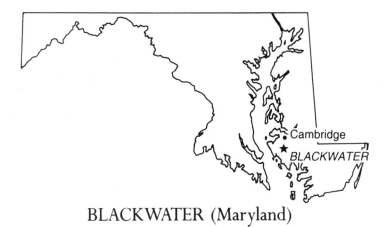

BLACKWATER (Maryland)

At least three endangered species and perhaps a fourth may well have shared a single tree in a remote part of this 16,667-acre refuge on the Eastern Shore of Maryland. It is the center of the largest nesting concentration of southern bald eagles along the East Coast north of Florida—usually 60 or so year-round of which a half-dozen or so bring off successful nests. There is also a sizable remnant population of the handsome Delmarva fox squirrel, readily seen and easily recognizable by its bushy, heavily furred tail, thick, light gray coat, and large size—at least twice that of its darker gray cousin.

But ducks and geese are the prime sight on this refuge, more than 70 percent water and marsh with 3,500 acres of mixed hardwood and pine woods. In mid-November up to 35,000 Canadas and 15,000 ducks may be here, including mallards, black ducks, gadwalls, pintails, green- and blue-winged teals, wigeons, shovelers, and mergansers. In winter peregrine falcons appear to take advantage of the good hunting. Both the five-mile auto-tour route and the fields next to refuge headquarters offer excellent vantage points for photographers—the tour route for sunset shots of flying waterfowl, the fields for geese (mostly Canadas but also snows) by the hundreds, sometimes thousands. (But don't try hunting season when there's a full moon; the wary, intelligent birds have learned to feed by night in order to avoid hunters in surrounding fields on private land, making them understandably inactive in daylight hours.)

Visitors can see the most wildlife if they go early and take their time—not only for eagles but also for red foxes, opossums, skunks, sometimes otters, and deer, both white-tailed and sika. The sika deer is a small Asiatic species, actually an elk, which was released on James Island in Chesapeake Bay about 1916, swam here, and prospered.

Nutrias, marsh-dwelling rodents native to South America unrelated to the beaver

71

but much like it in appearance, can also be sighted here. They were released in the southern United States in the 1930s and spread widely. This is the northern edge of their range—they literally freeze their tails off when it gets too cold, and older animals can be recognized in this way. The female mammary glands are so high on their sides that when the young ride on their mother's back they nurse while she swims along.

Most of the refuge wildlife can be seen at one time or another from the auto-tour route: pied-billed grebes, seven kinds of herons, ospreys, tundra swans, northern harriers, shorebirds, and quail, though the appearance of a visitor may cause a covey of these timid birds to disappear in an explosion of feathers. Visitors are asked to stay in their cars to lessen disturbance and maximize viewing for all.

Smaller birds are best seen from the walking trails: blue grosbeaks and indigo buntings, orchard orioles, and yellow-breasted chats, all of which are here in good numbers in season, along with some brownheaded nuthatches, Acadian flycatchers, and eight kinds of sparrows that nest here. The refuge also has an active nest box program that accommodates species ranging from wood ducks to bluebirds. The latter fledge more than 100 young a year and can be seen year-round.

How to get there: From Washington, D.C., take the Chesapeake Bay Bridge, then south on Route 50 to Route 16 (one mile beyond Cambridge), right or south onto 16 for six miles to the town of Church Creek, then left or south onto Route 335 for five miles and left onto Key Wallace Drive at the refuge.

Open: Wildlife drive open daily dawn to dusk, Visitor Center 8–4 weekdays, weekends 9–5 Labor Day through Memorial Day. Entrance fee.

Best times to visit: Mid-October through January.

What to see: Eagles; deer; Delmarva fox squirrels; waterfowl concentrations.

What to do: Auto and hiking trails; photography (no blinds but good opportunities).

Where to stay: Motels—in Cambridge, 12 miles north, and Easton, 27 miles north. Campgrounds—at Madison and Taylor's Island, 8 and 20 miles northwest on Route 16.

Points of interest nearby: Old Trinity Church, three miles west of Church Creek, active continuously since Revolutionary War, beautifully restored and maintained. Hooper Island, 25 miles southwest—interesting isolated fishing community with many migrating flickers, sharp-shinned hawks, harriers, and kestrels in September-October. But take a picnic—there's no restaurant.

For more information: Blackwater National Wildlife Refuge, 2145 Key Wallace Drive, Cambridge, Maryland 21613. Phone: (410) 228-2692.

Blackwater also administers two satellite refuges: *Martin Refuge,* a salt marsh island in Chesapeake Bay with habitat for ducks and wading birds; and *Susquehanna,* a one-acre island in the Susquehanna flats near Havre de Grace, formerly prime habitat for canvasbacks and redheads but altered by river damming and other factors. Both are remote and visitors are not permitted.

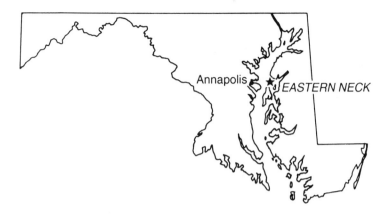

Annapolis

EASTERN NECK

EASTERN NECK (Maryland)

The essence of this 2,286-acre island refuge bordered by Chesapeake Bay and the Chester River is quickly discoverd by walking a short way out on the boardwalk into the marsh at Tubby's Cove, shortly to the right after crossing the old bridge that separates the refuge from the mainland.

As one passes through a small woods dominated by loblolly pine and American holly, small birds can be everywhere: nuthatches, chickadees, thrushes, flycatchers, jays, yellowthroats, and kinglets flying about, some resident and, in fall and spring, dozens of others stopping off on their way through.

From the woods one emerges to a point of land with an observation tower surrounded on three sides by marsh and, past that, open water and an entirely different world. Muskrat houses may be seen and, depending on the season, great numbers of Canada geese, mute and tundra swans, ducks of a dozen or so species, loons, grebes, and, farther out, black and white-winged scoters.

Northern harriers and red-tailed hawks glide by and perhaps one of the eagle pair that in recent years has nested on Eastern Neck and is frequently visible on a bare tree near refuge headquarters. Ospreys also nest regularly and successfully and wheel about overhead. Great blue herons, many from a colony of 75 nests just north of the refuge, prowl the edges.

Sandpipers, yellowlegs, and king and Virginia rails probe the grassy flats at low tide, and Forster's, common, and least terns dive for small fish in deeper water.

This is an exciting place where one can spend hours, and surely one of the most attractive small refuges in the system. Sometimes there are grand natural spectacles, as when small dark specks high in a mid-November sky drop down calling to their fellows until 10,000 great white tundra swans cover the nearby waters; or when 50,000 scaup ducks stop over in spring to feed en route to more northern nesting grounds. Fall migration regularly brings some 30,000 ducks and geese.

In summer rent or bring a small boat and go around the island, and if it is high tide explore Durdin, Shipyard, and Hail creeks (named in the early days when arriving boats were first hailed there). The entire six miles can be covered in a couple of hours, but stopping to observe the bank swallow colonies that produce some 1,200 young birds a summer and tying up at Bogle's wharf for a picnic lunch can provide many more hours of fascination.

On land six miles of auto and hiking trails give vantage points for the quiet and vigilant observer to watch white-tailed deer. The endangered Delmarva fox squirrel, whose large size and silvery coat easily distinguish it, are also here in good numbers. There are many pawpaws and consequently many zebra butterflies, which lay their eggs in August exclusively on this shrub. Thousands of migratory monarch butterflies sometimes cover the vegetation at the south end.

The secluded potholes and vast shoals of Eastern Neck covered with aquatic vegetation have been a haven for waterfowl for as long as anyone can remember. Kent County alone has an estimated half-million ducks and geese on its ponds and farm fields during the height of the fall migration.

Two structures on the refuge tell the story of its past and future. One, used now for youth groups and special projects, formerly was a spacious lodge known locally as the "millionaires' hunt club." The other is the refuge headquarters building, which was the first house in a planned development of part of the island, halted when the Fish and Wildlife Service at the last minute procured the land for a sanctuary.

How to get there: From Chestertown take Route 20 west and south to Rock Hall, then Route 445 south to the island and refuge signs.

Open: Sunrise to sunset.

What to see: Swans, geese, ducks, deer, Delmarva fox squirrels.

What to do: Observation tower; six miles of auto and hiking trails; photography (some fine flight shots of swans over bridge); good crabbing July to September (float a bushel basket on an inner tube and wade out and dip them up); boating (rentals of nonmotor boats nearby).

Where to stay: Motels—at Rock Hall, 8 miles north, and Chestertown, 21 miles north. Campgrounds—three miles north of refuge on bayshore.

Weather: January–February can have bad ice storms with alternate freeze-thaw, closing refuge roads, although one county road always stays open.

What to take and wear: Warm waterproof clothing in winter and when wet.

Points of interest nearby: Remington Farms, 12 miles north—an excellent wildlife and birding area with trails and self-guided tours, open from March to mid-October.

For more information: Eastern Neck National Wildlife Refuge, Route 2, Box 225, Rock Hall, Maryland 21661. Phone: (410) 639-7056.

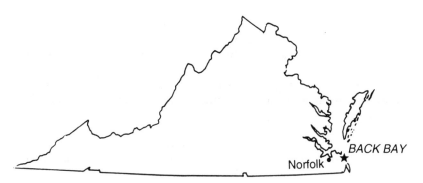

BACK BAY

Norfolk

BACK BAY (Virginia)

Back Bay confronts the Atlantic Ocean on one side and Virginia's Back Bay on the other, with 4,600 acres of fragile dunes, shrub community, upland woods, and bay habitat combining to support a wide variety of wildlife, including three endangered species. Loggerhead sea turtles crawl up on the beach on summer nights to dig sandy hollows in which they lay rubbery white eggs. Swift peregrine falcons streak through in migration, and shy, delicate piping plovers are given a special beach area to encourage their nesting.

Glistening white snow geese begin to drop down on the marshes in October and occupy them until mid-February, their numbers sometimes peaking near 35,000. The effect when they rise all at once, their nasal calls and strong wingbeats filling the air, is breathtaking.

Yellow-rumped warblers are present in the thousands in all seasons but summer (when they go north to breed), sometimes dozens in a single bayberry clump. A "pishing" sound made by blowing air through the lips may summon fifty or more.

Good wildlife observation is possible most of the year. Thousands of tundra swans come through in late November. Most of them are en route to nearby Mattamuskeet Refuge, but many stay at Back Bay.

Back Bay has reported the highest numbers on the National Audubon Society's Annual Christmas Bird Count for gannets (1,275), red-throated loons (549), and several other species. Winter storms may bring inshore long lines of pelagic birds such as surf and white-winged scoters, and northern harriers are abundant in midwinter, coursing back and forth in their mothlike flight as they search for prey.

White-tailed deer breed and then shed their antlers through February. Their burnished spotted fawns begin to appear in May, along with young nutria—beaverlike South American imports—which are frequently in the canals, sometimes riding atop their mothers, nursing from nipples high on her side.

By then downy duck broods are trailing in close lines behind their parents—gadwalls, black ducks, mallards, and wood ducks for which the refuge erects nest boxes. (Sometimes these are taken over by feisty screech owls, which also like this housing arrangement.)

Ospreys tend their young on platforms erected for them and sometimes atop duck blinds, occasionally in double-decker arrangements over barn owls in the blind beneath.

Gray foxes are seen on the dikes along with feral hogs, wild for generations now; muskrats; and, less visible, minks, otters, and weasels.

Brown thrashers sometimes seem to have families in every shrub; brilliant indigo buntings also nest commonly, as do prothonotary, prairie, and yellow warblers, flickers, and white- and red-eyed vireos.

Birds of the shore and marsh easily seen in this season include great blue, green, little blue, and black-crowned night herons; snowy and great egrets; yellow legs; sanderlings; turnstones; black-bellied plovers; and king and Virginia rails.

A stunning display of wildflowers begins in early spring: March hibiscus, creamy plume grass, splashes of pink meadow beauties and later acres of goldenrods and black-eyed Susans. Especially worth looking for are two exquisite orchids, the grass pink and tiny lady's tresses, and also the shiny, sticky insectivorous sundews.

Over 12 miles of beach, trails, and interior dikes are available for hiking; more may be added as the refuge gradually includes some 6,340 acres of marsh, swamp, and critical edge habitat ringing Back Bay, which has been approved for acquisition.

The plan calls for intensively managing these areas for wildlife in the hope of compensating for general deterioration of the surrounding area due to pesticide and siltation runoff from both agriculture and development. These have caused die-back of aquatic vegetation and lowered populations that depend on it—waterfowl and fish such as large-mouth bass, formerly abundant.

Despite these pressures, and the nearby presence of the populous Hampton Roads metropolitan area, this idyllic place continues to be a refuge for wildlife and humans alike, and visitors can find themselves walking stretches of beach entirely alone except for the sand, the sea, and the calling of seabirds.

How to get there: From Norfolk, Virginia, take I-64 south to Route 44 (Virginia Beach toll road), exit at Birdneck Road and turn right on General Booth Boulevard; continue to Princess Anne Road and turn left; continue to Sandbridge Road and turn left again; go three miles, then right on Sandpiper Road to refuge entrance.

Open: Daily, sunrise to sunset. Visitor Center open 8–4 Monday through Friday, 9–4 weekends, closed winter Saturdays and holidays. Admission charge $3 per vehicle or $1 on foot or bicycle. Duck stamp or Golden Eagle season passes honored. May be closed briefly if parking lot filled.

Best times to visit: Fall, winter, and spring.

What to see: Snow geese, waterfowl, shore and wading birds, sometimes warblers in large numbers.

What to do: Wildlife observation, photography from walks and roads; boating in Back Bay (cartop only); fishing in bay and surf.

Where to stay: Motels—many in Virginia Beach (crowded in season). Campgrounds—near Sandbridge and Knotts Island, six miles south; by permit in False Cape State Park, south of and adjacent to refuge and in Seashore State Park, 30 miles north.

Weather: Hot in summer but generally pleasant all year.

What to take and wear: Sturdy footgear for off-trail areas; sunscreen; insect repellent in summer.

Points of interest nearby: False Cape State Park; Seashore State Park, northern limit of Spanish moss; Great Dismal Swamp National Wildlife Refuge, 40 miles west; Mackay Island National Wildlife Refuge, six miles south; Virginia Marine Science Museum, on General Booth Boulevard in Virginia Beach; Pocahontas and Trojan state waterfowl management areas, adjacent to refuge.

For more information: Back Bay National Wildlife Refuge, P.O. Box 6286, Virginia Beach, Virginia 23456. Phone: (804) 721-2412.

Plum Tree Island Refuge, a 3,275-acre habitat for waterfowl, marsh-, and shorebirds, is also administered by Back Bay; however, public entry is prohibited because it was formerly a bombing range with unexploded ordnance considered dangerous.

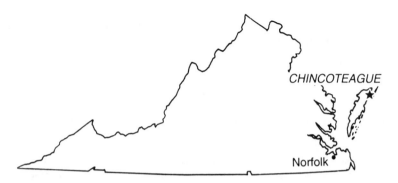

CHINCOTEAGUE *(Virginia)*

Chincoteague is one of the nation's outstanding refuges, both for the beauty and diversity of its wildlife and natural setting and for the many opportunities year-round for the visitor to observe and become quickly and actively involved.

During fall migration one can see up to 12,000 snow and Canada geese, dabbling ducks, and brant—this is one of the primary resting places for these interesting small geese from the Arctic, and like most of the creatures here they are easily visible, perhaps because they sense that they're protected.

Sika and white-tailed deer graze beside the trails along with the famous wild ponies that according to legend descended from a Spanish herd shipwrecked in the 1500s. Large, handsome, and endangered Delmarva Peninsula fox squirrels scamper through the trees. More secretive otters and foxes also are here.

Some 300 species of birds large and small are attracted to this varied 13,682-acre tract of marsh and dune, upland and woods centered on a barrier island bisected by the states of Maryland and Virginia and shared with the Assateague Island National Seashore. Chincoteague is a major stopover for hawks in spring and fall, one that coincides—since they offer a good meal opportunity—with the arrival of tens of thousands of shorebirds also pausing to rest and feed in migration.

A single water impoundment with its surrounding mud flats may hold 15,000 black-bellied plovers, sanderlings, dowitchers, dunlins, and red knots. Nearby, keeping an eye on them through the fall, are thousands of sharp-shinned, Cooper's, and red-tailed hawks; kestrels; northern harriers; and several hundred Peregrine falcons that come through, peaking in October. (A pair of peregrines has brought off a family of three in most recent years, so these swift predators are almost always visible.)

Piping plovers find their primary nesting refuge here. More than two miles of beach are set aside for the privacy of this tiny endangered shorebird.

The abundance of birds all year can only be hinted at. Many beautiful herons and egrets nest on small offshore islands and bring their families here. There are common and red-throated loons, horned and pied-billed grebes, shovelers, wigeons, gadwalls, buffleheads, black and wood ducks, nesting bobwhite quail, rails, oystercatchers, least and Forster's terns, skimmers, and, sighted offshore, eiders, scoters, and old-squaws.

Small birds commonly here include hermit, Swainson's and gray-cheeked thrushes; seaside sparrows (nearly always in winter some Ipswich sparrows, too); brown-headed nuthatches; both kinglets; pine and prairie warblers; blue-gray gnatcatchers; and white- and red-eyed vireos. One recent Audubon Christmas Bird Count turned up 133 species, including 265 water pipits, 360 tundra swans, and a long-billed curlew.

Chincoteague receives between 1.3 and 1.5 million visits a year from persons who come to view its natural blessings from a number of approaches. In summer a daily wildlife safari winds through quiet areas not otherwise open, and a boat cruises around the island to watch shorebirds feeding and large flights of herons and egrets leaving for their roosts, a stunning sight at sunset. For individual exploration there is a 3.2-mile wildlife loop open only to cyclists and hikers up to 3 p.m. and to vehicles as well after that. And there are ten miles of natural beach to walk.

The year's highlight for many is the roundup and auction of the wild ponies. The herd, which is maintained now at 150, is sent swimming over to Chincoteague Island the last week in July and a prescribed number of foals are auctioned off by the Chincoteague Volunteer Fire Company.

How to get there: From Dover, Delaware, take Route 13 south to Route 175 (about 5 miles beyond Pocomoke City, Maryland), east on 175 to Chincoteague Island, left at the light on North Main Street, then east on Maddox Boulevard to Assateague Island.

Open: Daylight hours for trails; office 7:00–4:30 M-F except holidays. Entrance fee.

Best times to visit: Spring and fall—but all seasons rewarding.

What to see: Snow geese; brant; sika deer; wild ponies; peregrine falcons; wide variety of other wildlife.

What to do: Auto, hiking, and cycling trails; summer boat cruises; photography (no blinds available but good opportunities from trails and drive).

Special events: Waterfowl Week at Thanksgiving with various activities.

Where to stay: Motels—a number on Chincoteague Island; also at Pocomoke, Maryland, 25 miles northwest. Campgrounds—several on Chincoteague, Assateague Island National Seashore, and Assateague State Park.

Points of interest nearby: Virginia Coastal Reserve, interesting chain of barrier islands owned by The Nature Conservancy, which can be visited by permission from TNC, Brownsville, Virginia; Assateague Island National Seashore and Assateague State Park, adjacent.

For more information: Chincoteague National Wildlife Refuge, P.O. Box 62, Chincoteague, Virginia 23336. Phone: (804) 336-6122.

Chincoteague also administers *Wallops Island,* a 373-acre refuge tract of marsh and woods habitat that is not open to the public.

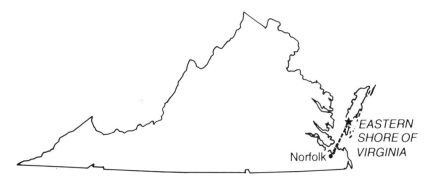

EASTERN
SHORE OF
VIRGINIA

Norfolk

EASTERN SHORE OF VIRGINIA (Virginia)

This refuge, located at the southern tip of the Delmarva Peninsula, is at its most dramatic in the fall when it acts as a geographic funnel for birds migrating south along the Eastern Seaboard. Sometimes millions of them—songbirds and waterfowl as well as raptors—may then stop and "stage" while waiting for favorable winds to assist them in crossing Chesapeake Bay.

Tree swallows may be everywhere, in the air and perched on every available shrub. Kettles of broad-winged hawks and other raptors may be swirling overhead. More than 100 peregrine falcons have been banded at a station on the tip of the refuge at this time. Several thousand acres of marsh in and around the refuge are filled with waterfowl, ducks, and geese of more than a dozen species as well as migrating wading birds—great blue herons and great and snowy egrets.

Songbirds move about in fields planted in millet, sunflowers, and various food plants. There may be flocks of southward-bound robins, as well as hundreds of others—bluebirds, meadowlarks, pine warblers, gold finches, seaside and Lincoln's sparrows, golden and ruby-crowned kinglets, Swainson's and hermit thrush, and cedar waxwings. Less visible but present are many thousands of shorebirds—dowitchers, knots, turnstones, and sanderlings.

It is one of the most important migratory bird habitats along the east coast.

The best way to see this refuge is by taking the self-guided wildlife foot trail or driving the paved road 1.5 miles around open fields. An observation platform on the wildlife trail rises 60 feet overlooking the barrier islands and ocean.

Several osprey nests are visible, and the resonant call of the clapper rail is audible even when this shy bird is hidden among the reeds. Bobwhite quail are common all year, as are white-tailed deer. Coyotes howl at night and occasionally are glimpsed pursuing small prey.

Flickers, Carolina chickadees, and eastern kingbirds nest, along with screech and great horned owls.

In winter a cold snap can bring together several hundred wintering American woodcocks, which close in on a thawed field to probe for earthworms.

During World War II, most of what is now the refuge existed as Fort John Custis. After the war this facility became Cape Charles Air Force Base; it closed in 1980. Some outlooks are former bunkers and gun emplacements but nevertheless it still reminds one of Captain John Smith's description of it in the 1600s as "a faire bay... heaven and earth never agreed better to frame a place."

How to get there: From Norfolk go north across Chesapeake Bay Bridge Tunnel on Route 13, take first right onto Route 600, and at the next intersection take another right. From Delmarva Peninsula go south on Route 13, take last left before bridge toll plaza onto Route 600.

Open: Dawn to dusk daily; office: 8–4 weekdays.

Best times to visit: Fall for migration flocks.

What to see: Migratory fall raptors, songbirds, waterfowl. Sometimes large groups of wintering woodcocks.

What to do: Walking trail, paved roadway, trips to Fisherman Island, October–April.

Where to stay: Motels—adjacent north on Route 13. Campgrounds—12 miles north on Route 13.

Weather: Summer can be muggy.

Points of interest nearby: Chincoteague National Wildlife Refuge, 60 miles north; Nature Conservancy Center at Brownsville, 30 miles north; Seashore State Park, 30 miles south across Chesapeake Bay; Back Bay National Wildlife Refuge, 40 miles south across Chesapeake Bay; Great Dismal Swamp, 60 miles south across Chesapeake Bay.

For more information: Eastern Shore of Virginia National Wildlife Refuge, R.F.D. 1, Box 122B, Cape Charles, Virginia 23310. Phone: (804) 331–2760.

Also administered by Eastern Shore of Virginia is *Fisherman Island* National Wildlife Refuge, located where the Chesapeake Bay Bridge Tunnel comes up for air. Also a staging area, this thousand-acre refuge is a nesting site for thousands of water birds, including brown pelicans; royal, common, and sandwich tern; skimmers; oyster-catchers; glossy ibis; willets; threatened piping plovers; gadwalls and black ducks; and ospreys on nesting platforms. In winter, rafts of 30 to several hundred sea ducks appear offshore. Public access is entirely through tours arranged with the Eastern Shore of Virginia National Wildlife Refuge office from October through early April.

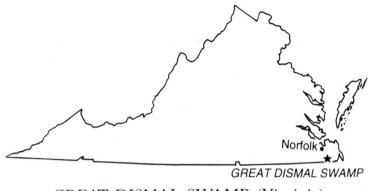

GREAT DISMAL SWAMP

GREAT DISMAL SWAMP (Virginia)

George Washington, who owned part of the Great Dismal Swamp and surveyed it in 1793, described it as "a glorious paradise" abundant with fowl and other wildlife. It still is. The 106,716-acre tract of brooding swampland, formed by forces active 10,000 years ago in this southeast corner of Virginia, is a unique ecosystem of natural inhabitants, some of them found nowhere else.

This is the only known habitat for the little Dismal Swamp short-tailed shrew and one of the few places where the rare dwarf trillium and silky camellia are found, sometimes in the thousands, in a remote section of the refuge.

Several hundred black bears are residents, along with bobcats, minks, white-tailed deer, gray foxes, and otters.

The bird life is remarkable. Ninety-seven species are known nesters, among the commonest the golden prothonotary warbler, flame-crested pileated woodpecker, and gorgeous wood duck—but also the elsewhere uncommon Swainson's warbler and an obscure race of the black-throated green warbler known as Wayne's.

There have been reported sightings that can only be called fantastic—like 10,000 pine siskins, a million robins, 25 million blackbirds.

As many as 30 male woodcocks might appear in a single evening in one area, "peenting" and performing their stunning courtship flights.

More hooded warblers can be seen here than at any other U.S. refuge. Belted kingfishers raucously dive everywhere along the extensive walking and biking trails that wind alongside waterways through the wooded swamps.

Some of the cypress trees are believed to be more than 1,500 years old, growing in peat soil firm enough for walking in most places but so malleable that a slim sapling can be thrust without effort 10 or 15 feet straight down into it.

In watery places are found the Brimley's chorus frog in the northern limit of its range, and (with sharp eyes) the little grass frog, our tiniest—a half inch long.

The Dismal Swamp fish, blind or nearly so with only vestigial eyes—related to the blind cave fish—slithers secretively through peat-stained swamp waters. There is also the lovely dwarf iridescent blue-spotted sunfish—and 73 species of butterflies.

This only begins to suggest the tremendous variety of sights and experiences available along the trails and in and around beautiful 3,100-acre Lake Drummond (whose origin, one story has it, was the work of an extremely active beaver family).

The swamp is steeped in history and lore as well. Patrick Henry once owned land here and Robert E. Lee's father nearly did (he failed to come up with the purchase price). Robert Frost, stung by the rejection of his poems by the woman he later married, came here contemplating suicide. Harriet Beecher Stowe set a novel here—one she liked better than *Uncle Tom's Cabin*—and poems were written about it by Thomas Moore and Henry Wadsworth Longfellow. Legends of the Lady of the Lake arose from lights seen at night now believed to be foxfire—a luminescence given off by certain fungi on rotting wood.

In its more recent history large tracts given by the Union Camp Company through The Nature Conservancy and later the Weyerhaeuser Company led to its establishment as a refuge in 1974 and formation of a citizens' National Great Dismal Swamp Society to ensure protection forever of its fragile and irreplaceable habitat.

How to get there: From Norfolk take I-64 east to its end, then 460 and 13 west about 6 miles, taking the Suffolk exit. At the first traffic light turn left on Washington Street (Route 13) and left again at White Marsh Road (Route 642) seven miles to the Washington Ditch entrance. For the refuge office, continue on White Marsh Road about a mile to Desert Road, left there about two miles.

Open: Daylight hours all year. Office 7–3:30 weekdays.

Best times to visit: Fall and spring (songbird migration peaks in May, also bloom of orchids, coral honeysuckle, and yellow jasmine).

What to see: Unique ecosystem including flora and fauna existing nowhere else. (But get out early; dense cover in much of this wooded swamp makes wildlife much more active and visible during early morning.)

What to do: Elevated boardwalk and more than 140 miles of trails and roads (foot and bike traffic only). Canoeing (boat rental nearby). Photography—along roads, and scenic spectaculars in lake sunsets.

Where to stay: Motels—in Suffolk and Chesapeake, five miles northwest and northeast. Campgrounds—in Feeder Ditch, boat access only; Merchants Millpond State Park, Gatesville, N.C.; private campground on U.S. 17 north of Feeder Ditch.

Weather: Summer can be hot, humid; winter roadways slippery and occasionally impassable.

What to take and wear: Insect repellent, sturdy walking shoes (waterproof for wet times); a compass could be handy.

Points of interest nearby: Back Bay National Wildlife Refuge, 50 miles east; Seashore State Park, 23 miles northeast; Northwest River Park, Chesapeake; Merchants Millpond State Park, Gatesville, North Carolina.

For more information: Great Dismal Swamp National Wildlife Refuge, P.O. Box 349, Suffolk, Virginia 23434. Phone: (804) 986–3705.

Also administered by Great Dismal Swamp is *Nansemond* Refuge, 206 acres of Nansemond River estuary and tidal marsh surrounded by a naval station and closed to access except for birds.

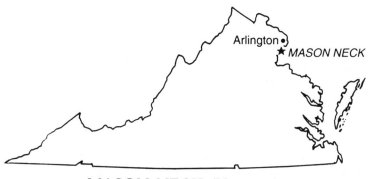

Arlington •
★ MASON NECK

MASON NECK (Virginia)

Mason Neck juts out on a peninsula in the Potomac River just 18 miles from Washington, D.C.—2,277 acres of woods and marsh that in 1969 became one of the first national wildlife refuges set aside under the federal Endangered Species Act, the first for the bald eagle. It gained its status mainly because private citizens, aided by The Nature Conservancy, were determined to protect the area containing an eagle nest site from development. First came the threat of a housing tract. Then refuge supporters resisted proposals to encroach on refuge land with an airport, a dredging project, a gas line, chemical aerosol spray tests, application of a chlorinated hydrocarbon insecticide aimed at eliminating an insect that proved all but nonexistent, and an eight-lane highway.

The battles probably are not over; but meanwhile the eagles have a place they can call their own—altogether more than 6,000 acres, for the whole peninsula is managed cooperatively to protect the eagles through the refuge, regional, and state parks, and a state historic site.

The results have been heartening. At least one pair of eagles has nested successfully in most recent years, and due to cleanup of the Potomac River overall numbers of eagles in the area have tripled in the past 10 years. The refuge wintering population is up to 30 to 40 birds, 10 to 20 in summer. Moreover, rafts of canvasback and redhead ducks, whose numbers had dropped to a few thousand nationwide during the sixties, can be seen here due to the return of submerged aquatic vegetation on which they feed.

Two nature trails wind through woodlands of towering, century-old oaks and beeches with trunks three feet in diameter, then open up to overlook a marsh where beavers maintain active workings. Pileated woodpeckers abound along with flickers, nuthatches and Carolina wrens, and seasonally scarlet tanagers, Acadian flycatchers, indigo buntings, yellow-billed cuckoos, and blue-gray gnatcatchers.

Four kinds of vireos nest—the white-eyed, red-eyed, solitary, and yellow-throated—and 11 warblers, including the cerulean and prothonotary; parulas, prairie, and Kentucky warblers, as well as redstarts and yellowthroats are around much of the year, as are yellow-breasted chats.

The refuge maintains a nest box program for wood ducks and bluebirds, but great blue herons fend for themselves with a colony of almost 600 nests—protected from public viewing. Individual birds can be seen almost anywhere about the refuge, their tall, graceful figures watching and feeding patiently, especially in the Great Marsh. It is one of the last large marshes remaining in otherwise urbanized and industrialized Fairfax County.

Barred and great horned owls are common, and woodcock, bobwhite, and a few turkeys are here. Deer are numerous and easily seen. There also are foxes, raccoons, and elusive river otters. Out on the river, scaup, bufflehead, and ruddy ducks sometimes are packed so closely together they appear to be islands.

A good way to see all this is by canoe at high tide; launch sites are limited. Environmental education groups, with permission, can put in from the refuge shoreline to explore the estuary and tidal guts and feel, as the marsh birds seem to, that there is no one else around at all.

How to get there: From refuge office on Woodbridge, take I-95 to Lorton exit 55, then left or east on Lorton Road, right or south on Route 1, left or east on Guston Road for 4¾ miles, right on High Point Road at refuge sign about ¾ mile to Woodmarsh Trail. To go to Great Marsh Trail, continue on Gunston Road another 1½ miles.

Open: Office (located in Woodbridge) open weekdays all year. Trails open daily dawn to dusk.

Best times to visit: April for spring migration; October–November for fall migration and January for wintering eagles.

What to see: Eagles (at binocular distance); deer, beavers, pileated woodpeckers in fall.

What to do: Trail birding. Great Marsh Trail marginally handicapped-accessible but being upgraded.

Where to stay: Motels—in Woodbridge, eight miles south of refuge. Campgrounds—Pohick Bay Regional Park, one mile north; Prince William Forest, 15 miles south.

Weather: Summer can be unpleasantly hot and humid; otherwise generally temperate.

What to take and wear: Sturdy waterproof footgear may be handy on trails; binoculars or telescope for eagle viewing.

Points of interest nearby: Pohick Bay Regional Park and Prince William Forest (see campgrounds)—attractive natural areas and trails, also in Mason Neck State Park. Gunston Hall Plantation, one mile north—state historic site, beautifully restored home of George Mason, "the pen of the Revolution."

For more information: Mason Neck National Wildlife Refuge, 14416 Jefferson Davis Highway, Suite 20-A, Woodbridge, Virginia 22191. Phone: (703) 690–1297.

Mason Neck administers two satellite refuges: *Marumsco*—63 acres of freshwater tidal marsh near Woodbridge; no visitor facilities but can be seen from adjacent Veterans Memorial Park. *Featherstone*—164 acres of hardwood bottomland bordering the Potomac, saved as it was about to become a garbage dump; currently restricted but visitor trails are planned.

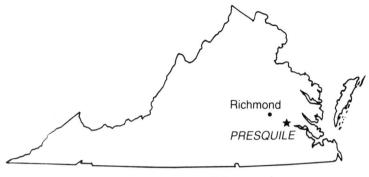

PRESQUILE (Virginia)

To get to Presquile the visitor must cross Turkey Island Creek by refuge-operated cable ferry or private boat—either should be arranged ahead of time. On the other side is a small natural oasis populated by some of America's most beautiful wild creatures.

Bald eagles are almost always visible, soaring or perching on a snag overlooking the water—the James River historically has been prime eagle territory.

Several of our most stunning birds are here in abundance—the eastern bluebird, vividly plumaged wood duck, and golden prothonotary warbler, lured by the inviting natural habitat enhanced by successful nest-box programs for all three.

Wandering along the three-quarter-mile East Marsh Trail one might surprise in spring a wild turkey hen gathering up a dozen little poults, or see racing across an upland field a red fox, its fur blazing in the sun.

There are stands of a curious and ancient silica-bearing plant called horsetail, which settlers used for scouring pots and which can serve as a nail file; white-tailed deer like to bed down in its thicker stands.

Presquile consists of 1,329 acres of upland farm fields, tidal woodland, and marsh, and was named "almost an island" when it was merely an oxbow bend in Virginia's historic James River. In 1934 a navigational cut across its narrow neck made it a separate entity and added to its attractions for wild and human creatures alike.

More notable than numbers of any species is the diversity and balance of flora and fauna here in an area increasingly marked by industrial and metropolitan development.

Numbers of waterfowl winter on the island, first arriving in September and reaching peaks of 4,000 Canada geese, 200 snow and blue geese, and 7,500 ducks, mainly puddlers but including small numbers of divers as well.

More than a dozen warbler species sweep over the island, including the prothonotary and a number that stay to nest: yellow-throated, Kentucky, black-and-white, parula, pine, prairie, and hooded. Along with them are many yellow-breasted chats, red- and white-eyed vireos, eastern meadowlarks, orchard orioles, pileated woodpeckers, indigo buntings, and grasshopper and field sparrows.

Barred and great horned owls are often visible during the day on shaded branches. Red-tailed and red-shouldered hawks hunt all year from overhead while great blue herons scout the marsh edges. Bank swallows are visitors—the only colony within 100 miles can be seen from a boat off Jones Point a few miles upriver. Forster's terns are common on the flats in all except winter.

Canoeists can put into the two creeks with permission and sometimes spot otters and muskrats. But others should stay on the nature trail—natives of the area can walk through without getting their shoe soles wet, according to legend, but those unused to its vagaries can sink down to the hips.

How to get there: From Richmond take I-95 to Exit 6E, east on Route 10 to Route 827 about 3 miles to the refuge ferry landing.

Open: All year; access by arrangement with the refuge office, open 7:30–4 weekdays.

Best times to visit: Spring for migrants and spring flowers, fall for waterfowl—special refuge open houses scheduled for each (check office for dates).

What to see: Deer, waterfowl, passerines—good diversity.

What to do: Nature trail; seasonal open houses (see *Best times to visit* above); picnicking; photography (no blinds); boating (bring own boat).

Where to stay: Motels—in Hopewell and near I-95, Exit 6E north of refuge. Campgrounds—at Petersburg, 20 miles southwest; also Pocahontas State Park, 15 miles north.

Weather: Generally pleasant all year.

What to take and wear: Boots—hip boots if you wish to explore the swamp.

Points of interest nearby: Petersburg National Battlefield, 10 miles west; two of the nation's earliest plantations, Shirley and Berkeley, 10 and 15 miles east; Harrison Lake National Fish Hatchery, 12 miles east. A monument near the ferry landing marks Bermuda Hundred, oldest incorporated U.S. town, where Pocahontas's husband, John Rolfe, was court recorder.

For more information: Presquile [pronounced "PRESS-keel"] National Wildlife Refuge, P.O. Box 189, Prince George, Virginia 23875. Phone: (804) 733–8042 (office); (804) 530–1397 (island phone).

Presquile also administers *James River* National Wildlife Refuge, 4,250 upland acres mainly devoted to preservation of the bald eagle. Not open to the public.

The Southeast States

The refuges of the Southeast harbor an extraordinary variety of wildlife, ranging from red wolves and Florida panthers to alligators, storks, and glorious roseate spoonbills. They stretch from *Roanoke River* on the Virginia–North Carolina border to a sanctuary for a diminutive deer in the Florida Keys, on down to islands ringed with reefs and beautiful tropical fish in the Caribbean.

NORTH CAROLINA

Only recently has the shivery howl of the red wolf in the wild been heard again. Now a dozen or so of these magnificent cinnamon-colored predators are living on *Alligator River* refuge in North Carolina, the first time ever that a species officially extinct in the wild has been successfully reintroduced.

The view crossing over the causeway to *Mackay Island* on a fall or winter morning can show dense white rafts of 30,000 or more greater snow geese packed together on the marsh. It's a high point of the year—but not the only one. Beautiful wood ducks breed here, as well as great blue herons, handsome pileated woodpeckers, and golden prothonotary warblers.

Few sights can be more stirring than a glowing sunset at *Mattamuskeet* surrounded by the whirring wings of tens of thousands of tundra swans—half the Atlantic flyway population, 80,000 or more—that winter here.

Pea Island is a birder's—and bird's—paradise, a fringe of land on the North Carolina Outer Banks where snow geese winter in flocks that can cover the refuge ponds with white, and thousands of shorebirds cover the sands in fall migration. More than 300 bird species have been listed.

Pee Dee was established as a wintering waterfowl area, but it has become a whole fascinating ecosystem with bobcats, gray and red foxes, beavers and nesting red-tailed and red-shouldered hawks. Northern harriers hunt low over the fields in winter. Endangered red-cockaded woodpeckers colonize the woods.

Some of the wildest country in the eastern United States is at *Pocosin Lakes,* where deer, black bears, otters, quails, yellow-rumped warblers, and thousands of ducks, geese, and tundra swans are at home on 111,000 acres of "pocosin"—upland shrub bogs resting upon spongy peat beds up to 12 feet thick.

Thirty or so Mississippi kites can wheel gracefully overhead at *Roanoke River,* a relatively new bottomland hardwood refuge so rich in habitat it attracts wildlife in large numbers. Deer herds of 50 or so browse. Up to 1,000 wood ducks roost together. On a spring morning 30 different songbirds can be heard in just a few minutes.

SOUTH CAROLINA

Ace Basin is another new refuge in one of the last and largest undeveloped estuaries along the Atlantic coast. Sometimes 300 endangered wood storks feed together at a single pool. Eagles and ospreys nest, and it's been estimated that one out of seven Atlantic Coast dabbling ducks take up winter residence here.

The wild, beautiful barrier islands of *Cape Romain* were the first spotted by arriving settlers. Now it attracts tens of thousands of water-oriented birds to its quiet sandy beaches, including the largest wintering population anywhere of American oyster-catchers. Others nest, some in great numbers, including royal terns and black skimmers. Alligators, otters, deer, and turkeys are here, too.

More than 100 colonies of rare red-cockaded woodpeckers cluster in aging longleaf pine woods at *Carolina Sandhills,* whose rolling sandhills are the remnants of a time when the Atlantic Ocean covered this whole area 55 million years ago. Deer, beavers, otters, and wild turkeys are also here.

Santee offers wonderful birding—more than 20 species from pileated woodpeckers to bald eagles (and an occasional golden), warblers, and waterfowl have been attracted to its diverse habitat, along with alligators, otters, gray and red foxes, and coyotes.

GEORGIA

Okefenokee is one of the great primitive areas of the world. Its brooding cypress swamps hold one of the larger alligator populations anywhere. Pileated woodpeckers hammer on ancient moss-hung trees. Thousands of herons and egrets nest and roost. Bobcats and possibly rare Florida panthers make their homes here, and orchids bloom in almost infinite variety.

Piedmont is an example of ravaged land restored to rich wildlife habitat, with wild turkeys, rare fox squirrels, deer, beavers, wood ducks, and 40 thriving colonies of endangered red-cockaded woodpeckers in its pine woods.

Spanish explorers called the *Savannah Coastal Refuges* the Golden Isles, their marshes rich in nutrients, nurseries for oysters, shrimp, and countless marine organisms that in turn attract great numbers of birds and other wildlife—eagles, brown pelicans, herons and egrets, otters, alligators, and minks, among others.

FLORIDA

Most of *Chassahowitzka* must be seen by boat—pristine salt marsh as far as the eye can see. At the river inlets are springs churning up millions of gallons of water a day. White ibis and many herons and egrets are home here, and, seasonally, endangered manatees, green sea turtles, and sometimes loggerheads.

No serious naturalist visiting southwest Florida should miss the *J. N. "Ding" Darling* refuge on Sanibel Island. Its varied accessible natural life of both subtropical and temperate climatic zones is incomparable: beautiful herons and egrets, shorebirds, otters, and alligators all are here.

Florida Panther protects one of the nation's most endangered species—the main remaining population east of the Mississippi for this member of the mountain lion family that has adapted to life in the swamps of south Florida.

Black bears and otters, eagles, ospreys, and alligators make their homes at *Lake Woodruff*, 19,000 acres of freshwater marsh, hardwood swamp, and scattered pinelands, most of which appears entirely untouched by human presence.

The beauty of the river on *Lower Suwannee* is undiminished today, especially for one with a boat to explore its 100 miles of navigable secondary streams. Otters, bobcats, and black bears are here, more than 150 nesting pairs of ospreys, and sometimes thousands of shorebirds, graceful herons, and egrets.

Loxahatchee is more than 145,000 acres of some of the most pristine remaining parts of the Everglades, with immense populations of wildlife and plants found nowhere else, including Everglade snail kites and limpkins, native orchids and ferns, and huge numbers of beautiful wading birds. One interior nesting colony supports up to 20,000 white ibises.

Merritt Island was a just-in-time idea during creation of the vast U.S. Cape Canaveral space center. It occurred to everyone that there might be room for both space exploration and wildlife here. Now this hospitable place has more endangered and threatened species than any other continental refuge—eagles, loggerhead turtles, and many more.

The diminutive animal for which *National Key Deer* was named is surely one of nature's most captivating creations—a fully antlered buck stands just over two feet high at the shoulders, a spotted fawn less than a foot—surviving now because nationwide concern was raised for their plight in 1957.

Eagles and black bears, alligators, otters, and spadefoot toads, along with hundreds of interesting birds, are a sampling of the tremendous wildlife array at *St. Marks'* 100,000 acres along northwest Florida's Big Bend coast. It's one of the few places north of Mexico where the secretive jaguarundi is known to live.

But for anyone who has ever wished to be on a beautiful, wild, uninhabited tropical island, *St. Vincent* is the place. Ospreys and eagles nest, skimmers ply the shallows, tall magnolias flower in gorgeous springtime display, and loggerhead sea turtles crawl up to scour out nests on moonlit summer nights.

PUERTO RICO

Streamer-tailed tropicbirds and colonies of thousands of seagoing sooty terns nest, and leatherback turtles weighing a half ton crawl up on beaches to lay their eggs on the *Caribbean Islands* collection of refuge units, some of the most beautiful in the national wildlife refuge system. Several are separate islands ringed by long undisturbed reefs where lovely tropical fish make their homes.

Following are birds of special interest found commonly at southeastern refuges at seasons indicated:

S: SPRING   s: SUMMER   F: FALL   W: WINTER

Horned Grebe: Cape Romain FW, Pea Island SW, Savannah W
Northern Fulmar: Pea Island SFW
Greater and Audubon's Shearwaters: Pea Island sF
Wilson's Storm-Petrel: Pea Island sF
Northern Gannet: Pea Island SFW, Savannah W
American White Pelican: Chassahowitzka SFW, "Ding" Darling SFW, Merritt Island
      SFW
Magnificent Frigatebird: Chassahowitzka SsF, "Ding" Darling SsF, Florida Keys SsFW
Wood Stork: Chassahowitzka s, "Ding" Darling SFW, Loxahatchee SFW, Merritt Island
      SsFW, Savannah s
Roseate Spoonbill: "Ding" Darling SsF, Merritt Island s
Tundra Swan: Mattamuskeet FW, Pea Island SFW
Fulvous Whistling Duck: Loxahatchee SW
Black Scoter: Pea Island SW
Surf Scoter: Pea Island SW
Bald Eagle: St. Marks W, St. Vincent SsFW
Sandhill Crane: Loxahatchee SFW, Okefenokee SsFW
Limpkin: Loxahatchee SsFW
Purple Gallinule: Loxahatchee SsFW, St. Marks s, Savannah s
American Oystercatcher: Cape Romain SsFW, Pea Island S, St. Vincent SsFW, Savannah
      SsFW
Whimbrel: Pea Island SF
Marbled Godwit: Cape Romain S, Pea Island F, Savannah W
White-rumped and Pectoral Sandpipers: Pea Island F, Savannah SF
Northern and Red Phalaropes: Pea Island SF
Gull-billed Tern: Cape Romain Ss, Pea Island Ss, Savannah s
White-crowned Pigeon: Florida Keys SsF

Red-cockaded Woodpecker: Carolina Sandhills SsFW, Piedmont Ss

Gray Kingbird: Chassahowitzka SsF, "Ding" Darling SsF, Florida Keys SsF, St. Marks Ss, St. Vincent Ss

Scrub Jay: Merritt Island SsFW

Black-whiskered Vireo: "Ding" Darling SsF, Florida Keys SsF

Painted Bunting: Cape Romain Ss, Loxahatchee SFW, Savannah s

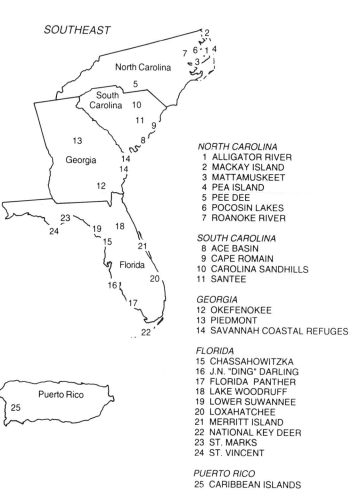

SOUTHEAST

North Carolina

South Carolina

Georgia

Florida

Puerto Rico

NORTH CAROLINA
1 ALLIGATOR RIVER
2 MACKAY ISLAND
3 MATTAMUSKEET
4 PEA ISLAND
5 PEE DEE
6 POCOSIN LAKES
7 ROANOKE RIVER

SOUTH CAROLINA
8 ACE BASIN
9 CAPE ROMAIN
10 CAROLINA SANDHILLS
11 SANTEE

GEORGIA
12 OKEFENOKEE
13 PIEDMONT
14 SAVANNAH COASTAL REFUGES

FLORIDA
15 CHASSAHOWITZKA
16 J.N. "DING" DARLING
17 FLORIDA PANTHER
18 LAKE WOODRUFF
19 LOWER SUWANNEE
20 LOXAHATCHEE
21 MERRITT ISLAND
22 NATIONAL KEY DEER
23 ST. MARKS
24 ST. VINCENT

PUERTO RICO
25 CARIBBEAN ISLANDS

Nags Head

ALLIGATOR RIVER

ALLIGATOR RIVER (North Carolina)

The howl of a red wolf in the night sends shivers of excitement up the spine. Until recently that sound had not been heard in the wild for a long time; this magnificent cinnamon-colored predator was officially extinct, the victim of habitat clearing, widespread slaughter, and aggressive predator control and poisoning programs.

Now it is heard again at Alligator River, the first time in history that a species officially extinct in the wild has been introduced back to the wild.

A dozen or so red wolves are living and having healthy pups, and more are being gradually introduced into this ideal habitat—141,253 acres of dense, wooded swamps, hardwood-pine forests, and fresh and brackish marsh making up most of a coastal peninsula bordered on one side by the Alligator River and on the other by Pamlico Sound, donated by the Prudential Insurance Company with help from The Nature Conservancy.

The social structure of these interesting animals is being studied for the first time. It's now known that a motherless weanling will be raised by its father alone—and a two-year-old female offspring may stay around to help her parents raise a new family.

The program is being watched around the country with a view to the possibility of returning other species that have become extinct in the wild; saving a wild area helps not only one species but whole ecosystems—and this one is home as well to one of the densest populations of back bears in the Southeast, perhaps up to 300. There are also deer, minks, otters, bobcats, red and gray foxes, and endangered red-cockaded woodpeckers. Alligators are here in the northernmost extreme of their range. Almost every warbler and songbird species found in the Southeast has used the refuge for nesting or during migration.

The refuge is full of marshes and old pocosins—the Indian word for "swamp on high ground"—which were drained for roads and canals when the area was logged. They are being returned to their former watery condition and more than 30,000 wintering ducks already have taken advantage of this—pintails, mallards, green-winged teals and ring-necks, plus hundreds of swans and Canada geese.

This is not a refuge that is easy to see. Its 250 miles of old logging roads are rough and cannot be covered by any but four-wheel-drive vehicles, and not always by them. The roads are open to hiking, but hikers should wear sturdy waterproof boots, long pants, long-sleeved shirts, and insect repellent. Off the roads, vegetation is so dense as to be impenetrable, so birdwatchers need to know their bird calls.

This is a refuge largely for the animals—and for visitors not easily daunted by natural obstacles.

How to get there: From Norfolk take Route 168-158 south to Nags Head, then U.S. Route 64-264 west to Manteo and refuge office.

Open: Dawn to dusk. Office 7:30–4 weekdays.

What to see: Wintering waterfowl concentrations are visible beside old logging road; others not easily seen.

What to do: Hiking or driving (with 4-wheel drive) on old logging roads.

Where to stay: Motels—in Manteo. Campgrounds—on Roanoke Island, seven miles east.

What to take and wear: Raingear for afternoon summer showers. Hiking boots and sometimes waterproof boots. Insect repellent (see text).

Points of interest nearby: Same as Pea Island National Wildlife Refuge.

For further information: Alligator River National Wildlife Refuge, P.O. Box 1969, Manteo, North Carolina 27954. Phone: (919) 473–1131.

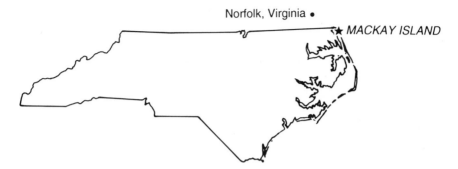

Norfolk, Virginia •

MACKAY ISLAND

MACKAY ISLAND (North Carolina and Virginia)

The causeway crossing to and over Mackay Island on an early fall or winter morning can be a wondrous experience. Up to 30,000 greater snow geese may be packed in dense white rafts on the marsh, all moving and conversing with one another about their imminent departure to daytime feeding areas. There may be 20,000 ducks—gadwalls, mallards, pintails, wigeon, blacks—dabbling in the water, while a scattering of wading birds, great egrets, and great blue herons stalk majestically about, getting their bearings. Up to 1,000 tundra swans may be among them.

It is a high point of the year—but not the only one—at this 7,900-acre refuge of marsh and hardwood-pine woodland that straddles Back Bay and Currituck Sound and is partly in Virginia, partly in North Carolina.

Several hundred beautiful wood ducks live here from spring to fall, bringing off downy broods in spring and sometimes turning over their nest boxes to screech owls, which like to gaze out in late afternoons. Great blue herons have a nest colony in snags on the east pool, where they share fishing rights with ospreys in summer.

The woodlands resound with the hammering of handsome pileated woodpeckers and the cheerful "bob-*white!*" of quail.

Golden prothonotary warblers nest in moist woodlands. The ascending trill of prairie warblers is heard through spring and summer. Shorebirds, peregrine falcons, merlins, and eagles stop by in migration. Northern harriers course mothlike over the marshes all winter.

A good way to see it all is from the refuge office/visitor center, which has a panoramic view of every habitat and both glorious sunrises and sunsets; also from the several walking or bike trails; or from the causeway, where it's possible to stop and pull off anywhere. Or, perhaps best of all, canoe quietly anyplace on the refuge (bring your own canoe, no rentals nearby).

Mackay Island has its historical side. Joseph Knapp founded Ducks Unlimited here, and *Birth of a Nation* was written here by Thomas Dixon.

How to get there: From Norfolk take I-64 to Highway 44 (Virginia Beach–Norfolk Expressway) east to Lynnhaven Parkway South exit, follow parkway to first light, Potters Road, left there to first light, London Bridge Road, right there 7 miles to General Booth Boulevard, right there to State Route 615, left or south there about 25 miles to refuge sign (1.3 miles past state line.)

Open: Daylight hours daily. Office 8–4:30 weekdays

Best times to visit: Spring, fall, winter (refuge interior waters are closed October 15– March 15).

What to see: Snow geese, waterfowl, wading birds.

What to do: Walking and bike trails, canoeing (no rentals).

Where to stay: Motels—in Virginia Beach, 30 miles north. Campgrounds—several within five miles north on Highway 615.

Points of interest nearby: Back Bay National Wildlife Refuge, 30 miles north. Cape Hatteras National Seashore, 125 miles south.

For more information: Mackay Island National Wildlife Refuge, P.O. Box 39, Knotts Island, North Carolina 27950. Phone: (919) 429–3100.

Currituck National Wildlife Refuge is a satellite refuge of Mackay Island—1,200 acres of marsh and upland on the North Carolina Outer Banks, part of one of the largest undeveloped coastal barrier ecosystems on the East Coast, with important wintering black duck habitat but no roads and no visitor facilities.

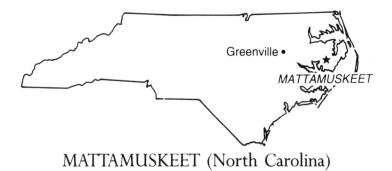

Greenville •

MATTAMUSKEET

MATTAMUSKEET (North Carolina)

Few natural experiences can be more moving than to sit quietly on the central canal levee east of Mattamuskeet refuge headquarters through a glowing sunset surrounded by the whirring wings of tens of thousands of swans, quite likely joined by 100,000 ducks of more than a dozen species and thousands of Canada and snow geese. The birds and their cries and wingbeats so literally fill the air and water that it is hard to imagine a world elsewhere.

Mattamuskeet is almost entirely covered with North Carolina's largest natural lake, which itself is almost covered at times with waterfowl, most spectacular being the tundra swans—half the Atlantic flyway population—that winter here.

It is the end of an almost 4,000-mile journey for these majestic once-rare white birds, formerly called whistling swans, which nest diagonally across the continent in the northwest Canadian Arctic. Everywhere they cause a stir, for no creature is more admired for its grace and beauty.

Here they stay from November to March and can be seen in large numbers— 30,000 or more—either from the many miles of auto and hiking trails that rim the lake or from Route 94, the seven-mile causeway that crosses over it.

The origin of Lake Mattamuskeet is a mystery. Some say it is a filled depression left after fires long ago burned out the upper peat layer. Others attribute its bowl shape to a meteor from outer space. Whatever, it is ideal feeding habitat now—18 by six miles and not much deeper than a swan's neck anywhere, filled with nutritious and succulent wild celery and redhead grass, a far cry from its sorry state after repeated attempts to drain and farm it before it became a refuge in 1934.

Despite its small land area, the remaining woods, marsh, and upland support a varied and interesting wildlife.

Great blue herons fish its fringes, and many of the beautiful wading birds roost in the flooded woods. Occasional bobcats and black bears appear along with otters, muskrats, and nutria playing in families on their feeding platforms.

Bald eagles visit and ospreys are around in all seasons, all but winter, edging the lake with dozens of nests in stunted cypresses.

103

Barred and great horned owls are common all year (sometimes quietly visible in tall pines), as are red-bellied, pileated, and occasionally red-headed woodpeckers, bobwhite quail, kingfishers, and yellowthroats.

There's often good birding right around refuge headquarters, with prothonotary warblers (they've nested in the mailbox), red-breasted and brown-headed nuthatches, red-eyed and white-eyed vireos, blue grosbeaks, indigo buntings, and sometimes crowds of cedar waxwings stripping the pyracantha bushes.

Highlights of some recent Audubon Christmas Bird Counts include 51,000 tundra swans, 9,500 snow geese, 3,062 wigeon, 2,145 Forster's terns, 253 golden-crowned kinglets, 4,520 robins, 51 orange-crowned warblers, 3,434 yellow-rumped warblers, and 800 green-winged teal.

How to get there: From Raleigh take Route 264 east about 150 miles to Swanquarter, then continue east on Route 264 to Route 94, then left or north 1.5 miles to refuge entrance road.

Open: Dawn to dusk. Office 7:30–4 weekdays.

Best times to visit: November through January.

What to see: Swans and other waterfowl, also passerines.

What to do: Many miles of driving and walking trails. Boating. Photography—no blinds but serious photographers can set up portable blinds; no one area— birds can be good anywhere.

Where to stay: Motels—at Swanquarter, seven miles east; Fairfield, seven miles north. Campgrounds—self-contained, in Engelhard, 15 miles west; also Fairfield. For camper-trailers, in Ponzer, 28 miles west.

Weather: Summers hot and humid, otherwise generally pleasant.

What to take and wear: Windbreaker for cooler winter days.

Points of interest nearby: Cape Hatteras National Seashore and Pea Island National Wildlife Refuge, 75 miles east; Swanquarter National Wildlife Refuge, 10 miles southwest; Cedar Island National Wildlife Refuge, 140 miles south; Pungo National Wildlife Refuge, 35 miles northwest.

For more information: Mattamuskeet National Wildlife Refuge, Route 1, Box N-2, Swanquarter, North Carolina 27885. Phone: (919) 926–4021.

Satellite refuges also administered by Mattamuskeet are *Cedar Island, Pungo,* and *Swanquarter.*

Cedar Island is an island refuge bordered by Core and Pamlico sounds, 12,500 acres, including one of the largest relatively pristine salt marshes on the East Coast, providing rest and feeding areas for many kinds of water birds—particularly noted as nesting habitat for black ducks but with representative mammal and songbird populations. A good refuge to see by boat. Bird enthusiasts have a good chance at black rails here. To get there take Route 70 from Morehead City to Atlantic, then Route 12 to the refuge. Picnic at the refuge office with a beautiful overview of Core Sound and in the distance the Outer Banks. Office open 8–4:30 weekdays, telephone (919) 225–2511. Motels at Cedar Island, Atlantic, and Beaufort.

Pungo is a little-known out-of-the-way gem composed of marsh, woodland, upland fields, and Pungo Lake, 12,350 acres once part of the Great Dismal Swamp, with peat soil a dozen feet deep where tens of thousands of tundra swans, snow and Canada geese, and ducks of a dozen species spend the winter and are easily visible along the 14 miles of roads (hard driving but passable) and 16 miles of trails open to hiking.

For a particularly fine walk drive to the north boundary, backtrack about 300 yards to the south side of the farm field and take the trail to the right about three miles to the east refuge boundary. Birding can be great—bluebirds flocking through the fields spring and fall, Cooper's hawks in the woods, white-tailed deer, and a good chance, if quiet, of spotting red and gray foxes and black bears.

To get there from Greenville take Highway 264 east to Pantego, then Highway 9 north to Highway 45, south on it to the refuge, office open 7:30–4 weekdays. (Call ahead, 919–926–4021, during limited hunt in September–October.)

Swanquarter is a satellite refuge about 10 miles southwest of Mattamuskeet—15,645 acres of beautiful pine and hardwood swamp and marsh bordering Pamlico Sound, an important sanctuary for diving ducks—redheads, scaup, canvasbacks, buffleheads, and ruddies, as well as brown pelicans, becoming more numerous here. Bears appear from time to time. Alligators are in one of the northernmost locations for that threatened species. Bald eagles and peregrine falcons visit in winter. The bird list is similar to Mattamuskeet.

This is a good refuge to see by boat, and small boats can be rented nearby. Launch at the Juniper Bay ramp and travel some of the lateral canals, especially in spring, to see alligators, rails, and perhaps nesting herons and a feeding eagle. But much can be seen from the 1,100-foot pier, including huge wintering rafts of scaup, ruddy ducks, and canvasbacks—up to 20,000 birds. And there's good birding along a lonely two-mile access road through scrub and pine from Highway 264 to the pier.

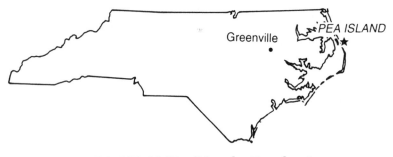

PEA ISLAND (North Carolina)

Pea Island is known far and wide as a birder's—and bird's—paradise, and indeed it is.

This 5,915-acre island is the end of the long journey south for the greater snow goose from its breeding grounds in the Arctic, and these large, once-rare birds can be seen here in winter in flocks that sometimes cover the refuge ponds with white.

Because they tend to stay in massed groups, their flights to and from feeding and resting places are spectacular, especially at dawn and sunset; and during the day they sometimes line the road through the sanctuary, their heads tinged with orange from iron oxide compounds in the tundra where they feed and nest in the summer.

They are only one of the great natural aspects of Pea Island refuge, a long finger of land located within Cape Hatteras National Seashore on the Outer Banks of North Carolina.

Only a little over a mile at its widest, the strip narrows down in places where, as the locals say, you can spit in the ocean on one side and Pamlico Sound on the other. In those places, it is little more than beach and dune held in place by sea oats—sand which can be almost covered in fall migration with thousands of ruddy turnstones, dunlins, marbled godwits, and sandpipers of a half-dozen species.

At its widest, it supports marshes and ponds that furnish food, shelter and breeding areas for avocets, stilts, barred owls, great blue herons, thousands of whistling swans and Canada geese, pintails, ring-necks, and a dozen other ducks, as well as nutria, minks, and frolicsome otters.

Thousands of brown pelicans are here near the northern edge of their range. Swallow-tailed kites are usually spotted at least once a year, as are purple gallinules and Eurasian wigeons and other rarities.

A chain of islands north of the refuge offers breeding habitat for a tremendous variety and number of water birds, which also are seen on the refuge at this time, and some—oystercatchers, skimmers—also nest on refuge beaches, sharing them with loggerhead sea turtles that crawl up at night to lay their eggs.

Peregrine falcons come through from mid-September to mid-October—50 sightings in one recent year—and sometimes several hundred sharp-shinned hawks in a single day. Huge rafts of cormorants can appear offshore in fall, along with such seabirds as gannets, fulmars, and shearwaters—visible with a spotting scope, especially after a storm—and in winter black and surf scoters.

Altogether more than 300 bird species have been identified on Pea Island. Among those listed as common or abundant at various seasons are magnolia, parula, and black-throated blue warblers, bobolinks, lark, sharp-tailed and seaside sparrows, ring-necked pheasants, ospreys, and clapper and king rails. Pea Island almost always heads the nationwide Audubon Christmas Bird Count for at least one species—in one recent year, 5,200 gannets and 8,840 yellow-rumped warblers.

How to get there: From Norfolk take Route 168-158 to Nags Head, then NC Highway 12 south to Pea Island. Office is six miles south of Oregon Inlet.

Open: Daylight hours all year. Office 9–4 weekdays April–September.

Best times to visit: Something interesting all year.

What to see: Broad spectrum of birdlife; otters, muskrats.

What to do: Wildlife observation from trails, platforms, and road. Special programs for bird hikes, etc., summer through fall.

Where to stay: Motels—in Nags Head, Kill Devil Hills, Manteo to the north, Rodanthe, Avon, Buxton, and Hatteras to the south. Reservations advisable in tourist season. Campgrounds—same, also on Roanoke Island.

Weather: Winter can be raw with constant wind; summer humidity uncomfortable when breeze dies.

What to take and wear: A light waterproof windbreaker at any time, warm clothing in winter.

Points of interest nearby: The refuge is within boundary of Cape Hatteras National Seashore Recreation Area. Historic Fort Raleigh, Sir Walter Raleigh's famed lost colony, is near Manteo, and a monument to the Wright brothers' first successful flight is at Kill Devil Hills.

For more information: Alligator River National Wildlife Refuge, P.O. Box 1969, Manteo, North Carolina 27954. Phone: (919) 473–1131 (Pea Island office open only seasonally).

Charlotte

★ PEE DEE

PEE DEE (North Carolina)

Pee Dee was established as a wintering area for ducks and Canada geese, and it furnishes an inland refuge that gathers birds from both the Atlantic coastal and Mississippi flyways.

But habitat once established furnishes refuge for a whole ecosystem, and Pee Dee now has bobcats; gray and red foxes; beavers; nesting red-tailed and red-shouldered hawks; harriers that hunt the fields in winter; and an array of interesting small birds including a colony of endangered red-cockaded woodpeckers.

Up to 12,000 ducks arrive in fall and spend the winter—mallards, blacks, pintails, gadwalls, wigeons, blue-winged teals, ring-necks, and occasional buffleheads, along with 1,000 or so Canada geese. Their presence usually attracts a few wintering bald eagles and rarely a golden eagle, preying on weak ones and fishing.

Bobcats often are around Arrowhead Lake early and late. Gray and red foxes are dispersed through the refuge. Beavers are on all the refuge waterways and are special favorites of school groups learning how these dam-builders create new habitat for waterfowl.

Birders come out in spring when warblers and songbirds arrive—bluebirds, orchard orioles, indigo buntings, and blue grosbeaks among others. Great blue herons and a good population of woodpeckers are around all year—pileated, red-headed, red-bellied, and flickers. Bobwhite quail coveys scurry through the woods in spring, and broods of wood ducks and a few resident geese follow their mothers closely over the ponds. Barred owls can be seen high in the pines, often by day, and screech owls often peer out of wood duck houses.

There's a hiking trail and auto tour route, and public roads circle much of the refuge boundary. A large photo/wildlife observation blind is behind the refuge office.

To get there from Charlotte take Highway 74 east to Wadesboro, then 52 north six miles to the refuge office. Office hours are 8–4:30 weekdays, the refuge open dawn to dusk every day. Town Creek Indian Mound, an interesting Indian burial site and museum, is 12 miles east. Motels are at Wadesboro and Albemarle; campgrounds at Norwood, 10 miles north, and Morrow Mountain State Park, 20 miles north.

For more information: Pee Dee National Wildlife Refuge, Route 1, Box 92, Wadesboro, North Carolina 28170. Phone: (704) 694–4424.

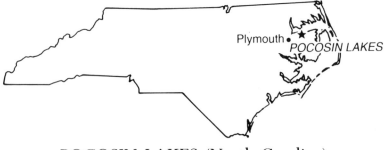

Plymouth
POCOSIN LAKES

POCOSIN LAKES (North Carolina)

Deer, black bears, otters, quail, yellow-rumped warblers, and thousands of ducks, geese, and tundra swans are at home on this fine new refuge of 111,000 acres of "pocosin"—upland shrub bogs overlaying spongy peat beds up to 12 feet thick.

It is some of the wildest country in the eastern United States, crisscrossed with canals, covered with sweet and loblolly bay, blueberries and huckleberries, so dense that visitors who set out hiking or driving its 100 miles of unimproved roads are urged to take a compass (also snakeproof hiking boots). If rains are heavy, usually January to March, roads can become impassable; if too little rain, the fire hazard to this sedge-covered peat soil (which has been ignited by sparks from a car's battery or catalytic converter, with devastating effect) may temporarily close the refuge.

That said, there is much to see here.

Concentrations of waterfowl between November and March may number up to 30,000 tundra swans, 20,000 snow geese, up to 5,000 Canada geese, and 30,000 ducks including mallards, pintails, wigeon, green-winged teal, and black ducks, also beautiful wood ducks which nest in boxes put up for them. Many of these are on the Pungo unit (formerly Pungo National Wildlife Refuge) where there are trails and an observation tower.

Visitor facilities on the rest, as well as complete wildlife inventories, are in the process of development. There can be good viewing from State Route 94 going south out of Columbia—the road is lined with pitcher plants in places—and from the Shore Drive along the west and south side of Lake Phelps.

A new office/visitor center is planned on the Scuppernong River in Columbia; on its completion the present office is planned for use as a field station.

How to get there: From Plymouth take Route 64 east to Roper, State Route 1126 (Newland Road) east to State Road 1183 (Shore Drive) and right on it 3 miles to refuge. To Pungo unit take Route 99 north 8 miles from Pantego, then turn right 2 miles at a church.

Open: Daylight hours. Office 7:30–4 weekdays.

Best times to visit: November–March for waterfowl concentrations.

What to see: Waterfowl, deer, black bears.

What to do: 100 miles of roads for driving, walking, in addition to public roads (see text); observation tower. Excellent fishing in Frying Pan unit for bass, bluegill, perch.

Where to stay: Motels—In Plymouth, Washington, Belhaven. Campgrounds—Near Pantego, also Pettigrew State Park.

Weather: Rains can make roads impassable, lack of it can create fire hazard (see text).

Points of interest nearby: Historic Somerset Plantation and Pettigrew State Park, both 20 miles north.

For more information: Pocosin Lakes National Wildlife Refuge, Route 1, Box 195-B, Creswell, North Carolina 27928. Phone: (919) 797–4431.

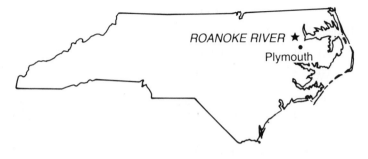

ROANOKE RIVER ★
Plymouth

ROANOKE RIVER (North Carolina)

The chorus of birdsong on a springtime morning at this magical new refuge in northeastern North Carolina is such that one can stand in one place and identify 30 different species in just a few minutes.

Black bears forage on berries. Bobcats hunt from the shadows. At dusk eight kinds of tree frogs chirp their own musical chorus, backed by barred owls booming "Who-cooks-for-you?"

Thirty or so Mississippi kites wheel gracefully overhead, sometimes somesaulting after dragonflies in midair, presumed nesting in what may be their northernmost East Coast appearance. Wild turkeys gobble, and flocks of 30 or so may gather in clearings.

Hardwood bottomlands like this are so rich in what wildlife need—not only solitude but an abundant food base for every level of life from microorganisms to top predators—that species survive in dense populations not otherwise possible.

Deer herds of 50 or so browse together. Brilliant wood ducks nest in natural cavities and later roost communally, sometimes around one of a half-dozen or so beaver ponds—perhaps 500 to 1,000 in one roost.

Great egrets and great blue herons nest in groups of a hundred or so pairs. Bald eagles hunt over the refuge.

Spawning habitat is protected for striped bass and a dozen or so other fish with special needs for clean, fresh running water in egg-laying and hatching.

Roanoke River was established for migrating and wintering waterfowl, and 20,000 may be here on the river and in refuge pools, including the black duck, a species of special concern.

Neotropical birds require for nest sites large old-growth forest tracts that are generally disappearing. Many find them here—redstarts, yellow-throated and warbling vireos, Kentucky and Swainson's warblers, and of special note, a good population of lovely cerulean warblers, usually seen in fewer numbers and considerably west of here.

Roanoke River saved one of the largest undisturbed hardwood bottomland swamps in the country, with planned acquisition boundaries covering 33,000 acres. Its beautiful cypress-tupelo wetlands are best seen by boat—either by canoe or 16-foot jonboat with a 25-horsepower motor—going quietly along and observing, stopping to tie up and hike through the woods. (Water levels can change suddenly and currents can be treacherous, so novices should not go out alone.) Otherwise, visitors can look around from pulloffs on U.S. Highway 13-17.

Visitor facilities are still in the planning stage. For advice on how to see what, consult refuge staff. Plan also to see nearby river tracts under the jurisdiction of the North Carolina Wildlife Resources Commission to preserve this same habitat. For information on these contact the commission at 512 North Salisbury Street, Raleigh, North Carolina 27604; telephone (919) 733–7291.

Motels are available in Williamston; campgrounds in Windsor and on nearby state land.

For further information: Roanoke River National Wildlife Refuge, P.O. Box 430, Bertie County Courthouse, Windsor, North Carolina 27983. Phone (919) 794–5326.

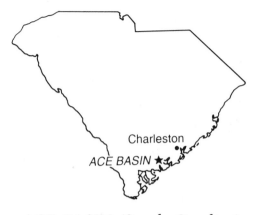

Charleston

ACE BASIN ★

ACE BASIN (South Carolina)

This relatively new refuge helps protect one of the largest undeveloped estuaries along the Atlantic coast, with rich bottomland hardwoods and fresh- and saltwater marsh offering food and cover to a wide variety of wildlife.

Endangered wood storks nest; sometimes 300 feed together at a single pool. At low water thousands of shorebirds—sandpipers, plovers, yellowlegs, dowitchers, dunlins—may be foraging on the pool's mudflats.

Several pairs of eagles nest either on the refuge or nearby, along with thousands of herons, egrets, and white ibis.

It has been estimated that up to one-seventh of Atlantic coast dabbling ducks may take up winter quarters here. Beautiful wood ducks and mottled ducks—a species of special concern—breed. The area is designated as high-priority habitat under the North American Waterfowl Management Plan.

Ospreys nest. Alligators bask on every sunny bank. Wild turkeys feed on acorns. White-tailed deer are everywhere in the uplands. There are raccoons, river otters, beavers, coyotes, gray foxes, and minks.

Ancient and endangered shortnosed sturgeon several feet long live in the rivers. Striped bass are being restored.

Ace Basin stands for the Ashepoo, Combahee, and Edisto rivers, which form the estuary and parts of the refuge boundaries. The basin is over 350,000 acres, of which the refuge will eventually cover 18,000. A State Wildlife Management Area and a National Estuarine Research Reserve also are located in the Ace Basin, and much of the rest will be protected by easements with private property owners, all as the result of citizen action through The Nature Conservancy, Ducks Unlimited, and over 60 other groups.

A single handful of earth taken at the water's edge indicates its value. Teeming with organic life and invertebrates, it is the base of a rich interconnected ecosystem that begins with microbiotic and invertebrate creatures and ends with top predators like the bobcat.

Visitor facilities (trails, visitor center, and observation tower) are in the planning stage, but hiking is permitted over the two refuge units (except during a limited deer hunt in October). Motels are in Charleston, Beaufort, and Walterboro, a campground in Green Pond.

Headquarters occupies a lovely 1828 plantation house on the National Register of Historic Places. To get there take Highway 17 south from Charleston 26 miles to State Highway 174, turn left and follow signs.

For more information: Ace Basin National Wildlife Refuge, Adam's Run, South Carolina 29426. For telephone, call Information.

CAPE ROMAIN

★

Charleston ●

CAPE ROMAIN (South Carolina)

Tens of thousands of water-oriented birds flock to nest or stay on quiet sandy beaches, open water sanctuaries, fresh and salt marsh, and live oak upland festooned with Spanish moss on this wild, beautiful 60,000-acre island refuge extending nearly 20 miles along the South Carolina coast.

Its barrier islands were the first land spotted by settlers coming to the South Carolina coast. In 1989 hurricane Hugo devastated parts of it—the maritime forest was set back from climax woods to first stage in its succession—but all is coming back.

The largest wintering population anywhere of showy black and white American oystercatchers feast in these unpolluted waters on abundant supplies of their favorite food, waiting until the wary crustaceans open up and then ripping in with crimson bills shaped like no other bird's to cut and paralyze the oyster's interior muscle.

Others nest, some in prodigious numbers—5,000 pairs of Royal terns; hundreds of pairs of snowy and great egrets and great blue, tricolored, yellow-crowned, and black-crowned night herons; 3,000 pairs of brown pelicans once endangered through much of their former range; 500 pairs each of least, sandwich, and gull-billed terns; and black skimmers that ply the water with their red and black bills agape to skim up small organisms, or rest on beaches, all facing into the wind. Many of these are on protected islands posted and patrolled during breeding season.

Clapper rails are abundant all year—sometimes 25,000 clattering away in the marsh. Whimbrels, dowitchers, and marbled godwits are common on the sandy shore.

Birders can sometimes spot 100 species during warbler-songbird migrations from mid-March to early May. Common at least seasonally are ruby and golden-crowned kinglets, brown-headed nuthatches, painted and indigo buntings, summer tanagers, ruby-throated hummingbirds, and parula warblers. Screech and great horned owls are around all the time as are yellow-throated warblers and flickers.

Alligators up to 14 feet long bask on the banks on all but chilly days, and otters frolic wherever there is water. White-tailed deer, wild turkeys, and black fox squirrels are everywhere. Raptors are attracted to the new openness of the woods, and there are red-tailed, red-shouldered, and Cooper's hawks; kestrels; and northern harriers.

A rarer sight but always a possibility are loggerhead sea turtles, which crawl up and lay eggs on beaches here in greater numbers than anyplace else on the South Carolina Coast. About 30,000 eggs were transplanted in the early 1970s to other quiet Atlantic beaches in the hope of restoring these great sea creatures with shells sometimes four feet across to their former range, once as far north as New Jersey. Visitors are unlikely to see adults, which come up at night (though sometimes their heads can be spotted in the bay), but occasionally a batch of young ones will explode from the sand and scamper to the water in early morning.

Handsome red wolves are an even rarer sight but a tantalizing possibility. The first pair were brought to Bull's Island in 1977 in a plan to see if a pure wild strain could be raised in an island situation and transplanted elsewhere. So far a half-dozen young have been sent to new locations, with a nucleus pair remaining here.

The only way to visit the refuge is by boat, so go first to refuge headquarters (or call) to arrange transportation. A concession boat goes to Bull's Island, which supports much of this varied wildlife (there are 17 smaller islands). The charge is $15 for adults, less for seniors and children, and for groups by prior arrangement; the boat goes mainly weekends, but sometimes other days, too. It also sometimes goes to the 17 smaller islands that otherwise are reachable only by small boat, best accompanied by guide (office can advise on this also—tidal areas can be hazardous).

How to get there: From Charleston go north 20 miles on Highway 17 to headquarters on the right.

Open: Daylight hours. Office 8:30–5 weekdays.

What to see: Birds of every kind, white-tailed deer, alligators, black fox squirrels; chance of otters, loggerhead sea turtles. Remains of two historic forts used as lookout for pirate ships.

What to do: More than 10 miles of trails, two miles interpretive; photography (photoblind planned); fishing (some say best anywhere for spot-tailed bass and others in surf; largemouth bass are coming back in freshwater lakes).

Where to stay: Motels—in Mount Pleasant, also Charleston. Camping—in Francis Marion National Forest.

Weather: Summers hot, humid; showers can occur anytime.

What to take and wear: Food, drinking water, insect repellent, raingear.

Points of interest nearby: Francis Marion National Forest—trails, one of the largest concentrations anywhere of endangered red-cockaded woodpeckers. Historic Charleston; Fort Sumter National Monument.

For more information: Cape Romain National Wildlife Refuge, 390 Bull's Island Road, Awendaw, South Carolina 29429. Phone (803) 928–3368.

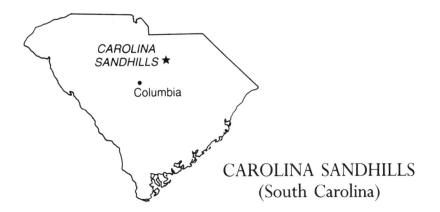

CAROLINA SANDHILLS ★

• Columbia

CAROLINA SANDHILLS
(South Carolina)

Rare red-cockaded woodpeckers, small black-and-white birds whose very particular breeding habits imperil their continued existence (and who flash their red cockades when excited or mating), find what they like here.

More than 100 colonies of this attractive endangered species—more than at any other national wildlife refuge—cluster in aging longleaf pine woods on this 45,586-acre tract of rolling sandhills that are remnants of dunes from an age when the Atlantic Ocean covered this whole area 55 million years ago.

Abuse of its resources by early settlers left this a wasteland. It was established as a refuge in 1939 and its reclamation has been remarkable. It now supports a rich and varied flora and fauna that include deer, beavers, otters, wild turkeys, foxes, bobcats, hundreds of gorgeous wood ducks, and a number of rare and endangered species, notably the eastern cougar.

The little Pine Barrens tree frog, called our most beautiful tree frog with its bright plum-striped green body, maintains isolated population pockets only here and in North Carolina, Georgia, and New Jersey—and its vigorous appearance here is a mystery. Sharing its wet hillside "seeps" are clumps of rare hooded pitcher plants, whose discarded trumpets with skeletal remains of small insects illustrate their carnivorous ways.

A tiny endangered pyxie-moss is also comfortably situated along with the large, handsome eastern fox squirrel, which can be almost the size of a small house cat and comes in various colors, though usually with a black face and white nose and eartips (often it is not initially recognized as a squirrel).

Visitors can easily view the red-cockaded woodpecker in the stands of 70- to 100-year-old pines, which it requires as a nest site. Only large old trees have heart wood cores large enough to contain the nests. A chamber in sapwood would fill with resin. The nest holes are marked by outpourings of sap from small exterior holes kept open by the birds, for reasons not certain, although it does repel some predators, especially snakes. Each nest is tended not only by the parents but by "helper" birds, so that each colony averages six birds.

Some of these are located along the hundred miles of refuge roads and trails, where they make good photographic subjects. One is at the picnic area, and another is right behind refuge headquarers, which in some years features not only nesting red-cockadeds but also red-headed woodpeckers and flying squirrels. (Nest trees are identified with white trunk bands.)

Wild turkeys are most easily seen when the males are gobbling and strutting in the fields on early spring mornings.

Several hundred Canada geese and mallards, wigeon, and ring-necked ducks winter here, plus good numbers of sharp-shinned hawks, hermit thrush, and ruby-crowned kinglets. Common all year are bluebirds, meadowlarks, brown-headed nuthatches, Carolina wrens, quail, red-tailed hawks, loggerhead shrikes, and screech owls; common in nesting season are orchard orioles, summer tanagers, chats, white-eyed vireos, nighthawks, ruby-throated hummingbirds, and hooded and yellow-throated warblers.

Birdfoot violets, sundews, golden clubs, dwarf irises, passion flowers, beauty berries, and trailing arbutus are among the many flowering plants, and excellent lists are available of all the interesting flora and fauna.

How to get there: From Florence take Route 52 northwest to Darlington; Route 151 west to McBee; then U.S. 1 north 4.5 miles to refuge headquarters.

Open: Daylight hours all year. Office 8–4:30 weekdays.

Best times to visit: December through early summer.

What to see: Red-cockaded woodpeckers, Pine Barrens tree frogs, carnivorous plants, deer, beavers.

What to do: Birdwatching can be especially good in spring migration; more than 100 miles of walking and auto trails; photography (blind available); picnic area; observation tower.

Where to stay: Motels—at Hartsville, 14 miles southeast. Campgrounds—at Cheraw State Park, 25 miles north; Sand Hills State Forest, adjacent northeast (primitive).

What to take and wear: Boots (will protect against sharp sandspurs), sturdy footwear for long hikes, waterproof for exploring bogs and seepage areas, insect repellent in spring and summer.

Points of interest nearby: Cheraw State Park (see Campgrounds); Sand Hills State Forest, adjacent northeast, with Sugar Loaf Mountain, unusual sandstone outcrop.

For more information: Carolina Sandhills National Wildlife Refuge, Route 2, Box 330, McBee, South Carolina 29101. Phone: (803) 335–8401.

Columbia

★
SANTEE

SANTEE
(South Carolina)

Santee offers wonderful birding. More than 290 species, from pileated woodpeckers to bald eagles (and an occasional golden), warblers, and waterfowl, have been attracted to its wide diversity of habitat.

Alligators, otters, bobcats, gray and red foxes, and coyotes as well have found homes around its 15,000 acres of mixed pine and hardwood forest, upland fields, marshes, ponds, and open water located in four tracts extending 18 miles along the northern side of Lake Marion. The refuge was established in 1941 after (and in mitigation of) construction of Lake Marion on the Santee River by the South Carolina Public Service Authority, which destroyed much of the area's natural waterfowl habitat.

Christmas is a peak time. Up to 30,000 wintering waterfowl may be here then (down from previous huge numbers due to drought and habitat loss that have diminished waterfowl populations nationwide)—mallards, wigeons, black ducks, ring-necked, blue- and green-winged teals, and hooded mergansers, plus some buffleheads, gadwalls, pintails, and Canada geese.

The Audubon Society's annual Christmas Bird Count regularly turns up 100 species or more, including orange-crowned warblers, red-cockaded woodpeckers, and dozens of pine warblers, brown-headed nuthatches, ruby-crowned kinglets, kingfishers, bluebirds, pileated woodpeckers, and hermit thrush.

Grizzled gray and some black eastern fox squirrels scamper about. Visitors who get to the observation tower early and late may see fox kits taught the finer points of stalking waterfowl (sometimes learning it's a mistake to take on a healthy Canada goose).

White-tailed deer show up with spotted fawns, iridescent purple gallinules tiptoe on lily pads, and a colony of endangered red-cockaded woodpeckers goes to work in an ancient pine in springtime (ask refuge staff for directions). Ospreys and eagles dive for fish and ospreys nest close by, as, elsewhere, do Cooper's, red-shouldered, and red-tailed hawks, and some Swainson's warblers and Bachman's sparrows.

Colorful wood ducks are permanent residents, sometimes turning over their nest boxes to screech owls when they're through. Wading birds, notably great blue herons, scout the water's edges and usually some nest as well.

The refuge contains one of the mysterious Carolina bays, odd egg-shaped earth depressions ranging from 200 feet to four miles in diameter occurring through Georgia and the Carolinas, all oriented in the same direction and having plant and soil types entirely different from their surrounding areas. A theory is that meteors formed them.

There is also a large mound where legend says a Santee Indian chief was buried standing upright, thus accounting for its height (others say it was a temple mound), on which the British built Fort Watson during the Revolutionary War, believed impregnable until soldiers under Francis Marion and Light-Horse Harry Lee in a single night built a tower overlooking it and overcame the fort in a surprise dawn attack.

How to get there: From Sumter take U.S. Route 15 south to Summerton, then eight miles south to refuge. From I-95 take Exit 102 and follow refuge signs .25 mile.

Open: Daylight hours. Office/Visitor Center 7:30–4 days except holidays.

Best times to visit: Fall through spring.

What to see: Alligators, red-cockaded woodpeckers, wide spectrum of birdlife.

What to do: Trails, boardwalks, observation tower. Boating (rentals nearby). Fishing can be superb—landlocked striped bass have been caught in Lake Marion weighing 55 pounds, largemouth bass 16 pounds, world's record black crappie and others, including catfish 74 pounds and more.

Where to stay: Motels—several in nearby Santee, also Summerton. Campgrounds—in Santee and North Santee, also Santee State Park, five miles south.

Weather: Summers hot and humid at times.

Points of interest nearby: Great Santee Swamp—huge, beautiful wild area five miles north of refuge; you need a guide from one of the marinas but it's worth it. Also Four-Hole Swamp (Beidler Forest), 50 miles southeast; Congaree Swamp National Monument, 35 miles northwest; Edisto Gardens, 25 miles west.

For more information: Santee National Wildlife Refuge, Route 2, Box 370, Summerton, South Carolina 29148. Phone: (803) 478–2217.

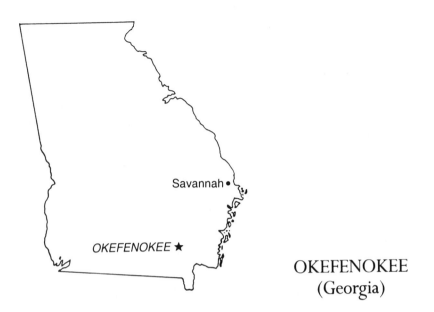

Savannah •

OKEFENOKEE ★

OKEFENOKEE
(Georgia)

Okefenokee is one of the great primitive areas of the world. Its dark, brooding cypress swamps hold one of the largest alligator populations anywhere, 10,000–12,000 of these primitive reptiles. Flame-crested pileated woodpeckers over a foot long hammer on its ancient moss-hung trees. Thousands of herons and egrets nest and roost.

It is one of the last strongholds of the black bear in the Deep South—up to 500 of these lumbering predators, which have been driven off former territories by persecution and development.

Bobcats and perhaps rare Florida panthers make their silent way along its forest paths—and a wildland corridor in process of completion links Okefenokee with Pinhook Swamp and the Osceola National Forest to the southwest to offer increased protection for these larger mammals that like to roam widely.

Orchids bloom in almost infinite variety in remote areas, and carnivorous sundews, butterwort, and pitcher plants set their sticky traps for insects.

The swamp is not all dark and moody. Crimson-crowned Florida sandhill cranes perform their courtship dances on the open, wet grassland prairies, celebrating their union with one of the wildest cries in the animal kingdom. Otters ply the waterways, snipe and killdeer visit their edges, and white ibises fly up by the hundreds from marshes that stretch golden in the sun as far as the eye can see.

Okefenokee is a mixture of freshwater marsh, pine uplands, and dense forest swamps extending over some 396,000 acres—about 620 square miles in the southeast corner of Georgia and north Florida with a tremendous range of natural inhabitants of all kinds, which can only be suggested here. Lists of those identified on the refuge show 233 birds, 42 mammals, 58 reptiles, 32 amphibians, and hundreds of plants of every description.

Great colonies of graceful long-legged herons and egrets, white ibises, and other wading birds can almost 20 acres and harbor up to 7,500 nests in a good year (lower in years of low water levels). Red-cockaded woodpeckers make homes in half-century-old pines, their trunks marked with white bands so biologists (and visitors) can keep a watch on this endangered small bird.

Golden prothonotary warblers nest numerously and visibly in moist woodlands, not far from parulas, brown-headed nuthatches, yellow-billed cuckoos, chuck-will's-widows, wood pewees, and Carolina wrens.

Everywhere are vistas that enchant the observant visitor and stimulate the photographer—dew-hung spiderwebs, spectacular sunsets with striking compositions of moss-hung cypress trees silhouetted against red skies in the Chesser Prairie while waves of birds cross over to their nightly roosts.

The wonder is not in any one of these but in their total effect, which is stunning—and its continued existence at all through a long history of attempts to denude its timbered areas and drain its wetlands (the abandoned canal symbolizing this effort was finally called Jackson's Folly). Fifteen-foot-deep peat beds continue to explode new islands to the water's surface. These eventually grow plants and trees that quake at a human footfall, a phenomenon that gave the swamp its Seminole Indian name, "Land of Trembling Earth." All this exists as a wilderness (353,000 acres so designated).

Three main entrances offer facilities for seeing the swamp on almost any knowledge level, with films, exhibits, tours, guides, auto and hiking trails, observation towers, and picture windows through which deer and egrets can be seen at the swamp fringes. Night boat riders listen to alligators bellowing, frogs chorusing, and pick out with flashlights the red eyes of the 'gators and the green and gold ones of the frogs, owls, spiders, and others. Overnight canoe-camping trips deep into the swamp are available by limited reservation (filled well in advance).

Okefenokee offers a bewildering array of possibilities. The visitor with time for just one might do well to go to the east-side visitor center entrance and there take boat or canoe, wildlife drive or boardwalk to view the vastness of thousands of grassy acres stretching to the horizon, where up to 1,000 sandhill cranes may be dancing, herons and egrets fishing, and alligators basking. Or go to the west entrance and see it all from the view of the cypress swamp. Either way is wonderful.

"One thing certain," said a man who has been everywhere in the swamp thousands of times, "it's different from anything else you'll ever see. If you went every day for the rest of your life, it would be different every time. There's always a little surprise. And always a beauty and serenity you can hardly convey—you have to see and feel it for yourself, like a beautiful painting."

How to get there: From Jacksonville take I-95 north to Kingsland exit, then Route 40 to Folkston. Refuge office and Visitor Center (east entrance at Camp Cornelia, Suwannee Canal Recreation Area) is 11 miles southwest of Folkston, just off Route 121/23. North entrance, Okefenokee Swamp Park, 10 miles south of Waycross off Route 1. West entrance, Stephen Foster State Park, a state-run park on leased federal property, 64 miles east of Valdosta on Route 94. Take spur 177 south of Fargo, Georgia, into the west entrance.

Open: Office 7–3:30 weekdays; Vistor Center 9–5 every day. Entrance hours vary seasonally; check with office.

Best times to visit: March through June and October through December (but always interesting).

What to see: Tremendous diversity—233 species of birds, 42 mammals, 90 reptiles and amphibians, hundreds of plant species, flowering all year—but mainly the swamp itself.

What to do: Walking and riding trails, boardwalks, observation towers, excellent interpretive exhibits, restored swamper's homestead, boat tours, photography, canoeing, overnight canoe camping (by prior arrangement up to two months in advance). Available for rental: shuttle service and equipment for canoe camping, boats, bicycles. Guided tours including at night for wildlife sounds, reflections of eyes.

Where to stay: Motels—at Waycross, Folkston, Fargo. Campgrounds—near Folkston, at Traders Hill Recreation Area 5 miles southwest. Also Stephen Foster State Park (west entrance); Laura Walker State Park, 10 miles southeast of Waycross; Crooked River State Park, 30 miles east of Folkston. Along refuge canoe trails by special prior arrangement (up to two months in advance).

Weather: Wide-ranging temperatures—summer can get up to high 90s, winter down to 20s. Be prepared. Summer may have sudden heavy showers, quickly clearing—also violent electrical storms when it's important to keep a low profile. Annual rainfall about 52 inches.

What to take and wear: Raingear, insect repellent, and a camera.

Points of interest nearby: State parks (see Campgrounds); Cumberland Island National Seashore, 30 miles east of Folkston. Fort Frederica near Brunswick, Georgia.

For more information: Okefenokee National Wildlife Refuge, Route 2, Box 338, Folkston, Georgia 31537. Phone: (912) 496–3331.

Banks Lake, a satellite refuge of Okefenokee located 2.5 miles west of Lakeland, Georgia, is 3,500 acres consisting of lake surrounded by marsh, habitat for bass and bream, wood ducks and cranes, wading and shorebirds, with no visitor facilities and few planned.

Atlanta
•

★
PIEDMONT

PIEDMONT (Georgia)

The little red-cockaded woodpecker whose choosy nest requirements drove it to the edge of extinction has more than 40 thriving colonies here. And there are hundreds of wild turkeys, rare fox squirrels, deer, beavers, wood ducks, and much other wildlife on land once so ravaged by poor management it was all but given up for lost.

When Piedmont was declared a refuge in 1939, erosion had left its 34,665 acres of rolling hills and bottomland in the Appalachian foothills denuded, infertile, and utterly depleted. A freight train, it is said, could have been driven through its eroded gulleys. The first Fish and Wildlife Service head, Ira Gabrielson, said if a wildlife refuge could be made here, it could be made anywhere.

It is a complete success story. Visitors come now from all over the world—from China, Russia, Europe—to get advice and learn how this can be done.

One of its first successes was the red-cockaded woodpecker which discovered just what it needed in some old trees which had escaped the axe: 70-year-old pines having trunks with the soft "red-heart" centers which this bird requires for its nest cavities. Visitors in spring can easily see (and photograph) them drilling holes and then pecking smaller holes around them so their nest openings are kept surrounded by sticky tree sap. Why they do this is uncertain but it may repel marauders such as snakes.

Lumbermen like to cut trees before they get this old, but Piedmont has signed agreements with adjacent Oconee and Hitchiti national forests to manage their trees cooperatively so habitat for this special small bird will continue to increase here and its population grow to a goal of 250 colonies.

Energetic beavers which can nearly always be seen early and late at Allison Lake have helped create many of the more than a dozen ponds which now offer wintering shelter for thousands of waterfowl—mallards, ring-necks, and some black ducks—as well as year-round fishing grounds for otters, ospreys, and great blue herons. White-tailed deer, gray foxes, bobcats, coyotes, and a few black bears come to drink at the water's edge.

Fox squirrels, two to three times the size of grays and sometimes colored coal black, are relatively tame and can be seen almost anywhere on the refuge.

Turkeys can be heard gobbling most spring mornings and the cocks give courtship displays at woods openings.

Large flocks of sandhill cranes go over bugling in V-formation in spring and often touch down overnight.

Warblers and songbirds flit through the woods, some en route to northern nesting grounds but hooded, pine, Kentucky and prairie warblers stay to raise families with indigo buntings, summer tanagers, bluebirds, and yellow-breasted chats.

Bachman's sparrows, rare elsewhere, can always be heard and often can be spotted by the assiduous birder. Flame-crested pileated woodpeckers hammer noisily.

The woods burst into bloom in April with dogwood, redbud and wisteria and wild lilies on streamsides. Thirty miles of roads are open for auto and foot travel. A lovely walk is along Falling Creek with a series of small natural dams and interesting mosses and wildflowers. The refuge office can give directions.

Indian habitation has been traced back 10,000 years. Sherman's troops marched through here on their way to the sea—and there are remnants from that time in rings still attached to trees where travelers tied their horses at old stagecoach stops.

How to get there: From Atlanta take I-85 south to Exit 61/Juliette Road, then east on Juliette Road 18 miles to refuge office/visitor center.

Open: Daylight hours all years. Office 8–4:30 weekdays, 9–5:30 weekends.

Best times to visit: Spring, fall and winter.

What to see: Red-cockaded woodpeckers, fox squirrels, deer, songbirds, waterfowl.

What to do: Nature trails. Photography (blind available).

Where to stay: Motels—At Forsyth, 18 miles west. Campgrounds—at Forsyth, also Indian Springs State Park, 22 miles northwest.

Weather: Summers hot, humid.

What to take and wear: Insect repellent a MUST—ticks with Lyme disease present. Hiking boots for off-trail exploring. Light waterproof windbreaker might be useful.

Points of interest nearby: Ocmulgee Indian Mounds near Macon (National Park Service). Jarrell Plantation adjoins refuge on west—historic working cotton plantation. Macon has many historic homes and periodic walking tours.

For more information: Piedmont National Wildlife Refuge, Route 1, Box 670, Round Oak, Georgia 31038. Phone: (912) 986-5441.

Bond Swamp, a relatively new satellite refuge of Piedmont, is 4,500 acres of bottomland hardwood swamp just six miles southeast of Macon with an active eagles' nest, three heronries, many beaver workings and thousands of wintering waterfowl located on the Tuscaloosa aquifer, which pumps 30 million gallons a day to supply its watery habitat. Visitor facilities in process of development.

SAVANNAH─────★
COASTAL Savannah •
REFUGES─────★

SAVANNAH COASTAL REFUGES
(Georgia and South Carolina)

Spanish explorers called them the Golden Isles, this sunlit chain of barrier islands along Georgia and South Carolina that form a protective buffer between the mainland and the ocean. The marshes behind them have been called the world's most productive acreage. Nutrients from both fresh- and saltwater make them nurseries for oysters, shrimp, and countless marine organisms, and because of this home to great numbers of birds and other wildlife.

Hundreds of pelicans fish off their beaches. Thousands of herons, egrets, and white ibises nest and roost. Tiny painted buntings flit about the undergrowth. Eagles and swallow-tailed kites catch warm thermal air currents and soar overhead. Peregrine falcons dive at breakneck speed on waterfowl to feed through the winter. And there are otters, alligators and minks, deer, bobcats, and much else.

The Savannah Coastal Refuges span 100 miles to create a wildlife corridor covering more than 53,340 acres on five island groupings anchored by Savannah and Harris Neck refuges on the coastal mainland. Some are accessible only by boat; some are partly or wholly off-limits to public use at various times. For information on schedules and reliable charters (boating can be hazardous with seven-foot tides) consult refuge headquarters in Savannah before planning an offshore trip.

Taking *Savannah* first—tremendous numbers of colorful wood ducks along with hawks, wading birds, and alligators in varieties and numbers occurring at few other places are at home on this 25,608 acres of freshwater marsh, tidal rivers, and bottomland hardwoods where the Savannah River borders Georgia and South Carolina.

Savannah is one of the nation's oldest refuges. It was started on lands occupied by century-old rice plantations. The miles of dikes now open to wildlife observation originally were built for rice cultivation and now provide a variety of habitat for a rich and diverse wildlife.

Up to 3,000 wood ducks may be present in winter. Cooper's hawks, along with red-tailed and red-shouldered hawks, nest.

Alligators are present on all the coastal refuges but especially here—and especially in April and October, when as many as 40 (the record is 100) can be seen at one time hauled out along the Laurel Hill Wildlife Drive.

Northern parula warblers flit through the live oaks at the refuge entrance from April through summer, and dazzling purple gallinules follow the same schedule wherever there are lily pads. In midwinter hundreds of snipe may be found probing the moist soils bordering the four-mile Laurel Hill Wildlife Drive. Graceful long-legged waders are here in great numbers—great and little blue herons, black-crowned and yellow-crowned night herons, glossy and white ibises. Great and snowy egrets nest in several colonies and fly in large V-formations to and from roosts and feeding areas seasonally, and in a good year 20,000 waterfowl of more than a dozen species spend the winter.

Bald eagles nest and ospreys soar. Flame-crested pileated woodpeckers frequent the woods. Birders find an impressive array of sparrows, including swamp, vesper, and, rarely, Henslow's and Bachman's.

White-tailed deer browse the dikes and otters occasionally course the waterways. Bobcats hunt secretively throughout the refuge's bottomland and marsh.

Interesting plants are here as well—an unusual introduced climbing fern, a varnish tree, and Chinese tallow trees descended from seeds shipped from Europe by Benjamin Franklin. Altogether more than 900 species have been catalogued.

But no sight is more awesome than the multihued wood ducks, sometimes 1,000 or so coming in at one time to roost in patches of maiden cane and water lily in the East Marsh in late afternoon. These and other freshwater-dependent species have been threatened by proposed harbor dredging and development, and resulting saltwater intrusion.

How to get there: Headquarters is in Federal Court Building in Savannah, 125 Bull Street. To get to Savannah Refuge take U.S. 17-A north across Savannah River, turn left on U.S. 17 and follow refuge signs.

Open: Daylight hours all year.

What to see: Alligators; wood ducks; snipe; purple gallinules; wading birds and waterfowl; 11 species of sparrows.

What to do: Four-mile nature drive, many miles of dikes for hiking, nature observation, photography.

Where to stay: Motels—in Hardeeville, South Carolina, and Savannah. Campgrounds—near Hardeeville; also Skidaway Island State Park, 15 miles south.

Weather: Midsummer hot, humid, buggy; midwinter occasional frost.

Points of interest nearby: Savannah has interesting Historic District Tours; Georgia Ornithological Society, P.O. Box 1278, Cartensville, Georgia 30120, has guide, checklists and advice for areas throughout state.

For more information: Savannah Coastal Refuges, P.O. Box 8487, Savannah, Georgia 31412. Phone: (912) 652–4415.

Taking the island refuges from north to south:

Pinckney Island—A spectacular late-afternoon sight is that of tremendous flocks of white ibises coming in to roost on a small pond just a mile from the refuge entrance on Route 278 five miles east of Bluffton, South Carolina. They nest in spring and summer along with hundreds of herons and egrets, while vast offshore oysterbeds attract oystercatchers and other shorebirds at low tide. Rafts of scaups spend the winter along with loons and red-breasted mergansers. Alligators, quail, and deer are here, and the endangered wood stork is common except in winter. Over 14 miles of trails are open to hiking and bicycling. Several smaller islands (some off-limits) are included in this 4,053-acre refuge.

Tybee—A 100-acre spoil island, closed to public use—but oldsquaw and black, surf, and white-winged scoters appear offshore in winter, and the best way to see them is with a telescope from nearby Fort Pulaski National Monument.

Wassaw—Believed by many to be the most beautiful of the Golden Isles, with 10,070 acres of pristine beaches, trails that wind through virgin stands of pine and live oak covered with resurrection fern, and thousands of acres of fertile and unspoiled saltwater marsh. Endangered bald eagles nest, as do ospreys and alligators. Clapper rails and painted buntings are abundant, along with most of the graceful wading and shorebirds common to the region. Loons are common fall and winter visitors.

Loggerhead turtles crawl ashore on summer nights to scour out nests and lay hundreds of eggs, monitored by researchers from the Savannah Science Museum (volunteers may sign up to assist with the research project). Erosion on the north end of the seven-mile beach has left a fascinating "boneyard" of live oak, pine, and palmetto skeletons, natural sculptures for the photographer.

Access is by boat only. Refuge office can advise on arranging trips.

Harris Neck—A tremendous variety of birdlife is at home in the refuge's 2,765 acres of varied habitat that includes grass and timberland, freshwater and salt marsh, mudflats and brush. The local Audubon Society holds its annual Christmas Bird Count here because it is likely to have the greatest species variety in the area.

When water conditions are optimal there may be dense concentrations of hundreds of ibises, herons, egrets, night herons, and endangered wood storks, some roosting but many—sometimes up to 40 stork pairs—nesting, throughout the season that starts in early spring and may go into September. When they fly en masse against the setting sun, the sight is unforgettable.

Painted buntings, bluebirds, and northern parulas delight the eye in summer—especially around the drive entrance—as do yellow-throated vireos, orchard orioles, summer tanagers, and yellow-billed cuckoos. Clapper rails, willets, sharp-tailed sparrows (winter only), and marsh wrens predominate in tidal marshland, and hundreds of wood ducks, wigeons, teals, gadwalls, and mallards spend fall and winter on the freshwater ponds. Otters are there, too. Large flocks of sparrows, including fox, grasshopper (uncommon), vesper, and, rarely, Lincoln's, winter around the old airstrip, which dates from World War II.

White-tailed deer and alligators are around all year.

Access to some fenced portions is not permitted and designated areas may be closed during the nesting season—check with refuge office. Otherwise get there by following U.S. 17 43 miles south from Savannah, then east on Route 131 to refuge entrance.

Blackbeard Island—This wild, beautiful 5,618-acre barrier island was named after the notorious pirate who reputedly buried treasure here (never unearthed). Blackbeard Island has been in continuous federal ownership since 1800, when President John Adams bought it for the Navy Department as a source of live oak timber for shipbuilding. Now loggerhead turtles crawl up on its seven miles of beach to lay eggs in summer; willets, oystercatchers, and black skimmers patrol its shores, and brown pelicans wheel and dive for fish. Large shorebird flocks rest and feed. Painted buntings nest in the wooded understory.

One of the densest alligator populations anywhere is at home in its freshwater ponds, apparently not interfering with large wintering flocks of waterfowl—ringnecks, canvasbacks, wigeons, and teals—or nesting colonies of herons, egrets, and ibises in the summer. Sometimes tremendous rafts of scaups—more than 20,000 birds—appear offshore in winter.

White-tailed deer (smaller than those on the mainland) wander along its trails and through the 3,000-acre designated wilderness area, which includes a stand of ancient pines and a beautiful "boneyard" of whitened tree skeletons left by erosion. Clapper rails and seaside sparrows nest in the marshes and pileated woodpeckers in the woods. A heronry at Flag Pond sometimes has more than 1,000 pairs of herons, egrets, ibises, and anhingas.

But it is the beautiful island itself and its remote, primitive feeling that provide the most memorable experience.

Access is by boat only. This can be arranged at Shellman's Bluff, on the eastern end of Shellman's Bluff Road, 51 miles south of Savannah on U.S. 17.

Wolf Island—Only the surrounding saltwaters are open to the public at this 5,126-acre refuge, which consists largely of salt marsh and a narrow beach strip on Wolf and neighboring Egg and Little Egg islands, heavily used by brown pelicans, herons and egrets, clapper rails, small numbers of oystercatchers and willets, and black skimmers and Wilson's plovers, which nest. For those who wish to view all this from a boat, charters can be arranged in Darien, Georgia.

CHASSAHOWITZKA

Tampa

CHASSAHOWITZKA (Florida)

Most of Chassahowitzka Refuge can be seen only by boat and it is a memorable experience—pristine salt marsh as far as the eye can see, interspersed with tidal streams and bars where graceful wading birds fish at low tide.

At the river inlets are springs that churn up millions of gallons of water a day (or sometimes in just an hour)—crystal clear as is all the water here, becoming bluish-green in the depths. White ibis and other lovely long-legged waders—great blue and little blue herons, snowy and great egrets, black-crowned and yellow-crowned night herons—are common along the river shorelines.

Green sea turtles and sometimes loggerheads hang around the mouths of the Homosassa and Chassahowitzka rivers, both of which flow through the refuge to the sea.

Endangered manatees, watery relatives to the elephant looking like lovable seagoing blimps up to 15 feet long, leave the rivers and come out into refuge waters when they warm up in spring and summer. Seasonal "slow speed" restrictions are strictly enforced; boating incidents are a chief cause of injury and death to this severely diminished species.

Bald eagles soar overhead and fish in marsh channels, sometimes stealing prey from the more numerous and slightly smaller ospreys that nest in the refuge.

A flock of 150 or so white pelicans and several thousand ducks winter in the refuge—mostly gadwall, wigeon, scaup, and ringneck.

Boaters going quietly along the rivers may see some of the mammal population—otters, bobcats, even black bears.

Passerines thrive in the wooded upland around refuge headquarters—prairie, pine, yellow-throated, and parula warblers; scarlet tanagers; brown-headed nuthatches; pileated woodpeckers; and seasonally, indigo and painted buntings. Flocks of thousands of wintering robins may appear.

Fishermen in tidal waters can angle for fresh- and saltwater fish simultaneously—and sometimes, with the extreme visibility, select which to go for ahead of time.

Boat and canoe rentals are available nearby. Visitors should consult with refuge staff before planning a trip both to avoid hazards and to get around and see everything.

How to get there: From Tampa take I-275 north to I-75, then north on U.S. 98, then right on Route 19, two miles to refuge office.

Open: Daylight hours year-round; office 7:30–4 weekdays.

Best times to visit: Wildlife always around; weather best spring and fall.

What to see: Herons, egrets, pelicans, alligators, ospreys, sometimes manatees, otter, sea turtles; crystal-clear springs.

What to do: Photography (scenics and wading birds); boating—boat and canoe rentals nearby.

Where to stay: Motels—Homosassa Springs. Campgrounds—Homosassa Springs and Chassahowitzka, also Withlacoochee State Forest, four miles east.

Weather: Midwinter can be damp and chilly, midsummer hot and humid.

Points of interest nearby: Homosassa Springs, which produces 2.5 million gallons of crystalline 74-degree water per hour to form the Homosassa River, where thousands of fish gather. Also Homosassa Springs State Park, where injured manatees are rehabilitated (see above). Crystal River archaeological site, 15 miles north. Crystal River National Wildlife Refuge, 12 miles north.

For more information: Chassahowitzka National Wildlife Refuge, 1502 Southeast Kings Bay Drive, Crystal River, Florida 34429. Phone: (904) 563–2088.

Chassahowitzka also administers four satellite refuges:

Crystal River—One of the world's most endangered species, the Florida (or West

Indian) manatee, makes winter quarters in the warm springs of Kings Bay at the headwaters of the Crystal River. Some 265 of these harmless, gentle water mammals, which can grow to be 15 feet long and weigh 1,500 pounds, browse on submerged vegetation from November through March, attracting 60,000 visitors yearly.

This attention, except as it focuses on their plight, has not been a plus for these appealing creatures whose greatest peril is from human waterborne activities. Once numerous, their state population is now around 1,200. With 150 to 200 dying every year—often injured by boats, others perishing because pregnant females are harassed and abort—their future is dim unless humans take greater care to protect them.

Even well-meaning swimmers do harm when they unintentionally interfere with feeding activities or the caring for their young, or drive them into colder water where these air-breathers are subject to pneumonia. (In one horrifying incident, a visitor carved his name on the side of one of these defenseless giants. Others try to ride them.) Harassment of ANY kind, including touching, is illegal and is prosecuted.

The refuge is made up of 20 small islands as well as underwater sanctuary areas in which humans are not permitted to enter. Dive shops rent snorkel and scuba gear.

Visitors should go by the nearby Chassahowitzka refuge office (address above) to learn where manatees have been seen and how best to go about visiting without harming them. (One tip: swim like a manatee, float quietly, unaggressively, and one is likely to swim up to you.)

Manatees and demonstrations of manatee behavior can be seen at nearby Homosassa State Wildlife Park (where injured manatees are rehabilitated).

Egmont Key—a 350-acre island in Tampa Bay where skimmers and least terns nest. Access by boat only, and no access to nest area during breeding season. Refuge open daylight hours only.

Passage Key—a 20-acre island in Tampa Bay where gulls, royal and sandwich terns, and pelicans nest. No access April to September.

Pinellas—a group of mangrove islands with difficult access, closed all year for nesting and roosting habitat.

Fort Myers

J.N. "DING" DARLING

J. N. "DING" DARLING (Florida)

No serious naturalist visiting southwest Florida can afford to miss the J. N. "Ding" Darling Refuge on Sanibel Island. Its wide variety of accessible natural life of both subtropical and temperate climatic zones is incomparable.

Wading birds are everywhere—herons, egrets, white ibises, wood storks, and sometimes 250 or so sensationally beautiful roseate spoonbills are along the five-mile wildlife drive, bordered on the left by brackish water and on the right by saltwater, drained by tides and interspersed by grassy, brush, and mangrove habitat to accommodate almost every kind of bird possible to these zones.

Alligators are here, too, and horseshoe crabs—a primordial species almost unchanged in 180 million years, mating sometimes in a spectacular shoreline display. Otters sport in the canals in early morning, and bobcats occasionally drink along the edges (an unwary one was taken by an alligator).

Hundreds of snowy and great egrets can gather in early-morning feeding frenzies when schools of small fish invade the shallows. Black skimmers ply the waters, bills agape. Reddish egrets, great blue herons, and yellow- and black-crowned night herons are common as well, the yellow-crowns courting and raising families in a colony at the end of the wildlife drive (in branches perilously low over cruising 'gators that

137

paradoxically protect the colony by preventing access by raccoons and other predators).

Shorebirds pass through by the thousands in spring and fall and many stay to nest—snowy and Wilson's plovers, willets, dowitchers, and others.

Bald eagles soar overhead, sometimes stooping to steal prey from ospreys that nest on the refuge as well as on channel markers and platforms erected by Sanibel citizens. The whole island is a declared sanctuary where red-shouldered hawks, pileated and red-bellied woodpeckers, and brown pelicans are common.

Warblers can appear by the thousands in April migration along with indigo and painted buntings, rose-breasted and blue grosbeaks, bobolinks, and northern and orchard orioles. A good place to see them is around the lighthouse (outside the refuge) and in the Bailey tract, where black-whiskered vireos and black-necked stilts come in spring. Large flocks of robins and cedar waxwings sometimes spend the winter, and the rare mangrove cuckoo is along the wildlife drive.

A canoe trail winds through the 4,975-acre refuge (rentals available). Wintering white pelicans can be there by the hundreds; frigate birds are overhead; and in spring there's an occasional swallow-tailed kite, along with porpoises, green and loggerhead turtles, and sometimes manatees.

For botanists there are orchids and air plants, strangler figs, gumbo limbo trees, mangroves, and in summer night-blooming cereus. Sanibel is famous for its shell-strewn beaches (a nonresident fishing license is required for live shelling, with two live shells the limit to preserve breeding populations).

Excellent guides are available to point out the island's wildlife—best seen on less-crowded weekdays. Visitation is over 700,000 some years and studies have shown wildlife, formerly approachable, has been severely impacted by thoughtless photographers and surging crowds that sometimes throw rocks and behave as if they were in a zoo rather than a sanctuary. Refuge staff will prosecute any visitor found disturbing birds or alligators.

To preserve the extraordinary wildlife experiences available here, photograph with long lenses from cars when possible; watch and appreciate but do not disturb.

How to get there: From Fort Myers airport and I-75 take Daniels Road to Six-Mile Cypress Road; left on it, cross U.S. 41 to Summerlin; left on it to Sanibel causeway (toll); turn right on Periwinkle Way to Palm Ridge Road and follow refuge signs.

Open: Sunrise to sunset daily except wildlife drive closed Friday. Visitor center 9–5 daily November to mid-April, 9–4 Monday-Saturday rest of year, closed some holidays.

Best times to visit: Interesting all year.

What to see: Ospreys, pelicans, great variety of wading birds, alligators; sometimes otters, manatees, sea turtles.

What to do: More than 10 miles of roads and trails for driving, hiking, photography (good from car windows). Boating and canoeing—rentals nearby. Interpretive tram tour (fee).

Where to stay: Motels—many on Sanibel (Chamber of Commerce can be helpful). Campgrounds—Koreshan State Park, 17 miles south of mainland (one small facility on Sanibel usually reserved months ahead).

Weather: Midwinter can be cool, cloudy; midsummer hot, humid. Hurricanes possible June–November.

Points of interest nearby: Sanibel-Captiva Conservation Foundation, nature center and trails; Corkscrew Audubon Sanctuary, sometimes nesting storks, 50 miles southeast; Everglades National Park, 90 miles south.

For more information: J. N. "Ding" Darling National Wildlife Refuge, One Wildlife Drive, Sanibel, Florida 33957. Phone: (813) 472–1100.

Ding Darling also administers three mangrove island refuges, *Matlacha Pass, Pine Island,* and *Island Bay,* which support sizable populations of pelicans, herons, and egrets. Public access to these is difficult and prohibited when it may disturb nesting birds. A river island subrefuge, *Caloosahatchee,* has limited wildlife use and no public facilities.

FLORIDA PANTHER
PANTHER

Naples

FLORIDA PANTHER (Florida)

This new 27,000-acre refuge protects one of the nation's most endangered species—the main remaining population east of the Mississippi for this member of the mountain lion family that has adapted to life in the swamps of south Florida.

Known as the Florida panther, it is the top predator of the south Florida food chain. The panther is a wilderness species, requiring hundreds of square miles for its territory and a steady diet of large prey such as deer and hogs to sustain itself. Because of these demanding needs, preserving the panther in its natural habitat virtually insures the survival of most other south Florida wildlife. The refuge is also home to black bears, bobcats, otters, alligators, endangered wood storks, and a wide variety of bird life.

The refuge includes the northern Fakahatchee Strand, largest strand swamp in the big Cypress Basin. The strand is dominated by a wetland forest of cypress trees and subtropical hardwoods and supports the largest concentration and greatest density of native orchids in North America. It adjoins the Big Cypress National Preserve and Fakahatchee Strand State Preserve. While the refuge is closed to most public use to protect the panther, these adjacent public lands are open to general public use.

For further information contact: Florida Panther National Wildlife Refuge, 3860 Tollgate Blvd., Suite 30, Naples, Florida 33942. Phone: (813) 353-8442.

Also administered from this office is the brand new *Ten Thousand Islands* National Wildlife Refuge, 20,000 acres of coastal estuaries just north of Everglades National Park. The refuge comprises one of the last remaining stretches of undeveloped Florida coastline, with marsh and mangroves protecting breeding and feeding grounds for fish, endangered manatees, bald eagles and sea turtles, and possibly crocodiles. Trails and observation platforms planned—contact office for latest information.

LAKE WOODRUFF
★

Orlando

LAKE WOODRUFF (Florida)

Lake Woodruff is a sparkling wonder of wildlife habitat completely encircled by 19,000 acres of freshwater marsh, hardwood swamp, and scattered pinelands where black bears and otters, eagles, ospreys, and alligators make their home. Most of it appears entirely untouched by human presence.

All the beautiful herons and egrets are here, nesting in the area and posing for photographers, and the glossy ibis population has been burgeoning.

Shy uncommon limpkins, with a wild cry described as one of unutterable desolation, prowl the reeds in greater numbers than at any other refuge—500 or so—because of the abundance of their sole food, the apple snail. For the same reason, the exceedingly rare and endangered snail kite makes an occasional appearance.

Ospreys are everywhere, 65 nests in cypress snags at one recent count. Bald eagles nest in greater seclusion but are seen soaring and fishing. Stunning swallow-tailed kites are overhead almost anytime between April and October. Red-shouldered hawks scream from the tops of longleaf pines to proclaim visitors' arrival.

Barred owls are common, sometimes seen on a shadowed limb in daytime. Warblers nest, especially the northern parula, pines, and yellowthroats. Birders may find Bachman's sparrows.

Wood ducks nest in wooded cavities and in April produce broods of downy young that leap out of the nest on hatching and fall unhurt 40 feet or so. Blue-winged teal and ring-necked ducks spend the winter.

Armadillos, gentle armor-plated mammals from the Southwest, lumber along after grubs on the dikes. The handsome little golden mouse builds its nest in trees, sometimes in thick "beards" of Spanish moss. Endangered gopher tortoises have an upland colony.

Several trails are open, and there are trails around the impoundments, where white-tailed deer and sometimes bobcats stroll (at different times).

But the best way to see the refuge is by boat, either small power boat or, better (quieter), by canoe.

Wild orchids and air plants grow on trees that overhang waterways like a canopy. Bears come to drink. Manatees forage alongside on water hyacinths. Otters emerge and bark at the intrusion. And alligators up to 14 feet or so climb out on mudflats, protected and seeming to know it.

How to get there: From De Land take Route 17 north to De Leon Springs and refuge sign, then left one block to Grand Avenue, left there .5 mile to refuge office. Trails are a mile west of office.

Open: Daylight hours. Office 8–4:30 weekdays.

Best times to visit: November through April.

What to see: Ospreys, alligators, red-shouldered hawks, herons, egrets, ibises, limpkins, sometimes otters and manatees.

What to do: Several walking trails (the dike path is best for wildlife); boating and canoeing (rentals nearby).

Where to stay: Motels—in De Land. Campgrounds—Blue Spring State Park, 10 miles south, and Ocala National Forest, adjacent to refuge.

Weather: Midwinter can be cool, midsummer hot, humid.

Points of interest nearby: Blue Spring State Park (see Campgrounds) often has wintering manatees; Ocala National Forest, fine natural area.

For more information: Lake Woodruff National Wildlife Refuge, P.O. Box 488, De Leon Springs, Florida 32130. Phone: (904) 985–4673.

Gainesville

LOWER SUWANNEE

LOWER SUWANNEE (Florida)

The beauty of the Suwannee River first celebrated by songwriter Stephen Foster is undiminished today. Its banks lined with hardwoods where alligators loaf on every exposed log, its byways where otters frisk and black bears and bobcats drink from its edges, are here to be celebrated by the visitor now—especially one with a boat to explore its 100 miles of navigable secondary streams, half of them fresh, half tidal salt creeks.

Lower Suwannee Refuge encompasses more than 40,000 acres that include on both sides of the river estuary virtually every kind of habitat in the state of Florida, from floodplain to upland—and consequently, every kind of wildlife, often in stunning congregations.

More than 150 nesting pairs of ospreys are here and several pairs of bald eagles.

In March and April migrating shorebirds can quite literally cover its oysterbars—tens of thousands of knots, dowitchers, oystercatchers, sandpipers, turnstones, and plovers shoulder to shoulder, fattening up for their northward trip to breeding grounds.

From April through mid-July as many as 3,000 wading birds together—1,000 white ibises in a single flock—may be feeding in the freshwater and salt marshes.

Great and snowy egrets and great blue, little blue, and tricolored herons are among them; these birds roost in the area all year and nest in a huge heronry on adjacent Cedar Keys refuge. Sometimes 20,000 may be roosting together.

The sight of these thousands of beautiful birds—plus several dozen endangered wood storks—flying between feeding and nesting or roosting grounds at daybreak or sunset, filling the air with their cries and wingbeats, can never be forgotten.

At least as spectacular are the gatherings of wintering waterfowl—sometimes thousands of redhead ducks in a convention of seagoing rafts in the Suwannee estuary, along with ring-necks, buffleheads, scaup, ruddies, goldeneyes, and mergansers, and in the freshwater interior, gadwalls, teals, mallards, pintails, shovelers, and mottled and wood ducks.

Limpkins, rare elsewhere, commonly prowl the water's edge for snails. Graceful swallow-tailed kites glide motionless overhead all summer on warm thermal air currents. Cooper's hawks and raptors of all kinds make a good living on smaller creatures. Pileated woodpeckers hammer and scream raucously.

Deer, wild turkeys, and quail forage commonly through the wooded uplands, watched silently by barred owls. Yellow-throated, pine, and prairie warblers nest, as do seaside sparrows, summer tanagers, red-headed woodpeckers, and loggerhead shrikes.

Endangered manatees from the Crystal River herd, eased out into the gulf by warm summer temperatures, have their calves in Suwannee sound and regather in the fall to seek out warmer water again. In the grass flats green sea turtles and Ridley's and occasionally loggerheads feed.

But Lower Suwannee is not so much for the spectaculars—though they exist— as for the naturalist who by quiet patient observation can come to appreciate the whole magnificent ecosystem here. This is the visitor who will see the brown-headed nuthatch gathering nesting material; the bobcat waiting in the shadows; the black bear coming quietly to the water's edge to drink; the sea turtle rising to the water's surface to breathe; and perhaps the gentle endangered indigo snake and gopher tortoise.

This broad river, almost a half-mile wide in places, can be navigated by power boat; but the tributaries are enjoyable in a quiet canoe, allowing unnoticed approach. However, be careful; get a map from refuge headquarters and tell someone your trip plans. One woman was lost for 36 hours and finally located by helicopter.

There is also a boardwalk and self-guided walking trail, 15 miles of refuge roads open to driving, plus 40 miles of old logging roads open to hikers that cover every type of wildlife habitat here.

And since the Suwannee has official status as one of Florida's Outstanding Waters, there is a good chance it will stay in its beautiful pristine state.

How to get there: From Gainesville take State Road 26 to Trenton, then Highway 129 south to Chiefland, then U.S. 19 south for 1 mile, then County Road 345 south 6 miles to County Road 347, and west on 347 for 12 miles to refuge sign.

Open: 24 hours daily; office 7:30–4 weekdays.

Best times to visit: All except mid- and late summer (hot and humid then, with voracious stinging insects).

What to see: Beautiful wading birds; shorebirds; bald eagles; ospreys; deer; other wildlife.

What to do: Boating, hiking, driving along roads; fishing is fantastic, both salt and fresh. Guides and charters available in Fowlers Bluff and town of Suwannee.

Where to stay: Motels—in Chiefland and Cedar Key. Campgrounds—Shell Mound County Campground, inholding on refuge; Manatee Springs State Park, 20 miles northeast; Shired Island County Campground, inholding on northwest refuge section.

Weather: Summer hot, humid.

Points of interest nearby: Cedar Keys National Wildlife Refuge, adjacent; Manatee Springs State Park, 20 miles northeast; Cedar Key Scrub State Park, adjoins to south, interesting scrub oak community.

For more information: Lower Suwannee National Wildlife Refuge, P.O. Box 1193-C, Chiefland, Florida 32626. Phone: (904) 493–0238.

Cedar Keys National Wildlife Refuge, administered by Lower Suwannee and located adjacent, is a collection of small subtropical islands supporting one of the largest nesting colonies of herons, egrets, brown pelicans, and other water birds in the South. In years past, there have been up to 200,000 birds, including 60,000 white ibises alone—along with perhaps the largest population of poisonous cottonmouth water moccasins of any place its size in the world. A doctoral candidate studying the cottonmouth tagged over 700 on the island. The two seem to exist in harmony, the snakes subsisting on fish leavings and eliminating rats as potential predators, the birds, which normally prey on smaller snakes, leaving them mostly alone.

Access to Cedar Key islands is by boat only, and only the beaches are open to public use (daylight only), but wonderful birding is possible from the beaches and from boats that can be rented in Cedar Key. Spring shorebirds are fantastic as at Lower Suwannee, and even warbler migrations can be observed from a boat in the channels.

Island interiors are closed to protect delicate flora and fauna, and Seahorse Key, which has the large heronry, is closed entirely (and patrolled) from January through June to protect the nesters. The town of Cedar Key is worth a visit, with its marine and nature museum—most of the birds that nest on the keys are seen around the town in large numbers.

LOXAHATCHEE
★
Fort Lauderdale •

LOXAHATCHEE (Florida)

The softly whirring wings of tens of thousands of beautiful herons and egrets calling to one another as they fly against a setting sun to roost for the night at Loxahatchee can hardly be described—it is overwhelming. It can be experienced at few places in the world.

Loxahatchee refuge encompasses more than 145,000 acres—221 square miles—of the legendary "River of Grass" that once covered the whole southern part of Florida as the Everglades. It is the northernmost remnant of that vast natural area and includes some of the most pristine remaining parts. It supports immense populations of wildlife and plants found nowhere else.

Thirteen endangered or threatened species find homes here.

Everglade snail kites only 14 inches long but with 44-inch wingspreads fly effortlessly over the marsh, settling so lightly that the smallest of branches will support them. They are one of the rarest birds in the United States. Here they share a lush population of apple snails (their sole food) with handsome brown limpkins, the "crying birds" of the marsh—rare elsewhere but common here. Here also are the Everglade minks, crested caracaras, bald eagles, and Florida sandhill cranes.

Plant life is fascinating. Native orchids and ferns are everywhere in the cypress swamp and along the boardwalk. A single cypress tree may support several hundred pink-blossoming bromeliads (air plants) along with the "baton rouge," a strawberry-colored lichen on its trunk.

But it is the huge numbers of beautiful wading birds that are the most memorable experience for most visitors. In a good year—which depends on water levels— there are as many as 270 rookeries on the refuge, each holding from a few up to 10,000 nesting pairs of herons, egrets, and ibises.

The most visible of these is along the Marsh Trail right behind the refuge office. It can hold up to 1,200 birds at the peak of breeding activity, and visitors can easily watch the entire breeding cycle, from the graceful dances and display of lacy nuptial plumage during courtship through incubation of eggs and feeding of the young birds.

Alligators are common, guarding their own yellow and black young ones in springtime and performing a useful task in patrolling the bird islands. They may snatch up a few young birds but they protect more than they get by preventing access to the roost by land predators such as raccoons.

An even larger rookery in the interior supports up to 20,000 white ibises, which spill out for their hunting into more visible refuge areas. (Water levels are all-important to nesting success: At three inches, food fish are condensed in pools. Under that, they dry up. Much over that, the fish disperse and adults find it difficult to catch enough to support a hungry nestful.)

In fact, there is much to see in any season. Anhingas—the southern "snakebirds" that can twist their necks in all directions—nest from early winter into summer. Fulvous whistling ducks are here winter, spring, and fall.

Gorgeous purple gallinules are always around, wood storks most of the time. As many as 45,000 ducks of 17 species spend the winter. And warblers are everywhere from mid-February through mid-April and again in fall, perhaps two dozen species, including the orange-crowned, Cape May, black-throated blue, yellow-throated, and prairie, plus indigo and painted buntings.

Bobcats and otters are here, and Florida panthers are believed to be present. But one must be prepared to spend some time and look carefully for any of these. Seen by only a few visitors, one bobcat whelped and raised a litter in a den on the Marsh Trail, so wary and quiet was it.

All this natural wonderland is under constant threat. Encroachment on or pollution of its water supply by agricultural runoff is destroying the habitat that makes possible its very existence. Once destroyed, even on the perimeter, this precious national treasure could be lost forever.

How to get there: From West Palm Beach take I-95 south to Boynton Beach Boulevard, exit west to U.S. 441, then two miles south on 441 to headquarters entrance.

Open: Sunrise to sunset year-round. May be closed during extreme drought periods but Visitor Center remains open 9–4 weekdays, 9–4:30 weekends, except closed Christmas Day and Monday–Tuesday mid-April to mid-October.

Best times to visit: Late fall, winter, spring.

What to see: Wading birds in large numbers; endangered snail kite; limpkins, alligators; ferns, orchids, air plants unique to the area.

What to do: Boardwalk; wildlife trails; boating (rentals available); 5.5-mile canoe trail; fishing popular for bass, bream; guided airboat tours; special events and tours scheduled throughout winter months.

Where to stay: Motels—in Royal Palm, 20 miles south; Delray, Boynton, 15 miles east. Campgrounds—John Prince County Park in Lake Worth.

Weather: Summer can be oppressive; January subject to cold snaps.

Points of interest nearby: Everglades National Park, 60 miles south; Hobe Sound Refuge, 40 miles north; Key Deer Refuge, 125 miles south.

For more information: Loxahatchee National Wildlife Refuge, Route 1, Box 278, Boynton Beach, Florida 33437. Phone: (407) 732–3684.

Hobe Sound Refuge, administered by Loxahatchee, on three and a half miles of shoreline supports the densest sea turtle nesting habitat of any national wildlife refuge on the Atlantic Coast. It is one of the last undeveloped stretches of barrier beach and dunes in a highly developed area—977 acres along the Intracoastal Waterway and Jupiter Island—and was preserved when residents donated it to the Fish and Wildlife Service through The Nature Conservancy.

Three species of endangered turtles use it for their crawls from May to August, the females emerging from the sea at night to scour out holes in the sand where they lay their eggs (weeping as they do so, for reasons not known). They may lay more than 100 eggs in a nest, then cover them with sand to be incubated by the sun's warmth. In recent years more than 1,000 nests have been recorded annually, most of them for the loggerhead sea turtle. But green sea turtles and leatherbacks also nest here, the leatherback the largest turtle in the world. It can weigh up to 1,500 pounds, its shell up to six feet across, its huge nest large enough to drive a small car into.

Summer visitors can join the Hobe Sound Nature Center for night turtle walks to observe all this.

Endangered least terns sometimes nest on the beach; when they do, the colony is roped off to protect them from disturbance (they sometimes also nest on the graveled roof of a nearby supermarket, where they find even less disturbance except when washed out by torrential rains).

The upland tract protects three endangered species—the gopher tortoise, indigo snake, and scrub jays.

Refuge headquarters is about six miles north of Tequesta on U.S. 1. Jonathan Dickinson State Park, ajdacent, has nature trails, camping, canoe rentals, and Florida's only wild and scenic river. At the south end of Jupiter Island is The Nature Conservancy's Blowing Rocks Preserve.

For further information contact Hobe Sound National Wildlife Refuge, P.O. Box 645, Hobe Sound, Florida 33475. Phone: (407) 546–6141.

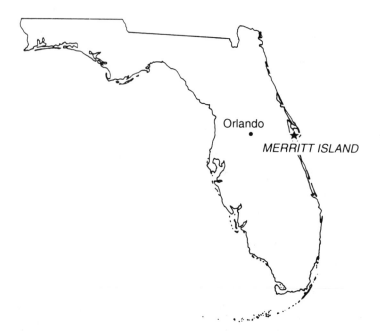

Orlando
•
★
MERRITT ISLAND

MERRITT ISLAND (Florida)

Merritt Island came about as a just-in-time idea during creation of the vast U.S. space center here. Housing and commercial construction had already begun (and by now would almost certainly cover this whole area, as it does much of this Florida east coast) when NASA began buying the land from which man first rocketed off to the moon.

Then it occurred to environmentalists and space people alike that there might be room for both here.

Merritt Island now is one of the great national wildlife refuges, with more endangered and threatened species than any other continental refuge, plus large concentrations of many nonendangered species—all on an overlay on Space Center land adjoining Canaveral National Seashore.

Nowhere is the ancient world juxtaposed so dramatically—and so harmoniously—with the modern world's technology as when prehistoric loggerhead turtles crawl up on a moonlit beach to dig nests and lay eggs in full view of a brightly lit shuttle on its pad. Biologists watched anxiously during the first shuttle launch for wildlife disturbance. They found that nesting eagles and ospreys barely turned their heads.

Many species here would be under extreme pressure but for this refuge, among them the southern bald eagle, which some years has seven active nests here. Sometimes 30 swift peregrine falcons have been here on a single day. Gentle manatees can be seen in refuge waters in all except midwinter. Brown pelicans nest here in even greater numbers than at nearby Pelican Island. The still-threatened American alligator is in safe numbers on this barrier island.

Endangered wood storks pair off here with greater nest success than anywhere else—for good reason. These majestic black-and-white birds require precise water depths to provide food both for themselves and their chicks. Too much or too little and they will abandon nests or even fail to develop breeding plumage. Here, water in the 77 ponds where they nest on over 25,000 acres can be adjusted to their exact needs.

Green and loggerhead sea turtles emerge from the sea to scour out nests on the sandy beach. There are also leatherbacks, largest of all living turtles. These weigh up to 1,500 pounds and have the unexplained ability to keep their cold-blooded bodies at warmer temperatures than the surrounding water. At least until recently visitors have been invited to go along on turtle watches to witness this moving nighttime summer event (check with refuge office and reserve early; spaces are limited).

At least 17 endangered or threatened animal species are here, including Florida scrub jays, which sometimes perch on visitors' shoulders; eastern indigo snakes; gopher tortoises; and numerous plants: the hand fern, pond apple, sea lavender, and others.

But equally interesting are the throngs of wild inhabitants that, if not rare as a species, are rare in most visitors' experience in the numbers in which they occur here—like wintering flocks of thousands of robins and tens of thousands of tree swallows.

Graceful long-legged wading birds colonize in heronries with thousands of nests—the greatest congregation of all these beautiful species on the U.S. East Coast, with great, tricolored, little blue, and green herons; black-crowned and yellow-crowned night herons; glossy and white ibises; snowy, cattle, and great egrets; and, here in their northernmost nesting occurrence, reddish egrets.

King, clapper, Virginia and sora rails are among the 310 birds on the refuge list—black rails, too, though these are so secretive they are hard to spot.

Bobcats, unusually large and husky ones here, are seen several times a week, sometimes with kits; and families of otters like to swim alongside the Black Point Wildlife Drive, frisking with young families, sliding down the banks, barking curiously at visitors who stop.

The Merritt Island tallies are usually among the highest in the nation in the annual Audubon Christmas Bird Count, both in numbers of species and numbers of individuals—merlins, palm warblers, kingfishers, and dozens of others.

Some species of birds—warblers, shorebirds, raptors, waterfowl—are migrating in some direction or arriving to spend a while almost anytime except during peak midsummer nesting. A visitor can almost count on seeing at least one rare peregrine falcon any day during October and November and often many more.

Large numbers of kestrels and sharp-shinned hawks might be stopping along the beach. Swainson's and worm-eating warblers and redstarts might be in brushy areas. Winter peaks of waterfowl often reach 70,000 or more of 23 species.

All this only suggests the wealth of wildlife here, much of which is visible to any visitor taking a little time to look quietly and carefully along the miles of walking trails or roads.

How to get there: From Orlando take the Beeline Expressway east to Route I-95, north to Route (state route) 406, and follow 406 through Titusville to the refuge, east of the Indian River Lagoon.

Open: Daylight hours all year (except when activities at Space Center close area). Office 8–4:30 weekdays. Visitor Center 9–5 weekends.

Best times to visit: All year has fine wildlife but June-August least advantageous, with many (including humans) seeking shelter from extreme heat.

What to see: More endangered and threatened plants and animals than any other continental U.S refuge, including eagles, manatees, alligators, peregrine falcons—plus large concentrations of nonendangered.

What to do: Self-guided walking and driving trails plus 100 miles of roads for on-your-own observation; photography (no blinds but photographers are encouraged to use their own and refuge staff is glad to advise where and how); boating (rentals nearby); fishing as good as any place in Florida for trout, redfish, pompano, whiting, blues. Films shown for groups by appointment.

Where to stay: Motels—at Titusville. Campgrounds—at Titusville; also Long Point County Park and Sebastian Inlet State Park, 50 miles south (near Pelican Island National Wildlife Refuge).

Weather: Summer hot, humid; mosquitoes ferocious and can last till Thanksgiving in a wet year. Some cool rainy days in January.

Points of interest nearby: Kennedy Space Center, with variety of interesting tours; Canaveral National Seashore; Pelican Island Refuge.

For more information: Merritt Island National Wildlife Refuge, P.O. Box 6504, Titusville, Florida 32782. Phone: (407) 867-0667.

Pelican Island, administered by Merritt Island, was the beginning in 1903 of the National Wildlife Refuge System. Even then for as long as anyone could remember it had been a roosting and nesting place for these large birds with huge feeding pouches in ponderous bills, so ungainly at rest but so graceful in the air, marvelously aloft on wings seven feet or so across. Like many birds in the 1800s there seemed such an inexhaustible number of them it mattered little if passing yachtsmen shot them for sport. But eventually the killing, particularly of birds at the nest, aroused nature groups such as the Florida Audubon Society and, through them, President Theodore Roosevelt. Despite criticism he took the unprecedented step of creating by Executive Order a national wildlife refuge to be a sanctuary and protected breeding ground for native birds.

Since then buffer zones have been added to the 3.5-acre island until the refuge now encloses thousands of acres of protected islands and water, where the pelicans, up to 500 nesting pairs, along with numbers of herons, egrets, cormorants, ibises, frigatebirds, and others gather all year to feed, roost, and raise young. It is an impressive sight—birds seeming sometimes to cover the tiny bit of land, hundreds soaring overhead almost anytime during daylight hours.

It can be seen from the mainland at the town of Sebastian (a spotting scope would be helpful) or from a planned visitor center. Boats can be rented nearby to view the island (from a distance) and also to explore the beautiful Indian River area, where almost any bird familiar to Florida is likely to be seen at one time or another.

St. Johns Refuge, also administered by Merritt Island, is a cordgrass salt marsh on the east side of the St. Johns River where the last dusky seaside sparrow was seen in the wild. It was one of the world's most endangered creatures and this refuge was established in the hope of saving it. Perhaps its population was too small to recover; at any rate it is now sadly reckoned to be extinct.

Key West

NATIONAL KEY DEER

NATIONAL KEY DEER (Florida)

The diminutive Florida Key deer, almost miraculously surviving today, is surely one of nature's most captivating creations. A fully antlered buck stands just over two feet high at the shoulders, a spotted fawn less than a foot. The sight of one of these teetering beside its mother from April to August inclines the onlooker to shake his head in disbelief. As recently as 1950 their total numbers were well below 100, brought near extinction by habitat destruction and poachers who used fire, packs of hounds, hatchets, bludgeons, and guns to kill and drive them from the Florida Keys, which had been their home since prehistoric times.

Excellent swimmers, they have been seen a mile or more at sea plowing the emerald waters between islands, a capability that may have contributed to their survival (as does the surprising fact that many of their wild foods here are equivalent in energy content to commercial animal feeds).

None would be alive today but for a handful of people who recognized their plight and publicized it, arousing nationwide concern that led to establishment of a national wildlife refuge for them in 1957.

Their survival is still uncertain. A recent estimate of 250–300 was down by about

100 from the 1970s. Important habitat is still being lost to commercial and residential development. Protected refuge lands are confusingly checkerboarded through the area and well-meaning residents illegally feed the deer, making them unwary of danger. Forty or so are killed every year by speeders on the roads. The Wilderness Society considers this one of the nation's ten most endangered refuges.

But visitors still can delight in the sight of Key deer almost anywhere in the area, especially on Big Pine and No Name keys, where solution holes in the oolite limestone hold the fresh water they need.

Key deer are but one of a remarkable array of rare creatures, some found nowhere else in the continental United States, that maintain a precarious existence on these tropical islands and in the clear blue-green water around them.

The American crocodile, sharper-nosed kin to the alligator, is found on Crocodile Lake Refuge and rarely elsewhere in Florida.

White-crowned pigeons, mangrove cuckoos, black-whiskered vireos, and great white herons are readily seen here (the last, now termed a color phase of the great blue heron, are distinguishable from the similar great egret by their large size and yellow, not black, legs).

Magnificent frigate birds inflate their breeding pouches like great scarlet balloons at their throats. Hundreds wheel overhead at any time of the year like black cutouts against the sky.

Several pairs of bald eagles nest as do dozens of ospreys—many on power poles along the main road. There are endangered yellow-and-black-striped Shaus' swallowtail butterflies; nesting loggerhead and green sea turtles; a few manatees in the clear inlets; and hundreds of beautiful wading birds of all species, many of which nest in large colonies on offshore mangrove islands. They fish in the shallows and mud flats along the roads, as do raccoons, the local tribe looking like bleached blondes with honey-colored pelts and indistinct or no rings on their bushy tails.

Brightly colored orchids and crimson bromeliads are among the exotic plants of which some, like the Florida tree cactus, are unique in the world.

How to get there: From Marathon take Route 1 south to Big Pine Key, turn right onto route 940 (Key Deer Boulevard) to Watson Boulevard and left at sign to National Key Deer headquarters. For visitors' contact point and nature trail continue on boulevard (1.25 miles) and turn off at refuge sign.

Open: Daylight hours. Office 8–5 weekdays.

Best times to visit: Fall, winter, spring.

What to see: Key deer; alligators; great white herons; ospreys; white-crowned pigeons; an array of flora and fauna occurring rarely or nowhere else in the U.S.

What to do: Walking trail and nearby Blue Hole, where alligators loaf; nature observation by walking, driving, or boat (rentals with guides available throughout area); photography; snorkeling in shallow, clear water or over reefs from boat.

Where to stay: Motels—in Marathon, Key West, or throughout the Keys. Campgrounds—Bahia Honda State Recreation Area, various others (marinas available for those coming by boat).

Weather: Summers seem burningly hot and humid to the uninitiated; otherwise beautiful year-round.

What to take and wear: Plenty of protective sun lotion and covering; insect repellent in summer. Take nautical charts when boating and consult an experienced boatman if going alone—it can be hazardous.

Points of interest nearby: Key West—interesting historic place with tram tours. Bahia Honda State Recreation Area, good shorebird viewing. Fine snorkeling and diving on North America's only coral reef at Looe Key National Marine Sanctuary, five miles off Big Pine Key, and Key Largo National Marine Sanctuary and John Pennekamp Coral Reef State Park, off Key Largo (also glass-bottom boats).

For more information: National Key Deer Refuge, P.O. Box 510, Big Pine Key, Florida 33043. Phone: (305) 872–2239.

National Key Deer Refuge (7,900 acres) administers two others: *Great White Heron* (7,407 acres) and *Key West* Refuge (2,019 acres and one of the oldest in the system, established in 1908). Their boundaries overlap and include many offshore islands. Together they extend 60 miles from Bahia Honda Key southwest to the Marquesas.

Refuge and private land boundaries are not too distinct, but for the most part well-behaved visitors can go anywhere.

National Key Deer also administers *Crocodile Lake* Refuge (4,205 acres) on North Key Largo, established in 1980 on critical crocodile nesting habitat that had been slated for development. Without this refuge the American crocodile might not exist today. This shy reptile is rarely seen and generally avoids contact with humans.

ST. MARKS (Florida)

Eagles, black bears, alligators, otters, and spadefoot toads are a sampling of the tremendous variety of wildlife on this refuge that protects 100,000 acres along the Big Bend coast of northwest Florida.

It is one of the rare places north of the Mexican border where the jaguarundi, a slender dark wildcat twice the size of a domestic type, is known to live.

Manatees and occasionally big sea turtles make summer homes in the 35,000 acres of water in Apalachee Bay, and at peak times up to 80,000 ducks spend the winter there—redheads, buffleheads, ring-necks, and scaup.

White-tailed deer, wild turkeys, bobcats, and armadillos find places they like in piney flatwoods, hardwood hammocks, and sandy oak country. Otters patrol more watery areas.

All the beautiful long-legged wading birds feed along the freshwater edges—great and little blue herons, snowy, reddish, and great egrets, white and glossy ibises, and sometimes endangered wood storks. Alongside them in the winter may be 25,000 wintering waterfowl—wigeons, pintails, gadwalls, shovelers, and green- and blue-winged teals.

Multihued wood ducks and pied-billed grebes are around all year, as are brown pelicans, belted kingfishers, and clapper rails. Here all but summer—when purple gallinules make their stunning appearance—are horned grebes, white pelicans, and loons.

Bald eagles start building (or reconstructing) nests in November—there are nine pairs here, one within binocular viewing, the others in remote areas. Eagles and ospreys can be seen fishing almost any time. There are usually about 100 osprey nests in old snags.

Endangered red-cockaded woodpeckers are not so easy to see; their four active colonies are in remote pine woods. But their numbers should increase as the woods age and more trees fulfill their exacting requirements—being at least 50 years old with soft "red heart" centers appropriate for these particular small birds' nest holes.

Other small birds can be here in great numbers, especially warblers and songbirds flitting through the shrubbery along the water and through the woodland understory in spring migration; many of the loveliest stay and nest—indigo buntings, prothonotary warblers, summer tanagers, orchard orioles, ruby-throated hummingbirds, seaside sparrows, and yellow-breasted chats.

In June and continuing well into autumn, whole sections of refuge waters are covered with 300 acres of white-blooming water lilies.

Monarch butterflies may appear en masse in late October—thousands clustered on shrubs and trees, staging for the dramatic migration of these fragile creatures over the Gulf to wintering grounds in Mexico.

St. Marks always ranks among top locales on the annual Audubon Society Christmas Bird Count for number of species—invariably over 150. Highlights of a recent count were 67 pileated woodpeckers, 23 red-tailed hawks, 1,341 double-crested cormorants, 10 endangered piping plovers, 16 barred owls, 39 brown-headed nuthatches, 316 ruby-crowned kinglets, and 48 belted kingfishers.

Most visitors see all this from the seven-mile road that ends up at the historic St. Marks lighthouse. But much more can be seen by getting out and bicycling or walking around. Forty-two miles of the Florida National Scenic Trail wind through the refuge. Or take a boat or canoe and explore the waterways. The refuge has 17,000 acres of designated wilderness area, where many of the wilder residents—and quite likely the jaguarundi—spend a good part of their time.

How to get there: From Tallahassee take Route 363 south about 20 miles to Route 98, east on 98 to Newport, then three miles south on Route 59 to refuge.

Open: Sunrise to sunset. Office and visitor center, 8–4:15 daily, 10–5 weekends. Entrance fee.

Best times to visit: Fall through spring (though interesting all year).

What to see: Ospreys, eagles, alligators, waterfowl, good assortment of small birds. Historic lighthouse.

What to do: Drive along lighthouse road; some 60 miles of roads for walking, observing; observation towers; boating and canoeing (rentals nearby); fishing good, both saltwater and fresh.

Where to stay: Motels—at Wakulla Springs, 10 miles northeast; also Panacea and Shell Point, to the west; also Tallahassee. Campgrounds—in nearby Newport; also Ochlockonee State Park and Apalachicola National Forest, to the west.

Weather: January is cool; summer hot, humid, with variety of biting insects.

Points of interest nearby: Fort San Marcos de Apalache, dating to 1500s, adjacent; Wacissa River nearby, a major canoe trail; Wakulla Springs (Edward Ball) State Park—a nature sanctuary with wildlife-viewing cruises (ospreys, limpkins, others) where the Wakulla River originates in a powerful spring flowing 83 million gallons a day, and mastodon bones have been found.

For more information: St. Marks National Wildlife Refuge, P.O. Box 68, St. Marks, Florida 32355. Phone: (904) 925–6121.

Panama City

ST. VINCENT

ST. VINCENT (Florida)

For anyone who has ever wished to be on a beautiful, wild, uninhabited subtropical island—here it is.

Named by Franciscan friars in 1633, St. Vincent is 12,358 acres of wide golden beaches, 10-foot-high dunes, sparkling freshwater ponds and tidal marsh, plus wooded and upland interiors that give it a wildlife and habitat diversity strikingly different from most barrier islands.

Tall magnolias flower in gorgeous springtime display, and great spreading live oaks are hung with Spanish moss along the north shore, along with a tremendous variety of other inland vegetation.

Ospreys and eagles nest and swoop down for fish in ponds and offshore waters. Skimmers ply the shallows, scarlet bills agape to glean small surface organisms. Shorebirds—oystercatchers and five kinds of plovers—congregate on oysterbars and nest (in protected areas) on the western shore. Swallow-tailed kites and brown pelicans soar overhead. Loggerhead sea turtles crawl up to scour out nests and lay eggs on moonlit summer nights.

And away from the shore, wild turkeys gobble up acorns, gray and red foxes prey on small rodents, white-tailed deer browse, and feral pigs, said to have Russian boar blood, root around for tubers. Small birds of the shrubs and woods nest—towhees, cardinals, brown-headed nuthatches, red-eyed vireos, red-bellied and downy woodpeckers, and a variety of warblers—northern parula, yellow-throated, yellow-rumped, and pine.

Bluebirds, eastern phoebes, and hermit and Swainson's thrush spend the winter.

Indians lived on St. Vincent centuries ago and left shell middens (it's illegal to disturb them). More recently it was stocked with exotic animals—zebras and such—of which only the sambur deer, sturdy beasts of Southeast Asian origin, remain. Related to our American elk, they weigh up to 700 pounds with large decorative antlers, and haunt marshy areas—which can get them into trouble with members of the island's large alligator population, known to bring down and make a meal of one.

Great blue and little blue herons and snowy and common egrets fish the water's edge and nest in rookeries in the dense interior. White ibises and endangered wood storks stop over.

Raptors pause in fall migration and a beachwalker in late October might see peregrine falcons, kestrels, and red-tailed, broad-winged, and sharp-shinned hawks, a half-dozen at a time stopping to rest and hunt.

Bronze gulf fritillary butterflies with silver-spotted underwings feed at purple-blooming blazing stars, joined by monarchs in their autumn flight south. Warblers stop by spring and fall.

Spring flowers abound—beach morning glories, marsh marigolds, swamp irises, rose mallows, salt-marsh hibiscus, small orchidlike blue sage, and fragrant rosemaries that scent the whole island.

Herpetologists enjoy the large snake population but visitors should step carefullly in dense areas and watch where they put their hands, lest a cottonmouth or rattler be lurking. Good lists are available of all the wild populations.

Access to St. Vincent is by boat only. Rentals are only sporadically available, so best bring your own. But on a calm day an inflatable rubber raft can negotiate the 500 yards from the mainland. And once there, more than 8 miles of shell-strewn beaches and 80 miles of sand roads (clearly marked) await to be explored on foot or bike. (If you think you see a red wolf, you might be right; St. Vincent is part of a repropagation program for this almost extinct species.)

How to get there: Headquarters: From Panama City take Route 98 65 miles to Apalachicola, go through town, turn left at the stoplight, and go one mile to the
marina; refuge headquarters is in the Harbor Master House on the right. The
refuge: From Apalachicola take U.S. Hwy 98-W approximately seven miles,
turn left onto County Road C-30 for 13 miles, turn left onto County Road
30-B (Indian Pass Road) three miles to end of road at the boat ramp (St.
Vincent Island is directly to the east across the pass).

Open: Refuge: daylight hours. Office: 8–4:30 weekdays.

Best times to visit: All but late summer, when heat, humidity, and insects are formidable.

What to take and wear: Sunglasses, hat (glare is intense), insect repellent; NEVER visit island without drinking water, even for a short stay.

What to see: Bald eagles, ospreys, pelicans, shorebirds and wading birds, alligators, deer, occasional foxes, otters, others.

What to do: More than 80 miles of roads for walking and biking (no motors). Beachcombing on eight miles of Gulf beaches. Photography—staff can suggest where and how to put up temporary blinds. Boating—this is the only island access; rentals and guides sometimes available.

Where to stay: Motels—Apalachicola. Campgrounds—at Indian Pass, 23 miles west; St. Joe Peninsula State Park, 30 miles west; St. George Island State Park, 21 miles east.

Weather: January–February can be cool, midsummer heat can seem unbearable.

Points of interest nearby: St. Joe Peninsula and St. George Island state parks—trails, beach (see Campgrounds); Apalachicola National Estuarine Research Reserve with visitor center in Apalachicola.

For more information: St. Vincent National Wildlife Refuge, P.O. Box 447, Apalachicola, Florida 32320. Phone: (904) 653–8808.

Mayaguez

★ *CARIBBEAN ISLANDS*

CARIBBEAN ISLANDS (Puerto Rico)

Streamer-tailed tropicbirds and large colonies of sooty terns nest, and leatherback turtles weighing a half ton crawl up on beaches and lay their eggs on this collection of refuge units, some of the most beautiful in the national wildlife refuge system.

Several are separate islands surrounded by long undisturbed reefs where spectacular tropical fish make their homes. Some are difficult or closed to public access, for reasons ranging from sensitive nesting areas to unexploded military ordnance.

Headquarters is at *Cabo Rojo* Refuge in Puerto Rico, where endangered yellow-shouldered blackbirds live along a loop trail and miles of service roads are available for birdwatchers to look around. It's best during the winter, when migrants come south and parula, prairie, Cape May, and unusual Adelaide's warblers may be here, along with smooth-billed anis and, all year, bananaquits, grassquits, warbling silverbills, nutmeg mannikins, and others.

This is not a prime birding area, however. Other nearby spots can be more productive: the Cabo Rojo salt flats, adjacent, where thousands of shorebirds—western and semipalmated sandpipers and others—can gather; and a Department of Natural Resources bird refuge with a variety of wading birds and waterfowl.

Laguna Cartagena, a new refuge unit five miles east, attracts purple gallinules, wading birds, and others to a large lagoon but until recently has been choked with cattails, and viewing has been all but impossible. Check for recent developments.

The refuge headquarters is a former Central Intelligence Agency listening post covered with a massive antennae system, gradually being removed, where peregrine falcons sometimes perch. To get there consult a map of Puerto Rico. From Mayaguez take Route 100 south to Boqueron, left there on Route 101, go one mile to Las Arenas, right on Route 301 to Km 5.1, where refuge office is located. There are places to stay in La Parguera, Mayaguez, and Boqueron, and a trailer park with cabanas nearby.

Visitors to all these tropical refuges should wear sunscreen, a hat, and other skin covering, and take water.

For more information on any of these, contact Caribbean Islands National Wildlife Refuge, P.O. Box 510, Boqueron, Puerto Rico 00622. Phone: (809) 851–7258.

Other refuge units are:

Buck Island—a 45-acre island, access by private boat only, with no trails or visitor facilities but a reef popular with snorklers and divers. Hawksbill sea turtles and red-billed tropicbirds nest here, also least terns. (Note: This is not the same as Buck Island Reef, a national monument near Green Cay.)

Culebra—one of the oldest U.S. refuges, established by proclamation in 1909 by President Theodore Roosevelt for migratory and nesting seabirds. It includes several units on the island of Culebra, also nearby Culebrita and 22 other islands and rocks including a series of tiny nesting islands. Culebra itself has a nesting colony of 15,000 pairs of sooty terns and 500 pairs of noddies on Flamenco Peninsula, where access is forbidden due to unexploded ordnance.

Other seabirds that nest on Culebra and on nearby refuge islands include both white-tailed and red-billed tropicbirds, bridled and roseate terns, and brown, masked, and red-footed boobies. Best way to see these is from a boat (access is not permitted during nesting season).

Sea turtles also nest—hawksbill, green, and the huge (up to 70 inches long, weighing a half ton) leatherbacks. Permission is sometimes granted to accompany research groups observing and tagging turtles laying their eggs on beaches at night.

Birding can be good around the island for wintering warblers and other species—ask at the refuge office. A bird list is available, as is information about the island, which is reachable by air or ferry from Puerto Rico. The islands are surrounded by many reefs where snorkeling and scuba diving are wonderful. Boat and car rentals can usually be arranged. Call ahead. Refuge headquarters telephone is (809) 742–0115.

Desecheo is a 360-acre rocky volcanic cone with three species of endemic lizards where brown boobies also nest. A special use permit can sometimes be obtained for research projects—otherwise unexploded ordnance keeps it closed to public access. But beautiful tropical fish inhabit the reefs around it, and hawksbill and green sea turtles nest.

Tiny 14-acre *Green Cay* is usually seen from a boat arranged in St. Croix and bound for nearby Buck Island Reef National Monument, a lovely place to observe the underwater world by snorkel or scuba. Green Cay's beaches are closed March 1 to September 30 to protect nesting shorebirds, especially endangered piping plovers, but its brown pelican roost is easily observed from offshore.

Least terns nest on *Sandy Point,* which has one of the prettiest and longest beaches on St. Croix. The colony is protected from access. Also, visitors should be warned of security problems there in recent years. Personal belongings should be protected. To get there from the airport take Route 66 to its dead end, then continue straight a half mile on a dirt road to the refuge. The Sandy Point beach is also a significant nesting area for huge leatherback turtles—highest density in the U.S.—as well as hawksbill and green sea turtles. Arrangements can sometimes be made to go out with those who monitor the nesting and watch these behemoths crawl out of the sea on warm nights from early March to mid-July and lay their eggs.

The Great Lakes States

The Great Lakes form the largest body of fresh water in the world, with surface area equal to almost a third of all the world's lakes together. Most of the refuges in this region are water-based.

MINNESOTA

Agassiz, for example, is named for Lake Agassiz, a huge prehistoric body of water that once covered an area larger than all the Great Lakes together. Now it combines open water, marsh, and woodland to harbor moose, a resident gray wolf pack, bobcats, coyotes, bears, fishers, and porcupines along with nesting sandhill cranes in an area of almost 100 square miles.

Big Stone has some of the oldest rocks on earth, formed two billion years ago. Now they form parts of beautiful hiking trails alongside marsh, swamps, woods, and tallgrass prairie where red fox go mousing and grassland birds flock in spring to nest.

Most refuges are set aside because they offer habitat to various wildlife species. *Minnesota Valley* became a refuge because citizens wanted one near their urban surroundings and worked to make it happen. Now coyotes howl, prothonotary warblers nest, and beautiful wood ducks raise young in this exciting new refuge along 34 miles of the Minnesota River.

Chippewa Indians harvest wild rice as they have for generations at *Rice Lake*—leaving some grains for more than 100,000 handsome ring-necked and other ducks and geese that stop here in fall. Black bears forage in the woods and porcupines climb aspens to nibble tender tips of bark and leaves.

Eagles nest and sandhill cranes leap up in courtship dances at *Sherburne,* 30,665 acres of lakes, woods, and grasslands not far from Minneapolis. White-tailed deer browse, leading spotted fawns in spring. Red fox sometimes den near refuge maintenance buildings.

Trumpeter swans, once near extinction, fly free at *Tamarac* in the company of bald eagles, deer, beavers, coyotes, and, in summer, several hundred white pelicans.

Upper Mississippi River extends along this great river system through four states and on the way offers habitat to some wonderful wildlife congregations—up to 60 percent of North America's tundra swans; up to 70 percent of the world's canvasback ducks; dozens of bald eagles; altogether 270 bird species, 50 mammals, 45 amphibians and reptiles, and 133 kinds of fish, plus fascinating plants.

WISCONSIN

Horicon's fame is based on its huge gatherings of Canada geese in the fall—but others make homes here, too: hundreds of graceful herons and egrets, white-tailed deer, red foxes, coyotes, minks, raccoons, and a half-dozen duck species.

Majestic greater sandhill cranes have made a comeback since their listing as endangered species and now perform high-leaping courtship dances at *Necedah*. Wild turkeys are also common now at this 43,656 acres of marsh, woods, and restored prairie.

Trempealeau is part of the Mississippi Flyway corridor and supports both upland and water-oriented wildlife, sometimes in large numbers—graceful black terns, great blue herons, double-crested cormorants, warblers, eagles, and ducks, as well as resident deer and beavers.

MICHIGAN

Seney shows what can be done to restore a ravaged area. Now eagles nest here, black bears raise families, sandhill cranes court and dance, loons nest in large numbers, and white-tailed deer browse with their spotted fawns.

Shiawassee is an oasis of wildlife habitat in a sea of agriculture. Waterfowl cover the ponds in fall migration, joined by bald eagles in late October and November. Some 1,000 tundra swans drop down in spring. And coyotes, red fox, and deer are around all year.

ILLINOIS

Chautauqua is an ancient wetland along the Illinois River that can attract huge numbers of water-oriented birds—up to a quarter-million waterfowl in fall and shorebird concentrations of up to 200,000 yellowlegs, sandpipers, and plovers. Dozens of eagles spend the winter feeding on waterfowl and fish. Red foxes are common, denning sometimes close by refuge headquarters.

Wildlife at *Crab Orchard* coexists comfortably with the nation's main federal maximum-security prison and such other human activities as industries making missile parts, sporting goods, and display cases. There are two active bald eagle nests, beaver workings everywhere around the lakes and ponds, wild turkeys, deer, and up to 200,000 Canada geese in migration.

More than a dozen state or federal champion trees are at *Cypress Creek,* along with flora and fauna seldom seen in this area because they are at the edge of their northern, western, or eastern range. Some cypresses are more than 1,000 years old and are virtual wildlife apartment houses, furnishing homes to owls, swifts, flying squirrels, and dozens of others.

Mark Twain refuge keeps "life on the Mississippi" viable for wildlife along 250 miles of the river that inspired the author for whom the refuge is named. More than 600 bald eagles winter on the refuge—and the river is a migration corridor for tens of thousands of raptors, warblers, and shorebirds.

INDIANA

Audubon called the wood duck with its dazzling colors "this most beautiful bird"— and it appears in abundance at *Muscatatuck.* But many others have learned about this place named in the Indian word for "land of winding waters": deer, beavers, coyotes, bluebirds, red-tailed hawks, and hundreds of warblers that come through in spring.

OHIO

Ottawa is a rich remnant of marsh that attracts a diversity of wildlife to its 8,316-acre oasis of habitat: tundra swans, eagles, deer, pheasants, and at peak times 100,000 waterfowl.

Following are birds of special interest found commonly at Great Lakes region refuges at seasons indicated:

S: SPRING   s: SUMMER   F: FALL   W: WINTER

Red-necked Grebe: Agassiz SsF, Tamarac SsF
Horned Grebe: Agassiz SsF, Crab Orchard SF, Ottawa S
American White Pelican: Agassiz SsF, Big Stone SsF, Minnesota Valley S
Yellow-crowned Night Heron: Mark Twain S
Tundra Swan: Agassiz SF, Horicon S, Minnesota Valley S, Ottawa SF, Shiawassee SF, Upper Mississippi River SF
Bald Eagle: Mark Twain W, Upper Mississippi River SFW
Sandhill Crane: Agassiz SF, Seney SsF
Lesser Golden Plover: Ottawa S
Upland Sandpiper: Big Stone S
Stilt Sandpiper: Chautauqua F
Long-billed Dowitcher: Agassiz SF, Chautauqua F
Wilson's Phalarope: Agassiz S, Big Stone S, Minnesota S

Gray Jay: Seney W

Northern Shrike: Agassiz W

Philadelphia Vireo: Ottawa SF

Prothonotary Warbler: Chautauqua Ss, Crab Orchard s, Mark Twain SsF, Upper Mississippi River Ss

LeConte's Sparrow: Agassiz Ss

Vesper Sparrow: Minnesota Valley SsF, Necedah SsF, Seney SsF, Sherburne SsF

Harris' Sparrow: Big Stone F

Lincoln's Sparrow: Big Stone SF

Lapland Longspur: Shiawassee W

Snow Bunting: Agassiz FW, Big Stone W, Necedah W, Ottawa SFW, Rice Lake W, Seney SFW, Shiawassee W, Tamarac W

GREAT LAKES

MINNESOTA
1 AGASSIZ
2 BIG STONE
3 MINNESOTA VALLEY
4 RICE LAKE
5 SHERBURNE
6 TAMARAC
7 UPPER MISSISSIPPI RIVER

WISCONSIN
8 HORICON
9 NECEDAH
10 TREMPEALEAU

MICHIGAN
11 SENEY
12 SHIAWASSEE

ILLINOIS
13 CHAUTAUQUA
14 CRAB ORCHARD
15 CYPRESS CREEK
16 MARK TWAIN

INDIANA
17 MUSCATATUCK

OHIO
18 OTTAWA

★ AGASSIZ

• Thief River Falls

AGASSIZ (Minnesota)

Gray wolves howl through the night and the Agassiz brushlands ring in the fall with the clash of five-foot antlers belonging to moose that may weigh 900 pounds and stand seven feet at the shoulder.

Otters slide down the dike banks and pop their heads out of the water to bark at visitors. Beavers industriously shore up lodges, and red fox pounce on rodents along grassy field edges. Bobcats, coyotes, badgers, bears, minks, porcupines, and fishers are here—and waterfowl peak during migration at more than 100,000 ducks of a dozen species and 30,000 Canada, blue, and snow geese.

No national wildlife refuge has a greater variety of spectacular wildlife than can be found on these nearly 100 square miles—61,449 acres—of marsh and woodland in the northwest corner of Minnesota, occupying part of what was a huge prehistoric glacial lake. Historically, Lake Agassiz—named after Swiss glaciologist Louis Agassiz—covered an area larger than the Great Lakes. Settlers were attracted to its teeming wild game. However, over the centuries it was so exploited by overlogging, overtrapping, overhunting, and ill-advised drainage attempts that it became tax-delinquent and a financial burden on the county, which led to its becoming a national wildlife refuge in 1937. Its comeback has been spectacular.

Now scarlet-crowned sandhill cranes dance and leap in the air during spring and 45 pairs nest on the refuge (their piercing "unison call" when male and female change incubation shifts is the way to count breeding couples). By fall, 2,000 of these stately birds congregate on the refuge.

Five species of grebes come to breed—red-necked on floating reed nests near the dikes. Later both the western and red-necked can be seen carrying fluffy young about on their backs.

Canada geese and more than a dozen species of ducks bring off broods—in a good year more than 18,000 ducklings—plus on the marsh edges Virginia, sora, and yellow rails, snipe, and Wilson's phalaropes; in grassy uplands the upland sandpiper and northern harrier; and on the edges of clearings woodcocks, which make soaring courtship flights in spring.

Several thousand black terns swoop in graceful swallowlike flight to scoop up millions of insects for their families. One heronry supports 75 pairs of great blue herons along with lesser numbers of great egrets; elsewhere on the refuge some 50,000 Franklin's gulls may nest.

Birders can usually locate LeConte's, sharp-tailed, and clay-colored sparrows, and other interesting nesters such as red-tailed hawks, great horned owls, sharp-tailed and ruffed grouse, Forster's terns, American and least bitterns, warbling vireos, marsh and sedge wrens, and among warblers the yellow, yellowthroat, Tennessee, and Nashville, and sometimes chestnut-sided and blackburnian.

Later hundreds of white pelicans come through in migration along with peregrine falcons, rough-legged hawks, and on mud flats golden plovers, marbled and Hudsonian godwits, avocets, dowitchers, yellowlegs, and sandpipers.

The first moose calf is usually observed around May 1 and white-tailed fawns three weeks later, along with the first waterfowl broods on the various ponds. This is where moose are often seen, chewing on aquatic plants and seeking respite from insects. The herd may number up to 400 and visitors can usually find these great beasts somewhere on the refuge, usually appearing even bigger than expected. "When you find one on the road," said one refuge employee, "you almost feel as if you could drive your truck under it." They look even larger when you are on foot.

Agassiz is the only refuge in the lower 48 with a resident gray wolf pack, but they are not easy to see. The reason is understandable: many people still hate and fear wolves and would kill them if possible, despite their protected, endangered-species status. To others their intelligence and organized social order inspire admiration and respect, and their howl (which sometimes can be called up by a refuge staffer) is thrilling like no other wild sound. In spring the young can sometimes be heard yapping while their parents teach them to hunt. Otherwise to most visitors they are a shadow swiftly fading back into the woods.

A fascinating area—though not easy to reach or navigate when there (and being fragile, requiring refuge permission)—is a quaking bog, a floating mat of mossy vegetation supporting tamarack and black spruce trees up to 40 feet tall that literally quake, bounce visibly, at a footfall. Amid the leatherleaf ferns are bog laurels, callas, pitcher plants, and orchids.

A herd of 20 to 30 elk is in the area, though usually seen on state or private areas five miles northeast.

More than 100 miles of trails are open to driving or hiking and refuge personnel can advise where they have seen wildlife recently.

Winter is inhospitable. Nearby Thief River Falls is often the coldest spot in the lower 48, and the refuge bird list goes down from 276 to 13, but those still around can be interesting: hoary redpolls, gray jays, snow buntings, crossbills, and snowy and sometimes great gray owls.

How to get there: From Thief River Falls take Highway 32 north to Holt, then east on County Road 7 about 11 miles to refuge headquarters.

Open: Daylight hours every day except when driving conditions do not permit. Office 7:30–4 weekdays.

Best times to visit: Spring and fall, for migrants, spring breeding plumage and fully antlered moose and deer in fall.

What to see: Moose, deer, waterfowl, beavers, Franklin's gulls, Forster's and black terns, wildflowers, quaking bog, and much more.

What to do: Auto and hiking trails; observation deck and tower; photography. Snow-shoeing, cross-country skiing in winter.

Where to stay: Motels—in Thief River Falls, 23 miles southwest. Campgrounds—in Thief River Falls and Old Mill State Park, 20 miles west; and other state parks (see *Points of interest* below).

Weather: Can be bitterly cold in winter and cool and rainy anytime. Check with office on road and trail conditions in wet or snowy weather.

What to take and wear: Warmest clothing in winter, windbreaker or sweater anytime. Waterproof footgear in spring and summer.

Points of interest nearby: Three state wildlife management areas adjoin the refuge; also Elm Lake Waterfowl Restoration Area, adjacent on southwest; also Old Mill State Park, 20 miles west; Lake Bronson State Park, 30 miles northwest; Hayes Lake State Park, 40 miles northeast; Itasca State Park—headwaters of the Mississippi—75 miles southeast. Lake of the Woods, 75 miles northeast, has wide-ranging recreational facilities.

For more information: Agassiz National Wildlife Refuge, Middle River, Minnesota 56737. Phone: (218) 449–4115.

BIG STONE (Minnesota)

The tall-grass prairie explodes in blooms of red and gold, purple and pink, and grassland birds flock in spring to nest and feed among them here against a background of granite outcrops known worldwide for their ruby-red hues.

They are some of the oldest rocks on earth, formed two billion years ago when deep earth pressures pushed up molten rock first exposed about 10,000 years ago. The last glacier receded then from ancient Lake Agassiz, which once covered a region larger than the Great Lakes, and the runoff cut a canyon leaving these great rosy stones visible—125 acres of them on the refuge.

Now, they form parts of beautiful hiking trails, with earth-filled fissures and shallow depressions once used by Dakotah Indians to grind corn and which now hold multicolored and unusual plants, and a gentle slope from which much of the interesting wildlife can be seen.

Trails pass through marsh, swamp, fields, and woodland. Along them red foxes go mousing, white-tailed deer drop spotted fawns in spring, and beavers and their constructions are everywhere along the river. Otters sport and slide down stream banks. Coyotes and badgers fade back if visitors come along, but a quiet observer might see one.

The first verified Minnesota sightings of yellow-crowned night herons, little blue herons, and snowy egrets were here, and the first nesting snowies. They were in a colony of some 2,500 great blue herons, black-crowned night herons, great egrets and up to 500 double-crested cormorants that nest on a floodplain island.

In another colony are 25 or so western grebe pairs and a convenient overlook from which the birds can be observed through their entire breeding cycle, from courtship water dances to fledglings riding about on their parents' backs.

Swainson's hawks nest; so do kestrels, northern harriers, red-tailed hawks, pheasants, woodcocks, screech and great horned owls, Forster's and common terns, and five kinds of swallows. Broods of wood ducks, mallards, pintails, shovelers, redheads, blue-winged teals, and ruddy ducks appear in June.

Warblers follow the floodplain forest along the river valley in spring, and migrating shorebirds are on the mudflats in spring and late summer—avocets, phalaropes, willets, marbled godwits, an assortment of sandpipers and plovers. Upland sandpipers nest.

Flowers burst forth in continual succession from snow-melt to freeze-up—ball cacti and prickly pears, unique for this area with purple and yellow blooms in early June; flameflowers with polypodium and adiantum ferns; and on the prairie, harebells, prairie clovers, pasqueflowers, coneflowers, gayfeathers. This is where birders find dickcissels and interesting sparrows—clay-colored, Harris', Lincoln's, grasshopper, LeConte's, Henslow's, vesper, and others.

April and May are best for spring migrants, September–October for fall. Flights of several hundred white pelicans appear (they nest in Marsh Lake, 20 miles southeast, where they can be seen from a bluff near Louisburg)—along with tundra swans, 20,000 Canada, blue, and snow geese, and 20 species of ducks, which peak at about 40,000 birds. Bald eagles are around the latter half of October, often feeding on weaker ducks.

Winter brings clouds of snow buntings, horned larks, sometimes lapland longspurs, crossbills, and redpolls, and every few years snowy owls.

Big Stone's existence is largely credited to one man—Lem Kaercher, editor and publisher of the Ortonville, Minnesota, *Independent*, who said it was a mistake to channelize the Whetstone River and cause severe siltation in Big Stone Lake and flooding downstream. He wanted to rectify it with better-planned water control and use the results to benefit wildlife. He won public and official support, and this 11,235-acre refuge is the satisfying result.

How to get there: From Ortonville (150 miles west of Minneapolis on Route 12) take Route 75 south two miles to railroad crossing, red barn, "Granite View Farm," and small sign, "U.S. Fish and Wildlife Tour Route." Turn right onto refuge auto-tour route.

Open: Daylight hours all year. Office, weekdays. Some areas have restricted use during nesting or hunting season and inclement weather—check with office.

Best times to visit: Spring and fall.

What to see: Deer, waterfowl, herons, egrets, beavers, good sparrow assortment. Unusual rose granite outcroppings and wild plants and flowers unique for this area.

What to do: Auto-tour route, many miles of roads for hiking; river canoe route in high water of spring and summer—check with office at other seasons.

Where to stay: Motels—several on Highway 12 near Ortonville, and in Milbank, South Dakota, nine miles west. Campgrounds—at foot of Big Stone Lake, Ponderosa; on Route 12 near Ortonville; at Meadowbrook State Park, nine miles northwest on Route 7.

Weather: Winter can be windy with weeks below zero, summer humid with temperatures over 100.

What to take and wear: Spotting scope for bird colony viewing. Footgear with nonslip soles for granite rocks. Heavy pants or tall boots to protect against cactus spines (or pliers to pull out spines!).

Points of interest nearby: Big Stone State Park, nine miles northwest. Lac qui Parle State Refuge and State Park, 35 miles south on Route 7. Nesting white pelicans on Marsh Lake, 20 miles southwest. Big Stone Lake has varied year-round recreational facilities.

For more information: Big Stone National Wildlife Refuge, 25 N.W. Second Street, Ortonville, Minnesota 56278. Phone: (612) 839–3700.

St. Paul
★•
*MINNESOTA
VALLEY*

MINNESOTA VALLEY (Minnesota)

Coyotes yip and howl at dawn and soon a whole chorus of coyotes is answering from various corners of this exciting and relatively new refuge that extends 34 miles along the Minnesota River.

Most refuges are set aside because they offer habitat to various wildlife species. Minnesota Valley became a refuge because citizens who live here felt the need for a wild place close to their urban surroundings. They worked with politicians and public officials and made it happen.

Now golden prothonotary warblers nest and beautiful wood ducks raise some 2,000 downy ducklings in natural tree cavities in swampy areas. More than 30,000 waterfowl stop in fall migration—mostly mallards but also blue-winged teals, ring-necks, shovelers, and redheads, along with Canada and snow geese and whistling swans. Coots pack together in huge rafts of several thousand each on Long Meadow Lake.

Bald eagles have nested and herds of white-tailed deer browse along the edge of the oak savannah within a few miles of high-rise hotels and the Minneapolis–St. Paul International Airport. Peregrine falcons have raised young on a ledge of the Control Data world center building next door.

Low-slung badgers, looking a little like thick rugs flowing over the ground, dig for ground squirrels with such efficiency they can seem to disappear into the ground as you watch. They have denned beside the Visitor Center.

A nesting colony accommodates more than 700 pairs of graceful great blue herons and great egrets that disperse over refuge wetlands seeking food for young families. There are several colonies of black terns' delicate floating nests.

Beavers slap their tails on the water to defend territories in Long Meadow Lake when they are challenged by refuge staff leaders slapping canoe paddles on the water during guided refuge field trips.

Eagles may stay all winter, depending on weather, feeding on fish and an occasional duck. A half dozen may gather in cottonwood trees in the Black Dog Lake area, where heated power plant discharge keeps the water open.

More then 250 bird species have been identified, of which 150 nest (birdwatchers take special note of warbler, shorebird, and raptor migrations) as well as 50 species of mammals—one of them the threatened harvest mouse—and 30 reptiles and amphibians, including handsome painted turtles that bask on logs and spring peepers whose high-pitched song is a first sign of spring.

Habitats include a beautiful native prairie remnant and a rare calcareous fen, a type of wetland where spring water passes through limestone with a change in acidity that supports unusual plant communities.

Wildlife is at home right around the splendid new Visitor Center, where deer sometimes browse, red foxes pounce on squirrels, and an outstanding slide show gives a fine overall introduction to this unusual refuge and how it works.

Located in a series of noncontiguous units totaling some 12,500 acres along the Minnesota River for which land is still being acquired, Minnesota Valley combines with similar units administered by state and local agencies to form a wildlife corridor extending 72 miles along the Minnesota River—a concept particularly valuable for wildlife which cannot fly from place to place but are limited to traveling on land. A hiking trail is under way that will link all these. The National Park Service is coordinating protection of an additional 50-mile stretch of land along the Mississippi River starting just a few miles away—a further extension of this protected corridor.

How to get there: From Minneapolis–St. Paul Airport take I-494 to 34th Avenue Exit, then south to 80th Street, then east and follow refuge signs.

Open: Daylight hours. Office 7:30–4 weekdays. Visitor Center 9 a.m.–9 p.m. every day.

What to see: Wildlife observation; photography, good at Bass Ponds and Old Cedar Avenue; 20 miles of walking trails; wildlife overlooks; Visitor Center with excellent slide orientation; biking; cross-country skiing in winter. Bulletin board lists special events.

Where to stay: Motels—Hilton, Holiday Inn, and Embassy Suites across the road, many others along I-494. Campgrounds—Lawrence Wayside State Park, near Jordan south of refuge, and at Shakopee, 25 miles southwest.

What to take and wear: Insect repellent, especially for ticks—Lyme disease present.

Points of interest nearby: Fort Snelling State Park and Historic Site, adjacent to Long Meadow Lake unit; Murphy's Landing, historic restoration, adjacent to Wilkie-Rice Lake unit.

For more information: Minnesota Valley National Wildlife Refuge, 3815 East 80th Street, Bloomington, Minnesota 55425. Phone: (612) 854–5900.

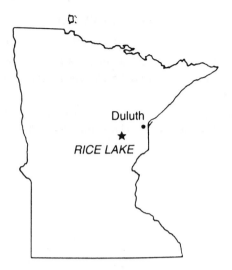

RICE LAKE (Minnesota)

Chippewa Indians harvest wild rice in the old way at Rice Lake—bending the stalks and stroking the seed heads with sticks so the ripe grains fall loose into the canoe. The grain remaining on the stalks and extensive unharvested rice beds provides seed for future years and feeds huge concentrations of waterfowl that congregrate here in fall on their southward migration.

It is a beautiful scene—perhaps 100,000 handsome ring-necked ducks plus 40,000 of other duck species and 5,000 Canada and snow geese against a backdrop of flaming scarlet maples and golden aspens, while around the lake up to 60 bald eagles prey on weaker waterfowl, sometimes perching atop a muskrat lodge to consume them.

They are part of a diverse ecosystem at this 18,104-acre refuge of flat bog laced with glacial moraine that is essentially a wilderness in east-central Minnesota.

In the woods black bears forage; often in fall a family group will climb an oak to eat acorns. Along with the eagles is a raptor migration that includes merlins, Swainson's, and rough-legged hawks and occasionally a peregrine falcon and golden eagle.

Porcupines lumber along and climb aspens, going out to the very tips for the tenderest bark and leaves, clinging precariously to supple branches that sometimes snap and drop them to the ground.

Beavers tend lodges in the Rice River and lake edges. White-tailed deer browse the fields and woods understory. Coyotes might be anywhere—but only briefly. Even briefer are glimpses of gray wolves, whose wariness is understandable—these intelligent animals are still widely hated and feared and sometimes hunted down despite their endangered species status.

Warbler and songbird migrations at spring bud-out can seem like a swarm of bees when thousands of small golden birds of a dozen or more species flit through the refuge, and many—the Connecticut, mourning, blackburnian, yellow, chestnut-sided and black-throated green—stay to nest.

Ruffed grouse drum in the woods and sharp-tailed grouse stamp about in grassland courtship dances before apparently indifferent females, which later lead broods along woods and upland edges. Great horned, screech, and saw-whet owls are common all year, the latter in low spruce branches.

Eagles congregate again at ice breakup to consume fish that have lain frozen in the ice over winter, then in late April or early May feed on spawning pike and buffalo fish.

Sandhill cranes touch down, and swans, upland sandpipers, and waterfowl rest briefly, their movements in their northward migration more dispersed than in fall, urgent to be on nesting grounds.

Others find the end of their northward journey here—yellow rails, yellow-billed cuckoos, scarlet tanagers, rose-breasted grosbeaks, bobolinks, northern orioles, ruby-throated hummingbirds, and five species of swallows, sometimes Brewer's blackbirds, and grasshopper and vesper sparrows. Occasionally there are western species at the easternmost edge of their range—western bluebirds, black-billed magpies, rarely a ferruginous hawk.

Two eagle pairs have raised families in recent years, plus such other raptors as red-tailed and broad-winged hawks, northern harriers, and a few Cooper's, sharp-shinned, and ospreys.

Loons nest on the shore of Mandy Lake and have their young out on the water by mid-June. Great blue herons and occasional great egrets fish the edge for frogs and bullheads. Phoebes claim the eaves at refuge headquarters.

Wildflowers begin at ice breakup in March with bloodroots, trilliums, gentians, yellow and showy lady's slippers, through tiger and Turk's-cap lilies and purple asters in fall.

Few visitors come in winter—it often amounts to breaking trail with cross-country skis or snowshoes but those who do are rewarded with a quiet beauty as at no other season, plus such hardy species as snowy owls, rough-legged hawks, crossbills, longspurs, redpolls, pine and evening grosbeaks, and clouds of snow buntings.

Rice Lake also administers two small boulder islands in Mille Lacs Lake, nest sites for gulls and terns, closed to the public, and the Sandstone Unit, 2,045 acres about 40 miles southeast, with grouse and waterfowl nest habitat where the public may be admitted but no trail development is planned.

How to get there: From Duluth take State Route 210 west 65 miles to McGregor, then State Route 65 south five miles to East Lake, then west two miles on gravel road to headquarters.

Open: Dawn to dusk daily year-round (some areas may be closed at times, as in breeding or hunting season—check with office). Office 8–4:30 weekdays.

Best times to visit: Fall is the favorite—especially late September and October, with migrants, foliage color, cool weather.

What to see: Great variety of wildlife including large concentrations of ring-necked ducks; eagles; deer; beavers; occasionally bears and coyotes; some western bird species; Indian burial mounds.

What to do: Wildlife observation; photography.

Where to stay: Motels—in McGregor, five miles north; Aitkin, 30 miles west; Cloquet, 35 miles east; Brainerd, 50 miles west; also in Mille Lacs resort area and Duluth. Campgrounds—north of McGregor and near Aitkin; also in Savannah State Park, 25 miles north, and Chippewa National Forest, 65 miles north.

Weather: Pleasant and cool most of year but unpredictable April-June; can be extremely cold in winter (40 below not uncommon).

What to take and wear: Insects can seem overwhelming in summer—repellent a must; raingear handy in spring; warmest clothing in winter.

Points of interest nearby: Savannah State Park, trails and historical points; Kimberly Wildlife Area, adjacent on west; Northwoods Audubon Center, 40 miles southeast; Boundary Waters Wilderness Area, 160 miles north.

For more information: Rice Lake National Wildlife Refuge, Route 2, Box 67, McGregor, Minnesota 55760. Phone: (218) 768–2402.

SHERBURNE
★
Minneapolis
•

SHERBURNE (Minnesota)

Eagles nest and majestic sandhill cranes leap up in pair-bonding exercises along with a wonderful assortment of other wildlife that have found their way to this 30,665-acre refuge of lakes, woods, and grasslands on a glacial outwash plain hardly more than an hour's drive from Minneapolis.

White-tailed deer with their spotted fawns browse along the many miles of roads and hiking trails. Red foxes have denned near refuge maintenance buildings. Coyotes lope across upland fields. Flame-crested pileated and red-headed woodpeckers hammer away in the woodlands. Black bears have been spotted (though rarely) feeding on berries.

Visitors on a good day in spring and fall might see 60 or so bald eagles dropping down in migration to rest and feed for a few days around some of the more than 20 small ponds and lakes. Two pairs have nested in recent years, one raising their young within view of the auto tour route.

Songbirds find Sherburne a welcome migration stopover, too, and the woods canopy and understory in May can be filled with thousands of them—easily 20 species of warblers, five kinds of vireos, a half-dozen kinds of thrush, 10 kinds of flycatchers.

Otters frisk along the water's edges. Beavers and muskrats build lodges on which Canada geese nest. Birds that prefer to raise families in hollow trees can choose among acres of dead timber with readily accessible cavities, and bluebirds, hooded mergansers, and beautiful wood ducks do just that. Thousands of ducklings are hatched out every year—woodies, mallards, blue-winged teals, and others.

Graceful black terns gather in loosely connected colonies on nests of floating vegetation and defend them with loud alarm cries if visitors pull off alongside Orrock Lake to view them through binoculars even at a distance of 100 yards. Coot and pied-billed grebe families are there, too, the grebes carrying downy young on their backs—and yes, those orange-headed chicks DO belong to those black coots.

Minnesota has a project for reestablishing trumpeter swans in the state and at least several appear every year with—it's hoped—the idea of settling down. Another plan is reestablishing once-plentiful sharp-tailed grouse so they can once again gather on ancestral springtime dancing grounds here.

Two or three dozen pairs of regal, crimson-crowned sandhill cranes find nest sites to their liking in grassy uplands, and their wild bugling calls fill the air for miles as they change places during incubation or fly out to feeding places. Dozens more gather with them on the refuge during fall migration.

Waterfowl numbers may peak in the tens of thousands, gathered in flocks spotted about the various lakes and ponds in October feeding on the nutritious wild rice that grows plentifully there.

Wildflowers are beautiful—whole fields of snowy pasqueflowers in spring followed by blue spiderworts, orange butterfly weeds, and purple and pink milkweeds, coneflowers in the prairie areas, and purple asters in fall.

Sherburne can be a fascinating place for birders year-round. More than 70 species breed, including indigo buntings, rose-breasted grosbeaks, great horned owls, red-tailed hawks, and others. Great blue herons and great egrets fan out from a sizable heronry near St. Cloud. Interesting sparrows migrate through and many stay for the summer—vesper, lark, field, clay-colored, grasshopper, and others as well as dickcissels.

Winter brings crossbills, purple finches, hoary and common redpolls, pine siskins, evening grosbeaks, and occasionally a snowy owl, a few Bohemian waxwings, or an invasion of pine grosbeaks.

Sherburne became a refuge because of citizen action when conservationists and sportsmen's organizations aware of its history as a lush wildlife area petitioned the government to set it aside and restore it to its original condition. This was done in 1965, and the land was finally accumulated and purchased ten years later. The results are a rich reward for all concerned.

How to get there: From Minneapolis–St. Paul take I-94 northwest about 40 miles to Rogers, then Highway 101 north to Elk River, where it becomes Highway 169; take 169 north to refuge sign 4.5 miles north of Zimmerman, and west five miles to refuge.

Open: Daylight hours. Office 7:30–4 weekdays.

Best times to visit: Spring and fall for migrants, summer for breeding birds. Fall colors peak first half of October.

What to see: Nesting bald eagles, waterfowl, sandhill cranes, white-tailed deer, foxes, loons, bluebirds; varied range of other wildlife. Prehistoric Indian mounds.

What to do: Auto and hiking trails as well as public viewing roads through refuge (auto tour route open weekends; weekdays drop by office for permission; not plowed in winter). Canoeing on St. Francis River when water conditions permit.

Where to stay: Motels—at Princeton, 10 miles northeast; Monticello, 15 miles south; Elk River, 20 miles southeast; St. Cloud, 25 miles west. Campgrounds—Sand Dunes State Forest, immediately south of refuge; several others within four miles on roads east, west, and south of refuge.

Weather: Spring is the last half of April through May—after that, weather can be hot and sticky. Can be quite cold in winter (propane gas sometimes solidifies in tanks) but beautiful.

What to take and wear: Prepare for heat, humidity, and full range of ferocious biting insects in summer, including ticks with Lyme disease. Well-insulated clothing in winter.

Points of interest nearby: Sand Dunes State Forest, just south of refuge.

For more information: Sherburne National Wildlife Refuge, 17076–293 Avenue, Zimmerman, Minnesota 55398. Phone: (612) 389–3323.

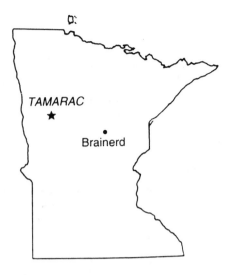

TAMARAC

★

• Brainerd

TAMARAC (Minnesota)

The trumpeter swan, whose name is synonymous with beauty in wildlife, was once common throughout the central and northern United States. Gunned down indiscriminately for feathers, meat, or simply target practice, "it has succumbed to incessant persecution in all parts of its range," wrote E. H. Forbush in 1912. "Its total extinction is only a matter of years."

Now this largest of North American waterfowl flies free at beautiful Tamarac refuge, the heartening result of a plan financed by Minnesotans who voluntarily checked off part of their income and property tax refunds to go to such nongame species recovery projects. Two-year-old swans raised in captivity for this purpose were brought here and successfully released to begin life anew in the company of bald eagles, white-tailed deer, beavers, and others.

Sixteen pairs of bald eagles nest at Tamarac, and a visitor to this 42,725-acre northwest Minnesota refuge can readily see them from its roads and walking trails.

Loons, handsome in black and white breeding plumage, dive and bring up fish for young families (which cling perilously to their parent's back) on sparkling lakes. Red-necked and pied-billed grebes also breed there and several hundred white pelicans visit in summer.

Tamarac is 40 percent watery habitat—21 lakes plus marsh and bog. More than 6,000 downy ducklings are produced every year: mallards, ring-necks, blue-winged teals, and colorful wood ducks that nest in tree cavities.

Coyotes and sometimes a gray wolf howl at night. Bobcats prowl uplands and otters slide down pond banks. Moose may wander in to cool off. Black bears lumber through the woods. Porcupines climb high to feed on pine bark. Beaver lodges are on most streams. Ospreys usually pick a waterside snag for nesting.

Such is the wilderness character of the place that standing at one of the historical spots where Indians lived and buried their dead, it almost seems as if nothing has happened since. Indeed, many of the wildflowers may be descendants of those that grew here two centuries ago—wood lilies, Indian paintbrushes, marsh marigolds, asters, showy lady's slippers—one 20-acre bog swamp may be covered with lady's slippers in the spring.

A census of ruffed grouse, taken by listening to the number of males drumming on logs to attract females, indicates over 1,000 breeding pairs. Great blue herons nest in three colonies accommodating more than 250 pairs, and these stately birds are usually fishing around the waterways.

More than two dozen kinds of warblers come through in May. Many stay to nest—chestnut-sided, black-and-white, and golden-winged warblers, along with red-eyed, warbling, and yellow-throated vireos, scarlet tanagers, rose-breasted grosbeaks, indigo buntings, and northern orioles.

Great horned and barred owls are in the woods year-round, along with flame-crested pileated woodpeckers.

The basis for much of this rich ecosystem is the abundant wild rice over which Dakota and Chippewa Indians fought. The Chippewas won and still harvest it in the ancient way—one man guiding the canoe, the other pulling the stalks over and tapping them with flails to let ripe kernels fall, filling a canoe with up to 300 pounds of grain—yet leaving some for waterfowl that come through in migration.

Fall brings foliage colors so brilliant with golden birches and aspens, crimson maples and sumac and maroon oaks that even longtime refuge hands say the sight in fall sunlight makes their eyes squint.

More than 35,000 ring-necked ducks may show up in mid-October, along with 12,000 other waterfowl—mallards, scaup, blue-winged teal—sometimes huge rafts of up to 30,000 coots, and an occasional golden eagle.

Winter can get down to 46 below, but it is dry cold with little wind and the birds can be worth it—colorful magpies, redpolls, crossbills, evening grosbeaks, snow buntings, and occasionally, if one is lucky, a hoary redpoll, Bohemian waxwing, or great gray or snowy owl down from the north.

How to get there: From Fargo, North Dakota, take Highway 10 for 45 miles east to Detroit Lakes, then Highway 34 for eight miles east to Becker County 29, then 10 miles north to refuge headquarters.

Open: 5 a.m.–10 p.m. all year, weather permitting. Office 7:30–4 weekdays, Visitor Center 12–5 summer weekends.

Best times to visit: Spring and fall.

What to see: Bald eagles, trumpeter swans, loons, ruffed grouse, deer, beavers, waterfowl. Spectacular fall foliage in late September. Profusion of wildflowers. Historical sites. Wild rice harvest mid-August to September.

What to do: Hiking trails, 10-mile auto tour route, over 40 miles of roads for driving, hiking. Auditorium with slide shows, films, talks. Summer weekend field trips. Fishing—walleye up to 10 pounds, northern pike up to 19 pounds (ice fishing in winter). Cross-country skiing trail (ungroomed). No snowmobiles.

Where to stay: Motels—a number in Detroit Lakes. Campgrounds—on Shell Lake and Island Lake, east of refuge (both tents and vehicles), also Buffalo Lake just west, and many in Detroit Lakes area.

Weather: Winter temperatures can go to minus 46 and frost possible any month. Short heavy thunderstorms possible June-August.

What to take and wear: Warmest clothing in winter, at least a windbreaker most of the year.

Points of interest nearby: Hubbel Pond State Wildlife Area, adjacent. Smokey Hills State Forest, just east. Itasca State Park (headwaters of the Mississippi), 20 miles northeast. Several other state forests within 30 miles.

For more information: Tamarac National Wildlife Refuge, HC 10, Box 145, Rochert, Minnesota 56578. Phone: (218) 847-2641.

Minneapolis
•

UPPER MISSISSIPPI RIVER ★

UPPER MISSISSIPPI RIVER
(Minnesota, Wisconsin, Iowa, Illinois)

Upper Mississippi River is a unique and stunning example of what a wildlife refuge can be: it surrounds and follows one of the world's great river systems as it flows through four states and shelters some of America's greatest and rarest wildlife congregations on its 200,000 acres.

Up to 60 percent of North America's population of tundra swans rest and feed on Weaver Bottoms north of Winona—a breathtakingly beautiful gathering of some 10,000 of these large white birds—en route from nesting territories on Alaska's west coast and northern Canada to Chesapeake Bay.

Up to 70 percent of the world's population of canvasback ducks feed on wild celery in pools near La Crosse, Wisconsin, in the fall.

Nesting colonies of hundreds of pairs of graceful herons and egrets are located every 20 miles or so along the refuge's 264-mile length.

A dozen pairs of bald eagles nest, and 80 may gather to rest and feed in spring and fall migration—sometimes with a golden eagle. A hundred or more fish around open waters near Reed's Landing, Minnesota, in winter.

Amid all this humans are welcome to hike, fish, boat, camp, and observe.

Visitors looking for spring warblers and songbirds find them everywhere in the spring, following the opening of green buds and hatching insects like a superhighway along the river's edge to northern breeding grounds. A birder sitting in one place on a good day might identify not only three dozen species but a dozen individuals of each species—palm, blackburnian, Wilson's, and Tennessee warblers, Bell's and solitary vireos, kinglets, Swainson's and hermit thrush, among many others.

For some it is the end of the nesting journey—for prothonotary and cerulean warblers, rose-breasted grosbeaks, indigo buntings, ruby-throated hummingbirds, dickcissels, whip-poor-wills, cuckoos, five kinds of swallows, five kinds of flycatchers, and seven kinds of woodpeckers, including the flashy crimson-crested pileated.

Five kinds of owls and five kinds of hawks are here all year and nest, and some winters snowy owls drop down from the north.

The river's central position between the Atlantic and Central flyways brings wildlife from both—eastern and western meadowlarks, red-winged and yellow-headed blackbirds. Because of the habitat diversity—deep water in pools behind the dams; wide marshes of sagittaria and bulrushes; timbered areas in the drier parts below the dams—both diving and dabbling ducks are attracted: teal, wigeon, shoveler, scaup, goldeneye, bufflehead. Terns and shorebirds come, too. Spotted sandpipers nest on shore, black terns in fragile floating constructs that they leave to skim across the water's surface for small organisms.

Fall colors are a blaze of scarlet maples, golden aspens, and wine-colored oaks on the high bluffs from mid-October to November.

Altogether there are some 270 species of birds, 50 mammals, 45 amphibians and reptiles, and 133 kinds of fish, plus uncounted interesting plants.

The best way to see it all is by boat—almost any kind of boat. A flat-bottomed motorboat is best in spring and summer's high waters, but with a canoe one can get back into deep quiet wilderness sloughs. Explore there in the company of muskrats, beavers, otters, and fishing herons and egrets, wandering in July and August among acres of gold and white lotuses and water lilies, near where colorful wood ducks nest in tree cavities. But it is possible to get lost, so be sure to take along one of the well-marked maps.

A houseboat can tie up to sandbars at night where camping is allowed for up to 14 days without a permit. White-tailed deer sometimes swim out from shore. There are boat ramps and rentals all along the way, and detailed information is available from all the various refuge district offices.

The refuge can also be seen very well from the continuous system of highways known as the Great River Road, which closely follows refuge boundaries with many pull-offs for observing wildlife (a spotting scope as well as binoculars can be useful here) as well as superb views in places where bluffs rise a sheer 600 feet from the riverbed. Especially notable outlooks are at Winona and La Crescent, Minnesota; Alma, La Crosse, Prairie du Chien, and Cassville, Wisconsin; Lansing, McGregor, Dubuque, and Clinton, Iowa; and Savanna, Illinois.

Nature trails are along the way, and there are good photographic opportunities (though a portable blind will assist serious work). Patience will allow fairly close-range observations—but everywhere it's a good idea to check with the district offices on what's been seen lately and where.

Upper Mississippi's establishment grew out of a tragic boating accident. The son of Will Dilg, founder of the Izaak Walton League, drowned in the river while the two were fishing. Dilg became a prime mover, understanding and pointing out the alternatives of failing to protect this area. The alternatives became clear when one considers places where the river is little more than a polluted ditch between farm fields, and asks the question: where except for such refuges would the swans and eagles and canvasbacks—and so many others—go?

How to get there: Refuge lands and waters extend on both sides of the Mississippi River from Wabasha, Minnesota, to Rock Island, Illinois. Boat landings are all along the river; district offices at four locations (see below).

Open: 24 hours daily. Offices 8–4 weekdays.

Best times to visit: Spring and fall for migrants. Early summer for nesting birds, midsummer best for flowering water plants. Early to mid-November for swans. Late fall for migrating eagles.

What to see: Great wildlife range—including swans, canvasbacks, herons, egrets, warblers, songbirds, deer.

What to do: Wildlife observation, trails, boating, camping, picnicking, swimming, photography. Visitor center at Winona planned. Fishing excellent year-round— bass run up to eight pounds, walleyes up to 15. Rental boats available nearby.

Where to stay: Motels—many in towns along river. Campgrounds—many, both public and private, along river, in state parks (see below), and on refuge islands.

Weather: Spring, summer best; summers can be sticky, especially in south; winters below zero with humidity and winds making it seem colder.

What to take and wear: Waterproof gear and protective covering for binoculars and photo equipment in boats.

Points of interest nearby: Many scenic outlooks—especially for fall colors; also state parks—as Perrot State Park, Trempealeau, Wisconsin; Pike's Peak State Park, and Effigy Mounds National Monument, McGregor, Iowa; O. L. Kipp State Park, Dresbach, Minnesota, all with great scenic views. Trempealeau National Wildlife Refuge, six miles east of Winona.

For more information: Upper Mississippi River National Wildlife and Fish Refuge, 51 East Fourth Street, Room 101, Winona, Minnesota 55987. Phone: (507) 452–4232.

District Offices:

Upper Mississippi River Refuge (Pools 4 through 6); 51 East Fourth Street, Room 100, Winona, Minnesota 55987. Phone: (507) 454–7351.

Upper Mississippi River Refuge (Pools 7 and 8); P.O. Box 415, La Crosse, Wisconsin 54601. Phone: (608) 784–3910.

Upper Mississippi River Refuge (Pools 9 through 11); P.O. Box 460, McGregor, Iowa 52157. Phone: (319) 873–3423.

Upper Mississippi River Refuge (Pools 12 through 14); Post Office Building, Savanna, Illinois 61074. Phone: (815) 273–2732.

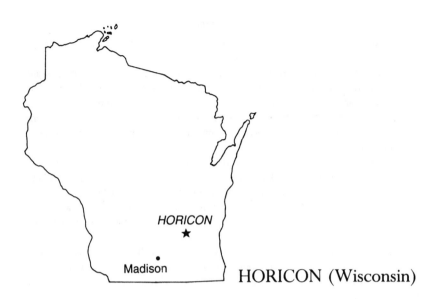

HORICON (Wisconsin)

Horicon is famous for its Canada geese, which congregate here in huge numbers, peaking around 200,000 in October and November. They fill the air with what the naturalist Aldo Leopold called "goose music," and just their physical presence overwhelms this great freshwater marsh.

Traffic can be bumper-to-bumper on the state road that traverses the refuge on all weekends when foliage color reaches its height and a significant proportion of the million or so Canadas that flock through on the Mississippi flyway are touching down in this immediate area.

But behind these spectaculars, it is the marsh itself—one of the largest cattail marshes anywhere—around which this refuge and its tremendously complicated and interesting ecosystem exist.

One of the largest heronries in the country is on an island in the southern third of the 31,000-acre marsh that is shared with the state of Wisconsin (the federal refuge administering the northern two-thirds). The nesting population can number 6,400 graceful wading birds—great blue herons, great egrets, and black-crowned night herons—which, along with bitterns, gallinules, pied-billed grebes, and others, fish throughout the marsh edges.

Redhead ducks nest here in their farthest east breeding population and along with blue-winged teal, mallards, and smaller numbers of ruddy ducks produce about 7,000 downy ducklings every year. These are swimming about refuge waters with their parents by early summer.

White-tailed deer browse around its edges, leading spotted fawns by early spring.

Red foxes and coyotes pounce on small rodents—and there are minks, raccoons, skunks, and others.

But the most important mammals in the marsh ecosystem are the muskrats, usually seen swimming about with mouthfuls of cattails, which they use both for food and home construction and furnishing. And this is their significant contribution—for in opening up areas in the cattails they create space for growth of seeding and fruiting aquatic plants and invertebrate organisms on which so many of the others depend for food as well as cover.

Among the beneficiaries of this are the ducks, which at Horicon in August can seem to be all of one species. This is because they are molting and therefore without their colorful display plumage and temporarily flightless. Many come from elsewhere for this purpose because at Horicon during this vulnerable time their survival chances are greatly enhanced—as are those of many other marsh residents—by this constant activity of their small furry neighbor.

Greater sandhill cranes nest—fifty breeding pairs of this stately gray bird with crimson crown and almost seven-foot wingspread, an arresting sight—and sound— as they graze in upland meadows or fly overhead with a bugling call that can be heard for miles.

Black terns are a state endangered species but here they commonly hover gracefully over the water and drop to pick up small minnows to take to delicate nests of floating vegetation.

Brilliant indigo buntings are here through the summer, as are flickers, red-headed woodpeckers, red-eyed and warbling vireos, yellow and yellowthroat warblers, and in the grasslands, dickcissels, meadowlarks, and vesper, grasshopper, and Henslow's sparrows. Both yellow-headed and red-winged blackbirds call from the cattails. More than 200 species are on the bird list.

Gorgeous ring-necked pheasants are around all year, as are great horned, screech, and short-eared owls and horned larks.

Winter temperatures can get down to 20 below but red-tailed hawks are still around and rough-legged hawks often hover over the fields. Juncos, tree sparrows, lapland longspurs, snow buntings, and evening grosbeaks usually visit and about every other winter there's a snowy owl.

All this is here largely because modern agricultural drainage equipment was not available a century ago. The marsh goes back 10,000 years when it was scoured out by the Wisconsin glacier. Indians used it first; then with settlers and lumbering a dam was built and it became the world's largest manmade lake—51 square miles. But farmers whose land was flooded opposed it, so it was removed in 1869 and drainage efforts began. With modern techniques this would all be farmland now. Luckily for the marsh, drainage efforts failed, and after a long fight by conservationists it was declared a refuge in 1941.

The result for those who appreciate the subtleties of the marsh is a web of life involving millions of creatures in "a magnificence that in its own small way compares to the Grand Canyon," said one refuge staffer—and just to sit quietly at dawn or dusk, watching and hearing the chorus of birds and frogs and crickets, is like listening to a great natural symphony.

How to get there: From Milwaukee take State Highway 41 north to State Highway 49, east on it 10 miles to County Road "Z," left on it and south four miles to refuge entrance road and follow signs.

Open: Dawn to dusk year-round, weather permitting—some areas can be closed for specific purposes during year; on these check with refuge office, open 7:30–4 weekdays.

Best times to visit: Spring and fall for migrants; summer for waterfowl broods.

What to see: Canada geese in large concentrations, also migrant ducks and swans; sandhill cranes; waterfowl; muskrats; deer.

What to do: A five-mile dike road is open to driving or bicycling in addition to viewing from late April to mid-September. Six miles of trails open to hiking and cross-country skiing. Photography (geese against sunset listed as one of outstanding photo opportunities on U.S. national wildlife refuges). Marsh overlook off Route 49. Short-range broadcast on 1610-AM tells of seasonal refuge activities. Parts of refuge open to cross-country skiing in winter.

Where to stay: Motels—in Waupun, Beaver Dam, Fond du Lac. Campgrounds—in Horicon; Fond du Lac County Park north of Waupun; Dodge County Ledge Park, two miles east.

Points of interest nearby: Horicon Marsh Wildlife area—southern third of Horicon Marsh, adjoining the refuge, managed by Wisconsin Department of Natural Resources, with hiking, canoeing, large heronry. Kettle Moraine State Park, east of refuge—unique geological features formed by glaciers. Horicon Ledge County Park, south of refuge—limestone outcrops with fine views of marsh and area.

For more information: Horicon National Wildlife Refuge, W4279 Headquarters Road, Mayville, Wisconsin 53050. Phone: (414) 387–2658.

Horicon also administers three small satellite refuges. *Green Bay* and *Gravel Island* in Lake Michigan are designated wilderness areas that support gulls, cormorants, and some waterfowl. Access is rocky and dangerous and only authorized by the refuge manager for scientific research. *Fox River* is 640 acres acquired in a court settlement brought against the owner for illegal marsh drainage. It supports waterfowl and sandhill cranes staging and breeding. No visitor facilities; special-use permits only.

NECEDAH (Wisconsin)

The greater sandhill crane, a majestic crimson-crowned gray bird standing four feet tall with wingspread up to 80 inches, was so reduced in numbers a few years ago that it was placed on the endangered species list. Its comeback since protection is such that flocks of more than 1,000 perform courtship dances at Necedah spring and fall in one of the larger concentrations of this still-rare bird on any national wildlife refuge.

The great birds gather in something like a square dance, crouching and springing into the air, waving their wings and opening their throats in great yodeling cries that can be heard for miles.

Their numbers peak in mid-October, when they may share the refuge with 24,000 or so Canada geese and 15,000 ducks of two dozen species, plus a dozen or so bald eagles resting and feeding on their way south.

Visitors can observe their gatherings in fields along the 11-mile self-guided auto tour route and from an observation tower that scans much of this 43,656-acre central Wisconsin refuge. The area was reclaimed by Presidential Order in 1939 from land ill-used in successive timbering and abortive drainage and agricultural attempts.

It is now a combination of marsh, woodland, and restored prairie that furnishes food and habitat for a wide variety of wildlife.

Wild turkeys in the northern fringe of their historic Wisconsin range are common here now. Sometimes three toms will strut and gobble before a single hen—who seems unimpressed, yet later will be leading a dozen or so poults scurrying through the woods.

Beautiful wood ducks nest—they have even colonized the nearby town of Necedah in cavities in the many silver maples there, and townspeople take the same pride in them that other communities do in robins and purple martins.

Warblers come through in good numbers in spring and also tundra swans, and at times several hundred swans may stay several weeks. Ruffed grouse drum on logs, and woodcocks take soaring flights at dawn and dusk to proclaim their territories and claim a mate. Deer appear with spotted fawns. Visitors may come long distances to pick delicious wild blueberries.

Coyotes prey on foxes which in turn prey on grouse and waterfowl. Beavers construct dams around the water control structures and otters fish the ponds, though not so visibly as in winter when the ice closes in and they can enjoy sliding down the snowy banks. Badgers try not to be seen at all and usually succeed, leaving only badger-shaped hemispheric holes that look as if a small tank went through.

Common and colorful summer nesters are scarlet tanagers, rose-breasted grosbeaks, indigo buntings, and red-headed woodpeckers whose scarlet heads and flashing white wing patches are highly visible throughout the year. Cooper's, red-tailed, and broad-winged hawks nest, as do northern harriers whose mothlike hunting flight is beautiful over the marshes and fields in late afternoon. The loon's wild cry is occasionally heard on larger ponds.

Fall foliage peaks in late September, when a feeder at the refuge office begins to draw small birds. The auto tour route is kept open in all but the most severe winter weather. Horned larks and snow buntings rise in clouds along with tree sparrows, evening grosbeaks, and rough-legged hawks, which hover over the windswept fields. One can sometimes sight two dozen in a single day's outing if snow cover isn't too deep. Snowshoeing and cross-country skiing are permitted.

Parts of the refuge may be closed during nesting and hunting seasons—check with the office on this.

How to get there: From I-90-94 at Tomah take Highway 21 east to the refuge, or from I-90-94 at New Lisbon go north to Highway 80. At the town of Necedah turn left on Highway 21 and follow refuge signs.

Open: Daylight hours except for seasonal closures; check with office, which is open 7:30–4 weekdays.

Best times to visit: April and October for migration.

What to see: Greater sandhill cranes, migrating eagles, grouse, waterfowl, deer, beavers, occasional otters. Variety of prairie wildflowers; lady's slipper orchids in woods.

What to do: Photography; auto-tour and hiking trails; observation tower; berry picking. Group guided tours can be arranged in advance.

Where to stay: Motels—in Tomah, Necedah, Mauston, and New Lisbon. Campgrounds—private campground east of Necedah on Highway 21; watch for signs.

Weather: Pleasant most of year; January-March can be quite cold with snow cover.

Points of interest nearby: International Crane Foundation near Baraboo, which studies cranes worldwide and has many live examples on the premises.

For more information: Necedah National Wildlife Refuge, Star Route West, Box 386, Necedah, Wisconsin 54646. Phone: (608) 565–2551.

TREMPEALEAU

★

•La Crosse

TREMPEALEAU (Wisconsin)

Trempealeau—named by French settlers "mountain with wet feet" for the high bluff along the Mississippi River—is a chance to see two diverse and interesting types of wildlife habitat that seasonally support migrating eagles and waterfowl as well as bluebirds, warblers, beavers, and white-tailed deer.

Much of this part of west south-central Wisconsin used to be the Trempealeau Prairie, a grassland with vegetation six feet tall supporting buffalos, elk, and prairie chickens. Remnants of those original grasslands remain on the 707-acre prairie section of this refuge; the rest are being restored to that condition, affording opportunities to observe this unique type of habitat where coneflowers and gayfeathers bloom and interesting sparrow species nest.

The rest of this 5,617-acre refuge is marshland that endured several ill-fated drainage and diking attempts in the interest of agriculture before these were finally given up and the land restored to its most appropriate function: that of a wildlife refuge. Separated from the main channel of the Mississippi River by a high railroad levee, it is part of the Mississippi flyway migration corridor and as such supports both upland and water-oriented wildlife, sometimes in large numbers.

Graceful black terns build delicate nests of floating vegetation. Beautiful wood ducks bring off downy broods in natural tree cavities. Eagles and ospreys nest (in secluded locations). Great blue herons and great egrets fish around the water's edges. Beavers build lodges, one along the hiking trail.

Double-crested cormorants nest on a mid-marsh structure erected for them out of telephone poles and sometimes gather to stage for fall migration in enormous numbers—up to 3,000 or more on the refuge in early October.

More than a dozen species of warblers may come through heading north in April and May, and several kinds, notably yellow and prothonotaries, stay to nest. Indigo buntings are bright spots around hedgerows, northern orioles weave pendulous nests into the ends of cottonwood branches, and bluebirds abound along the five-mile auto-tour route. Deer browse on the field edges, with their spotted young in summer. Northern harriers hover over the marsh.

Migrating eagles follow their food supply—fish and weakened waterfowl—ahead of ice freeze-up in the fall, and follow it again north in the spring. At such times several dozen may be around Trempealeau, roosting and feeding. Migrating ducks may peak at 24,000—mostly mallards, blue-winged teals, and scaups—through October, along with up to 5,000 Canada geese.

Much of this can be seen from a five-mile auto-tour route or along 10 miles of road open to hiking—especially School Bus Road. The western end of the state's Great River Trail for hiking and biking runs through the refuge.

How to get there: From Winona, Minnesota, cross river on Minnesota Highway 43 to Wisconsin Highway 35, then southwest eight miles and south one mile to entrance.

Open: Daylight hours. Office 7:30–4 weekdays except holidays.

Best times to visit: Spring and fall. Late summer for prairie wildflowers.

What to see: Deer; occasionally red foxes (often a den near the wildlife drive); distinctive prairie vegetation; migrating waterfowl, migrating and feeding eagles.

What to do: Auto and hiking trails; marsh observation platform; cross-country skiing, snowshoeing in winter.

Where to stay: Motels—in nearby La Crosse, Wisconsin, and Winona, Minnesota. Campgrounds—in Perrot State Park, three miles east.

Points of interest nearby: Weaver Bottoms and Lake Onalaska, part of Upper Mississippi National Wildlife Refuge, headquarters at Winona; also Perrot State Park.

For more information: Trempealeau National Wildlife Refuge, Route 1, Box 1602, Trempealeau, Wisconsin 54661. Phone: (608) 539–2311.

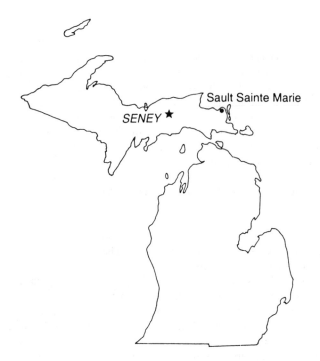

Sault Sainte Marie

SENEY ★

SENEY (Michigan)

E agles nest and black bears forage, sandhill cranes do elevated courtship dances, and beavers build lodges here on plenteous well-watered land once so misused it was given up for lost.

Michigan's Upper Peninsula was nearly stripped of its pine forests in 1870–90. Afterward uncontrolled fires, often deliberately set, all but destroyed the humus. Then unscrupulous developers drained and sold it for agriculture. When this failed the land reverted to the state for taxes. At last the state of Michigan recommended it be developed as a national wildlife refuge. Its restoration began in 1935, and the result shows how land all but ruined can be brought back to rich wildlife habitat.

Loons nest in one of the highest densities in Michigan. Their wild cries are heard at dawn and dusk through the summer, and they are a common sight along the auto-tour route, swimming along with downy young on their backs.

White-tailed deer with their fawns browse along the meadow edges. Porcupines nibble at jack pine bark and sometimes at the siding on refuge outbuildings. Six kinds of waterfowl nest, including beautiful wood ducks and hooded mergansers, within Seney's 153 square miles, which now contain over 7,000 acres of open water in 21 ponds, interspersed with pine and hardwood forest, meadows, bog and marsh.

The piercing "unison calls" of stately sandhill cranes, standing three feet tall with crimson crowns and wings that spread almost seven feet, are audible for miles as they head out in the morning to feed, and again in the evening as mated pairs reassure each other when they get together again for the night.

Ruffed grouse perform courtship rituals with whirring wings on "drumming logs" and woodcocks "peent" and spiral upward, feathers whistling, in woods openings to attract females in the spring.

Even the shy little yellow rail finds a home here, answering sometimes to stones tapped together, a sound similar to its own calls. Birders can arrange to go on "yellow rail tours" on early summer evenings.

There is a tremendous variety of wildlife here, much of it readily seen from the auto tour route or walking trails—or even from near refuge headquarters where northern orioles weave hanging nests at the ends of birch branches and Canada geese parade fluffy golden broods in April. Graceful black terns gather across the road in one of several colonies, swooping low over the water to scoop up tiny minnows for families hatched in delicate nests of floating vegetation.

Chicken wire protects trunks of birch trees on the visitor center lawn since a prize specimen fell to gnawings of an occupant of a beaver lodge behind the refuge manager's house.

A telescope along the auto-tour route is focused on one of three seven-foot eagle's nests so visitors can follow the breeding cycle from incubation, then when the young birds are flapping their wings in exercise routines, and finally when they take off.

More than 200 bird species are here as well as minks, muskrats, coyotes, bobcats, weasels, occasional moose, and a few endangered timber wolves. Common nesters are American bitterns, northern harriers—their mothlike flight a beautiful afternoon sight over the marsh—killdeer, snipe, black-billed cuckoos, great horned owls, hermit thrush, cedar waxwings, pileated woodpeckers, and a number of warblers—black-and-white, Nashville, yellow, magnolia, chestnut-sided, Canada—plus a few sharp-tailed and spruce grouse and rarely a black-backed woodpecker.

Visitors from Russia and China have traveled here to observe refuge techniques in raising sandhill cranes from egg to full-size bird—knowledge that may help save the Siberian crane as well as our own endangered whooping crane.

Several refuge ponds are open to fishing and contain large northern pike—not often caught, but the head of one captured by an otter measured 12 inches long. Almost a third of Seney is a wilderness area, including 9,500-acre Strangmoor Bog, a National Natural Landmark.

Fall foliage colors begin to peak in mid-September, brilliant when gold aspens and birches and scarlet maples mixed with evergreens are reflected in the quiet water against a blue sky.

Winters are relatively mild due to moderating influences of Lake Michigan and Lake Superior—an average low around 15 degrees, ideal for snowshoeing and cross-country skiing. Flocks of snow buntings are everywhere then, a long with redpolls, siskins, crossbills, and sometimes stunning groups of pine and evening grosbeaks. Moisture from the Great Lakes dusts the landscape every night with fresh snow so that each winter morning is a sparkling pristine vista.

A seven-mile self-guided auto tour is open from mid-May to mid-October (winter roads are not plowed), and there is a 1.4-mile self-guided walking trail. Special walks are scheduled through the summer—star walks, frog walks, evening bat walks. There are wildflower field trips in spring to see lady's slippers and wild orchids.

But one of the best ways to see Seney is as few visitors do: walk or bicycle on some 80 miles of gravel roads not open to motorized traffic, where one can see a bobcat or coyote, an otter family playing, an eagle consuming a fish on a low branch beside the road, a black bear with cubs.

How to get there: From Sault Ste. Marie take state route M-28 west about 80 miles to M-77 at Seney, then M-77 south five miles to refuge.

Open: Office 7:30–4 weekdays all year. Visitor Center 9–5 daily, May 15–September 30. Auto-tour route May 15–October 15 dawn to dusk.

Best times to visit: Memorial Day to mid-October (snow cover may limit general refuge access except on skis or snowshoes November 1–April 15).

What to see: Canada geese, sandhill cranes, loons, eagles, deer, otters; variety of others.

What to do: Auto-tour route; wildlife observation platform; hiking, self-guided or on 80 miles of gravel roads. Snowshoeing, groomed ski trails in winter.

Where to stay: Motels—limited in nearby Seney, Germfask; standard accommodations at Newberry 30 miles east, Manistique, 35 miles southwest. Campgrounds— several state forests within 10 miles of refuge. Excellent private campgrounds in Germfask and Newberry.

Weather: Moderate due to location between two Great Lakes—subzero unusual in winter—but snow accumulations may reach several feet.

What to take and wear: Insect repellent in summer a must. Waterproof gear might be handy.

Points of interest nearby: Pictured Rocks National Lakeshore; Hiawatha National Forest; Indian Lake, Big Spring, and Tahquamenon Falls state parks.

For more information: Seney National Wildlife Refuge, HCR #2, Box L, Seney, Michigan 49883. Phone: (906) 586–9851.

Seney also administers two satellite refuges:

Harbor Island is a 695-acre horseshoe-shaped island accessible only by boat in Potagannissing Bay, with interesting bird and mammal populations—deer, coyotes, red foxes, bobcats, bears, northern harriers, Cooper's hawks, white-winged and surf scoters, great blue herons—also wild orchids. Day use only. No visitor facilities.

Huron Islands is a group of eight small islands three miles offshore where pink and gray granite cliffs rise 200 feet and support nest colonies of herring gulls and cormorants. Only West Huron Island is open to the public and access is difficult due to turbulent surrounding waters.

SHIAWASSEE
(Michigan)

S ix rivers flow through Shiawassee, draining 6,000 square miles of what was once marshland teeming with wild creatures of all kinds. Now it is almost all agricultural. As a result this 8,984-acre refuge has become an oasis of habitat, a diked floodplain filled with food and places for cover, a situation wildlife recognize and respond to.

Waterfowl during the peak of fall migration cover the ponds and fill the air with their calls and feeding flights—50,000 ducks, mostly mallards and blacks but also wigeon, teal, mergansers, and others, and 25,000 geese, mostly Canadas with some snows and blues.

A dozen or more bald eagles join them in late October and November. Most are migrating and stopping to feed on weak or injured waterfowl but at least one family nests here and has been a familiar sight since June, fishing or carrying off an occasional unlucky muskrat.

A thousand or so tundra swans drop down in spring and usually stay for a month between mid-March and mid-April, feeding and resting en route from wintering grounds along the Atlantic coast to nesting areas thousands of miles to the northwest, some of them above the Arctic Circle.

White-tailed deer browse along the trails and woods understory, and because the habitat is so nutritious many show up in June with twin fawns, along with 10-point bucks, their spreading antlers still in soft "velvet" coverings.

Brilliant ring-necked pheasants cackle. Downy young broods of Canada geese as well as mallard, black, pintail, and wood ducklings appear on the ponds (most of the geese are the maxima or giant race of Canadas).

Coyotes and red foxes might be in any grassy field in summer, teaching their young how to pounce on rodents. Beavers build bank lodges along streams.

Large numbers of shorebirds—sometimes hundreds of dunlins, dowitchers, sandpipers, and yellowlegs—visit the mudflats in both spring and fall migration. Great blue herons fish the edges of all the streams and ponds along with great egrets and green-backed herons, the latter so common they sometimes have set up housekeeping in local backyards.

Indigo buntings nest; so do bobolinks, white-breasted nuthatches, redstarts, yellow and magnolia warblers, red-eyed and warbling vireos, northern harriers, black terns, and kingfishers, whose rattling call resounds everywhere. Red-tailed hawks, great horned owls, and screech owls are around all year, joined in winter by rough-legged hawks, snow buntings, lapland longspurs, sometimes redpolls and pine grosbeaks, and, every few years, a snowy owl.

How to get there: From Saginaw take State Route 13 south seven miles to Curtis Road, then west one mile to office.

Open: Dawn to dusk daily. Office 7:30–4 weekdays.

What to see: Congregations of geese and ducks; deer; great blue herons.

What to do: Observation tower. Nine miles of trails (can be closed during area hunt seasons; check with office). Photography of waterfowl, deer.

Where to stay: Motels—a number in Saginaw and nearby. Campgrounds—several in Saginaw but often crowded. Otherwise between Vassar and Mayville, 40 miles east.

What to take and wear: Sturdy waterproof footgear can be handy.

Points of interest nearby: Some say fishing for walleyed pike in the Saginaw River is the best in the country in late April–early May, ice fishing November–March.

For more information: Shiawassee National Wildlife Refuge, 6975 Mower Road, Saginaw, Michigan 48601. Phone: (517) 777–5930.

Shiawassee also administers two subrefuges:

Wyandotte—Three islands in the Detroit River, formerly an important waterfowl resting place; poor water quality and soil contamination have reduced use.

Michigan Islands—Six small islands established for herons, gulls, and terns. Three are designated wilderness. Access difficult and no public facilities.

Peoria

★
CHAUTAUQUA

CHAUTAUQUA (Illinois)

Chautauqua is an ancient wetland along the Illinois River where in good years up to a quarter of a million waterfowl stop en route to wintering grounds and some stay the winter. Shorebird concentrations have reached 200,000 birds—a carpet of yellowlegs, sandpipers, plovers, and others probing in the mudflats.

Dozens of bald eagles—sometimes 50 or more—spend the winter feeding on waterfowl and fish in the nearby river.

Warblers come through in spring, more than a dozen species flitting through the shrubbery and tree canopies in small flocks following budding out of leaves and hatching insects as they make their way north to nest. Songbirds follow closely upon them—rose-breasted grosbeaks, hermit and Swainson's thrush, golden and ruby-crowned kinglets and others.

Indigo buntings nest. So do warbling and red-eyed vireos, yellow and prothonotary warblers, redstarts and northern orioles, and seven kinds of woodpeckers, including the large flame-crested pileated.

Red foxes are common and have denned so close to headquarters of this 4,488-acre refuge that visitors have found fox kits playing in the parking area.

White-tailed deer are often along the edges; beavers have had a lodge along one of the walking trails; and fox squirrels, woodchucks, and bobwhite quail make themselves heard and usually seen.

Several hundred downy wood ducklings are hatched to their beautiful parents in natural tree cavities as well as nest boxes put up for them.

A large colony of great blue herons, black-crowned night herons, and great egrets are nearby, and hundreds of these graceful wading birds visit the refuge to feed through the summer and fall.

Whether eagles stay all winter depends on the weather. If the lake and river freeze over, they depart for open water farther south. But when it opens up again they return and are usually around in some numbers from October to February.

Whether the waterfowl—both geese and ducks of up to 26 species—and shorebirds are here in large or in greatly diminished numbers also depends on the habitat, in this case water levels. Chautauqua is a leveed lake and when the Illinois River flood levels are so high they go over the dikes, aquatic food plants cannot grow. Waterfowl come and stop over then, but do not stay. Similarly when water levels cover mudflats where shorebirds probe for replenishing food, they go elsewhere.

Projects have been proposed to remedy this, but they are expensive. Partial measures may help but not solve the problem completely. Waterfowl and shorebird use in the future depends on what happens to these.

But Chautauqua will remain a pleasant place for visitors wishing to see a good spectrum of wildlife of this region in any case.

How to get there: From Havana go north on Manito Blacktop 7 miles to refuge sign; follow signs to refuge headquarters.

Open: Sunrise to sunset. Office 8–4:30 weekdays.

Best times to visit: Winter for eagles; spring for warblers, songbirds; August for shorebirds; fall for waterfowl.

What to see: See above; also deer, foxes, muskrats, beavers.

What to do: Three hiking trails plus one self-guided interpretive trail. Observation tower over lake. Nut, mushroom, and berry picking in season.

Where to stay: Motels—in Havana eight miles southwest. Campgrounds—in Sand Ridge State Forest, eight miles east.

Points of interest nearby: Sand Ridge State Forest (see above), extremely sandy soil supports desert flora and fauna unique to this area; also has one of largest fish hatcheries in U.S. Dickson Mounds Indian museum across river on site of prehistoric Indian site. Mason State Tree Nursery, wildflowers, 6 miles southeast.

For more information: Chautauqua National Wildlife Refuge, R.R. 2, Box 61-B, Havana, Illinois 62644. Phone: (309) 535-2290.

Chautauqua also administers a satellite refuge, *Meredosia,* a 2,141-acre tract donated through The Nature Conservancy as waterfowl habitat, with no visitor facilities and not open to the public.

Marion
★
CRAB ORCHARD

CRAB ORCHARD (Illinois)

A herd of 4,000 white-tailed deer and flocks of waterfowl, up to 200,000 Canada geese and 40,000 ducks, coexist comfortably adjacent to the nation's main federal maximum-security prison here. They also share Crab Orchard's 43,000 acres with industries employing 1,500 persons making missile parts, explosives, sporting goods, and display cases.

Facilities for swimming, boating, camping, and waterskiing are here as well—and until recently Crab Orchard ran its own railroad. It is unique among U.S. refuges for its combination of high public use—more than a million visitors a year—and wildlife.

There are two active bald eagle nests and a former eagle nest that has been used by great horned owls. Gray and red foxes and coyotes are frequently along roadsides and scouting the edges of the three sizable lakes and 60 ponds that dot the refuge. Beaver workings are everywhere in the waterways.

Hawks nest through the woodlands—red-tailed, red-shouldered, broadwings, kestrels, and Cooper's, and northern harriers hunt over the marshes and restored native prairies. Wild turkeys have done so well that surplus birds are live-trapped to repopulate depleted areas elsewhere. Quail conveys scurry through the underbrush.

Bluebird houses fledge 340 or so young birds every year. Warbling and Bell's vireos nest; so do prothonotary and occasional cerulean warblers, chats, scarlet and summer tanagers, nighthawks, red-headed, red-bellied, and some pileated woodpeckers, upland sandpipers, and beautiful wood ducks in natural tree cavities.

It all works so well because the wild creatures keep mainly to the quieter parts of the refuge, and the main areas of overlap—the three sizable lakes and land around them—are used by wild and human visitors mostly at different seasons. The geese arrive in September after most warm-weather recreation is over and most of them stay until March, watched by a dozen or more golden and bald eagles that methodically flush the whole group, then prey on the weakest.

Photographers find relatively unwary subjects (using a telephoto lens) in deer along the roads and trails and in great blue herons spearing carp at the water's edge.

Even such shy birds as black- and yellow-crowned night herons breed, mostly on ponds in the half of the refuge that is closed to most public use. This is where the industrial residents are, in World War II structures built to make and store explosives; some still serve this purpose. After refuge establishment in 1947 local towns successfully resisted loss of jobs from their closure, and they could not now be easily separated—but they are gradually being phased out.

Visitors can see much of the refuge from 20-plus miles of roads open 24 hours every day (the wilderness area is open to foot travel only).

Because of the proximity of Southern Illinois University, the refuge is closely studied by students who have investigated its trees, vines, flowers, fish, reptiles, mammals, and almost everything else one might imagine. A deer you see wearing scarlet collars and streamers is doubtless part of a research project.

As a result, reports are available on everything from historic paddlefish in Crab Orchard Lake to the cucumber tree and lovely blooms of silky asters, trout lilies, purple trilliums, and stars-of-Bethlehem.

How to get there: From Marion take Highway 13 west to Route 148, then south 1.5 miles to refuge headquarters.

Open: Tour route 24 hours all year. Office 8–4:30 every day.

Best times to visit: March to mid-May and October-December.

What to see: Waterfowl; deer; eagles; songbirds.

What to do: Auto and hiking trails; observation tower; variety of recreation in public use areas—swimming, boating, waterskiing, picnicking and some of the best largemouth bass fishing in the Midwest (minimum 21 inches in some ponds).

Where to stay: Motels—at Marion, Carbondale, and numerous in area. Campgrounds—three on refuge; also Giant City State Park, three miles southwest.

Weather: July-August hot and humid; fall, early winter can be wet and cool.

What to take and wear: Waterproof gear might be handy, boots if hiking wet clay soil.

Points of interest nearby: Ferne Clyffe State Park, 10 miles south, and Giant City State Park (see Campgrounds)—unusual sandstone-limestone outcroppings. Shawnee National Forest borders refuge on south.

For more information: Crab Orchard National Wildlife Refuge, P.O. Box J, Carterville, Illinois 62918. Phone: (618) 997–3344.

Marion
•
CYPRESS CREEK ★

CYPRESS CREEK (Illinois)

More than a dozen state or federal champion trees are here along with dozens of plant and animal species seldom seen in this area because they are at the edge of their northern, western, or eastern range. Some of the cypresses are more than 1,000 years old.

One huge bald cypress is 73 feet tall, its trunk 34 feet around. There are champion green hawthorns, water locusts, overcup oaks, and ten others. Most can be readily seen by visitors.

The cypress swamp is stunning in itself—a place where a canoeist can see on a single stump a great blue heron fishing, painted turtles basking, golden prothonotary warblers foraging for insects, and bright green tree frogs in a wilderness scene that makes civilization seem far away.

Some ancient cypresses are wildlife apartment houses with several nests of beautiful wood ducks along with perhaps a pair of barred or barn owls, chimney swifts, barn swallows, pileated woodpeckers, flying and gray squirrels, bats and others. One big cypress cut down some years ago was home to more than 100 species.

It is all part of a newly established wetland reserve protecting not only waterfowl but bobcats, otters, deer, coyotes, and many others in a 30-mile corridor along the beautiful Cache River. Its protection is the result of citizen action through The Nature Conservancy and other groups worried about destruction of this natural treasure, resulting in a planned reserve of some 60,000 acres of which the designated refuge boundary covers about half.

Canada and snow geese, ducks of a dozen or so species, and bald eagles spend the winter. Bobwhite quail are common all year. The largest of several wading bird colonies nearby supports 400 great blue heron nests. Warblers come through in spring and ceruleans stay and nest along with orchard and northern orioles.

There are (and will be more) hiking, auto, and canoe trails with a visitor center in the planning stage. To see everything, stop at headquarters on the Shawnee College Campus, six miles east of I-57 Exit 18 (telephone 618–634–2231). There get maps and literature (or write ahead to Route 1, Box 53D, Ullin, Illinois 62992). There is much to see also on state lands adjacent. Motel accommodations are in Anna and Vienna, campgrounds in Ferne Clyffe State Park, 15 miles north.

MARK TWAIN

★
● Quincy

MARK TWAIN (Illinois, Iowa, and Missouri)

The author Mark Twain transformed *Life on the Mississippi* into vivid reality for generations of readers. Now this 125,000-acre refuge that bears his name and follows one of the world's great river systems for 250 miles through Iowa, Illinois, and Missouri does the same for visitors.

Commercial riverboats still travel its main channel—but some of the sloughs and backwaters are untamed and remote, still filled with wild creatures. Hundreds of bald eagles and tens of thousands of waterfowl can be present here in some of the country's greatest wildlife concentrations—along with wild turkeys, pheasants, swirls of golden warblers, foxes, beavers, coyotes, and others.

More than 600 bald eagles winter on the refuge in the greatest eagle gatherings in the lower 48 states—perhaps 150 at one time feeding in the trees or soaring and diving on fish in turbulent open water below the dams, lured by freeze-up of waters farther north.

Raptors in fall migration follow the river south like a superhighway. As many as 10,000 broad-wings have come through on a single spectacular October day.

Warblers can be the same in a northward direction in spring—a stream of small golden birds of two dozen or so species making the woods canopy come alive as they flit about following hatching insects among new green buds.

Thousands of shorebirds probe the mudflats for small organisms in late summer—sometimes 20,000 in one spot, covering the sandy bottom like a moving carpet of pectoral and least sandpipers, yellowlegs, black-bellied plovers, and others.

Autumn foliage colors reach a kaleidoscopic peak in mid- to late October, with breathtaking views of the entire river floodplain and its bluffs.

A half million or more ducks start to move through then: mallards, wigeons, pintails, blacks, redheads, scaups, ringnecks, more than a dozen species, along with beautiful wood ducks. A major function of the refuge is to protect the nest habitat of this lovely waterfowl, and more than 2,000 wood ducklings are hatched every year in cavities in riverine trees—along with exquisite golden prothonotary warblers that like similar surroundings.

Great blue herons and great egrets have a dozen nesting colonies along the river, mostly clustered in sycamore trees on islands. The largest colony contains some 250 nesting birds.

A walk into a field of sunflower-like Bidens in June may stir up dozens of blue flashes that turn out to be brilliant indigo buntings.

Quail, pheasants, and dickcissels whistle and call in the uplands. Redheaded, red-bellied, and pileated woodpeckers hammer away in the woods. Four kinds of swallows build mud nests, and bank swallows dig out colonial nest holes along the river's edge. Great crested and Acadian flycatchers hawk for flying insects. Barred, great horned, and screech owls hoot and twitter all year.

Up to 15,000 geese—Canadas and snows with some blues and white-fronteds—are on the river from early November to Christmas.

Many creatures are best seen in winter—they're hungrier and less wary then: a coyote crossing the frozen river; a flock of 100 wild turkeys pecking over a snowy field, then flying up to roost in a tall cottonwood; a red fox staring fixedly at bent-over grass, then pouncing on a hidden rodent.

The best way to see Mark Twain is by boat—by bringing a small boat or renting one along the way. But much can be seen from the hiking trails, observation platforms, or pull-offs from the miles of auto-tour routes.

Dates of the natural occurrences vary with weather and temperatures that can cause unpredictable river waters to freeze or to flood and rise several feet, changing the habitat so that eagles, waterfowl, or others change locations.

Refuge staff can be helpful in suggesting where to go and when. Refuge head-quarters is at Quincy, with offices at three other locations that administer the ten divisions and also General Plan Lands owned by the U.S. Army Corps of Engineers. Office hours are 7:30–4 weekdays.

One should consult the refuge staff before going out in a small boat. Sudden

storms or river traffic can stir up three- to five-foot waves. Take a refuge map AND
A COMPASS! It is true wilderness out there.

If possible, plan to visit several days—for this splendid refuge cannot be seen in
a quick day's tour. Motels and campgrounds are located all along the way, or ask
advice in some of the little river towns, which are worth a visit in any case—as is
Mark Twain's boyhood home at Hannibal, Missouri.

The lucky visitor will get into some of the back country and see the river and
its islands almost exactly as the first explorers and settlers did, or as Mark Twain
saw them—"utter solitudes [where] the dense, untouched forest overhung both
banks . . . and one could believe that human creatures had never intruded there
before."

For more information:

Mark Twain National Wildlife Refuge (Quincy Headquarters), 311 North Fifth
Street, Suite 100, Quincy, Illinois 62301. Phone: (217) 224–8580.

Mark Twain National Wildlife Refuge (Calhoun, Batchtown, and Gilbert Lake
divisions), HCR, Box 107, Brussels, Illinois 62013. Phone: (618) 883–2524.

Mark Twain National Wildlife Refuge (Louisa, Keithsburg, and Big Timber Divisions), R.R. 1, Wapello, Iowa 52653. Phone: (319) 523–6982.

Mark Twain National Wildlife Refuge (Clarence Cannon National Wildlife Refuge,
Gardner and Delair and Gregory Landing Divisions), P.O. Box 88, Annada,
Missouri 63330. Phone: (314) 847–2333.

Indianapolis
●

★
MUSCATATUCK

MUSCATATUCK (Indiana)

The wood duck, called by Audubon "this most beautiful bird" whose multihued plumage of scarlet, green, purple, blue-black, and gold "always affords pleasure to the viewer," affords that pleasure multiplied many times here.

Hundreds of colorful males and their less conspicuous mates make homes in natural tree cavities in this historic nesting place for them—Muscatatuck, named by Algonquin Indians "land of winding waters" because of the meandering, heavily wooded Muscatatuck River. It is ideal nesting habitat for this glorious bird whose survival was threatened in the 1930s by overhunting and habitat destruction.

It is plentiful here—its status no longer in question due to protection—and it is possible at certain times to sit quietly and see hundreds of these exquisite waterfowl resting on the water and flying back and forth to the woods and river beyond. Sometimes a thousand can take off at once, filling the air with plaintive cries and a rush of dazzling wings.

This diverse 7,724-acre refuge with bottomland stands of sweet gum, sycamore, and river birch, upland fields and woods of tulip, beech, maple, and oak, is home to a variety of wildlife.

White-tailed deer appear with spotted fawns in June. A hundred or so wild turkeys roam refuge woods and fields.

Coyotes howl at night. Beavers maintain a lodge on the auto tour route. Woodcocks zoom skyward in aerial nuptial flights. *"Bob-white!"* is proclaimed around old fence-rows. Ruffed grouse drum on logs. Minks, woodchucks, rabbits, squirrels, raccoons, and muskrats are all here.

Muscatatuck is known throughout the state of Indiana for its songbirds and occasionally uncommon wetland birds, including phalaropes and Wilson's plovers. Great blue and green-backed herons and least bitterns nest here. An alert summer visitor can hardly miss seeing numbers of brilliant indigo buntings.

Warblers come through in May and many stay and nest—cerulean, Kentucky, prairie, blue-winged, yellow, prothonotary, and some parulas, along with warbling vireos, chats, blue-gray gnatcatchers, and in the grasslands dickcissels, Henslow's sparrows, and sedge wrens.

Insects attracted by moist soil attract in turn eight kinds of flycatchers—olive-sided, wood-pewee, Acadian, willow, least, great crested, phoebes, and eastern king-birds.

Bluebirds nest in houses along the road and stay year-round as do cardinals, brown thrashers, goldfinches, kingfishers, and red-headed, red-bellied, and pileated wood-peckers.

Downy broods of Canada geese appear in April. Killdeer fearlessly nest in graveled parking areas and put on a "broken-wing act" to lure visitors away from eggs. Red-tailed hawks and an occasional osprey soar overhead. Barred and great horned owls may be seen on shadowed branches.

Waterfowl numbers peak in fall at around 10,000, including ring-necked ducks, gadwalls, mallards, blue and green-winged teals, and a dozen others. Muscatatuck is on the flyway for greater sandhill cranes, which gather in concentrations of up to 15,000 at Jasper-Pulaski State Fish and Wildlife Area in northern Indiana. Sometimes several hundred of these stop over, along with a few bald eagles.

Christmas Bird Counts have included tundra swans and up to 25 golden-crowned kinglets, 12 northern harriers, 136 white-crowned sparrows, and 222 Carolina chickadees.

How to get there: From Indianapolis take I-65 south to North Vernon exit, then Route 50 east three miles to refuge entrance.

Open: Dawn to dusk daily; office 8–4:30 weekdays.

Best times to visit: Spring and fall.

What to see: Wood ducks; deer; varied songbirds, waterfowl. Century-old settler's cabin.

What to do: Nature drives and hiking trails. Photography (blinds available, portable blinds permitted). Wildlife overlook. Gathering (for personal use only) of mushrooms, fruit, nuts, and antlers shed following mating season. Fishing for bass, catfish, bluegills, sunfish.

Where to stay: Motels—in Seymour, two miles west of refuge. Campgrounds—13 miles west on Route 258; Muscatatuck County Park, 15 miles east on Route 7; also Hardy Lake State Recreation Area, 25 miles south; Starved Hollow Lake State Area, 25 miles west.

What to take and wear: Waterproof footgear off trails.

Points of interest nearby: State areas (see Campgrounds); Clifty Falls State Park, on river bluffs, 30 miles southeast; Brown County State Park and Nashville, 35 miles northwest, artists' mecca famed for natural beauty, mid-October fall foliage (reserve accommodations well ahead). Jasper-Pulaski State Area (see text), about 150 miles northwest.

For more information: Muscatatuck National Wildlife Refuge, R.R. 7, Box 189A, Seymour, Indiana 47274. Phone: (812) 522–4352.

Toledo
OTTAWA

OTTAWA (Ohio)

Ottawa is a rich remnant of marsh that once covered 300,000 acres and stretched 75 miles along Lake Erie from Detroit to Port Clinton, Ohio. Now, with few other places to go, wildlife are attracted in large numbers to this 8,316-acre oasis of habitat, and visitors are treated to the sight of tens of thousands of waterfowl plus warblers, deer, pheasants, eagles, and many others.

During the peak of fall waterfowl migration, ducks and geese can seem to be everywhere—covering the water, calling, flying back and forth, filling the air. There may be up to 20,000 in a single pool, totaling on the refuge 100,000 ducks of a dozen or more species. Tundra swans and 25,000 Canada, snow, and blue geese join them from both the Mississippi and Atlantic flyways at this pivotal migration point.

More than a dozen bald eagles may concentrate their activities on the refuge then, soaring on eight-foot wings, largely family groups that have nested in the area—occasionally feeding on one of the weaker waterfowl. One eagle pair nests on the refuge, and refuge headquarters usually has a telescope focused on the nest so visitors can observe their activities.

Endangered peregrine falcons, which now nest successfully in Cleveland and Toledo, usually stop by on their way south.

Warblers in spring follow the Lake Erie shoreline onto the refuge, and birders from throughout the area come to glimpse these golden birds on their northward flights—magnolias, black-and-whites, bay-breasteds, and some two dozen other species, plus warbling, Philadelphia, and red-eyed vireos. They peak about Mother's

Day and a good viewpoint is right around refuge headquarters. Like much of the wildlife they are seen as well on adjacent 2,500-acre Crane Creek State Park, which has a boardwalk. Songbirds and raptors also come through then.

Wildlife viewing is highly accessible year-round. Along the entrance drive is a pond that may be lined with killdeer and yellowlegs, with geese and ducks in the field nearby. Young goslings can seem to be everywhere in early summer.

Nine miles of walking trails in the refuge's three separate lakefront units pass by white-tailed deer feeding in the fields or resting inconspicuously in wooded places. Brilliant male pheasants strut and cackle. Red foxes trot along the dikes and trail edges on the lookout for rodents. Muskrats, raccoons, minks, opossums, and skunks are there, too.

Shorebird migrations in mid- to late August depend on the wind direction off shallow Lake Erie. A southwest wind exposes mudflats to thousands of feeding dowitchers, sandpipers, peeps, and yellowlegs. A northeast wind can cover the flats with two feet of lake water, forcing the birds elsewhere.

Winter brings flocks of goldeneyes, mergansers, canvasbacks, and scaup plus such northerners as snow buntings, tree sparrows, and sometimes lapland longspurs, evening grosbeaks, and snowy owls.

Great blue herons are around all year, and great egrets in summer. Many of these nest on West Sister Island, nine miles out in Lake Erie, in the largest heronry in the Great Lakes, administered by Ottawa as a satellite refuge. It may have 1,500 pairs of great blues, 600 great egrets, and 1,300 pairs of black-crowned night herons, plus Ohio's only nesting little blues and snowy egrets, and 700 herring gulls.

How to get there: From Toledo take State Route 2 about 15 miles east to refuge entrance sign.

Open: Dawn to dusk daily. Office 8–4 weekdays.

Best times to visit: October and November, May.

What to see: Waterfowl, migrating in fall and with broods in summer. Great blue herons, deer, migrating warblers, bald eagles.

What to do: Nine miles of self-guided walking trails. Photographers can put up portable blinds with permission. Fishing (see below). Environmental education programs for students and teachers.

Where to stay: Motels—a number in Toledo or nearby Oregon, also Port Clinton, a lakeside resort area (these generally more expensive). Campgrounds—seven miles east off Route 2; also several at Port Clinton.

Weather: No extremes but winds off Lake Erie can be raw in early spring and fall.

Points of interest nearby: Crane Creek State Park, adjacent, excellent for warblers. Oak Openings Park, 18 miles west of Toledo—a little distant but worth it for amazingly varied habitat and wildlife. Lake Erie fishing can be wonderful for walleye and smallmouth bass—charter or rental boats available.

For more information: Ottawa National Wildlife Refuge, 14000 West State Route 2, Oak Harbor, Ohio 43449. Phone: (419) 898-0014.

Ottawa also administers *Cedar Point,* a 2,445-acre refuge 10 miles west, a waterfowl nesting and stopping place that may have concentrations of as many as 70,000 birds.

Access to Ottawa's satellite units is by special permit only. The best way to see them is to arrange with the refuge office to go along on a periodic survey and banding trip.

The Mid-South States

The mid-South has glorious coastal refuges where thousands of roseate spoonbills, purple gallinules, and—offshore—roseate terns and black skimmers live and breed. But its heart is the many thousands of acres of nutrient-rich bottomland hardwoods that have been saved for a great variety of wildlife.

Bottomland hardwoods, like estuaries and rainforests, teem with invertebrates and other organisms, supporting much more wildlife up and down the ecological scale than uplands.

The characteristic trees of this habitat, such as bitter pecan and overcup oak, provide rich forage for a variety of nut- and seed-eating creatures that in turn are food for predators like raccoons, bobcats, and occasional black bears and cougars. Intermittent flooding has kept these bottomlands unpeopled and wild. In some cases the visitor can see what the Indians saw—but only by the same means the Indians saw it, traveling on foot or by canoe.

ARKANSAS

Threading a small boat through *Big Lake*'s maze of waterways and virgin cypress trees, some of them more than 100 feet tall, can make civilization seem far away. Waterfowl like it, too, and their overflights in winter, sometimes to escape a hunting eagle, can fill the air with whirring wings and calling birds.

Cache River is a new refuge of mixed bottomland hardwoods interspersed with river channels and swamps, one of eight United States wetlands cited as of international importance. Deer, beavers, waterfowl, songbirds are here—even black bears and cougars from time to time.

Felsenthal's fertile basin was a wildlife paradise when Native Americans lived here.

It still is, a superb bottomland hardwood ecosystem supporting deer, beavers, waterfowl, turkeys, and, in surrounding pine stands, colonies of endangered red-cockaded woodpeckers.

Dozens of bald eagles follow waterfowl that congregate—up to 50,000 ducks and 25,000 geese—every fall and winter on *Holla Bend*, an old oxbow of the Arkansas River nestled beteween the Ozark Mountains on the north and the Ouachita Mountains on the south. Wood ducks and bluebirds nest in boxes alongside roads and ponds.

Some 150,000 ducks winter at *Wapanocca*, once a famous hunt club started after the Civil War because of the seemingly limitless wildlife in this rich bottomland just west of the Mississippi River. Deer are here, too, and bobcats, coyotes, beavers, and others.

Much of *White River* is a wilderness of bottomland, lakes, streams, and bayous that holds one of the healthiest populations of black bears in the eastern United States— also beavers, deer, wild turkeys, Mississippi kites, and nesting warblers. Sometimes the bears den 60 feet up in trees to avoid floodwaters.

TENNESSEE

Cross Creeks is a birding hotspot in the rich Cumberland River bottomland where eagles, bluebirds, Canada geese, and wood ducks nest, and tens of thousands of waterfowl winter. Deer and wild turkeys sometimes graze together in grassy fields.

Hatchie's swamp forest bordering the Hatchie River for 24 miles is a wildlife treasure, a rare remnant of the rich bottomland hardwoods that once covered 22 million acres of the lower Mississippi Valley. It supports deer, otters, beavers, wild turkeys, waterfowl, and—rare elsewhere—Swainson's and golden prothonotary warblers.

Devastating earthquakes in 1811 and 1812 caused the Mississippi River to rise 15 to 20 feet, then flow backward to fill the collapsed basin of *Reelfoot* Lake. The upper part of the lake is now this refuge on the Kentucky-Tennessee border, a seasonal home for spectacular numbers of bald eagles, waterfowl, and migrating songbirds.

Some of the largest waterfowl concentrations in the East gather to winter on *Tennessee* refuge, where the bandit Jesse James once farmed and Confederate general Nathan Bedford Forrest led his troops. Deer, foxes, coyotes, beavers, and songbirds also find homes here.

MISSISSIPPI

Mississippi Sandhill Crane refuge probably saved from extinction the endangered subspecies of the majestic bird for which it is named. Its population has been increasing, along with that of two other resident rarities, the Bachman's sparrow and gopher tortoise.

Noxubee's huge old pines have attracted colonies of endangered red-cockaded woodpeckers, which require old trees with soft "red-heart" centers for nest sites. Nowhere are they more visible than here. Turkeys and white-tailed deer also are around, plus some 20,000 waterfowl in winter.

St. Catherine Creek is a new refuge of great potential stretching for more than six miles along the Mississippi River. Thousands of wintering ducks nest and feed, white pelicans spend summer through early fall, and endangered wood storks roost. Otters frolic and beavers skirt places where alligators wait. Deer and coyotes feed in uplands.

Nowhere is the beautiful wood duck more brilliantly and abundantly visible than at *Yazoo*. About 10,000 wood ducklings are produced every year. There are also deer, wild turkeys, up to 25,000 herons and egrets, and up to 250,000 waterfowl in fall. Mississippi kites and nesting songbirds are around in spring and summer.

ALABAMA

Tens of thousands of migrating songbirds find *Bon Secour*—"safe harbor"—here on their first landfall migrating north in spring after a 600-mile flight across the Gulf of Mexico. The bird list has 369 species, as many as any national wildlife refuge. Ospreys nest, and alligators live in Gator Lake.

Wood duck houses at *Choctaw* are 20 feet high because the river can rise that much overnight. Refuge field headquarters then may be reachable only by boat. The periodic deluge can be inconvenient but it is one reason for the wildlife diversity. Wading birds nest. Thousands of ducks winter. Nutria swim. Deer and turkeys fatten on acorns and mast. Songbirds can fill the woods in spring.

Eufaula has been called one of the 10 best bird walks in the state. Endangered wood storks visit. Two nesting colonies support several thousand ibises and other beautiful wading birds. Wood ducks and bluebirds nest. Wild turkeys feed in the fields.

Up to 30,000 geese and 70,000 ducks of 22 species winter at *Wheeler,* the first national wildlife refuge overlaid on a power-dam project. It was an experiment followed throughout the U.S. and around the world. Nearby neighbors are the army's Redstone Arsenal and NASA's Marshall Space Flight Center. Wood duck predator guards are made of materials from Redstone scrap piles.

LOUISIANA

Flame-crested pileated woodpeckers hammer, river otters slide down mudbanks, and wild turkeys' rattling calls are heard for a mile or more through *Bogue Chitto*'s bottomland hardwoods. But take a compass when hiking or canoeing through its network of sloughs, oxbow lakes, and more than 50 miles of waterways within the refuge boundaries.

Bogue Chitto administers three other refuges. *Bayou Sauvage*'s 20,000 acres were acquired when developers' plans to drain them ended in bankruptcy court. Now

New Orleans schoolchildren come out to see marsh and wilderness and the beautiful creatures that live there. *Delta* and *Breton* are stunning marshes and barrier islands in and offshore from the delta where one of the world's longest rivers empties into the sea. Delta supports hundreds of thousands of wintering waterfowl and is landfall in spring for flocks of northward-migrating songbirds. Breton is over 10,000 acres of sandy beaches where tens of thousands of seabirds live and nest.

Until 1988 *Cameron Prairie* was an abandoned rice farm surrounded by marsh. It is on its way to becoming one of the South's great birding refuges, with roseate spoonbills, mottled and fulvous whistling ducks, purple gallinules, and sometimes a vermilion flycatcher or tiny black rail. Alligators and nutria are everywhere.

Catahoula shows how a misused area can be restored for wildlife use. Once overlogged and overgrazed, now prothonotary warblers and bluebirds nest, along with indigo and painted buntings. Wading birds colonize Catahoula Lake, and up to 75,000 waterfowl stay in winter.

The clear and scenic *D'Arbonne* Bayou winds through the refuge that bears its name, sanctuary for hundreds of long-legged herons and egrets and endangered red-cockaded woodpeckers. Beavers seem to enjoy the challenge of a refuge sometimes flooded over 80 percent of its area.

Huge populations of waterfowl explode from the water over *Lacassine's* marsh, filling the air with birds' calls and whirring wings. Roseate spoonbills nest and gorgeous purple gallinules make their way among an estimated 15,000 alligators, one of the densest populations anywhere.

Five thousand beautiful wading birds make their homes on two relatively new bottomland hardwood refuges, *Lake Ophelia* and its nearby satellite, *Grand Cote*. Several thousand young wood ducks hatch out every year, and there are bobcats, alligators, otters, beavers, minks, coyotes, and gray and red foxes.

Roseate spoonbills almost overwhelm the sunset when they fly from feeding grounds to nightly roosts for almost an hour every day at *Sabine*. Moorhens and brilliant purple gallinules parade their families, and there are an estimated 9,000 alligators.

Tensas River is a priceless remnant of bottomland habitat saved by citizen action, home to threatened Louisiana black bears, otter families, bobcats, barred owls, wild turkeys, and an array of waterfowl and songbirds.

Following are birds of special interest found commonly at Mid-South refuges at seasons indicated:

S: SPRING   s: SUMMER   F: FALL   W: WINTER

Horned Grebe: Wheeler FW
American White Pelican: Lacassine W, Sabine SFW
Northern Gannet: Bon Secour W
Olivaceous Cormorant: Lacassine SsFW, Sabine SsFW
Least Bittern: Eufaula S, Lacassine SsF, Sabine Ss, Yazoo s

Wood Stork: Catahoula sF, D'Arbonne s

White-faced Ibis: Lacassine Ss, Sabine SsFW

Roseate Spoonbill: Lacassine Ss

Fulvous Whistling Duck: Lacassine SF

Greater White-Fronted Goose: Lacassine SFW, Yazoo W

Wood Duck: Common or abundant at many mid-South refuges but extraordinarily abundant at Yazoo SsFW

Mottled Duck: Lacassine SsFW

Mississippi Kite: Tensas River S, Yazoo s

Bald Eagle: Reelfoot W

Purple Gallinule: Lacassine SsF, Sabine s

Mississippi Sandhill Crane: Mississippi Sandhill Crane FW

Black-necked Stilt: Lacassine SsF, Sabine SsF

Upland Sandpiper: Bon Secour SF

Wilson's Phalarope: Holla Bend SF

Scissor-tailed Flycatcher: Holla Bend SsF

Hermit Thrush: D'Arbonne FW, Eufaula W, Felsenthal W, Hatchie SFW, Wheeler FW, White River SFW

Swainson's Thrush: Big Lake S, Bon Secour SF, Cross Creeks S, Hatchie SF, Reelfoot SF, Sabine SF, Tennessee SF, Tensas River SF, Wapanocca SF

Gray-cheeked Thrush: Big Lake S, Hatchie SF, Reelfoot SF, Tennessee SF

Solitary Vireo: D'Arbonne FW

Bell's Vireo: Holla Bend Ss

Swainson's Warbler: Hatchie s, Tennesssee SsF

Hooded Warbler: Bon Secour SF, Eufaula s, Hatchie SsF, Mississippi Sandhill Crane s, Noxubee S, Reelfoot SF, Sabine S, Tennessee SF, Wapanocca SsF, White River Ss, Yazoo S

Cerulean Warbler: Hatchie SsF, Wapanocca SsF

Kentucky Warbler: Felsenthal SsF, Hatchie SsF, Reelfoot SF, Sabine S, Wapanocca SsF, Wheeler SF, White River Ss

Painted Bunting: Catahoula SsF

Seaside Sparrow: Sabine SsFW

Vesper Sparrow: Bon Secour F, Cross Creeks S

Lark Sparrow: Holla Bend SsF

Bachman's Sparrow: Mississippi Sandhill Crane Ss

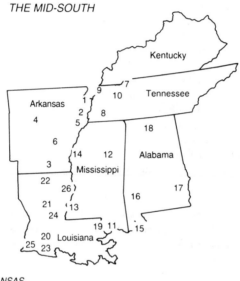

THE MID-SOUTH

ARKANSAS
1 BIG LAKE
2 CACHE RIVER
3 FELSENTHAL
4 HOLLA BEND
5 WAPANOCCA
6 WHITE RIVER

TENNESSEE
7 CROSS CREEKS
8 HATCHIE
9 REELFOOT
10 TENNESSEE

MISSISSIPPI
11 MISSISSIPPI SANDHILL CRANE
12 NOXUBEE
13 ST. CATHERINE CREEK
14 YAZOO

ALABAMA
15 BON SECOUR
16 CHOCTAW
17 EUFAULA
18 WHEELER

LOUISIANA
19 BOGUE CHITTO
20 CAMERON PRAIRIE
21 CATAHOULA
22 D'ARBONNE
23 LACASSINE
24 LAKE OPHELIA
25 SABINE
26 TENSAS RIVER

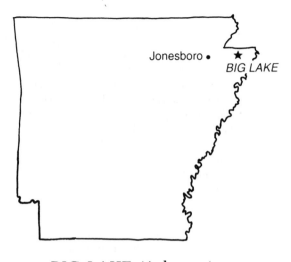

Jonesboro • ★
BIG LAKE

BIG LAKE (Arkansas)

Threading a small boat through the maze of waterways and virgin cypress swamps surrounding Big Lake can be a rare experience. Trees more than 100 feet tall and three feet in diameter seem to dwarf human observers. The only sounds are those of birds and an occasional beaver slapping its tail on the water, and the air is cool and refreshing on the steamiest day. (But do take a compass!)

Waterfowl have found this 11,038-acre refuge increasingly hospitable since a levee built around Big Lake has made possible control of water levels and also better wildlife-viewing for land-based visitors. Seasonal flooding and draw-down have encouraged growth of invertebrates and natural foods such as smartweed that furnish a nutritious diet attracting up to 5,000 geese and 80,000 ducks every fall and winter—mallards, pintails, blue-winged teals, and more than a dozen other species.

Flights at dawn and dusk in winter can be dramatic, filling the air with flying and calling waterfowl—and a dozen or so eagles may be here, too.

From the levee visitors can see not only birds but white-tailed deer, raccoons, opossums, squirrels, rabbits, and—if you look quickly—coyotes, which come out to prey on these (but which melt into the background when a visitor appears). Another good viewing point is the levee around Baker Island Mud Slough.

Multicolored wood ducks nest in natural cavities and in boxes put up for them, and handsome hooded mergansers sometimes take over these desirable spots, too.

Birders come out for spring and fall songbird and warbler migrations always with the hope of finding a rare Bachman's warbler, a bird widely believed but never verified to spend some time here. The refuge bird list does show 227 other species.

Common or abundant at least seasonally are pileated woodpeckers, barred and screech owls, great blue herons, killdeer (which often nest in the parking lot), northern harriers, dickcissels, indigo buntings, prothonotary warblers, and summer tanagers.

Big Lake is at the end of one of the world's largest drainage systems—the St. Francis River Basin Project, 215 miles long and 53 miles wide. Formerly five canals drained into it bringing silt and pesticide-laden water, which the levee now forces to bypass around the refuge in all but heavy flood times, greatly increasing water quality.

But visitors need to realize it's possible for the refuge to be flooded at any time but midsummer (sometimes it is 99 percent underwater), so it's always worth a check to see if roads are passable before coming.

How to get there: From Memphis take I-55 north to Exit 48, then Route 140 west to 181 and west on Route 18 to refuge headquarters, just past floodway bridge.

Open: Daylight hours all year (but waterways closed in winter as sanctuary to wintering waterfowl). Office 7–3:30 weekdays.

What to see: Wintering waterfowl; virgin cypress stands; songbirds, including— someday, it is hoped—the Bachman's warbler.

What to do: Boating (flat-bottomed jonboat with 10-horse motor is best, and it's necessary to bring your own); more than 10 miles of levee roads open to driving, hiking (can be flooded seasonally); fishing, some of the best in Arkansas for bass, bream, crappie.

Where to stay: Motels—Blytheville, 15 miles west, and West Memphis. Campgrounds—Big Lake State Management Area, adjacent to refuge.

Points of interest nearby: Big Lake State Wildlife Area, adjacent—includes Mallard Lake, which holds state record for largemouth bass. Also Wapanocca National Wildlife Refuge, 50 miles south; White River National Wildlife Refuge, 125 miles south.

For more information: Big Lake National Wildlife Refuge, P.O. Box 67, Manila, Arkansas 72442. Phone: (501) 564–2429.

CACHE RIVER ★

West Memphis

CACHE RIVER (Arkansas)

This new and wonderful refuge is like a little White River—mixed bottomland hardwood forest interspersed with meandering river channels, shallow sloughs, oxbow lakes, and shrubby swamps that make ideal wildlife habitat. As a critical wetland this area is one of eight in the U.S. designated as of international importance under the Ramsar Convention. Deer, beavers, waterfowl, eagles, and songbirds are here—even black bears and cougars from time to time.

It is a refuge in the process of acquisition, with a target of up to 40,000 acres, and the possibility exists of eventually having what would amount to a 60-mile wildlife corridor stretching to the White River refuge.

Until recently there have been few if any visitor facilities—these await further land acquisition. For more information write P.O. Box 279, Turrell, Arkansas 72384, or telephone (501) 343–2595.

El Dorado

FELSENTHAL

FELSENTHAL (Arkansas)

Felsenthal must have seemed a paradise to the Indians who once lived here. Its fertile basin around the confluence of the Saline and Ouachita rivers, 65,000 acres of uplands, open water, and rich bottomland hardwoods interspersed with lakes and sloughs, supports a superb wildlife ecosystem with many kinds of oaks and other fruited vegetation on which deer, waterfowl, turkeys, and a wide variety of other birds and mammals feed. Fish, reptiles, and amphibians are abundant.

Endangered red-cockaded woodpeckers find homes in over 25 known colonies in the surrounding upland pine stands. Wood ducks nest in its cypress-studded back-waters. Cormorants and anhingas hold out their wings to dry. Night herons stand like statues watching the water's surface for telltale ripples. Endangered wood storks visit in late summer in flocks of 100 or so.

Waterfowl start to arrive in October and peak in early January at around 100,000 ducks (primarily mallards and woodies) dispersed over the vast watered acreage of this 100-square-mile refuge. A dozen or so eagles usually spend the winter.

One of the best ways to see Felsenthal is by boat, ideally a 20-horsepower jonboat or a canoe which can explore quietly in the labyrinth of creeks and oxbows branching out from the rivers alongside old cypresses with trunks four feet in diameter on what was once a vast prehistoric lake. Beavers lounge about on their lodges, deer browse on acorns, and, common but more rarely seen, otters crunch mussels, and bobcats, gray foxes, or coyotes hunt and come to drink.

Hundreds of acres of pale-gold lotuses bloom in late summer in the open water.

Flame-crested pileated woodpeckers drum and call raucously throughout the woodlands. Golden prothonotary warblers nest.

There are also 15 miles of graveled roads and 65 miles of trails open seasonally to high-flotation all-terrain vehicles where hikers can go as well. Mayhaw picking is popular in early May among those who love this marble-sized fruit for its tart jelly. The excellent Visitor Center has museum-quality exhibits.

Felsenthal was established in mitigation of a series of locks and dams constructed by the Corps of Engineers on the Ouachita River. The result includes on this refuge the world's largest green-tree reservoir, 21,000 acres of seasonally flooded bottomland hardwoods that provide wonderful feeding and resting habitat for waterfowl and great blue and night herons, great egrets, and other wetland species as well.

Woodlands shelter large flocks of wild turkeys, barred and screech owls, and a half-dozen woodpecker species, plus such smaller varieties as nuthatches, chickadees, and titmice.

The refuge is rich in cultural history, with more than 200 identified prehistoric sites, some dating back to 8,000 B.C., overlooked from surrounding highlands by several mound-cluster ceremonial sites, some still little disturbed.

Felsenthal also administers *Overflow NWR*, one of the best wintering waterfowl refuges in the region. Up to 200,000 ducks and geese may winter there, plus numerous shorebirds in spring and fall migration. Passerines abound in bottomland hardwoods and edges. An ongoing acquisition program will bring acreage to over 18,000, and there are plans for facilities beyond the present minimal trails that will permit greater visitor usage. Overflow is located 30 miles east of Felsenthal, or 8 miles west of Wilmot on Route 52.

How to get there: From El Dorado take Route 82 east 45 miles to the refuge; from Crossett take Route 82 west five miles to the Visitor Center.

Open: Continuously year-round. Office/Visitor Center 7–3:30 weekdays, Visitor Center weekends 1–5, holidays except Christmas 9–5.

What to see: Waterfowl, wild turkeys, red-cockaded woodpeckers, deer, great blue and night herons, wood ducks, and a wide variety of songbirds. (Hunting can conflict with wildlife viewing during early October and six deer-hunt days in late October and November.)

What to do: Nature observation, boating, 15 miles of graveled roads plus 65 miles of ATV trails for hiking. Fishing fantastic in spring, very good all year for bream, crappie, largemouth bass, catfish.

Where to stay: Motels—in Crossett, five miles east. Campgrounds—Crossett Harbor, two miles west, Grand Marais, adjacent on south, and Moro Bay State Park, adjacent on west (but 30 miles by road). Primitive camping on refuge.

Weather: Seasonal flooding possible; mild winters, warm, humid summers.

What to take and wear: Waterproof footgear and insect repellent.

Points of interest nearby: Lake Georgia Pacific, adjacent to refuge—trails, fishing, good birding.

For more information: Felsenthal National Wildlife Refuge, P.O. Box 1157, Crossett, Arkansas 71635. Phone: (501) 364–3167.

HOLLA BEND

★

Little Rock

HOLLA BEND (Arkansas)

Holla Bend is an old oxbow in the Arkansas River nestled between the Ozark Mountains on the north and the Ouachita Mountains on the south. This river valley has become a prime focal point for bird activity in the south-central United States.

More than 50 bald eagles, and usually a few goldens, congregate every fall and winter when concentrations of up to 50,000 ducks and 25,000 geese are here—14 species of ducks along with Canada, snow, and a few Ross' geese that cover the ground and fill the air with their presence. They become so unwary in this hospitable place where they are not hunted (except by eagles) that visitors sometimes have to part them to pass through on the roads.

In a program to reestablish bald eagles as a nesting bird here young eagles have been "hacked out"—gradually introduced to the environment—and released on the refuge (conspicuous with large numbered wing tags), with the idea that they will join wild groups and return later to raise families.

Northern harriers and kestrels have built up to sizable populations during recent winters so that almost always a few and sometimes a dozen or so are hovering around moist soil areas and pouncing on rodents—the harriers on larger prey and kestrels on smaller ones.

Long-eared owls roost quietly in cedar thickets, standing tall and thin and hardly visible beside the tree trunks.

Great horned owls nest in lower forks of pecan trees alongside refuge roads. Barn owls have taken up residence in a box put up for them on an equipment shed.

Several birds are here on the easternmost edge of their range—beautiful scissor-tailed flycatchers, a common sight from spring through fall, perching and flying out and back for insects, long tail feathers streaming; roadrunners, usually seen running (what else?) down a road, with lizard in beak; and prairie falcons that soar over the wetlands for at least a few days each winter, usually after a cold front from the west.

Colorful wood ducks and bluebirds have taken enthusiastically to nest boxes put up for them alongside refuge roads and ponds.

Red-tailed hawks are a constant presence overhead.

Great blue herons and great egrets fish the water's edges.

Wild turkeys strut and gobble in upland fields, so common that a dozen or so are taken every year to repopulate other parts of the state.

Hundreds of shorebirds gather to probe for food on mudflats in April when water is drawn down from moist soil units—upland, pectoral, and spotted sandpipers, Wilson's phalaropes, snipe, and an occasional golden plover.

Flocks of golden warblers come through about the same time, sometimes sweeping in flocks over a field where insects have been hatching.

Holla Bend is good for dickcissels and sparrows, too—lark and field sparrows are common all year, and in fall and winter white-throats, white-crowns, Harris', fox, Lincoln's, and sometimes LeConte's and vespers are here, as well as Lapland longspurs.

Bell's vireos are common in the spring—listen for them singing down the slopes on the main road—as are the white- and red-eyed. Bright spots through the breeding season are northern orioles, summer tanagers, cardinals, goldfinches, and indigo buntings.

Birds are not the only attractive and interesting residents, however. Look for white-tailed deer with their spotted fawns browsing around field edges through the summer, armadillos rooting along roadsides, beaver lodges in the old river channel, fox squirrels scampering through the woodlands, and occasionally coyotes streaking through a field or, often in pairs, stalking snow geese. Black bears occur rarely, presumably moving between the mountain ranges.

Photographers have a treat here. Portable blinds can be put up and observers may get close views of the harriers and eagles as well as deer and waterfowl. At sunset the geese fly back for the night, the mountains a spectacular backdrop.

Holla Bend became a refuge largely through the efforts of local sportsmen and conservationists. Their efforts paid off for all concerned.

How to get there: From Russellville take Route 7 south; about two miles beyond Dardanelle turn left on Route 155, and proceed six miles to refuge entrance.

Open: Daylight hours all year. Russellville office 8–4:30 weekdays (closed federal holidays). Entrance fee.

Best times to visit: Fall through spring (but summer good, too).

What to see: Wintering bald and golden eagles; waterfowl concentrations; wild turkeys; scissor-tailed flycatchers; northern harriers and variety of other bird life; deer.

What to do: Sixteen miles of roads and trails for riding, hiking; photography (portable blinds permitted); fishing good spring and fall for largemouth bass, crappie.

Where to stay: Motels—in Russellville, Dardanelle. Campgrounds—Corps of Engineers campground, six miles south; also Mount Nebo State Park, 10 miles west, and Petit Jean State Park, 15 miles east.

Weather: Dry hot summers and wet cool winters can create poor road conditions.

Points of interest nearby: Ozark National Forest starts five miles north, Ouachita National Forest 10 miles south; Hot Springs National Park, 75 miles south, and the Buffalo River National Park, 60 miles north, can have outstanding birding; also Petit Jean and Mount Nebo State Parks (see Campgrounds)—good trails and scenic overlooks.

For more information: Holla Bend National Wildlife Refuge, P.O. Box 1043, Russellville, Arkansas 72801. Phone: (501) 968-2800.

Logan Cave is a satellite refuge administered by Holla Bend, established for the protection of a number of endangered species that live in what is called the "highest quality cave habitat in the entire Ozark region." Species include 25,000 endangered gray bats plus the blind Ozark cavefish, the rare troglobitic crayfish, the grotto salamander, and others. The cave is protected by a warden in residence, with admission by special permit for scientific research only.

WAPANOCCA (Arkansas)

Wapanocca was a famous hunt club started after the Civil War because of the seemingly limitless wildlife in this rich hardwood bottomland of north Arkansas just west of the Mississippi River. Memberships sold for $15,000 to the wealthy and notable (including cabinet members) from around the United States. Then agricultural drainage and stream channelization reduced the region's fertile habitat and wildlife to scattered remnants.

Descendants of original club members helped start this 5,484-acre refuge in 1961 to preserve a part of that rich area and bring back some of the wildlife concentrations once present.

Now some 150,000 ducks winter here—mallards, gadwalls, wigeon, pintails, blacks, and up to 50,000 geese, Canadas with some white-fronted and snows, flying in and out in great waves, and with them a half-dozen wintering eagles, bald and an occasional golden. Hundreds of nest boxes built by classes at the West Memphis and Earle high schools produce families of beautiful wood ducks and hooded mergansers.

White-tailed deer are here, along with bobcats, coyotes, squirrels, opossums, and raccoons, and in the waterways beavers, muskrats, and otters. One refuge visitor watched two bobcats stalk and try to corner a rabbit in a brush pile. Another reported an otter lying on his back consuming a large bass with four other otters gathered around, hoping to share the prize.

Beavers build lodges along the auto-tour route. Wild turkeys gobble and bobwhite quail whistle in the woods in spring. Screech owls sometimes peer from wood duck holes in the off-season, red-tailed hawks soar overhead, and barred owls call "Who-cooks-for-you" early and late.

Birders meet flocks of songbirds in the varied habitat in spring—orchard and northern orioles, bright indigo buntings, dickcissels, sometimes large flocks of handsome bobolinks, and more than two dozen kinds of warblers, including nesting Kentucky, cerulean, hooded, parula, and prothonotaries. Pileated and red-headed woodpeckers, horned larks, and Carolina wrens are around all year.

One of the best ways to see Wapanocca is by canoe or shallow jonboat out in Wapanocca Lake or through the beautiful cypress swamp. Thread through the flooded stands of trees sometimes 100 feet tall with trunks four feet in diameter where buttonbushes present feathery white blooms in spring and drop round balls and seeds for the ducks later on.

Beavers note human approach by slapping their tails on the water's surface. Great blue herons gaze intently into the water for prey, and a wood duck pair, sometimes with a brood in late spring, may appear around any curve.

How to get there: From Memphis take I-55 north about 15 miles to Turrell-Route 42 exit; refuge office is about two miles east on 42 just past railroad underpass.

Open: Daylight hours all year (parts close seasonally to offer hunting-season sanctuary to wintering waterfowl). Office 8–4:30 weekdays.

What to see: Wintering waterfowl, beautiful 1,200-acre cypress swamp, good assortment of small birds.

What to do: Seven miles of road for driving and hiking; walking in woods—but wear boots and long pants; boardwalk to observation platform; photography; boating (no rentals nearby). Fishing popular in spring for crappie, catfish.

Where to stay: Motels—West Memphis and Marion. Campgrounds—on I-55 about 10 miles south; also Shelby Forest, Lake Poinsett, and Village Creek State Parks, west of refuge.

Points of interest nearby: Crowley's Ridge, 40 miles west—interesting geological formations; Big Lake National Wildlife Refuge, 55 miles north; White River National Wildlife Refuge, 90 miles south; Cache River National Wildlife Refuge, 60 miles west.

For more information: Wapanocca National Wildlife Refuge, P.O. Box 279, Turrell, Arkansas 72384. Phone: (501) 343-2595.

WHITE RIVER
Pine Bluff

WHITE RIVER (Arkansas)

Black bears avoid flooding in their dens at White River by giving birth to cubs in holes 60 feet up in trees. They can do this because some of the ancient oaks and cypresses here have trunks five feet across.

The abundant beavers have made a similar adjustment, some of them building lodges on floating logs that become in effect beaver houseboats.

A wonderful assortment of wildlife is equally undeterred by seasonal flooding from the White, Arkansas, and Mississippi rivers that sometimes covers most of the refuge. Wild turkeys, eagles, deer, otters, and great congregations of waterfowl as well as songbirds find homes here on land so dense and wild humans rarely set foot on it.

Some of it is almost unchanged since before settlers came—112,500 acres of mixed bottomland hardwood forest with 169 natural lakes and 125 miles of streams and bayous just 20 miles west of the Mississippi River. But all of it is available to anyone willing to take a little time, and much can be seen even by the casual visitor on more than 100 miles of roads and trails.

One of the healthiest populations of black bears in the eastern United States is here—more than 200, quadrupled since the refuge was set aside in 1935.

Wild turkeys browse through the fields in flocks of 100 or more in a good year— their population is cyclical—and many have been transplanted to restock other areas.

White-tailed deer are everywhere, usually scattered about the refuge, but when

240

they seek high ground during flood times hundreds may herd together on upland fields.

The area calls itself the duck capital of the world, and when the sky over White River is full of up to 300,000 wintering ducks and up to 10,000 Canada geese (more in a severe winter), this seems no exaggeration. With them come bald eagles, sometimes up to 100, feeding on fish and weak or injured waterfowl. Two bald eagle nests have been active in recent years.

Reports of tawny long-tailed cats come in periodically, although there is no authenticated population of the rare panther or cougar.

White River contains one of the largest remaining tracts of bottomland hardwood forest in the lower Mississippi Valley, and with the Cache River and nearby state areas it has been designated a wetland of international importance. All this along with its grassy uplands makes it one of the best bird-finding places anywhere, especially for neotropicals of recent concern.

More than two dozen warbler species come through and many stay and nest, including the prothonotary, cerulean, hooded, and yellow-throated, as well as red-eyed, white-eyed, and yellow-throated vireos.

Open fields can be covered for a few weeks in spring with bobolinks and dickcissels, and the latter stay and nest. Shorebirds such as upland sandpipers en route elsewhere find these fields good places to fatten up on grasshoppers. Otherwise much of the wildlife can be seen from the east levee boundary and the Jacks Bay area.

Bright indigo buntings enliven summer roads and field edges. Mississippi kites hawk for insects, sometimes 50 or 60 soaring overhead. Flame-crested pileated woodpeckers command the woods noisily all year, but at dusk listen for the barred owl's "Who-cooks-for-you" along with the yips and howls of coyotes.

Recent Audubon Society Christmas Bird Counts have turned up 1,781 horned larks, 74 Carolina chickadees, 51 bluebirds, 50 Lapland longspurs, Bewick's wrens, and vesper, LeConte's, and Lincoln's sparrows.

Flooding can occur anytime but usually starts in December and continues through spring, when 90 percent of the refuge can be underwater. There is limited hunting in October and November. For these reasons and for wildlife protection, sanctuary sections may be closed, and the office should be contacted about how and when best to visit. Refuge staff are helpful in any case to learn what has been seen lately and where best to see it.

How to get there: The office is in DeWitt; new headquarters are planned on Route 1 in St. Charles. The refuge itself is accessible from Route 44 on the southwest end near Tichnor, on the north end from Route 1, and on the east from Route 85 and from Route 1 onto 316 and 318.

Open: All hours, but sections closed November to March for flooding or wildlife sanctuary—check with office. Office 8–4:30 weekdays.

Best times to visit: Fall and spring.

What to see: Waterfowl; deer; turkeys; wood ducks; possibly bears; eagles; good variety of birds, possibly even Bachman's warblers.

What to do: About 75 miles of roads and trails, many more unimproved trails for hiking; observation tower; photography—portable blind permitted; boating—rentals available, and a fine way to explore the White River and side chutes and ponds, but don't take a light boat out in flood waters, which can be unpredictably swift and dangerous; fishing can be fantastic in spring for crappie, also bass, bream, catfish; camping seasonally; guided group tours by prior arrangement; waterfowl banding—visitors invited to observe and participate.

Where to stay: Motels—in DeWitt, Stuttgart, Helena. Campgrounds—on the refuge March-October; also Lake Merrisach Corps of Engineers Park, south of refuge.

Weather: Winter can drop to zero; June-August steamy.

What to take and wear: Insect repellent a must spring-summer; waterproof footgear can be handy; bring compass if planning to get off the roads (visitors without one have had to spend the night out there).

Points of interest nearby: Arkansas Post National Monument, first white settlement west of Mississippi, 20 miles south; Louisiana Purchase Historical Monument, 25 miles north; beautiful old river bluff homes in Helena, 40 miles northeast; up to 400,000 snow geese can congregate in surrounding wheat fields—ask refuge staff where.

For more information: White River National Wildlife Refuge, P.O. Box 308, DeWitt, Arkansas 72042. Phone: (501) 946–1468.

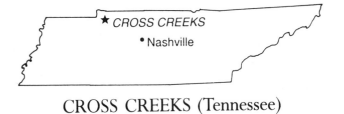

CROSS CREEKS (Tennessee)

Cross Creeks is a birding hotspot where eagles, bluebirds, Canada geese and wood ducks nest and tens of thousands of waterfowl spend the winter on 8,862 acres of rich Cumberland River bottomland, surrounded by rolling hills and high rocky cliffs in north-central Tennessee.

Barred owls, red-shouldered hawks, and bluebirds sometimes share the same territory—the owl and hawk using the bluebird house at the visitor center as a lookout perch in the day and late afternoon, the intrepid bluebirds slipping in at odd moments when the larger predators are away. Killdeer do their broken-wing act to lure visitors away from nearby nests, often in the barked landscaped area.

In summer, family groups of deer with spotted fawns, and bucks in racks of velvet, browse in grassy fields beside the 40 miles of roads and trails along with flocks of dozens of wild turkeys. The roadsides are not mowed often, so a whole ecosystem shares this habitat, too, ranging from foxes and coyotes looking for mice to minks and coveys of quail. Beavers are common on all the waterways, usually with a lodge just off one of the walking trails.

Waterfowl begin to arrive in October when the hills are suffused with color and build to a peak in December and January when there may be over 35,000 Canada geese and 55,000 ducks on the refuge pools, creeks, and reservoirs. When all these fill the sky flying in against a red sunset and fill the air with their calls, the effect is breathtaking (and highly photogenic).

Migrating bald and golden eagles are usually present in small numbers in winter, often in a dead tree from which they launch dives that cause the alarmed ducks to scatter in all directions. A few rough-legged hawks may be around, too, and harriers scout the marshes with their mothlike flight most of the year.

Two pairs of resident bald eagles have been nesting in recent years—one has produced triplet young most years since 1983. Nest sites are not easily visible but refuge staff can point one out, and adults are easily seen soaring and fishing about the refuge.

Birding groups come from a wide area at least three times a year: first in December and January for over 25 species of waterfowl—including Canadas with a few snow, blue, and white-fronted geese, and mallard and black ducks, but also gadwalls, wigeons, teals, pintails, wood ducks, shovelers, ring-necks, canvasbacks, redheads, mergansers, and scaups; then in March and April and again in mid-September and October for the migrant songbirds and shorebirds, plus a good assortment of sparrows, including LeConte's, vesper, lark, and Lincoln's in the foxtail grass.

Bright indigo buntings are a common and lively sight throughout the nesting season; around, too, are prothonotary and yellow-throated warblers, orchard orioles, chats, and blue grosbeaks. Great blue herons stalk the water's edges and seize crayfish, tossing them in the air and catching them a few times to soften them before swallowing them head-first. Black-crowned night herons fish at water-control structures.

Cross Creeks sets the birding hotline buzzing from time to time with such rarities as roseate spoonbills, wood storks, snowy owls, and cinnamon teals.

Part of the refuge is closed during the winter for waterfowl sanctuary—but guided van tours are scheduled there during that period, and wildlife is abundantly visible throughout the rest of the refuge, including excellent viewing from the Visitor Center.

How to get there: From Nashville take I-24 north to Clarksville Exit 4 or 11, then Highway 79 west to Dover, then left on Route 49 and follow refuge signs.

Open: Daylight hours all year (but portions closed in winter for waterfowl sanctuary). Office 7–3:30 weekdays. Visitor Center 7–5 weekdays, 9–5 Saturdays (part- or full-time volunteers welcome).

Best times to visit: Spring and October through January.

What to see: Waterfowl; eagles; deer; beavers; good wildlife assortment, and wildflowers are lovely spring through early fall.

What to do: Interpretive auto and hiking trails plus 40 miles available for driving, hiking. Boating and canoeing (no rentals)—Bull Pasture Creek an especially beautiful trip. Photography—excellent blind available on reservation basis. Group tours given by arrangement. Also permitted are biking, horseback riding, and grape, berry, and mushroom picking. Fishing—can be excellent for largemouth bass, bream, crappie, catfish—and striped bass have been stocked.

What to take and wear: Good walking shoes or boots for trails. Insect repellent, especially for ticks (Permanone is good)—Lyme disease is present.

Where to stay: Motels—in Dover, also Paris Landing State Park, 16 miles west (also has boats and marina). Campgrounds—Paris Landing State Park; also Land Between the Lakes, 10 miles west.

Weather: July to September can be very hot.

Points of interest nearby: Tennessee National Wildlife Refuge, 35 miles southwest; Fort Donelson National Battlefield Park, four miles northwest; Land Between the Lakes (see Campgrounds), numerous recreational facilities.

For more information: Cross Creeks National Wildlife Refuge, Route 1, Box 556, Dover, Tennessee 37058. Phone: (615) 232-7477.

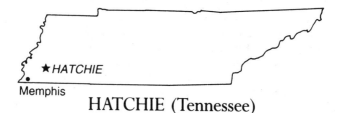

HATCHIE (Tennessee)

This swamp forest habitat is a wildlife treasure, a virtually unique remnant of the rich bottomland hardwoods that once covered 22 million acres in the lower Mississippi River Valley. Clearing has destroyed over 95 percent of it—habitat that like an estuary or rain forest is literally teeming with life, supporting five times more wildlife up and down the ecological scale than upland areas.

Here and in variant ways at Hatchie's two satellite refuges, Lower Hatchie and Chickasaw, it survives and supports populations of deer, wild turkeys, beavers, waterfowl—particularly nesting hooded mergansers—otters and a good variety of small birds in greater numbers than anywhere else in this part of the world.

The Hatchie River, which forms the northern refuge boundary for 24 miles, is one of the last unchannelized rivers in the lower Mississippi valley—a designated state scenic river that meanders about, functioning in a natural wetland cycle, absorbing overflow, cleansing the water, preventing abrupt flooding downstream. This untrammeled quality gives it not only a previously underestimated utility but a breathtakingly pristine beauty.

Otters, on the Tennessee threatened list, have a stronghold here and often sociably follow along after visitors to sloughs and oxbow lakes, frisking and splashing and sliding down banks, so numerous that some have been relocated to places in the state where they disappeared long ago.

Herds of deer graze in upland fields. When these fields are mowed in late summer, flocks of wild turkeys may appear to feed on disturbed insects, with broods of ten or so poults following the hens.

Swainson's warblers, rare elsewhere, are easily seen here, and with golden pro-thonotaries fill the swampy wooded areas with their territorial calls. Crimson-crested pileated woodpeckers are heard and seen everywhere in timbered places.

Colorful wood ducks and hooded mergansers are common all year, using natural tree cavities as well as 400 nest boxes put up for them to produce hundreds of downy ducklings that they parade on O'Neal's Lake (where ospreys sometimes dive menacingly on them, setting off a crippled-wing display by the agitated parents).

Migratory and wintering waterfowl reach peaks up to 45,000—about 75 percent mallards and an assortment of gadwall, black, pintail, teal, wigeon, and some can-

246

vasbacks and redheads. Geese, mostly Canadas plus a few snows and blues, peak around 5,000—but a severe northern winter can send up to 30,000 this way.

Members of the Memphis and Jackson Ornithological Societies come regularly, especially in spring and fall migrations when the refuge can be aswarm with two dozen species of warblers along with large numbers of bobolinks, Acadian flycatchers, redstarts, rose-breasted grosbeaks, hermit, gray-cheeked, and Swainson's thrushes, golden-crowned kinglets, vesper and Lincoln's sparrows, and northern orioles.

A breeding bird census in June shows that many of these stay and nest, including clouds of brilliant indigo buntings plus yellow-breasted chats, white-eyed vireos, yellow-billed cuckoos and resident quail, red-shouldered hawks, four kinds of owls, and five kinds of woodpeckers. Mississippi kites are summer visitors. More than 200 species are on the refuge bird list.

Coyotes, bobcats, and gray foxes are here as well but less easy to see. One of the best places to observe wildlife is in watered ditches along roads where duck broods find protection, yellow-crowned night herons stalk, and raccoons wash meals of crayfish.

Some roads may be flooded seasonally; also, hunting is allowed on the refuge during the fall, so visitors planning a trip from a distance should check with headquarters on these.

How to get there: From Memphis take I-40 east to Exit 56, then south on Highway 76 for .25 mile to refuge office, another 1.5 miles to refuge. From Jackson take I-40 west to Exit 56, etc.

Open: Daylight hours (but bad weather and floods can close roads). Office 7:30–4 weekdays except federal holidays.

Best times to visit: Spring through fall.

What to see: Waterfowl; deer; wild turkeys; otters; good assortment of small birds spring and summer, including Swainson's warblers; beautiful oxbow lakes and Hatchie River, designated state scenic river.

What to do: About 15 miles of roads for driving and hiking (can be mucky or flooded in wet weather). Boating (ramps on lakes and river; river sometimes obstructed after floods).

Where to stay: Motels—at junction of I-40 and Highway 76 at Exit 56. Campgrounds— near I-40 Providence Exit; also Chickasaw State Park, 40 miles southeast.

Weather: Winter can be damp, cold, with flooding; summer hot, humid.

Points of interest nearby: Chickasaw National Wildlife Refuge, 45 miles northwest;

Lower Hatchie National Wildlife Refuge, 45 miles north-northwest; Chickasaw State Park (see Campgrounds); Reelfoot National Wildlife Refuge, 70 miles north; Tennessee National Wildlife Refuge, 70 miles northeast.

For more information: Hatchie National Wildlife Refuge, P.O. Box 187, Brownsville, Tennessee 38012. Phone: (901) 772–0501.

Hatchie also administers two satellite refuges:

Chickasaw is more than 20,000 acres of bottomland hardwood habitat in the process of acquisition that historically has supported tremendous waterfowl populations— 250,000 mallards, for example—and in all probability will again. Located next to the Mississippi River, its uneven topography partly the result of the great 1812 New Madrid earthquake, it also has a large nesting colony of great blue herons and great egrets (and a few tricolored herons have been seen recently), with feeding habitat for endangered least terns and much else—wildlife similar to Hatchie, including large turkey and deer populations. To get there from Ripley take Highway 19 west through Arp, turn right at Wildlife Management Area sign and follow signs. County roads go through it and visitors can hike anywhere. Detailed information available from Hatchie.

Lower Hatchie is 4,138 acres of bottomland hardwood with open lakes and seasonally flooded wetlands, deer, otters, turkey—flocks up to 60 birds in the fields in spring— along with waterfowl concentrations and other interesting species: black rails, snowy egrets, feeding habitat for good numbers of endangered least terns and beautiful old-growth oaks and cypress trees up to 700 years old. To get there from Henning take Highway 87 west 19 miles to refuge office at Fulton. Much of refuge can be viewed from Highway 87, or walk or drive to Champion Lake. Managed as part of Lower Hatchie is Sunk Lake Natural Area, a remnant wetland with boating, fishing, and a boardwalk planned.

Union City

REELFOOT (Tennessee and Kentucky)

Reelfoot Lake, seasonal home for spectacular numbers of bald eagles, waterfowl, and migrating songbirds, was formed by devastating earthquakes in 1811 and 1812 that caused a 2,000-mile area to rumble for months and the lake basin, then part of the Mississippi floodplain, to fall 35 to 40 feet.

"The waters gathered up like a mountain 15 to 20 feet perpendicularly," according to an eyewitness. "Groves of trees disappeared and fissures in the earth vomited forth sand and water ... the atmosphere was so saturated with sulphurous vapors as to cause total darkness; trees cracked and fell into the roaring Mississippi."

Some said the Mississippi flowed backward three days to fill the 45-square-mile basin, the upper part of which is now 10,428-acre Reelfoot National Wildlife Refuge. Geologists say another major quake can be expected by the early twenty-first century. But for now Reelfoot, along with its notable natural inhabitants, is one of the beauty spots in this part of the United States.

Majestic stands of virgin bald cypress tower over shallow-watered inlets, their bulbous trunks ringed with thickly blooming wild roses in spring and later with golden lotuses and water lily pads where purple gallinules forage.

Waterfowl gather in wintering populations that peak at 100,000 geese and 250,000 or more ducks. Ruddies may cluster in groups of several thousand. In October a visitor might see 20,000 wood ducks or wigeon.

More than 56 species of fish inhabit its waters, including the curious and ancient paddlefish and bowfin. Mammals, though wary, are fairly readily seen early and late, including good numbers of white-tailed deer, beavers, raccoons, opossums, muskrats, foxes, coyotes, occasional bobcats and young mink families hunting along the waterways, and swamp rabbits, look-alikes for the familiar cottontail but larger and not averse to swimming. An outstanding array of snakes and lizards is resident (protected from collectors), including the yard-long amphiuma salamander.

Bald eagles appear in greater numbers than at any place of comparable size in the U.S.—between 100 and 200 almost every winter, roosting in swampy woodlands and going out to feed over the lake. They can be seen perched on snags and soaring overhead—or almost anywhere else in the area. It is not unusual to see 25 or 30 while driving Route 22 between Tiptonville and Samburg, and sometimes a few goldens.

Reelfoot is a superb birding spot. Naturalists come from all over the country for its spring warbler migrations, when 16 species may be seen commonly—and a dozen others less commonly—in waves starting in mid-March, peaking about mid-April, and continuing until June. There are also orioles, Swainson's thrushes, flycatchers, and many others along the Grassy Island wildlife drive.

Reelfoot has been highest in the nation in the Audubon Christmas Bird Count for ring-necked and wood ducks and others, and highest in Tennessee in number of species due to its varied habitat of wooded bluffs, upland, and swamp forest.

Red-tailed hawks are common; so are kestrels and northern harriers—sometimes dozens can be seen on a single late fall day in migration. Cooper's hawks nest near the bluffs. Ospreys nest, too; in recent years this has been their only breeding place in Tennessee. Mississippi kites are summertime familiars and believed to nest in remote areas. Wild turkeys are around all year.

Huge flights of blackbirds, sometimes a million or so, mostly red-winged but Brewer's and others, too, roost and scatter at dawn and return in broad ribbons 10 to 300 feet wide at dusk.

Ruby-throated hummingbirds flock around bird feeders. Woodpeckers—especially the large showy pileated—are common in woods.

Lovely long-legged wading birds, including great egrets and great blue herons, nest but not as formerly, when tens of thousands occupied a large section of the lake. They left when the 1957 movie *Raintree County* was made here. The film company set off dynamite charges in the heronry to make them fly up for dramatic effect, and they have never returned since in such large numbers.

How to get there: From Union City take Route 22 north about 15 miles to Route 157, then north one mile to sign. To Grassy Island unit (refuge has two units) go a mile past headquarters, left at Walnut Log and 1.5 miles to sign. To Long Point unit continue north on 157. It becomes Kentucky Route 311. Turn left at Route 1282 (first intersection) and go three miles to sign.

Open: Daylight hours, but parts close periodically for waterfowl sanctuary. Office/visitor center 8–4 weekdays and weekends January through March.

Best times to visit: All year.

What to see: Eagles, waterfowl, herons and egrets, wild turkeys, Mississippi kites, songbirds, warblers, beautiful vistas.

What to do: More than a dozen miles of roads and trails; photography (can be good from cars); fine fishing for crappie, bluegills, bass, catfish; boating (rentals nearby for jonboats and "Reelfoot lake boats" designed to cope with hidden snags here). Guided tours by prior arrangement.

Where to stay: More than a dozen motels, tent and trailer parks in the 10 miles along Route 22 between Samburg and Tiptonville, also good restaurants and accommodations at Reelfoot Lake State Park (but reserve ahead during peak times).

What to take and wear: Snakeproof boots if walking in heavy brush.

Points of interest nearby: Reelfoot Lake State Park, exhibits of Indian lore, good guided tours of natural areas, other recreational facilities.

For more information: Reelfoot National Wildlife Refuge, Route 2, Highway 157, Union City, Tennessee 38261. Phone: (901) 538–2481.

Lake Isom nearby is a subrefuge administered by Reelfoot, similar in natural inhabitants, open for hiking and (depending on weather) for driving. To get there from Samburg take Route 22 west to the spillway, then left at the first paved blacktop about 2.5 miles to refuge sign.

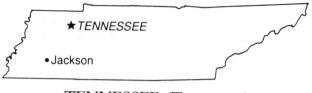

★ TENNESSEE

• Jackson

TENNESSEE (Tennessee)

Where the bandit Jesse James once farmed and Confederate general Nathan Bedford Forrest led his troops, some of the largest waterfowl concentrations in the East now gather in winter months with 100 or so eagles keeping an eye on them and preying on weaker ones.

Deer, foxes, coyotes, beavers, and songbirds also find a welcome here in large part because of work done to make the habitat receptive since it was established as a 51,358-acre wildlife refuge in 1945. It was an overlay on land bought and operated by the Tennessee Valley Authority for power and flood control in the 1940s, and when acquired it was an area depleted by disastrous land-use practices.

Now innovative uses of moist soil management—flooding and then drawing off water seasonally and at varying levels—have re-created ideal and dynamic marsh situations. Waterfowl now find not only open but nourishing land, with a variety of wild food plants and invertebrates growing and reproducing themselves in endless supply, so the birds return to breeding grounds in better condition to nest, lay eggs, and raise young. And the benefit is felt all up and down the food chain and by many other species.

Great blue herons now nest here in a colony of more than 1,000 birds. Wintering concentrations sometimes reach 100,000 Canada (with some snow) geese and more than 400,000 ducks of more than a dozen species. Sometimes so many mallards are in the flooded field areas that from the roads they appear almost as a solid shimmering green from their shining head plumage. With them and usually readily seen on cypress trees along the roads are the eagles, usually including at least several goldens. Bald eagles in recent years have raised three families on the refuge, and ospreys nest, too. Other raptors are also common—with ospreys, merlins, and red-shouldered, red-tailed, Cooper's, broad-winged, and sharp-shinned hawks.

Quail are common. Wild turkey gobblers fan out their tail feathers in courtly rituals in spring, and hens and poults appear in the fields in May and June. Hundreds of multicolored wood ducks nest.

Thousands of migratory shorebirds can appear along the 200 miles of shoreline in April and again in September, particularly on the flats at Pace Point, which has been designated a significant international shorebird site.

More than a dozen warblers are common or abundant in migration with a dozen others only a little less so, and many stay and nest: prothonotaries, yellowthroats, redstarts, chats, along with some Kentucky and hooded warblers and red-eyed, white-eyed, and warbling vireos. Bluebirds are common all year; so are killdeer, mourning doves, barred owls, Carolina wrens, loggerhead shrikes, and five kinds of woodpeckers.

Coyotes frequently forage along refuge roads in late afternoons; so do raccoons and opossums, more rarely bobcat and fox, and along the water beaver, muskrat, and mink.

Ginseng grows in back areas and in spring the hillsides are aglow with mountain laurels, wild azaleas and dogwood, redbud and serviceberry. Fall foliage peaks in vivid scarlet and gold in October.

The refuge includes three separate units with varying habitat but similar wildlife. Consult refuge staff on how best to see various aspects of the refuge.

Jesse James's old homestead was on the Duck River unit. No one knew he was anything but a farmer in those days, and neighbors only speculated as to why he always kept a mare saddled up and ready to go.

How to get there: Refuge headquarters is on Blythe Street in Paris (a new office/visitor center is planned). To get to the Big Sandy unit from Paris take Route 69A to Big Sandy, then northeast on Lick Creek Road to entrance. For Busseltown, Route 641 to Parsons, 100 east to Mousetail Road, left to entrance. For Duck River, take Route 70 east from 641, then Long Street south in New Johnsonville.

Open: Dawn to dusk. Office 7–3:30 weekdays.

Best times to visit: Fall, spring, winter.

What to see: Wintering eagles, waterfowl, wild turkeys, deer, songbirds, shorebirds.

What to do: About 50 miles of roads including self-guided tour route on Big Sandy unit, and trails, including boardwalk and self-guided Chickasaw Trail; photography (parts of refuge can be closed to visitation at times because of hunting pressure). Fishing can be fantastic on Kentucky Lake for crappie, bass, sauger, catfish.

Where to stay: Motels—many in Paris area, one each in Camden and New Johnsonville. Campgrounds—Paris Landing State Park; Mousetail Landing State Park near Busseltown; also Natchez Trace State Park, 30 miles southeast.

Weather: July-August hot, humid; January-February cold, damp.

What to take and wear: Warm waterproof clothing and footgear any winter day.

Points of interest nearby: TVA Land Between the Lakes, 40 miles northeast—many recreational facilities; the area is rich in state and national park natural areas and historic sites, such as Fort Donelson, 30 miles northeast, and Mount Zion National Historic Site on the refuge.

For more information: Tennessee National Wildlife Refuge, P.O. Box 849, Paris, Tennessee 38242. Phone: (901) 642–2091.

MISSISSIPPI
SANDHILL CRANE

Gulfport

MISSISSIPPI SANDHILL CRANE (Mississippi)

This refuge probably saved from extinction the endangered Mississippi subspecies of the sandhill crane, a majestic pearl-gray bird standing four feet tall with scarlet crown and wings that spread almost seven feet. Its trumpeting call can be heard for miles.

Its population has more than doubled from a low of 30 birds, and survival chances are good due to purchase of some 20,000 acres of savanna, swamp, and pine forest in southeast Mississippi, much of it through The Nature Conservancy.

This refuge has also made possible survival of at least 50 threatened gopher tortoises, free now to burrow on sandy ridges on land that would almost certainly have been lost as wild habitat by now, either to housing and commercial development or other habitat-destructive land-use practices.

Bachman's sparrows, a rarity on most bird lists, are here, as well as such notable plants of the pine-savanna wetlands as snakemouth orchids, grass pinks, pitcher plants, and sundews. Look for the reclusive sparrows when males proclaim territories on grasslands in April.

The best chance of seeing cranes is in winter—reserve a place on guided trips to an elevated blind in January and February, when the birds tend to flock. Even here they are not easy to see—but, as one visitor remarked philosophically, easier than if they were extinct.

A nature trail goes by tidal marsh where herons and egrets fish and back through savanna to interesting botanical specimens. Birding is good around headquarters and the entrance road for migrating warblers, brown-headed nuthatches, blue grosbeaks, and occasionally hooded warblers and Bachman's sparrow.

How to get there: From Gulfport take I-10 east to Exit 61, then north on Gautier-Vancleave Road .5 mile to entrance on right.

Open: Office, visitor center, trail 7:30–4 weekdays.

Best times to visit: Spring, winter.

What to see: Cranes, Bachman's sparrow, interesting plants.

What to do: Nature trail; observation tower; tours by appointment November-February.

Where to stay: Motels—at Moss Point, six miles east. Campgrounds—at Ocean Springs, 10 miles west.

Points of interest nearby: Gulf Islands National Seashore, 10 miles west.

For more information: Mississippi Sandhill Crane National Wildlife Refuge, 7200 Crane Lane, Gautier, Mississippi 39553. Phone: (601) 497–6322.

Grand Bay National Wildlife Refuge, about 12 miles southwest, is a new satellite refuge administered from here—4,000 acres (with more acreage planned) to preserve a unique tideland coastal marsh and plant community. Visitor facilities are still in the planning stage.

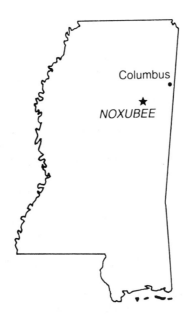

Columbus

★
NOXUBEE

NOXUBEE (Mississippi)

Most of Noxubee refuge is woodland—huge oaks and cypresses with trunks six feet in diameter and century-old pines that have attracted at least 17 colonies of rare red-cockaded woodpeckers. These small endangered birds require old pines with soft "red-heart" centers for their nest sites, which is one reason they have become scarce.

Nowhere are they more visible than here, where several colonies are seen or easily accessible from roads and trails.

Good populations of turkeys and white-tailed deer find welcome food and cover among the tall trees that in places form such a solid canopy that the forest floor is like a wilderness park. Indeed several thousand acres of bottomland hardwood are managed as a wilderness with no sign of human existence.

Some 20,000 waterfowl come to spend the winter on Bluff Lake, Green Timber reservoir, around some of the beaver ponds, and along the Noxubee River, which runs through the refuge. Wintering along with them usually are a half-dozen bald eagles.

A flock of 350 giant Canada geese, started with a captive flock but now free fliers, are almost always visible from the Canada goose overlook platform through the winter and later in spring nesting season, incubating their eggs and leading downy goslings to forage around the lake banks (keeping an eye out for basking alligators, here on the northern fringe of their range).

More than 100 pairs of beautiful wood ducks raise young in boxes put up by the refuge. There are three colonies of great blue herons and great and snowy egrets, the largest easily visible in cypress snags in Bluff Lake. Rare wood storks visit the lakes in August.

Flame-crested pileateds as well as red-headed, red-bellied, and downy woodpeckers and northern flickers are conspicuous through the woods. Bright indigo buntings are showy explosions of blue along the road and field edges in all but winter. Golden prothonotary warblers nest in moist surroundings; brown-headed nuthatches, Carolina wrens, yellowthroats and pine warblers, and white-eyed vireos on higher ground. Bluebirds find nest-box homes.

Barred owls and red-shouldered and red-tailed hawks raise families in tall tree forks. Wild turkeys start gobbling and shaking their scarlet wattles in the fields in February.

Coyotes yip and howl in early evenings and get every dog in the countryside stirred up.

Noxubee is an excellent example of how land can be reclaimed after erosion and depleted topsoil have taken a severe toll. Reforestation and good management practices since its acquisition in the 1930s have made it a garden for wildlife.

How to get there: From Starkville take Spring Street (or Oktoc Road) south off Route 12, bearing right at the fork, about 17 miles to the end of the blacktop. Turn right there and follow signs.

Open: Daylight hours all year. Office 8–4:30 weekdays.

Best times to visit: Late fall through spring.

What to see: Red-cockaded woodpeckers, deer, turkeys, resident giant Canada geese, wintering waterfowl, eagles.

What to do: Three hiking trails, observation platform, more than 40 miles of roads (some may be impassable in wet periods). Late fall hunting may conflict with wildlife observation but some areas around headquarters, trail, and overlook always open. Fishing excellent in spring for catfish, bass, crappie, bream.

Where to stay: Motels—in Starkville. Campgrounds—seasonal on refuge; also at Starkville, Oktibbeha County Lake nearby, and Tombigbee National Forest, adjoining refuge.

Weather: Hot, humid late summer, cool January-February with possibility of flooding through April.

Points of interest nearby: Tombigbee National Forest, trails (see Camping); in Columbus area, beautiful antebellum homes, tours, especially Waverly Plantation; scenic Natchez Trace Parkway, 24 miles west.

For more information: Noxubee National Wildlife Refuge, Route 1, Box 142, Brooksville, Mississippi 39739. Phone: (601) 323–5548.

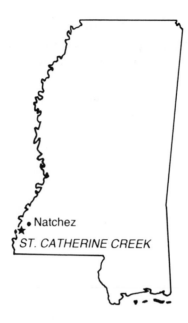

Natchez
★
ST. CATHERINE CREEK

ST. CATHERINE CREEK (Mississippi)

Thousands of ducks find winter welcome in the backwater sloughs of this new refuge of great wildlife potential that stretches for more than six miles along the Mississippi River. It was established for ducks as a feeding and resting place from which they can journey north in the spring in strong physical shape to take on arduous nesting activities. Much of this lush hardwood river bottomland was clear-cut and taken over by farming for which it was ill-suited. Now this tract is being restored and used for a purpose for which it is ideally suited: wildlife habitat.

The wildlife have responded. White pelicans spend summer through early fall here. Hundreds of wading birds, including endangered wood storks, feed and roost from the time the river's "spring rise" recedes until summer's end, and great blue herons are around all year. Shorebirds stop in migration. One recent January day found 22,000 ducks on the waterways, including 9,000 mallards and 8,000 pintails.

Northern harriers hunt over the marsh. Bald eagles have shown signs of nesting in a bald cypress. Bluebirds gather around headquarters.

Otters frolic and beavers industriously transport small limbs through waters where alligators wait. White-tailed deer browse the uplands. Wild turkeys hang about oak stands. Coyotes hunt in fallow fields.

Until recently at least, trails, auto-tour routes, and other visitor facilities have been mostly in the planning stage. Parts are open March 1–September 15 but flooding is unpredictable—in wet years the whole refuge can be underwater through June. Driving can be difficult on unimproved roads, built by oil companies that still hold mineral rights.

Birders can usually hike around, though, if they check in first at headquarters, open 7:30–4 weekdays.

To get there from Natchez take Route 61 south to Beltline Highway, right there to Cloverdale Road, left there to Bourke Road and right there to refuge entrance. Natchez has motels and campgrounds, also many historic antebellum homes. The Natchez-Trace Parkway originates there.

For more information: St. Catherine Creek National Wildlife Refuge, P.O. Box 18639, Natchez, Mississippi 39122. Phone: (601) 442-6696.

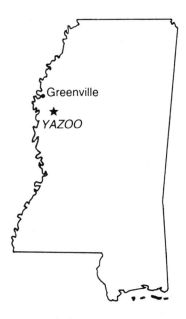

Greenville

★
YAZOO

YAZOO (Mississippi)

One glance at the wood duck in its breeding plumage of scarlet, green, blue, and bronze makes clear why it's described as the world's most beautiful duck. Nowhere is this spectacular bird more brilliantly and abundantly visible than at Yazoo National Wildlife Refuge.

Wood ducks sometimes seem to line the entranceway. They are common throughout the waterways, nesting in hundreds of houses as well as natural cavities. Refuge staff had to put hardware cloth over building chimneys to keep them from nesting there (after retrieving them unharmed from furnaces below).

Once a staff member left his shed for a few minutes while building a wood duck house. When he returned a female wood duck was inside staking out a prior claim while her mate stood guard outside. It is not uncommon for one box to be used for four broods in one season.

One huge dead cypress snag at Alligator Pond has held as many as 50 pairs of wood ducks, making it look like a decorated Christmas tree.

It would be hard to visit Yazoo without seeing a wood duck and more likely a good many of them—about 10,000 young ones are produced annually, between mid-February and mid-May.

But there is more to see at this 12,471-acre refuge of diverse habitat ranging from agricultural cropland, planted largely in wildlife food plants, to bottomland hardwood in the heart of the Mississippi delta country.

Herds of 50 to 60 white-tailed deer—occasionally up to 150, including well-antlered bucks—graze in the fields, which they share with flocks of wild turkeys. In spring a half-dozen gobblers may fan out their feathers and shake their red wattles in competitive display (even after the hens have gone off to lay eggs).

Up to a quarter-million waterfowl may gather here in the fall—mostly mallards but more than a dozen other duck species as well, along with Canada and up to 30,000 snow and white-fronted geese, and a few swans. Watching them from a stand of tall cypress are eagles, usually a few bald and sometimes a golden.

Up to 25,000 great and little blue herons, great and snowy egrets, and white ibis nest on low-lying buttonbush and willows in Alligator Pond, an overwhelming experience when they fly in and out just 20 feet overhead at dusk or early morning, joined by perhaps several dozen wood storks in late summer.

Several hundred alligators lie out on logs soaking up sunshine in March and April and the same before retiring to winter dens in fall.

Mississippi kites are here in large numbers in spring and summer—sometimes 60 observed in a single day, usually flying over wooded portions (they nest in dense, usually remote areas).

Songbird migrations bring dozens of species through in April. Interesting nesters include indigo and painted buntings, prothonotary warblers, summer tanagers, northern orioles, and dickcissels, along with pileated and red-headed woodpeckers, barred, great horned, and screech owls, purple gallinules, and least bitterns.

Reforestation has encouraged cottontail rabbits. Sometimes 200 of a population estimated at around 5,000 can be seen along the roads. Perhaps partly as a result, bobcats are common and, although wary, sometimes seen. Coyotes are occasionally spotted—some of them showing a heritage of red wolf strain—stalking rabbits or snow geese. And there are beavers, nutria (looking like beaver except for their round tails), minks, raccoons, opossums, and squirrels.

Wildlife is accessible here, seen fairly easily by the visitor willing to spend some time early and late on the roads and trails. Ask at the office for recent sightings. Permission is often granted to explore interior service roads. And best inquire if planning a visit during heavy hunting weekends in the fall.

How to get there: From Greenville take Route 1 south 29 miles to refuge sign, then left 2.5 miles to headquarters.

Open: Dawn to dusk. Office 7:30–4 weekdays.

Best times to visit: Fall through April.

What to see: Wood ducks; deer; wild turkeys; alligators; waterfowl; herons and egrets; Indian ceremonial mounds dating from A.D. 400.

What to do: Twenty-six miles of walking and driving trails (some may close in wet weather); photography (portable blinds permitted); no fishing in recent years due to heavy water pollution from agricultural chemicals.

Where to stay: Motels—in Greenville. Campgrounds—LeRoy Percy State Park, eight miles north.

Weather: Midwinter can be cold, blustery.

What to take and wear: Waterproof footgear during rainy periods.

Points of interest nearby: LeRoy Percy State Park, eight miles north; Delta National Forest, 30 miles south; Lake Washington, six miles west (good birding, also boat launches); Winterville Mounds Historic State Park, 35 miles north; beautiful antebellum homes throughout area.

For more information: Yazoo National Wildlife Refuge, Route 1, Box 286, Hollandale, Mississippi 38748. Phone: (601) 839-2638.

Yazoo also administers four satellite refuges—*Hillside, Mathews Brake, Morgan Brake,* and *Panther Swamp*—with similar bottomland hardwoods habitat and similar wildlife but with relatively few visitor facilities. Contact Yazoo office for details and directions.

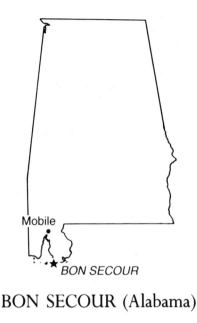

Mobile

BON SECOUR

BON SECOUR (Alabama)

The French words for "safe harbor" seem ideally appropriate for the tens of thousands of birds that find their first landfall here in spring after a 600-mile flight across the Gulf of Mexico.

Bushes and trees then can be literally filled with bright warblers and other songbirds, resting and feeding before continuing their northward migration to nesting grounds. Hummingbirds swarm by the hundreds around honeysuckle blossoms. Boats in the Gulf tell of being covered sometimes with small birds having difficulty completing the long flight. Here, they find food as well as rest. And they represent only a small percentage of the millions of birds on the Mississippi Flyway that flock through this part of the Gulf.

But there is even more at this beautiful, very special refuge on a narrow peninsula at the mouth of Mobile Bay, where red foxes scout at night for ghost crabs and retire by day behind dunes 30 feet high that protect beaches as white and crystalline as any in the Caribbean, and that harbor as well the engaging—and endangered—Alabama beach mouse.

The bird list has 369 species, as many as any national wildlife refuge. Of these, 135 are listed as common at one season or another, ranging from gannets, western kingbirds, and clapper rails to black skimmers that nest on a spoil island and great horned owls, brown-headed nuthatches, and pileated woodpeckers that raise young in the woods behind the sea oats and dwarf live oaks.

Beautiful wading birds of nine species nest colonially. Water pipits are common in all but summer. Alligators live in Gator Lake. The sparrow population seasonally includes the seaside, sharp-tailed, Lincoln's, LeConte's, and dickcissel.

Ospreys put on spectacular aerial courtship flights. Bald eagles have been hacked out on a platform here and it is hoped they, too, will become refuge regulars.

Loggerhead sea turtles have started nesting since mandatory use of TEDS (turtle exclusion devices) by shrimp fishermen have made the sea safer for them. A dozen or so used to be drowned every summer. Now they crawl up on summer nights and lay eggs on the beach as their species has done for 200 million years.

Southward migration in fall can be as spectacular as in spring. In addition to songbirds there are monarch butterflies, which can seem to cover late-blooming groundsel bushes, and raptors—sometimes hundreds of broad-winged hawks in an afternoon, and a half-dozen endangered swift-flying peregrine falcons.

Rarely, such unusual birds have been seen on the peninsula as a white-tailed tropicbird, black-legged kittiwake, Swainson's hawk, marbled godwit—even a snowy owl.

That's not all. Once the refuge manager looked out his window to see a black bear swimming toward the refuge from the Gulf. The bear was relocated to the mainland, where he was spotted a few days later back in the water a half mile from shore. Presumably he knew what he was doing and ended up in the Alabama woods.

Bon Secour covers 4,500 acres of beach, scrub oak, and woodland in four units along the peninsula and little Dauphin Island, with 10,000 planned to be acquired. It was established as a refuge as the result of citizens' fear that all this last pristine coast would be developed and lost to wildlife.

Stop in the refuge office to learn what has been seen lately, and report any good sightings of your own.

How to get there: From Mobile take I-65 to I-10, east on I-10 to Loxley exit, then south on state route 59 to Gulf Shores, west there on state route 180, 6.2 miles to refuge office.

Open: Daylight hours all week. Office 8–4:30 weekdays.

Best times to visit: October-November and March-April for migrations.

What to see: Tremendous array of birds, especially in migration; beautiful beaches and dunes.

What to do: Two miles of self-guided trails and lacework of old roads and trails for walking. Small boat for exploring Gator lake (first come, first served).

Where to stay: Motels—in Gulf Shores. Campgrounds—in Gulf State Park.

Weather: Sun can be burning at any season—always take sunhat and no.15 sunscreen lotion.

Points of interest nearby: Bellingrath Gardens and battleship *Alabama* near Mobile; Naval Air Station flight museum and Gulf Islands National Seashore, Pensacola.

For more information: Bon Secour National Wildlife Refuge, P.O. Box 1650, Gulf Shores, Alabama 36547. Phone: (205) 968–8623.

CHOCTAW

★

Mobile

CHOCTAW (Alabama)

Choctaw's wood duck houses are 20 feet high because the river can rise that much overnight here, forcing deer, raccoons, quails, wild turkeys, rabbits, bobcats, and even beavers to seek higher ground.

At such times the refuge field headquarters at Womack Hill may be reachable only by boat. A driftwood island can be entirely covered with creatures—including turtles and snakes—and refuge staff help some of them to dry land.

This periodic deluge is more blessing than inconvenience. It is one reason for the unusually rich wildlife diversity on this relatively small refuge of 4,218 acres of bottomland hardwoods and upland fields interspersed with lakes and sloughs.

When it is wet, thousands of wintering ducks of a dozen or more species find food in its flooded woodlands. When it dries out, deer, turkeys, squirrels, and others fatten on its acorns and mast.

Several thousand graceful wading birds raise families in cypress sloughs. One colony just off a northern refuge road accommodates hundreds of white ibis, little blue herons, and cattle egrets that engage in continuous courtship, incubation, and feeding flights back and forth from spring through summer. Alligators wait underneath for a young one to make a misstep and often themselves nest nearby, guarding their vegetation-covered eggs until black and gold offspring emerge.

Songbirds and warblers fill the woodlands in spring migration when hundreds of wood ducks are at the height of spectacular breeding plumage. Nutria—distinguished from beavers by their round tails—browse on aquatic vegetation. Red-tailed, red-shouldered, and broad-winged hawks nest. So do bluebirds, indigo buntings, and cardinals. Bald eagles spend the winter. Endangered wood storks visit. Black and turkey vultures share a colony.

Five miles of roads are open to driving and another 15 miles for hiking in dry weather. But one of the best ways to see Choctaw anytime is by boat. In summer when waters are low a canoe can pass silently alongside golden lotus blooms and water lilies where gallinules and rails inspect the underside of each lily pad for insects. In December cool temperatures and high waters find most wildlife foraging in the open on higher ground, not frightened by a boat with the motor on idle.

In floodtimes even fire ants show their survival instincts (which no one doubted), large clusters clinging together in floating clumps, the bottom ones drowning but the top ones making it through to form new colonies when waters recede.

How to get there: From Jackson (refuge office) go northwest on Route 69 to Coffeeville, west on 84; follow signs turning right or north to Barrytown and right at "T" through Womack Hill to Lenoir Landing turnoff, then right .5 mile to refuge.

Open: Daylight hours (but parts closed seasonally for waterfowl sanctuary or due to flooding—check with office, hours 7:30–4 weekdays).

What to see: Wood ducks, turkeys, beavers, alligators, deer, waterfowl.

What to do: Nature observation from refuge roads—or waterways as the case may be, since the entire refuge is flooded at times (usually dry May-September). Boating—rentals nearby. Fishing—some say the best in three states—in spring and fall for black bass, crappie, bream, catfish.

Where to stay: Motels—in Jackson and Butler, Alabama. Campgrounds—Corps of Engineers facilities two miles south or .5 mile north.

What to take and wear: Sturdy waterproof footgear.

Points of interest nearby: Stimpson State Fish and Game Sanctuary, noted for deer and turkey populations.

For more information: Choctaw National Wildlife Refuge, Box 808, 1310 College Avenue, Jackson, Alabama 36545. Phone: (205) 246–3583.

EUFAULA (Alabama and Georgia)

Birders can always find something of interest on these 11,160 acres of upland, woods, and marsh superimposed on Lake George, a Corps of Engineers reservoir in the Chattahoochee River at the southern boundary between Alabama and Georgia. It has been called by the Georgia Ornithological Society one of the ten best bird walks in that state.

Endangered wood storks visit, along with such rarities as the Ross' goose and occasional roseate spoonbills. Two sizable nesting colonies support several thousand birds, great blue herons along with great and cattle egrets, white ibises, and other graceful waders. One is visible to hikers; the other, in a closed area, is opened by request to organized groups.

Beautiful wood ducks and bluebirds have taken readily to a nest box program and are around all year; great crested flycatchers and screech and barn owls sometimes move into the houses after wood ducks vacate. Flocks of wild turkeys browse through the fields.

A field trip during warbler migration in spring and fall might turn up a dozen or so species, including pine, parula, prothonotary, and hooded; some stay the year. As many as 900 yellow-rumped have been present on the Audubon Society's Christmas Bird Count.

When water levels are low (which is unpredictable), mudflats attract shorebirds—yellowlegs, least sandpipers, dowitchers, dunlin.

In fall and winter, watch for large hawk populations—sometimes bald and golden eagles and peregrine falcons, along with red-tailed and red-shouldered hawks. Waterfowl populations peak around December with up to 15,000 ducks—mostly mallards but also blacks, gadwalls, pintails, teals, and some buffleheads, ruddies, and mergansers, along with snow and Canada geese (most of the resident Canadas are around all year).

Alligators reproduce here and bask on levee banks on warm days. A drive or hike around the refuge in the morning or evening may go by 20 or so white-tailed deer. Gray and red foxes hunt for mice in the upland fields. Bobcats scout warily along the field edges. Beavers keep their lodges in good repair alongside the trails.

Swallow-tailed and hairstreak butterflies feed on wild verbena—but the refuge has a constant display of wildflowers starting with bloodroot and trillium in spring through purple fall asters. A 40-acre marsh is covered with golden lotus bloom in late July.

One of the best ways to see this refuge is by canoe (bring your own)—paddling quietly along sloughs where otters fish and sora rails step delicately through willow thickets. Fish often can be seen feeding in the clear water—increasingly in this rapidly developing area Eufaula is an island of pristine water quality and a remnant of the lush oak savanna and riparian habitat once common here.

How to get there: From Eufaula take Route 431 north about 10 miles to Lake Point State Park information office, then right 2.5 miles to refuge office.

Open: Dawn to dusk. Office 8–4:30 weekdays.

Best times to visit: Fall, winter, spring all good.

What to see: Waterfowl; deer; alligators; good variety of birds.

What to do: 13 miles of roads for driving and hiking; fishing good in spring for bass, crappie.

Where to stay: Motels—in Eufaula. Campgrounds—Lake Point State Park, adjoining refuge.

Weather: Extremely hot and humid July-August.

Points of interest nearby: Lake Point State Park (see Campgrounds)—various recreational facilities, especially water-oriented. Beautiful historic homes in Eufaula (if there's time, go through the Shorter Mansion on the main street).

For more information: Eufaula National Wildlife Refuge, Route 2, Box 97-B, Eufaula, Alabama 36027. Phone: (205) 687–4065.

WHEELER (Alabama)

Tens of thousands of waterfowl and large numbers of graceful wading birds and other wildlife come to this 34,500-acre refuge nestled in the Tennessee River valley of north Alabama, the first national wildlife refuge overlaid on a power dam project.

It was an experiment begun in 1938 to see if waterfowl could be attracted to such places. Wheeler was assigned the middle third of the Tennessee Valley Authority's Wheeler reservoir. It has worked so well with waterfowl and other wildlife that its example has been followed not only throughout the United States but around the world.

Now up to 30,000 geese, mostly Canadas but also snows and blues, and 70,000 ducks of 22 species are here in winter resting on the refuge's 15,000 acres of open water and flying out to feed on its thousands of acres of cultivated upland and moist soil impoundments. A half-dozen eagles may be here, too. It is a prime example of how habitat can be created, for none of these existed as wildlife attractions when the refuge was established.

White-tailed deer have adapted to having space shuttle engines as neighbors— for two other government agencies, the army's Redstone Arsenal and NASA's Marshall Space Flight Center, occupy parts of this same government reservation. Some 2,000 young wood ducks hatch out yearly in nest boxes on poles, their predator guards constructed of materials from Redstone scrap piles.

Muskrat and beaver workings are visible on the waterways. Coyotes howl and yip early and late and sometimes even scout around the visitor center grounds. Raccoons and opossums forage along the trails; so do fox and bobcat, but they are warier and harder to see.

Bats of a dozen species roost in limestone caves. Two of these are endangered species—the Indiana and the gray, which has a nurse colony so sensitive to disturbance during reproduction that even refuge staff stay away. But at other times visitors may go and see 50,000 bats pour out at dusk (see Blowing Wind Cave below).

Bobwhites chirrup out from field and woods edges. Red-tailed and Cooper's hawks nest. Barn owls raise families in hollow trees as do screech owls when they don't take over a wood duck house.

Large numbers of graceful wading birds fish the water's edges. Wheeler has ranked highest in the nation for great blue herons and on the 1987 Audubon Society's Christmas Bird Count, 448 of these handsome birds were observed. In recent Christmas counts there have been 836 horned larks, 185 Carolina chickadees, 86 each of golden and ruby-crowned kinglets, 230 cedar waxwings, and 23 pileated woodpeckers.

Spring warbler migration peaks in mid-April with up to three dozen species, of which the hooded, prothonotary, and yellowthroat stay and nest. At that time the countryside is bright with blooming dogwood, redbud, wild plum, and azaleas.

Almost all the refuge wildlife can be seen at one time or another from an observation building with two-story one-way glass and microphone for hearing outdoor sounds—but there are also many roads and trails. Sit by a slough some evening and hear it come alive with whip-poor-wills, crickets, and frogs.

How to get there: From Decatur take highway 67 east one mile or from I-65 take Highway 67 west two miles.

Open: 24 hours year-round. Visitor Center 10–5 daily, November-February; 10–5 Wednesday-Sunday, March-October. Office 7–3:30 weekdays.

Best times to visit: Fall, winter, spring.

What to see: Waterfowl, wading birds, good variety of wildlife.

What to do: More than 100 miles of roads and trails; Visitor Center; observation building; boardwalk; boating (no rentals); photography; fishing. Guided group tours by arrangement.

Where to stay: Motels—in Decatur. Campgrounds—at Point Mallard Park, adjacent to refuge.

Weather: Winter temperatures can drop to near zero; midsummers so hot, humid that all life slows almost to a halt (except mosquitoes).

Points of interest nearby: Bankhead National Forest, 35 miles southwest; Joe Wheeler State Park, 30 miles west; Alabama Space and Rocket Center, 20 miles east; Mooresville, adjacent, one of the oldest incorporated villages in Alabama, unchanged for the past century—a treasure.

For more information: Wheeler National Wildlife Refuge, Route 4, Box 250, Decatur, Alabama 35603. Phone: Office (205) 353–7243; Visitor Center (205) 350–6639.

Wheeler also administers three satellite refuges: *Watercress Darter,* which protects the endangered watercress darter fish, and *Blowing Wind Cave* and *Fern Cave,* which protect endangered gray bats. None has any public use facilities, but visitors are permitted in summer to go to Blowing Wind and see spectacular flights of 400,000 bats going out to feed at dusk.

BOGUE CHITTO
Slidell

BOGUE CHITTO (Louisiana)

Wild turkeys issue territorial challenges from sandbars and cypresses on Bogue Chitto in rattling cries that can be heard for a mile or more up and down the river bottoms on spring mornings. Local people say the cries make their neck hairs stand on end and confirm their belief that the wild turkey "is more majestic than the eagle ever thought of being" and should have been, as Benjamin Franklin proposed, our national bird.

River otters slide and play on riverbanks, white-tailed deer browse, coyotes howl, and raucous pileated woodpeckers make the woods resound with their hammering on this 36,000-plus acres of mostly bottomland hardwoods, a precious remnant of rich wildlife habitat that once covered 25 million acres in the lower Mississippi valley.

But water levels can vary 15 feet—sometimes the refuge is 99 percent underwater—and a canoe or flat-bottomed jonboat is best for getting around the network of sloughs, oxbow lakes, and more than 50 miles of waterways within the refuge boundaries, stretches of which have been designated as state scenic rivers.

In any case, take a compass. Within a few minutes one can be out of sight or sound of civilization—a magical experience until one has to consider how to get back.

The self-guided canoe trail can take six hours, or it is possible to put in with a canoe or small jonboat and go out for a shorter distance. It is also possible to rent a canoe and guide from an outfitter in the area and go out for a day or several days, camping on the riverbanks and listening to the barred, great horned, and screech owls at dawn and dusk. Low water is hazardous with concealed stumps and other obstructions, so an experienced guide can be a good idea. Refuge staff are helpful in discussing plans.

Boardwalks and marked trails are planned around the lock areas, where it also is possible to launch a small boat.

Bogue Chitto also administers three subrefuges: Delta, Breton, and Bayou Sauvage National Wildlife Refuges (see below).

How to get there: From New Orleans take I-10 east to Slidell, exit at U.S. 190, go west a mile to NASA Computer Complex. Call ahead for a pass to gain entrance and proceed to refuge office. To get to the refuge itself take I-59 at Slidell north to Exit 3, then one mile west on U.S. 11 to state highway 41, then 8.6 miles north on 41 to Lock 1 road, right there two miles to public use area.

Open: Daylight hours. Office 7:30–4 weekdays.

Best times to visit: Low or high water may determine availability of refuge areas. Canoe trail normally passable January-June.

What to see: Wild turkeys, swallow-tailed kites, warbler migrations, beavers, deer, herons and egrets, wintering waterfowl.

What to do: Hiking (sturdy waterproof footgear can be helpful); canoeing; primitive camping (see text); fishing.

Where to stay: Motels and campgrounds—In Slidell and Picayune, Mississippi.

Points of interest nearby: Pearl River Wildlife Management Area, adjacent on south; Stennis Space Center on eastern refuge boundary in Mississippi.

For more information: Bogue Chitto National Wildlife Refuge, 1010 Gause Boulevard, Building 936, Slidell, Louisiana 70458. Phone: (504) 646–7555.

Bayou Sauvage is one of our newest refuges, more than 20,000 acres acquired when developers' plans to drain the marshes and build apartments ended in bankruptcy court. Now snowy egrets, glossy ibises, and tricolor herons nest within the New Orleans city limits and children—and adults—from the inner city can come see wilderness (or pretty close to it).

Wintering waterfowl concentrations can be spectacular.

Visitor facilities are still being developed, but it is possible to hike around or put in a canoe or small outboard for birding or fishing at an unimproved launch a half mile south into the refuge on U.S. 11 (interior access is closed for waterfowl sanctuary November-March). Or view alligators, white pelicans, and other refuge residents from shoulder pull-offs on U.S. 11, getting there from I-10 east from New Orleans. For further information contact Bogue Chitto NWR (see above).

Breton and *Delta*—Breton and Delta refuges are ample reason why Louisiana was John James Audubon's "favorite portion of the Union." Indeed they may not be very different today from what the great bird artist saw—hundreds of thousands of water- and shorebirds finding rest, food, and nesting sanctuary on marshes and barrier islands in and around the delta where one of the world's longest rivers empties into the sea.

To differentiate between the two: Breton Refuge is over 10,000 acres of sandy beaches that make up Breton Island and the chain of Chandeleurs 25 miles out in the Gulf of Mexico. Both are stunningly wild and beautiful, a world of blue sky and sea, white sands and sometimes tens of thousands of birds visible at one time— frigatebirds, royal terns, sooty and sandwich terns, laughing gulls, skimmers, reddish egrets, and many more.

Breton has the largest tern colony in North America, with over 60,000 nests, as well as the largest brown pelican colony, with over 2,000 nests—and much more. It became the second in the national wildlife refuge system in 1904 after a visit by Teddy Roosevelt.

Delta Refuge is 49,000 acres of shallow ponds, bayous, marsh, and a bit of upland located in the mouth of the Mississippi on which wintering waterfowl sometimes exceed a quarter million, including "blue" and snow geese and 13 duck species, as well as herons and egrets and alligators. In spring great numbers of small birds come in across the Gulf, sometimes to their first landfall in hundreds of miles, weary and highly visible—rose-breasted grosbeaks, indigo and painted buntings, scarlet and summer tanagers, and 25 warbler species, along with tremendous flights of tree swallows, sometimes 60,000 skimming over the inland ponds.

Visits to both refuges require an extremely seaworthy boat, preferably with sleep-aboard capacity, backup motor, and a supply of emergency food and water. At Delta, once there one can canoe about the small bayous and waterways. To get to Breton, one anchors offshore. Boats and guides can be arranged, and float planes will take visitors out to Breton for a visit or to camp for several days when it will not interfere with nesting. The refuge office can help arrange trips.

Fishing can be spectacular at both these refuges, especially in fall for redfish up to 10 pounds, speckled trout, striped and largemouth bass, and others.

Take sun lotion. As to weather, heavy fog can close in December through February, hurricanes can threaten July-September, and summer heat can be broiling.

For more information: Contact Delta-Breton National Wildlife Refuges, P.O. Box 924, Tidewater Road, Venice, Louisiana 70091. Phone: (504) 534–2235 (office hours irregular).

Lake Charles

CAMERON PRAIRIE

CAMERON PRAIRIE (Louisiana)

Louisiana's Cameron Parish is a birdwatcher's paradise and Cameron Prairie is a focal point for birders who may here add mottled ducks, roseate spoonbills, fulvous whistling ducks, purple gallinules, and sometimes even a vermilion flycatcher or black rail to their lists.

All these (except possibly the flycatcher and the black rail) as well as king rails, American and least bitterns, flocks of hundreds of white-faced and white ibises, and clouds of wintering waterfowl are regularly seen at this relatively new refuge, which until 1988 was an abandoned rice farm surrounded by freshwater marsh. Judging from the wildlife response to its conversion, it will be one of the South's great birding refuges.

Ducks reach a peak wintering population of 60,000 in fall and winter—mallards and green- and blue-winged teal along with wigeon, gadwall, and shovelers plus good numbers of ring-necks. Mottled ducks are year-round residents. Geese peak in late fall—up to 40,000, including 10,000 white-fronts and 30,000 snows and 80 or so lesser Canadas. They fly to and from adjacent feeding areas, filling the air with the rush of wings. Ask refuge staff for viewing advice.

Alligators are everywhere, best seen when they bask on levees in spring and fall. Nutria, beaverlike immigrants from South America, are easily spotted swimming in every waterway, and otters are seen occasionally. White-tailed deer browse in upland fields. Coyotes hunt the field edges.

Shrubby areas may be filled with warblers and other songbirds in spring and fall migration, and mudflats with migrating shorebirds—dowitchers, yellowlegs, stilts, western sandpipers, and others. Black-necked stilts stay and nest in good numbers as do scissor-tailed flycatchers. Wading birds such as snowy and great egrets, great blue and tricolored herons have several heronries and are easily seen around water's edge probing for food.

Because this refuge is relatively new, visitor facilities are relatively undeveloped. This refuge thus takes a little extra effort on the visitor's part, but it's well worth it.

How to get there: From Lake Charles take I-10 east to Chloe exit, then south on Route 397 about four miles to "T" with Route 14; east on 14 to Junction with Route 27; continue South on 27 and follow signs to refuge.

Open: 8–4:30 weekdays.

Best times to visit: Fall, winter, spring; November 15–February 15 for waterfowl concentrations.

What to see: Waterfowl, herons and egrets, roseate spoonbills, fulvous whistling ducks, mottled ducks, purple gallinules, others.

What to do: Several miles of roads along levees for driving, hiking. Photography— portable blinds permitted.

Where to stay: Motels—in Lake Charles. Campgrounds—Sam Houston State Park, north of Lake Charles.

What to take and wear: Sturdy waterproof boots, also repellent if hiking.

Points of interest nearby: Lacassine National Wildlife Refuge, 43 miles east; Sabine National Wildlife Refuge, 60 miles west; Rockefeller State Wildlife Refuge, 45 miles southwest; Holleyman Sanctuary, 40 miles west; Rock Jetty in Cameron— good birding. Also rice farms adjacent on Route 27, Creole Nature Trail, good birding.

For more information: Cameron Prairie National Wildlife Refuge, Route 1, Box 643, Bell City, Louisiana 70630. Phone: (318) 598–2216.

CATAHOULA (Louisiana)

Prothonotary warblers with orange-gold plumage, matching the robes of the Roman Catholic Church officials from which their name derives, sometimes nest in boxes vacated by bluebirds outside refuge headquarters here.

These small colorful birds of wet woodland—along with indigo and painted buntings—are only a few of the numbers of wild creatures attracted to these 5,308 acres of river delta hardwood bottomland bordering Catahoula Lake in south-central Louisiana, a refuge which exemplifies how a misused area can be restored and made a haven for wildlife.

When acquired it had been logged and overgrazed, its forest understory gone, a bare remnant of the bottomland hardwoods that once covered the area.

Now waterfowl concentrations through winter months fill the air with birds—at their height up to 75,000 moving between Duck Lake on the refuge and neighboring Catahoula Lake, beginning with pintails, mallards, blue- and green-winged teals, gadwalls, wigeons, and later divers such as ring-necks, canvasbacks, and scaups, along with snow and a few white-fronted geese.

In addition hundreds of pairs of wading birds of all species nest in a rookery on Catahoula Lake—great blue and little blue herons, great and snowy egrets, white ibises, and others—and are a noisy and beautiful sight every summer's dawn flying out from the lake to feed at water's edge over the whole surrounding area.

Wood storks and anhingas, uncommon here, visit through the summer and fish for crayfish and other small prey along the bayous.

Beautiful wood ducks are abundant. They nest both in boxes put up by the refuge and in natural tree cavities along Cowpen Bayou and can be seen with broods of downy young in early summer. Deer browse about the edges. Red foxes and coyotes sometimes streak across fields—common but wishing to avoid seeming so. Nutria—like beavers in appearance but more sociable—can be seen feeding on vegetation and swimming along borrow ditches. Alligators bask on the logs.

Pileated woodpeckers, summer tanagers, red-shouldered hawks, and barred owls are among the other interesting and colorful birds that frequent woods, roadsides, and shrubbery.

Catahoula Lake is an historic waterfowl area as piles of bones in Indian middens show. Hundreds of thousands of birds have wintered here every year in memory because of Catahoula Lake's unique situation as a backwater of the Red and Ouachita rivers. It floods in winter when the birds are here, then drains later to allow growth of food plants such as millet and chufa. In recent years control structures have regulated flows to ensure ideal water levels.

In a special situation, local law allows livestock such as cattle and hogs to graze freely over portions of the parish, including the seasonally drained lake bottom—with an effect on waterfowl that some say is detrimental, others say not. Another feature that may startle visitors is the presence of oil wells along with saltwater injection wells, pipelines, and oil storage tanks, because original purchase of refuge land unfortunately did not include mineral rights.

Fencing keeps out local livestock but the refuge must coexist with oil drilling. And seasonal flooding may leave some refuge roads impassable from January through June.

Roads and trails are beautiful here, winding along the bayous through old trees hung with Spanish moss. They are always open to foot travel—just bring boots, which are handy anyway for getting off and hiking the fenceline right-of-ways to see small birds that seek more densely covered areas.

How to get there: From Alexandria take state highway 28 north to state highway 84, left on 84 (1.5 miles) to refuge entrance.

Open: Daylight hours. Office 7–3:30 weekdays.

What to see: Waterfowl; deer; nutria; alligators; large cypress trees; good assortment of small birds.

What to do: Walking and driving trails; observation tower; boating on Duck Lake (ramps available, 10 hp limit); excellent fishing, especially in spring when timberlands flood, bass move in to spawn and minnow populations explode.

Where to stay: Motels—in Jena, 12 miles west, and Alexandria, 30 miles southwest. Campgrounds—west two miles on Highway 84; also in Alexandria-Pineville area. Primitive camping in Saline Wildlife Management Area off Highway 28.

Weather: Summers hot and humid; any heavy rainfall upstream creates possibility of river backup and flooding.

What to take and wear: Waterproof footgear, especially for off-trail hiking.

Points of interest nearby: Adjoining Catahoula Lake, historic waterfowl area; Saline Wildlife Management Area off Highway 28; Kisatchie National Forest, near Alexandria. Catahoula Lake Festival in late October.

For more information: Catahoula National Wildlife Refuge, P.O. Drawer Z, Rhinehart, Louisiana 71363. Phone: (318) 992–5261.

D'ARBONNE ★ • Monroe

D'ARBONNE (Louisiana)

The clear and scenic D'Arbonne Bayou winds through 17,421 acres of pinelands, hardwood bottomlands, and small lakes and ponds that make up D'Arbonne Refuge, sanctuary for the endangered red-cockaded woodpecker as well as for hundreds of long-legged herons and egrets and such notable smaller birds as the golden prothonotary warbler, which nests commonly in its moist woodlands.

Colonies of beavers live in its wet areas, which are considerable since 80 percent of D'Arbonne can be flooded at times with backup from the Ouachita River. The water level fluctuates as much as 30 feet—mostly in the spring but it can be anytime between November and July. For this reason it's always a good idea to consult the refuge office about access to roads, trails, and boat ramps according to current water conditions.

White-tailed deer feed in upland areas—also, less visibly, bobcats, coyotes, and gray foxes. There is a small alligator population.

For birders there are interesting spring songbird migrations, sometimes with thousands of warblers of a dozen or more species moving through in April, and shorebird movements with large flocks of plovers, sandpipers, and others probing the mudflats in spring and again in early fall. Roadrunners are here in the easternmost edge of their range. Barred owls' "who-cooks-for-you" call is heard in early mornings.

Wild turkeys strut in spring. Crimson-crested pileateds are only the most conspicuous of eight common woodpeckers. Mississippi kites visit in midsummer. Songbird nesters include indigo and a few painted buntings, chats, summer tanagers, and hooded, pine, parula, and black-and-white warblers along with yellow-throated and warbling vireos. Sparrows include Bachman's, Henslow's and Lincoln's.

Large numbers of wading birds gather to gorge on crayfish when waters recede later in summer—great and little blue herons, great and snowy egrets, and sometimes hundreds of endangered wood storks.

The several clans of red-cockaded woodpeckers are easily visible from trails, especially in April and May when adults are feeding young. Photographers can set up temporary blinds.

Bald eagles are usually present when waterfowl build to peaks up to 70,000 in fall and winter, mostly mallards and woods, scaup and gadwall, with some canvasbacks, pintails, ruddies, and ring-necks.

The beautiful wood ducks nest and produce some 1,500 ducklings, which usually can be seen about the waterways in May. Flocks of several hundred white pelicans stop by in spring and fall en route to and from nesting grounds.

Herpetologists follow the mass breeding of hundreds of spotted salamanders in roadside ditches in April.

There are 13 miles of roads and 50 miles of trails for driving, hiking, or biking. But one of the best ways to see the refuge is from a small boat. Even better, canoe down the D'Arbonne Bayou, which winds along 15 miles of twists and turns through the entire refuge, between high banks of mosses and ferns and areas timbered with tall cypress and bitter pecan, overcup oak and tupelo gum, with an occasional glimpse of some of the wildlife residents in a serene semi-wilderness setting that is restorative for the soul.

How to get there: From Monroe take I-20 west, exit at Mill Street (Route 143), go north about 13 miles to refuge entrance. Refuge office is at 201 Jackson Street in Monroe.

Open: 24 hours. Office 7:30–4 weekdays.

Best times to visit: Spring and fall.

What to do: Nature observation (best avoid heavy fall hunting weekends); boating— rentals available in Monroe; fishing—can be fantastic for bream, catfish, also bass when flood waters recede in early summer.

Where to stay: Motels—in Monroe. Campgrounds—in Monroe; also Kisatchie National Forest, west of refuge, and Cheniere State Park, south of refuge.

Points of interest nearby: Felsenthal National Wildlife Refuge, 40 miles north; Tensas River National Wildlife Refuge, 50 miles east; Upper Ouachita National Wildlife Refuge, 34 miles north.

For more information: D'Arbonne National Wildlife Refuge, 201 Jackson Street, P.O. Box 3065, Monroe, Louisiana 71210. Phone: (318) 325–1735.

Upper Ouachita is a satellite refuge administered by D'Arbonne—20,905 acres with similar wildlife and bottomland hardwood habitat bordering along the Ouachita River for 18 miles. A beautiful drive when water is down (check with office) is along the River Road, cool and shaded by tall trees hung with Spanish moss that gives an almost cathedral-like effect, where much of the wildlife can be seen. To get there go four miles east from Haile on Parish Road 2204.

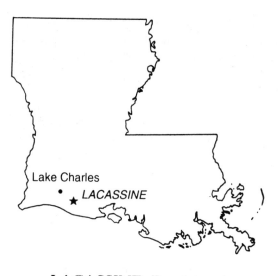

Lake Charles

LACASSINE

LACASSINE (Louisiana)

Some of the largest gatherings of waterfowl anywhere explode into the air over Lacassine's marsh, filling it with eager calls and the rustle of whirring wings. Their huge flights between sunset and dark and again at daybreak during the fall and winter are an unforgettable and heart-stirring spectacle.

Nesting roseate spoonbills are here as well, with great numbers of gorgeous purple gallinules and graceful wading birds and perhaps the densest population anywhere of American alligators—estimates run as high as 15,000 on this 32,624-acre refuge in southwest coastal Louisiana.

Yet the visitor who first sees 16,000-acre Lacassine Pool may think, "How peaceful it is!" Contrasted to sounds of traffic and civilization it seems dead quiet—almost like another world with its great expanse of water and islands of marsh vegetation shining gold and dark green against the clear water and blue sky as far as the eye can see.

Then one becomes aware of an undercurrent murmur that may build until it is almost a dull roar. Some of the masses of vegetation show themselves to be in fact rafts of ducks and geese that lift and then settle again like a great blanket, and the dull roar is their continuous "conversation" among themselves.

Sometimes the marsh is covered with white water lilies or bull's tongue flowers. Stay until dusk and it becomes a jungle with various creatures muttering and moving about, punctuated by the shrieking of a gallinule or the bellow of a bull alligator.

It is a wondrous place. Those who have lived and worked here for years feel it is one of the most beautiful on earth.

Wintering populations of ducks and geese sometimes reach 500,000—more than a dozen species of ducks and four of geese, settling in at the southern end of both the Mississippi and Central flyways. White-fronted geese are here in their largest concentrations in the Mississippi flyway. Fulvous whistling ducks are here in spring and fall in the largest numbers of any U.S. refuge, and black-bellied tree ducks in recent years have started nesting and spending the entire year here.

The list of common and abundant wading and other waterbirds includes white-faced and white ibises; snowy, cattle, and great egrets; great blue, little blue, tricolor, green-backed, black- and yellow-crowned night herons; least and American bitterns, olivaceous cormorants, black-necked stilts, and many others.

In summer there may be more than 5,000 white-faced ibises alone and tens of thousands of other long-legged waders, most of them nesting colonially, the great blue herons and cormorants preferring tall cypress trees, the roseate spoonbills taking to medium-sized willows, and ibises using low-growing buttonbushes and willows. Colonies of courting birds, flaring their feathers and exchanging nest material, may contain 10,000 birds in an area as small as five acres.

Eagles are occasional winter visitors; so are peregrine falcons. Nutrias, a beaver-like South American immigrant, forage along through the canals; armor-plated armadillos root through vegetation on the levees and particularly around refuge headquarters.

All of this may be seen from four miles of roads open to driving or hiking and another 25 miles of levee roads open to hiking. Some roads through the heaviest waterfowl concentrations are closed to cars in winter when birds pack into safe refuge territory during hunting season, but these will be opened on request for wildlife-viewing, weather permitting (they can be all but impassable in wet weather).

How to get there: From Lake Charles take I-10 to Exit 54 (Welsh), then south on Highway 99 to Highway 14, east three miles to Highway 3056; headquarters is at the end of that road. To go to Lacassine Pool go west five miles from intersection of Highways 99 and 14, left to Parish Road 7-5, and follow signs.

Open: Daylight hours. Office 7–3:30 weekdays.

Best times to visit: Determined by weather and personal preference—something to see all year.

What to see: Huge concentrations of waterfowl and wading birds, including large numbers of roseate spoonbills. Purple gallinules. Nutrias. Armadillos. Alligators.

What to do: Nature-viewing from drive and walkways; photography (portable blinds permitted with refuge approval); bass fishing is popular. Refuge has about 100 miles of canals and boat trails but best take something larger than a canoe and consult refuge staff on plans.

Where to stay: Motels—in Jennings or Lake Charles. Campgrounds—adjacent (not on) headquarters tract, or at Sam Houston State Park, 50 miles northwest— or anywhere along the beach in Cameron Parish.

Weather: Summer is humid; winter can dip below freezing but it doesn't hold there (consult great blue herons—they don't start nesting until cold weather is over for the year).

What to take and wear: Water-repellent gear; insect repellent.

Points of interest nearby: Cameron Prairie National Wildlife Refuge, 35 miles west; Sabine National Wildlife Refuge, 80 miles west; Rockefeller Wildlife Refuge, 60 miles west; Avery Island, 75 miles east; Kisatchie National Forest, 75 miles north; Atchafalaya National Wildlife Refuge, managed by the state of Louisiana, 80 miles east on Route 10; Holleyman-Sheely Sanctuary, 100 miles west.

For more information: Lacassine National Wildlife Refuge, HCR 63, Box 186, Lake Arthur, Louisiana 70549. Phone: (318) 774–5923.

Also administered by Lacassine is *Shell Keys* Refuge, established in 1907, an eight-acre nesting colony offshore. Access is limited and difficult, by special permit only.

Alexandria

LAKE OPHELIA

LAKE OPHELIA (Louisiana)

L ake Ophelia and its nearby satellite refuge, Grand Cote, are two beautiful and relatively new refuges in central Louisiana—Lake Ophelia with a planned total of 30,000 acres of bottomland hardwood swamps, meandering sloughs and some upland; Grand Cote planned for a total of 12,000 acres of bottomland hardwood that was cleared but is being reconverted to forest and natural wetlands.

Bobcats, alligators, otters, beavers, minks, coyotes, and gray and red foxes make their homes here, along with some 5,000 pairs of beautiful wading birds—great blue and yellow-crowned night herons, glossy and white ibis, great, snowy, and cattle egrets. Sandhill cranes and wood storks visit. Several thousand young wood ducks are hatched out every year, and about 100,000 ducks of several species overwinter on each refuge, accompanied by bald eagles that prey on weak or injured ones. A hacking program has begun, gradually introducing young birds to the environment, whereby it is hoped that young eagles raised on platforms here will return to nest.

Wildlife is similar on both refuges but Lake Ophelia, surrounding a lovely clear cypress-lined lake by that name (actually a wide meander area of the Red River), has more upland types. Snow and white-fronted geese prefer the openness of Grand Cote. Fishing is permitted at Lake Ophelia from March to October, and no better refuge trip could be imagined than taking a small flatbottom boat with a 10-horsepower motor out for a day in this pristine place.

Both are relatively undeveloped. The refuge office until recently has been on the

Tunica-Biloxi Indian reservation on Highway 1 near Marksville (marked by a conspicuous eight-foot blue goose)—office hours 8–4 weekdays, telephone (318) 253–4238. A visitor center is planned on Grand Cote, with nature trails and an observation tower.

Both of these fine new wildlife reserves were made possible by The Nature Conservancy.

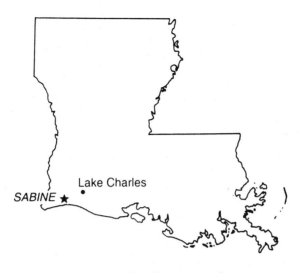

Lake Charles

SABINE ★

SABINE (Louisiana)

For about an hour almost every afternoon of the year glorious roseate spoonbills fly overhead from feeding grounds to nightly roosts at Sabine refuge, their brilliant plumage matching if not overpowering the sunset.

To many this is the memorable sight here. To others the prize goes to the alligators, which certainly are no longer an endangered species on this 142,846-acre expanse of tremendously rich and productive fresh, brackish, and saltwater marsh in the southwest corner of coastal Louisiana. Sabine's alligator population is estimated at about 9,000; visitors to the 1.4-mile marsh walking trail (wheelchair-accessible) will see at least a half dozen, often many more.

But there is much more, most of it visible at one time or another along the trail, which offers a microcosm of the whole refuge wildlife population. Moorhens and brilliant purple gallinules parade families of improbable-looking bald chicks. Usually secretive king and clapper rails peep out of the phragmites. Muskrats and nutrias forage on marsh vegetation, leading young ones in spring and summer (the nutria nurse babies from mammary glands on the sides of their backs). Even a coyote is remotely possible—and if it looks like a red wolf, it might be one that carries some red wolf blood in its background.

Large numbers of wading birds—white-faced and white ibis and all the beautiful herons and egrets common to this part of the country—fish along the edges, spillovers from several rookeries that accommodate thousands of them on more remote sections. Thousands of cormorants, both double-crested and olivaceous, nest here, too.

This is a primary waterfowl refuge at the southern end of the eastern and Mississippi flyways. Sometimes tens of thousands of wintering ducks of a dozen or so species are here—blue- and green-winged teals, shovelers, gadwalls, scaups, and others, with an occasional ring-necked and cinnamon teal.

Snow geese come in daily, sometimes hundreds of them, at a site near headquarters to gather grit, necessary for their digestive processes. Usually one or two wintering merlins and peregrine falcons are hanging around the same site.

Warbler and songbird migrations can be lively, especially in late April and into May after a frontal weather passage, when they come down to feed and rest in their first landfall north of the Gulf. An oak grove near headquarters can be full of small birds, one tree holding 16 warbler species.

Sabine always registers one of the nation's highest in the Audubon Society's Christmas Bird Count with close to 200 species, including perhaps 5,000 white pelicans, 3,613 olivaceous cormorants, 26,392 snow geese, 15 Ross' geese, 480 black-necked stilts, and 2,583 yellow-rumped warblers, along with such unususal inclusions as rufous and black-chinned hummingbirds, varied thrush, vermilion flycatchers, Lapland longspurs, a Virginia's warbler and Bewicks's wren, and 280 seaside sparrows.

Route 27 goes through the refuge and is part of the Creole Nature Trail through various state natural areas. Refuge staff are glad to direct visitors to other places in the area that are rich in birdlife—like beaches where 10,000 hawks can sometimes be seen in a day's migration.

How to get there: From Lake Charles take I-10 west to Sulphur, then south on route 27 about 27 miles to refuge signs.

Open: Daylight hours. Visitor center 7–4 weekdays, 12–4 weekends and holidays.

Best times to visit: Much to see all year.

What to see: Alligators; roseate spoonbills; wading birds, waterfowl; nutria; much else.

What to do: Excellent Visitor Center; marsh walking trail; observation tower; ten miles of State Route 27 on refuge is part of Creole Driving Trail (maps available); photography, good on walking trail; boating on 125 miles of canals and bayous March 15–October 15.

Where to stay: Motels—in Sulphur and Lake Charles. Campgrounds—in Ward Four Parish Park, 14 miles north; Sam Houston Jones State Park, 27 miles north; or anywhere along the beach in Cameron Parish.

Weather: August hot and humid with deer flies; January to March can be rainy, blustery.

Points of interest nearby: Cameron Prairie National Wildlife Refuge, 10 miles east;

Lacassine National Wildlife Refuge, 80 miles east; Audubon Society's Holley-man-Sheeley Bird Sanctuary, 15 miles south, can be fantastic during spring and fall migration; Creole Nature Trail (see above) follows many points of interest including Rockefeller Wildlife Refuge. Refuge staff will advise on other good birding spots open by permit—oil company roads, Hackberry and Peveto Woods, and numbers of others.

For more information: Sabine National Wildlife Refuge, Highway 27 South, 3000 Main Street, Hackberry, Louisiana 70645. Phone: (318) 762–3816.

Monroe •

TENSAS RIVER

TENSAS RIVER (Louisiana)

This priceless remnant of wildlife habitat, more than 57,000 acres of rich bottomland hardwood forest and oxbow lakes such as once covered 25 million acres of the Mississippi Valley, was saved when citizens banded together to protest after plans were announced to clear-cut and farm it.

Conservationists, sportsmen, and schoolchildren all joined in the effort to preserve the last of the woods along the Tensas River where the red wolf, the cougar, and ivory-billed woodpecker once lived. The Army Corps of Engineers was persuaded to buy the land in mitigation of several detrimental water projects and turn it over to the U.S. Fish and Wildlife Service.

Now a healthy population of threatened Louisiana black bears roams free (this is the original "teddy bear" named after Theodore Roosevelt when he visited and admired this forest's "towering majesty").

Otter families frisk in streams. Scarlet-crested pileated woodpeckers hammer and call raucously. Barred owls call "Who-cooks-for-you" and the answer can re-echo from dozens of other barred owls at varying distances.

A bobcat pounced on a visitor covered with camouflage cloth who called the abundant wild turkeys too realistically. Coyotes yip and howl early and late. Sometimes a young litter can be heard welcoming their mother returning with a midday meal.

Up to 40,000 ducks and several thousand geese congregate in winter, attended by bald and an occasional golden eagle, spectacular when they return from feeding and funnel down in wave after wave in late afternoon.

Songbird migrations attract birders from a wide area in spring and fall for warblers of more than two dozen species, including the Swainson's, which stays and nests along with good numbers of prothonotaries, parulas, hooded, and, it's believed, the rare Bachman's. Bright indigo buntings are along every road and field edge along with painted buntings, summer tanagers, dickcissels, and others. (A good assortment of what's around is usually the excellent Visitor Center—and check with refuge staff about what's been seen lately.)

Watch for hawks in fields approaching the Visitor Center—red-tails and kestrels perched in trees and harriers in mothlike flight low over the ground. White-tailed deer browse the field and road edges.

Great blue herons and great egrets with other graceful wading birds feed at the water's edges. One rookery not far from a trail holds up to 10,000 cattle egrets along with little blue herons and white ibis. Mississippi kites nest, too, and soar overhead in spring and summer, flipping on their backs sometimes for a large insect.

Birds noted on recent Audubon Christmas Counts include 301 ruby-crowned kinglets, 249 yellow-rumped warblers, 15 winter wrens, 293 Carolina chickadees, 135 bluebirds, 232 Lapland longspurs, 1,269 horned larks, 9,492 snow geese, 4,432 killdeer, and 3,646 wood ducks.

Alligators bellow on spring mornings and bask on banks of the Tensas River, a lovely waterway on the refuge unmarked by human interference. A beautiful way to see the refuge is by canoe (bring your own), passing through every wildlife habitat, overhung by giant trees with Spanish moss and vines as thick as your arm.

Or hike through the woods where handsome black-phase fox squirrels leap from branch to branch of oak and cypress trees up to 100 feet tall, some with trunks up to 10 feet in diameter, where almost any of this refuge's interesting wildlife could appear at any time.

How to get there: From Monroe take I-20 east to Waverly exit, then north on Highway 577 for 1.5 miles, east on Highway 80 for four miles, turn right at refuge sign and go 10 miles to office/Visitor Center.

Open: 24 hours. Office/Visitor Center 8–4 weekdays, 10–4 September-December weekends.

Best times to visit: Summer hot, humid, but lots to see then, too (bring insect repellent).

What to see: Deer, wading birds, songbirds, alligators, waterfowl, beautiful Tensas River and woodlands.

What to do: Boardwalk across wooded slough to observation deck; five-mile primitive hiking trail; 25 miles of roads for hiking, bicycling or driving; canoeing; fishing on two small lovely lakes for bream, perch, catfish (no gasoline motors).

Where to stay: Motels—at Tallulah and Welhi. Campgrounds—several adjacent to refuge.

Points of interest nearby: D'Arbonne and Upper Ouachita National Wildlife Refuges, near Monroe; Vicksburg National Military Park, 18 miles east; Poverty Point National Monument, interesting Indian area, at Epps.

For more information: Tensas River National Wildlife Refuge, Route 2, Box 295, Tallulah, Louisiana 71282. Phone: (318) 574–2664.

The North-Central States

The north-central refuges lie within the Great Plains, once a region of seemingly endless prairies and lakes, now mostly given over to intense agricultural activity, predominantly in corn, wheat, and cattle. They include some notable migratory waterfowl refuges along the Missouri River and on natural and man-made lakes, but the glory of this region lies in its nesting refuges for water birds and waterfowl. Nowhere else in the country are there so many places so well suited to this activity. Throughout the Dakotas and Nebraska (and also in Minnesota and Montana in neighboring regions) there are thousands of ponds and wetlands ranging in size from less than a hundred acres to many square miles, each providing nesting habitat for ducks and often for wading and shorebirds and geese as well.

These are called by the homely name of "prairie potholes." For the most part they are left over from the last glacier, scoured out by the retreating ice that left a hardpan or clay depression holding water even in dry periods. Some of them are on named refuges; other are administered by wetland management districts under the U.S. Fish and Wildlife Service. Still others are privately owned, but subject to nondrainage easements sold to the government. Most are open to the public, but except for parking most have few if any visitor facilities.

"Potholes" hardly describes them adequately—for they are jewels of marsh and water, small areas of remnant beauty that the first settlers saw in profusion. They represent one of the great assets of these north-central states, and it is to the credit of their citizens that many have been saved, for those not under such protection are steadily lost to drainage, this extraordinary wildlife habitat gone forever.

NORTH DAKOTA

Western grebes perform graceful courtship ballets on the waterways while on the shortgrass prairie sharp-tailed grouse inflate lavender throat sacs—all to impress females in breeding season at *Arrowwood,* where prairie chickens are making a comeback.

Giant Canada geese, once believed extinct, now are plentiful nesters at *Audubon.* So are great blue herons, western and pied-billed grebes, and other water-oriented species on more than 120 refuge islands in 11,000-acre Lake Audubon.

Des Lacs has such wildlife riches on its lake, marsh, mixed prairie, and woodlands one hardly knows where to start. A quarter-million snow geese fly up against a backdrop of golden leaves in fall. Sharp-tailed grouse have courtship dances. Several hundred white pelicans visit. Ruddy ducks bob bright-blue breeding-colored bills. And birders come for Sprague's pipits and LeConte's and Baird's sparrows.

The high resonant bugling of up to 25,000 majestic sandhill cranes can fill the crisp fall air over *Long Lake.* They succeed thousands of rusty-hooded avocets and tens of thousands of dowitchers and "peeps" that line the shores in August and September.

More than 250 bird species have been noted at *J. Clark Salyer,* of which half have nested, some in great numbers—colonies of hundreds of double-crested cormorants and great blue and black-crowned night herons, for example. This refuge has one of the nation's richest and most exciting bird populations from spring to fall, including unusual pipits and sparrows. Sometimes 150 Swainson's hawks are in a single field in late September.

Sullys Hill was set aside when the buffalo had been driven to the edge of extinction. Nucleus groups of buffalos, elk, and white-tailed deer were introduced and all now are highly visible residents, along with frisky prairie dogs.

The constant calls of 100,000 or so waterfowl are audible spring and fall at *Tewaukon,* and summer brings such nesters as grebes, phalaropes, great blue herons, and others. Omnipresent are "flicker-tails"—Richardson's ground squirrels, the North Dakota state animal.

Upper Souris is a spectacular birding refuge, where a quarter-million geese gather in fall. Eagles follow them and the 50,000 ducks that come. Of the 250 bird species noted here, 150 nest, including five kinds of grebes, 17 kinds of ducks, marbled godwits, avocets, red-tailed hawks, great horned owls, and interesting pipits and sparrows. Mammals are present, too—deer, beavers, foxes, porcupines.

SOUTH DAKOTA

Trumpeter swans, largest North American waterfowl, once close to extinction, nest at *Lacreek* (though more easily seen when not seeking privacy for nesting activities). White pelicans breed—2,500 nests packed on two small islands. Shy American bitterns are abundant. Up to 10,000 ducklings are produced annually. Mule and white-tailed deer bring out spotted fawns in June.

Wintering eagles prey on fish and weakened waterfowl at *Lake Andes,* then roost at nearby *Mundt* refuge. Tens of thousands of ducks and geese gather in spring and fall. Iridescent ring-necked pheasants cackle in every field, and red foxes sometimes den alongside the road.

About two million of the mid-continental population of snow geese come through *Sand Lake* in spring migration—sometimes a million are there at once. Numbers of nesting birds are equally impressive. By fall, counting both nesters and migrants, Sand Lake may have a half-million Franklin's gulls, a quarter-million mallard ducks, 5,000 tundra swans, and 12,000 huge white pelicans.

Waubay in Sioux Indian language means "nesting place for birds," appropriate since more than 100 species are recorded nesters at this lovely small refuge in the prairie pothole region, including American bitterns, five kinds of hawks, 15 species of ducks, and five kinds of grebes, including the red-necked grebe and common goldeneye duck, both at the southernmost edge of their range.

NEBRASKA

Bald and golden eagles soar over beautiful *Crescent Lake*'s 18 jewellike ponds and lakes and surrounding grasslands where sharp-tailed grouse display lavender throat sacs in courtship dances. Long-billed curlews and upland sandpipers—among many others—nest. Both white-tailed and mule deer graze.

Elk and bison roam as they did 400 years ago on the prairie grasslands of *Fort Niobrara.* So do white-tailed and mule deer. A prairie-dog "town" covers 20 acres. Texas longhorns amble about. Coyotes yip to each other early and late, and porcupines lumber along almost anywhere.

IOWA

A blizzard of birds can overtake *Desoto* in fall and winter—a half-million waterfowl, including hundreds of thousands of snow geese, tens of thousands of ducks, and the eagles that prey on weakened ones. Red-headed woodpeckers perch on nearly every refuge sign in warm months, and red-tailed hawks soar overhead.

Union Slough is a preglacial remnant so flat that a strong gust of wind can determine the direction of its water's flow. Waterfowl come, ring-necked pheasants are abundant, deer graze in the fields, and great blue herons scout the water's edges.

If plans go well, bison and elk will be grazing on Iowa's tall grass prairie at the new *Walnut Creek* refuge for the first time since the state's native herds were extinguished more than a century ago. Restoration is just beginning.

KANSAS

Dozens of bald eagles are around *Flint Hills* in fall and winter, preying on weakened members among the 150,000 or so ducks and geese that stay till spring if there's no hard freeze. Prairie chickens "boom" on cool spring mornings, and wild turkeys gobble to proclaim breeding territories. Coyotes howl at dusk, and bobcats warily stalk field edges for rodents.

At least six subspecies of Canada geese arrive at *Kirwin* in great honking V-formations every fall and many stay the winter, along with several dozen eagles. This diverse refuge also has deer and pheasants, wild turkeys and quail, and several thousand tall vociferous sandhill cranes both spring and fall.

Half the shorebirds in North America are believed to stop at *Quivira* or nearby Cheyenne Bottoms during annual migrations. The importance of these places to these birds—as well as to thousands of sandhill cranes, white pelicans, waterfowl, and others—cannot be overstated. Without them, continued existence of many of these birds would be in jeopardy.

MISSOURI

Mingo has something for naturalists of almost any persuasion—nesting eagles, wild turkeys, deer, otters, large waterfowl concentrations, and some of the largest specimen trees in existence.

More than 200 bald eagles—one of the largest wintering eagle concentrations in the country—are sometimes on *Squaw Creek* in winter following the large concentration of waterfowl present then. Does bring out spotted fawns in summer, muskrats build domelike lodges, and coyotes hunt along the roads.

Swan Lake is not about swans but Canada geese. The nearby town calls itself Wild Goose Capital of the World because 100,000 or so of the Canadas occupy the refuge by late October. But there are also deer, coyotes, wild turkeys, sometimes 250,000 ducks, 2,000 white pelicans, and 30,000 snow geese, along with impressive hawk migrations in fall.

Following are birds of special interest found commonly at North-Central refuges at seasons indicated:

S: SPRING   s: SUMMER   F: FALL   W: WINTER

Trumpeter Swan: Lacreek SFW
Mississippi Kite: Quivira SsF
Golden Eagle: Lacreek SFW
Bald Eagle: Flint Hills SFW, Lacreek W, Lake Andes W, Mingo FW, Quivira SF, Squaw Creek FW, Swan Lake FW

Prairie Falcon: Quivira W

Gray Partridge: Arrowwood SsFW, Audubon SsFW

Greater Prairie Chicken: Flint Hills SsFW

Sharp-tailed Grouse: Arrowwood SsFW, Audubon SsFW, Crescent Lake SsFW, Fort Niobrara SsFW, Lacreek FW, Long Lake SsFW

Sandhill Crane: Audubon SF, Lacreek SF, Long Lake SF, Souris Loop Refuges SF

Snowy Plover: Quivira Ss

American Avocet: Audubon Ss, Crescent Lake SsF, Long Lake SsF, Quivira SsF, Sand Lake Ss, Souris Loop Refuges SsF

Long-billed Curlew: Crescent Lake Ss, Fort Niobrara Ss

Marbled Godwit: Audubon Ss, Lacreek S, Long Lake SsF, Sand Lake Ss, Waubay Ss

Red-Necked (Northern) Phalarope: Crescent Lake S, Souris Loop Refuges SsF, Waubay SF

California Gull: Arrowwood SsF

Least Tern: Quivira Ss

Least Flycatcher: Crescent Lake S, Waubay SF

Scissor-tailed Flycatcher: Flint Hills Ssf, Quivira SsF

Bohemian Waxwing: Souris Loop Refuges SFW

Bell's Vireo: Flint Hills SsF, Quivira sF, Squaw Creek Ss, Swan Lake Ss

Lark Bunting: Audubon Ss, Crescent Lake SsF, Lacreek Ss, Long Lake SsF

Common Redpoll: Sand Lake W, Souris Loop Refuges SFW

Baird's Sparrow: Arrowwood Ss, Souris Loop Refuges SsF

LeConte's Sparrow: Souris Loop Refuges SsF

Sharp-tailed Sparrow: Souris Loop Refuges SsF

Lapland Longspur: Arrowwood SF, Audubon F, Flint Hills SF, Lake Andes W, Long Lake SFW, Quivira FW, Souris Loop Refuges SF, Tewaukon SFW

Chestnut-collared Longspur: Audubon Ss, Lake Andes S, Long Lake SsF, Quivira W, Tewaukon S

Snow Bunting: Arrowwood W, Audubon W, Tewaukon W, Souris Loop Refuges SFW

NORTH-CENTRAL

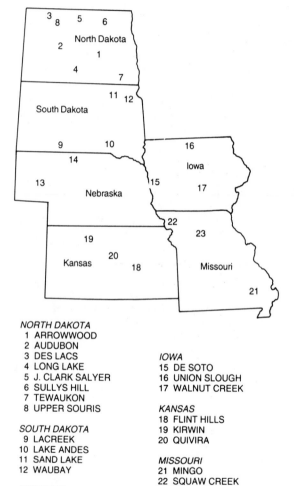

NORTH DAKOTA
1 ARROWWOOD
2 AUDUBON
3 DES LACS
4 LONG LAKE
5 J. CLARK SALYER
6 SULLYS HILL
7 TEWAUKON
8 UPPER SOURIS

SOUTH DAKOTA
9 LACREEK
10 LAKE ANDES
11 SAND LAKE
12 WAUBAY

NEBRASKA
13 CRESCENT LAKE
14 FORT NIOBRARA

IOWA
15 DE SOTO
16 UNION SLOUGH
17 WALNUT CREEK

KANSAS
18 FLINT HILLS
19 KIRWIN
20 QUIVIRA

MISSOURI
21 MINGO
22 SQUAW CREEK
23 SWAN LAKE

ARROWWOOD ★

• Jamestown

ARROWWOOD (North Dakota)

Western grebes perform graceful courtship ballets, skittering over the water's surface in pairs on this wonderfully diverse east-central North Dakota refuge.

Sharp-tailed grouse gather at dawn on more than a dozen dancing grounds in spring where 250 or so ardent males stomp down the grass, spread their wings and tails, and inflate lavender gular sacs, seeking to impress females.

Prairie chickens, extirpated from the area by inhospitable farming practices, are making a comeback.

Badgers and red foxes raise families in dens often alongside the 5.5-mile auto-tour route. White-tailed deer browse in wooded coulees along with smaller numbers of long-eared mule deer. Coyotes hunt small rodents, and lustrous minks fish the water's edges and consume their catch on the banks.

Eared grebes with golden ear tufts sometimes gather in colonies to build up to 3,000 nests of floating vegetation on the edge of Arrowwood Lake behind refuge headquarters.

Endangered piping plovers have nested on islands in Jim Lake along with avocets and marbled godwits.

Wood ducks, often called our most beautiful waterfowl, nest—as do handsome hooded mergansers—in boxes put up for them in the waterways, producing hundreds of downy young.

Eagles follow migrating waterfowl to prey on weak or injured ones, and 15 or 20 can be around in late October when duck numbers may peak at 40,000, geese at 35 to 40,000, before ice freeze-up. There have been as many as 6,000 tundra swans, up to 6,500 canvasbacks.

Small numbers are here in spring, though 50 or so eagles may come to feast when lake waters thaw in April after a hard winter has killed large numbers of fish.

Birders come from afar to see gray partridges, here in pairs in spring and coveys in fall, and Baird's and LeConte's sparrows and Sprague's pipits, which can be hard to see but usually can be located with help and advice from the refuge staff (as can most of the interesting wildlife inhabitants).

Common at various seasons are Tennessee warblers, red-tailed and Swainson's hawks, northern harriers, clay-colored and Harris' sparrows, ring-necked pheasants, Lapland and chestnut-collared longspurs, and large colonies of bank and cliff swallows. White pelicans are around through the warm seasons, sometimes in huge numbers.

Giant Canada geese nest as do American bitterns and 15 species of ducks, including wigeons, blue-winged teals, shovelers, pintails, and some redheads, ring-necks, and canvasbacks.

The hills and valleys, which were caused not by upthrust but by centuries of erosion from snowmelt runoff, display wildflowers from spring to frost—prairie roses, black sampsons, gaillardias. Yellow bladderworts bloom in the marsh.

The auto-tour route winds through all the varied habitat—tall and shortgrass prairie, over softly green slopes, beside watered potholes, and alongside prairie dog burrows where litters of young "dogs" appear in May, leaping over each other in play and sometimes stopping to wash their mother's and each other's faces.

There are 28 miles of trails for hiking, but visitors are free to walk anyplace on the 15,934-acre refuge

How to get there: From Jamestown take Route 281 north 22 miles to refuge sign, just north of Edmunds; turn right six miles to headquarters.

Open: Auto tour always open unless impassable due to weather—rest of refuge daylight hours but parts can be closed for sanctuary during hunting. Office 7:30–4 weekdays.

What to see: Waterfowl; sharp-tailed grouse; prairie chickens; Baird's sparrows; prairie dogs; deer; prairie wildflowers. Reserve ahead for grouse and prairie chicken viewing blinds.

What to do: Auto-tour route; hiking; picnicking; photography—see viewing blinds above, and refuge staff can advise on how best to photograph other wildlife, with portable blinds permitted. Cross-country skiing and snowshoeing in winter.

Where to stay: Motels—Jamestown, 30 miles southwest. Campgrounds—Jamestown Dam Recreation Area and Carrington, 25 miles north.

Weather: Winters harsh—60-below wind chill—and refuge roads can be impassable.

Points of interest nearby: Northern Prairie Research Center, Jamestown; Valley City National Fish Hatchery, 40 miles southeast; Chase Lake Prairie Project Headquarters, 25 miles west; Alkali Lake Audubon Sanctuary, 25 miles southeast.

For more information: Arrowwood National Wildlife Refuge, 7745 Eleventh Street, S.E., Pingree, North Dakota 58476-8308. Phone: (701) 285-3341

Arrowwood also administers a number of subrefuges and waterfowl production areas, mostly of a water orientation though with varying wildlife, and most with few visitor facilities. Notable is *Chase Lake,* with (in most years) the largest breeding colony of white pelicans in North America—up to 10,000 pairs—and many other birds, too. Visits are restricted during nesting season, but the spectacle can be viewed from a distance, and plans are under way for a visitor center and tour route. To arrange a visit, talk with Arrowwood refuge office.

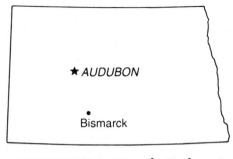

★ AUDUBON

•
Bismarck

AUDUBON (North Dakota)

In 1843 Audubon journeyed up the Missouri River to explore the native creatures of central North Dakota and make sketches for his paintings. This 14,735-acre refuge named for him is still superb habitat for water birds of all kinds. The rolling prairie is dotted with pothole ponds dating from the last glacier.

The 11,000-acre lake in the refuge holds more than 120 islands, beautiful against the sparkling blue water and harboring thousands of nesting birds.

Audubon Refuge includes the south side of Lake Audubon while the state fish and game land are on the north—both established as mitigation for wildlife habitat destroyed by construction of the Garrison Dam. Mitigation work for a later irrigation project, the Garrison Diversion Irrigation Project, is ongoing in the form of riprapping islands and building shoreline marshes.

Giant Canada geese—largest race of this handsome bird—were believed extinct until a sizable group was rediscovered on a pond in Rochester, Minnesota, in 1962. Audubon Refuge is one of the places where they were first returned to North Dakota, successfully propagated, and the young released back into the wild. Now they are plentiful and visitors can see them nesting each spring along the eight-mile auto-tour route in predator-proof nesting structures.

Other nesters include western and pied-billed grebes, avocets, marbled godwits, Wilson's phalaropes, great blue herons, cormorants, rails, black and common terns, and 11 kinds of ducks.

Several of the green, moundlike islands are dotted in spring with white birds—nesting California and ring-billed gulls (take a spotting scope for a better look).

White pelicans visit in summer. Migrating shorebirds may drop down by the thousands on mudflats, including endangered piping plovers that also nest. Sandhill cranes circle and bugle in fall, and sometimes hundreds stop to rest and feed. Ducks peak at 35,000 in October, geese at 40,000, and bald eagles are not far behind, preying on weak or injured ones.

Red foxes sometimes den near the tour route road. Richardson's ground squirrels, aptly called "flickertails," scurry around headquarters, where some of the best small birding is also in the shelterbelts of trees and shrubs that shield against the strong winds.

The grasslands are fascinating, too. Ring-necked pheasants cackle. Marbled godwits call *"godwit! raddica-raddica!"* as they take wing. Birders can find chestnut-collared longspurs, upland sandpipers, lark buntings, vesper, clay-colored, and often Baird's sparrows, yellow warblers, and marsh wrens. Wildflowers bloom from early spring— pasqueflowers, blazing stars, purple coneflowers, and pincushion cacti suggest the great variety.

A fine way to experience the prairie is to leave your car and sit quietly on a hilltop on a calm morning (or dusk) and wait for the wildlife to visit YOU—an unwary deer grazing, a snipe winnowing, or coyotes yipping.

How to get there: From Minot go south 46 miles on Highway 83, then east at refuge sign .7 mile on gravel road to headquarters.

Open: Daylight hours; office 8–4:30 weekdays. Tour route open every day except afternoons only during fall waterfowl hunting season.

What to see: Pelicans, waterfowl, shorebirds, white-tailed deer, bald eagles in late fall.

What to do: Eight miles of roads for driving, hiking (with sturdy shoes, hike off roads, too).

Where to stay: Motels—Garrison, 12 miles northwest; Underwood, 12 miles south. Campgrounds—Fort Stevenson State Park, 15 miles northwest; Lake Sakakawea State Park, 19 miles southwest; others in Garrison reservoir area.

Weather: Winters harsh, roads often impassable.

Points of interest nearby: Fort Mandan, Lewis and Clark campsite, 20 miles south; Garrison Dam National Fish Hatchery, 14 miles southwest; Garrison dam and dam outwash, 12 miles southwest, for winter eagle-watching; Lake Sakakawea shoreline, nesting piping plovers.

For more information: Audubon National Wildlife Refuge, Route 1, Box 16, Coleharbor, North Dakota 58531. Phone: (701) 442–5474.

Audubon also administers *Lake Ilo* Refuge near Dunn Center, which is completely different—more like an Old West range land, with golden eagle and pronghorn antelope habitat surrounding a lake that was drawn down when its dam was found to be hazardous. Since then waterbird use has burgeoned. Endangered piping plovers have nested and endangered whooping cranes have visited, among others. Significant archeological sites have been discovered. A new environmental study will determine the future use of this interesting small refuge. For details consult the Audubon office.

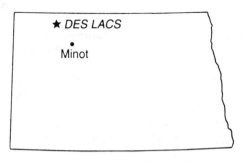

★ *DES LACS*

•
Minot

DES LACS (North Dakota)

A quarter-million snow geese fly up in swirling white clouds calling tumultuously against a backdrop of golden leaves here in fall. In spring, sharp-tailed grouse stomp about and inflate lavender gular sacs to attract females on their courting grounds.

Flocks of several hundred white pelicans stay until fall, coursing back and forth in breathtaking formations, dipping and rising in long columns behind the lead bird.

Descendants of a captive flock of Giant Canada geese raise families in 100 or so flax bales in the marsh that turn out to be waterfowl apartment houses when mallards nest simultaneously in hollows in the side. (Hundreds of these have been placed on private land for farmers who wish to provide nest facilities on their own wetlands.)

In fact, one hardly knows where to start with the abundance of wildlife riches, and especially birds, at this 19,544-acre refuge of lake and marsh, mixed prairie grass and woodland following along the Des Lacs River north to the Canadian border, from ice breakup in April until winter closes in again in November.

The approach to the refuge from the tiny town of Kenmare gives a springtime hint: ruddy ducks bobbing bright blue bills in courtship display; mallard, scaup, canvasback, and redhead ducks incubating eggs nearby; handsome western grebes, nicknamed "swan grebes" for their grace, preparing for the water ballets with which they woo their mating partners.

Visitors can watch the sharp-tailed grouse in their mating displays from blinds on two of the 30 or so leks (courting grounds). Reserve ahead and arrive before dawn while coyotes are still howling and great horned owls still hooting.

Several hundred whistling swans stop by in spring and fall, and, rarely, a half-dozen majestic endangered whooping cranes.

Ducks of a dozen or so species go through in fall, peaking at 25,000 or so, followed by golden and bald eagles who feed on the weak and stragglers; and 50,000 come by in spring and wait until ice breaks up to continue farther north to nest.

Birders almost certainly can add Sprague's pipits and LeConte's and Baird's

308

sparrows to their list. They are common, along with Bohemian waxwings, Wilson's phalaropes, and raucous black-billed magpies all year.

Of the more than 250 species on the bird list, at least 140 have nested, some in great numbers. They include three other grebe species, 16 kinds of ducks, black-crowned night herons, upland sandpipers, Wilson's phalaropes, avocets, Franklin's gulls, black terns, gray partridges, and red-tailed, Cooper's, and Swainson's hawks.

In addition, the Audubon Christmas Bird Count usually turns up redpolls, horned larks, snow buntings, pine and evening grosbeaks, and sometimes a goshawk, hoary redpoll, or snowy owl.

Visitors on the trails early and late will probably see white-tailed deer and quite likely coyotes and snowshoe hares, possibly even a bobcat or red fox.

But most visitors come here for birds of a water orientation, and go on to Lostwood for wildlife of the prairie.

How to get there: From Minot go north on Route 52 to Kenmare, then west on County Road 1-A, 1.5 miles to headquarters.

Open: Daylight hours (closed briefly for sanctuary during hunting). Office 8–4:30 weekdays.

Best times to visit: Spring, summer, fall.

What to see: Waterfowl, sharp-tailed grouse, pelicans, shorebirds, deer, raptors, Sprague's pipits, Baird's and LeConte's sparrows.

What to do: Fifteen miles of roads for driving, hiking; roads not plowed in winter but open then to snowshoeing, cross-country skiing; blinds for viewing, photography; canoeing on calm mornings and evenings can be beautiful (bring your own canoe); Tasker's Coulee Recreation Area, picnicking, comanaged with Kenmare city parks.

Where to stay: Motels—in Kenmare, or wider selection in Minot. Campgrounds—in Kenmare and Bowbells, 16 miles west.

Weather: Winters severe (yearly temperatures can range from 40 below to 105 above).

Points of interest nearby: Lostwood, Salyer, Upper Souris National Wildlife Refuges (see these listings).

For more information: Des Lacs National Wildlife Refuge, P.O. Box 578, Kenmare, North Dakota 58746. Phone: (701) 385–4046.

Lostwood, administered from Des Lacs but with its own manager, is a gem—a unique area of almost 27,000 acres of beautiful, wild, remote prairie grasslands spotted with some 4,000 sparkling blue glacial lakes and potholes, becoming known worldwide as a birding hotspot. Species rare elsewhere are seen easily here— grasshopper and Baird's sparrows, Sprague's pipits, and others. It has the highest per-acre population of sharp-tailed grouse anywhere, with a blind (reserve ahead) near one of the 35–40 spring dancing grounds where visitors can hear males "wooing" females and watch them dance and click their tail feathers.

One of the highest nesting populations of Wilson's phalaropes is here; also several pairs of threatened piping plovers, along with marbled godwits and upland sandpipers.

Originally bison and natural wildfires maintained the native prairie habitat. Now this effect is replicated by carefully controlled fires and planned grazing that have increased nesting of Baird's sparrows, pipits, and sharp-tailed grouse, among others.

Eared grebes with golden mating headgear are here in great numbers. So are avocets, willets, and a dozen or more duck species.

Nesting raptors include northern harriers, red-tailed and sometimes Swainson's and ferruginous hawks, and short-eared owls. White pelicans visit in warm months. Tundra swans and sandhill cranes stop by in migration. Up to 30,000 snow geese are here for about two weeks in October. Migrating peregrine falcons come by in May, and gyrfalcon and snowy owl sightings are rare winter treats.

The beauty of this wild place can hardly be described. Going along the roads or trails in early spring, the air is filled with waterbirds calling and circling over their new nesting territories. White-tailed deer and jackrabbits graze. Ground squirrels scurry about through a seasonal succession of wildflowers, from crimson prairie lilies to brilliant purple gayfeathers and blazing stars.

Atop a rise, the wind swirls the mixed needle and wheatgrass prairie like waves at sea, green in June, golden in late summer, and pink to purple in fall. Sudden prairie thunderstorms can send billowing dark clouds and lightning flashes, drop six inches of rain in an hour, sometimes hail, then leave bluebird skies again.

There is a seven-mile, self-guided auto-tour route and a seven-mile hiking trail. It's possible to hike off the road anywhere in the 5,577-acre wilderness area (but take a compass). In winter when there's snow, cross-country skiing and snowshoeing are lovely (but prepare for extreme cold, sometimes 70 below with windchill).

Lostwood is 18 miles west of Des Lacs, and can be reached from Kenmare via County Highway. To get there take Highway 2 to Stanley, then Highway 8 north 21 miles. The field station is open irregular weekday hours; write ahead to Route 2, Box 98, Kenmare, North Dakota 58746, or telephone (701) 848–2722.

Des Lacs also administers wetland management districts which include *Lake Zahl* and *Shell Lake* refuges. These contain varied wildlife, mostly of the wetland type, and limited visitor access. For information on arranging a visit, consult refuge head-quarters.

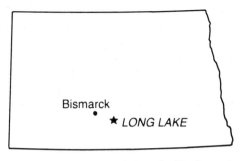

Bismarck
● ★ *LONG LAKE*

LONG LAKE (North Dakota)

The high resonant bugling of sandhill cranes fills the crisp, cool air every fall when up to 25,000 of these impressive birds stop over—along with flocks of waterfowl and others—at this 22,310-acre North Dakota refuge.

August to late November can be a wondrous time. First come thousands of rusty-hooded avocets, and tens of thousands of dowitchers, peeps, and other shorebirds, which gather on the mudflats from August to mid-September.

Then the great gray sandhills, standing four feet high with wingspreads up to seven feet, dominate the early dawn and sunset with the loud excitement of their comings and goings—sharing the refuge sometimes with 10,000 or so Franklin's gulls, 20,000 geese, mostly Canadas, and 40,000 ducks, mallards, wigeons, teals, and more than a dozen other species. Sometimes one or two endangered whooping cranes join them.

By late November they are gone—leaving the refuge to the thousands of ring-necked pheasants and white-tailed deer that are here all year, along with sharp-tailed grouse and horned larks plus occasional snowy owls that show up in the dead of winter.

The migrants go through in less spectacular groupings in spring. Male grouse gather on a courtship dancing ground where the refuge sets up a viewing/photography blind (reserve ahead). When there is ample water, western grebe couples dance graceful courtship ballets.

More than a dozen duck species, including canvasbacks, pintails, redheads, and ruddies, bring off families. There are handsome lark buntings, clay-colored sparrows, and sometimes northern orioles. Birders may find chestnut-collared and Lapland longspurs and others.

In recent years endangered piping plovers have nested. Black-crowned night herons prowl the water's edges at dusk and often have a rookery.

Picnickers have a fine view from a butte overlooking the west end of the refuge and the mixed prairie and rolling hills alongside it.

Photographers can set up temporary blinds with permission. Ask refuge staff where wildlife have been seen lately and they will often permit hiking in closed areas. Be sure to report afterward what you have seen.

This refuge was established around this long shallow lake—now divided in sections—to solve a botulism sickness among waterfowl. There has been partial success, but a lack of water management capability on the lake itself prevents total control of the disease.

How to get there: From Bismarck take I-94 east to Sterling exit, then Highway 83 11 miles south through Moffit, turn east at refuge sign.

Open: Refuge—daylight hours (much of the refuge can be seen from public roads open 24 hours—listen for coyotes at dusk). Office—7:30–4 weekdays.

Best times to visit: August-November for spectacular fall migrants.

What to see: Sandhill cranes, pheasants, deer, waterfowl and shorebirds, Franklin's gulls, sharp-tailed grouse.

What to do: Wildlife viewing; photography; picnicking.

Where to stay: Motels—Bismarck, 35 miles west, or Steel, 30 miles northeast. Campgrounds—in Bismarck.

For more information: Long Lake National Wildlife Refuge, R.R. 1, Box 23, Moffit, North Dakota 58560. Phone: (701) 387–4397.

Long Lake also administers 72 waterfowl production areas that are open to the public—consult the office on how to visit. It also administers two satellite refuges, *Slade* and *Florence Lake,* with geese, waterfowl, and deer; closed to the public but permission to visit can sometimes be arranged.

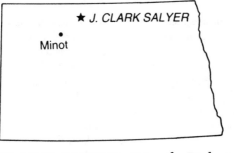

J. CLARK SALYER (North Dakota)

This refuge has one of the nation's richest and most exciting bird populations from spring to fall. More than 250 species have been noted here, ranging from sharp-tailed grouse on their dancing grounds in spring to Swainson's hawks in great numbers in fall—sometimes 150 in a single field in late September, to water birds of all kinds, including five species of nesting grebes, and small birds rare elsewhere, such as Sprague's pipits and Baird's and LeConte's sparrows.

More than 125 species nest, some in great numbers—up to 17,000 Franklin's gulls and colonies of hundreds of double-crested cormorants and great blue and black-crowned night herons. An average year produces more than 18,000 ducklings—pintails, mallards, gadwalls, and others.

White pelicans are here all summer, and thousands of sandhill cranes and whistling swans go through in migration.

The reason for all this is clear from a look at this 58,693-acre north-central North Dakota refuge with its tremendous diversity of habitat—36,000 acres of native and introduced grasslands, dense nesting cover and thick woodlands, together with one of the outstanding waterfowl marshes in the Central Flyway winding along 55 miles of river bends and oxbows north to the Canadian border.

Fall often is spectacular, beginning with migrating shorebirds—northern phalaropes abundant, along with least, pectoral, and semipalmated sandpipers, yellowlegs, and others. Later there can be up to 150,000 geese—snows, white-fronts, and Canadas—and nearly a quarter of a million ducks of more than a dozen species. Aerial views then remind the visitor of olden times with seemingly countless birds in the air, on land and water, every place the eye can see.

Lapland longspurs are common nesters, as are upland sandpipers, avocets, marbled godwits, Wilson's phalaropes, northern harriers, and, among smaller birds, lark buntings, least flycatchers, northern orioles, and an unusally fine array of sparrows. Common all year are sharp-tailed grouse (with two dozen dancing grounds on the refuge), gray partridges, horned larks, black-billed magpies, and in winter redpolls (with occasional hoaries), snow buntings, and Bohemian waxwings. Hikers on the Sandhills Walk on spring mornings will hear ruffed grouse drumming and wild turkeys gobbling. Bald and golden eagles may be around at any time.

This refuge is a prime example of land restoration after drainage, drought, poor farm practices, and market hunting left it close to a wildlife desert when it was acquired in 1935. Nesting islands were built, the marsh restored, and vegetation offering food and cover was reintroduced.

The visitor can see all this along with white-tailed deer, coyotes, beavers, minks, foxes, and others of the mammal population from two excellent trails (look down at and through the grasses for a botanist's trove of interesting plants) and a fine five-to-thirteen-mile canoe route.

The refuge was named after J. Clark Salyer II, an early leader in establishing the national wildlife refuge system. Both are honored thereby.

How to get there: From Minot take Route 83 north 25 miles to Upham turnoff, then east 27 miles (partly graveled road) to Upham, then Route 14 north two miles to headquarters.

Open: 5 a.m. to 10 p.m. daily. Office 8–4:30 weekdays.

Best times to visit: Spring through fall.

What to see: Migrating and breeding waterfowl; wild turkeys; sharp-tailed and ruffed grouse; shorebirds; white pelicans; Sprague's pipits; Baird's and LeConte's sparrows; deer.

What to do: 27 miles of auto-tour routes; canoe trail (rentals in Minot); whole sandhill area open to hiking. Photography—reserve ahead for blind on dancing ground or to put up portable blind. Fishing can be good for walleye and northern pike.

Where to stay: Motel—at Westhope, adjacent on north; Bottineau, 27 miles northeast; Minot, 50 miles southwest. Campgrounds—in Towner; Bottineau City Park (trailers); county park west of Bottineau; Upham City Park; and Lake Metigoshe State Park, 43 miles northeast.

Points of interest nearby: Lake Metigoshe (see Campgrounds); International Peace Garden, 58 miles northeast; Upper Souris National Wildlife Refuge, 50 miles west.

For more information: J. Clark Salyer National Wildlife Refuge, Box 66, Upham, North Dakota 58789. Phone: (701) 768–2548.

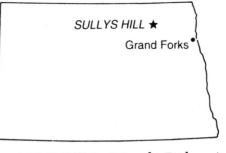

SULLYS HILL ★
Grand Forks

SULLYS HILL (North Dakota)

Sullys Hill is one of the oldest refuges in the United States, set aside by President Theodore Roosevelt in 1904 when the buffalo, once one of the most numerous hooved animals in the world, had been driven to the edge of extinction.

By 1917 nucleus groups of six buffalos, fifteen elk, and four white-tailed deer were introduced, all of which had disappeared from the area. All have flourished and can be seen from May 1 to October 31 along the auto-tour route, as can a sizable "town" of frisky black-tailed prairie dogs, these, too, persecuted and driven from much of their historic western range.

Sullys Hill is becoming a well-known birding refuge as well, with good numbers of water, shore, and marsh birds of all kinds along the shores of 12-acre Sweetwater Lake and on Devils Lake adjoining the refuge. There are snow and blue geese—up to 250,000 in fall migration—white pelicans in all the warm months, double-crested cormorants sharing rocky nesting islands with Canada geese, and some of the various nesting ducks, including shovelers, mallards, gadwalls, blue-winged teal, pintails, mergansers, and beautiful wood ducks that use boxes put out by the refuge.

Bitterns, grebes, godwits, and great blue and black-crowned night herons are here as well—the lake shore can be alive with birds on early spring and summer mornings—and a representative group of all the wildlife can be seen at a feeding area where grain is put out daily for a captive flock of Giant Maxima Canada geese (their young are free to join wild flocks) plus waterfowl that have been injured and are no longer able to fly, including several tundra swans. Wild turkeys and deer often show up. It is a fine photographic spot.

There is also a bluebird trail, and one of the area's most impressive migrations of small birds, especially warblers, through the woods, grasslands, and brushy areas of this 1,674 acres of rolling glacial moraine in northeast North Dakota. On a good day in May an observant birder can sit quietly in one spot with binoculars and count 40 species without moving: magnolia, prothonotary, black-throated blue and black-and-white warblers, tree swallows, fox sparrows, vireos, and others, many of which nest as well. (Refuge staff often can suggest where to find particular species such as piping plovers, bank swallows, and others either on or off refuge.)

But it is the four-footed creatures that attract most summer visitors when young animals come into view in late spring and early summer and when bison contend for mates in late summer, pawing the ground and assuming threatening stances, while elk bugle in calls that can be heard for miles.

The auto-tour route closes in winter months when weather often is poor and terrain impassable. Roads are not maintained and the animals are allowed to roam freely. Access can sometimes be arranged by scheduling well ahead, depending on staff availability and weather conditions.

But the nature trail is always open, with excellent birding all along Sweetwater Lake and on a boardwalk through the wetlands. Birdwatchers are allowed to walk in before the 8 a.m. opening during prime warbler days.

A dozen or more eagles, mostly bald but some golden, begin to appear with the waterfowl in fall and stay until freeze-up. Even in winter horned larks, redpolls, gray partridge, Lapland longspurs, and occasional snowy owls and golden eagles are here.

How to get there: From Devils Lake take Highway 57 south 13 miles to Fort Totten, then follow refuge signs one mile east.

Open: 8 a.m. to sunset May to October. Auto tour closes down then but headquarters area, picnic area, and nature trail open all year.

Best times to visit: Spring through fall.

What to see: Bison, elk, white-tailed deer, prairie dogs, wild turkeys, variety of water-oriented birdlife as well as passerines.

What to do: Four-mile auto-tour route with scenic overlooks (closed in winter); nature trail; picnicking; photography; snowshoeing and cross-country skiing in winter. Fishing can be good in Devils Lake just off refuge for walleyes, northerns, white bass.

Where to stay: Motels—Devils Lake, 13 miles northeast. Campgrounds—many surrounding Devils Lake, both private and state parks.

Weather: Winters bitterly cold.

Points of interest nearby: Fort Totten State Historic Site, one mile west.

For more information: Sullys Hill National Game Preserve, Devils Lake Wetland Management District, Box 908, Devils Lake, North Dakota 58301. Phone: (701) 766–4272 or (701) 662–8611.

Sullys Hill is administered from the Devils Lake Wetland Management District, which also manages 41,000 acres on 190 Waterfowl Production Areas and 150,000 acres of wetland easements in eight counties—natural areas maintained for waterfowl production, the former open to the public but with few facilities besides parking. For more information contact the district office, P.O. Box 908, Devils Lake, North Dakota 58301. Phone: (701) 662–8611.

Lake Alice Refuge, 11,335 acres, is also administered from this office. It has an observation tower with spectacular views of migratory waterfowl concentrations. When water conditions are right, it is one of the area's best duck nesting marshes. Otherwise few facilities besides parking. Check with office before planning a visit.

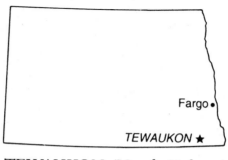

Fargo •

TEWAUKON ★

TEWAUKON (North Dakota)

The constant calls and gabbling conversation of migrating birds here in fall—higher-pitched by geese, low murmurs punctuated by strident quacking by ducks—and the gale-force sound of their thousands of wing beats can overwhelm the senses. There is no visible end to the flocks both in the air and on the water when their populations peak in October.

It is equally so in spring—although less spectacular because snowmelt and other moisture fill wetlands to the brim and birds fan out over a wider area. There may be up to 100,000 ducks and similar crowds of snow and Canada geese in the area—birds from both Mississippi and Central Flyways.

Coming in as well may be 8,500 tundra swans and 1,000 or so white pelicans, and sometimes 200,000 Franklin's and ring-billed gulls—white birds everywhere.

Snow geese move on to summer breeding grounds near the Arctic Circle but many other waterfowl stay and nest. Tewaukon is perfect habitat, 8,363 acres of native prairie grassland, marsh, and wetland with over 100 bodies of water ranging from small clay-bottomed glacial potholes to 1,200-acre Lake Tewaukon.

In spring each pothole may have a brightly colored courting pair of ducks—or several, of different species: shovelers, mallards, pintails, redheads, canvasbacks, blue-winged teal, and others.

Western grebes patter across the water's surface in graceful courtship ballets. Dull-colored male phalaropes, reversing usual sex roles, incubate eggs while the bright females whirl about to stir up water organisms. Up to 700 double-crested cormorants may nest colonially, their roosts visible from refuge roads.

And there are great blue, green-backed, and black-crowned night herons, black terns, bitterns, Virginia rails, and in the grasslands bobolinks, dickcissels, upland sandpipers, chestnut-collared longspurs, and an assortment of sparrows, including vesper, clay-colored, lark, Savannah, and a few LeConte's. Swainson's and red-tailed hawks nest.

Sandpipers stop in spring and again on the mudflats heading south in August—commonly Baird's, least, pectoral, and white-rumped.

Pheasants, gray partridges, horned larks, and great horned owls are around all year. So are white-tailed deer, appearing with spotted fawns in May. Beavers sun themselves on domed lodges. Thirteen-lined ground squirrels are omnipresent as are little Franklin's and Richardson's ground squirrels—the latter North Dakota's state animal, their shorter tails held erect, giving them the nickname "flickertail."

Red foxes sometimes den near the road and may be spotted streaking across a field after rodents (for recent sightings of these and others, ask at headquarters).

Beautiful wood ducks gather in colorful flocks of up to 100 in fall. A notable migration of bald eagles takes place in spring and fall—sometimes 17 are seen in a single tree in October.

Winters can be so harsh that almost everything hibernates or flies away. But heavy snows can bring herds of 1,000 or so deer to feed on the refuge, and hardy souls can usually find Lapland longspurs, snow buntings, redpolls, Bohemian waxwings, and perhaps a snowy owl.

Also administered from Tewaukon are Waterfowl Production Areas and small easement refuges that serve as valuable wildlife nesting and resting areas. Ask at the office for information on how to visit these.

How to get there: From Fargo take I-29 south to Highway 11 exit, then west 28 miles to Cayuga and south six miles on Sargent County Road 12 to headquarters.

Open: Sunrise to 10 p.m. daily. Office/Visitor Center 8–4:30 weekdays. Portions of the refuge are closed to the public. Detailed public-use information is available at the Visitor Center kiosk when the center is closed.

What to see: Water birds; deer; beavers; eagles; native prairie vegetation; Indian burial mounds.

What to do: 11 miles of roads and trails including interpretive drive and walk; picnic area; photography (temporary blinds by permit); fishing good seasonally for northern and walleyed pike.

Where to stay: Motels—Lidgerwood and Milnor. Campgrounds—Silver Lake County Park, 11 miles west, and Forman City Park.

Points of interest nearby: Tewaukon State Game Management Area, adjoining on north; Sheyenne National Grasslands, 25 miles north.

For more information: Tewaukon National Wildlife Refuge, R.R. 1, Box 75, Cayuga, North Dakota 58013. Phone: (701) 724–3598.

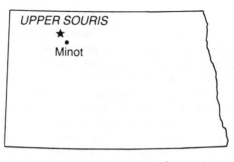

UPPER SOURIS
★
• Minot

UPPER SOURIS (North Dakota)

Great horned owls hoot and coyotes yip in the sharply cool predawn April air—
spring comes late on this 32,000-acre refuge of lakes, marsh, prairie, and
woodlands extending over 30 miles along the Souris River, which loops down from
Canada. But soon the action unfolds and a dozen or more male sharp-tailed grouse
are stomping about—"dancing"—and inflating lavender throat sacs in guttural calls
audible to any female within a half mile.

It is one of the wildlife spectaculars here—indeed like nothing else in nature—
but it is far from the only one.

More than a quarter-million geese gather in fall, mostly snows but also Canadas
and white-fronted, flying back and forth like great roaring clouds of birds that can
be almost deafening to an onlooker on the shoreline. Eagles follow them, and 50,000
ducks that also come through, and prey on weaker ones. A half-dozen or so bald
and golden eagles are here during spring and fall.

Birders come to add Baird's and LeConte's sparrows and Sprague's pipits to their
lists—but there is more. The bird list has more than 250 species, of which 150 are
known to nest, including five species of grebes, Wilson's phalaropes, marbled godwits,
avocets, 17 kinds of ducks, and cormorants and great blue and black-crowned night
herons in several colonies. More than 3,000 ducklings are produced yearly.

Upper Souris may be the prettiest of the "Souris Loop" national wildlife refuges
located on or near the Souris or Mouse River, which got its name from the great
numbers of mice that early French fur trappers saw here (the others are Des Lacs,
Salyer, and Lostwood). Upper Souris's wildlife trail winds over softly rolling hills,
green and sprinkled with wildflowers when the prairie awakens in spring, with long
vistas of sparkling pools interspersed with golden marsh vegetation.

Visitors may spot some of the mammal population as well—white-tailed deer,
porcupines, minks, foxes, beavers, plus the engaging "flickertail" or Richardson's
ground squirrel, North Dakota's state mammal. Even elk, antelope, and moose are
seen on rare occasions. In fall the wooded coulees turn brilliant yellow.

White pelicans are here all summer. Hundreds of tundra swans go through in spring and fall, and sometimes thousands of sandhill cranes, though the latter are more often seen overhead than on the ground. Raptors, perhaps because of the rodents, are common—Swainson's and red-tailed hawks, northern harriers, rough-legged hawks in fall, and occasional prairie and gyrfalcons. Short-eared owls hunt in late afternoons.

Volunteers are welcome to help with nest drag studies in May and June, spotting and recording data on nesting harriers, partridges, grouse, upland sandpipers, ducks, and others. Contact the refuge ahead. Volunteers can also participate in the Christmas Bird Count each December, when snowy owls, snow buntings, northern shrikes, Bohemian waxwings, and common redpolls are likely sightings, with hoary redpolls present some years.

Photoblinds are available on three of 25 or so grouse leks, or dancing grounds, in April; reserve three weeks ahead to be sure of space.

Anyone wishing information on North Dakota birding would do well to contact the state's premier birder, Dr. Gordon Berkey at Minot State University, who assembled the refuge bird list (Phone: (701) 857–3078 [office] or 838–1513 [home]).

How to get there: From Minot take Route 83 north about 15 miles, then west on County Road 6 (marked Lake Darling) for 12 miles to headquarters.

Open: 5 a.m.–10 p.m. daily. Office 8–4:30 weekdays except holidays.

Best times to visit: Spring and fall.

What to see: Sharp-tailed grouse; waterfowl concentrations; tundra swans; white pelicans; Baird's and LeConte's sparrows, Sprague's pipits.

What to do: Self-guided auto tour route; six miles of roads for driving; hiking; photography; picnicking; canoeing; boat and shore fishing can be excellent for northern and walleyed pike, smallmouth bass; cross-country skiing and snow-shoeing when there's enough snow.

Weather: Spring and fall can be cool, cloudy, windy; winters harsh, with roads impassable.

Points of interest nearby: Theodore Roosevelt National Park, 100 miles southwest; Lake Metigoshe State Park, 90 miles northeast; J. Clark Salyer National Wildlife Refuge, 55 miles east, and Des Lacs National Wildlife Refuge, 35 miles northwest (see individual entries).

For more information: Upper Souris National Wildlife Refuge, R.R. 1, Box 163, Foxholm, North Dakota 58738. Phone: (701) 468–5467.

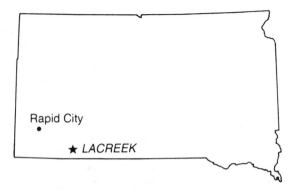

Rapid City
•

★ *LACREEK*

LACREEK (South Dakota)

Glistening white trumpeter swans, largest North American waterfowl and once close to extinction, nest here and demonstrate their majestic strength and beauty in territorial and courtship displays from November to May.

Pair-bonded for life, they preen and greet one another with showy wingflapping and resonant honks that can be heard for a half mile or more. They are seen most easily in winter when they gather in deep open water near refuge headquarters, sometimes 200 or more in March; then they fan out to nest in the Nebraska sandhills and western South Dakota. They are secretive and require large breeding territories. In June, they reappear with cygnets—refuge staff can sometimes direct visitors where.

There is much else as well on this 16,410 acres of marsh and grassland at the edge of the rolling sandhills of southwest South Dakota. Lacreek is one of the richest areas in bird life in the country. And perhaps because of its remote location, most of the wildlife, including the mammals, is highly visible. It is hard to imagine going through the auto tour or hiking around without interesting sightings.

Magnificent white pelicans, whose nine-foot wingspreads exceed the trumpeters' by only a little, pack together—a spectacular sight—on two small islands, their 2,500 or so nests within a few inches of each other, at one of the few places in the United States where they breed.

Their nests sometimes are intermingled with those of double-crested cormorants and great blue herons, and are preceded in early spring by Canada geese of the Giant race, a grouping once thought extinct, which also sometimes use muskrat or beaver lodges as nesting structures.

American bitterns, shy denizens of the high marsh grass, are so abundant here that visitors with a sharp eye can easily spot them.

Nesting of water birds of all kinds is phenomenal. Up to 10,000 young ducks can be produced in a year—mostly blue-winged teal but also mallard, pintail, redhead, gadwall, wigeon, green-winged teal and canvasback. There are nesting Virginia and sora rails, Forster's and black terns, avocets, coots, western grebes, and black-crowned night herons.

The grasslands are equally productive with breeding long-billed curlews, upland sandpipers, thousands of ring-necked pheasants (a single photograph once included 137 of these striking birds), and sharp-tailed grouse, which tend to relocate their courtship and dancing grounds from year to year.

Northern harriers, Swainson's, and a few ferruginous hawks nest as do great horned owls, burrowing owls (many in prairie dog holes), and short-eared owls— a dozen or so are sometimes hunting low over fields on late fall afternoons.

Handsome lark buntings are abundant; so are yellow warblers and cliff swallows, which build solid mud dwellings on headquarters buildings and bridges.

Sandhill cranes go through in migration, sometimes dropping down to spend a week or two in October in huge numbers—up to 12,000. A dozen bald and golden eagles spend the winter feeding on fish, weakened waterfowl, and various creatures that perish during the harsh winters.

Mule and white-tailed deer including bucks with impressive racks browse, and does bring out spotted fawns in June. One can hear and often see coyotes in early morning and evening. Muskrats and beavers build marsh lodges. Black-tailed prairie dogs have a 15-acre colony along the auto-tour route. The tiny swift fox, once feared extinct, now lives here in small numbers.

How to get there: From Rapid City take I-90 east to Kadoka exit, then Highway 73 south to Highway 18, east two miles on 18 to refuge sign, south four miles on gravel road to Tuthill and west one mile to refuge entrance.

Open: Sunrise-sunset daily. Office 7–3:30 weekdays.

What to see: Trumpeter swans, white pelicans, Canada geese, sharp-tailed grouse, waterfowl, short-eared owls, deer, prairie dogs, sandhill plant associations— many others.

What to do: 12 miles of roads for driving, hiking; self-guided tours; observation tower; photography (permits may be granted for temporary blinds); picnicking; fishing, especially through winter ice for northern pike. Refuge staff are helpful in directing visitors with special objectives.

Where to stay: Motels—in Martin. Campgrounds—in Martin, also (primitive) at Little White River Recreation Area on refuge.

Weather: Blizzards and severe cold in winter; roads may be muddy spring and fall— check ahead for conditions.

Points of interest nearby: Bowring Ranch Nebraska State Park, 15 miles south, restored pioneer ranch; Wounded Knee National Historic Site, 30 miles west; Badlands National Monument, 60 miles northwest; Fort Niobrara National Wildlife Refuge, 70 miles southeast.

For more information: Lacreek National Wildlife Refuge, HWC 3, Box 14, Martin, South Dakota 57551. Phone: (605) 685–6508.

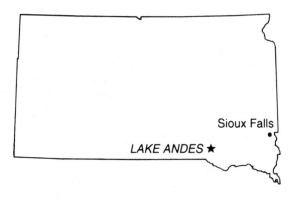

Sioux Falls
•

LAKE ANDES ★

LAKE ANDES (South Dakota)

With one powerful swoop a bald eagle deftly plucks a walleyed pike from the tailwaters of the Missouri River below Randall Dam and rises to consume its catch in a tall cottonwood tree—a thrilling winter sight in and around Lake Andes and adjacent Karl Mundt Refuge.

Tens of thousands of waterfowl gather in spring and fall. Up to 3,000 white pelicans may be here in April and May, some staying the summer, traversing the refuge in waves of undulating flight on nine-foot wingspreads, later packing into tight islands of shining white on the water.

Iridescent ring-necked pheasants cackle in every field, gathering in flocks of several thousand in fall on the Owens Bay tract.

White-tailed deer drop spotted fawns in May, and bucks hold impressive racks of antlers above the marsh grass later (identify less common mule deer by their bigger ears and bouncier lope).

Red foxes sometimes den alongside the road. Coyotes track small prey through the grasslands. More secretive but here, too, are badgers, raccoons, and opossums.

Lake Andes is a natural prairie lake dependent on snowmelt and rainfall runoff, which is cyclical. Every 20 years it is dry. Wildlife varies depending on conditions.

Eagle concentrations occur from November to mid-February in and around Lake Andes and adjacent Karl Mundt Refuge. There can be up to 100 birds (there have been as many as 280) feeding around Lake Francis Case and the spillway of the Fort Randall dam on fish and on weak or injured waterfowl.

The waterfowl themselves are a stunning sight—and sound—sometimes almost 200,000 of them in the Lake Andes area, the 70,000 or so geese mostly Canadas with some white-fronted and snows, the 100,000 ducks mostly mallards with some teal, wigeon, pintails, and others, filling the air with their calls and whirring wings when they take off at dawn to go out to feed and return again at dusk.

325

All are in fine view from several points about the water areas.

The eagles spend the night on the Mundt Refuge, established specifically as an eagle roost and sanctuary on land bought with funds from public sale of endangered-species drinking cups in a "Save a Living Thing Project." It is closed to public use because roosting eagles are so sensitive to disturbance. But a public road bisects it from which visitors can sometimes see the eagles as well as deer, wild turkeys, prairie-chickens, sharp-tailed grouse, quail, and others. The adjacent Corps of Engineers park and nature trail also affords excellent sightings.

In wet years not only waterfowl but tundra swans stop at Lake Andes in migration, and there are bitterns, pied-billed grebes, cormorants, great blue and black-crowned night herons, nesting yellowlegs, and spotted and upland sandpipers.

There are in all years northern harriers coursing over the grasslands, Swainson's, red-tailed and rough-legged hawks, red-headed woodpeckers, and dickcissels. A delightful nature trail winds through marsh, woods, brush, prairie, and pothole ponds. Bobolinks call territorially. Great horned and screech owls take off from shelter belts at dusk. In wet years mallards, teal and redhead ducks nest and sedge and marsh wrens chatter from the cattails.

Lake Andes also administers over 110,000 acres of small parcels of natural prairie marsh and upland in 20 counties, acquired as Waterfowl Production Areas and owned or held in perpetual easement, supporting a varied wildlife and open to the public but with no facilities other than parking areas. Consult staff on how to arrange a visit.

How to get there: From Yankton take Highway 50 west to Lake Andes, go north past grain elevators one mile to unmarked paved road, east there six miles to refuge.

Open: Daylight hours. Office 8–4:30 weekdays.

Best times to visit: Spring and fall.

What to see: Eagles; waterfowl; deer.

What to do: Nature trail; photography; five miles of public roads for viewing.

Where to stay: Motels—Lake Andes, Wagner, Pickstown. Campgrounds—at Lake Francis Case, eight miles south.

Weather: Winter can be harsh with poor driving conditions; summers extremely hot.

Points of interest nearby: Fort Randall Dam and Lake Francis Case Recreation Area—eagle-viewing, various nature-oriented facilities—eight miles south; Gavins Point National Fish Hatchery at Yankton.

For more information: Lake Andes National Wildlife Refuge, R.R. 1, Box 77, Lake Andes, South Dakota 57356. Phone: (605) 487–7603.

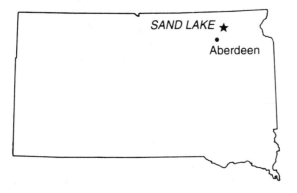

SAND LAKE ★
• Aberdeen

SAND LAKE (South Dakota)

About two million of the mid-continental population of snow geese come through Sand Lake in spring migration and sometimes almost half of them are here at once (1.2 million one recent spring)—a presence that overwhelms the senses. When a bald eagle makes a pass at the flock 80,000 may take off at once, filling the air with whirring white wings, the unison of their one-note calls a constant roar.

Tens of thousands of other water-oriented birds come through and many of them—more than 100 of the almost 250 bird species seen here—stay to nest on this 21,498-acre South Dakota refuge of marsh, lakes, prairie, and woodland, including Canada geese of the Giant race, ducks of 13 species, great blue and black-crowned night herons, double-crested cormorants, Forster's and black terns, and many others.

Handsome black-and-white western grebes with ruby eyes, called "swan grebes" for their grace, rise on webbed feet and perform courtship ballets and later carry downy young about on their backs (the youngsters hang on even when parents dive for food)—readily seen, along with golden-tufted eared grebes, from the Mud Lake spillway along Houghton Dam.

There are large colonies of great blue herons alongside the auto-tour route, snowy and cattle egrets, smaller numbers of white-faced ibis and others in tremendous colonies out in the marsh.

By fall, with both nesters and visitors heading south, there may be a half million Franklin's gulls, a quarter million mallard ducks, 5,000 or more tundra swans, and up to 12,000 white pelicans spiraling upward in great undulating flights, their nine-foot wingspreads glistening in the sun.

Sometimes it seems that if any more birds arrived they could not be accommodated. Indeed this wildlife oasis in a sea of intensive agricultural development illustrates the importance of such refuges. Without it much of the marvelous wildlife here simply could not continue.

Sand Lake exemplifies as well a new nongame species emphasis. There is a trail of bluebird nest boxes; also nesting upland sandpipers, marbled godwits, avocets, phalaropes, marsh wrens, orchard and northern orioles, swallows, horned larks, dickcissels—and among the predators, four owls—screech, great horned, burrowing, and long-eared—and seven hawks, the Swainson's, sharp-shinned, Cooper's, red-tailed, ferruginous, northern harriers, and kestrels.

Sometimes 20 species of warblers and altogether 60 kinds of songbirds can be spotted in shrubby wooded areas at the height of passerine migration in May.

Ring-necked pheasants cackle in the fields. White-tailed deer show off spotted fawns in early summer—mostly twin sets here—and almost every small watering area has a den of red foxes. Badgers are plentiful but shyer.

Sand Lake has been so successful in reproducing Giant Canada geese, a separate race once thought extinct, that a captive flock in a pond near headquarters reproduces young that are transported to start new flocks elsewhere.

Appearance of many species such as shorebirds depends on water conditions. Less rainfall and mudflats attract thousands of shorebirds; more water enhances nesting conditions for others.

Up to 200 eagles, mostly bald with some golden, are usually here fall through spring. Winter brings Lapland longspurs, snow buntings, Bohemian waxwings, and usually a snowy owl or two.

How to get there: From Aberdeen take U.S. 12 east eight miles, then north 20 miles on County Road 16 to refuge sign.

Open: Daylight hours. Office/Visitor Center 8–4:30 weekdays, open summer weekends (check hours).

What to see: Sometimes huge concentrations of various water-oriented birds, nesting and in migration in fall and especially spring; pheasant; deer; red foxes.

What to do: Self-guided auto tour and hiking trail; 40 miles open seasonally for driving, hiking, and in winter cross-country skiing (interior roads closed during fall hunting season and during harsh winter weather); observation tower; picnicking; photography.

Where to stay: Motels—In Aberdeen, also Hecla, just northeast of refuge, and Houghton, on the east. Campgrounds—Richmond Lake State Recreation Area, 25 miles west-southwest.

Weather: Winters harsh; even April can be cold and windy with poor road conditions.

Points of interest nearby: Sand Lake Recreation Area, adjacent; Ordway Prairie, owned by The Nature Conservancy, 35 miles west—a fascinating wildlife and habitat area; Dacotah Prairie Museum, Aberdeen; Waubay National Wildlife Refuge, 55 miles southeast.

For more information: Sand Lake National Wildlife Refuge, R.R. 1, Box 25, Columbia, South Dakota 57433. Phone: (605) 885–6320.

Sand Lake also administers:

Pocasse Refuge, 2,585 acres, mostly marsh and open water, just north of Pollock. Up to 10,000 sandhill cranes come through in spring and fall along with waterfowl, pelicans, and usually a few whooping cranes. Beavers and deer are also present. Route 10 bisects the refuge, which is open dawn to dusk.

Waterfowl Production Areas comprising more than 100 units of wetland habitat in nine counties totaling more than 200,000 acres are owned or under easement— natural areas maintained for waterfowl production, the former open to the public but with few visitor facilities besides parking. For more information ask at refuge office.

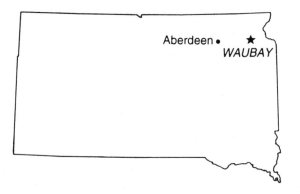

Aberdeen • ★
WAUBAY

WAUBAY (South Dakota)

Waubay in Sioux Indian language means "nesting place for birds," an apt designation for this lovely small refuge in the prairie pothole region of northeastern South Dakota since, of the almost 250 bird species that have been seen here, more than 100 are recorded as nesters.

These include two which are unusual in this latitude but present sometimes in fairly good numbers: the red-necked grebe and common goldeneye duck. Here is one of the southernmost breeding records for both of these handsome birds.

Four other grebes nest as well: the horned and eared, with golden ear tufts highlighting their breeding plumage; pied-billed; and the western, whose graceful courtship water ballets are often visible from refuge headquarters.

Secretive American bitterns nest in good numbers here—also double-crested cormorants, great blue and black-crowned night herons, Giant Canada geese, 15 species of ducks, and five kinds of hawks (the sharp-shinned, red-tailed, Cooper's, Swainson's, and northern harrier).

The reason for all this is the great variety of habitat, which includes two dozen ponds and lakes along with marsh, upland, and woods, a rarity in this area where prairie wildfires historically burned off all but the grasses. But here are not only tall cottonwoods and bur oaks but prickly ashes, ironwoods, and basswoods, some over a century old.

A bluebird trail winds through all the habitat types. Marbled godwits and upland sandpipers are common nesters; so are black terns, ring-necked pheasants, great horned owls, bobolinks, white-breasted nuthatches, three kinds of woodpeckers, clay-colored and vesper sparrows, yellow warblers, and small numbers of endangered piping plovers.

White-tailed deer bring out their fawns in June and young beavers and muskrats can sometimes be seen atop their domed houses. Thirteen-lined ground squirrels are everyplace. Richardson's and Franklin's ground squirrels prefer overgrazed grasslands and roadsides where they scamper about like miniature prairie dogs (Richardson's have short tails, Franklin's long).

Prairie bloom reaches a peak in August with Maximilian sunflowers, orange wood lilies, bottle gentians, and masses of goldenrod.

Migrations of waterfowl, shorebirds, and passerines can be interesting both spring and fall—in spring up to 300,000 snow geese are in the area, along with sandhill cranes and tundra swans. And there can be up to 20,000 ducks—blue-winged teals, gadwalls, redheads, shovelers—and 10,000 Giant and other Canada and greater white-fronted geese. Flocks of several dozen beautiful male wood ducks gather in nesting season. Diving ducks visit in late October—up to 25,000 ring-necks, scaup, and redheads, and sometimes 5,000 to 10,000 spectacular tundra swans.

By winter the birds have dwindled to a mere dozen or so species and refuge roads can have snowdrifts 25 feet deep. But for the hardy there are redpolls and snow buntings to see, along with Lapland longspurs, Bohemian waxwings, and sometimes a gray partridge or snowy owl.

Waubay also administers 39,000 acres of Waterfowl Production Areas in six counties, small tracts averaging 200 acres maintained for nesting habitat and largely as natural areas, open to the public but with few visitor facilities besides parking. For information on how to visit these, consult the refuge office.

How to get there: From Watertown take I-29 north 31 miles to Summit exit, then 11 miles west on Route 12 to County Road 1, and seven miles north there to refuge sign.

Open: Sunrise to sunset. Office/Visitor Center 8–4:30 weekdays, 11–5 Sundays, Memorial Day to Labor Day.

Best times to visit: March-April for spring migration, August-September for wildflowers and fall migration.

What to see: Giant Canada geese, grebes, deer, pheasants, bluebirds, wood ducks, and a variety of others.

What to do: 10 miles of public roads through refuge; self-guided walking trails; observation tower; picnicking; photography (consult staff about possibilities); cross-country ski trails.

Where to stay: Motels—Webster, 20 miles southwest. Campgrounds—Pickerel Lake State Park, five miles north; also Roy Lake State Park, 20 miles northeast.

Weather: Winters can be brutal, cold, snowy, roads blocked.

Points of interest nearby: Fort Sisseton State Park, 35 miles northwest, Sieche Hollow

State Park, 25 miles northeast (camping at these also); four good birding areas—
Rush Lake, eight miles south, Bitter Lake, 15 miles south, Hedke's Pass, five
miles southwest, Cormorant Island in South Waubay Lake. Also Blue Dog State
Fish Hatchery, five miles south.

For more information: Waubay National Wildlife Refuge, R.R. 1, P.O. Box 79, Waubay,
South Dakota 57273. Phone: (605) 947–4521.

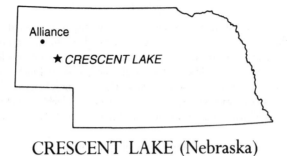

Alliance
★ CRESCENT LAKE

CRESCENT LAKE (Nebraska)

Once the sea washed over this wild and remote region and huge crocodiles lived here, and later camels and rhinoceros. Now it is one of our most interesting and beautiful refuges, where bald and golden eagles soar, and deer and pronghorn antelopes roam.

Trumpeter swans have nested. Sharp-tailed grouse display on their dancing grounds, and long-billed curlews and many others find sanctuary on this remote 45,818 acres in the rolling, grass-covered Nebraska sandhills, the largest continuous dune area in the western hemisphere.

Its moisture-retaining soil supports nutritious vegetation in meadows and marsh. Eighteen jewellike ponds and lakes, most of them surrounded by dense nesting cover, attract and support a widely varied wildlife population.

Male sharp-tailed grouse gather in spring to stomp about, inflate violet gular sacs, and throatily entreat mates on at least 41 known leks. A blind is located so visitors who reserve ahead can get a close look as well as take good pictures.

Upland sandpipers, with hearing so acute they are said to orient themselves to their nesting area by detecting surf vibrations from both Atlantic and Pacific oceans, are abundant. So are Wilson's phalaropes—but look for the brightly plumaged female bird because these reverse their sex roles. The males are dun-colored and incubate the eggs (sometimes 45,000 phalaropes are here in early May).

Long-billed curlews, showing reddish wing linings and greatly extended bills when they fly, breed commonly, as do avocets, striking black and white shorebirds with russet heads and necks in spring.

Eared grebes show up with golden ear tufts and build nests of floating vegetation. Double-crested cormorants colonize an island in Goose Lake with 150 or so nests.

As many as 40 bald eagles sometimes hang around to prey on weakened waterfowl when 20,000 ducks and geese are scattered around the refuge in fall.

Raptors are wonderful. Golden eagles might be here any time, atop a post or mound, looking for rodents. So might peregrine or prairie falcons. Swainson's and red-tailed hawks nest. Ferruginous hawks appear in summer, and rough-legged at other times of year. Northern harriers course over the marshes, and short-eared owls over the meadows at dusk (sometimes dipping down to investigate a visitor).

Striking lark buntings are common in warm months—so are grasshopper and lark sparrows, Forster's and black terns, Baird's sandpipers, and nighthawks nasally "peenting" while hawking for insects at dusk. This transitional location brings both eastern and western meadowlarks, eastern and mountain bluebirds, and red-winged and yellow-headed blackbirds. Townsend's and MacGillivray's warblers occasionally show up.

Canada geese and a dozen other kinds of ducks nest. Several hundred white pelicans come through seasonally.

Coyotes are likely to be seen hunting for rodents such as the common pocket gophers and kangaroo rats. Both mule and white-tailed deer are here, the former in smaller numbers but more apparent (their curiosity leads them to investigate the visitor). Watch for pronghorns' white rear ends as they graze together on the east side of the refuge.

Horned larks are everywhere and sometimes ring-necked pheasants, too. The excellent bird list tells not only numbers and seasons but where to find various species.

Wildflowers abound, from endangered blue blow-out penstemons to blazing stars and masses of prairie coneflowers and sunflowers. Interesting reptiles and amphibians include ornate box turtles, prairie race runners, and barred tiger salamanders.

One can marvel at such vast areas seemingly untouched by human existence, and the best way to do it is to start out driving slowly, getting out and walking trails and around ponds and brushy areas and looking closely (a limited number of binoculars and scopes are available on loan at the office).

How to get there: From Oshkosh go north on West Second Street for 28 miles from intersection of Routes 27 and 26, following refuge signs all the way (winter weather or heavy rains can make some stretches difficult).

Open: Daylight hours. Office 7:30–4 weekdays.

What to see: Wonderful wildlife spectrum including waterfowl, sharp-tailed grouse, long-billed curlews, upland sandpipers, raptors, also deer, antelopes, coyotes, interesting sandhill formations.

What to do: Fifty miles of roads for driving, hiking, including two designated hiking trails and a self-guided auto tour (some roads may require 4-wheel drive). Photography (vehicle is a good blind). Fishing, good through ice for bass, perch, bluegills.

Where to stay: Motels—Oshkosh and Alliance. Campgrounds—Oshkosh and Alliance, also Smith Lake State Recreation Area, 50 miles north. None on refuge.

What to take and wear: 4-wheel drive if planning to explore back roads; canteen if hiking cross-country.

Points of interest nearby: Scottsbluff National Monument, 105 miles west—ruts left by Oregon Trail still visible; Chimney Rock Historical Park, 85 miles west; Ash Hollow Historical Park, 60 miles southeast; Wildcat Hills Big Game Refuge (also fine birding) near Scottsbluff.

For more information: Crescent Lake National Wildlife Refuge, HC 68, Box 21, Ellsworth, Nebraska 69340. Phone: (308) 762–4893.

Also administered by Crescent Lake is *North Platte* Refuge, 5,047 acres of lakes and grassland northeast of Scottsbluff, which offers resting habitat to large seasonal waterfowl concentrations—up to 200,000 ducks and 12,000 geese, plus up to 40 eagles. Sandhill cranes stop by to loaf in spring, and great blue herons and cormorants have a nesting colony. Habitat is different but wildlife species are similar to those at Crescent Lake, and there are several miles of roads for driving and hiking (parts of the refuge are closed seasonally to provide wildlife sanctuary). Best fishing in the state for walleye; good for bluegills, striped bass, others.

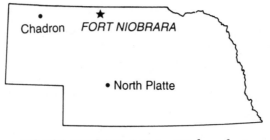

Chadron · ★ FORT NIOBRARA

· North Platte

FORT NIOBRARA (Nebraska)

Fort Niobrara is a mid-country natural treasure. Elk and bison roam in herds as they did 400 years ago on the prairie grasslands of north-central Nebraska— their numbers not equal to those before white men came, although it will almost seem so to a visitor looking out over the free-roaming herds at this 19,130-acre refuge.

White-tailed deer are here as well, showing fluffy white "flags" of tails as they lope up the rolling sandhills—mule deer, more curious, edging closer to see what is going on.

One prairie dog "town" covers 20 acres—its attractive playful residents, which once numbered in the millions but were exterminated over much of the West, fearless here as they scamper among their burrows (which they share with burrowing owls).

Texas longhorn cattle, evolved from descendants of Spanish fighting bulls and brought over by explorers and settlers—a steer can weigh a ton with record horn length of nine feet—amble about for the most part peacefully (but don't get out of your car in their close presence!).

Coyotes are out and around early and late. Porcupines lumber along almost anywhere, anytime.

Once in prehistory great herds of camels, rhinoceros, mastodons, and three-toed horses wandered here—their fossil remains still turn up—and before that, vast seas covered this lush grazing vegetation on which cattle in the Sandhills can gain three pounds a day.

Now the bison, their numbers once estimated at 60 million but reduced nearly to extinction by 1900, renew their hold on the land with calves born in May. So do the massive-antlered elk whose ancestors came over from Siberia. Contesting bison bulls raise clouds of dust in August, pawing the ground in courtship and mating to start the whole process over again, and bull elk start their stentorian bugling displays in September.

Birding is excellent, too. Large flocks of sharp-tailed grouse, wild turkeys, and prairie-chickens are here, and blinds are set up in April where visitors can watch their courtship dancing (reserve ahead).

Upland sandpipers and long-billed curlews are common and nest. So are pheasant, red-tailed hawks, great blue herons, and such interesting smaller birds as black-headed grosbeaks, chats, rock wrens, Say's phoebes, horned larks, grasshopper and lark sparrows, and occasionally a Townsend's solitaire.

Prairie wild flowers peak in June, with blazing stars and 20 other species blooming at once.

The beautiful Niobrara River flows through the refuge, and canoeing along its fast-running (but not dangerous) winding course through deep canyons and wooded breaks is a wonderful way to see the refuge and its wildlife. So is the nature trail beside the waterfall.

In the fall surplus animals, beyond the healthy number for the range, are rounded up and auctioned off, a popular October event. It is no easy trick for a man on horseback to move a one-ton bull buffalo—"Generally we herd them just about anywhere they want to go," said one herdsman.

How to get there: From Valentine take Route 12 east four miles to Fort Niobrara.

Open: Dawn to dusk. Visitor Center 8–4:30 daily Memorial Day through Labor Day, 8–4:30 weekdays rest of year.

Best times to visit: April through October.

What to see: Bison, elk, longhorn cattle, deer, prairie dogs, turkeys, sharp-tailed grouse, prairie-chickens, upland sandpipers; prehistoric wildlife relics.

What to do: 15 miles of roads for driving, hiking (also 4,630-acre Wilderness Area, but check with office first); horseback riding; self-guided trail; canoeing (rentals available nearby); picnicking; photography (vehicle is a good blind).

Where to stay: Motels—in Valentine. Campgrounds—in Valentine; also Ballards Marsh State Park, 20 miles south; Merritt Reservoir, 26 miles southwest.

Weather: Winters can be harsh, snow and rain can make roads impassable.

Points of interest nearby: Merritt Reservoir, 26 miles southwest; Halsey National Forest, 50 miles southwest; Valentine National Wildlife Refuge, 25 miles south.

For more information: Fort Niobrara National Wildlife Refuge, HC 14, Box 67, Valentine, Nebraska 69201. Phone: (402) 376–3789.

Valentine is more a birder's refuge—administered from Fort Niobrara—and a wonderful one, where sharp-tailed grouse and prairie-chickens inflate colorful gular sacs and display on dancing grounds (visitors can watch from blinds). Shorebirds and grassland species such as avocets, phalaropes, killdeer, upland sandpipers, and long-billed curlews come by the thousands, some to stop and rest in migration, many to stay and nest.

One can see why. Valentine, a National Natural Landmark, is covered with welcoming habitat—71,516 acres, of which 10,000 are water, distributed among dozens of potholes, lakes, and marshes with the rest grassland, meadows, and rolling sandhills, beautiful and quiet and vast, seeming to stretch on forever.

Walking along in the spring, one hardly leaves one pair of long-billed curlews before another flies up, defending its breeding territory. The boom of male prairie-chickens in the mornings can be heard for a mile or more. Canada geese have a nest atop every muskrat house. A pair of great horned owls presides over every tree grove.

American bitterns nest, along with black-crowned night herons, eared, western, and pied-billed grebes, black and Forster's terns, and numbers of ducks—mallards, pintails, blue-winged teal, gadwalls, shovelers, redheads, and canvasbacks.

Up to 5,000 white pelicans spend the summer. So do lark buntings, red-eyed and warbling vireos and chestnut-collared longspurs. Short-eared owls hunt in late afternoons.

Mule and white-tailed deer are around all the time, as are coyotes (though less readily seen) and occasionally antelope.

More than 40 miles of roads are open to driving and hiking. Fishing is popular for bass, perch, bluegills, and northern pike, through the ice in winter.

To get to refuge field headquarters take Route 83 south from Valentine 17 miles to Spur Route 16B, then west 13 miles. Weather and other information is similar to Fort Niobrara.

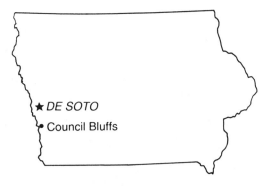

★ DE SOTO
● Council Bluffs

DESOTO (Iowa)

The swirling flight and din of a half-million waterfowl—hundreds of thousands of snow geese and tens of thousands of ducks—have been likened by visitors to this 7,832-acre southwest Iowa refuge to a blizzard of birds, and the sight of them all together almost a religious experience.

Nowhere are they closer and more dramatic than at the DeSoto Visitor Center viewing gallery in fall where eagles, which follow the waterfowl south to prey on weaker ones, may come crashing down from a height of 1,000 feet to take a goose on the water, or coyotes stalk the fringes of a group resting on the meadow, sending them all wildly aloft with a sudden run on the flock.

The clamoring white birds may come by the refuge viewing gallery only a few yards away; the eagles glide in sometimes at eye level.

But there is much here throughout the year.

Eagles may stay from November through March—sometimes up to 120 of them, feeding on waterfowl and fish in this 750-acre oxbow lake that was cut off when the Missouri River was channelized by the U.S. Army Corps of Engineers.

The geese include blues (a snow goose color phase), along with Canadas and white-fronteds—and alert birders will spot Ross', which make up about 4 percent of the group, plus occasionally such rarities as eiders and scoters. Canadas include the starting nucleus of a breeding flock of Greater Canadas. Ducks are mostly mallards but a dozen other species are present, too.

Hundreds of white pelicans with huge nine-foot wingspreads visit sporadically from late August into October.

White-tailed deer graze in fields early and late, sometimes herds of 50 or 100 in winter. Raccoons and rabbits forage along roadsides and muskrats, minks and beavers along the lake.

Early mornings resound all year with cackling pheasant, whistling quail, and gobbling wild turkeys. Up to 1,500 pheasants may feed in late fall on corn and soybean fields where ongoing studies show how to farm with least environmental stress, using sludge from the city of Omaha for natural fertilizer. Springtime brings thousands of dickcissels to the alfalfa fields, and dozens of woodcocks in their dramatic courting flight to woods openings, here on the western fringe of their breeding range.

Red-headed woodpeckers perch on nearly every refuge sign during warm months. Red-tailed hawks soar overhead. Great blue herons and great egrets scout the water's edges. Great horned and barred owls are here—though not often seen in daylight.

Common to abundant small nesters include rose-breasted grosbeaks, northern and orchard orioles, redstarts, yellow warblers, eastern kingbirds, grasshopper sparrows, and warbling vireos.

Endangered piping plovers and least terns nested here historically, and shorelines and sandbars have been cleared to encourage their return. They have nested in the area.

The curious and endangered paddlefish, a primordial creature that can grow up to six feet and weigh over 100 pounds, is here. Population numbers were brought low by oversnagging (the only way it can be caught), but the waters have been restocked. If you see a swirl of something huge in the water, it could be a paddlefish.

Horsetail or scouring rush grows in refuge lowlands—an ancient plant containing so much silica you can file your nails on it.

Scoters and common and king eiders drop down occasionally in winter along with goldeneyes, mergansers, and a few Townsend's solitaires. Visitors at headquarters have seen coyotes take a deer on the frozen lake.

The excellent Visitor Center features not only wildlife displays but over 200,000 artifacts from the steamboat *Bertrand,* which sank in 1865 on what was then the Missouri River, now refuge land. Clothing, equipment, even food supplies en route to the minefields of Montana were preserved almost perfectly in the river silt until unearthed in 1968.

Wildlife have always been attracted here, as have humans. Indians probably hunted the area, and the explorers Lewis and Clark camped on or near what is now the refuge on their way west.

How to get there: From Council Bluffs/Omaha go north on Interstate 29 to Exit 75 (Missouri Valley, Iowa) and refuge sign, then west about five miles on U.S. 30 to refuge entrance.

Open: 6 a.m.–10 p.m April 15–September 30, 8–6 rest of year. Visitor Center 9–4:30 daily, except major holidays. Office 8–5 weekdays.

What to see: Waterfowl, eagles, white pelicans, deer, coyotes, pheasants, wild turkeys; Visitor Center with wildlife exhibits and artifacts from 1865 steamboat *Bertrand.*

What to do: 12 miles of roads for driving, hiking (parts can be closed seasonally). Nature trails. Observation platform (wheelchair-accessible). Photography (blind available by reservation). Boating, picnicking, mushroom-gathering, and fishing (especially for northern and largemouth bass in summer and through winter ice, conditions permitting).

Where to stay: Motels—at Blair, Nebraska, five miles west, Missouri Valley, six miles east. Campgrounds—at Wilson Island (Iowa) State Recreation Area, adjacent on south.

Points of interest nearby: Wilson Island (see Campgrounds); Neale Woods and Fontenelle Forest, privately endowed nature centers 25 miles south; Fort Atkinson at Fort Calhoun, historic site with trails, nature center, south in Nebraska; Henry Doorly Zoo in Omaha, outstanding nature exhibits including black-footed ferrets. Large bank swallow colony near Ponka, 30 miles north.

For more information: DeSoto National Wildlife Refuge, Route 1, Box 114, Missouri Valley, Iowa 51555. Phone: (712) 642–4121.

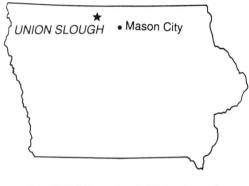

UNION SLOUGH (Iowa)

U nion Slough is a remnant of a preglacial period, a finger-shaped refuge nine miles long and a half-mile wide in land so flat that a strong gust of wind— 35 miles an hour or more—determines the direction of the slough's water flow.

Indians called it Mini Okaoan Kaduza, "water which runs both ways."

In this state, which is given over almost completely to agriculture, it has become a small wildlife mecca offering welcoming habitat ranging from marsh and woods to prairie uplands.

Waterfowl coming through in spring and fall migration may peak at 25,000 birds, including up to 4,000 geese—mostly Canadas but with some snow, blue, and white-fronted, and more than a dozen duck species, of which good numbers of mallards, blue-winged teal, and beautiful wood ducks stay to nest.

Ring-necked pheasants are abundant and gray or Hungarian partridge common all year. Their downy broods are around the refuge roads and trails, and in a stand of native prairie grassland on the north end in early summer. About this same time broods of ducklings and a few Canada goslings appear on the ponds—especially on Gabrielson Pool, where sometimes a dozen or so wood duck families can be seen from the bridge by a quiet visitor. Pied-billed grebes build floating nests there.

A few tundra swans and sometimes up to 2,000 white pelicans touch down in spring and fall.

White-tailed deer browse at dawn and in late afternoons, especially around deer-watching areas marked on the refuge map. There are also foxes, raccoons, squirrels, rabbits, and a few beavers, their workings visible along the nature trail.

Great blue herons and great egrets scout the water's edges. Thousands of shorebirds may stop by on mudflats in August and early fall.

Common nesters among small birds are sedge and marsh wrens, red-headed woodpeckers, eastern bluebirds, yellow-billed cuckoos, dickcissels, and horned larks. Screech and great horned owls are around all year.

Blanding's turtles are here along with snapping turtles weighing up to 50 pounds. The latter are prolific—79 eggs were once found in a single nest.

How to get there: From Algona take Routh 169 north about 15 miles toward Bancroft; turn right on County Road A-42 at the south edge of Bancroft (a cemetery is on the northeast corner) and continue six miles to the refuge sign.

Open: Office 7:30–4 weekdays; parts of refuge may be closed seasonally to protect sensitive nesting areas or in severe weather—check with office.

What to see: Waterfowl; upland birds; deer.

What to do: Several miles of public roads cross refuge and are always open. Interior roads open intermittently; also prairie grasslands area; Deer Meadow picnic area-nature trail.

Where to stay: Motels—several in Algona. Campgrounds—several near Algona, including Call State Park and Smith Lake.

Weather: Winter snow can close refuge roads.

Points of interest nearby: Ingham State Wildlife Area, 40 miles west. Pilot Knob Park at Forest City, 25 miles east.

For more information: Union Slough National Wildlife Refuge, Route 1, Box 52, Titonka, Iowa 50480. Phone: (515) 928–2523.

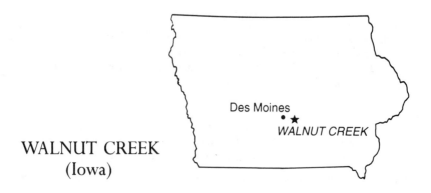

Des Moines
• ★
WALNUT CREEK

WALNUT CREEK
(Iowa)

For the first time since Iowa's native bison and elk were extinguished more than a century ago, these large impressive animals will be grazing on natural tallgrass prairie here.

Walnut Creek became one of the newest of our national wildlife refuges after plans were scrapped to develop the area for a nuclear power plant. Its concept is not to save habitat but to recreate it on these 8,654 acres where, as elsewhere, Iowa's native grasslands are long gone to another grass—corn—and with them the great herds that once lived on them.

Intensive research developed a plan to reconstruct the original prairie and oak savanna around tiny remnants still existing, with 30 to 50 of the plant species that originally grew here. Blazing stars, compass plants, coneflowers, purple prairie clovers, and others will get a new foothold in a landscape dominated by big and little bluestem and Indian grass; when they do a whole ecosystem is expected to rally—bluebirds, wild turkeys, and woodcocks in the savanna, upland plovers, prairie-chickens, meadowlarks, and grasshopper sparrows in the prairie.

Skipper butterflies are expected back, too, with wood ducks and blue-winged teal pairing off in the wetlands. Coyotes, gray and red foxes, and great blue herons are already responding.

An Education and Visitor Center has been in the planning stage southeast of Prairie City, with hiking trails and an auto-tour route. Motels are available in Prairie City and in Des Moines, 20 miles west, and camping in Lake Red Rock Recreation Area, adjacent on the south.

For more information: Walnut Creek National Wildlife Refuge, P.O. Box 399, Prairie City, Iowa 50228. Phone: (515) 994–2415.

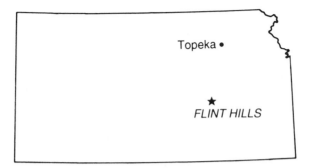

Topeka •

★
FLINT HILLS

FLINT HILLS (Kansas)

U p to 10,000 white pelicans stop by Flint Hills in spring and fall migration, covering the waterways with white. Beautiful wading birds feed in the marsh alongside both sides of the Highway 130 approach to the refuge in warm months—great and little blue herons, snowy and great egrets—and nest in sycamore trees by Lebo Creek.

Dozens of bald eagles accompany the southward journey of ducks and geese, preying on injured or vulnerable ones. There may be up to 100,000 ducks, chiefly mallards but also wigeon, gadwall, and blue-winged teal, later common mergansers, and 70,000 geese, mostly snows but also Canadas and some white-fronteds. Many stay the winter if there's not a hard freeze-up.

An Eagle Tour is held jointly with the Audubon Society every January to view the eagles here then, but something of wildlife interest goes on every month of the year.

Flint Hills was named for the rolling fossil-filled limestone range just to the west that was formed when seas washed across this area in ancient Permian times. This range runs the length of Kansas and often holds the largest concentrations of greater prairie-chickens in the United States. Many of these wander over to the refuge when there is sufficient upland, although, as the refuge lies in the flood pool of the John Redmond Dam and reservoir, up to 90 percent of its 18,463 acres can be inundated at times.

April and May are the best times to see prairie-chickens. They can be heard "booming" any cool spring morning throughout the area from a half hour before to an hour after sunrise. Refuge staff can advise where they have been lately, and the Kansas parks department usually sets up a blind where they can be viewed on their lek, or "dancing" ground.

Wild turkeys can be heard gobbling to proclaim nesting territories. Coyotes howl at dusk. Bobcats scout about for rodents on the woods and field edges. White-tailed deer graze almost anywhere.

The usually uncommon upland sandpiper is common to abundant and visible on fence posts in spring. Red-tailed hawks and northern harriers are around all the time, as are barred and great horned owls. Sometimes thousands of Franklin's gulls and Forster's terns go through.

Among smaller species indigo buntings and dickcissels are common in warm seasons as are northern and orchard orioles, Bell's and warbling vireos, grasshopper sparrows, red-headed woodpeckers, and the lovely scissor-tailed flycatchers. There are usually some LeConte's sparrows in migration and sometimes many warblers, including Tennessee, Nashville, orange-crowned, and yellow-rumped.

Birding is not always easy. Tall grass can be hard to see through, and rains can make roads and trails impassable. Check with the office to learn what has been seen lately and how best to see it.

How to get there: From Emporia take I-35 north to Route 130 (Exit 141) then south to Hartford High School and turn right 3.5 blocks to refuge.

Open: 24 hours (some areas closed in fall). Office 8–4:30 weekdays.

What to see: Waterfowl; eagles; prairie-chickens; wading birds; deer.

What to do: 40 miles of roads for driving, hiking; interpretive trails; observation tower; fishing good spring and fall for white bass, channel catfish.

Where to stay: Motels—in Emporia, 20 miles northwest. Campgrounds—primitive on refuge; also on John Redmond Reservoir land, 15 miles southeast.

Weather: Tornadoes possible spring and summer; rains can make roads, trails impassable—check with office.

Points of interest nearby: John Redmond Reservoir with various recreational facilities; home and newspaper office of famed Pulitzer Prize–winning editor William Allen White in Emporia.

For more information: Flint Hills National Wildlife Refuge, P.O. Box 128, Hartford, Kansas 66854. Phone: (316) 392–5553.

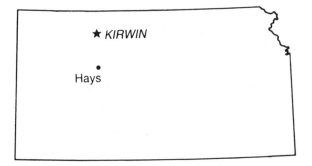

KIRWIN (Kansas)

The largest flocks of Canada geese in Kansas's well-traveled section of the Central Flyway, including at least six subspecies of this handsome bird, arrive in great honking V-formations every October and many spend the winter on this diverse 10,778-acre refuge, an overlay on a Bureau of Reclamation project just 30 miles west of the geographical center of the contiguous United States.

Several dozen eagles follow them, mostly bald but some goldens, and they, too, stay through the cold months.

And there are white-tailed deer and pheasants, wild turkeys and quail, pairing up in springtime, appearing with young ones in early summer and coming together in feeding groups of 100 or so in late fall and winter.

Visitors sometimes see 40,000 Canadas during fall migration, and many more come through, with some white-fronted geese as well. In a good year—when ideal weather combines with sufficient water—mallards, gadwalls, pintails, blue-winged teals, and shovelers nest here.

Several thousand sandhill cranes are noisy, spectacular spring and fall visitors, with sometimes a few endangered whooping cranes en route from northern Canada breeding grounds to south Texas.

White pelicans herd fish in the shallows spring through fall. Red-headed woodpeckers and brown thrashers seem to be every place. Other interesting regulars are Swainson's hawks, Wilson's phalaropes, avocets, black terns, Baird's sandpipers, dickcissels, vesper and lark sparrows, eastern and western kingbirds, and thousands of Franklin's gulls. Great blue herons have a rookery on the edge of the refuge.

Birding is good along brushy areas and shelter belts—there are probably more trees in Kansas now, as a result of planting programs, than a century ago. Raucous, colorful black-billed magpies are common all year. So are horned larks, flickers, and great horned owls. All raptors find good hunting in the grasslands—northern harriers, red-tailed hawks, prairie falcons, occasional peregrines, and rough-legs and sometimes snowy owls in winter.

Black-tailed prairie dogs delight onlookers in a 35-acre "town." Badgers are nocturnal but their badger-shaped hemispheric burrows are always visible. Beavers are all around the lake. Coyotes pursue rodents in the fields and stalk geese on the winter ice. More elusive but also here are bobcats and red foxes.

Kirwin has had water problems caused by drought and changing farm practices. More terraces and small ponds plus more irrigation have meant less water going into the lake. This can mean less waterfowl habitat. Yet more prairie chickens and turkeys have appeared recently so such changes can mean a broadening of general wildlife habitat—and wetland protection projects of the North American Waterfowl Council including many on private lands may help in the future to restore past waterfowl populations.

How to get there: From Phillipsburg take Route 183 south to Glade, then east on Route 9 for six miles to refuge sign.

Open: 24 hours. Office 7:30–4 weekdays.

What to see: Waterfowl, prairie dogs, pheasants, deer, turkeys, plus beautiful restored prairies and prairie wildflowers.

What to do: 29 miles of roads for driving, hiking, including self-guided interpretive drive and trails; picnic areas; fishing can be the best in Kansas for walleyes.

Where to stay: Motels—in Phillipsburg, 12 miles northwest. Campgrounds—in Phillipsburg, also on refuge (primitive).

Weather: Can change quickly with extremely high winds; winters can drop to 30 below.

Points of interest nearby: Hansen Museum at Logan; old Fort Bissell, Phillipsburg; Big Barn, a huge old restored barn now a national historic landmark, 15 miles southeast.

For more information: Kirwin National Wildlife Refuge, Route 1, Box 103, Kirwin, Kansas 67644. Phone: (913) 543–6673

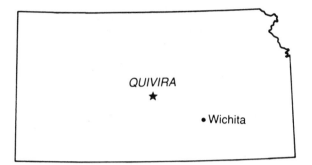

QUIVIRA (Quivira)

★

• Wichita

QUIVIRA (Kansas)

Half the shorebirds in North America are believed to stop at Quivira or nearby Cheyenne Bottoms during annual migrations.

The importance of these places to these birds—as well as to tens of thousands of sandhill cranes, white pelicans, waterfowl, and others, including endangered species—cannot be overstated. Without such islands of habitat where they can rest and feed while traveling between wintering and breeding grounds, their continued existence would be in jeopardy.

As it is, visitors here are treated to overwhelming sights and experiences, as when great flocks of the majestic cranes fly low over marsh and fields each spring and fall, filling the air with high bugling cries audible for miles as they go out to the fields to feed in early morning and return to roost in the salt marshes at dusk.

Among them may occasionally be seen rare white whooping cranes. There may be 75,000 waterfowl—Canada and white-fronted geese and ducks of more than a dozen species, some of which stay the winter.

On the mudflats are Wilson's phalaropes whirling in circles to stir up prey, long-billed curlews, pectoral, white-rumped, and Baird's sandpipers, Hudsonian and marbled godwits, and a tremendous variety of others. Many stay to nest—including avocets and delicate black-necked stilts, threatened snowy plovers and upland sandpipers with hearing so sensitive they are said to locate their midcontinental nesting grounds by sensing surf vibrations from both Atlantic and Pacific oceans.

This is raptor country, too. Cooper's, Swainson's, rough-legged, and red-tailed hawks are a common sight perched atop utility poles and tall cottonwoods, swooping down on mice or prairie voles or for a larger meal, rabbits or the equally common bobwhite quail and ring-necked pheasants. Bald eagles follow the waterfowl and a dozen or so are here in all but summer. Sharp-shinned hawks snatch an occasional meal at the headquarters bird feeder.

Mississippi kites, instantly recognizable by their swift swallowlike flight, take large insects well into the evening. They are common and nest—but have moved their main colony to the nearby town of Stafford, which could lay claim to being the Mississippi kite capital of the world. Most streets have at least one nesting pair. Quivira regularly gets calls from townspeople asking what to do when kites defending nest territories dive on cats and small children (reply: wait till nesting season is over and don't worry, they won't hurt either pets or youngsters).

Up to 6,000 white pelicans soar here in great columns, the sun glinting off their nine-foot wingspreads.

Endangered least terns dip down for minnows to feed a colony whose success has increased since the refuge built up nesting sandbars protected from floods and surrounded them with electric fence to keep out predators.

Wild turkey gobblers display before hens in April and cluster in flocks of 100 or so in winter.

White-faced ibis and great blue herons nest. So do some greater prairie chickens. Other common nesters are beautiful scissor-tailed flycatchers, red-headed woodpeckers, Bell's vireos, dickcissels, and lark sparrows. Bewick's wrens, Say's phoebes, lazuli buntings, and Lapland and chestnut-collared longspurs are here, too. The bird list of more than 250 species reflects Quivira's location, almost exactly in the geographical center of the country. For example, both eastern and western meadowlarks are here.

Prairie dogs sit up and take notice of the visitor as do burrowing owls, which take over some of their holes. White-tailed deer browse in fields. Coyotes hunt for rodents and howl to one another in the evenings.

Coronado was here searching for the fabled Seven Cities of Gold in 1541, when he found a tribe of handsome seven-foot natives whom he called, adapting an Indian word, Quivira, which symbolized for him the plenteous natural life he saw. A rich reminder of that life remains for the visitor today.

How to get there: From Hutchinson take Route 50 west to Zenith, then north on Zenith Road for eight miles (continuing as it becomes dirt) to refuge headquarters.

Open: Daylight hours. Office 7:30–4 weekdays.

Best times to visit: Spring and fall but good all year.

What to see: Shorebird and waterfowl concentrations, least terns, Mississippi kites, pheasants, eagles, white pelicans, sandhill cranes and occasional whoopers, deer, prairie dogs.

What to do: 20 miles of roads for driving, hiking; photoblinds (first come, first served); group guided tours by arrangement. Hikers may roam over the entire refuge.

Where to stay: Motels—in Stafford, 13 miles southwest; Great Bend, 35 miles northwest; Hutchinson, 28 miles east. Campgrounds—at Great Bend and Hutchinson (a few in Stafford).

Weather: Severe thunderstorms likely May-June (western Kansas is one of the windiest places in the interior U.S.).

Points of interest nearby: Cheyenne Bottoms State Waterfowl Management Area at Great Bend—one of the greatest waterbird concentrations of the central flyway spring and fall; Kansas Cosmosphere and Space Center, Hutchinson; Fort Larned National Historical Site, 50 miles northwest.

For more information: Quivira National Wildlife Refuge, Route 3, Box 48A, Stafford, Kansas 67578. Phone: (316) 486–2393.

MINGO (Missouri)

Mingo has something to fascinate anyone with a serious interest in nature, from denizens of an ancient swamp where once the mighty Mississippi flowed, to wild turkeys, deer, otters, large waterfowl concentrations, and some of the largest specimen trees in existence.

Bald eagles are here and have two active nests. Birders come to explore around the boardwalks during spring migration for the arrival of songbirds including seven kinds of vireos and more than two dozen species of warblers of which many stay to nest—warbling and Bell's vireos, parula, prothonotary and hooded warblers, chats, summer tanagers, rose-breasted grosbeaks, indigo buntings, and numbers of others.

Fall migration brings up to 100,000 mallards and thousands of gadwalls, pintails, wigeons, and wood ducks, which also nest here, producing dozens of broods every May and June. Up to 50,000 Canada geese and a few blues and snows arrive in October and many stay the winter (ducks move on south at freeze-up). Eagles follow the waterfowl and prey on weaker ones; 25 or so usually stay through the winter and are featured periodically in "Eagle Weekends" at the refuge.

Great blue, little blue, and yellow-crowned night herons are common and nest. So are barred owls and red-shouldered and red-tailed hawks; occasionally there are also Cooper's hawks.

A quiet walk, drive, or canoe trip at early morning or dusk will usually provide the visitor with sights of white-tailed deer and perhaps also beavers or a family of playful otters, rarely a fox, mink, or bobcat.

Spring flowers are beautiful and a special tour is held in April to view them— bluebells, redbuds, wake-robin trilliums, rue anemones, Dutchman's breeches, dog- wood, yellow rockets, and swamp buttercups, and in isolated areas spider lilies and purple fringeless orchids. Later there are large tracts of golden-blooming lotuses. In summer, trumpet creepers attract hummingbirds from everywhere, and scarlet car- dinal flowers follow the roadsides in fall.

The trees are magnificent. Six specimens are of champion size, including a Carolina buckthorn, green hawthorn, water oak, planer tree, water locust, and an overcup oak 72 feet tall with a trunk 174 inches around.

The whole history and ecology of Mingo's mammals, reptiles, amphibians, and almost everything else has been listed, recorded, and catalogued and is available to the visitor for reference.

This 21,676-acre refuge in Missouri's southeastern bootheel has been a swamp and haven for wildlife since the river changed course 18,000 years ago. Shawnee and Osage Indians camped here but it inspired in them the fear that swamps often still do, and they gave it its present name, which means treacherous and unreliable. A Confederate colonel, Jeff Thompson, hid here and earned the Civil War nickname "Swamp Fox."

It became a refuge after fires, overtimbering, and unsuccessful drainage attempts made it useless for any other purpose. Now those same drainage ditches with pumps have been used to return it to its present lush state.

How to get there: From Cape Girardeau take Route 74 west to Dutchtown, left on Route 25 to Advance, turn right there at 91 to get on Route C, take C to Arab, then south on 51 to Mingo.

Open: Dawn to dusk. Visitor center 8–4 weekdays, 9–4 weekends March 15–No- vember 30.

What to see: Deer; waterfowl; eagles; wild turkeys; large trees; great variety of plant and other natural life.

What to do: Nature trails and drives; special wildlife tours in April, October, November; canoeing (no rentals available); photography (portable blinds permitted); fishing for bass, bluegills, crappies, catfish.

Where to stay: Motels—at Poplar Bluff, 25 miles southwest; Dexter, 24 miles southeast; Wappapello, 10 miles west. Campgrounds—at Wappapello; also Duck Creek State Management Area, adjacent on north.

Points of interest nearby: Duck Creek and Wappapello Lake (see Campgrounds); Big

Oak Tree State Park, 40 miles west, good birding; University State Forest, south of Wappapello.

For more information: Mingo National Wildlife Refuge, Route 1, Box 103, Puxico, Missouri 63960. Phone: (314) 222–3589.

Mingo also oversees 90-acre *Pilot Knob,* habitat for the endangered Indiana bat, but there are no public facilities or access at present.

SQUAW CREEK (Missouri)

Anyone who wishes to see America's majestic national bird can fairly well count on doing so at Squaw Creek National Wildlife Refuge in late fall and winter.

Sometimes more than 200 bald eagles—one of the largest wintering eagle concentrations in the United States—are here then on this 7,178-acre tract of marsh, woods, and upland in the northeast corner of Missouri. They are following the spectacular flocks of waterfowl that are also here on their way south—up to 350,000 snow and blue geese and 100,000 ducks that can all but cover the refuge waters from October to December.

It is a dramatic sight—the huge concentrations of waterfowl gabbling among themselves in a roar that seems to overwhelm the senses, then going absolutely silent at the appearance of an eagle; then the roar reaches an even greater crescendo as the birds lift off in a huge milling cloud, rolling about like a giant white wave that subsides as the birds resettle.

It is a spectacle that will be repeated until the eagle finds a weaker one and captures it for a meal, then again when another eagle arrives, and so on through the several-month stay of the tremendous flocks. The waterfowl finally leave when cold blustery weather settles in, though some weaker ones remain usually into February, providing a continuing food source for the raptors.

The refuge holds Eagle Days over a weekend in early December, with programs and tours to view the great birds, sometimes 30 in a single tree, or soaring in high circles or, if the main pool is frozen over, perhaps 100 eagles resting on the ice, feeding on birds, or sunning themselves if it is a pleasant day.

They are often visible from refuge headquarters as well as on the 10-mile auto-tour route. Photoblinds are permitted along hiking trails and photo chances are excellent, especially along the auto-tour route where visitors must stay in cars so that close-by wildlife viewing of eagles, waterfowl, deer, and others is possible. Squaw Creek has been listed as one of the Audubon Society's "Best Bets" for photography at national wildlife refuges.

Deer appear with dappled fawns in summer, resting in the woods and grazing in herds of 100 or so. Alongside the roads are pheasants and hunting coyotes. Muskrats build domelike lodges in the water that offer resting and sometimes nesting places for birds and keep the marsh open with their foraging.

Huge white pelicans with nine-foot wingspreads come through, sometimes up to 2,000 or so, in fall and spring. Birders come to see thousands of shorebirds on mudflats in spring migration—long-billed dowitchers, Wilson's phalaropes, Hudsonian godwits, and lesser yellowlegs.

Great horned and barred owls are common all year; in summer there are orchard and northern orioles, yellow-breasted chats, indigo buntings, great blue herons, and red-eyed, warbling, and Bell's vireos.

The endangered massasauga rattlesnake is here, and motorists should give it safe passage on the roads.

Of special interest are the loess bluffs—strange unstratified rockless hills of yellow windblown soil formed in glacial times that later became hard, almost crystalline. They are found along the river basin from Squaw Creek to Sioux City but at few other places in the world. They are topped with native prairie grasses, including a number of state endangered plants.

The bluff trail offers a spectacular view of three states.

How to get there: From St. Joseph, Missouri, take Route I-29 35 miles north to the Rulo, Nebraska, exit (no. 79), then Route 159 west two miles to refuge headquarters.

Open: Sunrise to sunset daily. Office 7:30–4 weekdays, and fall weekends.

What to see: Wintering eagles; large waterfowl concentrations; deer; muskrats; unusual loess bluffs.

What to do: Auto-tour route; walking trails; observation tower; photography.

Where to stay: Motels—Squaw Creek Truck Plaza, two miles east on Route 159; at Mound City, five miles north; Big Lake State Park, eight miles east on Route 159. Campgrounds—Big Lake State Park (see Motels).

Weather: Spring and fall rains can make refuge driving difficult.

Points of interest nearby: Big Lake State Park (see Motels)—white pelicans in migration. Bluff Woods State Area, 35 miles south, and Honey Creek State Area, 15 miles south, good birding and natural spots. St. Joseph Natural History Museum, extensive collections and information.

For more information: Squaw Creek National Wildlife Refuge, P.O. Box 101, Mound City, Missouri 64470. Phone: (816) 442–3187.

Chillicothe
★
SWAN LAKE

SWAN LAKE (Missouri)

The name is Swan Lake but no one knows why anymore; swans are almost never seen here and this northwest Missouri refuge of 10,670 acres is held in thrall by the Canada goose. The nearby town of Sumner, population 200, proudly calls itself Wild Goose Capital of the World and each fall holds a Wild Goose Festival with queen, parades, and dances. Its Bicentennial project was erection of the world's largest statue of a Canada goose—40 feet high with a 61-foot wingspread and an audiovisual presentation in the base.

Objects of all this attention start arriving in mid-September from nesting grounds in the tundra and by late October may number 100,000. Their calls are heard for a mile or more and they seem to be everywhere filling land, water, and sky.

It is an awesome sight and though it is shared with other species—deer, wild turkeys, sometimes up to 250,000 ducks, 2,000 white pelicans, and 30,000 snow geese—the Canadas clearly dominate the scene.

It has been somewhat unexpected. Swan Lake was established in 1937 to offer rest and feeding grounds for ducks. Geese then were only occasional visitors. Only 25 came in 1940. By 1945 there were 10,000, and more and more came until it became clear they like it here, to put it mildly.

Interest in the species is not aesthetic but rooted in the Canadas' being a prime trophy for waterfowl hunters. After the birds' numbers increased, hunt clubs bought or leased most of the surrounding area until individual hunters complained, and state and federal authorities carved out the "Swan Lake Zone"—a move that aroused controversy—whereby the refuge is ringed by a belt of land in which 50 pit blinds have been constructed for use by hunters during a controlled, reservation-only season that starts in late October and continues until a given quota (in recent years 10,000 birds) has been taken.

But their quarry have lived up to a reputation for intelligence. When gunfire starts they fly high, many out of gun range, when over the hunt zone, and only drop down when safely over refuge land. Several times in recent years the quota has not been reached. (Still, reports show that 40 percent of adult geese banded here carry some shot in their bodies and of those killed, official statistics add 20 percent to the mortality figures for those that die later from their wounds. These and other wounded or weakened waterfowl are a primary food source for up to 100 bald eagles that winter on the refuge.)

Despite focus on the geese, other interesting wildlife are present and other activities offered—and though the auto-tour route is closed in fall and winter to offer quiet sanctuary, the masses of waterfowl can be seen almost equally well from the observation tower, the dike road, and the nature trail.

Bobwhites are commonly present all year as are horned larks, cardinals, flickers, red-headed and red-bellied woodpeckers, and screech, barred, and great horned owls. Seasonally common to abundant are great blue and green-backed herons, great egrets, coots (as many as 10,000), hermit and wood thrushes, and five kinds of swallows.

Hawk migrations in spring and fall can be impressive, with common to abundant sightings of Cooper's, red-tailed, red-shouldered, rough-legged, and broad-winged, along with northern harriers and a few merlin.

The refuge supports a herd of about 500 deer and some 60 coyotes, which have sometimes denned along the walking trail. Smaller numbers of red foxes are here—hard-pressed by the coyotes—and otters, which slide and frisk along the waterways, though shy and not easy to see.

How to get there: From Kansas City (about 100 miles) take I-35 north to Route 36, east on 36 to State Route 139, south there to Sumner, and south on Swan Lake Drive about three miles to refuge.

Open: Office/Visitor Center 8–4:30 weekdays; interior of the refuge dawn to dusk March 1–October 15; nature trail, observation tower open all year.

Best times to visit: Spring (March) and fall for great waterfowl concentrations.

What to see: Massive groups of Canada geese, also ducks, snow geese, white pelicans, deer.

What to do: Nature trails; auto-tour drive; photography (hunters' blinds can be used by permission); observation tower.

Where to stay: Motels—in Chillicothe, 30 miles northwest, and Brookfield, 25 miles northeast. Campgrounds—Pershing State Park, five miles northeast.

Points of interest nearby: World's largest statue of a Canada goose at Sumner, three miles away; Fountain Grove State Wildlife Area, five miles northwest (waterfowl concentrations) and Pershing State Park, five miles north—both attractive natural areas with trails, the latter featuring the boyhood home of World War I General John J. Pershing at Laclede.

For more information: Swan Lake National Wildlife Refuge, Route 1, Box 29A, Sumner, Missouri 64681. Phone: (816) 856–3323.

The Southwest States

Eagles and mountain lions, stately endangered whooping cranes and secretive ocelots only suggest the sweep of wildlife at these southwestern U.S. refuges, which offer habitat ranging from prairies to mountains to parched desert.

ARIZONA

Settlers likened *Buenos Aires*'s lush prairies to a sea of flowing grass and then largely destroyed them by overgrazing. They have been restored on these 116,000 acres in southwest Arizona to support a magnificent wildlife spectrum ranging from deer, pronghorn antelopes, and kit foxes to brilliant vermilion flycatchers and rarities like beardless tyrannulets seldom seen elsewhere.

Cabeza Prieta was set aside to save the desert bighorn sheep from extinction in 1939, largely at the instigation of the Boy Scouts of America. Its 1,000 square miles of spectacular mountains and desert are one of the wildest, most desolate places in the country.

Cibola is one of the three national wildlife refuges on the lower Colorado River, critically important riverine habitat for migrating and wintering geese—largest such concentrations in the desert Southwest—as well as for hundreds of species of shorebirds and songbirds.

Another is *Havasu*, which has some of the most spectacular scenery and diverse and interesting wildlife in the valley, ranging from waterfowl to desert bighorn sheep and, in spring, western grebes performing graceful courtship ballets.

Still another is *Imperial*, stretching for 30 miles along both sides of the Colorado in California and Arizona, harboring bighorn sheep of the Sonoran desert. A stone's throw away, mule deer and great blue herons fish in lush green riparian habitat.

Kofa's jagged peaks rise abruptly several thousand feet from the desert floor. More than a half-million acres of this thousand-square-mile refuge is designated Wilderness Area where desert bighorns make their homes. Like *Cabeza Prieta,* it was set aside after troops of Boy Scouts wrote President Franklin D. Roosevelt asking that he do so.

Water amid parched surroundings makes *San Bernardino* a special place for more than 230 bird species as well as mule and white-tailed deer, javelinas, shy coatimundis, ring-tailed cats, and the endangered fish for which it was established.

NEW MEXICO

Bitter Lake's skies in fall can be filled with snow geese and a large portion of the world's lesser sandhill cranes—but every season can be interesting. In spring endangered interior least terns and threatened snowy plovers nest, and northern harriers are a common sight hunting low over the grasslands.

Hauntingly musical cries of 12,000 or so scarlet-crowned greater sandhill cranes fill the air over *Bosque Del Apache* starting in October and through the winter. You can tell how cold it is on winter mornings by whether they trail their long legs in flight or tuck them in. At 15 degrees, they tuck them in. Snow geese, turkeys, coyotes, porcupines, and other wildlife are here.

Swift prairie falcons—faster than peregrines at high altitudes—perform spectacular aerial courtship gymnastics and nest on the ledges in steep canyons at *Las Vegas,* ideal raptor habitat. It's not unusual to see a half-dozen kinds of birds of prey in a single tour of the interpretive loop drive here.

More than 60 bald eagles may spend the winter at *Maxwell* feasting on rainbow trout and weaker members of the flocks of 10,000 or so Canada geese and 12,000 ducks that are here then. Burrowing owls nest in holes excavated by prairie dogs. Handsome bufflehead drakes flare white crown feathers to entice a mate.

San Andres in the San Andres Mountains exists for protection of desert bighorn sheep. Located in the White Sands Missile Range, it is closed to public access.

TEXAS

Rails, "rather hen-shaped marsh birds of secretive habits and mysterious voices" (as Roger Tory Peterson describes them), like *Anahuac* refuge—six species of them (kings and clappers are easiest to see). Alligators are here by the thousands, and beautiful roseate spoonbills are around all year.

Aransas is winter home to what is probably the world's best-known endangered species: the majestic white whooping crane. This is where we saw it brought back from the edge of extinction. But there is much else—collared peccaries, alligators, armadillos, bobcats, mountain lions. Aransas claims one of the longest bird lists of any refuge: 389 species and still counting.

One of the world's most endangered birds maintains a precarious hold in the grasslands of *Attwater Prairie Chicken*, a southeast Texas refuge named after it. The refuge is shared with caracaras, white-tailed hawks, and sometimes 95 percent of the world's white-fronted geese.

Some of the country's best birding is at *Brazoria/San Bernard*. Hundreds of bright warblers and other songbirds "fall out" in April. Some 150,000 snow geese and thousands of ducks spend the winter. And tens of thousands of beautiful herons and egrets gather in summer nesting islands.

Badgers resembling small fast-moving tanks share *Buffalo Lake* with mule deer, diminutive swift foxes, and raptors of a half-dozen species—and, when there is enough water, the birds that require it. Burrowing owls share a 100-acre prairie dog town.

Pirouetting scissor-tailed flycatchers share the diverse habitat of *Hagerman* with thousands of migrating waterfowl, clouds of white pelicans, and dashing roadrunners. It's known among birders for an assortment of interesting sparrow types. Dickcissels sing on every post in summer.

Spotted ocelots and rare jaguarundis, like small dark panthers, prowl the brush and marsh of *Laguna Atascosa*. Mountain lions stalk white-tailed deer. This refuge has the densest population of wild cats in the country—but birding can be fantastic, too, including 80 percent of the continent's population of redhead ducks.

One of the largest gatherings of stately sandhill cranes in North America spends the winter at *Muleshoe*—more than 100,000 in some years. Swainson's hawks are common nesters, and it's not unusual in midwinter to see eight or more raptor species in one day, including bald and golden eagles and possibly a prairie falcon.

Santa Ana is known as the jewel of the national wildlife refuge system and even a brief look shows why. Orange and black altamira orioles and brilliant green jays fly out of the mesquite. Hummingbirds with bright orange bills hover about scarlet turk's cap lilies. Ocelots and a few mountain lions prowl back in the junglelike vegetation.

OKLAHOMA

Hundreds of resplendent wood ducks fly in to roost at *Little River*, a relatively new refuge with, as well, red-shouldered hawks, pileated woodpeckers, wild turkeys, Mississippi kites, alligators, white-tailed deer, and large nesting colonies of herons and egrets.

Indians fought over *Salt Plains*'s largest salt flat in mid-America. Settlers loaded their wagons with it to preserve food. Now it is a significant migratory stopover for thousands of shorebirds as well as stately endangered whooping cranes. Threatened snowy plovers and endangered least terns nest.

Sixty bald eagles can be arrayed in tall cottonwoods on a fall or winter day at *Sequoyah* waiting to prey on weakened or injured members of the 50,000 or so ducks and 60,000 or so geese that spend cold months here. Lovely scissor-tailed flycatchers, the Oklahoma state bird, come for warmer months, sometimes nesting on power pole crossbars.

Sometimes 100 bald eagles spend the winter at *Tishomingo*—feeding on weakened or injured waterfowl as well as catfish and crappie on Lake Texoma. There are also interesting raptors—kestrels and northern harriers as well as Swainson's, ferruginous, and Cooper's hawks—and a large deer herd.

One of the largest waterfowl concentrations in Oklahoma is at *Washita*—up to 50,000 geese in winter, mostly Canadas but also snows and white-fronteds with an occasional Ross', and perhaps 20,000 ducks of more than a dozen species. Prairie dogs occupy a "town" of 50 or so near the refuge office.

Wichita Mountains was our first national wildlife refuge, set aside in 1901 (though first designated as a Forest Reserve), and it is a showplace of the system, with herds of buffalo, elk, Texas longhorns, prairie dogs, stunning scenery, and a breathtaking variety of interesting birds, plants, reptiles, and rocks—all easily accessible to the visitor.

Following are birds of special interest found commonly at Southwest refuges at seasons indicated:

S: SPRING   s: SUMMER   F: FALL   W: WINTER

Least Grebe: Laguna Atascosa S
Reddish Egret: Laguna Atascosa SFW
Least Bittern: Anahuac SsF, Havasu SsF, Imperial s
Wood Stork: Anahuac sF, Brazoria s
White-faced Ibis: Anahuac SsF, Aransas SW, Brazoria SF, Laguna Atascosa SF, Las Vegas S
Roseate Spoonbill: Anahuac SsF, Brazoria SsFW
Fulvous Whistling Duck: Anahuac F
Black-bellied Whistling Duck: Laguna Atascosa Ss, Santa Ana s
Ross' Goose: Bitter Lake SFW, Bosque del Apache W
Black-shouldered Kite: Brazoria SFW, Santa Ana s
Mississippi Kite: Salt Plains SsF, Washita Ss, Wichita Mountains SsF
White-tailed Hawk: Attwater Prairie Chicken SsFW
Bald Eagle: Las Vegas W, Maxwell F, Salt Plains SFW, Sequoyah FW, Tishomingo W
Golden Eagle: Maxwell FW, Muleshoe FW, San Andres SsFW
Crested Caracara: Attwater Prairie Chicken SsF
Plain Chachalaca: Laguna Atascosa Ss
Gambel's Quail: Cabeza Prieta SsFW, Cibola SsFW, Havasu SsFW, Imperial SsFW, Kofa SsFW
Scaled Quail: Muleshoe SsFW
White-winged Pheasant: Bosque del Apache SFW
Attwater's Greater Prairie Chicken: Attwater Prairie Chicken SW
Purple Gallinule: Anahuac Ss

Sandhill Crane: Attwater Prairie Chicken FW, Bitter Lake W,
  Bosque del Apache FW, Brazoria FW, Laguna Atascosa FW, Las Vegas W,
  Muleshoe SFW, Salt Plains SF, Washita SF
Whooping Crane: Aransas SFW, Bosque del Apache FW
Snowy Plover: Aransas SF, Bitter Lake SF, Buffalo Lake s, Havasu sF, Muleshoe Ss, Salt
  Plains SsF
Wilson's Plover: Laguna Atascosa SsF
Long-billed Curlew: Brazoria SFW, Laguna Atascosa SFW
Marbled Godwit: Anahuac SF, Havasu s
Baird's Sandpiper: Buffalo Lake Ss, Hagerman SF, Washita S
Red-necked Phalarope: Havasu s
Gull-billed Tern: Anahuac SsF, Aransas S, Laguna Atascosa SsF
California Gull: Havasu S
Black Skimmer: Aransas SsFW, Brazoria Ss, Laguna Atascosa Ss
Inca Dove: Havasu Ss
White-tipped Dove: Santa Ana SsFW
Greater Roadrunner: Bitter Lake Ss, Bosque del Apache SsFW, Cibola SsFW, Havasu
  SsFW, Imperial SsFW, Laguna Atascosa SsF
Elf Owl: Cabeza Prieta Ss, Santa Ana Ss
Common Pauraque: Laguna Atascosa SsF, Santa Ana SsFW
Common Poor-will: Bosque del Apache s, Kofa SsF, Las Vegas Ss
White-throated Swift: Havasu W, Las Vegas SsF
Buff-bellied Hummingbird: Santa Ana s
Black-chinned Hummingbird: Havasu Ss, Las Vegas s
Anna's Hummingbird: Havasu Ss
Broad-tailed Hummingbird: Las Vegas Ss
Rufous Hummingbird: Las Vegas s, Maxwell s
Costa's Hummingbird: Cabeza Prieta sW, Cibola Ss, Havasu S, Imperial Ss, Kofa S
Golden-fronted Woodpecker: Laguna Atascosa SsFW, Santa Ana SsFW
Gila Woodpecker: Cabeza Prieta SsFW, Cibola SsFW, Havasu SsFW, Imperial SsFW,
  Kofa SsFW
Ladder-backed Woodpecker: Bosque del Apache SsF, Cibola SsFW, Havasu SsFW, Imperial
  SsFW, Laguna Atascosa SsFW, Muleshoe SsFW, Santa Ana SsFW
Wied's Crested Flycatcher: Imperial Ss
Black Phoebe: Bosque del Apache s, Cibola SFW, Havasu SsFW, Imperial SFW
Say's Phoebe: Bosque del Apache SsFW, Cabeza Prieta SFW, Cibola SFW, Havasu
  SFW, Kofa SFW, Las Vegas SFW
Vermilion Flycatcher: Brazoria SFW
Ash-throated Flycatcher: Bosque del Apache Ss, Cibola SsF, Havasu Ss, Imperial SsF,
  Kofa Ss
Brown-crested Flycatcher: Havasu s, Laguna Atascosa Ss, Santa Ana SsF
Great Kiskadee: Laguna Atascosa s

Couch's Kingbird: Santa Ana Ss

Scissor-tailed Flycatcher: Anahuac SF, Aransas SsF, Attwater Prairie Chicken SsF, Brazoria SsF, Buffalo Lake F, Hagerman SF, Laguna Atascosa SF, Muleshoe SFW, Salt Plains SsF, Santa Ana SF, Sequoyah SsF, Tishomingo SsF, Washita SsF, Wichita Mountains SsF

Violet-green Swallow: Bosque del Apache SF, Havasu S, Las Vegas SsF, Maxwell sF

Steller's Jay: Las Vegas SsF

Scrub Jay: Las Vegas SsF, San Andres SsFW

Pinyon Jay: San Andres SsFW

Green Jay: Santa Ana SFW

White-necked Raven: San Andres s

Verdin: Cibola SsFW, Havasu SsFW, Kofa SsFW

Mountain Chickadee: Bosque del Apache W

Black-tailed Gnatcatcher: Cabeza Prieta SsFW, Cibola SsFW, Havasu SsFW, Imperial SsFW, Kofa SsFW

Long-billed Thrasher: Santa Ana SsFW

Curve-billed Thrasher: Cabeza Prieta SsFW, Laguna Atascosa SsFW, Muleshoe SsFW, San Andres SsFW

Crissal Thrasher: Cibola SsFW, Havasu SsFW, Imperial SsFW

Sprague's Pipit: Attwater Prairie Chicken SW

Phainopepla: Cabeza Prieta SFW, Cibola SFW, Havasu SW, Imperial SFW, Kofa SFW

Bell's Vireo: Salt Plains SsF, Tishomingo Ss

Virginia's Warbler: Las Vegas s

Lucy's Warbler: Bosque del Apache s, Havasu SsF, Imperial Ss

Black-throated Gray Warbler: Cabeza Prieta S

Townsend's Warbler: Cabeza Prieta S, Kofa S

MacGillivray's Warbler: Cabeza Prieta SF, Cibola SF, Havasu SF, Imperial SF, Kofa S, Muleshoe S

Black-headed Grosbeak: Cabeza Prieta SF, Cibola SF, Havasu SF, Las Vegas S

Lazuli Bunting: Kofa S

Painted Bunting: Aransas SsF, Attwater Prairie Chicken S, Hagerman Ss, Laguna Atascosa S, Santa Ana S, Tishomingo SsF, Wichita Mountains Ss

Green-tailed Towhee: Bitter Lake S, Las Vegas SF

Brown Towhee: Kofa SsFW, Las Vegas SsF

Abert's Towhee: Cibola SsFW, Havasu SsFW, Imperial SsFW

Rufous-crowned Sparrow: Wichita Mountains SsFW

Olive Sparrow: Laguna Atascosa SsFW, Santa Ana SsFW

Botteri's Sparrow: Laguna Atascosa Ss

Cassin's Sparrow: Bitter Lake SsF, Buffalo Lake s, Laguna Atascosa SsF, Muleshoe Ss

Brewer's Sparrow: Cabeza Prieta SFW, Cibola SF, Havasu SF, Kofa SF

Lark Sparrow: Aransas SsF, Bitter Lake SsF, Bosque del Apache SF, Buffalo Lake s,

Hagerman SsF, Las Vegas SsF, Salt Plains SsF, Sequoyah Ss, Tishomingo SsF, Washita s, Wichita Mountains SFW

Lark Bunting: Las Vegas s, Maxwell SsF, Muleshoe SsF, Washita W

Black-throated Sparrow: Bosque del Apache SsF, Cabeza Prieta SFW, Havasu SsFW, Kofa SsFW, San Andres SsFW

Sage Sparrow: Bosque del Apache SFW, Cabeza Prieta SFW, Havasu W

LeConte's Sparrow: Attwater Prairie Chicken SW

Seaside Sparrow: Anahuac SsFW, Brazoria SsFW

Harris' Sparrow: Hagerman SFW, Salt Plains SFW, Tishomingo SFW, Washita SW

McCown's Longspur: Muleshoe W

Chestnut-collared Longspur: Wichita Mountains FW

Bronzed Cowbird: Laguna Atascosa Ss, Santa Ana Ss

Hooded Oriole: Havasu s

Altamira Oriole: Santa Ana Ss

Scott's Oriole: Cabeza Prieta Ss, Kofa Ss

Lesser Goldfinch: Bosque del Apache SW, Las Vegas S

SOUTHWEST

ARIZONA
  1 BUENOS AIRES
  2 CABEZA PRIETA
  3 CIBOLA
  4 HAVASU
  5 IMPERIAL
  6 KOFA
  7 SAN BERNARDINO

NEW MEXICO
  8 BITTER LAKE
  9 BOSQUE DEL APACHE
 10 LAS VEGAS
 11 MAXWELL
 12 SAN ANDRES

TEXAS
 13 ANAHUAC
 14 ARANSAS
 15 ATTWATER PRAIRIE CHICKEN
 16 BRAZORIA / SAN BERNARD
 17 BUFFALO LAKE
 18 HAGERMAN
 19 LAGUNA ATASCOSA
 20 MULESHOE
 21 SANTA ANA / LOWER RIO GRANDE
    VALLEY COMPLEX

OKLAHOMA
 22 LITTLE RIVER
 23 SALT PLAINS
 24 SEQUOYAH
 25 TISHOMINGO
 26 WASHITA
 27 WICHITA MOUNTAINS

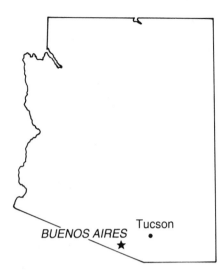

BUENOS AIRES
Tucson
•
★

BUENOS AIRES
(Arizona)

L ush prairies that settlers likened to a sea of flowing grass and then largely destroyed by overgrazing have been restored on this 116,000 acres in southwest Arizona—and with it a magnificent spectrum of wildlife including masked bobwhite quail that were brought back from extinction here.

Mule and white-tailed deer and Chihuahuan pronghorn antelopes graze, attracted by streams and 130 ephemeral ponds in a valley that turns bright green after late summer storms. These gully-washers send lightning crackling from peak to peak in surrounding mountains, clearing afterward to spectacular sunsets of crimson, lavender, and gold.

Birds can be seen here that are found at few other refuges, especially along the Arivaca Creek riparian corridor: rose-throated becards, tropical and thick-billed kingbirds, green kingfishers, and beardless tyrannulets.

Mountain lions cross from the San Luis mountains to the Baboquavari and Las Guajas ranges on the west and some are permanent residents, along with one of the largest populations of desert mule deer in southern Arizona. There are Coue's white-tailed deer, javelina, coyotes, bobcats, kit foxes, badgers, coatimundis, and hooded and spotted skunks. In drier sections beautiful but venomous Gila monsters and three species of rattlesnakes can be found.

Brilliant vermilion flycatchers flutter about streamsides in summer, and only a little less abundant in their habitats are Gila and ladderbacked woodpeckers, dusky-capped, ash-throated, and brown-crested flycatchers, greater pewees, lazuli buntings, and four kinds of hummingbirds: the broadbilled, black-chinned, broad-tailed, and Anna's. Interesting winter sparrows include Cassin's, Brewer's, and black-throated.

Gray hawks nest. Hundreds of white-faced ibises can come through in fall when thousands of ducks fill the ponds and hundreds of sandpipers, yellowlegs, and dowitchers line the shores. A visitor in winter might see 25 or 30 raptors along the auto-tour route—red-tailed, rough-legged, and ferruginous hawks, and occasional golden eagles. Common all year everywhere are Chihuahuan ravens and roadrunners.

This is the only place in the U.S. with four species of quail: the Gambel's, scaled, Montezuma (Mearn's), and the masked, which was reinstated with a foster-parent program using young hatched in captivity in Maryland and parented here by male Texas bobwhites.

All this only suggests the avian and other wildlife riches, and there are also archeological sites from early Native American civilizations and historic buildings.

How to get there: From Tucson take I-19 south toward Nogales, then Ajo Way/Route 86 west 20 miles to Robles Junction; there take Route 286 south 38 miles to refuge sign and left to headquarters. A new visitor center is planned nearby for 1994.

Open: Daylight hours (police patrol at night for border drug smugglers). Office 7:30–4 weekdays.

Best times: All seasons interesting (see weather below).

What to see: Wonderful bird array including masked quails; mule and white-tailed deer; pronghorn antelope; historic and archeological sites.

What to do: Auto-tour routes; walking and hiking trails. Group slide shows by arrangement.

Weather: Torrential rains in July–August can make driving difficult on ungraveled roads. NEVER drive into running water during flash flood—wait till it subsides.

Where to stay: In Arivaca; also Rancho de la Osa, historic site in Sasabe; camping and RV hookups in Arivaca; primitive camping on refuge.

Points of interest nearby: Arizona Sonoran Desert Museum, 55 miles north; many outstanding birding spots—Madera Canyon, 55 miles east (sulphur-bellied flycatcher, elegant trogon); Sycamore Canyon, 35 miles east (five-striped sparrow, varied bunting, elegant trogon); Ramsey Canyon, 150 miles east (12 species of hummingbird); Sabino Canyon 75 miles north (beautiful birds, riparian corridor); Patagonia Preserve 100 miles east (gray hawk, becard); San Bernardino NWR at Douglas.

For further information: Buenos Aires National Wildlife Refuge, P.O. Box 109, Sasabe, Arizona 85633. Phone: (602) 823–4251.

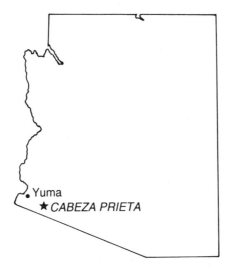

Yuma
★ *CABEZA PRIETA*

CABEZA PRIETA (Arizona)

Cabeza Prieta is one of the wildest, most desolate places in the country, a spectacular mountain and desert refuge of more than 1,000 square miles, most of which is designated Wilderness Area. It was set aside in 1939 largely at the instigation of the Boy Scouts of America to save the desert bighorn sheep from extinction.

It has helped serve that purpose not only for the sheep but for the extremely rare Sonoran pronghorn antelope and for a number of rare-to-unique plants—the massive scaly-barked elephant tree, on which bighorns like to practice their charges; organ pipe and senita cacti (which means old man's whiskers in Spanish); and the limberbush, whose slender branches can be tied in a knot.

Wildlife is not plentiful. The lower Sonoran desert climate is too harsh. Two of its inhabitants, the bighorn and the little kangaroo rat, have learned to subsist virtually without drinking water, getting sufficient moisture from seeds, dew, and forage plants.

A visitor should go with a view toward appreciating the desert ecology and be prepared to deal with its harshness (refuge staff have suggestions).

Find a place with a beautiful view (almost anyplace) and some shade and settle down and wait. Eventually things will start to happen. Horned toads will begin to move about, then ground squirrels and some of the other smaller mammals and birds. (Don't wait near water. Wildlife can die if kept away long from this precious resource.)

Red-tailed hawks soar overhead. Prairie falcons course swiftly along, looking for prey.

Noisy cactus wrens scold and showy Gambel's quail stroll along the roadsides and in the washes. Costa's hummingbirds appear for nectar when paloverdes burst into yellow bloom and desert ironwood (which may be 700 years old) into pink.

Verdins build conspicuous ball-shaped nests in cacti. Elf owls and Gila woodpeckers make homes in the giant saguaro cactus and white-winged doves eat the saguaro fruit. Any shrub might hold black-tailed gnatcatchers, curve-billed thrashers, dark cardinallike phainopeplas, black-throated sparrows and a variety of flycatchers, especially the western and brown-crested, western kingbird, and western wood pewee. Scott's and northern orioles are a possibility on the eastern end.

Javelinas or collared peccaries might appear. Less likely, especially in daytime, when they seek shelter from the sun, are coatimundis, kit foxes, ringtailed cats, bobcats, mule deer, and coyotes, though campers will probably hear these last yipping at night. Wary bighorns will be seen by lucky chance or by a visitor who minutely scans the mountains with spotting scope. Antelopes and mountain lions are here but even less likely to be seen.

Brilliant flowers of the barrel and hedgehog cactus as well as dune primroses, desert sunflowers, verbenas, catchfly gentians, and pink penstemons often appear on the Pinta Sands beyond Tule Well.

A visit to Cabeza Prieta is not for everyone. The beautiful rugged landscape in which mountains jut abruptly 3,000 feet above the flat desert floor can be hazardous. Temperatures can stay at or over 100 degrees for 100 straight days from June to October. Annual rainfall varies from two to six inches.

The rocky road, in many places just a trace, was named El Camino de Diablo— devil's highway in Spanish—because so many over its long history have died there of thirst and exposure.

Consult staff at the headquarters/Visitor Center—this is necessary in any case because permits are required. Cabeza is used as a military gunnery range and refuge personnel must check on the practice schedule before anyone, including themselves, can enter.

Four-wheel drive is required—preferably two four-wheel drives each with two spare tires in case of breakdown. Strongly recommended are two gallons of water per day per person, plus enough for an extra 48 hours, as well as broad-brimmed hats, long sleeves and pants, sun protection, and charcoal if building a campfire (DON'T burn refuge wood). Drive SLOWLY, without a dust plume if possible, to minimize road erosion and preserve the delicate desert ecology. Plan at least a two-day trip to see everything.

How to get there: From Yuma take Route 8 east to Gila Bend, then Route 85 south to Ajo. Office/Visitor Center is on north end of town.

Open: 24 hours (with limitations, see text). Office 7:30–12, 1–4:30 weekdays.

What to see: Unique desert wilderness—desert birds, invertebrates, small mammals; chance of bighorns, antelope.

What to do: Driving, hiking, photography—mostly scenic.

Where to stay: Motels—in Ajo, larger selection in Gila Bend. Campgrounds—primitive on refuge; also at Organ Pipe Cactus National Monument, adjacent.

Weather: Comfortable in winter, cool at night—rest of year hot to the point of hazardous.

What to take and wear: Plenty of water (see text), spare tires, 4-wheel drive vehicle (no rentals locally), brimmed hat, long-sleeved shirt and long pants, sun lotion.

Points of interest nearby: Organ Pipe Cactus National Monument, adjacent southeast; Painted Rock State Park, just west of Gila Bend; Kofa National Wildlife Refuge, 160 miles west.

For more information: Cabeza Prieta National Wildlife Refuge, 1611 North Second Avenue, Ajo, Arizona 85321. Phone: (602) 387–6483.

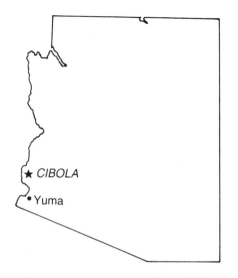

CIBOLA (Arizona and California)

On late fall afternoons hundreds of tall, graceful sandhill cranes fill the air with their melodious bugling as they glide in low formations, necks outstretched, to nightly roosts here. Shortly afterward, just at dusk, thousands of Canada geese follow them, overwhelming onlookers with their honking calls and whirring wings and the sheer presence of their numbers.

More than 25,000 Canadas along with some snow and white-fronts and a dozen or more species of ducks winter here—the largest such concentrations in the desert Southwest—along with up to 1,000 majestic sandhills.

This riverine habitat running through a desert environment is the critically important southern end of winter migration for many of them as well as for hundreds of shorebirds—dowitchers, spotted and least sandpipers, yellowlegs, and others, and some songbirds as well—yellow-rumped and orange-crowned warblers, western meadowlarks, ruby-crowned kinglets, and pine siskins, as well as such others as are present all year, among them yellowthroats, Abert's towhees, loggerhead shrikes, and Savannah and song sparrows.

Cibola is one of the three national wildlife refuges on the lower Colorado River, its 16,667 acres bordering alluvial river bottom and desert mesa in Arizona and California with a dense growth of salt cedar, mesquite, and arrowweed surrounded by areas farmed largely for wildlife food.

A fine way to see it is to put in a canoe and paddle or simply float down through the old river channel—about nine miles, a leisurely one-day trip. Or put in at Blythe to the north, float down through Cibola and on through Imperial Refuge on the south to Martinez Lake—about 60 miles, with campgrounds along the way (though not on the refuges). It is an unforgettable experience.

On land, there is an auto-tour loop, plus miles of very rough roads where one can take a high-clearance vehicle and then hike—ask staff for suggestions on what to see, when and where.

Showy Gambel's quail are common all year on the edges of fields and washes. Great blue herons and snowy egrets fish in shallow waters. Western Clark's grebes forget themselves in watery courtship ballets in late April and, with pied-billed grebes, carry young on their backs later.

Mesquite thickets attract verdins, Abert's towhees, black-tailed gnatcatchers and phainopeplas—which like to find mistletoe there—and furnish sunset perches for great horned owls. Endangered Yuma clapper rails nest—a recent count turned up 50 birds. Say's phoebes sometimes nest in a headquarters loft. Red-tailed hawks raise families atop giant saguaro cacti.

Roadrunners frequent the roads, dashing into the brush to snatch lizards. White pelicans can show up almost anytime. Fall can bring huge flocks of white-winged and mourning doves—sometimes up to 20,000 white-wings.

Mammal populations are similar to Imperial's. Rare sightings of bighorn sheep are more likely at Imperial; others like bobcats, coyotes, burros, and mule deer might be more likely to be seen while driving or walking the dike roads early and late at Cibola.

How to get there: From Blythe, California, take I-10 west to Neighbours Boulevard exit, then south on Neighbours, cross Sprawl's Farmer's Bridge and go south 3.5 miles on Cibola Road to headquarters.

Open: Dawn to dark. Office 8–4:30 weekdays.

Best times to visit: October through February.

What to see: Waterfowl; cranes; roadrunners; good variety of small birds; interesting old pioneer cottonwood log cabin on bluff (off refuge).

What to do: Auto-tour loop; other roads are rough for all but high-clearance vehicles but can be hiked; canoeing (rentals nearby). Hunting October–January can restrict morning wildlife observation mostly to headquarters and auto-tour loop.

Where to stay: Motels—in Blythe; also Ehrenberg, Arizona. Campgrounds—a number of private, county, and state facilities within 25 miles—three adjacent to refuge.

Weather: Summer can be extremely hot and dry until August, then hot and humid until mid-September.

What to take and wear: Hiking boots if doing much walking; sun protection; high-clearance vehicle with plenty of gas, food, water (in case of breakdown—roads are little traveled).

Points of interest nearby: Glamis Sand Dunes, 40 miles south; giant desert intaglios—huge figures of men and animals scoured out by Indians in desert north of Blythe. Also Imperial, Havasu, and Kofa National Wildlife Refuges.

For more information: Cibola National Wildlife Refuge, P.O. Box AP, Blythe, California 92226. Phone: (602) 857–3253.

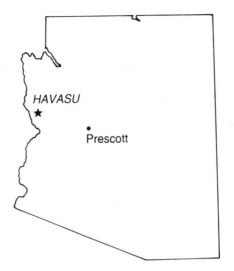

HAVASU   (Arizona and California)

Havasu has some of the most spectacularly beautiful scenery and diverse and interesting wildlife of any place in the lower Colorado River valley, ranging from geese and ducks to desert bighorn sheep.

Reddish-orange basalt cliffs rise sheer and rugged hundreds of feet from clear blue-green waters (that's what "havasu" means in Indian) in 18-mile Topock Gorge, where great blue and black-crowned night herons visit.

Western grebes perform graceful courtship ballets where the Colorado River and Lake Havasu meet, and endangered Yuma clapper rails breed in 4,000-acre Topock Marsh.

But perhaps most remarkable is the unit named after legendary mountain man Bill Williams, containing habitat that ranges through a half-dozen life zones—from high rocky desert to mesa, desert floor, and a creosote-ocotillo association, pockets of saguaro cactus and blue-green paloverde, to river-bottom delta with marsh and open water and a dense forest of 50-foot Fremont cottonwood trees.

Access to these is not effortless. One can set out by vehicle and go into the Bill Williams unit, but to see most of it, one must hike—and to experience Topock Gorge, it is necessary to go by boat. This can be managed by canoe or houseboat without difficulty—the waters are not dangerous and boat rentals are available at concessions near the refuge—and the effort is rewarded many times over (particularly at a time other than a crowded summer or holiday weekend).

Canada and snow geese arrive in late October, peak around year's end, and stay

377

until February, occasionally with a few Ross'. Bald eagles are usually around then, too.

Gambel's quail can be everywhere in the uplands, and roadrunners running along the roads. Birders have a good chance of seeing verdins, crissal thrashers, black-throated sparrows, Abert's towhees, black-tailed gnatcatchers, and an assortment of flycatchers: black phoebes, ash-throated, western, Say's, and sometimes the brilliant little vermilion. The bird list has 292 species.

Thousands of doves sometimes appear in late August.

Coyotes are common and in summer sometimes even swim and wade in the river after coots, carp, and turtle eggs. Beavers and muskrats are there, too. Feral burros whose ancestors accompanied mining prospectors pick their way on the cliffsides along with an occasional desert bighorn sheep.

Porcupines nibble on cottonwood and willow twigs. Gray foxes, western pipistrel bats, antelope squirrels (with markings and speed like antelopes), and desert kangaroo rats (which are adapted to live without drinking water) thrive along with a few desert tortoises and beautiful but poisonous Gila monsters.

Havasu is one of three national wildlife refuges set aside along the lower Colorado River to provide wildlife habitat where native areas were altered by dam construction or artificial river channels. The others are Cibola and Imperial, 100 miles south. A visit to all is a fine idea.

How to get there: Havasu has three district units. To get to Pintail Slough in the Topock Marsh unit, cross the river in Needles and take Harbor Avenue north, turn right on Highway 95 and continue on 95 to refuge signs. Topock Gorge is entered by water from Lake Havasu to the south or at the Topock bridges from the north. For access to Bill Williams unit take Route 95 five miles north from Parker Dam; just before bridge over Bill Williams River take dirt road adjacent to the cliff on the right heading southeast.

Open: 24 hours all year. Office 8–4 daily.

Best times to visit: Late fall to early spring.

What to see: Fantastic scenery. Wide variety of birds and animals appropriate to habitat ranging from open water to desert.

What to do: Boating (rentals available); photography (blind available); hiking; observation towers; fishing for catfish, bluegills, crappie, striped bass, and in spring rainbow trout.

Where to stay: Motels—in Needles and Havasu City. Campgrounds—a concession at Five-Mile-Landing, several at Lake Havasu City state parks.

Weather: Needles is often the hottest place in the nation—highs can AVERAGE 115 degrees June–September.

What to take and wear: Brimmed hat; sun lotion; long sleeves and pants. A water supply on extended excursions.

Points of interest nearby: London Bridge, brought over from England, Lake Havasu City; Joshua Tree National Monument at Twenty Nine Palms, California; Mitchell Caverns, 40 miles west. Cibola, Imperial, Kofa Refuges to the south.

For more information: Havasu National Wildlife Refuge, 1406 Bailey Avenue, Suite B, P.O. Box 3009, Needles, California 92363. Phone: (619) 326–3853. Bill Williams Sub-headquarters Phone: (602) 667–4144.

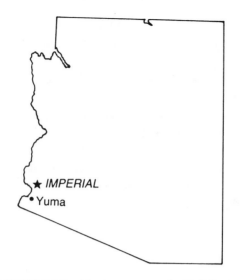

IMPERIAL (Arizona and California)

Mule deer drink and great blue herons fish in green riparian habitat on one of the last untrammeled stretches of the lower Colorado River, while a stone's throw away, rainbow-hued mountains and the lower Sonoran desert shelter bighorn sheep.

Imperial covers 25,765 acres stretching for 30 miles along both sides of the Colorado River in California and Arizona. Exploring its waters by canoe or raft and its desert uplands on the Painted Desert hiking trail and in side trips along the four-mile Red Cloud Mine Road (best by high-clearance vehicle) offers both scenic loveliness and an entrancing range of plant and animal life.

Gambel's quail are everywhere—broods scurrying along the roads, handsome males calling from atop small boulders.

Roadrunners scamper along sunny ridges and pounce on unsuspecting basking lizards.

Coyotes yip early and late.

Mule deer find cover in desert washes where they browse among paloverde and ironwood trees on their way down to the river to drink. So do small troops of wild Appaloosa horses and feral burros, descendants of ones that once accompanied gold miners.

Low-growing creosote and brittlebush shelter blue grosbeaks, phainopeplas, verdins, crissal thrashers, yellow-breasted chats, and warbling vireos, along with black-tailed gnatcatchers, abundant Abert's towhees, and other interesting smaller birds.

White-winged and mourning doves nest in droves in willows along the river, and sandbars may attract large associations of water birds—a single bar may have avocets and stilts at one end, Caspian and Forster's terns at the other, an assortment of sandpipers around the edges, and endangered Yuma clapper rails clattering at dawn and dusk.

Beavers slap the water with their tails and there could still be a few endangered Colorado River squawfish—our largest American minnow, sometimes reaching a length of five feet and weight of 80 pounds.

Tremendous flights of tree, cliff, and barn swallows go through in spring and fall. Warblers make a bright migratory appearance in spring, especially if stopped by a cold front. More than 2,000 white pelicans may come down at various watering holes and swirl overhead in flocks of 100 or so.

Costa's hummingbirds zoom in spring courtship flights over crimson-trumpeted chuparosa shrubs so fast the tiny birds cannot be seen, only the whistling of their tailfeathers heard.

Wintering waterfowl find their way here—flocks of Canada geese along with pintails, mallards, redheads, and cinnamon and green-winged teal. Shorebirds come through in early spring and August. Migrating turkey vultures put on a spectacular show, up to 600 spiraling up from roosts adjacent to headquarters in March and April.

Flowering plants can be stunning in a year with enough rain. Paloverdes burst forth in yellow bloom, smoketrees and ironwood in lavender. Beavertails are pink, prickly pears varying shades of red. Bellyflowers—so-called because you have to get down on your belly to examine them—can cover whole hillsides in purple and gold.

But hikers who strike off on their own should be warned: parts are so remote that refuge staff have to rescue at least a half-dozen visitors each year. Take a compass, a map, and especially drinking water.

On the river, one can put in a canoe at the upper end and float or paddle down the entire refuge, stopping to camp overnight halfway down at Picacho State Recreation Area. Or if the schedule permits a two-day trip, start at upper Cibola National Wildlife Refuge and continue on through both refuges to Imperial Dam. It was Imperial Dam that led to the establishment of these two refuges, to manage and protect wildlife at once displaced by its construction and attracted by backwaters formed thereby.

It is easy traveling—no raging whitewater here, only the wide river lined with canes and willows to which most of the refuge wildlife come at one time or another. (Be sure to stop at an interesting restored watchman's cabin at a former silver and lead mining camp. It's off a riverside trail, so ask directions.)

How to get there: From Yuma take Route 95 north 25 miles, then west on Martinez Lake Road 14 miles and follow signs to refuge.

Open: 24 hours a day, all year. Office/Visitor Center 8–4:30 weekdays, Visitor Center 10–4 weekends October to March.

Best times to visit: Mid-October to late May.

What to see: Wide variety of desert and water wildlife; stunning wildflowers in wet years.

What to do: Boating on Colorado River (rentals available, and guided float trip outfitters at Martinez Lake); self-guided hiking trail; driving on Red Cloud Mine Road, hiking on off-road trails; photography—consult staff on opportunities; observation tower; fishing excellent for bass, catfish, crappie, bluegills.

Where to stay: Motels—many in Yuma. Campgrounds—in and near Yuma and at Picacho State Recreation Area on California side of river.

Weather: Summers hot and dry, often 110 degrees.

What to take and wear: High-clearance vehicle sometimes needed for refuge roads, and be sure to take spare tire and jack. TAKE DRINKING WATER, map, and tell someone of your plans. Sun lotion and insect repellent are important, especially for water trips.

Points of interest nearby: Picacho State Recreation Area (see Campgrounds); Mittry Lake State Area, on Arizona side—fine birding; Cibola, Havasu, Kofa, and Salton Sea National Wildlife Refuges.

For more information: Imperial National Wildlife Refuge, P.O. Box 72217, Martinez Lake, Arizona 85365. Phone: (602) 783-3371.

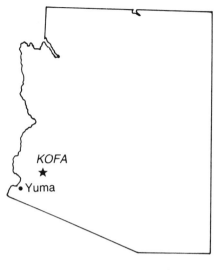

KOFA (Arizona)

The first sight of Kofa is awesome—jagged peaks rising abruptly several thousand feet from the desert floor, altering in hue with every light change. It is stunning during a springburst of brilliant fuchsia and gold cactus and paloverde bloom, with one of Kofa's famed bighorn sheep marked out against the sky, the distant mountains receding in shades of purple and blue sunset.

Old-timers say it is a spectacle that never palls.

Desert bighorns are the noted residents of this thousand-square-mile refuge, of which more than a half-million acres is designated Wilderness Area. Magnificent descendants of wild sheep of Asia that crossed the land bridge from Siberia 500,000 years ago, they were overhunted to the point of near-extinction before citizens pressed for a refuge to be set aside to protect them. Troops of Boy Scouts wrote President Franklin D. Roosevelt, who proclaimed the beginnings of Kofa in 1939.

With protection from poaching and work to enhance waterholes, the sheep population has increased to upwards of 1,000—and other wildlife, through always sparse in this harsh dry habitat, has benefited, too.

Two pairs of golden eagles nest regularly on the cliffs, and the canyons and washes shelter such interesting species as verdins, black-tailed gnatcatchers, Costa's hummingbirds, Gambel's quail, black-throated and Scott's orioles, brown towhees, cactus, rock, and canyon wrens and dark cardinallike phainopeplas—and preying on them, sharp-shinned hawks.

A variety of desert mammals are about, too—mule deer, gray foxes, coyotes, bobcats, ringtails, rarely a mountain lion, also kit foxes and kangaroo rats—both the latter adapted to live without free water, extracting it from prey, forage and their own life processes.

The bighorns are not easily seen—even getting to the point where one might spot them is a feat one should not undertake without preparation (see *What to take*).

Having prepared, go to Kofa Queen Canyon, enter the narrow pass, scan with binoculars over the horizon line atop the highest mountains, and continue to do this as you proceed along. This is where these remarkably adapted animals, whose hooves are like horny grippers with tough rubbery pads, like to spend their time. The young are adept soon after birth in leaping from crag to crag at breathtaking speed. The sheep may also be at lower elevations but they are more readily visible against the sky.

They have keener eyesight than a man's enhanced with eight-power binoculars and will see you before you see them. But they are supremely self-confident—rams have been known to challenge a refuge helicopter taking their census—and so curious, they come closer just to get a better look.

The other way to see sheep during dry periods is to go to one of the blinds, set up near waterholes to count wildlife populations, but available to the public by permission to observe or photograph. This should be undertaken only by those who can stand heat—wildlife come only to drink during hot, dry extremes. One should go before dawn prepared to stay concealed in the blind all day—and not snap a shutter until after the animals have relieved their thirst.

If possible camp overnight (following refuge directives). Desert denizens repose out of sight in the heat of day but some will creep up curiously around the edge of a campfire at night.

Native California fan palms are visible in a grove from the Palm Canyon trail. Giant saguaro cactus, which can grow 50 feet tall, weigh 12 tons, and live 250 years, provide food and shelter for elf owls and Gila woodpeckers. (Rattlesnakes are here—don't plunge your hand quickly into a thicket or a pack-rat nest.)

Kofa, incidentally, is not an old Indian name but a contraction of "King of Arizona," named for an abandoned mine on the refuge.

How to get there: From Yuma, take Route 95 north toward Quartzsite, Arizona, which passes four well-signed entrances on the right. At the refuge boundary, look for leaflet boxes just beyond the signs. Another entrance into the northeast corner is from Exit 45 off I-10, east of Quartzsite.

Open: 24 hours all year. Yuma office at 356 West First Street, 8–12, 1–5 weekdays.

What to see: Desert bighorn sheep, phainopeplas, saguaro cactus, a wide spectrum of interesting desert life and spectacular views.

What to do: Explore more than 300 miles of primitive roads and trails. Photography— waterhole blinds available by permission, best before August, which tends to be stormy.

Where to stay: Motels—in Yuma, also Quartzsite, Parker. Campgrounds—primitive camping on refuge (important to follow refuge directives); also at Quartzsite, and on BLM land (primitive) south of Quartzsite.

Weather: Summers searingly hot, 110 degrees or more.

What to take and wear: Sun lotion and broad-brimmed hat, long sleeves and pants; spotting scope; if going any distance, 4-wheel drive or high-clearance vehicle, flashlight, food, WATER, compass, extra gas, hiking boots, snakebite kit; notify someone of expected return in case you get lost or stuck (as did the writers).

Points of interest nearby: Imperial National Wildlife Refuge, 40 miles north of Yuma, Arizona; Cibola National Wildlife Refuge, 20 miles south of Blythe, California; Cabeza Prieta National Wildlife Refuge, 40 miles south of Gila Bend, Arizona. Annual Quartzsite Pow-Wow (Rock and Mineral Show and reputedly world's largest flea market) first weekend in February.

For more information: Kofa National Wildlife Refuge, P.O. Box 6290, Yuma, Arizona 85366-6290. Phone: (602) 783–7861.

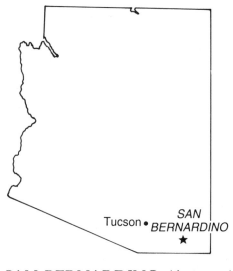

Tucson • SAN BERNARDINO ★

SAN BERNARDINO (Arizona)

Water in parched surroundings makes San Bernardino a scenic attractant to more than 230 recorded bird species, as well as to mule and white-tailed deer, javelinas, shy and nocturnal coatimundis, and ringtailed cats and the endangered fish for which it was established.

Mountain lions and bobcats prowl the environs of streams and ponds supplied by springs and artesian wells from an aquifer that dates to an 1887 earthquake. Here—and almost nowhere else—live the Yaqui chub and Yaqui topminnow, the latter a coppery-sized little fish visible from most water's edges.

Gray hawks nest. Bright vermilion flycatchers flaunt brilliant plumage wherever there's water. Great blue herons are around all year, as are red-tailed hawks, road-runners, loggerhead shrikes, black phoebes, pyrrhuloxias, cardinals, and their sooty look-alikes, phainopeplas.

Birders find seasonally common green-tailed towhees, lark buntings, chats, Lucy's, Townsend's, and black-throated gray warblers, and Brewer's, vesper, and black-throated sparrows, plus occasional rarities such as tundra swans and bearded tyrannulets. There can be fulvous and black-bellied whistling ducks and assorted other waterfowl.

The best way to visit is to go first to refuge headquarters in Douglas (open 8–4 weekdays) and there get literature and directions for the two refuge units, which have similar but not identical wildlife and habitat. A county road bisects the Leslie

Canyon unit and San Bernardino has a road and trails. Be warned; summer can get to 100 degrees or more. Take a sunhat, lotion, and drinking water.

Points of interest nearby include the Slaughter Ranch and museum adjacent (Slaughter was a famous Old West sheriff) plus such excellent birding spots as Guadalupe Canyon, 10 miles east (private but access usually given for birdwatching); Ramsey Canyon, 45 miles west; San Pedro (BLM) Riparian Area, 35 miles west; and Chiricahua National Monument, 65 miles north.

Douglas has motels and RV parks; Coronado National Forest, just north, has campgrounds.

For further information contact San Bernardino National Wildlife Refuge, 1800 Estrella, Douglas, Arizona 85607. Phone: (602) 364–2104.

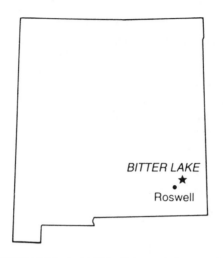

BITTER LAKE
★
Roswell

BITTER LAKE (New Mexico)

The skies are sometimes filled with snow geese and a large portion of the world population of lesser sandhill cranes over this 24,526-acre refuge in southeastern New Mexico—a wonderful sight when all are silhouetted against Capitan Mountain during a gold and crimson sunset.

Snow geese numbers may peak at 40,000 during November and December, along with several thousand ducks of 16 different species and up to 20,000 cranes. The refuge notifies nearby Cannon AFB at Clovis of peak numbers and locations so that their pilots can avoid refuge airspace and possible collisions. The U.S. Air Force schedules flight training at the Roswell Airport for squadrons stationed throughout the United States, since the Roswell airstrip is one of the longest in the world. Because the refuge lies within this practice area, aircraft can prove hazardous to birds, and vice versa.

There is something of interest in the natural world during every season at Bitter Lake, a well-watered oasis on the edge of the Chihuahuan Desert. Its name dates back to the early cattle drives of the late 1800s, when cattlemen found Bitter Lake and the springs that feed it to be "bitter" to the taste. Some think the alkaline water to be more sweet than bitter. While it is not suitable for human consumption, this does not deter its use by waterfowl and other wildlife.

Birding can be excellent. Due to its location near the 100th meridian, on the plains rimmed by mountains, Bitter Lake gets representatives from the east, west, and both high and low elevations—eastern, western and mountain bluebirds, for example.

Endangered interior least terns are found only at Bitter Lake within New Mexico, where they share the salt flats for nesting sites with another threatened species, the snowy plover, and with avocets and black-necked stilts. The Air Force is cautioned that even the shadows of overhead aircraft may terrorize these nesting birds, perhaps suggesting birds of prey.

Common species year-round are Say's phoebes, roadrunners, scaled quail, loggerhead shrikes, killdeer (which protect their nests on roadways and shoulders with a broken-wing act), horned larks, and the introduced white-wing pheasant. Interesting sparrows that are seasonally common include the Cassin's, white-crowned, savannah, lark, clay-colored, and Brewer's. Hundreds of white pelicans and snowy egrets provide the main event in early fall.

Northern harriers are a common sight as they hunt low over the grasslands. Great horned owls sometimes take over nest boxes built for Canada geese over the open water. Their hooting can often be heard late on winter evenings, advertising their presence.

Just off refuge, black-tailed prairie dogs have hundreds of burrows, which are sometimes shared with burrowing owls. Large, colorful ferruginous hawks also visit the colonies during migration. The observant visitor may see mule deer on the refuge when they leave the shelter of trees along the Pecos River to visit farm fields. Coyotes, badgers, and bobcats are common in the refuge, although more secretive and less likely to be seen.

The Lake St. Francis Natural Area consists of a series of strikingly blue gypsum sinkholes, some measuring as much as 90 feet deep. These provide habitat for the endangered Pecos gambusia, a mosquito fish, and the threatened Pecos pupfish, two tiny species of desert fish. An unusual marine algae is also found in these inland salt waters. Due to its sensitive nature, the natural area is open only by special permission for scientific research.

How to get there: From Roswell, take U.S. 380 (Second Street) east about three miles to a highway sign directing you to the refuge. From the highway turnoff, it is eight miles to refuge headquarters, following directional signs. The eight-mile auto-tour road starts there.

Open: One hour before sunrise to one hour after sunset daily. Office hours are 7:30–4:00 weekdays.

Best times to visit: October through February for snow geese and sandhill cranes; early fall for white pelicans and snowy egrets.

What to see: Large numbers of sandhill cranes, waterfowl, white pelicans, snowy egrets; also basking red-eared and spiny softshell turtles, coachwhip snakes, and both prairie and diamondback rattlers.

What to do: Eight miles of self-guided auto tour, with free leaflets; observation platforms; two hiking trails; picnicking; Salt Creek Wilderness Area.

Where to stay: Motels—in Roswell. Campgrounds—in Roswell and at Bottomless Lakes State Park, 10 miles east.

Points of interest nearby: Carlsbad Caverns National Park, 90 miles to the south; Lincoln National Forest, 70 miles west; Dexter National Fish Hatchery (endangered fish), 25 miles southeast; Bottomless Lakes State park, 10 miles east.

For more information: Bitter Lake National Wildlife Refuge, P.O. Box 7, Roswell, New Mexico 88202. Phone: (505) 622–6755.

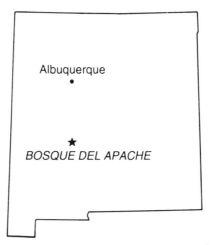

Albuquerque
•

★
BOSQUE DEL APACHE

BOSQUE DEL APACHE (New Mexico)

The hauntingly musical cries of 12,000 or so scarlet-crowned greater sandhill cranes, birds which have been on earth for 40 million years but numbered fewer than 1,000 in this flyway when this refuge was established in 1939, begin in October and continue through the winter here—the largest winter concentration of these birds in the world, two-thirds of the world population. They stay until some of those which are pair-bonded begin spectacular spring courtship dances before heading back north.

Joining them in dawn and sunset flights when skeins of calling birds sometimes fill the rosy sky are up to 60,000 white snow geese down from their Arctic breeding grounds, smaller numbers of Canada and Ross' geese, and 25,000 ducks of 14 species, some of which stay when spring comes and nest.

(You can tell how cold it is on winter mornings by whether cranes fly with their long legs trailing or tucked up in their feathers. At around 15 degrees, they tuck them in.)

Up to eight majestic white whooping cranes are usually with the sandhills, offspring of an experiment to see if their gray cousins could act as foster parents to start a new flock of this beautiful endangered species. (There have been setbacks but the program has not been abandoned.)

Along the 15-mile auto-tour route coyotes stalk stragglers among the geese. Twenty or so wintering bald eagles watch from cottonwoods for likely prey. Golden eagles could appear any time during the year.

Turkey gobblers strut. White-winged pheasants—an introduction that has thrived—cackle. Roadrunners dash this way and that. Mule deer browse. Gambel's quail can be everywhere.

Porcupines doze in tree forks or nibble on bark and twigs. Beavers nibble closer to the ground. Bobcats and badgers are here, though wary. Mountain lions are rarely seen but one pair of visitors found one awaiting their descent from an observation deck. They exchanged uneasy stares until, curiosity satisfied, the lion ambled off.

Handsome black-necked stilts and rusty-hooded avocets nest, usually within view but inconspicuous, on small islands of vegetation. Young ducklings of 11 species follow closely behind their mothers in the waterways in May.

Most of the interesting wildlife on this 57,191-acre refuge of marsh, grasslands, and wilderness in the shelter of the Magdalena Mountains in central New Mexico can be seen readily by the visitor along the miles of roads and trails open to nature exploration. (Walk carefully in brushy areas or you might meet a western diamondback rattlesnake, too.)

Clouds of nighthawks wheel overhead at dusk, snatching up insects, and just as they leave hundreds of bats of 14 identified species take over, catching their breakfast in the same way.

Shorebirds stop by in spring and fall—yellowlegs, long-billed dowitchers, Wilson's phalaropes, snipes, and others.

Red-tailed hawks and northern harriers are common and ferruginous and rough-legs are around frequently. Great blue and black-crowned night herons and snowy egrets forage in summer around the water's edges.

Common at least seasonally are flickers and ladder-backed woodpeckers, black and Say's phoebes, western kingbirds, violet-green swallows, rock and marsh wrens, lesser goldfinches, common yellowthroats, blue and black-headed grosbeaks, mountain chickadees, lark, sage and black-throated sparrows, and horned larks. In lesser numbers are verdins, bushtits, curve-billed and crissal thrashers, vermilion flycatchers, olivaceous cormorants, pyrrhuloxias, and Chihuahuan ravens.

Pueblo Indian ruins dating back to 1300 are here. So are remnants of El Camino Real, the historic route from Mexico City to the Spanish frontier in New Mexico from the 1500s to the 1800s. Apaches camped in the woods along the river, giving the refuge its name.

How to get there: From Socorro take I-25 south to San Antonio Exit 139, then Route 380 east .5 mile to Route 1 (at Owl Cafe) and right eight miles to refuge.

Open: One hour before sunrise to one hour after sunset. Office 7:30–4 weekdays. Visitor Center 7:30–5 weekdays in winter, 7:30–4 April–September, 8–5 weekends except closed weekends April–September.

Best times to visit: November–February for cranes, waterfowl, but all year interesting.

What to see: Sandhill cranes; snow geese; great variety of others.

What to do: Fifteen miles of roads for nature observation; interpretive trails, 30,000 wilderness acres open to hiking; observation decks (tour route closed during eight-day hunting season in November but secondary route open—check with office). Photography—listed by Audubon Society as one of refuge "best bets" photographically, good from road but portable blinds can be set up with permit, sometimes in back areas for special purposes.

    Fall Crane Festival over weekend in late November with special tours, workshops, crafts, study groups in natural history, geology, history, culture, on refuge and surrounding area.

Where to stay: Motels—in Socorro. Campgrounds—in Socorro; also on Route 1 just north of refuge; primitive on refuge for organized youth groups, and Cibola National Forest, 25 miles west. Several area bed-and-breakfasts cater to bird-watchers—fact sheet available from refuge.

Points of interest nearby: Old San Miguel Mission in Socorro; Salinas National Monument, 70 miles northeast; VLA Laboratory (world's largest radio telescope), 70 miles west; Elephant Butte Reservoir, 60 miles south.

For more information: Bosque del Apache National Wildlife Refuge, P.O. Box 1246, Socorro, New Mexico 87801. Phone: (505) 835–1828.

    Also administered from this office is *Sevilleta* National Wildlife Refuge, 228,000 acres north of Socorro acquired with help from The Nature Conservancy, supporting populations of antelopes, deer, Rocky Mountain bighorns, mountain lions, bears, bobcats, and others. It is used intensively for scientific research but otherwise no public access.

LAS VEGAS (New Mexico)

Swift prairie falcons, flying faster than peregrine falcons at high altitudes because of lighter wing-loading (they are official mascots of the U.S. Air Force Academy) spend all year here, performing spectacular courtship gymnastics and nesting on ledges in steep canyons on the nature trail.

Las Vegas is ideal raptor habitat—8,671 acres of prairie grasslands and piñon juniper woodlands at 6,500 feet elevation backed up against the beautiful Sangre de Cristo mountains.

It is not unusual to see a half-dozen species of birds of prey in a single tour of Las Vegas's interpretive loop drive. Northern harriers course over the grasslands in low mothlike flight. Kestrels hover, sometimes motionless in a head-on wind, then dive on a small rodent. Ferruginous, redtails, and roughlegs take up lookouts on a pole or tall cottonwood.

Merlins, Cooper's, Swainson's, and sharp-shinned hawks are around most of the time. Endangered peregrines zoom through in migration.

And bald eagles, a dozen or more, with a few golden eagles feed on fish and an occasional duck on Lake McAllister in fall and winter.

But there is more—Las Vegas can be a wonderful birding refuge, despite water problems in the past. With 15.3 inches average yearly rainfall, it depends on runoff from winter snowpack in the mountains. When water is plentiful more than 2,000 sandhill cranes may drop down in fall alongside 10,000 Canada geese, 3,000 or so snow geese, a few white-fronts and Ross', and 15,000 ducks, mainly mallard, gadwall, pintail, and blue-winged teal.

Long-billed dowitchers and an assortment of sandpipers—western, least, Baird's, and stilt—stop by on mudflats in August. They come through in spring, too, but like the others are more dispersed then and anxious to get to breeding grounds. Eared and pied-billed grebes build nests of floating vegetation; avocets, colorful in bronze hood plumage, lay olive-buff eggs among tufts of vegetation on pond banks. Long-billed curlews with eight-inch decurved beaks raise families in grasslands.

Las Vegas has one of the loveliest nature trails anywhere between sandstone and granite bluffs rising 200 feet along the winding and verdant Gallinas Creek (pace yourself; it's steep in places). There the visitor feels the remoteness of this wild place where Indians left pictographs showing wildlife of that time and cliff swallows build tubular mud nests by the thousands.

Small mammals abound—pocket gophers, voles, ground squirrels—part of the attraction for raptors, as are numerous horned larks. Bobcats and badgers are elusive but listen for coyotes howling in the early mornings. Pronghorn antelopes graze, often in view of the refuge office.

Along the nature trail and in the Lake McAllister area a careful birder can find rock and canyon wrens, green-tailed towhees, mountain and western bluebirds, scrub and Steller's jays, Say's phoebes, Cassin's kingbirds, and when wild columbine blooms, black-chinned, rufous, and broad-tailed hummingbirds.

How to get there: From Las Vegas take Route 104 east two miles to Route 281, then south four miles to refuge entrance.

Open: Daylight hours. Office 8–4:30 weekdays.

Best times to visit: Fall and winter.

What to see: Raptors, sandhill cranes, waterfowl, relics of old Spanish ranches on nature trail.

What to do: Eight miles of public road loops through refuge with interpretive leaflet; nature trail (get permit at office); wildlife overlook; good fishing for brown and rainbow trout—22 inches not unusual—on Lake McAllister (600-acre state-owned refuge inholding).

Where to stay: Motels—in Las Vegas, including historic Hotel Plaza. Campgrounds— Storrie Lake State Park, also McAllister State Waterfowl Area (primitive).

Weather: High winds, dust storms in spring, otherwise generally pleasant.

Points of interest nearby: Fort Union National Monument, 25 miles north; Pecos Pueblo National Monument, 40 miles southwest; Maxwell National Wildlife Refuge, 85 miles north; many historic buildings in Las Vegas.

For more information: Las Vegas National Wildlife Refuge, Route 1, Box 399, Las Vegas, New Mexico 87701. Phone: (505) 425–3581.

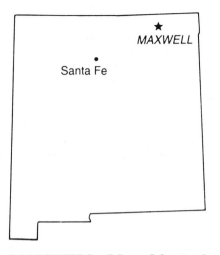

MAXWELL (New Mexico)

Something of wildlife interest goes on all the time on Maxwell's 3,600 acres of lakes and open prairie in northeastern New Mexico.

Up to 62 bald eagles spend November to March feasting on rainbow trout and weaker members of the flocks of some 10,000 Canada geese and 12,000 ducks—a dozen or more species come through in fall and smaller numbers in spring.

Burrowing owls nest in holes excavated by black-tailed prairie dogs that bark and frisk in a "town" of 50 acres or so.

Handsome bufflehead drakes flare white crown feathers and bob up and down in courtship. Hundreds of beautiful Wilson's phalaropes—females are the better-looking in this species—whirl around to stir up watery prey, some while stopping in migration, others staying to nest along with avocets and yellowlegs.

Raptor and songbird populations are notable—prairie falcons and golden eagles may be seen all year, red-tails in fall and winter, and kestrels, Swainson's hawks, and northern harriers nesting, with songbirds finding welcoming habitat in clumps of shrubs and fruiting trees that dot the terrain around a dozen former homesites.

In dry periods Maxwell is inhospitable but most years there is sufficient moisture for five species of grebes—western, Clark's (similar to the western), horned, eared, and pied-billed, which nest. There are great blue herons, snowy egrets, white-faced ibises, and migrating flocks of 70 or so stunning white pelicans going through in early fall.

Black-billed magpies and horned larks are everywhere, as are ring-necked pheasants and rock wrens. Seasonally present are kingbirds—eastern, western, and some Cassin's—Say's phoebes, ravens, roadrunners, violet-green swallows, lark buntings, and rufous hummingbirds (often attracted to visitors wearing red). Perching eagles are readily seen thanks to man-made "trees"—power poles festooned with branches, ideal as lookouts.

Pine siskins and mountain bluebirds like the 6,000-foot elevation as well as the horseshoe of mountains that surrounds the refuge and makes its weather almost impossible to predict—the wind can blow from four directions in any two-hour period, sometimes bringing snow or rain.

Coyotes are always around, scouting lake edges and prairies; also cottontails, jackrabbits, and long-tailed weasels, which shed their brown coats in winter and turn entirely white except for black tail tips.

How to get there: From Raton take I-25 south to Maxwell, then north .8 mile on NM 445 and west 2.5 miles on NM 505 to entrance.

Open: 24 hours year-round; office/Visitor Center 7:30–4 weekdays.

What to see: Raptors, waterfowl, songbirds.

What to do: Seven miles of roads, most areas open to hiking by permit (check with office). Guided group tours by arrangement. Fishing can be outstanding for rainbow trout.

Where to stay: Motels—in Raton. Campgrounds—primitive, on refuge (three-day limit); also Cimarron Canyon Wildlife Area, 37 miles southwest.

Weather: Can be erratic and down to 32 below in winter.

Points of interest nearby: Philmont Scout Ranch—field headquarters of the Boy Scouts of America, museum, trails, 29 miles southwest; Kit Carson's home, 35 miles southwest; Las Vegas National Wildlife Refuge, 85 miles south; many historic spots and outstanding trout fishing in area (ask at office).

For more information: Maxwell National Wildlife Refuge, P.O. Box 276, Maxwell, New Mexico 87728. Phone: (505) 375–2331.

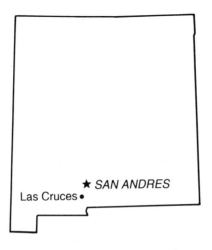

Las Cruces ● ★ *SAN ANDRES*

SAN ANDRES (New Mexico)

San Andres is 57,215 acres northeast of Las Cruces in the San Andres Mountains established for protection of desert bighorn sheep, located entirely within the White Sands Missile Range and closed to public access. For more information: San Andres National Wildlife Refuge, P.O. Box 756, Las Cruces, New Mexico 88004. Phone: (505) 382–5047.

ANAHUAC (Texas)

Anahuac is famous for its rails, those "rather hen-shaped marsh birds of secretive habits and mysterious voices, more often heard than seen," as Roger Tory Peterson describes them. There are six different species here for the expert birder to ferret out (kings and clappers are relatively easy to see, the others more challenging).

Once-endangered alligators are here by the thousands, easily visible except during cold spells or extreme heat and humidity when even they seek shady respite.

Beautiful roseate spoonbills are here all year, as are great numbers of other tall, graceful wading birds—flocks of hundreds of white and white-faced ibis, great blue, little blue, and green-backed herons, snowy and great egrets, and in summer and fall, stately white wood storks.

Raptors are notable—northern harriers coursing low over the marsh, small colorful kestrels hovering over the fields, red-tailed hawks perching atop fenceposts and in trees, with a few bald and golden eagles and occasionally black-shouldered kites wheeling overhead in fall and winter.

One of the great sights is the takeoff and landing in late fall and winter of up to 80,000 snow and blue geese and sometimes over 100,000 ducks, including mallards, gadwalls, pintails, teals, and more than a dozen other species. Not only the sight the sound of thousands of whirring wings as they leave in wave after wave for feeding areas and return again in the early evening is memorable.

More solitary are the mottled ducks, common here within their extremely limited U.S. range.

Stunning purple gallinules frequent the roadside waterways in spring and with young families in summer, along with common moorhens and delicate, lovely black-necked stilts. Strikingly marked masked ducks are here from time to time—their first authenticated U.S. nesting was on Shoveler Pond.

Spring migration can be a fantastic sight when small warblers and songbirds fly over the Gulf in April and drop down, exhausted, to feed and rest in shrubs and trees before continuing their northward push—Tennessee and magnolia warblers, redstarts, orioles, sometimes eye-filling groups of exquisite vermilion and scissor-tailed flycatchers (see High Island below).

Thousands of shorebirds also stop in spring and fall on tidal mudflats and shallow exposed marsh—marbled godwits, golden plovers, long-billed curlews, pectoral, stilt, and upland sandpipers.

Anahuac was the last natural stand of the extremely rare red wolf. Now all animals of pure red wolf strain have been captured as part of a plan to raise animals in captivity and then release them again in the wild. Some of Anahuac's wolf descendants have been released at Alligator River and Cape Romain National Wildlife Refuges. But occasionally bigger-than-usual coyotes with reddish fur hark back to wolf ancestors here.

It is hard to imagine going out on this refuge without seeing numbers of interesting natural inhabitants, including some of the mammals—perhaps raccoons, bobcats, muskrats, and nutria, which swim along with their young on their backs (alligators have been observed doing the same thing, giving a young one a ride on an adult's big flat scaly forehead).

How to get there: From Houston take I-10 east to Highway 61, then south to FM 562, south to FM 1985, and four miles east to refuge entrance. Refuge headquarters are in Anahuac at 509 Washington Avenue, opposite the courthouse.

Open: 24 hours all year. Office 8–4:30 weekdays.

Best times to visit: April for migrations; November–January for waterfowl concentrations.

What to see: Rails; wading and shorebirds; raptors.

What to do: 15 miles of roads for walking or driving. Photography. Fishing from bayshore, excellent for flounder, redfish, trout, others.

Where to stay: Motels—in Baytown, Winnie, High Island, and Anahuac. Camp-

ANAHUAC

grounds—Fort Anahuac and White's County Parks, northwest of refuge; also along bayshore on refuge, primitive, three nights only.

Weather: Summers extremely hot, humid.

Points of interest nearby: Big Thicket National Preserve, 70 miles northeast—last U.S. habitat of ivory-billed woodpecker, if any still exist; Sea Rim State Park, 45 miles southeast; High Island Audubon Sanctuary, southeast 20 miles—wonderful birding, especially in spring. For general nature-watching, contact the helpful Houston Audubon Society, 440 Wilchester, Houston, Texas 77079, telephone (713) 932–1392; or the Outdoor Nature Club, 10602 Cedarhurst, Houston, Texas 77096, telephone (713) 723–8559.

For more information: Anahuac National Wildlife Refuge, P.O. Box 278, Anahuac, Texas 77514. Phone: (409) 267–3337.

Also administered by Anahuac are two satellite refuges, *McFaddin* and *Texas Point*—coastal marshes offering habitat to wintering waterfowl and migrants, with, until recently at least, relatively few visitor facilities. To arrange a visit contact the McFaddin/Texas Point National Wildlife Refuges, P.O. Box 609, Sabine Pass, Texas 77655. Phone: (409) 971–2909.

ARANSAS ★
●
Corpus Christi

ARANSAS (Texas)

The majestic whooping crane is perhaps the world's best-known endangered species and Aransas, one of America's premier national wildlife refuges, is where we have seen it brought back from the edge of extinction.

Once seen, the whooping crane can never be forgotten. Strong and graceful, our tallest North American bird stands up to five feet with a seven-foot wingspread. Partly it is this regal presence that has inspired worldwide desire for their survival, partly a dramatic life-style that exemplifies beauty confronting great hazard at every turn.

When a pair of the tall white birds with scarlet crowns and black wingtips bow and leap in courtship dances, their "bugling" calls are heard for miles.

"When we hear this call we hear no mere bird," said the naturalist Aldo Leopold. "He is the symbol of our untamable past."

The call resounds along a 2,600-mile migration route from nesting grounds in remote northwest Canada (only discovered in 1954 after a forest fire) to winter quarters at Aransas on the Texas Gulf Coast. It is a perilous trip undertaken mostly in twos and threes—two adults with a lone chick between them.

Reported to be extinct in 1923, the species has shown a gradual increase since only 21 were known to exist in the wild in 1941. A recent count showed 146; about

60 survive in small captive groups and there are a dozen or so in an experimental flock in Idaho and New Mexico. All this is watched carefully and uneasily, for a single disastrous mishap—such as an oil or chemical spill on their winter feeding grounds—could cause losses beyond recovery.

"We live 15 seconds away from disaster" from $23 billion in petrochemical cargoes passing yearly through the refuge via the intracoastal waterway, says refuge manager Brent Giezentanner.

But for now, this is one of few places where the beautiful cranes can be seen from early November to late March, either from the 40-foot observation tower equipped with telescopes or from one of the tour boats operating in refuge waters out of the nearby Rockport-Fulton area, which guarantee sightings or your money back.

But Aransas's fame would be justified even without the cranes, whose marsh habitat takes up but a fifth of its almost 55,000 acres. The rest is grassland and oak-brush with a large, seasonally flooded lake on which exist a tremendous variety of flora and fauna that can only be suggested here.

Countless thousands of rolls of visitors' film depict the stately white-tailed deer posing with fine racks of antlers in fall and spotted fawns in spring beside the trails and 15-mile auto-tour loop. Collared peccaries, alligators, armadillos, and bobcats are fairly common—about 250 alligators are here, including a 13-footer that haunts Thomas Slough—and although rarely seen, coyotes and mountain lions are around, too.

Aransas claims one of the longest bird lists of any national wildlife refuge—389 species. Common at various seasons are such stunning and interesting varieties as reddish egrets, roseate spoonbills, wood storks, sandhill cranes, long-billed curlews, white and brown pelicans, white-tailed hawks, scissor-tailed flycatchers, and various waterfowl.

Bird migrations can be spectacular. In April and May warblers and other songbirds in bright breeding plumage—such as tanagers and indigo buntings—can be present in huge numbers, especially in a "fallout" after a norther. At such times 33 species have been counted in 15 minutes in the immediate area around the refuge wildlife interpretive center, the oaks and shrubs reminding onlookers of decorated Christmas trees. Similar numbers can appear in fall.

Hundreds of shorebirds—avocets, stilts, yellowlegs, and a full range of plovers and sandpipers—appear in spring migration and again in fall on flats near the picnic area or the tower. Cormorants occasionally move along offshore in rafts of 1,000 or more, so closely packed they appear to be black islands in the water.

All nine American members of the rail family are here, along with least, eared, and pied-billed grebes and 15 kinds of beautiful herons, egrets, and other wading birds.

Wildflowers can be glorious, the headquarters lawn sometimes is solid with orange

Indian blanket, and there are Christmas berries and brilliant purple beautyberries in October.

Staff at the wildlife interpretive center are prepared to enhance the visitors' stay with fine informative leaflets and advice on where, when, and how best to see everything (and a superb Aransas natural history guidebook prepared by two volunteers can be purchased).

How to get there: From Rockport go north on Route 35, turn right on Route 774 and follow refuge signs.

Open: Every day sunrise to sunset. Wildlife interpretive center 8–4:30 daily except Thanksgiving and Christmas.

Best times to visit: October to May (most wildlife here then and weather generally best).

What to see: Whooping cranes, deer, great variety of others.

What to do: Many miles of walking and driving trails; wheelchair-accessible observation tower; photography—excellent, especially for deer, from car; boat tours out of Rockport to view cranes in refuge marshes. (The refuge does not arrange boat tours—contact individual boat operators directly.) Excellent interpretive center with films, slides, educational packets for schoolchildren.

Where to stay: Motels—in Rockport and Port Lavaca. Campgrounds—in Rockport, also Goose Island and Port Lavaca state and county parks, and on refuge by permission for organized educational and youth groups.

Weather: Summer can be extremely humid, hot, insect-ridden; usually some cold rains January–February.

What to take and wear: Boots if walking off-trail, insect repellent a must in warm months, also long-sleeved shirts and pants. Bring container for drinking water in summer.

Points of interest nearby: The whole Rockport area has wonderful birding, and refuge staff are happy to suggest spots where special things can be seen—prairie chickens, caracaras, others; also contact the Rockport Chamber of Commerce, which can be helpful and publishes a birders' guide. Also Welder Wildlife Refuge at Sinton (open once a week); Padre Island National Seashore; Second Chain of Islands Audubon Sanctuary, best seen from excursion boat out of Rockport. Many interesting historic sites in area.

For more information: Aransas National Wildlife Refuge, P.O. Box 100, Austwell, Texas 77950. Phone: (512) 286–3559.

Also administered by Aransas is *Matagorda Island* State Park and Wildlife Management Area, a 38-mile-long coastal barrier island newly acquired to be managed jointly with the Texas Parks and Wildlife Department. It is home to badgers, white-tailed deer, coyotes, and 19 state or federally listed threatened or endangered species, including whooping cranes. There are 320 species on its bird list. A passenger ferry to the island currently operates on weekends from Port O'Connor, and the Texas Parks and Wildlife Department operates a shuttle service on the island. Check with refuge or Matagorda State Park Superintendent, Port O'Connor, Texas 77982. Phone: (512) 983–2215.

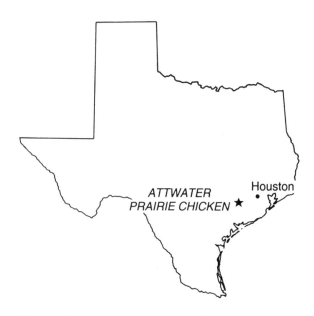

ATTWATER
PRAIRIE CHICKEN ★

Houston

ATTWATER PRAIRIE CHICKEN (Texas)

The beleaguered Attwater prairie chicken, one of the world's most endangered birds, maintains a precarious hold in the grasslands of this southeast Texas refuge that it shares with a number of other interesting species such as caracaras, white-tailed hawks, nesting mottled and black-bellied whistling ducks, and sometimes 95 percent of the world population of white-fronted geese.

Attwater prairie chickens are small henlike birds so inconspicuous you might not notice one right beside you in its chosen habitat. But that changes when spring courtship starts and males gather on short-grass booming grounds (called leks) to advertise their readiness to mate.

They stomp and leap in the air, vibrate stiffly erected head feathers and inflate orange throat sacs to make booming sounds like a foghorn, or wind blowing over the neck of an empty bottle. Their leaping and stamping can be heard and felt for 50 feet or more and in favorable weather the booming is audible for a mile. Plains Indian headdresses and dances may have originated in these performances.

Once Attwater prairie chickens were so numerous in Texas coastal prairies that old-timers said the booming caused pain to sensitive eardrums. As if to lessen this, gunners practiced marksmanship using them as clay pigeons and held team competitions to kill as many of these attractive, inoffensive little fowl as possible; the party that killed the smallest number would then pay the outing expenses. Tallies made, piles of sometimes thousands of birds were left to rot or be eaten by vultures.

Irresponsible shooting caused the loss of great numbers of birds, but the major cause of their decline was habitat destruction. By 1937 their range had been reduced 93 percent, their population down an estimated 99 percent, and they were believed close to following their near relative, the heath hen, into extinction.

It has not happened. Hunting them was stopped in 1937 and despite subsequent setbacks and a report in 1941 that nothing could save them, they are still here, and this refuge, established in 1972, is dedicated to preserving habitat to ensure their survival. The Nature Conservancy and the World Wildlife Fund originally bought 3,500 acres, the Fish and Wildlife Service bought more to bring total acreage to 7,980, and plans are to enlarge it to 15,000—plus imaginative plans to improve and preserve habitat on private land.

So while Attwater prairie chickens are not here in large numbers—fewer than 100 out of perhaps 500 over the state of Texas—there is hope.

And anyone wishing to see one almost certainly can do so during their courtship in April from an observation blind set up near their booming ground.

Other interesting birds and mammals enjoy this island of habitat amid rice and other agricultural fields. White-tailed deer browse. Skeins of wintering geese fill the sky from mid-October to March—up to 120,000 snow geese, 60,000 Canadas, and 80,000 white-fronts. Up to 60,000 ducks are here—in fall, blue and green-winged teals, pintails, wigeons, and gadwalls; in winter, hooded mergansers, cinnamon teals, lesser scaups, and redheads. (Avian cholera from drought and overcrowding has caused problems in some recent years.)

Scissor-tailed flycatchers are common; so are Sprague's pipits, loggerhead shrikes, painted buntings, dickcissels, orchard and northern orioles, vesper and LeConte's sparrows, great blue herons, snowy egrets, and white-faced ibis.

Trees along the waterways can be filled with warblers and migrant songbirds in April, when a bluebird nest-box trail along the entrance road becomes active amid a carpet of bluebonnets, Indian paintbrush, primrose, and coreopsis.

The refuge tries to prevent disturbance during prairie chicken courtship but northern harriers like to harass males at their dancing, swooping down though never actually striking. Apparently it's only sport for the hawks and after a few minutes the chickens usually resume their strutting and booming. It was thought aberrational until an old account revealed harriers have been doing this for generations with no discernible gain to the hawks and no more than temporary agitation to the chickens.

How to get there: From Houston take I-10 west to Exit 720, then south on Texas Highway 36. Turn right on Texas Farm Road 3013, go 10 miles to refuge sign and two miles farther on gravel road to headquarters.

Open: Sunrise to sunset. Office/Visitor Center 7:30–4 weekdays.

What to see: Attwater prairie chickens; also waterfowl, caracaras, white-tailed hawks, wildflowers, interesting sparrows and songbirds.

What to do: Two self-guided trails, a four-mile auto-tour route. Observation blind. Permission for individual photoblinds given for special projects.

Where to stay: Motels—in Columbus, 22 miles northwest; Sealy, 13 miles northeast; Eagle Lake—the Farris 1912, a restored Victorian hotel and south Texas landmark (reserve ahead). Campgrounds—Stephen F. Austin State Park, 18 miles northeast.

Points of interest nearby: The Eagle Lake area has some of the largest concentrations of wintering geese in Texas—thousands can usually be seen feeding in fallow rice fields along public roads. Eagle Lake has an annual wildflower celebration in March with self-guided auto tours through carpets of colorful bluebonnets, paintbrush, others. For recent local information call the Houston Audubon Society, (713) 932–1392, or the Outdoor Nature Club, (713) 723–8559.

For more information: Attwater Prairie Chicken National Wildlife Refuge, P.O. Box 519, Eagle Lake, Texas 77434. Phone: (409) 234–3021.

Houston •

★

BRAZORIA /
SAN BERNARD

BRAZORIA/SAN BERNARD (Texas)

Some of the best birding in the United States is here. Warblers and other songbirds sometimes "fall out" by the hundreds in April, dozens of species in bright breeding plumage, in trees and shrubs, borne by south winds over the Gulf of Mexico and stopped by a wind shift to the north. (They return in fall but in duller feathers.)

This is an ancestral wintering spot for snow geese; 150,000 or so may be here from November through January, a dawn spectacular when they rise at first light and fly out to feed or return against a rosy sunset, swirling and filling the air with loud calls and wingbeats, finding places to roost for the night.

There are thousands of wintering ducks—green-winged teals, shovelers, wigeons, gadwalls, pintails, perhaps 700 mottled ducks—and Moccasin Pond is one of the best places on the Texas coast to see cinnamon teal.

Nesting islands accommodate tens of thousands of beautiful herons and egrets, including the relatively rare reddish, along with hundreds of roseate spoonbills and once-rare brown pelicans, which have made a strong comeback here. All these fan out to feed throughout these refuges and may be joined by a thousand or so endangered wood storks.

Alligators loaf on the banks almost anyplace.

Brazoria is part of the annual Audubon Society Freeport Christmas Bird Count, which often is highest in the nation in the number of species seen at that time—and San Bernard, with a separate count, is not far behind.

Birders might spot six hard-to-see rail species in April, including the rare yellow rail, while black-shouldered kites hover overhead.

Brilliant vermilion flycatchers sometimes set up territories around the shop at Brazoria.

Up to 4,000 sandhill cranes spend the fall and winter with bobwhite quail in the upland areas. Lovely scissor-tailed flycatchers are common then, and short-eared owls can often be found around the salt grass.

These two refuges, San Bernard and Brazoria, are administered from the Brazoria Refuge Complex office in Angleton. They are similar but with different visitor access. San Bernard has eight miles of gravel road of which three miles encircle Moccasin Pond, and is open dawn to dusk daily.

Brazoria has more diverse habitat. Six miles of road go along freshwater ponds, salt mudflats, woods, and upland prairie ridges. It is open only on the first full weekend of every month, when an open house is held. Otherwise there is only intermittent visitation, unscheduled, whenever a work crew happens to be on the refuge (inquire).

The refuge staff plus a knowledgeable volunteer corps are helpful in suggesting where visitors might seek special birds—everything from yellow rails to vermilion flycatchers—as well as a look, if they have a shallow-bottomed boat, at one of the spectacular nesting islands. There are also three fine local naturalist groups that are a fund of information (see below—*Points of interest nearby*).

How to get there: The Refuge Complex office is at 1212 North Velasco (Business Route 228) in Angleton. To San Bernard from Houston take Highway 288 south to Lake Jackson, turn west or right on FM 2004 and follow 11 miles to refuge sign. To Brazoria turn east or left on FM 2004, follow about five miles to FM 523, turn right there 5.5 miles to refuge sign.

Open: Office 7:30–4 weekdays. San Bernard dawn to dusk daily. Brazoria first full weekend in month (see text above).

Best times to visit: October through April (but summer good, too).

What to see: Waterfowl; wading birds; variety of others.

What to do: Nature observation; photography can be good.

Where to stay: Motels—in Angelton and Lake Jackson. Campgrounds—near Brasosport; also permitted on public beaches and Brazoria County Parks (interesting in themselves; Phone: [713] 849–5711).

Weather: Humid, subject to sudden downpours anytime.

What to take and wear: Raingear, strong insect repellent.

Points of interest nearby: This is a great birding area, especially in winter. For information on good spots contact Houston Audubon Society, 440 Wilchester, Houston, Texas 77079, phone (713) 932–1392; Outdoor Nature Club, 10331 Longmont, Houston, Texas 77042; Brasosport Birders has maps and data on interesting county places available at refuge office. Also visit the Brasosport Museum of Natural Science and adjacent Nature Center and Planetarium in Lake Jackson—and black skimmers often colonize a nearby parking lot on private land, opened to view in late June (inquire).

For more information: Brazoria/San Bernard Refuge Complex, P.O. Drawer 1088, Angleton, Texas 77516. Phone: (409) 849–7771.

Another refuge, *Big Boggy,* is administered from this office—similar to the others in habitat and wildlife but with no public use. A visitor center is planned, and an additional 30,000 acres recently acquired for Brazoria includes rare coastal prairie habitat and with it the possibility of reintroducing the endangered Attwater's prairie-chicken.

Amarillo
•
★
BUFFALO LAKE

BUFFALO LAKE (Texas)

Badgers resembling small, fast-moving hairy tanks share Buffalo Lake with mule deer, prairie dogs, diminutive swift foxes, and raptors of a half-dozen species—and, when there is sufficient water, the birds that require it.

This 7,664-acre refuge leads a double life. It was established when Buffalo Lake covered 2,000 or so acres, fed by rainfall and Tierra Blanca Creek and springs as well. But irrigation use has diverted creek water, lowered the water table, and dried up the springs, so the refuge has evolved to furnish habitat largely to dry-land creatures—and these have been responsive.

Burrowing owls share a 100-acre prairie dog town with those appealing rodents. Swainson's hawks nest commonly and good numbers of ferruginous, red-tailed, and rough-legged hawks and northern harriers are around in fall and winter, along with a few bald and golden eagles—more of these if heavy rains fill the lake bed.

Horned larks, meadowlarks, bobwhite quail, and ring-necked pheasants can be every place, and wild turkeys often browse in fields along the auto-tour route, along with mule deer. Vesper, lark, and Cassin's sparrows visit the grasslands. Orchard and northern orioles nest. Killdeer lay eggs in the drive or even the parking lot where they're protected with a sawhorse until hatching, if discovered soon enough.

Highlights of recent Audubon Christmas Bird Counts have included ladder-backed woodpeckers, scrub jays, Lapland and McCown's longspurs, 160 sandhill cranes, and 2,225 lark buntings.

Sometimes a torrential rainfall fills up to 300 acres of the former lakebed and the refuge undergoes an overnight change. Thousands of waterfowl come—snow and Canada geese, teal, shoveler, mallard and pintail ducks and others, and shore and wading birds such as great blue and black-crowned night herons, Baird's sandpipers, and Wilson's phalaropes.

It is always a beautiful refuge, with its rose-colored limestone outcrops almost like a small Grand Canyon in places, and spring flowers of many hues cover the rolling hills.

How to get there: From Amarillo take I-27 south to Canyon, then Route 60 west to Umbarger and Route FM 168 south two miles to refuge.

Open: 8 a.m.–10 p.m. daily. Office 8–4:30 weekdays.

Best times to visit: Fall through spring.

What to see: Mule deer; prairie dogs; good small birding in canyons and draws; numerous wintering waterfowl and migrating shorebirds when water conditions permit.

What to do: Ten miles of roads open to foot and vehicular traffic including 4.5-mile interpretive auto tour and two trails (entire refuge is open to hiking); picnicking; camping (see campgrounds); horseback riding.

Where to stay: Motels—in Canyon, 10 miles east, also Hereford, Amarillo. Campgrounds—on refuge (groups should reserve ahead); also at Palo Duro Canyon State Park, 22 miles east.

Weather: Summers hot, dry, windy. Spring rainstorms with 50-mph winds can occur suddenly.

Points of interest nearby: Palo Duro Canyon State Park—scenically beautiful, good birding (see Campgrounds); Lake Meredith, 75 miles northeast—good birding; Panhandle-Plains Historical Museum, Canyon.

For more information: Buffalo Lake National Wildlife Refuge, P.O. Box 179, Umbarger, Texas 79091. Phone: (806) 499–3382.

HAGERMAN (Texas)

Pirouetting scissor-tailed flycatchers along with thousands of migrating waterfowl, clouds of white pelicans, dashing roadrunners, and much else are part of the highly visible scene at this 11,319-acre north Texas refuge.

But the emphasis is not so much on numbers as diversity and accessibility of the various wildlife to visitors. Most can be seen from a road that bisects the refuge with beautiful rolling prairie dotted with wildflowers on the left and on the right, waters of the Big Mineral Arm of Lake Texoma, which was formed by construction of the Denison Dam on the Red River bordering Texas and Oklahoma.

Most of the waterfowl species common to the Central Flyway settle here for at least part of the year—more than a dozen kinds of ducks and up to 10,000 geese, Canadas, snows, white-fronteds, and Ross'. Most move farther south for the winter but a few thousand usually stay on, with a bald eagle or two keeping a lookout for stragglers.

Hagerman is known among area birders for its assortment of interesting sparrow types. Dickcissels sing on every post in summer. Field and lark sparrows nest commonly and other seasons can bring crowds of white-throated, white-crowned, and Harris' along with fox, LeConte's, Lincoln's, and others. Outbreaks of chestnut-collared and other longspurs follow hard winters up north.

Colorful indigo and painted buntings, blue grosbeaks, and cardinals are common nesters, and golden prothonotary warblers in wet and woodsy situations. Here all year are bluebirds, mockingbirds, bobwhite quail, killdeer, and meadowlarks. Great blue herons have a rookery on dead osage orange trees visible by spotting scope.

Mississippi kites nest and soar after insects in the summer skies. Wild turkeys have been reintroduced.

The prairie shelters rodents, which in turn attract raptors. Red-tailed, red-shouldered, and broad-winged hawks nest commonly.

Migrating shorebirds can be impressive when mudflats are exposed, depending on lake levels: sometimes hundreds of Baird's sandpipers as well as western, least, upland, pectoral, stilt, and solitary along with Wilson's phalaropes, dowitchers, occasional golden plovers, and long-billed curlews.

Some 50,000 white pelicans funnel through the area spring and fall, their nine-foot white wings glistening silver as they rise in great swirling clouds of hundreds of birds catching the thermals.

But the refuge beauties are the streamered scissor-tailed flycatchers fluttering and wheeling after flying insects, sometimes massing in flocks of hundreds preparing for fall migration.

The clowns are the roadrunners dashing frantically about, disappearing in the brush to reappear with a writhing snake or lizard.

Visitors who get out at dawn will get the best looks at mammals—grazing white-tailed deer, bobcats (sometimes with young in summer), minks, armadillos rooting about in leaves, beavers, raccoons padding along a creek bed, or coyotes whose yips punctuate the day early and late.

The prairie itself can be breathtakingly beautiful, undulating like sea waves in the breeze, covered with a succession of colorful wildflowers—larkspurs, daisies, coneflowers, pink penstemon.

More than 100 oil wells pump over 5,400 barrels a day—the refuge was established in 1946 and oil discovered in 1951 (the refuge does not own underground mineral rights). They are spotted throughout the marsh, water, and upland habitat.

But offensive as the derricks are to many visitors, the geese and deer browse alongside and eagles perch on willows and oaks overlooking them, apparently unconscious of any unnatural intrusion. To many Texans they are an appropriate if not downright beautiful part of the native scene along with bluebonnets, Indian paintbrush, and spring-flowering redbuds.

How to get there: From Dallas go north 60 miles on U.S. 75 to Sherman–Farm Market 1417 exit, then north 13 miles on 1417 to refuge sign and left six miles to entrance.

Open: Daylight hours. Office/Visitor Center 7:30–4 weekdays, Visitor Center 8:30–3:30 weekends.

Best times to visit: October through spring.

What to do: Five miles of roads for driving, four miles for foot travel only; photography (portable blinds permitted); fishing in Lake Texoma for striped bass, also crappie, bream, channel cat. Ask staff about local birding hotspots. Guided birding tours Tuesday and Thursday mornings.

Where to stay: Motels—in Denison and Sherman. Campgrounds—many operated by Corps of Engineers in area, also Eisenhower State Park, nine miles northeast.

Weather: July–August hot, humid; January–February possible icestorms.

Points of interest nearby: Denison Dam, recreation, museum, tours, nine miles north; Eisenhower State Park, various recreation facilities; Eisenhower birthplace in Denison; Heard Natural History Museum, McKinney, 45 miles south; Tishomingo National Wildlife Refuge, 70 miles north.

For more information: Hagerman National Wildlife Refuge, Route 3, Box 123, Sherman, Texas 75090. Phone: (903) 786–2826.

LAGUNA
ATASCOSA

Harlingen

LAGUNA ATASCOSA (Texas)

Spotted ocelots and rare jaguarundis, like small dark panthers, prowl the brush and marsh of this 45,187-acre refuge, a former delta of the Rio Grande River where birds and other wildlife riches almost beggar description. Many species are exceedingly rare; others appear in large numbers seldom seen elsewhere.

It is the only place in the United States where endangered ocelots are known to have denned.

Powerful mountain lions take on prey as large as the statuesque white-tailed deer. Bobcats prey on the omnipresent cottontail rabbits—and sometimes seem omnipresent themselves. One birdwatcher returned to his car to find one sitting in the driver's seat. Another visitor was watching some redhead ducks, felt something brush against his leg, and looked down to see a tawny bobcat.

Laguna Atascosa has the densest population of wild cats in the country. But that's only the beginning. This refuge is a bridge between tropical and temperate biotic zones and therefore home at various seasons to a tremendous variety of all kinds of wildlife from both.

Birding here is truly fantastic. Unusual and impressive sightings can only be suggested rather than listed here in their entirety.

Eighty percent of the continent's population of redhead ducks winters here. When they fly over, sometimes a quarter-million birds, it can take five minutes during which most onlookers stop all conversation and just watch and listen to the whirring wingbeats.

With crowds of other waterfowl here as well—pintails, wigeons, shovelers—there can be more than a million birds taking to the air from Laguna Madre and flying back and forth over Redhead Ridge. Sometimes they seem to stretch across the whole horizon. One refuge staffer recalls seeing a flight five miles long. (Redhead Ridge was a famous hunting spot in the 1700s where tens of thousands of redheads were killed during traditional overflights solely for fat deposits. These were cut out and rendered for saddle ointment, the rest of the bird discarded.)

Endangered aplomado falcons are here throughout the year. Once these swift long-tailed falcons nested here. Now a hacking program has released young birds that it is hoped will one day restore a breeding population.

Harris' and white-tailed hawks, rarities elsewhere, have nested.

Black-bellied whistling ducks, showy long-legged fowl with bright red bills, pink feet, and large white wing patches, abound in spring and summer. They nest in boxes put out by the refuge, and those they pass up for natural cavities are taken by barn owls for their families.

Spectacular green jays, roadrunners, and others are common at feeders and brushy areas around headquarters, where yellow-billed cuckoos seem to be everyplace, along with long-billed thrashers, brown-crested flycatchers, and Couch's kingbirds. Small families of javelinas might rush out of the brush at any time, or an armadillo come lumbering along rooting about for grubs.

In recent years three pairs of yellow-green vireos have nested at headquarters, their only known breeding place in the U.S.

Familiars are here alongside the rarities—cardinals and meadowlarks along with border species seldom seen in this country such as plain chachalacas, pauraques, white-tipped doves, least grebes, kiskadee flycatchers, golden-fronted woodpeckers, and Botteri's and olive sparrows.

The "fall-out" of songbirds when they hit a "norther" here en route to breeding grounds can seem almost incredible—trees and shrubs coming alive with small yellow, red, and blue birds everyplace, dropping down to rest before resuming migration. It happens two or three times each spring during March through early April with stunning scissor-tailed and vermilion flycatchers, painted and indigo buntings, blue grosbeaks, northern orioles, dickcissels, four kinds of swallows, numbers of small warblers, and many others.

Shorebirds can appear in tremendous numbers—long-billed curlews, yellowlegs, dowitchers—and threatened piping plovers spend winters along the Bayside tour loop. A huge heronry on an island to the north is protected from public access but its birds feed on the refuge and are commonly seen most of the year—graceful tricolored, great blue, and little blue herons, reddish, snowy, and great egrets sharing the marsh and tidewater shallows with occasional roseate spoonbills.

Laguna's bird list notes some 389 species—but this only hints at the wealth of bird and other life here, as does the annual Audubon Christmas Bird Count in which Laguna almost always counts more than 150 species.

White-tailed deer appear with fawns in spring browsing in groups of 20 to 40; bucks with imposing racks appear later.

Photographic opportunities are one of the best in the refuge system. Special-use permits may be granted for temporary blinds, but these are limited to special purposes to avoid wildlife impact. However, many subjects are relatively unwary, and a vehicle makes an excellent blind; with a telephoto lens and a little care, good pictures can be taken without one.

In spring trees and shrubs blossom in succession, beginning in February with fields of creamy yuccas, followed by fragrant sweet acacia with yellow globes filling the small trees. By April prickly pear cactus show off large flowers of yellow, red, and every shade between. Purple cenizo and orange lantana also bloom in April. And for herpetologists, there are 29 snake species, including rattlers, coral snakes, and gentle indigos.

How to get there: From Harlingen take Farm Road 106 east 25 miles to refuge sign, follow to headquarters on Buena Vista Road.

Open: Sunrise to sunset. Office 8–4:30 weekdays. Visitor Center 10–4 daily October–April, weekends September and May (closed June–August and Thanksgiving, Christmas, New Year's).

What to see: Great variety and numbers of birds and mammals, with largest concentrations of waterfowl in October–January. (Visitors should call the rare-bird alert—[512] 565–6773—to get the latest sightings.)

What to do: About 25 miles of roads and trails including six walking trails and two auto-tour routes; excellent visitor center; photography; guided bird tours in winter.

Where to stay: Motels—in Harlingen, also South Padre Island (fine beaches, birding). Campgrounds—Cameron County Parks on South Padre Island and Arroyo City.

Weather: Mild winter temperatures make wildlife watching most enjoyable October–April.

Points of interest nearby: Santa Ana National Wildlife Refuge, 45 miles west. The drive north to Kingsville is good for spring wildflowers. The Brownsville dump is the place to see Mexican crows and white-necked ravens.

For more information: Laguna Atascosa National Wildlife Refuge, P.O. Box 450, Rio Hondo, Texas 78583. Phone: (512) 748–3607.

MULESHOE (mule shoe)

MULESHOE (Texas)

The stirring spectacle of tens of thousands of sandhill cranes—one of the largest aggregations of that stately species in North America—flying overhead and calling to one another against a red sunset (sometimes with a rising full moon) is unforgettable. It is almost an everyday occurrence at Muleshoe Refuge in the northwest Texas high plains from late September through February.

These are the same birds that spread across the Platte River bottoms in their migrations to and from more northerly nesting grounds. Their numbers vary with moisture and temperature conditions. They usually arrive the third week in September, peak in December, and some stay into February. In years of severe weather some may move farther south. There are seldom fewer than 10,000 of these majestic birds, which can stand four feet tall with wingspreads up to seven feet.

Muleshoe often has the nation's highest number of cranes in the National Audubon Christmas Bird Count, more than 100,000 in some years. The highest number ever recorded here was 250,000 in February 1981.

The best place to see them is on one of Muleshoe's three lakes, especially spring-fed Paul's Lake, which often has water when others are dry. The birds generally roost in the center of these shallow lakes, ideal crane habitat with long exposed shorelines that they can watch for enemies. A visitor should arrive before daybreak as the cranes awaken and take off with a trumpeting *gar-r-oo* and whir of wings, sometimes flying 15 miles to feed (ask refuge staff for likely places to see them).

For a panoramic view against the sky, go to the pull-off on Highway 214, equally dramatic in the evening. Sometimes the birds perform extraordinary leaping courtship dances in late afternoon and continue until sunset and dark.

In a good year for water, thousands of ducks and geese also may winter here—mostly mallards but also pintails, wigeons, gadwalls, and others, and 1,000 or so Canada and snow geese.

Small birding can be excellent. No observant visitor could fail to see horned larks and handsome lark buntings along the fields and roads, and songbirds can be attracted in large numbers to an area of trees and shrubs near refuge headquarters, especially in spring and fall migration.

Ladder-backed woodpeckers, curve-billed thrashers, loggerhead shrikes, and meadowlarks are common all year. So are scaled quail—often around headquarters—and bobwhites in draws and brushy areas. Seasonally common are scissor-tailed flycatchers, lark sparrows, blue grosbeaks, and Cassin's sparrows. An alert birder can often find McCown's longspurs in winter.

Shorebird migrations can be good in August and early fall when moisture is sufficient—sometimes 1,000 or more Wilson's phalaropes and good numbers of Baird's, western, and least sandpipers, dowitchers, avocets—which nest—and others.

Raptors are impressive always. Swainson's hawks are common nesters. It is not unusual in midwinter to see eight or more raptor species in one day—harriers, bald and golden eagles, kestrels, merlins, red-tailed, Cooper's, sharp-shinned and rough-legged hawks, and possibly a prairie falcon.

Burrowing owls hole up at several prairie dog towns that they share with those engaging small frolicsome mammals, as do some less engaging rattlesnakes.

Visitors who get out early and late might see coyotes or one of the wary bobcats.

How to get there: From Lubbock take Route 84 northwest to Littlefield, then Route 54 west 19 miles to Route 214, then north five miles to refuge sign.

Open: Daylight hours all year. Office/Visitor Center 8–4:30 weekdays.

Best times to visit: October–February.

What to see: Sandhill cranes, waterfowl, prairie dogs, good assortment of raptors and small birds.

What to do: Five miles of roads for driving, many more for hiking; photography (portable blinds by permit); picnicking.

Where to stay: Motels—in Muleshoe. Campgrounds—primitive on refuge.

Weather: Summers hot, wind and thunderstorms possible anytime in spring and summer.

Points of interest nearby: National monument in Muleshoe to the beast that "without ancestral pride or hope of offspring . . . [has] helped all over the world to bear the burdens of mankind."

For more information: Muleshoe National Wildlife Refuge, P.O. Box 549, Muleshoe, Texas 79347. Phone: (806) 946–3341.

Grulla Refuge, 30 miles west in New Mexico, is also administered by Muleshoe. It has similar habitat plus an interesting sand dune area visible at one end. Thousands of sandhill cranes and shorebirds visit when water is sufficient. There's an entrance road and a half-mile drive and observation area.

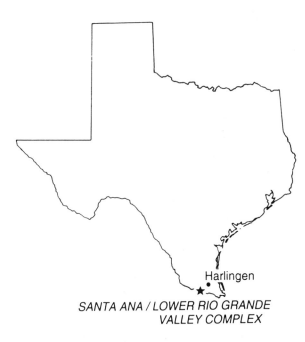

SANTA ANA / LOWER RIO GRANDE
VALLEY COMPLEX

SANTA ANA/LOWER RIO GRANDE VALLEY
(Texas)

Santa Ana is known as the jewel of the national wildlife refuge system and even a brief look shows why. Orange and black altamira orioles and brilliant green jays fly out of the mesquite. Buff-bellied hummingbirds with bright orange bills hover about scarlet turk's caps.

Chachalacas resembling small hen turkeys call "cut-it-out! cut-it-out!" as one leaves the winding tree-lined drive and enters the exquisite natural setting of this relatively small 2,088-acre sanctuary.

Back in the junglelike vegetation live rare and secretive ocelots and small, dark, pantherlike jaguarundis, and a few mountain lions.

Once much of the Texas-Mexico border along the Rio Grande River was like this—a wildlife paradise with rich bottomland and tangled semitropical woodland in which plant and animal species found nowhere else in the United States thrived at this northernmost limit of their range.

Agricultural and urban development have left only a remnant of the original lush habitat and ecosystem. But in 1980 a creative plan was launched to establish a Lower Rio Grande Valley National Wildlife Refuge with land acquired for a wildlife corridor

423

stretching for 190 miles along the northern edge of the river and including all its prime habitat types. (Wildlife corridors benefit four-footed creatures such as ocelots that, unlike birds, cannot fly between islands of refuge habitat.)

The goal is 107,500 acres of which almost half have been acquired. Plans for visitor access are not complete but meanwhile Santa Ana is a window on what this wondrous area will be.

To mention only a few of the rarest wild creatures to be seen here—and for the most part readily seen—is a matter of difficult selection. There are so many. But among birds present in this part of south Texas that naturalists come from around the world to observe are the least grebe, black-bellied whistling duck, gray hawk, hook-billed kite, ringed kingfisher, Couch's kingbird, great kiskadee, long-billed thrasher, and tropical parula. And there are many, many more.

The bird list totals more than 380 species, extraordinary for such a tiny refuge. Rare vagrants such as the crane hawk and elegant trogon arrive unexpectedly every year.

Hidalgo County reputedly has more butterfly species than any other in the nation, and the refuge holds annual July Fourth and Christmas butterfly counts.

Bobcats and coyotes are best seen early and late but they can vanish in thick vegetation that furnishes complete cover even a few feet away. Armadillos are more easily spotted, rooting for grubs alongside the trails. Look sharp for an ocelot looking down at you from a forked tree branch where his spots blend perfectly with the dappled shade.

Two national champion trees grow here, a saffron plum and Texas lignum vitae, plus other interesting types such as sandpaper trees, leadtrees, and ebonies—a century-old specimen of the latter, now dead, was a national champion with a 131-inch diameter.

The growing season averages 327 days; spring blooming starts in mid-February and a constant show of flowering plants continues (in normal rainfall years) until year-end.

Rocks are rare so if you think you see a gray rock about eight inches across, it might be a giant toad weighing a pound or more. A rustle of leaves could be a least shrew, at 2.2-plus inches our shortest and hungriest mammal, often eating more than its weight daily.

Huge flights of white-winged doves can roost in the refuge in mid- to late September—thousands may pour over in a half hour at dusk. Great numbers of broad-winged hawks go through in late March—once 73,000 in just a few days, stopping overnight and boiling up in kettles of hundreds to be on their way again early the next morning.

All these creatures converge here because it is the meeting of two major migratory bird flyways—the Mississippi and Central—and four major climatic zones, the subtropics, temperate, Chihuahuan desert, and coastal zone of the Gulf of Mexico.

How to get there: From McAllen take Expressway 83 east to Alamo, then south on FM 907 to end of road at U.S. Military Highway 281. Turn left to refuge sign, .3 mile.

Open: Hiking trails sunrise to sunset daily. Visitor Center 8–4:30 weekdays, 9–4:30 weekends and holidays, closed Thanksgiving, Christmas, New Year's. Seven-mile auto-tour route 9–4:30 except when interpretive tram operates, November through April (five trips a day; fee).

Best times to visit: Winter and spring (go early, try to avoid peak holidays and weekends).

What to see: Great variety and numbers of flora and fauna found seldom if at all elsewhere in the U.S.—green jays, altamira orioles, buff-bellied hummingbirds, occasionally endangered ocelots, jaguarundis, many, many more.

What to do: 12 miles of hiking trails with blinds for wildlife observation, photography. Auto-tour route (see *Open* above). Wheelchair-accessible trail.

Where to stay: Motels—at McAllen, 16 miles northwest; Harlingen, 35 miles east (midpoint between Santa Ana and Laguna Atascosa refuges). Campgrounds—Bentsen Rio Grande State Park, 25 miles west.

Weather: Summer can be hot, humid, with daily highs near or over 100, early fall rainy.

What to take and wear: A field guide to birds of Texas and Mexico is useful, though Visitor Center has one for reference.

Points of interest nearby: Falcon State Recreation Area, 90 miles west; Bentsen Rio Grande State Park, 25 miles west; Sabal Palm Grove Sanctuary, 60 miles east; Laguna Atascosa National Wildlife Refuge, 60 miles east—all are windows on Rio Grande Valley National Wildlife Refuge Complex. Also South Padre Island, 90 miles east.

For more information: Santa Ana/Lower Rio Grande Valley National Wildlife Refuge Complex, Route 2, Box 202A, Alamo, Texas 78516. Phone: (512) 787–3079.

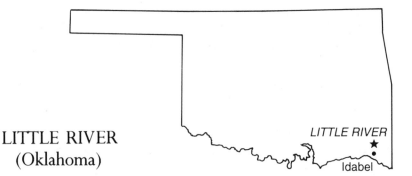

LITTLE RIVER
(Oklahoma)

Hundreds of resplendent wood ducks and mallards fly in to roost, a beautiful sight at sunset during their winter stay here. This relatively new 15,000-acre refuge was established for wintering waterfowl, to furnish nutritious habitat in bottomland hardwood wetlands from which they can return to northern nesting grounds in good shape for arduous nesting activities.

A visitor center and formal trails are currently in the planning stage. But much can be seen from 10 miles of roads. There are many white-tailed deer and a few alligators and wild turkeys. Bobcats and beavers are common (though wary). A few bald eagles winter along Little River, which forms the south boundary of the refuge. Common and more easily spotted are red-shouldered hawks, pileated woodpeckers, and a good assortment of smaller birds. Northern and orchard orioles nest. So do barred owls, Swainson's warblers, and Mississippi kites.

The largest of five heronries supports 80 great blue heron nests, 30 pairs of great egrets, and a dozen pairs of anhingas. A variety of woodland warblers come through and a fine array of wildflowers appears in the woods in spring—bloodroot, wake robins, may apples.

A small isolated population of bird-voiced tree frogs has been found; these join in spring evening chorales with gray and green tree frogs, and leopard, bronze, and chorus frogs.

To get there from Idabel go north on Highway 70, cross Little River, and four miles north of the bridge turn right at a crossroads; after one mile turn right again, go another mile, and turn left onto a gravel road; go .5 mile to a fork, turn right, and follow to refuge.

Roads can be impassable during spring floods. Best check with headquarters, 635 Park Drive, P.O. Box 340, Broken Bow, Oklahoma 74728; phone (405) 584–6211. The refuge is always open, the office 8–4:30 weekdays. Broken Bow has motels and Beavers Bend State Park, 15 miles north, has campgrounds.

Little Sandy NWR is a satellite easement refuge of bottomland hardwood waterfowl habitat north of Tyler, Texas, closed except by special permission.

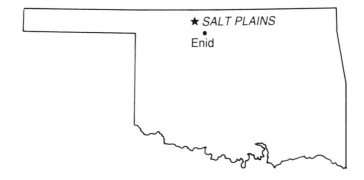

★ *SALT PLAINS*
•
Enid

SALT PLAINS (Oklahoma)

Indians fought battles over this largest salt flat in mid-America. Settlers loaded their wagons with it to preserve food. It produces selenite crystal formations found nowhere else in the world.

It has attracted wildlife in variety and sometimes spectacular numbers because of its diverse combination of open water, grassland, river delta, and dense brush and woods.

Salt Plains is a significant Central Flyway stopover for shorebirds, especially of the short-legged variety—sometimes 15,000 or so Baird's, western, and least sandpipers and 20 other species out on the flats (ask the office where best to see them). Franklin's gulls may peak at 30,000 or more.

Threatened snowy plovers and endangered least terns nest on the salt flats and are visible from the observation tower.

Stately whooping cranes, one of the world's most endangered birds, drop down here in greater numbers than at any other refuge on their 2,600-mile migration route (causing anxiety when they coincide with goose-hunting season).

Lovely scissor-tailed flycatchers can be everywhere from April to October. Wild turkeys, quail, and ring-necked pheasant are abundant.

More than 150 bald eagles may show up in fall and winter to feed on fish and weakened waterfowl among the 40,000 geese present then, including Canadas, white-fronted, and snows in both blue and white forms, and up to 36,000 ducks of more than a dozen species.

White pelicans in huge rafts adding up sometimes to 10,000 or more may stay from mid-September to mid-October.

More than 30,000 stately crimson-crowned sandhill cranes come from mid-October through November. A hundred or so turkey vultures take up a summer roost, in recent years on Cottonwood Point.

Hundreds of little blue herons and snowy and great egrets nest colonially on an island in the Great Salt Plains Lake (which is no more than several feet deep anywhere in its 10,000 acres) along with fewer great blues, green-backed and black-crowned night herons, and up to 30,000 cattle egrets, all of which fan out over the refuge to feed.

Swainson's hawks are common in all but winter, northern harriers in all but summer. Here at various times are rough-legs, Cooper's, and red-tails, including the Krider's and Harlan's verson of this species.

Colorful flocks of 50 or so cardinals are around in winter, and singles all year. Bewick's wrens are permanent residents; so are bluebirds, horned larks, loggerhead shrikes, meadowlarks, and screech and great horned owls. Common seasonally are Bell's and warbling vireos, Harris' and grasshopper sparrows, indigo buntings, dick-cissels, red-headed woodpeckers, and yellow and yellow-rumped warblers. Giant race Canada geese have been reintroduced and nest here.

White-tailed deer browse on the headquarters lawn in evenings. Coyotes hunt the road and trailsides. A smooth six-inch-wide trail across the nature walk marks where a beaver dragged its tail.

The crystals, which have an hourglass formation, can be dug in specified areas April 1 to October 15. It's delicate work—they are easily broken. But since they constantly break down and re-form (for reasons not well understood), there's no permanent loss.

Wear sun lotion against brilliant reflections off the white salt flats—and don't drive on nondesignated areas, which are underlain by a quagmire of quicksand where horses, wagons, even an airplane have sunk and been forever lost.

How to get there: From Enid take Route 81-60-64 north and west to Jet, then right 14 miles on Route 38 to refuge sign and west a mile to headquarters.

Open: Daylight hours all year. Office/Visitor Center 7:30–4 weekdays.

Best times to visit: Something happening all year but activity dips in July–August heat.

What to see: Good assortment of birds from eagles, sandhill cranes, and waterfowl to passerines and migrant whooping cranes; white-tailed deer; coyotes; selenite crystals; largest salt flat in midcontinent.

What to do: Auto-tour route; self-guided walking trail; observation tower; camping, picnicking, swimming, boating (no rentals) in designated areas April 1–October 15; photography (portable blinds permitted by advance arrangement); digging for selenite crystals; fishing can be good for catfish, sand bass.

Where to stay: Motels—in Cherokee, Alva, larger selection in Enid, 50 miles southeast.

Campgrounds—on refuge in summer; year-round at Great Salt Plains State Park, adjacent.

Weather: Spring can bring sudden thunderstorms, tornadoes, and temporarily impassable roads; summer, many mosquitoes.

What to take and wear: Protective sun lotion against brilliant reflections from white salt flats a MUST. Bring sunglasses.

Points of interest nearby: Museum of Cherokee Strip, in Enid; Byron State Fish Hatchery, four miles north; original homesteader's sod house, 40 miles southwest; Great Salt Plains State Park, adjacent.

For more information: Salt Plains National Wildlife Refuge, Route 1, Box 76, Jet, Oklahoma 73749. Phone: (405) 626–4794.

SEQUOYAH (Oklahoma)

Sixty or so eagles can be arrayed in tall cottonwood trees on a fall or winter day on this 20,800-acre east-central Oklahoma refuge that nestles in the confluence of the Arkansas and Canadian rivers, which once formed the border between the Cherokee and Choctaw Indian nations.

The eagles prey on weak or injured waterfowl that come through in fall and spring and sometimes stay the winter—up to 50,000 ducks, mostly mallards (their main Central Flyway wintering area) but also gadwall, pintail, teal, wigeon, shoveler and wood ducks, and up to 60,000 geese—snows, Canadas, and white-fronteds. It is the largest concentration of snow geese in the state. And the refuge produces up to 100 beautiful young wood ducks every year in boxes as well as natural tree cavities.

Scissor-tailed flycatchers, the lovely Oklahoma state bird with long tail streamers and pearl and salmon plumage, perch on power lines and poles through warmer months, sometimes nesting on the crossbars.

Hundreds of shorebirds migrate through in April and May, stopping around any low place that holds water—golden plovers, spotted, pectoral, white-rumped, and least sandpipers, sometimes ruddy turnstones and Hudsonian godwits. In recent years endangered least terns have nested on sandbars.

Warbler migrations are irregular but in a good year tiny golden birds can seem to be everywhere in the woods and brush when may apples come up and redbuds and dogwoods bloom.

Up to 6,000 white pelicans stop by spring and fall, with similar numbers of double-crested cormorants.

Raptors like it here—five species nest, including kestrels and red-tailed, red-shouldered, broad-winged, and Swainson's hawks. A hacking program for young bald eagles gives hope that species may nest here, too.

Barred and great horned owls bring off families; flickers, red-headed, red-bellied, and some pileated woodpeckers are here all year; and common at least seasonally are yellow-billed cuckoos, great blue herons, great egrets, Carolina wrens, bluebirds, both kinglets, chats, and indigo buntings.

Bobcats are perhaps more readily seen than at most refuges, occasionally with their kits, by the visitor who goes out early and wends his way quietly. Coyotes howl, beaver workings are always evident, and river otters are making a comeback, fishing around ponds and fallen floating trees.

Armored gars churn the water dramatically when spawning, sometimes leaping from the surface like porpoises.

Sequoyah is named for the Indian who invented the Cherokee syllabary—comparable to our alphabet but symbolizing syllables, not letters—which enabled the Cherokees to write and record their history. The area was visited by the famed early naturalist Thomas Nuttall, who wrote about it in his *A Journal of Travels into the Arkansas Territory During the Year 1819*.

Quiet moments on the refuge even now recall the wildness of when these historic predecessors were present.

How to get there: From Fort Smith, Arkansas, take Route 64 west to Roland, Oklahoma, then I-40 west to Vian exit and south three miles on county road.

Open: Sunrise to sunset. Office 7:30–4 weekdays.

Best times to visit: October–March for waterfowl, eagles; April–June for shorebirds, waders.

What to see: Waterfowl, waders, shorebirds, raptors, scissor-tailed flycatchers, white pelicans, occasional bobcats.

What to do: Walking trail, six-mile auto loop. Photo blind over marsh (best reserve ahead). Films, tours, slide shows available on advance request for groups. Fishing can be excellent in good water conditions for crappie, bass, channel catfish. Limited hunt in fall can restrict wildlife observation; check with office.

Where to stay: Motels—in Sallisaw, Vian, Muldrow, Roland, Fort Smith. Campgrounds—KOA south of Sallisaw; also Brushy Lake State Park, 12 miles northeast.

Points of interest nearby: Sequoyah's home, 20 miles northeast; Cookson Hills State Game Refuge, 18 miles northeast; beautiful scenic Talimena Drive on Route 1 from Talihina, Oklahoma, to Mena, Arkansas; George Miksch Sutton Avian Research Center near Bartlesville.

For more information: Sequoyah National Wildlife Refuge, Route 1, Box 18A, Vian, Oklahoma 74962. Phone: (918) 773–5251.

Also administered from Sequoyah is *Oklahoma Bat Caves,* for preservation of the Ozark big-eared bat plus the endangered gray bat and other obscure cave species. Closed to public access.

Oklahoma City
•

TISHOMINGO
★

TISHOMINGO (Oklahoma)

Sometimes 100 bald eagles come to spend the winter at Tishomingo, feeding on catfish and crappie as well as injured or weakened waterfowl on Lake Texoma, the Corps of Engineers project on which this 15,464-acre refuge of water, woods, grass, and croplands is overlaid.

Up to 40,000 geese—mostly Canadas but also white-fronteds and snows—and 80,000 ducks of 20 or so species are here then, along with various raptors—kestrels and northern harriers as well as some Swainson's, rough-legged, ferruginous, and Cooper's hawks (the Cooper's are nesters as are the broad-winged, red-shouldered, and red-tailed).

A favorite sight for visitors is the deer herd. Hundreds are on the refuge. It's not unusual to count 150 in a 20-acre field in the headquarters area, wearing thick coats in winter. Does become scarce in early spring, then reappear with spotted fawns in May.

Scissor-tailed flycatchers are abundant spring through fall, as are painted and indigo buntings, dickcissels, lark and Harris' sparrows, and good numbers of blue grosbeaks, orchard orioles, and red-headed woodpeckers. Birders will find summer tanagers, Carolina and Bewick's wrens, blue-gray gnatcatchers, and an assortment of vireos—white-eyed, Bell's, red-eyed, and warbling.

Great blue and little blue herons and great egrets spend summer at the water's edges. Wood storks occasionally drop by. Sometimes 30,000 or more Franklin's and ring-billed gulls are there.

White pelicans make dramatic appearances unannounced in great rafts of several thousand in October.

Shorebird migrations can be lively when moisture conditions encourage their stopovers with Baird's and upland sandpipers and occasional long-billed curlews and golden plovers.

Beautiful wood ducks feed on the acorn crop and hang around wooded stumps in the East Flat. Up to 50 wild turkeys are sometimes seen in spring in Big Bottom along the entrance road. Great horned and barred owls start hooting a half hour before sunset.

Beavers gnaw at twigs and saplings and attempt to plug up water-control structures. Raccoons are adept at opening fishermen's baitboxes. Armadillo root for grubs along the roadsides. Bobcats are here but usually unseen.

Indian paintbrush and devil's poker bloom colorfully in spring along with redbud and dogwood trees through the woodlands.

Occasionally in September and October a spectacular several million blackbirds of seven species, including red-winged, yellow-headed, rusty, and Brewer's, come in to roost in great black funnel clouds across the western sky. Later in the fall a half-million crows may roost.

A good way to see Tishomingo is by jonboat. Siltation has formed a delta in Lake Texoma on which trees and other vegetation have grown to become a new 5,000-acre de facto wetland wilderness area (at no cost to taxpayers).

How to get there: From Ardmore take Route 70 east to Route 12, north there to Route 22 east and through Tishomingo to refuge sign, turn right there onto blacktop three miles to headquarters.

Open: 24 hours all year (daylight hours only to vehicles). Office 7:30–4 weekdays.

Best times to visit: Mid-October through early spring.

What to see: Deer, waterfowl, variety of others.

What to do: 15 miles of driving and hiking roads including interpretive nature trail (parts are closed October–February for wildlife sanctuary); spectacular Jemison's lookout; observation tower with spotting scope; picnicking; boating (no rentals); fishing can be excellent March to October for crappie, catfish.

Where to stay: Motels—at Tishomingo and Ardmore. Campgrounds—on refuge; also Murray State Park, Ardmore.

Weather: Spring is tornado and flood season until about May. Severe flooding can close trails and refuge buildings.

Points of interest nearby: Chickasaw National Recreational Area, 35 miles northwest; historic Chickasaw Council House in Tishomingo (still in use as the county courthouse); Hagerman National Wildlife Refuge, 70 miles south; Tishomingo Wildlife Management Unit, adjoining on west, jointly managed with state.

For more information: Tishomingo National Wildlife Refuge, Route 1, Box 151, Tishomingo, Oklahoma 73460. Phone: (405) 371–2402.

★ *WASHITA*

• Oklahoma City

WASHITA (Oklahoma)

U p to 50,000 geese fly overhead filling the air with their honking—a thrilling dawn and dusk spectacular during winter months at this 8,084-acre refuge of native grassland, farm fields, wooded creeks, and open water in west-central Oklahoma.

It is one of the largest waterfowl concentrations in Oklahoma, mostly Canada geese but with good numbers of snows and white-fronteds and an occasional Ross', and perhaps 20,000 ducks of more than a dozen species.

Keeping an eye on them all from November to January are a dozen or so bald eagles (with some goldens)—roosting in cottonwoods along the lake, feeding on fish and then, after the water ices up, on waterfowl, dipping down to harass them and discover when they fly up which are the weaker ones.

Black-tailed prairie dogs occupy a "town" of 50 or so near the refuge office— adults foraging on grasses, pups coming out to play in spring, all scampering for their holes when a sentry spots a hawk or the shadow of one and barks an alarm.

Grazing deer are conspicuous in families and flocks all year. Beavers den along the creeks.

Several thousand stately sandhill cranes and sometimes a pair of endangered whooping cranes touch down in spring and fall migration. Several hundred white pelicans usually visit for a few weeks.

The native prairies support a sizable rodent population that in turn attracts their predators—coyotes, bobcats and hawks.

On one day, October 9, 1973, 600 Swainson's hawks were counted on refuge fields, and almost every year up to 200 migrating Swainson's are counted in some field on some day in October.

Red-tails, northern harriers, and kestrels are common to abundant all year, and others in fair to good numbers in all except summer—Cooper's, sharp-shinned, rough-legged, ferruginous, and from time to time the falcons—merlin, prairie, and peregrine. Ospreys appear frequently over the waterways, and sometimes 40 or so Mississippi kites nest in trees along the watercourses and soar in the summer sky.

Streamered scissor-tailed flycatchers pair off by the hundreds and perch on every high wire through the warm months, looking for insects. Cliff and barn swallows colonize abundantly under bridges.

Shorebird migrations can bring sizable groups of Baird's, least, and western sandpipers and Wilson's phalaropes, as well as upland sandpipers and long-billed curlews, which come when lake levels are down, leaving mudflats exposed, or when heavy rains flood grasslands, Franklin's gulls appear in large numbers to devour insects on newly tilled fields.

Common all or part of the year are red-headed and red-bellied woodpeckers, great blue herons, bobwhite quail, killdeer, yellow-billed cuckoos, Bewick's wrens, and Harris' and lark sparrows. Birders come, too, for less common varieties— Sprague's pipits, ladder-backed woodpeckers, sage thrashers, lark buntings, and black-headed grosbeaks.

The native prairies are beautiful in themselves, waving and verdant in summer, golden later, abloom with Indian paintbrush and coneflowers.

The entire refuge is open March 15 to October 15 for walking. The south end is closed the rest of the time to offer waterfowl sanctuary but all the wildlife is accessible for viewing through the year, often best seen by walking along the river— ask refuge staff where things have been spotted lately.

How to get there: From Clinton take Route 183 north nine miles to Route 33, then follow signs west 18 miles to refuge.

Open: Daylight hours all year. Office 7:30–4 weekdays.

Best times to visit: November–March for waterfowl concentrations.

What to see: Waterfowl; deer; prairie dogs; sandhill cranes; Mississippi kites; eagles; scissor-tailed flycatchers; beavers; sometimes coyotes.

What to do: Five miles of roads for driving, hiking; observation towers; photography; boating (limited rentals in adjacent state park); fishing can be good for bass, crappie, walleye, sand bass.

Where to stay: Motels—in Clinton, 28 miles southeast; Elk City, 28 miles southwest. Campgrounds—Foss Lake State park, adjacent.

Weather: Sometimes violent thunderstorms and tornadoes in April and May.

Points of interest nearby: Western Trails Museum, Clinton; Foss Lake State Park, adjacent;

Boiling Spring State Park, 50 miles north; Little Sahara State Park (with sand dunes and wild camel population!), 80 miles northeast.

For more information: Washita National Wildlife Refuge, Route 1, Box 68, Butler, Oklahoma 73625. Phone: (405) 664–2205.

Washita also administers *Optima* National Wildlife Refuge, 4,333 acres of sand sage, grassland, and woods in the Oklahoma Panhandle which supports many raptors attracted to an abundant small mammal population. Public roads run through it; otherwise few visitor facilities; consult Washita office.

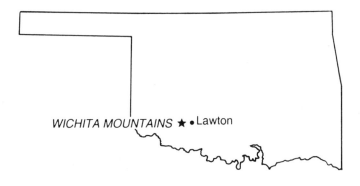

WICHITA MOUNTAINS ★ •Lawton

WICHITA MOUNTAINS (Oklahoma)

Wichita Mountains is a showplace of the national wildlife refuge system. Herds of buffalos, elk, Texas longhorns, a prairie dog town, stunning scenery, and a breathtaking variety of interesting birds, plants, reptiles, and rocks are all here.

This is where it all began, set aside by proclamation by President William McKinley in 1901, just before tiny Pelican Island refuge in Florida—the first of more than 400 U.S. refuges which now cover more than 33 million acres and protect thousands of species of wildlife, including most of our endangered species. (Pelican Island remains the first official wildlife refuge; Wichita Mountains was at first called a Forest Reserve).

Wichita Mountains was set aside for the plains buffalo, or bison, monumental beasts that can stand six feet at the shoulder and weigh more than a ton. Once they were among the most numerous animals on earth; their herds, estimated at 60 to 70 million, darkened the plains for miles around.

By 1900 hide hunters and "sport" killers had almost exterminated them, sometimes shooting thousands and leaving the carcasses to rot. The New York Zoological Society saved a small number and offered to donate a nucleus of 15 on condition Congress appropriate $25,000 to build a fence around them. In 1907 the great Comanche chief Quanah Parker came with other mounted braves to watch the release in this protected area of the remnant of these animals that had provided meat and tepee skins for generations of their ancestors.

The bison prospered. In 1911–12 elk, which had been eliminated from the Wichitas in the late 1800s, were successfully reintroduced. In 1927 the refuge received a foundation herd of 20 Texas longhorn cattle, a historically significant breed descended from cattle brought over by early Spaniards. These great rangy animals, whose horns can measure eight feet tip to tip, are preserved in the Wichitas with management aimed at maintaining the integrity of the breed, which in the 1870s and 1880s were driven within sight of the refuge up to the Great Western Cattle Trail.

Prairie dogs, once even more numerous than the bison—gregarious, frolicsome little rodents that once existed in the billions on the prairies, their burrow colonies spread over tens of thousands of square miles—were allowed to repopulate here away from farmers and cattlemen who nearly poisoned them out of existence. White-tailed deer and wild turkeys, once all but gone from the region, are common here now, too.

Here as well is the mixed native prairie that supported all these populations and now is gone from much of the Plains. Some of the grasses are six feet tall with roots almost as long, hoarding water and nutrients against dry times, intermixed in season with brilliant wildflowers. This is land that has never seen a plow, strewn with huge lichen-covered boulders, weathered granite mountains over five million years old, a rugged rocky island upthrust visible for many miles in the otherwise rolling and featureless plains of southwestern Oklahoma.

Looking out over the 59,019 acres of this refuge you see the country as it was before Europeans came—"nothing except what God put here," as one staffer put it—for much of it is unfenced and the herds roam free (some places are closed to permit protective management of animals and habitat).

There are 35 miles of roads from which all this can be readily viewed, 15 miles of hiking trails, and other varied habitat—canyons, streams, woods, mountains, more than 20 lakes, and two wild and beautiful wilderness areas.

Handsome green and yellow "mountain boomers" or collared lizards are common on the red granite rocks.

Streamered scissor-tailed flycatchers nest. So do Mississippi kites, as anyone around will attest (they dive-bomb intruders). Bald and golden eagles spend the winter. Numerous ducks of a dozen or more species visit refuge lakes in spring and fall migration. Colorful wood ducks nest in tree cavities near the lakes. Bobwhite quail are common all year, as are rufous-crowned sparrows, eastern bluebirds, red-tailed hawks, white-breasted nuthatches, red-bellied woodpeckers, Bewick's wrens, and some rock and canyon wrens. Seasonally present are painted buntings, summer tanagers, pine siskins, American goldfinches, Harris' and Lincoln's sparrows, chestnut-collared longspurs, and chuck-will's-widows.

Endangered black-capped vireos nest in a few remote difficult-to-visit areas.

Campers almost certainly will hear coyotes and great horned owls, and unless they put food away securely will probably meet a raccoon personally. Buffalos have been known to wander through picnic grounds or campsites, and these big creatures should be given a wide berth. Mountain lions and bobcats are present but so wary they are unlikely to be seen.

Young animals begin to appear in mid-March. Adult bison and longhorn cattle are very protective of their newborn calves—enjoy them at a distance! Indian blanket,

Venus' looking-glass, false indigo, and other colorful wildflowers burst into bloom a few weeks later.

Elk tours are led through areas where males start their "bugling" during mating season, beginning in September (yard-long windpipes produce bellows heard for miles). Reserve ahead; tours are limited to 25 persons. Many fine tours are scheduled throughout the year to see wildflowers, stars, stream life, eagles, and other natural elements.

Auction sales of surplus bison and longhorns, determined by carrying capacity of the land for healthy herds, are held in September and November; the public is welcome.

There are wonderful things all year. No visitor should leave without visiting the top of Mount Scott, where a large part of Oklahoma stretches out in all directions and you can stand eye to eye with a red-tailed hawk or Mississippi kite, sometimes only 20 feet away, hovering motionless in a northwest wind.

How to get there: From Lawton take Route 62 west to Cache, then north 12 miles on Route 115 to refuge headquarters; or take the Route 49 West exit of Interstate 44 just north of Lawton, then west eight miles into the east entrance of the refuge.

Open: 24 hours all year. Office 8–4:30 weekdays. Visitor Center 10–6 Fridays, weekends, holidays March through November.

Best times to visit: Spring and fall ideal for migrating birds, wildflowers, young animals, colorful foliage.

What to see: Free-roaming herds of bison, Texas longhorns, white-tailed deer, also elk and great variety of birds, mammals, and reptiles. Bald and golden eagles in winter.

What to do: 35 miles of roads for driving, 15 miles of hiking trails; photography; fishing, best in spring for channel cat, black bass; picnicking; camping, limited backpacking (see below); scenic overlook from Mount Scott; guided tours and programs through the year on wide range of natural history subjects.

A limited elk hunt to keep the herd within carrying capacity of the land is held, usually nine days over several weeks in November and December during which some areas are closed to public use—check ahead for schedule.

DRIVE SLOWLY AT NIGHT because of all the wildlife around. Don't feed any of them—you won't provide the nutrients they need, and with feeding they can become aggressive toward humans.

Where to stay: Motels—in Lawton. Campgrounds—on refuge, first come, first served (often filled on major holidays). Limited backpacking by permit in Charons Garden Wilderness Area; arrange ahead. Youth group camp area; arrange ahead.

Weather: Can be extremely changeable with oppressive heat July–August, ice storms in winter.

What to take and wear: Hiking boots on rocky terrain, compass if going off-trail in wilderness area.

Points of interest nearby: Quartz Mountain State Park, 50 miles northwest; Fort Sill Historical Museum; Museum of the Great Plains, in Lawton.

For more information: Wichita Mountains Wildlife Refuge, Route 1, Box 448, Indiahoma, Oklahoma 73552. Phone: (405) 429–3222 or 429–3221.

The Mountain States

M ountain states refuges combine spectacular scenery with some of our most impressive wildlife in wild, remote surroundings often almost unchanged since the early days of this country. Mammals include bison, elk, bighorn sheep, pronghorn antelopes, moose, and mountain lions. Birds include raptors such as bald and golden eagles, goshawks, prairie, peregrine, and gyrfalcons, along with trumpeter swans and great colonies of nesting white pelicans.

IDAHO

One of the largest nesting colonies of white-faced ibises anywhere is on the Dingle Swamp in the scenic *Bear Lake* valley—up to 5,000 of them, along with great blue and black-crowned night herons, snowy egrets, and sometimes thousands of Franklin's and California gulls fanning out over the area in conspicuous feeding flocks.

Camas, named for a blue lily whose bulb Indians once gathered as a staple food, is a beautiful 10,578-acre refuge where moose forage on willow shoots. In years of good water, 200,000 ducks fly up against a backdrop of the snowy Lemhi mountain range. Rare trumpeter swans and peregrine falcons nest.

Hundreds of handsome white pelicans and tens of thousands of other water-oriented birds are attracted to *Deer Flat*'s 11,430 acres which surround Lake Powell and islands stretching for 113 miles along the Snake River.

Greater sandhill cranes perform high-leaping courtship dances and nest at *Grays Lake,* on a remote high plateau that is mostly marsh and water surrounded by national forest and the lofty Caribou Mountains.

Kootenai is a small refuge of unusually diverse habitat—woods, ponds, marsh, streams, and upland backing up to the Rocky Mountains. The wildlife is diverse, too: mule and white-tailed deer, otters, coyotes, occasionally larger mammals, and a variety of birds ranging from killdeer and grouse to swallows and warblers.

Minidoka is the only place in Idaho where white pelicans are known to nest. Western grebes perform graceful courtship ballets and ruddy ducks show off robin's-egg-blue bills in the breeding season.

MONTANA

The nutrient-rich marshes at *Benton Lake* are one of the most productive waterfowl-nesting refuges in the country. Graceful swans, geese, ducks, and other water-oriented birds can literally fill the water and sky from spring to late fall.

Sharp-tailed grouse inflate lavender throat sacs to contest for mates and pheasants puff out scarlet cheeks at *Bowdoin*'s 15,437 acres of marsh, water, and native grasslands, where thousands of water birds of many species also come each spring. White-tailed deer and pronghorn antelopes graze.

One of the largest nesting colonies of white pelicans in the country takes to the air over *Medicine Lake*'s 31,457 acres of meadows, pasture, lakes and ponds. Eared and horned grebes build floating nest colonies. Sharp-tailed grouse gather on a dozen or more dancing grounds.

Ospreys share tree nests with majestic Canada geese (though not at the same time) at *Metcalf,* along the Bitterroot River. Coyotes den, and bald eagles have nested in recent years.

Much of the wildlife that roamed *National Bison Range* before settlers came is here today—bison, elk, pronghorn antelopes, mountain goats, and bighorn sheep—and great numbers of smaller interesting mammals—yellow-bellied marmots and pine chipmunks, among others.

The trumpeter swan, largest waterfowl in North America and one of the most beautiful, came back from the edge of extinction at beautiful *Red Rock Lakes* in the remote wild Centennial Valley at the foot of the snowy Continental Divide.

The Missouri River meanders through rugged *Charles M. Russell* Refuge looking much as it did when the explorers Lewis and Clark saw it here in 1805. Pronghorn antelopes hurtle along at speeds up to 40 miles an hour. Bighorn sheep clamber up rocks. Sage and sharp-tailed grouse gather in dawn courtship dances.

WYOMING

The largest wintering elk herd in the world—up to 10,000—gathers at *National Elk* against a backdrop of snowy peaks rising to 13,000 feet—a spectacle reminiscent of elk herds 200 years ago. Coyotes and bald eagles are usually around then too and, in open water, trumpeter swans.

The Oregon and Mormon Trails went through the Green River Valley, and so undisturbed is this land that a visitor to *Seedskadee* can stand on the bluffs and see their wagon ruts. Wildlife have left their own trails here—sage grouse, moose, mule deer, prairie dogs, pronghorn antelopes, and, overhead, golden eagles.

NEVADA

Desert bighorn sheep once close to extinction roam the crags of wildly beautiful *Desert* refuge, the largest population of these majestic animals on the largest national wildlife refuge outside Alaska. A fascinating variety of other flora and fauna also find ecological niches on these 1.5 million acres that cover six altitudinal life zones rising from the desert floor to 10,000 feet.

More than 200 springs, some so hot they can burn the hand, feed *Ruby Lake*'s marshy acres. Mountain lions prey on mule deer that come down from the Ruby Mountains. White-faced ibis nest. Greater sandhill cranes leap up in courtship dances.

Sheldon was established for the pronghorn antelope. Sometimes hundreds of these swift animals gather in summer at its watering places.

The greater *Stillwater* marsh once covered 10,000 square miles. Human development almost destroyed it, but it is being restored and wildlife has responded. Up to 78 percent of the continental population of long-billed dowitchers is here in migration, and a third or more of the Pacific Flyway population of canvasback ducks.

UTAH

Bear River fell on hard times due to record floods, but it is coming back and can be an unbelievable gathering point for birds—sometimes millions altogether of golden-tufted eared grebes, tundra swans, ducks, geese, shorebirds, and others.

A sparkling wildlife oasis attracts deer, coyotes, swans, ibises, and a whole spectrum of creatures to *Fish Springs* on the southern fringe of the Great Salt Desert at the base of mountains that rise to 8,000 feet.

Dinosaurs once dominated the wildlife at *Ouray*. Only relics of their time remain, replaced by mule deer, golden eagles, sandhill cranes, waterfowl, Lewis' woodpeckers, Say's phoebes, and a fine assortment of other small birds.

COLORADO

Up to 10,000 scarlet-crowned sandhill cranes spread seven-foot wings in spring courtship dances at *Monte Vista*, where the nearby town holds the annual March Crane Festival. It is also a major waterfowl mating ground.

Nearby at its companion refuge, *Alamosa*, bald eagles gather then to feast on fish winter-killed in frozen oxbows of the Rio Grande River.

Visitors to *Arapaho*, highest of any refuge outside Alaska, are almost certain to see fleet-footed pronghorn antelopes, so keen-eyed they can look in all directions at once and pick out a small object four miles away. Moose and elk are here, too, and birds that migrate not seasonally but vertically up and down the surrounding mountains.

Browns Park has been a haven for wildlife since before the dawn of history—some of it human, when cattle rustlers hid out. Now antelopes, mule deer, elk, and sometimes mountain lions and black bears are here, along with eagles, hawks, sage grouse, and many kinds of water birds.

Following are birds of special interest found commonly at Mountain States refuges at seasons indicated:

S: SPRING   s: SUMMER   F: FALL   W: WINTER

White-faced Ibis: Bear Lake Ss, Bear River SsF, Bowdoin Ss, Browns Park Ss, Camas sF, Fish Springs s, Ouray Ss, Stillwater s

Trumpeter Swan: National Elk SsFW, Red Rock Lakes SsFW

Barrow's Goldeneye: National Elk SsF, Red Rock Lakes SsFW

Golden Eagle: Arapaho SW, Bear River SW, Browns Park SW, Camas SW, Charles M. Russell SsFW, Desert S, Metcalf W, Minidoka SW, National Bison SsFW, Ouray SsFW, Seedskadee SsFW, Sheldon SsF

Bald Eagle: Alamosa/Monte Vista FW, Bear River SW, Bowdoin S, Browns Park W, Camas SW, Charles M. Russell SW, Deer Flat W, Kootenai SFW, Metcalf W, Minidoka SW, National Elk SsFW, Ouray W, Red Rock Lakes SsFW, Seedskadee W

Prairie Falcon: Seedskadee SW, Sheldon SsF

Goshawk: National Elk SsF

Chukar: Sheldon SsF

Sage Grouse: Arapaho SF, Browns Park SsF, Camas F, Charles M. Russell SsFW, National Elk SsFW, Ruby Lake SsFW, Seedskadee SsFW, Sheldon SsFW

Sharp-tailed Grouse: Charles M. Russell SsFW, Medicine Lake SsFW

Gray Partridge: Benton Lake F, Bowdoin SsFW, Charles M. Russell SsFW, Medicine Lake SsFW, Minidoka sF, National Bison SsFW

Sandhill Crane: Alamosa/Monte Vista SF, Bear Lake SFW, Camas SsF, Charles M. Russell SF, Grays Lake SsF, Medicine Lake SF, National Elk SF, Ouray SF, Red Rock Lakes SsF, Ruby Lake Ss

Whooping Crane: Grays Lake SsF

Long-billed Curlew: Bear River Ss, Camas Ss, Minidoka s, Red Rock Lakes Ss, Ruby Lake Ss

Marbled Godwit: Benton Lake SF, Bowdoin SsF, Medicine Lake SsF, Seedskadee S

Red-necked (Northern) Phalarope: Browns Park S, Metcalf SF, Stillwater SsF

Flammulated Owl: Desert s

Vaux's Swift: Kootenai Ss

White-throated Swift: Browns Park SsF, Desert s, Ouray s, Pahranagat s

Black-chinned Hummingbird: Browns Park SsF, Grays Lake Ss, Ouray s, Pahranagat s

Calliope Hummingbird: Grays Lake s, Kootenai Ss, National Elk SsF

Broad-tailed Hummingbird: Desert s, Ouray s
Rufous Hummingbird: Desert s, Kootenai Ss, Ruby Lake sF
Lewis' Woodpecker: National Bison Ss, Ouray Ss, Ruby Lake s
Ladder-backed Woodpecker: Desert SFW
Olive-sided Flycatcher: National Elk SsF
Dusky Flycatcher: Desert s, Kootenai S, National Elk SsF, Ruby Lake SsF
Gray Flycatcher: Desert s
Gray Jay: National Elk SsFW
Pinyon Jay: Browns Park SsFW, Charles M. Russell SsF, Desert SsFW
Steller's Jay: Kootenai SFW, National Elk SsFW
Clark's Nutcracker: Desert SsFW, National Elk SsFW, National Bison SsFW, Red Rock
    Lakes SsFW
Mountain Chickadee: Desert SsFW, National Elk SsFW, National Bison SFW, Red Rock
    Lakes SsFW
Plain Titmouse: Ruby Lake SsFW
Bushtit: Desert SsFW, Ruby Lake SsFW
Pygmy Nuthatch: Desert SsFW, National Bison SFW
Sage Thrasher: Alamosa/Monte Vista Ss, Browns Park SsF, Camas s
Mountain Bluebird: Alamosa/Monte Vista S, Arapaho Ss, Browns Park SsF, Charles M.
    Russell SsF, Grays Lake Ss, National Elk SsF, National Bison SF, Ruby Lake SF,
    Seedskadee SsF
Varied Thrush: Kootenai S
Sprague's Pipit: Bowdoin Ss, Charles M. Russell Ss
American Dipper: Kootenai sF, National Elk SsFW, Red Rock Lakes SsF
Bohemian Waxwing: Bowdoin SFW, Charles M. Russell SFW, National Bison SF
Phainopepla: Desert SsFW
Northern Shrike: Red Rock Lakes SFW
Loggerhead Shrike: Charles M. Russell SsF, Stillwater SsFW
Virginia's Warbler: Desert s, Ouray Ss
Lucy's Warbler: Pahranagat s
Black-throated Gray Warbler: Desert s
Grace's Warbler: Desert Ss
MacGillivray's Warbler: Desert F, Kootenai s, National Elk Ss, National Bison Ss, Red
    Rock Lakes Ss
Blue Grosbeak: Pahranagat s
Lazuli Bunting: Deer Flat F, National Bison Ss
Green-tailed Towhee: Desert SsF, Sheldon s
Cassin's Finch: Desert SsFW, National Elk SsF, Red Rock Lakes SsF
Pine Grosbeak: Red Rock Lakes SsFW
Rosy Finch: Arapaho SW, Red Rock Lakes SW, Seedskadee W, National Elk Ss
Common Redpoll: Red Rock Lakes SW, Seedskadee W, National Elk S
Red Crossbill: Charles M. Russell s, Kootenai S, National Bison s

Lark Bunting: Benton Lake SsF, Bowdoin SsF, Charles M. Russell Ss, Medicine Lake
    Ss

Lark Sparrow: Bear River F, Fish Springs s, Medicine Lake SsF

Black-throated Sparrow: Desert SsF, Pahranagat SsF

Sage Sparrow: Desert SF, Sheldon s

Lapland Longspur: Charles M. Russell sFW

Chestnut-collared Longspur: Benton Lake SsF, Bowdoin Ss, Medicine Lake SsF

Snow Bunting: Benton Lake F, Medicine Lake FW, Red Rock Lakes W

THE MOUNTAIN STATES

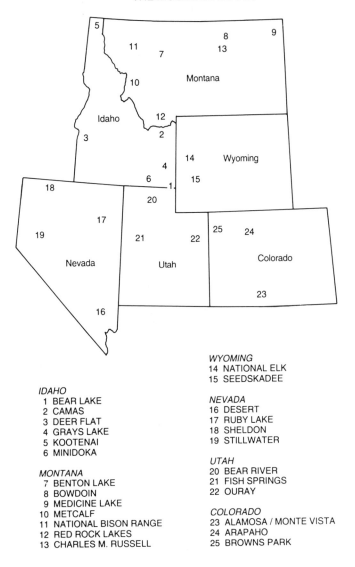

WYOMING
14 NATIONAL ELK
15 SEEDSKADEE

IDAHO
1 BEAR LAKE
2 CAMAS
3 DEER FLAT
4 GRAYS LAKE
5 KOOTENAI
6 MINIDOKA

NEVADA
16 DESERT
17 RUBY LAKE
18 SHELDON
19 STILLWATER

UTAH
20 BEAR RIVER
21 FISH SPRINGS
22 OURAY

MONTANA
7 BENTON LAKE
8 BOWDOIN
9 MEDICINE LAKE
10 METCALF
11 NATIONAL BISON RANGE
12 RED ROCK LAKES
13 CHARLES M. RUSSELL

COLORADO
23 ALAMOSA / MONTE VISTA
24 ARAPAHO
25 BROWNS PARK

BEAR LAKE

Pocatello

BEAR LAKE (Idaho)

One of the largest nesting colonies of white-faced ibises anywhere is here on what was historically a wonderful waterfowl area, Dingle Swamp. But to a visitor coming here in spring and early summer the whole scenic Bear Lake valley, flooded naturally and artificially to assist wild hay crops, can seem filled with wetlands and water birds.

The ibises, up to 5,000 of them, nest deep in the marsh of this 18,000-acre refuge but fan out over the area in conspicuous feeding flocks as do other species that share their nest site—great blue and black-crowned night herons, snowy egrets, and sometimes thousands of Franklin's and California gulls. Forster's and a few Caspian terns nest nearby.

Great Basin Canada geese nest here in large numbers and both geese and up to 3,000 downy goslings can seem to be everywhere, covering the water, marsh, and even the roads (drive carefully) in May.

Redhead ducks, another species of special concern, nest here along with mallards, gadwalls, cinnamon teals, pintails, canvasbacks, and others, producing altogether up to 7,000 ducklings yearly, visible around the waterways later than the goose families, usually in June and July.

Sandhill cranes also nest as do avocets, willets, and pied-billed, eared, and western

449

grebes, the latter performing lovely courtship water ballets, all the grebes carrying young about on their backs afterward.

Graceful black terns build loose colonies of floating nests. Dozens of American bitterns nest among the reeds—but one must look carefully at every reed to spot these well-camouflaged birds.

White pelicans with nine-foot wingspreads are about in nonbreeding groups through the warm months. Sometimes 200 or so gather in group fishing parties. Migratory birds are best seen in April and September. Bald and golden eagles stay through the winter, a half dozen or so usually around the refuge and Bear Lake as long as there is open water.

Red foxes and coyotes hunt in the uplands—not simultaneously, as these two don't get along well together. Porcupines lumber along the roads. Occasionally mule deer come down from the surrounding hills, rarely a moose, elk, or bear—the deer in greater numbers in winter, sometimes hundreds browsing along Merkley Ridge.

Bear Lake also oversees Oxford Slough, a waterfowl production area 60 miles northwest, with large numbers of white-faced ibis as well as waterfowl. Ask staff about a visit.

How to get there: From Montpelier go west 2.5 miles on Highway 89, then left at sign five miles on gravel road to refuge.

Open: Daylight hours. Office 7–4:30 weekdays (staff is small; call ahead or pick up material at information station).

Best times to visit: Spring through fall.

What to see: White-faced ibis, other wading and shorebirds and waterfowl, especially redhead ducks.

What to do: Auto-tour route, other roads and dike trails (some closed until after July 1 to minimize nesting disturbance; miles of county roads are always open from which to view most of the area); photography; canoeing (no rentals, and only after July 1).

Where to stay: Motels—in Montpelier. Campgrounds—East Beach State Park on east side of lake, also Caribou National Forest, four miles west of Montpelier on Highway 89. Paris, Bloomington, and St. Charles canyons all have campgrounds in close proximity to the refuge.

Points of interest nearby: Bear Lake and Bear Lake State Park, south of refuge, and Minnetonka Cave, impressive formations, near St. Charles.

For more information: Bear Lake National Wildlife Refuge, 370 Webster, Box 9, Montpelier, Idaho 83254. Phone: (208) 847–1757.

CAMAS ★
• Idaho Falls

CAMAS (Idaho)

Camas, named for the blue lily whose bulb Indians once gathered here as a staple food, is a beautiful 10,578-acre southeast Idaho refuge where moose forage on willow shoots and, in years of good water, up to 200,000 ducks fly up against a mountain backdrop of the snowy Lemhi range to the west and the Tetons to the east.

Rare trumpeter swans and peregrine falcons nest, the latter a successful outgrowth of a Peregrine Fund "hacking out" program for young falcons, some of which have returned in recent years to raise families on a tower visible by spotting scope.

Visitors can watch mule deer in early morning and evening—up to 200 may gather in snowy fields near headquarters from October to February—as well as beavers and muskrats in the waterways and pronghorn antelopes in uplands.

Camas is a wonderfully diverse habitat, offering semi-desert rangeland to irrigated meadows, marsh, and open lakes where, again depending on water supply, white-faced ibises can share an impressive colony of several hundred nests with great blue and black-crowned night herons, snowy and great egrets, double-crested cormorants, and sometimes several hundred pairs of Franklin's gulls.

Sandhill cranes nest—sometimes atop muskrat houses.

When young long-billed curlews hatch in the uplands in late May their big-billed parents may gather in agitated groups of a dozen or so calling loud musical "curlee" warnings at visitors walking or driving too near their hatchlings.

Duckling broods, primarily redheads but also mallards, gadwalls, shovelers, and cinnamon teal with some Canada geese, are on the waterways from early June on; but the prime waterfowl sights are in early April when breeders and migrants combined can seem to cover every water surface and fill the air when they take flight.

Raptors are always around. Kestrels and ferruginous hawks nest, sometimes in trees just east of headquarters. Great horned owls are usually in trees near the canal. Short-eared owls skim marsh grasstops hunting in late afternoons. Great grays show up occasionally in winter. Eagles visit then, too—a dozen or so roost in cottonwoods around headquarters November to March.

Migrating tundra swans stop in migration, sometimes up to 1,000. A dozen or so nonbreeding white pelicans usually stay through warmer months.

Refuge trees and shrubs are a conspicuous feature in this semi-arid agricultural area. Birds notice them and come down, especially small birds in migration spring and fall when sometimes 20 or 30 species can be counted in a few hours including warblers, mountain chickadees, kingbirds, rufous hummingbirds, thrushes, orioles, and others.

Nighthawks wheel and kite about for insects. Pheasants and sage grouse are most noticeable in uplands in the fall.

Most of all it is the solitude and intimacy of this remote and undisturbed setting that strikes visitors driving or walking along the marshes or paddling a canoe.

How to get there: From Idaho Falls take I-15 north to Hamer exit, then follow signs three miles north and two miles west to headquarters.

Open: Daylight hours. Office irregularly weekdays (hunting season can limit access October–January; check ahead).

Best times to visit: Each season has interesting features.

What to see: Waterfowl, wading birds, long-billed curlews, mule deer, moose.

What to do: 20 miles of improved roads for driving, hiking (plus 15 unimproved); canoeing around marsh units (not during nesting season); look, if you wish, but don't dig for gold taken in a stagecoach robbery, reportedly hidden along Camas Creek and never recovered.

Where to stay: Motels—Idaho Falls, 36 miles southeast. Campgrounds—at Roberts, 20 miles south; also in Targhee National Forest, 30 miles north.

Weather: Snow can block access mid-December to March.

Points of interest nearby: Mud Lake Wildlife Management Area, five miles southwest; Market Lake Wildlife Management Area, 20 miles south (can have large pintail groups); wind-sculptured sand dunes, 20 miles east; Yellowstone and Teton National Parks both within 100 miles.

For more information: Camas National Wildlife Refuge, 2150 E. 2350 N., Hamer, Idaho 83425. Phone: (208) 662–5423.

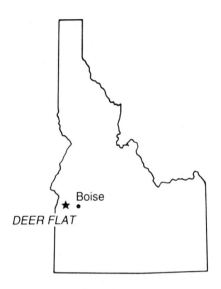

Boise
★ •
DEER FLAT

DEER FLAT (Idaho)

U pward-spiraling white pelicans, majestic bald eagles, and tens of thousands of waterfowl come to Deer Flat's welcoming 11,430 acres that surround Lake Lowell and Snake River Islands stretching for 113 miles along the Snake River from Walter's Ferry, Idaho, to Farewell Bend, Oregon.

In recent years an eagle pair has nested and up to 500 great white pelicans have spent the warm months resting on the lake and taking off to catch warm air thermals on a sunny day.

The Snake River section includes 107 islands ranging from a half to 40-plus acres that accommodate nesting Canada geese as well as great blue and black-crowned night herons, California and ring-billed gulls, Caspian and black terns, avocets, stilts, and, among the ground-dwellers, beavers and minks. Western grebes are occasional nesters and in years of high water can be seen in graceful courtship water dances.

Several thousand goldeneyes may rest there in winter. On the lake 40 or so bald eagles follow the appearance (and prey on weaker members) of waterfowl concentrations—up to 90,000 ducks of which 80,000 are mallards along with pintails, mergansers, wigeon, cinnamon and green-winged teal, and up to 12,000 Great Basin Canada geese. Waterfowl rest on the lake at night and forage by day in nearby fields making spectacular flights to and from feeding grounds.

About 80 wood duck boxes are occupied by kestrels and screech and saw-whet owls when the beautiful waterfowl are not in residence.

Shorebirds congregate on sand and mudflats around the New York Canal at the southeast end when water is drawn down for irrigation. In the spring and fall snipes, western sandpipers, long-billed dowitchers, and long-billed curlews visit these areas. Several hundred pairs of curlews nest in most years on Bureau of Land Management land just west of the refuge (ask staff where).

The best time to see waterfowl as well as eagles is from mid-September to March, though in a hard December freeze many may move to the river. But patient visitors can see a dozen eagles on almost any winter day in cottonwoods around headquarters and another dozen or so along the lower embankment at the northwest end. Coyotes may be out on the frozen lake looking for a hapless bird.

Small birding also is best in these two places with ruby-crowned kinglets, cedar waxwings, yellow warblers, yellow-headed blackbirds, lazuli buntings, juncos, and violet-green swallows common at various seasons.

Red-tailed hawks and northern harriers are common nesting raptors. Rough-legged hawks, goshawks, and prairie falcons are often present in winter. Handsome black-billed magpies, ring-necked pheasants, and California quail can be seen everywhere—often from the Visitor Center viewing window.

Mule deer hang around the south side. Red foxes have denned next to the observation tower.

Visitors should realize that wildlife appearances can be cyclical. White pelicans only began to appear after drought elsewhere, which in turn led duck populations to decline.

How to get there: From Nampa go south on 12th Avenue to Lake Lowell Avenue, then four miles west to refuge sign, then onto Upper Embankment Road. Headquarters/Visitor Center at west end of this road. To see the refuge turn right at Orchard Avenue off Lake Road and follow it left past various access points.

For Snake River sector take Route 45 from Nampa south 12 miles to Walter's Ferry and follow river past various access points.

Open: Daylight hours. Office/Visitor Center 7:30–4 weekdays.

Best times to visit: March–April and October–December (but others good, too).

What to see: Waterfowl; eagles; shorebirds; white pelicans.

What to do: County roads encircle Lake Lowell unit with 10 miles of internal roads for hiking, biking; fishing can be good in spring for bullhead, crappie, largemouth bass; recreation area for picnicking, general water-oriented activities. See the river unit by driving along adjacent roads and entering at various access points (consult staff on these) or by canoe or shallow-draft jetboat.

Where to stay: Motels—in Nampa and Caldwell. Campgrounds—municipal camping in Homedale and Marsing, and Boise National Forest, 30 miles north.

Points of interest nearby: Birds of Prey Natural Area set aside for raptors, especially nesting golden eagles and prairie falcons, 55 miles southeast; Bogus Basin Mountain, 40 miles north; Indian pictographs just north of Snake River unit.

For more information: Deer Flat National Wildlife Refuge, 13751 Upper Embankment Road, Nampa, Idaho 83686. Phone: (208) 467–9278.

GRAYS LAKE
★
Pocatello●

GRAYS LAKE (Idaho)

Pairs of greater sandhill cranes arrive in April and immediately start high-leaping courtship dances at this refuge on a remote high plateau that is mostly marsh and water surrounded by national forest and the lofty Caribou Mountain. Then they nest—more than 200 pairs, the largest breeding colony in the world of this stately gray bird. By fall, with other cranes migrating south, they may number 3,000 or so.

Among the gray cranes may be a few white whooping cranes, part of an attempt to start another breeding group of this large rare crane that stands up to five feet tall with wingspread up to seven feet. These whoopers were raised by sandhills, their close cousins, in the hope they would breed and establish a flock that would take the shorter, safer migration route of the sandhills—850 miles from Idaho to New Mexico, as compared with the hazardous 2,600 miles from whooper breeding grounds in the far Canadian north to south Texas wintering grounds. Several approaches have been taken in this effort but final results are uncertain.

Two other rare and spectacular birds make their homes here: trumpeter swans and peregrine falcons.

Trumpeters, largest waterfowl in the world, historically nested over much of the United States. Their numbers were so reduced by killing both for food and feathers (thousands of swan-feathered robes were sent to Europe) that by 1912 they were believed extinct or nearly so.

Then a remnant population was discovered in the Yellowstone ecosystem. From there they have been reintroduced to this excellent habitat and have nested, so it is hoped a new population group will thrive. These are birds of such wild habits that they cannot usually be seen except by spotting scope, but they are here.

The same is true of swift peregrines that have been clocked at 180 miles an hour when "stooping" on prey but whose numbers were laid low by DDT, which resulted in thinning eggshells. Since DDT was banned in the U.S. their situation has improved, and birds have been transplanted from the Idaho Birds of Prey Center and "hacked out" at a tower here. They have nested, and peregrines are almost always visible by spotting scope around the hacking tower through the breeding season.

Among other wildlife—Franklin's gulls have a huge nesting colony of 10,000 to 15,000 birds, which they share with several hundred white-faced ibises. There are nesting colonies of eared and western grebes and graceful black terns. Canada geese lead broods of youngsters through the meadows in June.

Red-tailed hawks soar and pause on lookout posts. So occasionally do Swainson's. Northern harriers hunt flying low over the marshes and grasslands. Long-billed curlews and 13 species of ducks nest. Mountain bluebirds often are seen around headquarters.

Moose are here, too, along with mule deer, red foxes, coyotes, and an occasional elk—but these can be wary and hard to see.

Camas lilies can turn meadows briefly purple—and there is a succession of blooming lupine, flax, and Indian paintbrush.

Best ways to see the refuge are, first, along the county roads that border it on all sides, with several (unmarked) observation pull-offs; and second, from a platform on a hill behind refuge headquarters, 150 feet above the valley floor. Much of the wildlife can be seen from these vantage points, especially with a spotting scope.

How to get there: From Soda Springs go north on Route 34 about 34 miles to refuge sign (just before Wayan); turn left three miles to headquarters.

Open: Viewing areas and Visitor Center 24 hours (closed December–April). Office 8–4:30 weekdays.

Best times to visit: Late April through October 15.

What to see: Sandhill cranes, possibly whooping cranes; peregrine falcons; trumpeter swans; Canada geese; variety of others.

What to do: Observation platform; 25 miles of roads (mostly county roads) for driving, looking.

Where to stay: Motels—Soda Springs, 37 miles south. Campgrounds—Forest Service:

Gravel Creek, five miles south, also Tin Cup and Pine Bar, 10 and 15 miles east.

Weather: Frost recorded in every month, six feet of snow cover most of winter. Spring, fall can be cold, icy, too.

Points of interest nearby: Forest Service land adjoining—trails and good birding; ruts left by Oregon Trail in Caribou National Forest adjacent, and on Soda Springs Golf Course; National Elk Refuge and Teton National Park, 65 miles northeast.

For more information: Grays Lake National Wildlife Refuge, 74 Grays Lake Road, Wayan, Idaho 83285. Phone: (208) 574–2755.

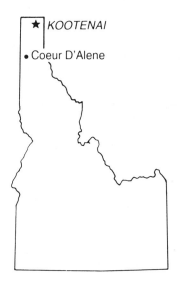

★ KOOTENAI

● Coeur D'Alene

KOOTENAI (Idaho)

The extraordinarily diverse habitat of this small refuge in the beautiful Kootenai River valley just 18 miles south of the Canadian border—woods, ponds, marsh, streams and upland backing up to the Selkirk Range of the Rocky Mountains—has wildlife to match.

Mule and white-tailed deer live here as well as coyotes, beavers, playful otters, and occasional moose and elk. There is always a chance of seeing a black bear or moose and rarely a mountain lion (one was spotted on the road by the refuge workshop). The adjacent Selkirk Mountains have been designated as critical habitat for endangered woodland caribou (which were transplanted there not long ago) and the threatened grizzly bear, and there's a remote possibility of seeing either of these in the Selkirks.

Fearless killdeer nest on the auto-tour route and try to warn off cars by doing a "broken-wing" act. Rufous, calliope, and black-chinned hummingbirds visit headquarters feeders as well as a succession of nectar-bearing wildflowers—wild clematis, mountain hollyhocks, columbines, paintbrush, lupines, and mariposa lilies.

Ruffed grouse can be heard in courtship "drumming" and snipe are "winnowing" in spring—males flying upward until they are only a tiny speck, then darting downward, wind whistling through their feathers.

A pair of endangered bald eagles nests where they can be seen with spotting scope from the auto-tour route. Ospreys feed in the ponds in summer. Coyotes have a litter every year and the pups learn to hunt in fields along the tour route.

All the natural life here, including interesting amphibians, reptiles, and plants, are notable more for diversity than large concentrations, though migrating ducks can peak at up to 40,000 in fall.

More than 225 bird species have been identified. Nesters include Canada geese, beautiful wood ducks and 13 other waterfowl species, kestrels, harriers and red-tailed hawks, pileated woodpeckers, five kinds of flycatchers, six kinds of swallows, Swainson's and varied thrushes, and five kinds of warblers, including MacGillivray's.

Dippers nest under bridges and ledges along Myrtle Creek, flying through waterfall spray and striding unhesitatingly under the water for small prey. Steller's jays and Clark's nutcrackers nest at higher elevations and come back to winter in the valley.

The 1.5-mile Island Pond trail passes close by creatures of the marsh environment—and be sure to take the short trail up through tamaracks and cedars, ferns, mosses, Indian pipe, and shining mica-filled rocks to Myrtle Falls. It is cool and pleasant on the hottest day, and beautiful all the time.

How to get there: From Bonners Ferry take Riverside Road on the south bank of the Kootenai River heading west five miles; continue through refuge to headquarters.

Open: Daylight hours. Office 8–4:30 weekdays.

Best times to visit: Spring and fall.

What to see: Waterfowl, pileated wodpeckers, raptors, migrating tundra swans, mule and white-tailed deer, chance of coyotes, moose, bears; broad wildlife spectrum.

What to do: County roads through and around refuge; 4.5-mile auto-tour route; 1.5-mile interpretive trail, short wheelchair-accessible headquarters trail and observatory at cascade pond, several miles of unimproved foot trails; two observation/photography blinds. Some restrictions during fall hunting season.

Where to stay: Motels—Bonners Ferry, five miles east. Campgrounds—Forest Service for 10–25 miles north along Route 95.

Weather: Roads can be blocked by winter snow, slippery in spring rains.

Points of interest nearby: Creston Valley Wildlife Area, 40 miles north—nature walks, canoe trails; MacArthur Lake State Wildlife Area, 15 miles south.

For more information: Kootenai National Wildlife Refuge, HCR 60, Box 283, Bonners Ferry, Idaho 83805. Phone: (208) 267–3888.

Pocatello

MINIDOKA ★

MINIDOKA (Idaho)

This is the only place in Idaho where lordly white pelicans are known to nest—100 or so on an island in Lake Walcott. There also are nesting western grebes, which court in graceful water ballets and later carry young about on their backs; ruddy ducks that show off robin's-egg-blue bills when in the mating mood; eared grebes with golden ear tufts.

Many waterfowl stay and nest, especially mallards, redheads, and Canada geese. Visitors can see many of these and their fuzzy youngsters on Lake Walcott near the headquarters of this 20,721-acre refuge in southern Idaho.

The pelicans share their island with nesting California gulls and double-crested cormorants. On the shore nearby great blue herons and snowy egrets share nest trees.

Nighthawks wheel about for insects. Ospreys show up in late winter/early spring, golden eagles wheel and soar all year, and bald eagles feed opportunistically in winter on fish and injured waterfowl stragglers.

Look for songbirds in shrubby-grassy woods behind headquarters as well as sandy sagebrush tracts where there are often sage thrashers, larks, sage and Brewer's sparrows, western tanagers, eastern and western kingbirds, and sometimes lazuli buntings, black-headed grosbeaks, and yellow-rumped warblers.

Mule deer and occasionally pronghorn antelopes appear here also. Great horned owls often nest in the trees.

Ruts left by wagons heading west on the Oregon Trail still mark Minidoka, one of the nation's oldest refuges, set aside by President Theodore Roosevelt in 1909 after construction of the Minidoka Dam across the Snake River created Lake Walcott.

This dam pioneered use of hydroelectric power to pump irrigation water and as such is on the National Register of Historic Places. A side effect has been Lake Walcott's attraction for waterfowl in this formerly desertlike area.

The lake with its many bays and inlets has become a valued molting sanctuary for ducks and geese that hide safely there while growing new flight feathers.

Long-billed curlews nest in the uplands—usually readily visible along old Highway 30, as are pronghorns (ask refuge staff). Handsome black-billed magpies are omnipresent. Agile minks forage on rocks in the spillway below the dam. Hundreds of tundra swans congregate on the river and lake in spring and fall.

Except for the headquarters area and a stretch of road open seasonally, this is not an easy refuge to see. The terrain is rough and lava strewn, requiring 4-wheel drive or sturdy hiking boots (hiking is permitted anywhere on the refuge). If possible bring a boat (rentals are sometimes available in the area) and go quietly about observing water-oriented wildlife. A canoe is ideal. Refuge staff can suggest ways to see particular species.

How to get there: From Burley take I-84 east to Burley-Rupert exit, north onto State Highway 24 through Rupert to refuge sign, then six miles northeast on State Highway 24 via Acequia to another refuge sign, then six miles east on County Road 400 North, to Minidoka Dam.

Open: Dawn to dark. Office 8–4:30 weekdays, closed if staff are out in field (brochures available in box; call ahead with special questions).

Best times to visit: Spring and fall.

What to see: Migratory waterfowl; nesting water birds; songbirds; mule deer; interesting lava formations.

What to do: Limited driving, hiking (see above); boating from April 1 through September 30 (portions of the refuge closed to protect nesting birds); picnicking; trout fishing can be good.

Where to stay: Motels—in Burley, 17 miles southwest. Campgrounds—at Declo I-84 interchange, nine miles south; Massacre Rocks State Park, 30 miles east; and Bureau of Reclamation facilities (refuge is an overlay on Bureau land).

Weather: Wet winter snows can make roads impassable.

Points of interest nearby: Massacre Rocks (see Campgrounds)—historic exhibits, old Oregon Trail, good birding; pioneer hydroelectric irrigation project, tours. This is a good stop to and from Craters of the Moon and Yellowstone, about 200 miles north.

For more information: Minidoka National Wildlife Refuge, Route 4, Box 290, Rupert, Idaho 83350. Phone: (208) 436–3589.

★ BENTON LAKE
•
Great Falls

BENTON LAKE (Montana)

Graceful swans, geese, ducks and a multitude of other water-oriented birds literally fill the water and sky at Benton Lake from spring to late fall in a beautiful glimpse of what Montana wetlands and prairies were before civilization came.

This expanse of nutrient-rich marshes is one of the most productive waterfowl refuges in the United States. More than 20,000 ducklings reach flight stage each year—more in a good year: gadwalls, pintails, shovelers, lesser scaups, blue-winged teals, and others. In the general throng one mother sometimes will adopt another's babies—one female lesser scaup was seen leading a long weaving line of 50 fuzzy ducklings.

Up to 100,000 ducks and 2,500 Canada geese may be here in spring and fall migration.

Uplands teem with nesting marbled godwits, upland sandpipers, willets, and gray partridges. Short-eared owls fly low in hunting forays in late afternoons. Burrowing owls are often seen perched atop earthen mounds above subterranean nesting chambers.

Fifty or so sharp-tailed grouse display lavender throat pouches and dance in April just off the auto-tour route (reserve space in a blind to see them more closely).

Handsome lark buntings call from every small rise, and the native prairie grasses can be full of chestnut-collared longspurs, horned larks, vesper and often grasshopper and Baird's sparrows.

Franklin's gulls raise young families on 10,000 nests in two great floating marsh colonies and gold-festooned eared grebes construct similar accommodations.

It can be a stunning, almost bewildering experience to drive or hike down the dike surrounded by birds—the eared grebes in their nest colonies, rusty-hooded avocets incubating eggs at the water's edge, Canada geese followed by downy broods, phalaropes in grand whirling array.

Black-crowned night herons nest and white-faced ibises often stay through early fall; then when the prairie is at its bleakest in earliest spring and late fall, up to 7,500 tundra swans show up to fill the refuge with their graceful white presence.

Raptors can be splendid, too. Bald eagles come spring and fall looking for weakened waterfowl; peregrine and prairie falcons zoom through then along with a few ferruginous hawks, and it's not uncommon to see magnificent gyrfalcons looking over the frozen marsh in March and April—one beautiful white female captured a sharp-tailed grouse on the auto-tour route.

Rough-legged hawks and golden eagles and occasionally a few snowy owls appear in fall and winter. Spectacular numbers of Swainson's hawks appear in late summer and fall—as many as 150 in a single day.

Mudflats attract impressive migratory shorebirds—thousands of dowitchers, a variety of smaller sandpipers, plovers, and sometimes rarities like a whimbrel or Hudsonian godwit.

Swift pronghorn antelope have their fawns here. Badgers are common though too wary to be seen easily—but burrows with young ones are numerous in spring. Coyotes den, and these "little prairie wolves" are out in the fields and on the ice in winter early and late scouting about for small prey.

Benton Lake also administers Waterfowl Production Areas and wetland easements in ten counties, some quite spectacular but maintained principally for their wildlife habitat and with few visitor facilities. To arrange a visit consult a refuge headquarters.

Outstanding areas are: Blackfoot—nesting sandhill cranes, blue grouse, denning bobcats, wintering elk; Furnell—prairie pothole country at the base of the lovely Sweetgrass Hills with pronghorns, mule deer, sharp-tailed grouse, waterfowl; Jarina—against a sheer rise of the Rockies where winds can reach up to 90 mph, raptors nest on the cliffs and wolves, grizzly bears, and mountain lions are transient visitors.

How to get there: From Great Falls take 15th Street (Route 87) north across Missouri River to Bootlegger Trail; follow it north 12 miles to refuge office.

Open: Dawn to dusk; office 8–4:30 weekdays.

Best times to visit: Spring through fall.

What to see: Waterfowl, shore and marsh birds in nesting and migration; raptors, especially Swainson's hawks in fall; coyotes.

What to do: Wildlife observation, on foot or along auto-tour route (parts can be closed seasonally due to bad weather or to prevent wildlife disturbance); photography—good from car window, or reserve space in blind for sharp-tailed grouse dancing.

Where to stay: Motels—in Great Falls. Campgrounds—commercial in Great Falls; Thane Creek Forest, 50 miles east; Lewis and Clark National Forest, 60 miles southeast.

Weather: Can be frozen mid-November to April.

Points of interest nearby: Giant Springs, world's largest freshwater spring, in Giant Springs State Park, 15 miles south; Freezeout State Wildlife Area, 40 miles west—good birding, upwards of 100,000 snow geese spring and fall; Charles M. Russell studio/gallery in Great Falls; spectacular 80-mile drive along Missouri River cliffs between Great Falls and Helena, either on freeway or adjacent recreational road.

For more information: Benton Lake National Wildlife Refuge, P.O. Box 450, Black Eagle, Montana 59414. Phone: (406) 727–7400.

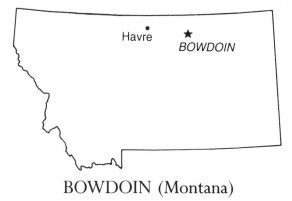

Havre
★
BOWDOIN

BOWDOIN (Montana)

White pelicans with nine-foot wingspreads, delicate rusty-hooded avocets, and in recent years endangered piping plovers come together with thousands of water birds of many species every spring to nest and bring up families at this 15,437-acre refuge of marsh, water, and native grassland in north-central Montana.

Sharp-tailed grouse shake inflated lavender throat sacs, contesting for mating partners on prairie dancing grounds. Bronze ring-necked pheasants puff out scarlet cheeks. White-tailed deer and fleet-footed pronghorn antelopes bring out long-legged young ones in June.

Porcupines nibble on green shoots and in winter on new-formed Russian olive bark, their 30,000 hollow quills providing insulation and warmth as well as buoyancy for swimming if necessary. Engaging "flickertails"—Richardson's ground squirrels— look like small prairie dogs at their holes.

Great blue and black-crowned night herons fish the water's edges. Buff-brown marbled godwits with long upturned bills nest in large numbers. Conspicuous in prairie areas are such notable smaller breeding residents as Sprague's pipits, Baird's sparrows, lark buntings, and chestnut-collared longspurs.

"Land of the Big Sky" this is called, because the clarity of sun-filled atmosphere stretches like a great airy bowl around the entire horizon seeming to take up far more space in one's vista than the subdued rolling landscape beneath. As a result the whole world except for a token foothold can seem to be composed simply of a huge blue sky filled with birds—black and common terns, Wilson's phalaropes, white-faced ibises, and a great many others—calling, demonstrating bright breeding plumage, and later herding youngsters along to flight stage before starting a fall southward trek.

Most can be seen along a 15-mile auto-tour loop that wanders around Lake Bowdoin and through various habitats. Ask refuge staff for suggestions on how to see particular species.

More than 2,000 white pelicans colonize islands in Lake Bowdoin, along with double-crested cormorants, and California and ring-billed gulls. Franklin's gulls (favorites of farmers for their insect consumption) nest in Bowdoin's extensive bulrush marshes.

Eared grebes with gold-accented head plumage build floating nests in the marshes. Yellow-headed and red-winged blackbirds flare brilliant colors from every patch of bulrush. Cliff swallows construct colonies of tubular mud nests under every bridge. Short-eared owls appear for late afternoon hunting forays.

Hundreds of young Canada geese and thousands of ducklings of a dozen or more species come off nests every year joined in fall by southward migrating snow and some Ross' geese and up to 1,000 tundra swans. Southward-moving waterfowl can build up to fall concentrations of 70,000 or so.

Raptors can be impressive both spring and fall. Common almost every year are sharp-shinned, Cooper's, red-tailed, rough-legged, Swainson's, and a few ferruginous hawks, northern harriers, and transient bald and golden eagles.

Winters can be bitterly cold with snow and rain making roads hazardous—but black-billed magpies, snow buntings, and horned larks don't seem to mind. Russian olive berries attract flocks of 50 or 100 Bohemian waxwings, and Audubon Christmas Bird Counts can turn up sage grouse, gray partridge, great horned owls, prairie falcons, mountain chickadees, redpolls, goshawks, and an occasional snowy owl.

How to get there: From Malta take Route 2 one mile east to refuge sign on right (old U.S. 2) and follow six miles to headquarters.

Open: Daylight hours. Office 8–4:30 weekdays.

Best times to visit: Spring and fall.

What to see: White pelicans, nesting waterfowl and marsh birds, sharp-tailed grouse, and many others in large numbers; deer, antelopes.

What to do: 15-mile auto-tour loop; photography (grouse dancing grounds can be good from car—consult staff—and portable blinds are permitted). (Limited fall hunt on parts of refuge.)

Where to stay: Motels—in Malta, seven miles west; also Sleeping Buffalo, 15 miles northeast. Campgrounds—in Malta; also Nelson State Park, 15 miles northeast.

Points of interest nearby: Nelson Reservoir, 15 miles northeast; Charles M. Russell National Wildlife Refuge, 70 miles south.

For more information: Bowdoin National Wildlife Refuge, P.O. Box J, Malta, Montana 59538. Phone: (406) 654–2863.

Bowdoin also administers four smaller refuges, *Black Coulee, Creedman, Hewitt Lake,* and *Lake Thibadeau,* with similar habitat but no visitor facilities.

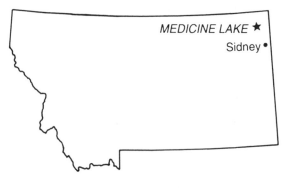

MEDICINE LAKE ★
Sidney •

MEDICINE LAKE (Montana)

One of the largest nesting colonies of white pelicans in the United States takes to the air over this 31,457 acres of meadows, pasture, lakes, and ponds in northeast Montana. In a good year they produce up to 3,000 young birds whose impressive and handsome parents have wings that spread almost nine feet in soaring flight.

Eared and horned grebes in striking gold head-feathering build floating nest colonies, and handsome black-and-white western grebes perform breathtaking courtship water ballets that visitors can see in spring (when water is high enough) from road pull-offs. Altogether they bring off sometimes thousands of young grebes that ride about on their parents' backs, clinging even when they dive for food.

Double-crested cormorants and great blue herons sometimes share breeding sites with the pelicans, and sometimes settle amid nests of California and ring-billed gulls that whiten the islands on which they raise up to 6,000 families. All can be seen from the lake shore along the auto-tour route.

Sharp-tailed grouse gather on a dozen or more dancing grounds. Males rise in early morning to stomp and shake inflated lavender gular sacs to attract females (which sometimes, studies show, choose mates not so preoccupied with dancing and mate with THEM). A blind is available by prior reservation for watching and photography.

It is a prodigious waterfowl nesting area. Hundreds of Canada geese and sometimes more than 30,000 ducklings are hatched out in spring and early summer—shovelers, gadwalls, blue-winged teal, pintails, and others.

Threatened piping plovers nest on graveled shores—ask at the office where they might be seen (and other species, too).

Along the 14-mile auto-tour route and around Sayer Bay a visitor can usually spot such nesting shorebirds as marbled godwits, rusty-hooded avocets, and Wilson's phalaropes, and in the prairies, upland sandpipers, chestnut-collared longspurs by the hundreds, plus McCown's longspurs, Sprague's pipits, lark buntings, and Le-Conte's, Baird's, lark, and clay-colored sparrows.

In summer pheasants and gray partridges pick up grit and insects along the roads. If a hawk goes by so fast you can't tell what it was, it was probably a prairie falcon. Short-eared owls and northern harriers cruise along the grasstops in late day, especially after a snowy winter has left meadow vole populations high.

White-tailed deer are here in the largest numbers in this section of the country—groups of 50 or so graze in fall and winter, and occasional antelope appear.

Several coyote pairs usually den near the auto-tour route and pups are out learning to hunt from July on.

Bald and golden eagles might be anywhere along the auto-tour route—especially bald, sometimes 60 in fall and in spring just after ice breakup.

In fall birds that stopped briefly en route north to breeding grounds come through again and, unpressed by such urgent purpose, stay longer—sometimes 2,000 tundra swans, buildups of up to 20,000 Franklin's gulls and 100,000 waterfowl (perhaps 50,000 shovelers alone), and up to 10,000 sandhill cranes, plus occasional ferruginous hawks.

All depends on water. Drought means fewer birds—but if it is not too long, it benefits habitat, returning nutrients to soil for release later in aquatic vegetation and invertebrate food.

Hiking is permitted anywhere except critical nesting sites (hiking boots can protect against cactus), especially in the beautiful 11,366-acre wilderness area where a visitor can feel something of the isolation from civilization that pioneers experienced here.

Four research areas are set aside for study of Indian archeological sites, significant nesting areas, and unique botanical groups.

How to get there: From Williston, North Dakota, take U.S. 2 west 35 miles to Culbertson, then north 25 miles on MT 16 to refuge sign.

Open: Sunrise–sunset. Office 7–3:30 weekdays.

Best times to visit: May through October.

What to see: White pelicans, cormorants, waterfowl, shorebirds, sharp-tailed grouse, bald eagles, Sprague's pipits, longspurs, deer.

What to do: 14-mile auto-tour route (can be closed first days of limited hunting, also by snow November–March); observation tower; photo blind; canoeing; picnicking.

Where to stay: Motels—in Culbertson, 24 miles south; Plentywood, 25 miles north.

Campgrounds—in Plentywood; also Lewis and Clark State park, 90 miles southeast.

Weather: Winter temperatures can fall to 40 below.

Points of interest nearby: Theodore Roosevelt National Park, 90 miles southeast; Fort Union Trading Post Historical Site, 40 miles south.

For more information: Medicine Lake National Wildlife Refuge, HC 51, Box 2, Medicine Lake, Montana 59247. Phone: (406) 789–2305.

Medicine Lake also administers *Lamesteer* Refuge, an 800-acre wetland easement, and 40 waterfowl production areas, open but with few facilities. To arrange a visit, consult staff.

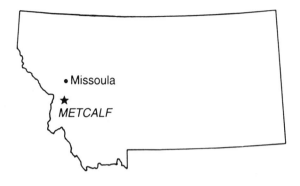

• Missoula
★
METCALF

METCALF (Montana)

Ospreys share tree nests with majestic Canada geese (though not at the same time) along with much other highly visible wildlife at this fine small refuge of woods, fields, marsh, and open water along the Bitterroot River in western Montana.

Bald eagles have nested in recent years. Coyotes den and bring out pups in summer, the parents leaping high over the grass to locate meals for growing families. Dappled fawns follow their mothers and sometimes 100 or so white-tailed deer graze in fields at the south end.

Pheasants cackle through the uplands. Otters have begun to appear with pups in recent years. Muskrats stack up mounds of vegetation for underwater dwellings that waterfowl use above the waterline for resting and sometimes nesting.

Great horned owls come out at dusk around the picnic area, hooting and flying back and forth to fuzzy owlets in the spring. Moose occasionally wander over from the river. This is a favorite spot in August for beautiful wood ducks, sometimes beavers, and in the shrubby areas, passerines.

Flame-crested pileated woodpeckers are a spectacular resident and rosy-breasted Lewis' woodpeckers can usually be found in warm months. So can flickers, kingbirds, yellowthroats, three kinds of hummingbird (rufous, calliope, and black-chinned), and six kinds of swallow. White-breasted and pygmy nuthatches are around all year but seem noisier and more numerous when it's cool.

Yellow-bellied marmots scamper through the uplands and sun themselves on logs in warmer months. An extremely lucky visitor might spot an elk, bobcat or bear.

Northern harriers and short-eared owls both hunt in late afternoon flights over the marshes. Rough-legged hawks come in winter along with a dozen or so bald eagles and a few goldens. Migrating waterfowl stop by spring and fall, peaking around 10,000. (More than a dozen species nest.) A year's highlight is 600 or so transient tundra swans and occasionally a lordly trumpeter. Great blue herons are common all year.

Ospreys arrive in early April and immediately begin to harass the geese that have taken up family duties in bulky nests left by the big "fish hawks" the previous year in dead cottonwoods and ponderosa pines. Luckily the geese are about finished by then and the downy young drop perhaps 100 feet to the ground, bounce and dash unhurt to the water.

Ospreys then take over and are a delight to visitors who can easily watch them hunting, catching fish, and "changing the guard" as one takes over incubating and brooding chores from another.

Much wildlife can be seen from the county road without getting out of the car— otherwise at the picnic area or on the several walking trails (see three-foot harvester ant piles there).

This is a beautiful refuge, too. When a rising or setting sun in spring or fall casts a pink glow on snowy peaks of the Bitterroot Range reflected on the water (St. Mary's rises to 9,000 feet), it seems no wonder the Salish-Kootenai Indians made this their home.

How to get there: From Stevensville take East Side Highway to Wildfowl Lane and refuge sign, then north 1.5 miles to south refuge boundary.

Open: Daylight hours year-round. Office 8:30–4:30 weekdays.

Best times to visit: All year can be interesting.

What to see: Nesting ospreys; resident and migratory waterfowl; deer; raptors; pheasants; tree-nesting geese; historic homestead.

What to do: County road through refuge and along south boundary for driving, hiking; several walking trails; picnic area.

Where to stay: Motels—Stevensville; also Missoula, 25 miles north; Hamilton, 25 miles south. Campgrounds—Bitterroot National Forest, just west.

Points of interest nearby: Bitterroot National Forest surrounds refuge and includes the Sapphire Mountains, four miles east (you really can find sapphires); 1.2-million-acre Selway-Bitterroot Wilderness Area, just west; beautiful river float trips from Hamilton to Missoula; excellent information kiosk at junction of Routes 93 and 269; historic Stevensville, St. Mary's Mission/Fort Owen, oldest white settlement in Montana.

For more information: Metcalf National Wildlife Refuge, P.O. Box 257, Stevensville, Montana 59870. Phone: (406) 777–5552.

NATIONAL BISON RANGE
★
• Missoula

NATIONAL BISON RANGE (Montana)

National Bison Range sits in a gentle verdant valley on the west slope of the Rockies in a range called "land of the Shining Mountains" by the Indians. Once an island in a prehistoric lake, it remains a treasure island for naturalists with its varied and abundant wildlife of all kinds, including mammals, birds, wildflowers, and great scenic beauty.

Many of the creatures that roamed this part of northwest Montana before people were here are present now. Bison, once one of the most numerous mammals on earth with perhaps 70 million in great herds on the western plains, were reestablished here after their numbers had been reduced by overkilling to fewer than 100 in the wild. President Theodore Roosevelt set this refuge aside in 1908, and the newly formed National Bison Society found a nucleus herd (which had been saved by an Indian named Walking Coyote) and financed their transfer here by popular subscription. Now their descendants thrive.

Elk, with antlers that can be more than four feet across, live here along with swift and beautiful pronghorn antelopes, mountain goats and bighorn sheep, white-tailed deer, coyotes (the "little prairie wolf"), badgers, minks, and great numbers of smaller interesting animals—yellow-bellied marmots, Columbian ground squirrels, and yellow pine chipmunks.

Black bears come to feed on berries in season.

And, while most visitors come for the impressive large animals, the bird population alone would make this a great refuge: golden eagles common all year and nesting; and common to abundant at one season or another are a wonderful array that can only be suggested by mentioning lazuli buntings, Lewis' woodpeckers, Clark's nutcrackers, dusky flycatchers, grasshopper and vesper sparrows, Townsend's solitaires, red-breasted and pygmy nuthatches, mountain chickadees, mountain bluebirds, Bohemian waxwings, red crossbills, common goldeneyes and short-eared owls.

Less common but still readily seen from time to time are ospreys, prairie falcons, blue and ruffed grouse, pygmy and long-eared owls, calliope and rufous humming-birds, and black-headed and pine grosbeaks. Raucous handsome black-billed mapgipes are everywhere. Canada geese and mallards nest along Mission Creek, where bank swallows colonize.

The refuge, which rises 2,100 feet in the three miles from headquarters to the spectacular lookout at High Point on the auto-tour route, is also a botanist's (as well as photographer's) delight with the varied habitat. Its 18,500 acres range through streambeds, prairie grasslands, deep woods of Douglas fir and ponderosa pine, and heavily shrubbed areas of prairie roses, hawthorns, chokecherries, and serviceberries. Here small birds are abundant and the wildflowers nothing short of awesome. Visitors seeing lupine fields in the distance sometimes take out binoculars to be sure the shimmering blue is not a sparkling lake.

Visitors can see a great deal around headquarters, including some of the large mammals. Marmots are common and there is a short walking trail. But the best way to see it all is to take the 19-mile auto tour. Everything can be seen there at one time or another. Drive slowly and plan to spend at least two hours, more if possible—most interested naturalists find that days could be consumed looking at everything here. For small birds stop by a thicket, especially along Pauline Creek, listen and wait. The wait will not be long—the area can be alive with buntings, warblers, and orioles.

Stay in or near the car. Stay on the road—one-ton buffalo can be unpredictable and dangerous. It is best to go early when the gate opens or just before the tour route closes in the evenings to see the most. Scan the tops of slopes for bighorns, remembering that camouflage colors can make them look like a large rock (in late evening they can appear in large numbers on the roads). Young calves and fawns begin to show up in May; bison mating behavior starts in late July when bulls start fighting, bellowing, and pawing the earth around cow herds.

How to get there: From Missoula take State Highway 93 north 35 miles to Ravalli, then Route 200 west six miles to Dixon, then Route 212 north four miles to refuge entrance, following signs.

Open: Daylight hours weather permitting (heavy winter snows can make travel difficult). Office 8–4:30 weekdays, Visitor Center 8 a.m.–8 p.m. daily mid-May through September, otherwise 8–4:30 weekdays.

Best times to visit: Interesting things to see all year, but best before and after heavy summer traffic. Long tour route is closed from late October through mid-May.

What to see: Bison; elk; deer; bighorn sheep; pronghorn antelopes; golden eagles; great variety of interesting animals, birds, plants; magnificent scenery.

What to do: 14-mile self-guided auto-tour route (several short loops available for those with less time); short walking trail (including handicapped-accessible); photography (good from car—rated as a photographic "best bet" by the *Audubon Guide*); picnicking.

Where to stay: Motels—Charlo, Polson, Ronan; large selection in Missoula. Campgrounds—near Ravalli, Ronan, Charlo; refuge has list of others.

Weather: Midsummer can be hot and dusty.

Points of interest nearby: St. Ignatius Mission, 15 miles east—historic Jesuit mission with unique, beautiful murals. Mission Mountain Wilderness Area and adjacent Tribal Wilderness (only wilderness area set aside by an Indian tribe) just east of refuge. Flathead Lake is 30 miles north; Glacier National Park, 120 miles north.

For more information: National Bison Range, 132 Bison Range Road, Moiese, Montana 59824. Phone: (406) 644–2211.

National Bison Range also administers *Ninepipe* Refuge, 12 miles north; *Pablo* Refuge, 30 miles north; and *Swan River* Refuge, 60 miles northeast—largely waterfowl refuges, sometimes with up to 50,000 birds in migration, good birding generally, good fishing for largemouth bass but no visitor facilities. It also manages a number of smaller refuges and waterfowl production areas, mostly open but with few facilities. To arrange a visit consult refuge office.

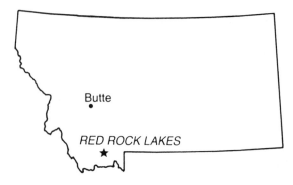

Butte

RED ROCK LAKES
★

RED ROCK LAKES (Montana)

One of the most beautiful birds in the world came back from the edge of extinction in one of the most beautiful places in the world. The bird: the stately trumpeter swan. The place: Red Rock Lakes Refuge in the remote, wild Centennial Valley at the foot of the snowy Continental Divide, part of the greater Yellowstone ecosystem.

The trumpeter swan is the largest waterfowl in North America. Over five feet long with a wingspread up to eight feet, it can weigh almost 30 pounds and can live about 20 years. It mates for life and is distinguished from all other swans by an extra loop in the windpipe that makes possible a deep, clear call that can be heard for miles.

Once it ranged over much of the United States. But pressure to kill it both for meat and feathers (thousands of swan-feather robes were shipped to Europe) so reduced its numbers that in 1912 the noted ornithologist Edward Howe Forbush wrote, "Its trumpeting call will soon be locked in the silence of the past . . . total extinction is only a matter of years." Some believed it gone already.

Then a small group was discovered in the Centennial Valley and, with only 68 known still in the wild, steps were taken in 1935 to establish this refuge where it recovered and now survives in a stable population of 250 to 300. That is not very many but it is saturation level here for this solitary bird that insists on a minimum breeding territory of 15 and sometimes as much as 640 acres within which it will tolerate no other large bird, even of a different species, to enter, driving away geese, cranes, all others.

But transplant pairs have been taken from the population here to other parks and refuges around the country and to nearby states in a program to expand its range to areas of better winter forage, and a large population was discovered in Alaska and western Canada. As a result the beautiful trumpeter, while still rare, is no longer endangered; its numbers in the lower U.S. are about 2,000 and worldwide a comfortable 13,500.

The visitor to Red Rock Lakes cannot always be sure of seeing trumpeters—they often nest in remote marshes. But usually he can catch a glimpse of them, perhaps with gray cygnets in summer. Ask at the office where they've been seen lately (and investigate Shambo Pond).

A trip to Red Rock Lakes is a superb experience in any case. Sandhill cranes nest and can be seen in high-leaping spring courtship dances anywhere on these 68 square miles, of which 50 square miles is designated wilderness and 13,000 acres are covered with shallow lakes, marshes, and meadows fed by snowmelt from mountains that rise to nearly 10,000 feet.

Moose nibble on willow bottoms all year. Swift pronghorn antelopes graze and drop their fawns on the open grasslands in June. Porcupines climb up aspens and snooze in their notches.

Fields, foothills, and mountain slopes offer a colorful profusion of wildflower bloom through the growing season—shooting stars, paintbrush, mallows, columbines, blue lupines, and many others. In the streams are rare Arctic grayling.

Badgers dig burrows conveniently near those of the Richardson's ground squirrels on which they like to dine. White-tailed deer browse the willow bottoms, mule deer in more mountainous terrain. Coyotes yelp across the valley at one another early and late.

Exceedingly rare but always exciting possibilities are visits by black and grizzly bears, mountain lions, lynx, and timber wolves.

White pelicans spend the summer. So does, rarely, an endangered whooping crane. Tundra swans come in fall. Seventeen duck species breed, including the Barrow's goldeneye. Bald and golden eagles nest; so do peregrine falcons, great horned and great gray owls, great blue and black-crowned night herons, long-billed curlews, ruffed, sage, and blue grouse, and among the smaller types, Clark's nutcrackers, mountain chickadees, Cassin's finches, Townsend's solitaires, pine grosbeaks, and rosy finches.

Winter is forbidding. Roads are closed most of the time. But if one can get through, moose and white-tailed deer are more visible then, and the scenery, always stunning, is absolutely breathtaking (trumpeters more readily seen at that season at Harriman State Park, 35 miles southeast).

How to get there: From Lima take I-15 south 14 miles to Monida exit "0" and refuge sign, then 28 miles east on gravel and dirt road to headquarters at Lakeview.

Open: 24 hours. Office 7:30–4 weekdays.

Best times to visit: Mid-May through October.

What to see: Trumpeter swans, sandhill cranes, eagles, waterfowl, wading birds, moose, variety of others plus wildflowers, spectacular scenery.

What to do: About 30 miles of roads for driving, hiking (walking permitted almost everywhere); canoeing (restricted during nesting); photography; fishing for rainbow, brook, cutthroat trout; some cross-country skiing, snowshoeing.

Where to stay: Motels—guest ranch adjacent, resort ranch 1.5 miles northeast; also in Lima, 50 miles northwest. Campgrounds—limited facilities on refuge; commercial 45 miles east near West Yellowstone, Montana; BLM land adjacent on southwest open to primitive or backpacking campers.

Weather: Sudden rains can make roads difficult through June (sometimes even later), and snows November–April may block roads to all but over-snow vehicles (average 151 inches snow yearly). Bring warm clothing spring and fall, frost possible even in midsummer.

Points of interest nearby: Yellowstone National Park, 50 miles east; Harriman State Park (see text); Beaverhead National Forest, adjacent on north.

For more information: Red Rock Lakes National Wildlife Refuge, Monida Star Route, Box 15, Lima, Montana 59739. Phone: (409) 276–3536.

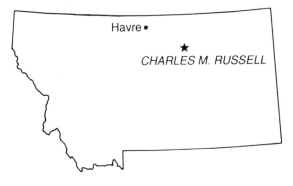

Havre •

★
CHARLES M. RUSSELL

CHARLES M. RUSSELL (Montana)

Climb to the valley's edge at this spectacular refuge and you will see the Missouri River meandering through rugged "breaks" looking as it did when the explorers Lewis and Clark came in 1805—or even, so little has changed, earlier when duck-billed dinosaurs and *Tyrannosaurus rex* were the dominant wildlife.

But now a cow elk grazes with her calf on river-bottom grasses. White-tailed deer forage on skunkbrush sumac. A mule deer finds shade under a juniper bush and fluffy Canada goose broods follow close behind their stately parents.

Sage and sharp-tailed grouse males gather at dawn in spring mating season to inflate and shake gold and lavender throat sacs and stamp the ground on traditional booming and dancing grounds. Coyotes skirt through open places and slip into cover again.

Pronghorn antelopes hurtle across the grasslands at speeds approaching 40 miles an hour and bighorn sheep clamber up rocks—sharing this million-or-so acres with 40 other mammals and a tremendous variety of interesting birds, reptiles, plants, and fossil remains of prehistoric residents. Paleontologists continue to make new discoveries of prehistoric activity.

Prairie dog "towns" cover thousands of acres where these captivating little animals once were almost extirpated from the refuge—and with them exist whole interesting interlocking ecosystems. Sometimes sharing the burrows they dig are burrowing owls, desert cottontails, and occasional rattlesnakes. Mountain plovers seek out the open gravelly substrate around their homes as nesting sites.

Black-footed ferrets, one of the world's rarest animals, are no longer found on the refuge, but reintroduction of members of this scarce species is planned.

Preying upon the little "dogs" are coyotes, badgers, bobcats, and a whole range of raptors including golden eagles and ferruginous hawks. One golden eagle family grew up in a cottonwood tree a quarter mile from a "town" where an eagle parent would go every day as if to the neighborhood supermarket and bring back dinner.

Elk, killed off in early settlement days, have been reintroduced and now grow racks of record size, spreading five feet and more in late summer. In September upwards of 200 gather along the river bottoms. The bulls bugle and challenge each other, contending for mates and protecting their harems, a wildlife spectacular at early morning and dusk.

Raptors are attracted to this wild area—swift rare prairie falcons spring through fall and at various seasons merlins, sharp-shinned, red-tailed, Swainson's, and rough-legged hawks, northern harriers, bald eagles, and ospreys, with occasional ferruginous, goshawks, peregrines, and gyrfalcons and five common species of owl—great horned, saw-whet, long-eared, and short-eared (sometimes everyplace in the grasslands late on a fall afternoon), and the snowy in winter.

Fifty or more bald eagles may gather in the waters immediately below Fort Peck dam in December and January to feed on fish stunned or injured in passage.

White pelicans come through, as do common loons, in spring, and there are nesting great blue herons, large numbers of migratory waterfowl and shorebirds, sandhill cranes, and such interesting common to abundant small birds as pinyon jays, red-breasted nuthatches, rock wrens, sage thrashers, mountain and western bluebirds, Bohemian waxwings, lark buntings, and Lapland and chestnut-collared longspurs. Endangered piping plovers and least terns nest.

Spring can produce carpets of prairie roses, penstemons, and blue lupines—and there is bloom until freeze-up.

Strange paddlefish, huge ancient specimens with no true bones, grow up to 140 pounds and are sometimes snagged by fishermen.

The refuge is named after the great cowboy artist who, with no instruction, magnificently painted the life he saw here in the last century against backgrounds much like these seen here today.

Much of this wild area still is not fully explored. That is partly what makes it fascinating to visit, either by the winding 20-mile auto-tour route, hiking out over the badland "breaks," following some of the less-traveled trails by horseback or 4-wheel drive (take a compass, though a new map road-numbering system makes it less likely you'll get lost) or go as Lewis and Clark did, following the waterways through unaltered wilderness, camping along the way.

How to get there: Headquarters is in west Lewistown on Airport Road. Enter the auto-tour route by all-weather gravel road from Route 191, 55 miles south of Malta. For other entrances 4-wheel drive is recommended. Get a map and consult refuge office.

Open: 24 hours year-round. Headquarters 7:30–4 weekdays.

Best times to visit: Late spring and fall; summer is fine early and late in the day.

What to see: Elk, antelopes, deer, prairie dogs, grouse, raptors, many others; excellent birding, interesting botanicals.

What to do: 20-mile auto-tour route; 400 miles of roads open to 4-wheel drive and hiking; boating (free-flowing parts of refuge on west end are suitable for rafting and canoeing, motorized boats recommended for impounded waters of Fort Peck Lake); fishing, excellent for walleyes, smallmouth bass, lake trout; photography—many opportunities, especially elk in fall; horseback riding; also cross-country skiing and snowshoeing depending on snow conditions.

Where to stay: Motels—Fort Peck, Glasgow, Malta, Lewistown, Jordan. Campgrounds—permitted throughout the refuge and at Corps of Engineers and state park areas within refuge.

Weather: Montanans keep one eye on the horizon; winters are harsh, temperatures can change 50-plus degrees in 24 hours any time from late fall through early spring—all seasons changeable; even a sudden thunder shower can make roads quickly impassable and leave travelers stranded.

What to take and wear: Jack, chains, shovel, food, water, hiking boots, and compass when venturing off main roads.

Points of interest nearby: Montana State Fish Hatchery, Lewistown; Fort Peck Museum and Visitor Center, east end of refuge.

For more information: Charles M. Russell National Wildlife Refuge, P.O. Box 110, Lewistown, Montana 59457. Phone: (406) 538–8706.

Ul Bend Refuge adjoins Charles M. Russell and is administered by it. Its wildlife and habitat are similar. If anything, it is more remote and difficult of access. Charles M. Russell also administers four satellite waterfowl production refuges—*Halfbreed, Hailstone, Lake Mason,* and *War Horse*—which emphasize waterfowl and have similar habitat but no elk or bighorn sheep. Consult the refuge office about a visit to these.

★ NATIONAL ELK
•
Jackson

NATIONAL ELK (Wyoming)

The largest wintering elk herd in the world—up to 10,000—gathers here against a stunning backdrop of snowy mountain peaks rising 13,000 feet. It is an unforgettable spectacle reminiscent of elk herds 200 years ago.

The elk begin gathering in mid-November. Then, from mid-December to late March, visitors can ride horse-drawn sleighs to get a wonderful view of the herd.

Coyotes and bald eagles are usually around then, too, and sometimes mule deer, moose, bighorn sheep, and in open water, trumpeter swans.

Bull elk can weigh up to 700 pounds with antlers up to six feet across. Once millions of these great beasts, like the bison, roamed over much of the United States, but they competed with ranchers for winter range. They were killed in large numbers also for trophies as well as for tusklike teeth that were made into charms and ornaments. Antlers were ground up for sale in Asia, some say for aphrodisiacs, others for vitamin supplements.

One year 10,000 died of starvation here and local people appealed for emergency feed to tide them over. Finally their numbers were so reduced and their condition so deplorable that wide national support developed for a national wildlife refuge.

The original refuge was established in 1912. Later the Izaak Walton League with nickels and dimes from thousands of schoolchildren bought more acreage. Now there are 37 square miles set aside and elk are the focus of this small western town where they can be seen by schoolchildren from classrooms, by patients from hospital beds, and housewives through kitchen windows.

Antlers, shed annually, are gathered by Boy Scouts and piled in high arches around the town square, decorated with colored lights at Christmas and later auctioned off with 80 percent of the proceeds going to pay for elk's supplemental winter feed.

But though elk are the star attraction here, they are not the only ones nor is winter the only interesting season.

Rare trumpeter swans—largest waterfowl in North America—nest. So do large numbers of other waterfowl—mallards, mergansers, green-winged and cinnamon teal, and Canada geese. Barrow's and common goldeneyes are around in winter. So are rough-legged hawks.

Golden and bald eagles nest nearby; so do prairie falcons and red-tailed hawks along with blue, sage, and ruffed grouse, long-billed curlews, and sandhill cranes (these are along the county road from mid-May through August).

Small birds common at various seasons include calliope hummingbirds, Clark's nutcrackers, mountain chickadees, mountain bluebirds, Townsend's solitaires, Steller's and gray jays, western tanagers, Lewis' woodpeckers, and Williamson's sapsuckers (birding can be good along Flat Creek or around the picnic area).

Dippers walk through and under the water of valley streams. Gray-crowned and black rosy finches gather in large winter flocks at feeders in town.

A few antelope graze in summer. Coyotes can be almost anywhere anytime. Sometimes they hunt with badgers, the latter flushing ground squirrel colonies and each finding prey among the disturbed group.

The elk mistakenly can be perceived as living inside a fence because of the high wire barrier around the west refuge boundary—but the fence only separates them from populated places. Behind and beyond are millions of acres of national park, forest, and wilderness where they can roam. They leave to spend summers at higher elevations up to 90 miles away; visitors then will find them elsewhere, including around the Timbered Island area of Grand Teton National Park 20 miles north. There males bugle challenges audible for miles in the September rut.

In November they settle down and return. Sometimes several hundred bulls can be seen then, calmly feeding and resting together in refuge fields along Highway 89.

How to get there: Located next to Jackson. Go east on Broadway a mile to headquarters. Refuge entrance is one-quarter mile east at base of mountain. (New visitor center is planned along Route 89.)

Open: Daylight hours year-round. Office 8–4:30 weekdays.

Best times to visit: December through March for elk.

What to see: Elk in large wintering concentrations; coyotes; trumpeter swans; raptors, possibly eagles, bighorn sheep, moose, mule deer.

What to do: Sleigh rides into elk herds mid-December to late March; nine miles of county roads through refuge for driving, biking (parts can be closed in winter); pull-outs on Route 89 overlooking Flat Creek and marshes (swans, others there in summer); photography—blind available (get permit from office); picnic area with children's trout-fishing pond. Trout fishing can be excellent in season (up to 22-inch native cutthroats).

Where to stay: Motels—many in Jackson area. Campgrounds—many in and around Jackson, including adjacent national forest and national parks.

Weather: At 6,200-foot elevation, nights cool even in summer and sometimes 50 below in winter (dress warmly on sleigh rides).

Points of interest nearby: Grand Teton National Park, adjacent north and west; Bridger-Teton National Forest, east; Yellowstone National Park, 55 miles north; National Fish Hatchery, on refuge. Stop at Jackson Hole, Wyoming, Travel Information Center near picnic area for more information on scenic and natural areas.

For more information: National Elk Refuge, 675 East Broadway, P.O. Box C, Jackson, Wyoming 83001. Phone: (307) 733–9212.

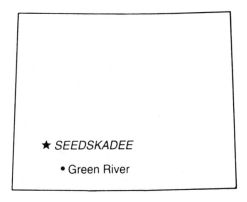

★ *SEEDSKADEE*

• Green River

SEEDSKADEE (Wyoming)

Seedskadee is rich in both history and wildlife. The Oregon and Mormon Trails both went through the Green River Valley, and so undisturbed has the land been that a visitor to this 14,455-acre refuge in southwest Wyoming can stand on the bluffs and see wagon ruts left by those pioneers.

Wildlife have left their own trails. Sage grouse, for which the refuge is named— the word means River of the Prairie Hen in Shoshone Indian—are more numerous in this area than anywhere else. So are golden eagles, those raptors of remote places soaring with six-foot wingspreads looking out for sage grouse as well as prairie dogs and jackrabbits in the sagebrush-covered fields and salt-grass bottomlands. They are common all year and nest here, and their wintering population on the refuge may be 40 or so.

Gray-crowned and black rosy finches, which show rosy wings and rumps both in flight and at rest, come in flocks of 100 and more to headquarters feeders in all but summer when these hardy small birds leave to nest in mountains above the timberline.

A herd of 300 or so mule deer are here, many of them around headquarters where the large handsome bucks have learned they will not have to dodge hunters' gunfire. Swift pronghorn antelopes graze. Bobcats are common though not readily seen—coyotes more so, racing across the sagebrush.

The Green River is the heart of this refuge, beautiful and verdant, winding 20 miles through it and attracting wildlife for miles around in this sparse, desolate country—all readily visible from the auto-tour route that follows the benchlands. A map shows various historic sites.

A herd of 300 or so moose are photographers' favorites, nibbling on willows in fall and winter and on succulent marsh greens in summer. Anyone driving observantly along the auto-tour route is likely to see at least one red fox.

The numerous beavers keep most of the willows chewed down to low shrubs, and ones they overlook are used by porcupines for browse and resting places.

White-tailed prairie dogs colonize almost 2,000 acres where these attractive, playful little mammals attract interesting neighbors: burrowing owls, which take over some of their holes; mountain plovers, which like the gravelly ground for their surface nests; and badgers, which dig their own holes nearby to have a ready source of dinner.

More than half the 227 bird species occurring here nest.

Birds of prey can be remarkable. Red-tailed, Swainson's, and ferruginous hawks, northern harriers, and prairie falcons nest on ground, trees, or bluffs overlooking the river. Rough-legged hawks are here in winter, and up to 30 bald eagles gather to feed on fish where the river is open from November through March.

In recent winters trumpeter swans have fed on aquatic vegetation in the river's Dodge Bottom area.

Great blue herons nest in cottonwoods, visible from the bluff road. White-faced ibis are common. Several hundred sandhill cranes stop spring and fall in the shallow bottomlands. Mountain bluebirds raise families along a bluebird nest-box trail.

Sage grouse are always here, leading young broods, flying back and forth to food and water, their courting grounds usually on the edge or just off the refuge. Staff can say where they have been seen recently.

Canada geese nest on river islands and platforms and docks nearby. Some 2,000 ducklings grow up every year—blue-winged and cinnamon teal, redheads, ruddies, pintails, and others, on ponds near headquarters where they are readily seen.

How to get there: From Green River take Route I-80 west seven miles to LaBarge Road cutoff, then Route 372 north 30 miles to refuge sign and east two miles to office.

Open: 24 hours year-round. Office 7:30–4 weekdays.

Best times to visit: Spring through fall.

What to see: Sage grouse, deer, moose, antelopes, waterfowl, prairie dogs, eagles.

What to do: 20 miles of roads and trails including auto-tour route; whole refuge open to horseback riding and hiking except during nesting season; canoeing; photography; fishing (fall best) for rainbow, brown trout.

Where to stay: Motels—in Green River, 39 miles southeast. Campgrounds—12 miles north below Fontenelle Dam.

Weather: Winters at this 6,100-foot elevation can be cold, snowy, with roads impassable.

Points of interest nearby: Names Hill, 43 miles north (Jim Bridger scratched his name here); Fossil Butte National Monument, 40 miles west; Flaming Gorge Recreation Area, 60 miles south.

For more information: Seedskadee National Wildlife Refuge, P.O. Box 700, Green River, Wyoming 82935. Phone: (307) 875–2187.

DESERT
★
• Las Vegas

DESERT (Nevada)

Desert bighorn sheep once close to extinction roam the crags of this wildly beautiful refuge—the largest population in existence of these majestic animals on the largest national wildlife refuge outside Alaska.

A fascinating variety of other flora and fauna also find ecological niches on these 1.5 million acres (almost 2,400 square miles) that cover six different altitudinal life zones rising from the hot desert floor to snowy mountains at 10,000 feet.

Small birds can migrate here not by flying to distant places but by moving up to a more comfortable elevation to nest in summer and back down in winter.

Mountain lions are here, and little kit foxes and endangered desert tortoises. Golden eagles nest on rocky ledges. Bristlecone pines—one of the oldest and hardiest plants on earth—survive as do a forest of Joshua trees and another of ponderosa pines.

The annual Audubon Christmas Bird Count often shows several species in greater numbers here than anywhere else in the nation—most frequently the sage sparrow, hepatic tanager, and LeConte's thrasher.

These and numbers of other small birds enjoy the Corn Creek field headquarters with its springs, ponds (where the endangered Pahrump poolfish lives), remnants of old fruit and nut orchards, and fruiting mulberry trees, along with an assortment of elms, cottonwoods, locust, Russian olives, and mesquite.

It is a lush oasis in this arid state and any bird that spots it while going through is going to stop. The concentrating effect of this inviting habitat is indicated by a sample year when 21 species of vireos and warblers were recorded in this one spot in April–May and September–October migration including Hutton's vireos, Tennessee, blackburnian, and blackpoll warblers as well as ovenbirds and indigo buntings.

On a good May morning when trees are fruiting, especially the mulberries, birder M. Vincent Mowbray found "it is not unusual to observe 55 species in less than two hours." In addition there are occasionally truly extraordinary sightings such as a wood stork, purple gallinule, and Mississippi kite.

Among interesting birds listed as common seasonally are flammulated and northern pygmy owls, pygmy nuthatches, lesser nighthawks, poor-wills, black-throated gray and Grace's warblers, and green-tailed towhees. Residents include Gambel's quail, verdin, moorhens, Bewick's wrens, phainopeplas, black-throated sparrows, blue grosbeaks, gray flycatchers, and ladder-backed woodpeckers.

The Mormon Well Road goes through all the life-zone elevations. Going out from Corn Creek it forks right to the picnic area and left through desert valleys en route to higher elevations where the sheep are most often found. It comes out at Route 93 toward the Pahranagat Refuge. The Mormon Well way is regarded hereabouts as a nice Sunday drive but it requires a pickup truck or preferably 4-wheel drive to be sure of getting through. Small birds and some of the other refuge inhabitants, including some of the small mammals, congregate at the attractive picnic area in the ponderosa pines.

The Alamo Road passes side roads to various springs in the mountains where the sheep are—but to see these, it is necessary to hike or go on horseback; and while it can be done in a day (a very FULL day), it is better if possible to camp out. This is a marvelous experience in any case. Stars seem to blaze. Coyotes howl, owls twitter, and sometimes a kit fox comes to investigate.

Here one is believed to have an 80 percent chance of seeing the sheep by hiking up higher than they are, usually at least 6,000 feet (3,000 feet above the road), finding a comfortable spot, and sitting quietly for a few hours, binoculars at hand. If a bighorn doesn't show you might spot one of the other interesting residents— a cliff chipmunk, bobcat, badger, desert tortoise, or one of the 12 species of bats.

Sheep as well as other wildlife come to the springs in the hottest part of the summer—but as a refuge leaflet warns, don't let your presence keep them away from the springs. They urgently need it to survive.

How to get there: From Las Vegas take Route 95 north 22 miles to refuge sign, then four miles to Corn Creek subheadquarters.

Open: 24 hours daily. Las Vegas office 7:30–4:30 weekdays.

Best times to visit: September–October and early spring except summer for sheep when concentrated near water.

What to see: Desert bighorn sheep, mule deer, flora and fauna appropriate to six separate altitudinal life zones from 2,600 to nearly 10,000 feet.

What to do: 150 miles of auto, hiking, and backpacking trails; primitive camping; photography—temporary blinds by permit; picnicking (note: about two-thirds of refuge is an air force gunnery range and off-limits).

Weather: Mean temperature is 60 degrees but this reflects elevational range from 120 on valley floor to below zero at 10,000 feet.

What to take and wear: Warm clothing for high elevations; high-clearance or 4-wheel drive (depending on destination); flashlight, compass, plenty of food and water, including water for your horse if riding; hiking boots—this is rocky desert; spotting scope for distant sights.

Where to stay: Motels—in Las Vegas. Campgrounds—for RVs in Las Vegas, also Lake Mead Recreation Area, 40 miles southeast. Primitive on refuge.

Points of interest nearby: Lake Mead (see above); the Las Vegas wash, southeast of town, excellent birding; Charleston Range in Toiyabe National Forest, opposite refuge on Route 95; Red Rock National Recreational Area, just west of Las Vegas.

For more information: Desert National Wildlife Refuge, 1500 North Decatur Boulevard, Las Vegas, Nevada 89108. Phone: (702) 646–3401.

Also administered from the Desert office are:

Ash Meadows—12,736 spring-fed acres and desert uplands 90 miles northwest of Las Vegas, cited under the Ramsar convention as a wetland of world significance, providing habitat for at least 26 plants and animals found nowhere else in the world, including the endangered devil's hole pupfish, which can be seen 12 feet down in the clear spring water. It has hiking trails but no other public-use facilities; field office open 7:30–4 weekdays.

Moapa Valley—34 acres 50 miles northeast of Las Vegas, no public facilities, maintained largely as a springhead outflow channel where one rare fish species, the Moapa dace, occurs.

Pahranagat—5,380 acres of water and marsh that attract a wonderful range of wildlife. Drive or walk in from Route 93. Common at least seasonally are—to note a few—green-tailed towhees, black-throated sparrows, violet-green swallows, pine siskins, Bullock's orioles, MacGillivray's warblers, northern harriers, great blue herons, and eight species of ducks.

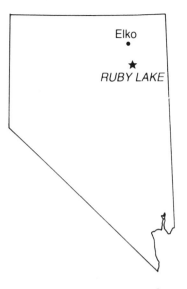

Elko •

★
RUBY LAKE

RUBY LAKE (Nevada)

More than 200 springs, some cold, some so hot they can burn the hand, feed Ruby Lake's 37,632 marshy acres, supplemented in spring by snowmelt from the beautiful white-crowned Ruby Mountains that border the refuge and harbor one of the largest mountain lion populations left in the West.

Mountains and refuge both were named for red stones that settlers found here and misidentified. They were garnets, and some are still here.

Mountain lions are wary and seldom seen. They prey on mule deer that come down to fresh water from the adjoining mountains. (Sometimes 100 or so of the deer are seen trekking along behind refuge headquarters on their way to nearby wintering areas.)

Greater sandhill cranes leap up in courtship dances in upland meadows from March to April, and nest here. So do trumpeter swans, the world's largest waterfowl. Canada geese and ducks of a dozen species show off broods in May, June, and July. This is one of the most important breeding areas in the Intermountain West for canvasback and redhead ducks, which in a good year produce 3,000 or more ducklings.

The marsh holds nesting colonies of white-faced ibis—up to 300 pairs—along with great and snowy egrets, great blue and black-crowned night herons, and American bitterns, which feed along the dikes (and like to hang around the state-run trout hatchery here where rainbows, brooks, browns, and a new hybrid tiger trout are hatched and grow up to six pounds).

Rusty-hooded American avocets nest; so do black-necked stilts, Wilson's phalaropes, long-billed curlews, and sage grouse (a dozen cocks may gather on courtship dancing grounds in April and May).

Northern orioles sometimes nest around headquarters. Lewis' woodpeckers are usually in wooded Harrison Pass. Bushtits like brushy places around springs as do plain titmice, mountain bluebirds, lazuli buntings, Cassin's finches, black-headed grosbeaks, sage thrashers, marsh wrens and sometimes Townsend's solitaires, interesting flycatchers, and an assortment of swallows and sparrows, especially the sage, lark, Brewer's, and black-throated. Dippers sometimes duck into hatchery raceways.

Northern harriers are the most common raptor, flying low over the marshes, but prairie falcons are almost always here as are red-tailed and rough-legged hawks. Golden eagles nest nearby and bald eagles sometimes appear in winter. Dozens of turkey vultures roost behind headquarters. Tundra swans and white pelicans visit seasonally.

Coyotes will be spotted by most visitors who get out early and late, and around dusk their yips join the hoots of great horned owls. Pronghorn antelopes graze on sagebrush flats year-round. Sometimes porcupines graze the sagebrush, too, eating the tops. Muskrats perform a valuable service keeping bulrushes open to waterfowl, and their houses are resting and nesting platforms for ducks, geese, cranes, and swans.

The refuge serves both the Pacific and Central Flyways, and in fall up to 25,000 ducks can be here.

Water comes rushing out of Cave Creek behind headquarters at up to 27 cubic feet per second and a constant 42 degrees—cold in summer but above freezing in winter—attracting (as do other springheads) those still around then: pine siskins, magpies, pinyon jays, Clark's nutcrackers, juncos, ravens, and mountain chickadees.

How to get there: From Elko take Lamoille Highway east seven miles to Highway 228, then south 27 miles to Jiggs; four miles south of Jiggs turn left at fork, go 15 miles through Harrison Pass onto Ruby Valley Road and refuge sign, then eight miles south.

Open: Daylight hours year-round. Office 7–3:30 weekdays.

Best times to visit: April through October.

What to see: Nesting and migrating water birds; trumpeter swans (especially in fall); sandhill cranes; pronghorn antelopes; mule deer; lovely spring wildflowers; historic homesteader cabin.

What to do: 10 miles of dike roads for driving, hiking, also 18 miles of adjacent county roads; photography; small boating and canoeing (permitted seasonally in limited areas); fishing for trout and largemouth bass. Slide shows and guided tours can be arranged for groups.

Where to stay: Motels—in Elko: also Wells and Ely. Campgrounds—in Humboldt National Forest adjoining refuge.

Weather: Harrison Pass can be closed by winter snows—consult refuge on possible alternative route.

Points of interest nearby: Historical museum in Elko; fine hiking, good birding in national forest and mountains adjacent where mountain goats are sometimes seen; Franklin Lake just north is an outstanding marsh when there's water; also Great Basin National Park, 170 miles southeast; raptor migration September-October at Goshute Mountain, 170 miles northeast.

For more information: Ruby Lake National Wildlife Refuge, Box 60-860, Ruby Valley, Nevada 89833. Phone: (702) 779–2237.

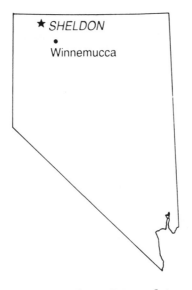

★ *SHELDON*

•
Winnemucca

SHELDON (Nevada)

Pronghorn antelopes gather sometimes by the hundreds in summer watering places here. But most of the time the wildlife at this ruggedly beautiful half-million acre refuge are scattered, and the visitor can look 15 or 20 miles in all directions to the mountains and see no other living thing but a golden eagle soaring in the sky, and lovely wildflowers if there's been enough rain.

Only with binoculars and spotting scope, carefully and patiently scanning every crag and sagebrush clump, might one make out more—anything from burros and wild horses, sage grouse foraging along the ground, a prairie falcon flying back and forth to a nest on a bluff ledge, grazing mule deer or a coyote, bobcat, even a rare mountain lion stalking one of the omnipresent jackrabbits. Bighorn sheep are in remote areas.

Sheldon, like its sister refuge, Hart Mountain, 30 miles north, was established for the pronghorn antelope, that swift strong animal that can run 40 miles an hour for six miles—and up to 8,000 may spend the winter, usually moving into lower sections on the eastern end then (the refuge rises from 4,100 feet on the east to over 7,000 feet on the western end with a range of habitats and wildlife communities in between).

Highway 140 goes through the refuge and is paved, though snowdrifts may cover it in winter; from it 50 miles of graveled county roads wind through the various habitats; off the graveled roads go dirt roads that in some places are merely tracts and require 4-wheel-drive high-clearance vehicles. Graveled roads may be impassable after sudden rain or snow storms—best check ahead if there's any question. Snow is possible from October to June. Evenings can be cool all year.

Best places for birds like Say's phoebes or green-tailed towhees are the riparian areas or around ponds at the Dufurrena field station where waterfowl stop in spring and fall migration and some nest, including Canada geese and mallard, gadwall and pintail ducks. Nighthawks circle for insects at dusk, and poor-wills forage along roads in the dusk and evening. Mountain bluebirds are common in spring; horned larks just about anywhere, anytime.

Rock hounds are permitted to look for opals and sunstones and take seven pounds home (but not to dig or blast for them).

State hunting rules apply in the fall but the original 35,000-acre refuge tract, known as "little Sheldon," is a no-hunting sanctuary. With that proviso the whole refuge is open all year to the hiker, backpacker, and horseback rider with 19 primitive campsites available. The Desert Trail Association has established a hiking corridor.

How to get there: From Lakeview go four miles north on Route 395, then east 65 miles on Route 140 to state line and refuge land, 19 miles later refuge sign; right there one mile to field station, one mile farther to information kiosk.

Open: 24 hours. Refuge office 7:30–5 weekdays, not always manned. Complex office for Sheldon and Hart Mountain Refuges in Lakeview, Oregon, is open weekdays 8–5.

What to see: Pronghorns, mule deer, wild horses, burrow, sage grouse, beautiful wild landscape.

What to do: 40 miles of paved road, 50 miles of graveled, many miles of dirt track for driving, hiking; fishing can be good for bass, bluegills.

Best times to visit: Spring through fall.

Where to stay: Motels—in Winnemucca, Denio, and Lakeview. Campgrounds—primitive on refuge.

Weather: Spring extremely unpredictable.

What to take and wear: Sturdy footgear, layered clothing for extremely variable temperatures, full tank of gas, extra food and water, at least one spare tire (sharp obsidian rock fragments are hard on tires).

For more information: Sheldon National Wildlife Refuge, P.O. Box 111, Room 308, U.S. Post Office Building, Lakeview, Oregon 97630. Phone: (503) 947–3315; or Sheldon National Wildlife Refuge Field Station, (702) 941–0200.

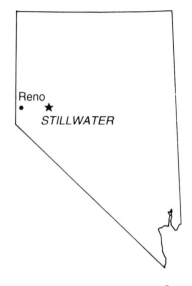

Reno
★
STILLWATER

STILLWATER (Nevada)

This great marsh teeming with wildlife once covered a closed mountain basin of almost 10,000 square miles during the Pleistocene epoch. It attracted prodigious numbers of water birds. The birds were followed by human settlement that archeologists date back 3,000–4,000 years.

Human intervention in this century almost doomed this natural marvel when the government's first Bureau of Reclamation project diverted water to "reclaim" the desert for agriculture. Wiser human intervention now is restoring it, the result of a landmark congressional act that authorized funds to buy water rights (from willing sellers) to restore these wetlands that are a crucial link in shorebird migrations and have been recognized as an essential site in the Western Hemisphere Shorebird Reserve Network.

The first water has started to flow and more will come. It is the exciting result of joint efforts by the U.S. Fish and Wildlife Service and a wide-ranging amalgam of groups including The Nature Conservancy, Audubon Society, Environmental Defense Fund, Defenders of Wildlife, and others—naturalists, hunters, trappers, humane societies, working together as the Lahontan Wetlands Coalition. (Studies continue on water source contaminants).

Wildlife has responded. Up to 78 percent of the continental population of long-billed dowitchers are here in spring and fall migration. One-third to half of the Pacific Flyway population of canvasback ducks are here seasonally, 90 percent of the snow geese in Nevada, up to 13,000 tundra swans, and the world's largest colony of white-faced ibis.

Hundreds of avocets, black-necked stilts, and phalaropes come through in spring and in August, and many stay through the summer to nest. Flocks of hundreds of white pelicans come down to feed and rest from April to October. Several hundred thousand waterfowl of a dozen or more species spend the winter and many stay through the year, raising 15,000 ducklings in a good year.

Great blue and black-crowned night herons and snowy and great egrets are common to abundant through the warm months. Red-tailed hawks and northern harriers nest and feed in uplands. So do great horned owls. Bald eagles are here in winter whenever there's open water—sometimes up to 70. All can be seen from the refuge's hundred miles of roads.

How to get there: From Reno take Interstate 80 to Fernley, then Alternate U.S. 95 to Fallon, then 50 east to Stillwater Road and follow signs to refuge.

Open: 24 hours year-round. Office 7–4:30 weekdays.

Best times to visit: Spring through fall (see *Weather* below).

What to see: White pelicans, wading birds, cormorants, waterfowl, tundra swans, bald eagles.

What to do: Drive or hike up to 100 miles of refuge roads (see *Weather* below); photography—can be good from car, and beautiful sunsets.

Where to stay: Motels—in Fallon. Campgrounds—in Fallon; also primitive campground on refuge.

Weather: Check weather reports—rains can make ungraveled alkali roads slippery and impassable. Summer temperatures get up to 100 degrees and are hot and dry—fill up gas tank, carry a gallon of drinking water, wear a hat and sun lotion (roads are solitary and not patrolled).

Points of interest nearby: Churchill County Museum, Fallon (a must); Grimes Point archeological area (petroglyphs), 10 miles east; Lahontan Dam/Reservoir, water-oriented recreation, 15 miles east; Carson Lake, excellent for shore and marsh birds; historic Pony Express trail, just south of Fallon.

For more information: Stillwater National Wildlife Refuge, P.O. Box 1236, Fallon, Nevada 89406-1236. Phone: (702) 423–5128.

Stillwater also administers *Anaho Island* Refuge in Pyramid Lake, Nevada, the site historically of one of the largest nesting colonies of white pelicans in the country—sometimes more than 10,000 of the great white birds along with hundreds of nesting cormorants, gulls, terns, and great blue herons, sometimes more than 16,000 in all. This, too, has been endangered by loss of water, threatening to expose a land bridge, thereby permitting entry by predators that would destroy this valuable nesting site. This, too, has been saved by acquisition of water rights, which will keep lake levels at a safe depth. (Anaho is closed to public access to prevent disturbance to nesting birds.)

Funds have been assured to purchase sufficient water to restore 25,000 acres of wildlife marsh permanently in the valley: 14,000 on Stillwater National Wildlife Refuge, 10,200 acres on Carson Lake state wildlife area, and 800 acres on the Fallon Indian Reservation.

It is a heartening victory by citizens of diverse interests working together.

BEAR RIVER

★ BEAR RIVER

• Salt Lake City

BEAR RIVER (Utah)

The explorer Captain Howard Stansbury said of Bear River in 1849, "I have seen large flocks of birds before . . . but never did I behold anything like the immense numbers here congregated together . . . as far as the eye can see."

In the mid-1980s this great sanctuary seemed all but lost, flooded out after five years of record snowmelt and runoff. But this was followed by five years of drought and receding waters, and while work remains to be done on water control and visitor facilities, Bear River Refuge is productive again. The 12-mile auto-tour route is open and plans are under way for refuge expansion and enhancement.

Again almost unbelievable numbers of beautiful and interesting birds gather here so visibly that a visit to these ponds and salt marshes where the Bear River empties into the Great Salt Lake is a stunning treat for novice and seasoned naturalist alike.

Sometimes in spring and fall migration millions of birds of all kinds may stop by, their low babbling "conversations" never halting, even at night. Some of the spectacles seen then can only be called amazing: thousands of golden-tufted eared grebes covering the Bear River, a half-million swallows like a tremendous windborne cloud, hundreds of marbled godwits and long-billed dowitchers.

The largest concentrations of tundra swans anywhere—around 12,000 of these most graceful of snowy waterfowl—may come through in fall. There can be a half-million or more ducks, including shovelers, green-winged teal, and pintails plus canvasbacks, cinnamon teal, and others—all against a stunning backdrop of the blue Promontory Mountains on the west and snowy crests of the Wasatch Range on the east. Stay until dusk—local people claim "the West's most gorgeous sunsets" and it's hard to dispute.

In May hundreds of young bird families may be along the auto-tour route, in the water, on the edges of the dikes, or in the roadways—killdeer doing their "broken-wing" act to distract attention from nests of babies, willets, coot, lovely pink-legged, black-necked stilts, and downy Canada goslings. Some of the goslings' parents volunteer for extra duties so that diligent pairs sometimes are seen leading lines of 20 or more young, theirs and their neighbors'. Of the 222 species of birds identified as visiting Bear River at one time or another, at least 60 species have nested.

Sometimes up to 5,000 breeding pairs of delicate, graceful avocets, their heads and necks russet with breeding color, are present on the dikes. Ruddy ducks bob their heads toward their mates in frantic excitement, showing off bright blue bills freshly colored for the occasion. Western grebes, called the "swan grebe" for their graceful curving white necks, perform remarkable courtship "water ballets," later build floating nests and carry their young about on their backs, their offspring managing to hang on even when the parents dive for food. Huge rolling carp weighing 20 to 35 pounds are an impressive sight in May and June.

White pelicans with nine-foot wingspreads are here throughout the warmer months; so are long-billed curlews and sometimes thousands of Wilson's phalaropes, spotted sandpipers, and Forster's terns. Northern harriers are common all year. So are black-billed magpies and ravens. Bald and golden eagles abound in late fall, winter, and early spring, sometimes a hundred or more.

Great blue and black-crowned night herons have had sizable nesting colonies in the past and it is hoped will again. So have white-faced ibises, snowy egrets, California and Franklin's gulls, double-crested cormorants, Caspian terns, and many others.

The airboat was first developed here so refuge personnel could oversee over 100 square miles of shallow water and marsh. The staff are knowledgeable in suggesting how best to see everything, with excellent leaflets about the refuge and related nature subjects.

How to get there: From Brigham City turn west on Forrest Street, which becomes Bird Refuge Road, go 15 miles to beginning of auto-tour route. (New visitor center planned about two miles west of I-15.)

Open: Daylight hours. Office 8–4:30 weekdays.

Best times to visit: Mid-April through December (but all year interesting).

What to see: Wide spectrum of birds, especially water-oriented, many in great numbers.

What to do: 12-mile auto-tour route; photography—fine opportunities from car window but permits granted for temporary blinds.

Where to stay: Motels—in Brigham City. Campgrounds—Cache National Forest, three miles east of Brigham City, also KOA and private in Brigham City; Willard Bay State Park, just south of refuge; others.

Points of interest nearby: Golden Spike National Monument, 25 miles northwest; Cache and Wasatch National Forests, east and southeast; Mormon Tabernacle in Salt Lake City; interesting old buildings in Brigham City.

For more information: Bear River Migratory Bird Refuge, 866 South Main Street, Brigham City, Utah 84302. Phone: (801) 723–5887.

FISH SPRINGS (Utah)

Powerful springs gushing out of the earth at up to 43 cubic feet per second at a constant 70 degrees have created a sparkling oasis for wildlife here on the southern fringe of the Great Salt Desert at the base of mountains that rise to 8,000 feet.

Birds and other wildlife are attracted—thousands of ducks, swans, ibis, herons, and others, including rarities not usually seen in these parts (green-tailed towhees, snowy plovers, white-throated swifts, McCowns' longspurs; for these consult the hotline through refuge headquarters).

Human visitors should be warned: except for the marsh, there are few more aridly inhospitable places anywhere. Though archeologists date human use of this area back 6,000 years, it's over 100 miles to the nearest motel and 45 miles to the nearest gas station.

Up to 20,000 ducks crowd the pools in spring and even more in fall migration, along with such showy shorebirds as Caspian terns as well as least and western sandpipers and long-billed dowitchers.

Canada geese and nine kinds of ducks, including pintails, redheads, wigeon, and ruddies, parade downy broods in early summer. Delicate black-necked stilts, rusty-hooded avocets, and coots nest on the 100 or so islands in the pools. Pied-billed grebes carry young on their backs.

Several hundred white-faced ibis build colonial nests joined by snowy egrets and black-crowned and great blue herons. Ring-necked pheasants are common in the uplands.

Trumpeter swans, transplanted from Red Rock Lakes Refuge, are here during the winter now, as are northern harriers and red-tailed hawks. Golden eagles nest in nearby mountains.

Coyotes don't seem to mind visitors. Mule deer graze readily visible along the 38 miles of refuge roads and trails (as well as on roads leading to the refuge). Jackrabbits are everywhere—the staple food base for eagles, coyotes, bobcats, and other carnivores, including, rarely, mountain lions. Thousands of muskrats keep bulrushes open for ducks and shorebirds. Kit foxes keep a low profile but are here, too.

Small birds hang around the shrubbier wooded areas, either around headquarters—sometimes five species of hummingbirds at feeders there—or the picnic area, where trees were planted when it was a Pony Express station. (When the Pony Express operated, it was the fastest route between St. Joseph, Missouri, and Sacramento, California, but so dangerous riders were paid the then-large sum of $125 a month plus two revolvers, one rifle, one bowie knife, and a Bible.)

Canoeing (bring your own) can be a pleasant way to see wildlife when water is sufficient (nesting areas off-limits). A warning when driving: watch for flash floods, which can occur without warning after even a half inch of rain and leave a foot of water and boulders in slippery, muddy dips in the road. Locals always carry at LEAST two spare tires.

But what a place! Climb up to the mountainside on a clear day and you can see over 60 miles, usually with no other human being in all that space. You can even, looking closely, discern the curvature of the earth.

How to get there: From Tooele follow State Road 36 south to Pony Express route, then west 65 miles on gravel road to refuge.

Open: Sunrise to sunset. Office 7:30–4 weekdays.

Best times to visit: May/June for shorebirds, wading birds, waterfowl broods. September/ October for waterfowl concentrations.

Where to stay: Motels—in Tooele, 105 miles northeast. Campgrounds—primitive on BLM land 1.5 miles north; at rebuilt Pony Express station on BLM land, 42 miles east.

For more information: Fish Springs National Wildlife Refuge, Box 568, Dugway, Utah 84022. Phone: (801) 831–5353.

Salt Lake City
•

★
OURAY

OURAY (Utah)

Dinosaurs once dominated the wildlife here. In frontier days Kit Carson hunted and John Wesley Powell explored this area. Now Ouray furnishes a verdant oasis in a dry land. Only seven inches of rain fall annually on these 11,961 acres in northeast Utah, but the Green River meanders for 12 miles through it. Sooner or later every creature for miles around comes here to get a drink.

Mule deer scramble up sandstone and clay bluffs that turn green, gold, pink, and red with changing light and humidity and have been sculptured by erosion into fantastic shapes.

Migrating bald and golden eagles feed on weaker members of waterfowl flocks in winter, sometimes congregating by the dozens at ice breakup in mid- to late February. Golden eagles nest on cliffs on the north end, northern harriers in or on the ground in marshes or fields, and red-tailed hawks in cottonwood trees near headquarters; various other raptor species, including Swainson's and Cooper's hawks, come through in good numbers in spring and fall.

Stately scarlet-crowned gray sandhill cranes stop and feed on the marshes and in farm fields on the refuge en route to far northern nesting grounds, occasionally accompanied by an endangered whooping crane.

Birders come to find Lewis' woodpeckers and they almost always do, foraging and nesting in cottonwoods, often right around headquarters. They can also find marbled godwits and rusty-hooded avocets and delicate pink-legged black-necked stilts in most warm months, as well as Say's phoebes, western kingbirds, yellow and yellow-rumped warblers, vesper sparrows, and sometimes chats, lazuli buntings, blue grosbeaks, Virginia's and orange-crowned warblers, and green-tailed towhees.

Great blue herons have a colony of 100 or so nests in cottonwoods on the other side of the river (they don't seem to mind visitors so ask at office for directions on getting a close look).

Handsome ring-necked pheasants and colorful, raucous black-billed magpies—which build huge nests—are heard as well as seen almost everywhere.

Fourteen species of ducks nest—cinnamon, green-winged and blue-winged teal, mallards, lesser scaup, gadwall, pintails, shovelers, ring-necks, wigeon, buffleheads, canvasbacks, redheads, and ruddy ducks sporting bright blue bills for the occasion. Canada geese also nest on the refuge and are around all year.

Prairie dogs have burrows scattered through the refuge—two small groups along the entrance road, another on the way to the overlook (these are the white-tailed, which do not colonize in such tight gatherings as their black-tailed cousins). Some of them have been appropriated by burrowing owls that stand guard, small erect figures, during the day.

Porcupines like to spend afternoons in tree forks.

Many visitors come just to see the big buck mule deer, which not uncommonly carry 10-point racks in fall. Coyotes hunt the uplands—bobcats also but they're hard to see—and endangered fish also live here, especially the Colorado squawfish and razorbacked sucker (the refuge has an endangered fish hatchery for propagating and returning them to the wild).

Some of the rocks date back to the time when dinosaurs and other prehistoric creatures—turtles and small mammals that no longer exist—were common here. Their relics can be seen in these rocks.

There are several ways to see the refuge. Drive or hike the miles of roads and trails, or take a canoe or raft in the Green River and watch beaver at work, ducks loafing on sandbars, swallows skimming along the steep banks, and an entirely different peaceful perspective.

How to get there: From Vernal take Route 40 west 14 miles to refuge sign, then south on Route 88 for 15 miles to entrance. Office is in Vernal.

Open: Daylight hours. Office 7:30–4:30 weekdays.

Best times to visit: Spring through fall.

What to see: Waterfowl, eagles, hawks, migrating sandhill cranes, pronghorns, mule deer, striking scenery.

What to do: 40 miles of roads open to driving, hiking, including auto-tour route, scenic overlook; canoeing (no rentals); good fishing for channel catfish.

Where to stay: Motels—in Vernal and Roosevelt. Campgrounds—primitive on Dinosaur National Monument, 23 miles southeast; on BLM land at Pelican Lake, adjoining; at Ashley National Forest/Flaming Gorge Recreational Area, 60 miles north.

Weather: Summer can be desert-hot, with sudden strong thunderstorms in spring.

Points of interest nearby: Pelican Lake, access by BLM land (see Campgrounds) can be good birding for grebes, ducks, some bald and golden eagles; Browns Park National Wildlife Refuge, 90 miles northeast; Flaming Gorge and Dinosaur Monument (see Campgrounds), also Jones Hole National Fish Hatchery, 45 miles northeast, beautiful scenery, trout, hiking trail into Dinosaur; plus river trip, walking tours in Vernal—the area has many points of interest.

For more information: Ouray National Wildlife Refuge, 1680 West Highway 40, Suite 112-C, Vernal, Utah 84078. Phone: (801) 789–0351.

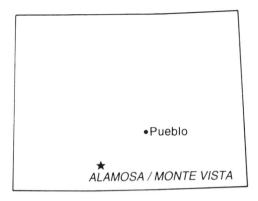

●Pueblo

★
ALAMOSA / MONTE VISTA

ALAMOSA/MONTE VISTA (Colorado)

Ten thousand majestic scarlet-crowned sandhill cranes spread seven-foot wings and leap high in courtship dances at Monte Vista in spring—a spectacle around which the town of Monte Vista in south-central Colorado has built an annual March Crane Festival (altogether some 20,000 cranes stop by the whole San Luis Valley in migration). With them may be a few endangered whooping cranes.

But another festival could be held focusing on the bald eagles on Monte Vista's close-by companion refuge, Alamosa, where 70 or so of these magnificent birds of prey gather from early March to April to feast on fish winter-killed in frozen oxbows of the Rio Grande River.

These two refuges share some of the same wildlife but in other ways are quite different, and their accessibility and the visitor experience can be quite different, too.

Alamosa is a scene of wild untrammeled scenic beauty where the visitor looks upon one of the last remaining unspoiled riparian stretches of the Rio Grande River from an 80-foot bluff, often standing at eye level with the northern harriers, golden eagles, and hawks—Swainson's, rough-legged, and red-tailed—that hunt in this meadow (the first two species also nest).

Three miles of road along the Rio Grande River are open to walking or biking. Thousands of ducks and geese are here—mallards, gadwalls, pintails, shovelers, cinnamon, and blue- and green-winged teal, along with Canada geese, many with young broods in early summer. There is a nesting colony of snowy egrets, black-crowned night herons, and white-faced ibis that fan out over the refuge to feed.

Great horned owls can be spotted in the trees at dusk—they sometimes take over black-billed magpies' large nests. Horned larks are common all year, in summer sage thrashers and barn swallows. Sometimes cliff swallows seem to build their tubular mud nest structures on every convenient vertical surface. Yellowthroats and yellow-rumped warblers nest along the river.

Beavers build dens in the riverbank. Muskrats swim along with large mouthfuls of grass to munch on and line winter dwellings. Ravens croak from higher perches.

Monte Vista is readily accessible by vehicle with a three-mile auto-tour route plus 12 miles of county roads through the refuge, its 100 or so small ponds surrounded by magnificent high mountains and national forests. It also is a major waterfowl nesting ground. Many of the mallards and Canada geese do not go elsewhere but spend most of their lives in this valley. When joined by migrants in spring and fall their populations, along with those of a half-dozen other waterfowl species, sometimes peak around 40,000.

Prairie falcons can be seen all year by anyone who seeks them out, as can peregrine falcons from May to November.

Mule deer are around browsing all year. So are smaller numbers of pronghorn antelopes, and in winter a herd of 500 or so elk come down from the mountains to forage. Photography can be excellent from the auto-tour route and country roads.

Coyotes are out stalking rodents or ring-necked pheasants early and late. Bobcats and badgers are around but warier and less visible.

Golden eagles hover and glide high all year over both refuges. Avocets in russet-headed breeding plumage raise young as do Wilson's phalaropes in which the sexes reverse their roles as well as their breeding plumage, males incubating eggs and females wearing the bright colors and whirling in mad circles as they feed in shallow waters (sometimes it's hard to understand why they don't drop from dizziness).

The worry for these refuges and especially Monte Vista is precious water, which comes from the Rio Grande River and ground water from artesian wells. Increased demand for irrigation and development has lowered the water table, and proposed future demand threatens to lower it even more. This confrontation over use of a critical resource will not be resolved easily.

But for now, waterfowl and snipe and great blue herons find welcoming habitat here.

How to get there: To Alamosa, go east from the town of Alamosa on Route 160 four miles to El Rancho Lane and refuge sign, then right 2.5 miles to headquarters. To Monte Vista, take state highway 15 south from the town of Monte Vista six miles to visitor contact station, which is open March-April, otherwise intermittently.

Open: Daylight hours all year. Office open 7:30–4 weekdays.

Best times to visit: Spring, fall for migrants—but all year interesting.

What to see: Cranes; bald and golden eagles; peregrine falcons; waterfowl; herons; egrets; shorebirds.

What to do: Driving, hiking, wildlife observation, photography.

Where to stay: Motels—in towns of Alamosa and Monte Vista; Campgrounds—in Alamosa and Monte Vista; also Forest Service campgrounds in nearby mountains.

Weather: Spring can be extremely dusty, windy—even snowy (refuge is at 7,500 elevation with 90 frost-free days a year; winter temperatures can drop to 50 below).

What to take and wear: Warm clothing in winter, a jacket even in summer. Bug repellent in warmer months.

Points of interest nearby: Great Sand Dunes National Monument, 25 miles northeast; Rio Grande State Wildlife Area, five miles north; excellent trout fishing in surrounding Rio Grande National Forest.

For more information: Alamosa/Monte Vista National Wildlife Refuge Complex, 9383 El Rancho Lane, Alamosa, Colorado 81101. Phone: (719) 589–4021.

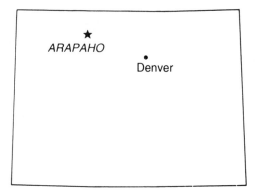

ARAPAHO (Colorado)

Visitors to this highest of any refuge outside Alaska can be almost certain to see fleet-footed and keen-visioned pronghorn antelopes, handsome beasts that can look in all directions at once, pick out a small object four miles away and have been clocked at speeds of 70 miles an hour.

Moose are here, too, and elk, and birds that migrate seasonally not north and south but vertically up and down the mountains surrounding Arapaho's 18,000-plus acres that spread out in a glacial bowl 8,300 feet high alongside the Continental Divide in north-central Colorado.

Rosy finches are here—the gray-crowned, black, and brown-capped, of which the last are found only in a relatively small range in this part of the United States. These hardy little birds spend the winter here—sometimes hundreds around feeders at the refuge office—and leave in spring along with some of the gray and Steller's jays, red crossbills, mountain chickadees, and mountain bluebirds to nest at even higher elevations. Mountain bluebirds are seen in late summer as high as 12,000 feet.

Sage grouse are common in summer and fall when dozens of broods forage along the edges of upland meadows. The males' colorful courtship displays strutting and inflating orange throat sacs occur off the refuge proper but refuge staff can advise on good places to see (and often photograph) them.

Waterfowl arrive as soon as the ice melts in late March or early April, and many stay and nest around small ponds and marshes fed by the Illinois River in this area known as North Park—the historical meaning of "park" in this sense being a mountain meadow.

The refuge produces up to 400 Canada goslings every year and some 6,000 ducklings, mostly gadwall and scaup but also mallards, pintails, redheads, and ruddies, the male ruddies conspicuous during breeding season with robin's-egg-blue bills that they bob rapidly up and down.

Wilson's phalaropes—the females wearing the bright plumage in this species—nest; so do willets, sora rails, and avocets. Black-crowned night herons have a substantial rookery and great blue herons a small one along the Illinois River. Dippers, which manage somehow to walk underwater, are here occasionally.

Golden eagles are present through the warmer months, soaring or atop power poles along Route 125 looking for ground squirrels or prairie dogs.

Swainson's hawks are common spring through fall as are kestrels and northern harriers and, somewhat less so, ferruginous hawks and prairie falcons.

Moose graze among the willows by the river, often with twin calves in summer. Porcupines nibble on the bark. Badgers lumber along, stopping at the slightest vibration to dig out prey—they can displace more earth for their size than any other animal. They can strike terror among white-tailed prairie dogs in their "towns," often shared with Richardson's ground squirrels, beside the auto-tour route.

Coyotes are out early and late pouncing on rodents in upland meadows. Long-tailed weasels streak through sagebrush after the same prey.

A resident herd of 30 to 50 elk are joined in winter by several hundred more that move down then from the mountains. Mule deer winter here as well, along with white-tailed jackrabbits that turn all white then except for black eartips, which sometimes seem to bob like hundreds of black dots against the snowy background as they congregate around refuge field headquarters, scolded by omnipresent black-billed magpies.

How to get there: From Denver take I-70 west to Route 40, through Granby, then north on Route 125 to refuge sign eight miles south of Walden.

Open: Daylight hours. Office 8–4:30 weekdays.

Best times to visit: Late spring through early fall (other times roads can be muddy and in winter snowy and icy).

What to see: Pronghorn antelopes; moose; rosy finches in winter; waterfowl and shorebirds; prairie dogs; raptors.

What to do: Self-guided auto-tour route; nature trail for handicapped; 14 miles of roads open to driving, hiking—and entire refuge open to walking over pleasant terrain. Fishing excellent in some years for brown trout. Group guided tours by arrangement.

Where to stay: Motels—in Walden. Campgrounds—north of Walden; also various national and state forests in area.

Weather: Only 30 frost-free days a year here, and winters can drop to 50 below.

What to take and wear: Waterproof hiking boots; always a jacket.

Points of interest nearby: Rocky Mountain National Park, 60 miles southeast; Mount Zirkel Wilderness Area, 20 miles west; Colorado State Forest and Park, 22 miles east; Routt National Forest, 25 miles southwest.

For more information: Arapaho National Wildlife Refuge, P.O. Box 457, Walden, Colorado 80480. Phone: (303) 723–8202.

Arapaho also administers three satellite refuges:

Pathfinder—16,807 acres southwest of Casper, Wyoming, used by waterfowl and shorebirds. Antelopes and mule deer make their home here as do many rattlesnakes. No visitor facilities; public access is extremely difficult.

Bamforth—1,160 acres of mostly salt flat, periodically flooded, visited by waterfowl, shorebirds, pronghorn antelopes; surrounded by private land with no public access.

Hutton Lake—1,969 acres of five small lakes surrounded by marsh and upland at a 7,150-foot elevation 12 miles southwest of Laramie, Wyoming—not staffed but it can be an extremely interesting place to visit. Migrating ducks sometimes peak at 20,000 in April, including 7,500 redheads. A dozen species commonly nest, including ruddies, canvasbacks, cinnamon teal, also eared grebes, avocets, phalaropes, Forster's and black terns, Virginia rails, and various wading birds. Golden eagles are common all year. Common in warm months are mountain bluebirds, cliff swallows, Say's phoebes, and ash-throated flycatchers, and in winter three kinds of rosy finches. Pronghorns and mule deer visit.

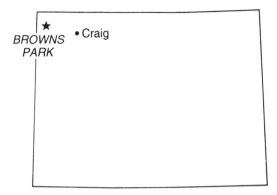

BROWNS PARK (Colorado)

Browns Park has been a haven for wildlife since before the dawn of history, when dinosaurs roamed here. Later came Indians and fur trappers and in the 1890s outlaws who took advantage of its relatively mild climate and advantageous location, in a remote vastness where three states meet, to operate a sort of triangle trade—rustling cattle in one state, fattening them a while on Browns Park, and selling them to the third, then reversing the process if necessary to hide out when difficulties arose. They were known as the Hole in the Wall Gang because they used a hidden mountain pass.

Now a wonderful assortment of wildlife is here. Antelopes, mule deer, wintering elk, and a few moose find it hospitable. So do eagles, hawks, sage grouse, great blue herons, and many kinds of water birds and mammals.

Mountain lions, like bobcats and black bears, are wary but present—a lion pair was spotted walking up the headquarters road and a bear family down by the Green River at this 13,455-acre refuge in the northwest corner of Colorado—surely one of the most remote of our national wildlife refuges and one of the most fascinating.

Browns Park was established in 1965 to restore habitat lost through construction of the Flaming Gorge Dam upstream (its canyons do seem almost to flame in the morning sun) and its roads, in past times barely passable, have been improved and are now one of the most striking wildlife drives anywhere. The beautiful scene seems untouched by the hand of man, with marshes and old oxbows of the Green (really green) River paralleled by bluffs of 50 to several hundred feet where from overlooks most of the refuge wildlife can be seen.

Deer swim across the river, passing beavers carrying building material in their jaws for dams and lodges. Otters play on the banks. Canada geese nest on river islands and on platforms in adjacent marshes—but sometimes break with tradition and raise broods on canyon ledges or in an old red-tailed hawk's nest high in the cottonwoods alongside. Great horned owls are frequently spotted in these same trees, where they nest as well.

A half-dozen or more golden eagles make this their permanent home and nest in cliffs, as do cliff swallows, which sometimes gather with others of their fleet-winged family in huge migration groups. Thousands of swallows of a half-dozen species are sometimes whirling around in Swallow Canyon just west in Utah, from which they funnel through on the refuge (a canoeist or rafter gets a fine view of the spectacle).

Several dozen pairs of white-faced ibises usually summer in the bottoms. Black-crowned night herons take up residence on Hog Lake. Great blue herons and their nest activities can be observed from a lower campground area. Tundra swans and occasional trumpeters go through.

Badgers lumber along like small tanks on upland meadow edges. White-tailed prairie dogs have loose colonies of several hundred along the roads and scuttle among their burrows.

Ruddy ducks bob robin's-egg-blue bills at mating time, and a dozen other duck species nest. Black-chinned hummingbirds sip at globe mallows and a succession of nectar-bearing wildflowers, as do their broad-tailed and rufous cousins. Pinyon jays scream from pinyon junipers in the benchlands above the river floodplain.

Curious little dippers that can walk under water—even turbulent mountain streams—nest and forage all along Beaver Creek in warm months. Turquoise male mountain bluebirds proclaim upland territories. Poor-wills can be heard and occasionally seen toward evening along meadows. Brilliant and vocal magpies seem to be everywhere all year.

Winter brings bald eagles and gray-crowned rosy finches, and thousands of deer and elk descend from hip-deep snow in higher elevations to feed more easily here both in meadows and along the open river where, it is said, Jim Bridger and Kit Carson came to sell their pelts.

Just west of the refuge is the cabin site where the outlaw Butch Cassidy could look out and call much of this—for a while at least—his own, sometimes with a female associate, Josie Bassett. Josie's sister was the famous "Queen Ann" Bassett, never convicted of rustling herself but only, local belief has it, because she was tried by a jury of her peers.

How to get there: From Craig take Route 40 west 31 miles through Maybell, then right or north on Route 318, 60 miles to refuge entrance.

Open: 24 hours all year. Office 8–4:30 weekdays.

Best times to visit: Interesting happenings all year.

What to see: Antelopes, waterfowl, shore- and wading birds, eagles, landmarks from old rustler and outlaw era.

What to do: Auto-tour loop and 30 miles of unimproved roads (some best with high clearance vehicle) for driving, hiking. Photography. Fishing, sometimes good for rainbow, cutthroat, and brown trout. Limited hunting. Float trip through the refuge on rafts or canoes on Green River (rentals nearby) takes a day, or for a beautiful three-day 85-mile trip go from Flaming Gorge to Split Mountain.

Where to stay: Motels—Craig, 85 miles southeast. Campgrounds—on refuge in specified areas; at Browns Park Store, five miles east; or Flaming Gorge Recreational Area, 50 miles northwest.

Weather: Winters fairly mild with sudden blizzards; mosquitoes can be fierce in summer.

Points of interest nearby: Bighorn sheep can often be seen in Beaver Creek Canyon on BLM land adjacent on north, and Dinosaur National Monument adjoining on south; Flaming Gorge Recreation Area (see Campgrounds); Jones Hole National Fish Hatchery, 45 miles south, hiking, fishing, striking scenery; Ouray National Wildlife Refuge, 90 miles southwest.

For more information: Browns Park National Wildlife Refuge, 1318 Highway 318, Maybell, Colorado 81640. Phone: (303) 365–3613.

The West Coast States

The refuges of the west coast stretch from Puget Sound in Washington to Tijuana Slough near the Mexican border and include some of the wettest and driest habitats anywhere—river deltas, mountains, deserts, volcanic remnants, and great marshes. Several are critically important links in the Pacific Flyway.

WASHINGTON

A spectacular structural web of buttes, basins, rock mesas, and cataracts known as the Drumheller Channels—a National Natural Landmark with rocks up to 60 million years old—is the dramatic setting for *Columbia*'s wildlife: coyotes and mule deer, sandhill cranes and swans, and more than 100,000 ducks and geese in fall and winter.

Few places are deer and elk so readily seen as at *Columbian White-Tailed Deer/Julia Butler Hansen,* especially in fall. Bull Roosevelt elk are bugling, charging, and locking antlers while contesting for mates, with some of the same activity (less spectacular) going on among the small subspecies of the white-tailed deer for which this refuge was established.

Nisqually is a pure and unpolluted river delta refuge on Puget Sound where thousands of shorebirds and waterfowl live and stop during migration, along with harbor seals, river otters, and beavers and on land coyotes, occasional black-tailed deer, and literally more cottontail rabbits than you can shake a stick at.

A striking winter scene at *Ridgefield* takes place when tens of thousands of waterfowl fly up at dawn or sunset against the distant backdrop of Mount St. Helens. This is a major sandhill crane winter roost as well, and in summer, up to 400 pairs of great blue herons nest in the cottonwood trees.

White-tailed deer graze in open meadows among more than 100 lakes and marshes where quaking aspens turn gold in fall at *Turnbull,* a beautiful refuge as well as wonderful wildlife habitat. A herd of 60 or so elk bugle for mates along the auto-tour route and later young elk trail in spring behind mothers shedding shaggy winter coats.

Willapa is a secret national treasure with more diverse wildlife habitat for its size (11,500 acres) than any other U.S. refuge. On it are black bears, huge Roosevelt elk, nesting bald eagles, blue and ruffed grouse, and great numbers of waterfowl, shor-ebirds, and songbirds of many kinds, including occasional rarities seldom seen else-where.

OREGON

Pronghorn antelopes, swiftest of North American mammals—clocked at seventy miles an hour—are the reason *Hart Mountain* became a refuge. But bobcats and mountain lions, coyotes, elk, mule deer, and golden eagles find refuge, too, in these wild, remote surroundings. As varied and fascinating wildlife as any U.S. refuge is found on *Malheur's* 289 square miles. Up to 5,000 white pelicans nest on islands in the lake. Golden eagles nest in rimrocks. Over 100 bald eagles spend the winter, and greater sandhill cranes leap up in spring courtship dances. Huge bucks with 40-inch antlers graze in the Blitzen Valley.

Long-billed curlews have made *Umatilla* their refuge, arriving every March 14 in one of the largest populations in the Pacific Northwest. But others are here, too—up to 450,000 waterfowl stop in migration and spend the winter, and some nest. Great horned owls fly at dusk. Mule deer graze in the fields.

It is easy to see why pioneers on the Oregon Trail liked the green and fertile land that is now the *Western Oregon Complex*—land that on these refuges now safeguards the entire wintering population of the dusky Canada goose.

CALIFORNIA

California condors came as close to extinction as any species still alive. Now once again they fly free over *Hopper Mountain,* which adjoins and acts as a buffer for the 53,000-acre Sespe Condor Sanctuary in Los Padres National Forest and is the staging area for their reintroduction.

More than 200,000 shorebirds and waterfowl winter over when water is plentiful in rainfall-scarce *Kern's* marshes and wetlands. Burrowing owls prefer the semi-arid uplands, which they share with three endangered species—blunt-nosed leopard lizards, Tipton's kangaroo rats, and the diminutive kit fox.

Concentrations of waterfowl at the *Klamath Basin* refuges of California and Oregon are some of the largest on the North American continent—millions of ducks and geese, seeming almost to darken the skies as in old stories when they arrive in fall migration. Bald eagles gather then, too—sometimes up to 1,000 flying to and from winter roosts. Both bald and golden eagles nest, as do large numbers of white pelicans and handsome western grebes.

Modoc is a high oasis filled with attractive habitat for water-oriented birds on the edge of California's Great Basin desert—almost 200 small islands in more than two dozen lakes and ponds. Around them is sagebrush upland where pronghorn antelopes migrate and sandhill cranes perform courtship dances.

Sacramento is one of the most important wintering areas in the Pacific Flyway for waterfowl that nested and first took wing around prairie potholes and as far north as Siberia. Over half the North American pintail ducks can be among the million and more here at least part of the time then. It's also a good nesting area for dowitchers, rails, and others.

Tens of thousands of shorebirds can turn the mudflats at *Salton Sea* to living carpets of birds in April—sometimes 36,000 western sandpipers, 10,000 whimbrels, and 6,000 avocets on the edge of this 46,991-acre refuge, most of which is undersea. Passerines also can go through in great numbers.

San Francisco Bay, the country's first urban refuge, supports large numbers of all kinds of water-oriented birds both in migration and nesting—70 percent of all Pacific Flyway shorebirds in winter or migration, as well as delicate and beautiful avocets and black-necked stilts all year.

Waterfowl and shorebirds can also flock together in spectacular numbers at *San Luis,* a beautiful sight against a sparkling marsh and gently rolling grasslands. Bald eagles are here, too, also Tule elk, stately sandhill cranes, and sometimes 150 lovely black-shouldered kites in a single clump of trees.

Little *Tijuana Slough* with 1,056 acres saves one of the last and best remaining estuarine habitats in southern California. It has a long and wonderful list of birds— over 350 species and still counting, including several endangered and threatened species that can be readily seen.

Following are birds of special interest found commonly at West Coast refuges at seasons indicated:

S: SPRING   s: SUMMER   F: FALL   W: WINTER

Arctic Loon: Willapa SW
Red-throated Loon: Dungeness W, Nisqually SFW
Red-necked Grebe: Dungeness W, Willapa W
Sooty Shearwater: Willapa SW
Brandt's Cormorant: Dungeness SsFW, Willapa SFW
Pelagic Cormorant: Dungeness FW, Willapa SFW
Trumpeter Swan: Willapa W
Harlequin Duck: Dungeness SFW
Surf Scoter: Dungeness SFW, Nisqually SFW, San Francisco Bay FW, Willapa SFW
White-winged Scoter: Dungeness SFW, Nisqually SFW, Willapa SFW
Ross' Goose: Salton Sea FW, Sacramento FW, San Luis FW

Brant: Nisqually S, Willapa SW

White-faced Ibis: Salton Sea FW

Wood Stork: Salton Sea s

Black-shouldered Kite: Kern SsF, San Francisco Bay SsFW, San Luis FW

Goshawk: Willapa W

Bald Eagle: Dungeness W, Klamath SW, Modoc SW, Salton Sea F

Golden Eagle: Hart Mountain SsFW, Klamath SW, Malheur SsFW

Prairie Falcon: Hart Mountain SsF

Chukar: Hart Mountain SsFW

Sage Grouse: Hart Mountain SsFW

Sandhill Crane: Hart Mountain SsF, Malheur SsF, Modoc SsF, Ridgefield F, San Luis
     FW

Snowy Plover: San Francisco Bay s

Surfbird: Dungeness W

Black Turnstone: Dungeness SFW, Willapa W

Long-billed Curlew: Umatilla Ss

Whimbrel: Dungeness SF, Willapa SF

Red-necked (Northern) Phalarope: Dungeness W, Salton Sea SF, San Francisco Bay SsF

Long-billed Curlew: Klamath S, Malheur Ss, Salton Sea SFW, San Francisco Bay SFW,
     San Luis SFW

Marbled Godwit: Salton Sea SF, San Francisco Bay SsFW

Yellow-footed Gull: Salton Sea S

Glaucous-winged Gull: Dungeness SsFW, Nisqually SsFW, Ridgefield SW, San Francisco
     Bay SFW, Willapa SFW

Thayer's Gull: Dungeness W

Bonaparte's Gull: Nisqually SFW, Salton Sea S, San Francisco Bay SsFW, Willapa SF

Mew Gull: Dungeness SW, Willapa SFW

Heermann's Gull: Dungeness sF, Willapa FW

Black-legged Kittiwake: Willapa F

Common Murre: Nisqually W, San Francisco Bay S, Willapa SF

Pigeon Guillemot: Dungeness W, Willapa SF

Rhinoceros Auklet: Dungeness s, Nisqually W

Tufted Puffin: Dungeness s

Band-tailed Pigeon: Nisqually SsF, Western Oregon Complex s, Willapa Ss

Flammulated Owl: Hart Mountain SF

Lesser Nighthawk: Kern Ss

Calliope Hummingbird: Hart Mountain s

Rufous Hummingbird: Hart Mountain s, Malheur s, Nisqually Ss, Western Oregon
     Complex Ss, Willapa SsF

Allen's Hummingbird: San Francisco Bay Ss

Olive-sided Flycatcher: Dungeness s, Willapa Ss

Dusky Flycatcher: Hart Mountain SsF

Gray Flycatcher: Hart Mountain SsF
Black Phoebe: Kern FW, Salton Sea SFW, San Luis Ss
Ash-throated Flycatcher: San Luis s
Gray Jay: Dungeness SsFW
Steller's Jay: Dungeness SsFW, Klamath SsFW, Western Oregon Complex SsFW, Willapa SsFW
Yellow-billed Magpie: Sacramento SsFW, San Luis SsF
Mountain Chickadee: Hart Mountain SsFW, Klamath SsFW, Modoc SF, Turnbull SF
Chestnut-backed Chickadee: Dungeness SsFW, Nisqually SFW, San Francisco Bay SsFW, Willapa SsFW
Verdin: Salton Sea SsFW
Bushtit: Nisqually SsFW, Ridgefield SsFW, San Francisco Bay SsFW, Western Oregon Complex SsFW
Pygmy Nuthatch: Hart Mountain SsFW, Turnbull SsFW
Mountain Bluebird: Hart Mountain SsF, Malheur SF
Sage Thrasher: Hart Mountain SsF, Malheur sF, Hart Mountain SsF
Black-throated Gray Warbler: Dungeness s, Nisqually SsF, Salton Sea S
Townsend's Warbler: Dungeness s
Hermit Warbler: Klamath s
MacGillivray's Warbler: Dungeness s, Hart Mountain SsF, Modoc S, Nisqually SsF
Black-headed Grosbeak: Dungeness s, Hart Mountain SsF, Klamath s, Nisqually s, Ridgefield Ss, Salton Sea S, San Francisco Bay Ss, Western Oregon Complex Ss
Lazuli Bunting: Hart Mountain SsF, Salton Sea S, Western Oregon Complex s
Green-tailed Towhee: Hart Mountain SsF
Abert's Towhee: Salton Sea SsFW
Lark Sparrow: Umatilla SsF
Sage Sparrow: Hart Mountain SsF, Malheur SF
Golden-crowned Sparrow: Klamath SF, Nisqually W, San Francisco Bay SFW, San Luis SFW, Western Oregon Complex SFW
Rosy Finch: Hart Mountain SFW
Cassins' Finch: Hart Mountain SsF
Lesser Goldfinch: San Francisco Bay SsF

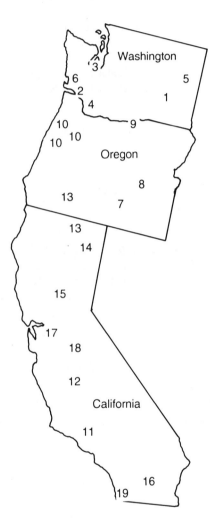

THE WEST COAST

WASHINGTON
 1 COLUMBIA
 2 COLUMBIAN WHITE-TAILED DEER /
   JULIA BUTLER HANSEN
 3 NISQUALLY
 4 RIDGEFIELD
 5 TURNBULL
 6 WILLAPA

OREGON
 7 HART MOUNTAIN
 8 MALHEUR
 9 UMATILLA
 10 WESTERN OREGON COMPLEX

CALIFORNIA
 11 HOPPER MOUNTAIN
 12 KERN
 13 KLAMATH BASIN
 14 MODOC
 15 SACRAMENTO
 16 SALTON SEA
 17 SAN FRANCISCO BAY
 18 SAN LUIS
 19 TIJUANA SLOUGH

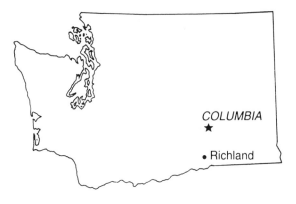

COLUMBIA
★

• Richland

COLUMBIA (Washington)

Columbia is as fascinating and beautiful geologically as it is noted for its ducks and geese, sandhill cranes and swans, coyotes and mule deer.

Some of its rocks are 60 million years old, predating earthquakes that opened cracks 30 to 50 miles deep from which volcanic eruptions sent molten rock pouring over the basin here. Layers 10,000 feet thick in places now form the Columbian Plateau, one of the world's great lava fields.

A second cataclysm followed a million years ago when the Cascade Range to the west was upthrust; then 12,000 years ago during the Pleistocene Ice Age glacial dams collapsed and released enormous walls of water in the world's greatest documented flood. According to the U.S. Geological Survey it was 10 times the flow of all the rivers in the world, and may have happened up to 80 times.

It scoured a spectacular complex of buttes, basins, rock mesas, and cataracts known as the Drumheller Channels, a starkly scenic and dramatic National Natural Landmark that can be seen along the auto-tour route.

After creation of the nearby Columbia Basin Irrigation Project in the late 1950s, seepage water formed more than a hundred ponds, sloughs, streams, and wet meadows, a visual oasis in this arid land that normally gets only 7.5 inches of rainfall a year.

More than 100,000 ducks and geese are attracted here in the fall and winter, including Canada geese and tundra swans and up to 5,000 sandhill cranes that stay up to six weeks in spring. In summer, 11 species of ducks in bright breeding plumage stay to nest, including cinnamon teal, mallards, redheads, and ruddy ducks.

Great blue herons scout the water's edges. Pugnacious coots with bright-colored chicks take loud squawking issue with one another.

Raucous and spectacular magpies are everywhere. Here seasonally, especially in riparian areas along Crab Creek, are Say's phoebes, rock and marsh wrens, lazuli buntings, northern orioles, and (rare elsewhere) ash-throated flycatchers. In uplands are an assortment of sparrows—vesper, sage, lark, Brewer's, and grasshopper, and in migration a few white-crowned and golden-crowned.

Long-billed curlews nest at Columbia. So do avocets and black-necked stilts. A few bald eagles spend the winter.

The cliffs are nest sites for red-tailed hawks and prairie falcons, barn and great horned owls—some of whose fuzzy young can be seen on the rock ledges in spring—and thousands of cliff swallows that swarm like bees when they fly in and out of their mud nests while feeding their young.

Coyotes might be seen almost anytime, especially hunting early and late in the day. Yellow-bellied marmots bask on sun-warmed rocks. Porcupines leave stripped branches on Russian olives. Beavers build lodges in banks and swim along cattail edges.

Many animals not seen during the day leave tracks in ash from the Mount St. Helens eruption, now crusted over with lichens and mosses. You may see signs here of mule deer, California quail, pheasants, and rabbits. Rattlesnakes are not aggressive, but common here—watch where you put hands and feet, and do not attempt to touch, harass or harm them; they are protected as are all the wildlife.

How to get there: From I-90 at Moses Lake take State Route 17 south to refuge signs and follow to refuge.

Open: Daylight hours. Office in Othello open weekdays but staff often afield; call ahead or get information leaflets from dispensers on the refuge. Much of refuge closed October-March to offer sanctuary during hunting seasons (but wildlife still can be viewed from some areas).

Best times to visit: Spring is best—whole refuge is open, wildflowers blooming, birds in bright plumage, both residents and those migrating through.

What to see: Waterfowl, sandhill cranes, tundra swans, coyotes, spring wildflowers (hillsides can be blanketed with pink phlox, mariposa lilies, blue larkspur); spectacular scenery.

What to do: 25 miles of roads for driving and hiking including auto-tour route, interpretive trails, also viewing from public roads; good fishing for rainbow trout (season opening is crowded), bass; photography; beautiful wildernesslike canoe trail (bring own canoe).

Where to stay: Motels—in Othello, Moses Lake. Campgrounds—on refuge in Soda Lake campground, also Potholes State Park, two miles northwest, and surrounding state wildlife land.

Weather: Temperatures can reach 100-plus in summer.

Points of interest nearby: Potholes State Park; Potholes Reservoir, adjacent on north; Gingko State Park (petrified forest), 40 miles west; Grand Coulee Dam Natural Recreation Area, 100 miles north.

For more information: Columbia National Wildlife Refuge, 735 East Main Street, P.O. Drawer F, Othello, Washington 99344. Phone: (509) 488–2668.

Also administered by Columbia is *Saddle Mountain,* a refuge of 30,000-plus acres of sagebrush-grasslands and sand dunes along the last free-flowing stretch of the Columbia River, a wintering and nesting waterfowl area with a number of endangered species. In the past it has been partly closed to public use, located in a nuclear-reactor control zone, but it is proposed to be enlarged and developed for public use, to include 49.5 miles along the Columbia River including the river's last spawning area for fall Chinook salmon, large nesting islands, wintering eagles, and a name change to *White Bluff.* Consult on current status.

COLUMBIAN WHITE-TAILED DEER/JULIA BUTLER HANSEN (Washington and Oregon)

At few places are deer and elk so readily seen as here—especially in fall when the bull Roosevelt elk are contesting for mates by bugling, charging, and locking antlers (a few with eight-by-eight prongs).

The deer, a small subspecies of white-tailed deer for which this refuge was established, also are sparring for mates then, neither species deterred by visitors watching them in October and November from the refuge road.

Lewis and Clark were the first white men to document Columbian white-tailed deer, abundant when the explorers arrived in 1806. But this lovely animal with the flashing white tail has such a limited range that it may live its entire life within half a square mile—a life-style ill-suited for survival when settlers cleared much of the land for farming.

By the 1930s it was believed extinct. Then a remnant herd of 200 was found and this refuge of 4,800 acres was set aside for them in 1972. The population now is considered stable and today this graceful deer can readily be seen against woods edges most mornings and evenings.

This relatively small refuge of mixed grasslands interspersed with sitka spruce, red alders and willows, and Columbia River bottomland has other interesting wildlife as well.

Black-shouldered kites are here through warm months and are believed to have nested. Red-tailed hawks and northern harriers are here year-round. Bald eagles nest in the area in summer and fish all year. Rough-legged hawks and peregrine falcons migrate through. Ospreys come in May, nest and stay until fall.

Coyotes hunt through the fields. Minks leap along the edges.

Great blue herons and Steller's jays are around all year. Rufous hummingbirds sun themselves in summer. Flocks of hundreds of goldfinches flit through fields. Golden-crowned sparrows and warblers migrate through. Here until fall are varied thrushes, Bewick's wrens, and Wilson's warblers.

Migrant waterfowl build up to 5,000 geese in fall—mostly dusky, western, and lesser Canadas—and several thousand ducks.

An early spring smelt run attracts tens of thousands of gulls—herring and ring-billed, western, glaucous-winged, California, and a few Bonaparte's—when these silvery foot-long fish swim up the Columbia River to spawn from January to March. Seals come, too, and more than 100 eagles that steal from the gulls or, if they have to, catch their own. Ask at the office where best to view this.

How to get there: From Longview take Route 4 west 22 miles; two miles beyond Cathlamet is refuge sign.

Open: Daylight hours. Office 7:30–4:30 weekdays.

Best times to visit: Spring, fall, winter.

What to see: Columbian white-tailed deer, elk, waterfowl, raptors.

What to do: 12 miles of roads (including public road loop around refuge) for driving, hiking, bicycling; photography (can be good from car window); fishing for chinook and silver salmon in fall, all year for sturgeon.

Where to stay: Motels—in Longview, 22 miles west, bed-and-breakfasts in Cathlamet. Campgrounds—at Skamokawa, one mile west.

Weather: Rainy and overcast much of the time, especially in winter (annual precipitation 106 inches). Boots can be handy.

Points of interest nearby: Historic Redmen Hall, Skamokawa; two state salmon hatcheries, five and seven miles north; Willapa National Wildlife Refuge, 30 miles west.

For more information: Columbian White-Tailed Deer/Julia Butler Hansen National Wildlife Refuge, P.O. Box 566, Cathlamet, Washington 98612. Phone: (206) 795–3915.

Also administered from this office is *Lewis and Clark,* 38,000 acres of largely islands, sandbars, and open water in the Columbia River estuary, with minks, beavers, river otters, and nutrias, also wintering and resting areas for swans, waterfowl, and shorebirds. It is accessible only by boat, which in these windy tidal waters can require an expert boatman. Best consult office before planning trip.

NISQUALLY *★* Olympia

NISQUALLY (Washington)

Nisqually is a pure and unpolluted refuge of 2,817 acres on a 4,000-acre river delta on Puget Sound where thousands of shorebirds and waterfowl live and rest during migration with mammals of both marine and terrestrial orientation—in the water harbor seals and river otters, on land, coyotes, beavers, occasionally black-tailed deer and literally more cottontail rabbits than you can shake a stick at. The only native steelhead run on Puget Sound is here within view of beautiful snow-capped Mount Rainier, source of the snowmelt that feeds the Nisqually River—all within a few miles of metropolitan populations of more than two million persons.

But more than anything else, Nisqually is a bird (and birder's) refuge. Here all year round in saltwater are western and horned grebes, white-winged, surf and common scoters, and common and Barrow's goldeneyes. Glaucous-winged, Bona-parte's, Heermann's, and mew gulls also are here all year. Freshwater nesters include mallards, colorful wood ducks, and Canada geese.

In fall they are joined by up to 6,000 green-winged teal, 15,000 American wigeon, and during the shorebird migration up to 6,000 dunlin, along with western sandpipers, northern phalaropes, long-billed dowitchers, and yellowlegs. Black brant winter here, feeding on eelgrass; short-eared owls hunt over winter marshes. Other raptors here year-round include rough-legged, Cooper's, and Swainson's hawks, and bald eagles, which nest and feed on the winter steelhead run. Great horned owls spend spring and summer.

That Nisqually is a refuge at all is due to the efforts of citizens who worked against proposals to turn it into either a sanitary landfill or deepwater port. Their protective efforts against constant intrusive threats continue through the Nisqually Delta Association. Meanwhile inventories still are being made of the rich variety of flora and fauna that exist on the many habitat types here ranging from fresh and saltwater marshes through riparian zones to uplands and deciduous/coniferous forests.

Three trails wander through it all from which visitors can see the nesting Canada geese, white-winged, surf and common scoters, loons, grebes (with an occasional red-necked), and altogether 19 species of dabbling and diving ducks.

In uplands, hundreds of bright goldfinches feed on swaying thistles. Warblers flit through riparian and wooded zones in migration, and eight species stay to nest, including the orange-crowned, black-throated gray, and MacGillivray's—along with Bewick's wrens, Bullock's orioles, varied, Swainson's, and hermit thrushes, chestnut-backed and black-capped chickadees, bushtits, and black-headed grosbeaks. Tree swallows raise families in bluebird nest boxes.

Red-tailed hawks and great horned owls nest in cottonwoods, northern harriers on the ground in high marsh, kestrels in boxes put out by the refuge.

Great blue herons have a colony of 80 or so nests along McAllister Creek. Band-tailed pigeons are seen all summer.

How to get there: Take I-5 to Nisqually Exit 114 and follow the signs one-half mile to the refuge parking lot.

Open: Daylight hours. Office 7:30–4 weekdays. Education center weekends. Entrance fee.

Best times to visit: Spring, fall, winter.

What to see: Passerines, raptors, waterfowl, shorebirds, bald eagles.

What to do: Three hiking trails through various habitats (dike trail partly closed during state fall waterfowl hunting); observation tower; boating (but bring your own boat); fishing can be good for steelhead and sea-run cutthroat trout, coho and chum salmon.

Where to stay: Motels—in Olympia, also Lacey, Tumwater, 5–10 miles west; Tacoma, 20 miles north. Campgrounds—off I-5 near Nisqually exit, also four state parks within 40 miles.

Weather: Late fall, winter can be cool and rainy.

Points of interest nearby: Seattle Aquarium; Tacoma's Point Defiance Zoo; Northwest Trek, Eatonville (animals in natural habitat); Mount Rainier National Park, 80 miles southeast; Olympic National Park, 70 miles northwest (don't miss the rain forest); Olympic Peninsula Scenic Drive circling the Puget Sound peninsula.

For more information: Nisqually National Wildlife Refuge, 100 Brown Farm Road, Olympia, Washington 98506.

Several outstanding refuges are also administered by Nisqually:

Dungeness is the largest natural sand hook in the nation, a fantastic birding spot and a visual spectacular as well winding almost five and one-half miles out to sea. Visitors come from all over the world to see some of the species on its long list, many not easily seen elsewhere, especially pelagic types. This is due largely to its unique habitat situation—631 acres of upland and sandspit in the Strait of Juan de Fuca, all at the foot of the beautiful Olympic Mountains.

Winter is the best time for birding here, though fog sometimes doesn't burn off until noon. Common then are such rarities on most birders' lists as Arctic and red-throated loons, double-crested and pelagic cormorants, red-necked and three other kinds of grebes, black turnstones, glaucous-winged gulls, black-legged kittiwakes, surfbirds, pigeon guillemots, bald eagles, and more than a dozen species of ducks including harlequins, surf and white-winged scoters, common and Barrow's golde-neyes, and up to 6,000 black brant feeding on the eelgrass.

Summer can be crowded with vacationers on the periphery, but there are nesting waterfowl and a number of interesting birds, including rhinoceros auklets and tufted puffins. Among small birds are chestnut-backed chickadees, gray and Steller's jays, and many warblers, including the black-throated gray, MacGillivray's, and orange-crowned, and warbling and solitary vireos in the shrubs and woods.

Refuge mammals include black-tailed deer, harbor and elephant seals hauling out on Graveyard Spit, river otters, killer whales in the outer bay, and an occasional red fox family.

Dungeness also provides habitat for the rosy day moth and golden sulphur butterfly (collecting forbidden) as well as 10 species of salmon and four of trout (steelhead, rainbow, cutthroat, Dolly Varden) plus the justly famed Dungeness crab.

The refuge must be seen on foot, allowing a good two hours each way, best at low tide. To reach the parking area, take Route 101 west from Sequim to Kitchen-Dick Lane. Go north three miles and follow the road to the right onto Lotagesell Road. Immediately turn left and go through Dungeness Recreation Area until it dead-ends on the refuge parking lot. Camping, pets, and bicycles are permitted in Dungeness Recreation Area but not on Dungeness Refuge. Sequim has motels, and sight-seeing trips, both land and water, can be arranged there.

Gray's Harbor is newly authorized, with visitor use still being planned. It will surely be one of the most outstanding in the country, with one of the largest concentrations of shorebirds in the lower 48 states. Up to a million shorebirds stop at Bowerman Basin every year in mid-April, a stunning natural event. A visitor center is planned near Hoquiam, Washington. Viewing is from parking areas near the airport or from openings along the trail to the top of the peninsula during the peak shorebird season in April.

Protection Island—a 316-acre coastal island providing nesting habitat for 75 percent of the seabird population of Puget Sound, including some 17,000 pairs of rhinoceros auklets as well as tufted puffins and others. It was set aside by citizen action led by Eleanor Stopps, who earned the nickname "tiger in tennis shoes" for her tireless efforts to marshal support to save this irreplaceable habitat after a "for sale" sign had been put up dividing it into 800 housing lots. The island is closed to the public but private boat tours can be arranged, staying at least 200 yards from shore.

San Juan Islands are a group of 83 islands in northern Puget Sound. Some are minute—only a few rocks—but even these are useful to large numbers of seabirds. Most are designated wilderness areas, inaccessible and, because of their sensitive nature, closed to public access. Two that are open—Turn and part of Matia—are managed cooperatively as state marine parks. The rest must be viewed by boat, at least 200 yards offshore (as with all these sensitive nesting islands). Ferries and sightseeing boats run in the area, and small boats can be rented with or without guide (at least 19-foot minimum is suggested and expert handling can be required in the severe riptides).

Birding is impressive with double-crested and pelagic cormorants, tufted puffins, pigeon guillemots, rhinoceros auklets, black oystercatchers, and up to 10,000 glaucous-winged gulls. There can be 40 or more bald eagle nests, and seals, otters, and sometimes killer whales.

Winter days can be cool and foggy but otherwise there's much to see at any season. To get there, take a ferry from Anacortes to Friday Harbor and there charter or rent a boat. Motels are there also, and camping is permitted on both Matia and Turn Island (neither has potable water). Waters are regarded as a fisherman's paradise.

Washington Islands refuge include some 870 rocks, seastacks, reefs, and islands stretching more than 100 miles along the coast from Cape Flattery and Quillayute Needles to Copalis Beach. This unusual refuge supports enormous numbers of nesting and resting seabirds—more than a million occupy these islands and nearby waters in the various seasons, including tufted puffins, Leach's and fork-tailed petrels, rhinoceros auklets, black oystercatchers, pigeon guillemots, Brandt's and pelagic cormorants, sooty shearwaters, sometimes peregrine falcons, along with harbor seals and sea lions, sea and river otters, and gray, piked, and killer whales. Access to all islands is forbidden except by special permit, and boaters are asked to stay 200 yards offshore. Indeed, the approach to many is so difficult it is likely they have never been visited by humans.

But many are visible from various shore points (a spotting scope is helpful); one of the best viewpoints is at La Push, 15 miles west of Forks. Boat services take pelagic observation trips from time to time; ask the refuge office about these.

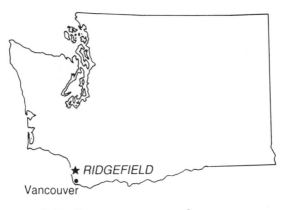

RIDGEFIELD
Vancouver

RIDGEFIELD (Washington)

Tens of thousands of waterfowl—geese and ducks and tundra swans—winter here and can be a spectacular sight flying up at dawn going out from nightly roosts to feed and returning again at sunset against a backdrop of Mount St. Helens rising in the distance.

It is a major sandhill crane winter roost as well, up to 1,000 of the stately gray birds with scarlet crown patches flying overhead in early morning and late afternoon, filling the air with their bugling calls in late October and November and again in March and early April, viewable from an observation-photographic blind (handicapped-accessible). Tundra swans are here from November into February.

Up to 400 pairs of great blue herons nest in cottonwood trees on Bachelors Island, their largest colony in the Pacific Northwest. It is obscured from view by summer foliage but the birds are easily seen as they forage along water's edges, sometimes with visiting great egrets.

The Columbia River is the western boundary of this 5,150-acre refuge, and Lake River's backwater slough and ponds form the eastern boundary. Fields planted with high-quality food crops provide maximum wildlife habitat on this relatively small refuge.

Up to 20,000 ducks and 40,000 geese winter here, including many of the dusky Canada subspecies that has been in need of special protection because of its limited range. Its total population, about 12,000, winters in this area and nests solely on Alaska's Copper River delta.

At least 10 duck species nest on the refuge—mostly wigeon and mallards, but also gadwalls, pintails, shovelers, and cinnamon, blue, and green-winged teals.

Raptors are notable—especially bald eagles, four nesting pairs within a few miles and one on the refuge in a remote area, and a dozen or so feeding on fish and weakened ducks in winter. Red-tailed hawks are common nesters. Great horned owls often roost along Bower Slough in the River "S" unit and nest elsewhere on the refuge.

Common snipe sometimes pose for photographers on fence posts alongside the marsh. Bewick's wrens are seasonally common; so are scrub jays, common yellow-throats, black-headed grosbeaks, tree and violet-green swallows, chestnut-backed chickadees, and savannah sparrows. Flocks of band-tailed pigeons usually move through in fall.

The Oaks-to-Wetlands interpretive trail winds alongside wetlands, a beaver lodge, and through groves of massive Oregon white oaks, some with trunks 12 feet around and canopies of 60 feet or more.

How to get there: From Vancouver take I-5 north 10 miles to Ridgefield exit 14, then west on Route 501 three miles into Ridgefield. Refuge headquarters is at 301 N. Third Street.

Open: Daylight hours. Office 7:30–4 weekdays.

Best times to visit: Spring, fall, winter.

What to see: Wintering waterfowl, sandhill cranes, bald eagles, great blue herons.

What to do: Auto-tour route; interpretive walking trail; observation-photo blind; blackberry picking; limited waterfowl hunting in fall can close River "S" unit. Consult refuge office.

Where to stay: Motels—in Vancouver, also Woodland, seven miles north. Campgrounds—Paradise Point State Park, three miles north; Battle Ground State Park, 15 miles south (closed in winter).

Points of interest nearby: Fort Vancouver National Historic Site, 15 miles south; Mount St. Helens National Monument, 65 miles northeast; Columbia River Gorge Scenic Area, 30 miles southeast.

For more information: Ridgefield National Wildlife Refuge, P.O. Box 457, 301 North Third Street, Ridgefield, Washington 98642. Phone: (206) 887–4106.

Four satellite refuges are administered by Ridgefield:

Conboy Lake NWR—a spectacularly beautiful valley of forest and mountain meadow at the foot of snow-covered Mount Adams with marvelous wildlife—many kinds of birds, especially those of higher elevations, along with black-tailed deer, beavers, coyotes, and (though not easily seen) elk and black bears and sometimes river otters. Sandhill cranes nest (the only place in Washington). Bald eagles are around most of the year, 15 or 20 in winter or early spring feeding on waterfowl whose concentrations in fall and spring sometimes approach 10,000.

Ruffed grouse are common and blue grouse are here also as are wild turkeys. There are usually several nests of red-tailed hawks as well as screech and great horned owls. Common at least seasonally are rufous and calliope hummingbirds, hairy woodpeckers (occasionally pileated and Lewis' also), mountain chickadees, mountain and western bluebirds, varied thrushes, and red crossbills.

Facilities until recently at least have been minimal (though some are in the planning stage) and most waters freeze in winter. However, county roads divide and skirt the refuge perimeter and afford good views. For further information contact Conboy NWR, 100 Wildlife Refuge Road, Box 5, Glenwood, Washington 98619. Phone: (509) 364–3410.

Franz Lake NWR—Some 500 lowland acres along the Columbia River 30 miles east of Vancouver, Washington, with naturally occurring wapato, favorite food of tundra swans, which winter there—no public access but viewable from state highway 14.

Pierce NWR—Canada goose resting and wintering habitat 35 miles east of Vancouver; no public use facilities.

Steigerwald NWR—600-acre wetland 15 miles east of Vancouver; no public use facilities.

TURNBULL (Washington)

More than 100 lakes and marshes interspersed with Ponderosa pine and quaking aspens that turn gold in fall make this 15,468-acre refuge beautiful as well as wonderful wildlife habitat.

White-tailed deer graze in open meadows. Porcupines look down from tree notches. A herd of 60 or so elk may be observed along the auto-tour route, males bugling for mates in the fall and youngsters appearing in spring when their mothers are shedding shaggy winter coats. Coyotes scout the wetland edges and yip back and forth to one another.

Beavers construct lodges when there's enough water—drought can alter conditions for all the wildlife. Winslow Pond is a good place to stop near the entrance road to see Canada geese and some of the 16 species of ducks that breed here, especially the handsome redheads but also mallards, cinnamon teal, scaup, and ruddies—Turnbull is one of the best waterfowl nesting grounds in eastern Washington.

In fact, birding enthusiasts will find something of interest over a wide variety of species and in almost every season.

Pygmy nuthatches are abundant through the Ponderosa pines along with their white-breasted and red-breasted cousins as well as mountain chickadees, downy woodpeckers, and flickers. Western and mountain bluebirds nest in boxes along bluebird trails (as do flying squirrels occasionally). Willow flycatchers and western wood pewees are conspicuous all the time.

Great horned owls sometimes flush from the tops of thickets where pygmy owls occupy the understory.

Black terns hunt in graceful hovering flight over the water and build floating nests as do eared and pied-billed grebes. Great blue herons have a secluded colony. Red-tailed hawks soar and nest, goshawks occasionally, and bald and golden eagles usually arrive with the waterfowl that peak—depending on water supplies—at up to 15,000 in October. Barrows' and common goldeneyes stay the winter except when ice closes the waters.

Tundra swans migrate through both spring and fall, in greater numbers in spring.

A visitor can spend hours on the five-mile auto-tour route, especially stopping to walk some of the trails marked off it and noting the wildflowers—purple camas lilies, pink bitterroot, yellow balsamroot, lupines, wild delphiniums, sticky geraniums, and others that bloom from early spring through much of the summer.

Turnbull also has interesting rock formations, part of the "channeled scablands" created when a monstrous wall of water overwhelmed this part of east-central Washington 10,000 years ago.

Local people are proud of the refuge because they are responsible for it. The wetlands now so hospitable to wildlife of many kinds had been mostly drained for abortive agricultural projects when citizens decided it should be restored, petitioned the government until this was done in 1937, and supported it over the years until it became the fine place it is today, with student groups and teachers coming through the school year to see and learn.

How to get there: From Spokane take I-90 west to Cheney/Four Lakes exit; west on state highway 904 to Cheney; turn left on Cheney Plaza Road and go four miles south to entrance.

Open: Daylight hours. Office 7–4 weekdays.

Best times to visit: April through November.

What to see: Waterfowl, deer, wildflowers, possibly coyotes.

What to do: Seven miles of roads including self-guided auto tour, with short marked hiking trails off it (but visitors can walk anywhere in the public-use area); photography for scenic wetlands, waterfowl; slide shows for groups by arrangement.

Where to stay: Motels—in Cheney, and large selection in Spokane area. Campgrounds—one mile west of Cheney; also in Riverside State Park, 25 miles northeast.

Points of interest nearby: Mount Spokane State Park, 55 miles northeast; Fince Arboretum, Coeur d'Alene Park, many others in Spokane area; Little Pend Oreille State Wildlife Refuge near Colville, 100 miles north.

For more information: Turnbull National Wildlife Refuge, S. 26010 Smith Road, Cheney, Washington 99004. Phone: (509) 235–4723.

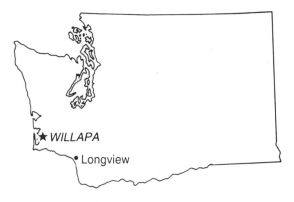

★ WILLAPA
• Longview

WILLAPA (Washington)

Willapa is a secret national treasure in the southwest corner of Washington with more diverse wildlife habitat for its size than any other U.S. refuge.

Black bears, huge Roosevelt elk, nesting bald eagles, blue and ruffed grouse, and great numbers of waterfowl and shorebirds as well as songbirds of many kinds are on these 11,500 acres. There are also occasional rarities seldom seen in the conterminous U.S. Habitats range from fresh and tidal salt marsh to virgin forest with red cedar trunks up to 12 feet across.

Black brant dine on eelgrass. Great rafts of thousands of dabbling ducks—wigeon, pintails, mallards, and green-winged teal—concentrate on feeding grounds in September and October. This is a key wintering area for canvasbacks.

Up to 300,000 shorebirds stop by northbound in spring, sometimes all at once, a dramatic sight when a great flock flies in unison against a dark cloudy sky, then turns so their light wing undersides flash a bright reflection from a slit of sun at the horizon; or a peregrine falcon or merlin dives on such a group to single out a vulnerable member.

Willapa is composed of several units mostly in and around Willapa Bay, open only to foot travel in order to preserve its wilderness quality—but one can stop at pull-offs along Highway 101 and see large numbers of waterfowl.

Leadbetter Point is the northern end of the peninsula of Long Beach separating the bay from the Pacific Ocean and has long been known among birders for outstanding sightings of godwits, whimbrels, oldsquaws, and surf and white-winged scoters. Threatened snowy plovers nest and masses of sooty shearwaters go through in August en route from Alaska to islands off New Zealand.

The mainland unit at the south end of the bay offers miles of dikes between the salt marsh and freshwater marshes where goldeneyes and buffleheads dive and thousands of Canada geese feed.

Long Island is more than 5,000 acres of meadow, marshland, and Sitka spruce, western hemlocks, and virgin red cedar stands believed to be 4,000 years old. Black bears are here—males swim across to mate with females in estrus in June, also impressive Roosevelt elk with bulls up to 700 pounds, black-tailed deer, coyotes, beavers, river otters, nesting eagles, pygmy owls (and eight other owl species), Cooper's hawks, pileated woodpeckers, and many songbirds. Long Island is accessible only by boat, and though it is a short trip it can be hazardous, with swells rising quickly to six feet or more. Lives have been lost here so the crossing should not be undertaken by any but an expert boatman after consultation with the refuge office. In any case much of the island wildlife can be seen on other refuge units.

There are great blue heron colonies and, common at least seasonally on one or another of the refuge tracts, Brandt's and pelagic cormorants, tundra and trumpeter swans, black turnstones, band-tailed pigeons, western and mew gulls, black-legged kittiwakes, common murres, pigeon guillemots, chestnut-backed chickadees, red crossbills, and black-throated gray warblers, to mention but a few, along with commonly wintering rough-legged hawks and snowy owls.

How to get there: From Portland take I-5 north to Longview, Washington, then west on Route 4 to Route 101, thence south five miles to headquarters. There get maps and directions for various refuge units.

Open: 24 hours. Office 7:30–4:30 weekdays.

Best times to visit: Spring and fall (migration peaks April 15 and October 1).

What to see: Great variety and numbers of water-oriented birds, some seldom seen elsewhere, also black-tailed deer, possibly bears, Roosevelt elk, otters.

What to do: 26 miles of hiking roads and trails; observation pond at headquarters where sampling of wildlife often seen; beachcombing on Long Island for agates, driftwood.

Where to stay: Motels—at Long Beach and throughout peninsula. Campgrounds—throughout peninsula; also Fort Canby and Fort Columbia State Parks, 15 miles south, and primitive on Long Island.

Weather: Snow is rare but winter months each average 15 inches of rain, tapering off in March, April.

What to take and wear: Raingear, rubberized hiking boots, spotting scope.

Points of interest nearby: Oysterville historic village; Nahcotta State Shellfish Laboratory;

Leadbetter Point State Park, adjoining refuge on south; Lewis and Clark Interpretive Center at Fort Canby, also excellent birding for murres, pelagic cormorants, sometimes wandering tattlers.

For more information: Willapa National Wildlife Refuge, HC 01, Box 910, Ilwaco, Washington 98624. Phone: (206) 484–3482.

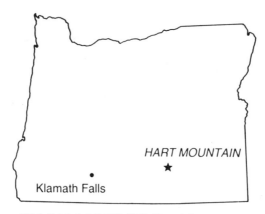

HART MOUNTAIN
★

Klamath Falls

HART MOUNTAIN (Oregon)

Pronghorn antelopes, with the keenest vision of any North American mammal and swiftest of them all—clocked at 70 miles an hour—are the reason Hart Mountain became a refuge. But there is much more here amid surroundings so wild and remote that civilization seems far away.

Bobcats and mountain lions, wary and secretive, prowl the rimrocks. This is one of the few places where California bighorn sheep can be seen in the wild. Mule deer are found in bitterbrush and aspen groves throughout the refuge. Elk are moving in from surrounding mountains.

Coyotes yip across the canyons at night and pounce on rodents and small mammals. Badgers guard hemispheric badger-shaped burrows.

Golden eagles and prairie falcons nest on cliff ledges, and birders find such interesting passerines as sage thrashers, Cassin's finches, green-tailed towhees, and pygmy nuthatches. Sage grouse stage spectacular spring courtship dances.

The sturdy pronghorn, with protruding eyes that can see both forward and backward and discern small moving objects four miles away, was once almost as abundant as the buffalo. Its population in the early 1800s was estimated at 40 million. Within 75 years its numbers were so reduced—thousands killed to use as poison bait for wolves and coyotes—that some felt it was already extinct.

But a few pronghorns remained in the Great Basin Desert, and private citizens worked to establish this 250,000-acre refuge for them. It was set aside in 1936. Hart Mountain is a massive fault-block where some 2,500 antelopes spend the spring, summer, and fall and have their young during the months of May and June. Many of these same antelopes travel to Sheldon refuge, 30 miles southeast, where herds spend the winter (altering their habits in milder or harsher weather cycles).

Antelopes at Hart Mountain are found in low sagebrush sites and meadows throughout the refuge in spring, summer, and fall. They can best be viewed in summer and fall along the 20-mile Blue Sky Road that runs from field headquarters south into the refuge, and near the dry lakebeds located in the southeast of the refuge.

Several graded roads traverse the high desert plateau that rises 4,000 feet from lake-strewn Warner Valley to an elevation of 8,065 feet. Other trails can be followed if one has a 4-wheel drive or high-clearance vehicle "and steel nerves," according to a refuge staffer (new maps are being drawn to show these). Horseback riding and hiking are permitted anywhere. Mountain bikes are permitted on open established roads only.

Reintroduced in 1954, the California bighorn sheep herd on Hart Mountain serves as a transplant source for reestablishing this handsome species elsewhere in Oregon and Nevada. Hikers to higher elevations have come across herds of 80 or more ewes and lambs and 20–25 rams. Refuge staff usually know where they have been seen lately.

Stop frequently and scan the area carefully with binoculars. Check out large rocks to be sure they are not a resting antelope, or one of the wild horses. Watch out for nighthawks basking on the road at midday, or sleepy yellow-bellied marmots looking like rocks themselves.

A great variety of smaller birds are in aspens and willows around field headquarters, in a large grove of ponderosa pines 20 miles south of headquarters at Blue Sky, and along riparian areas through the canyons—among them dusky and gray flycatchers, calliope and rufous hummingbirds, red-naped and red-breasted sapsuckers, sage and Brewer's sparrows, plain titmice, lazuli buntings, black-headed grosbeaks, and MacGillivray's warblers.

Goshawks and Swainson's hawks have nested at Blue Sky. Flammulated owls are sometimes around, great horned owls always. Rough-legged hawks are common in winter as are rosy finches.

The whole Warner Valley from which Hart Mountain ascends is an outstanding ornithological area where water birds stop in migration and some nest—grebes, white pelicans, sandhill cranes, snowy and great egrets, white-fronted and Ross' geese, and 19 duck species. This is cyclical depending on water. One visitor looked back over the valley on a spring day to see an estimated 10,000 tundra swans covering one small lake. So keep an eye out—but at least one eye on that twisting road!

How to get there: From Lakeview (headquarters is in the post office building) take Route 395 north five miles, then east 25 miles on Route 140 to Plush cutoff and refuge sign, north on Route 313 to Plush; just after Plush follow pavement east then north along base of Hart Mountain and continue on the gravel road ascending the mountain to the field office.

Open: 24 hours. Lakeview office 8–4 weekdays.

Best times to visit: Late May to late October.

What to see: Pronghorn antelopes, mule deer, California bighorn sheep, Indian petroglyphs in rimrocks, sage grouse, golden eagles, peregrine falcons from hack site southwest of refuge.

What to do: 20-mile Blue Sky Road (120 miles of 4-wheel-drive roads); picnicking; hiking; horseback riding; photography; rockhounding (opals, jasper, blue agate for personal collections, seven-pound limit); limited big-game hunt several weeks August-October. Hot springs for dusty travelers, a constant 99 degrees.

Where to stay: Motels—in Lakeview and Burns. Campgrounds—primitive camping available in designated sites on refuge. Permits are available at field headquarters for overnight backpacking, horsepack trips. Other primitive camping on area BLM and Forest Service land; RV camping six miles east of Frenchglen and Lakeview.

Weather: Freezing likely any month; winter snow can close many roads and mud, washouts in spring and early summer—ask ahead about conditions.

What to take and wear: Sturdy footgear, layered clothing, extra water, full gas tank, good tires—two spares on 4-wheel-drive secondary roads.

Points of interest nearby: Warner Wetland, 15 miles southwest; Sheldon NWR, 90 miles southeast; Malheur NWR, 45 miles northeast; Fremont National Forest, 40 miles southwest; 150-mile Oregon High Discovery Tour Route including refuges, others.

For more information: Hart Mountain National Antelope Refuge, P.O. Box 111, Lakeview, Oregon 97630. Phone: (503) 947–3315.

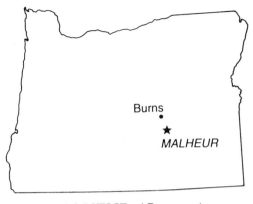

MALHEUR (Oregon)

Golden eagles nest in rimrocks where bobcats and mountain lions also look out over this beautiful 289 square miles in southeast Oregon that have as diverse and fascinating wildlife as any U.S. refuge.

Greater sandhill cranes leap up in spring courtship dances and later lead chicks about the marsh. By fall most of the Central Valley population—up to 3,000 of these majestic gray cranes with scarlet crown patches—gather here in preparation for fall migration.

Over 5,000 delicately beautiful avocets and black-necked stilts come through the Malheur basin along with thousands of least and western sandpipers, dowitchers, long-billed curlews, marbled godwits, and concentrations of waterfowl—sometimes 50,000 snow geese and 100,000 ducks.

But Malheur is remarkable not so much for tremendous numbers as for a wonderful variety of wildlife with something interesting to see in all but midwinter—sometimes even then, when over 100 bald eagles roost in the trees and fly out over the marsh to feed on fish or weakened waterfowl.

Canada goose broods appear in late April, duck broods in July—in a good year more than 10,000 cinnamon teal, gadwalls, redheads, and others. Hundreds of herons and egrets nest on islands in Malheur Lake and can be seen over most of the watered areas—it was the threatened status of these graceful birds, slaughtered for their lovely courtship feathers, that caused President Theodore Roosevelt to establish Malheur refuge in 1908.

Birding can be wonderful for smaller types as well. In spring migration a careful observer may spot 100 or more species over a weekend around P-Ranch and headquarters, including western tanagers, sage thrashers, lark, sage, and Brewer's sparrows, bobolinks, mountain bluebirds, rock and canyon wrens, Wilson's warblers,

Say's phoebes, and many warblers. During the spring and fall migration hundreds of birders flock to Malheur looking for eastern United States species that are rare in Oregon. Among those seen have been hooded, Tennessee, chestnut-sided, Cape May, northern parula, magnolia, black-throated blue and green, Blackburnian, yellow-throated, worm-eating, palm, bay-breasted, and prothonotary, as well as ovenbirds and indigo buntings.

Researchers have reported the densest nesting population anywhere of willow flycatchers in thickets along the tour route in the south Blitzen Valley. Dippers forage underwater in Blitzen River tributaries near Page Springs.

Once-rare trumpeter swans, transplanted from a flock at Red Rock Lakes Refuge, live here year-round, their nest sites sometimes visible from the Buena Vista overlook (also at Benson Pond). As many as 10,000 tundra swans are here in the fall. Up to 5,000 white pelicans nest on Malheur Lake islands when conditions are right and fly overhead in great white squadrons.

Gorgeous cock pheasants herd harems along in spring. On cool mornings chukar partridges warm themselves on dark south-facing rocks. California quails pick up grit on roadsides. Prairie falcons nest along with ferruginous, Swainson's, and red-tailed hawks and five species of owls, the great horned in tall cottonwood trees near headquarters. Peregrine falcons come through occasionally.

Herds of 40 or so deer graze in the Blitzen valley, including huge bucks with 40-inch antlers. Occasionally these fall prey to mountain lions. Coyotes prey on rodents in the meadows.

These and most of the other wildlife can be seen from the tour route starting either at refuge headquarters, at Frenchglen (where an old hotel is a designated state historic spot) or at either of two midway points. One can continue on from Frenchglen in summer on a Backcountry Byway over Steens Mountain through alpinelike terrain with beautiful spring wildflowers, dramatic views, and sometimes elk, antelopes, and bighorn sheep.

Don't hurry. Stop frequently to look around, listen, and let the beauty of one of the nation's largest inland marshes seep in, or much will be missed.

Keep a lookout for beavers along the East Canal Road, porcupines trudging in the meadows, yellow-bellied marmots on rocky cliffs, long-tailed weasels along the roads, historic ranch buildings, old lava beds, and minks and otters in the Blitzen River. Watch carefully also on the road between the refuge and Burns; much of that privately owned area is managed in a way to attract wildlife, and some of the most spectacular sights may be there, especially in spring.

How to get there: From Burns take Route 78 east two miles, then Route 205 south 24 miles to refuge sign and left six miles to headquarters.

Open: Dawn to dark. Office 7–3:30 weekdays.

Best times to visit: April through mid-October but all year is interesting.

What to see: Concentrations of waterfowl, shorebirds; sandhill cranes; trumpeter and tundra swans; songbirds; mule deer; bald eagles; others.

What to do: Drive 42-mile tour route (Center Patrol Road); visit Benson Museum at refuge headquarters; photography; slide shows for organized groups. Migratory Bird Festival first April weekend, on refuge and nearby Burns.

Where to stay: Motels—at Burns, 32 miles north; B&Bs at Diamond; also historic Frenchglen Hotel by reservation. Campgrounds—Page Springs BLM campground and Camper Corral on south refuge boundary; also at Steens Mountain, national forests, and BLM lands.

Weather: Can be cold into June, and summer nights usually cool; heavy rain and snow can close tour route and make driving difficult over Steens Mountain. In summer carry drinking water, insect repellent, and sunscreen.

Points of interest nearby: Steens Mountain loop drive (seasonal), up to 10,000-foot elevation, remarkable scenic and wildlife view; Hart Mountain NWR, 42 miles southwest (but road sometimes impassable in bad weather); Ochoco National Forest, 45 miles northwest; Malheur National Forest, 50 miles northeast. Many of these, including Malheur Refuge, are on new 150-mile Oregon High Desert Discovery Tour Route.

For more information: Malheur National Wildlife Refuge, HC-72 Box 245, Princeton, Oregon 97721. Phone (503) 493–2612.

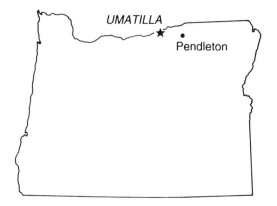

UMATILLA
★
• Pendleton

UMATILLA (Oregon and Washington)

Every March 16 the word goes around: "Curlee! Curlee!" has echoed over the marsh and uplands signaling the return of spring with that of the long-billed curlews in one of the largest populations in the Pacific Northwest.

For 20 miles along both sides of the Columbia River, the Umatilla Refuge offers in this arid desert steppe country a variety of welcoming habitat not available elsewhere—woods, islands, backwater sloughs, and croplands, which attract a remarkable array of wildlife through most of the year.

Up to 450,000 waterfowl winter and stop over in migration and some breed here, including up to 50,000 Canada geese and more than a dozen duck species. Keeping an eye on them in winter and feeding on weak ones are several dozen bald eagles. Tundra swans visit in spring and fall.

A herd of 40 to 80 mule deer browse in the fields and raise fawns. Coyotes scout the brush and marsh edges pouncing on rodents and small mammals—and the same prey base that supports them attracts many raptors.

Great horned owls fly at dusk; so do short-eared owls over the marsh. Long-eared, barn, and screech owls nest, as do northern harriers and red-tailed and Swainson's hawks. Rare western burrowing owls raise families in badgers' discarded upland burrows. Prairie falcons zoom through spring and fall.

Great blue herons share nest colonies with double-crested cormorants on river islands (sometimes they choose Coast Guard channel markers). Ring-billed gulls and Caspian terns occupy other islands in one of their few breeding sites in this part of the country, alongside beaver lodges and small numbers of otters.

This 22,885-acre refuge was set aside to replace wildlife habitat inundated by construction of the John Day Dam, a loss compensated in part by formation of the McCormack and Paterson backwater sloughs on the refuge. Dense Russian olive thickets have grown up and one covering more than 60 acres shelters, according to an Oregon State University study, the densest wintering small-bird population in the northwest, as well as, in other seasons, lark and Harris' sparrows, warblers, and chats.

Pheasants and California quail forage around brushy areas. Horned larks fly up in scattered clouds of thousands in the winter.

But the stars of Umatilla are the long-billed curlews, medium-sized marbled brown shorebirds with improbable eight-inch curved bills whose prompt arrival every year causes great excitement. No one can call in by telephone because people are all calling each other to report the first sighting. There has been a move to declare an official Curlew Day; in any case this interesting bird is conspicuous here from mid-March through the June nesting of at least 500 pairs in both dry and moist uplands, and many stay around afterward loafing and feeding on grasshoppers.

There is also a desert area of moving sand dunes with dry-land reptiles, plants, insects, and birds that can be fascinating—observing tracks where, for example, a black-billed magpie has swooped down and carried off a wriggling snake. Not far away the river cuts a sparkling blue slash through the arid land and in the distance one can see the Blue Mountains and on a clear day, snow-covered Mount Hood in the Cascade Range.

How to get there: Take Paterson Ferry Road exit from I-84, follow Paterson Ferry Road north four miles to refuge entrance. Office is in post office building in Umatilla.

Open: 5 a.m.–10 p.m. Office in Umatilla 8–4 weekdays.

What to see: Waterfowl, mule deer, raptors, long-billed curlews, coyotes, passerines.

What to do: Driving, hiking—best way to see refuge is driving or hiking along entrance road and access trails and roads marked along it; also from pull-offs from Highway 14 on the Washington side. Also boating—trips can be arranged with guides in Umatilla and Boardman. Parts are open to hunting in state season on fall Wednesdays and weekends. Fishing can be good for bass, sturgeon, walleyes.

Where to stay: Motels—in Umatilla, Hermiston, also Boardman adjacent to refuge. Campgrounds—in Boardman; also Crow Butte State Park and Plymouth Corps of Engineers Park on Washington side.

Weather: Frequent spring dust storms; summer 100-plus, dry.

Points of interest nearby: McNary Dam, with windows for viewing salmon and steelhead trout on the fish ladders on the Washington side.

For more information: Umatilla National Wildlife Refuge, P.O. Box 239, Umatilla, Oregon 97882. Phone: (503) 922–3232.

Also administered by Umatilla are:

Cold Springs—Large winter waterfowl concentrations, including most species common to the Pacific Flyway. Many also breed at this lovely 3,117-acre refuge superimposed on an irrigation reservoir seven miles east of Hermiston, Oregon. There's a large and varied raptor population as well. Migrating shorebirds use mudflats in fall. Swans and pelicans visit in winter, and mule deer are here all year. Several miles of gravel roads and trails can be followed to view wildlife but take a refuge map—visitors get lost sometimes.

McKay Creek—Also superimposed on an irrigation project, these 1,837 acres eight miles south of Pendleton provide wintering habitat for some 12,000 ducks and 2,000 geese, as well as a good raptor population. Visitor facilities are not highly developed and the refuge is mostly closed in winter.

McNary—These 3,631 acres of fields, marsh, and open water with several islands in the Columbia and Snake Rivers are a wildlife oasis amid increasing land development in this part of southeast Washington. American white pelicans and tundra swans are common in spring and fall migration along with 60,000 ducks and 40,000 geese. Many stay through the winter—and nesters in summer include Canada geese, mallards, gadwalls, pintails, and others. Northern harriers and red-tailed hawks are here; also pheasants and great blue herons. Forster's terns nest near a large ring-billed and California gull colony on the Hanford Islands. A one-mile interpretive walking trail around the pond near refuge headquarters in Burbank provides opportunities to see many species of birds, especially waterfowl. For further information, contact McNary National Wildlife Refuge, P.O. Box 544, Burbank, Washington 99323. Phone: (509) 547–4942.

Toppenish—Still in a state of acquisition and development but there is much to see on this small refuge reached by going south seven miles on Route 97 from Toppenish, turning right at base of hill. There are waterfowl, wading birds, raptors, including eagles and prairie falcons in winter, and among smaller birds, sage thrashers, sage sparrows, and a fine breeding colony of bobolinks; also an observation tower and walking trail.

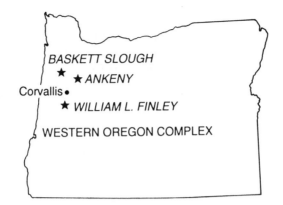

WESTERN OREGON COMPLEX (Oregon)

It is easy to see why settlers on the Oregon Trail ended their long trek in this green and fertile Willamette Valley—from Independence, Missouri, to Independence, Oregon—and why numbers of waterfowl have always found it so hospitable. Historically one of these has been the dusky Canada goose, an uncommon subspecies distinguished by its slightly smaller size and noticeably darker breast.

The attractive little dusky's whole population winters in the Willamette and along the lower Columbia River (it nests in an equally restricted area on Alaska's Copper River delta) where hunting and land development in this century have gradually diminished its numbers and the areas open to it.

To safeguard its remaining population these three refuges were set aside in 1964–65. The dusky responded well and initially its numbers increased slightly. Unfortunately, continued hunting losses and predation on its breeding ground have brought it down again from close to 40,000 to around 12,000, which divide roughly between the 2,800-acre Ankeny Refuge, 2,500-acre Baskett Slough Refuge, and 5,325-acre William Finley Refuge, which administers all three.

Certain areas are set aside for quiet sanctuary for these sometimes nervous birds (especially in hunting season), but they can almost always be seen from refuge and county roads, sometimes fairly close by, when they venture into the fields to feed, along with up to 50,000 Taverner's Canada geese, a more numerous subspecies with lighter gray breast.

The three refuges, located not far apart, are similar, but Finley, with varied habitat and an interpretive walking trail, probably holds the most interest for visitors. A herd of 50 or so elk moved in after forest management practices pushed them out of accustomed habitat to the west and can be commonly found grazing just north of headquarters. Bobcats are around occasionally and most of the animals indigenous to the coast range have been seen at one time or another, including pileated woodpeckers and the first nesting record for the white-tailed kite in Oregon.

Common all year at all three refuges are red-tailed hawks, kestrels, ruffed grouse, California quails, great horned owls, great blue herons, and a variety of smaller birds, including bushtits, Bewick's wrens, scrub and usually Steller's jays, white-breasted and often red-breasted nuthatches, killdeer, flickers, and handsome wood ducks, which nest in boxes set out for them.

Band-tailed pigeons spend fall feeding in most cornfields (the population of this interesting bird is under pressure because of overhunting). Best times for warbler and other songbird migrations is April through June 15. Common seasonally are tundra swans, Swainson's and varied thrushes, black-headed grosbeaks, lazuli buntings, yellow-breasted chats, golden-crowned sparrows, and orange-crowned and Wilson's warblers, which also nest.

Black-tailed deer browse and coyotes hunt small rodents. All three refuges have trails that can be hiked in summer but only Finley and Basket Slough have areas open to public use during the winter period. Most of Finley and Ankeny are closed November 1–April 15 and Baskett Slough October 1–May 1 to keep geese on refuge land during hunt seasons and when they might graze on surrounding farmland (which has caused problems), but they can be seen from the roads. Best way to visit all three is to get maps, directions and other pertinent information from the Finley office and plan from there.

How to get there: From Corvallis take Route 99 W, 8.5 miles south to refuge sign, then two miles west on a gravel road.

For more information: Western Oregon Refuge Complex, 26208 Finley Refuge Road, Corvallis, Oregon 97333. Phone: (503) 757–7236 (open weekdays).

Also administered from this office is *Bandon Marsh* Refuge, an undisturbed 289 acres of salt marsh north of Bandon, Oregon. Otters live here, also beavers, harbor seals, black-tailed deer, waterfowl, and occasional rare visitors such as Mongolian plover and Hudsonian and bar-tailed godwit. No facilities—consult office on how to visit.

Hundreds of thousands of seabirds come ashore in spring and summer to nest on several wild uninhabited rocky coastal and island refuges also administered from the Western Oregon Refuge Complex.

Cape Meares Refuge, the main land-based one, is located on a headland just south of Tillamook Bay two miles north of Oceanside. *Three Arch Rocks* Refuge is a group of arched rocky islands two miles south of Cape Meares, and *Oregon Islands* Refuge consists of a string of islands, some only a few rocks themselves, scattered for 300 miles from the north Oregon coast to the California border.

Huge concentrations of common murres, tufted puffins, guillemots, petrels, and

Brandt's and pelagic cormorants use these, as well as sea lions and harbor seals. Except for the land portion of Cape Meares, all are inaccessible (and off-limits to all but scientific study by special permit), but some can easily be seen—and a fantastic sight they are, with birds packed shoulder to shoulder on every available rock space, sometimes 100,000 or more, occasionally diving to the water or flying low overhead.

The best view of Three Arch Rocks is from a pleasant motel on a hill just beside Oceanside where the proprietors seem to enjoy having birdwatching visitors. For a closer look go to the lighthouse parking lot two miles north adjoining the Cape Meares tract.

The various holdings in the Oregon Islands Refuge range from rocks awash in rough weather to the fairly substantial Goat Island, and can be viewed from the many state parks and waysides that line the Oregon coast (camping is often available at these, too). Consult the refuge suboffice at Newport for advice on which present the best sights when. As with all these, a spotting scope is a must for a really good look.

A coastal suboffice of the Western Oregon Refuge Complex is at the Marine Science Center, 2030 South Marine Science Drive, Newport, Oregon 97365. Phone: (503) 867–4550.

HOPPER MOUNTAIN (California)

Once California condors flew free over this 2,457-acre tract of rugged mountains—and now they are here again. Captive breeding of the majestic bird with nine-foot wingspread, which has come as close to extinction as any species still alive, has been successful beyond expectations, and in January 1992 two California condors were released to the wild.

Hopper Mountain adjoins and acts as a buffer for the 53,000-acre Sespe Condor Sanctuary in the Los Padres National Forest and is the staging area for the project. After this has been accomplished and a stable free population exists, plans call for public viewing areas. But for the foreseeable future, visits to this sensitive tract will be by special arrangement only.

For more information: Hopper Mountain National Wildlife Refuge, P.O. Box 3817, Ventura, California 93006. Phone: (805) 644–1766.

★ *KERN*

• Bakersfield

KERN (California)

More than 200,000 shorebirds and waterfowl may visit and winter over at Kern's marshes and wetlands when water supplies are plentiful. Birders like to check around the six miles of riparian habitat along an old slough channel to find black and Say's phoebes, water pipits, white-crowned sparrows, and any of four species of owls that frequent that area, including great horned, long-eared, short eared, and barn owls.

Burrowing owls prefer the semi-arid uplands that they share with three interesting endangered species—the diminutive kit foxes, Tipton's kangaroo rat, and the blunt-nosed leopard lizard, most visible in summer when, looking like a small, spotted dinosaur, it runs rapidly about on two hind legs after insects and even small lizards.

Black-shouldered kites are one of the beauties of the refuge, common all year in hovering flight or nesting in trees.

Kern is a remnant of a once-fabulous waterfowl area. Tulare Lake, just north, at one time covered 800 square miles and was the largest freshwater lake west of the

Mississippi River, with abundant wildlife—millions of waterfowl, trout weighing up to 40 pounds, and great herds of elk and deer. In the late 1800s land was "claimed" from it by levees, and in a few years the lakebed was completely dried up.

Kern was established in 1960 to restore these 10,618 acres as part of this once vast waterfowl and wildlife habitat. But rainfall is scarce in this valley, which lies in the rain shadow of the coast ranges, and wetlands must be maintained most of the time with water from deep wells or purchased from the California aqueduct, which is costly. This is done in fall and winter but not in summers, which are hot and dry and less interesting for visitors.

In fall and winter concentrations of ducks include mallards, gadwalls, pintails, green-winged and cinnamon teal, and ruddy ducks. There are also eared and pied-billed grebes, snowy and great egrets, great blue herons, and impressive groupings of shorebirds—yellowlegs, long-billed curlews, dowitchers, avocets, stilts, and least and western sandpipers.

Raptors generally follow the waterfowl, which provide meals for peregrine and prairie falcons as well as Swainson's hawks, harriers, and sometimes even red-tailed hawks and golden eagles.

Roadrunners dash along the auto-tour route looking for lizards or large insects. Pheasant cackle in brushy areas. Coyotes hunt opportunistically wherever ground squirrels and other small prey hang out. Bobcats are around but seldom seen.

Kern also supports interesting rare plants—the giant slough thistle, considered for endangered status, and brilliant blue phacelias—in such numbers when moisture is sufficient that they can appear at a distance as sparkling bodies of water.

How to get there: From Bakersfield take I-99 north to second Delano exit, then left (west) at second stop sign for about 20 miles on Garces Avenue, which dead-ends at refuge headquarters.

Open: Daylight hours except Saturdays and Wednesdays in hunting season October-January. Office 8–4:30 weekdays except 7–3:30 in summer.

Best times to visit: September through April.

What to see: Waterfowl, shorebirds, pheasants, coyotes, black-shouldered kites.

What to do: Auto-tour route; hiking.

Where to stay: Motels—in Delano, Lost Hills, Corcoran. Campgrounds—Buena Vista County Park, 24 miles south; KOA at Lost Hills.

Points of interest nearby: Sequoia National Forest, 65 miles northeast; Tule Elk State Refuge, 40 miles south; Lake Isabella, reservoir recreation, 42 miles east; various Nature Conservancy properties—contact TNC office in Bakersfield.

For more information: Kern National Wildlife Refuge, P.O. Box 670, Delano, California 93216. Phone: (805) 725-2767.

Also administered by Kern are:

Pixley, 20 miles northeast, similar to Kern in wildlife and habitat; open to visitors obtaining a permit from Kern.

Bitter Creek, 14,000 acres south of Maricopa; acquired as traditional feeding, resting, and loafing areas for California condors. No public use except by special permit.

Blue Ridge, 897 acres acquired as summer roosting area for California condors because it is adjacent to their traditional feeding and resting sites; no public access.

KLAMATH BASIN

★

• Klamath Falls

★

KLAMATH BASIN (California and Oregon)

The Klamath Basin refuges of California and Oregon are among the most exciting in the world, with stunning gatherings of millions of ducks and geese, hundreds of eagles, as well as intimate glimpses of natural life of all kinds against a background of spectacular scenic beauty in the six refuges in this complex covering 151,000 acres.

The concentrations of waterfowl, largest on the North American continent, seem almost to darken the skies as in old stories when they arrive in fall migration.

Up to 500 bald eagles fly to and from winter roosts (sometimes up to 1,000) in the largest numbers outside Alaska, sometimes moving visitors to tears at this sight of so many of our majestic national bird that once seemed headed for extinction. Sometimes more than 100 can be counted from a single vantage point.

Both bald and golden eagles nest, along with 10 species of hawks and 10 kinds of owls. Winter may bring thousands of northern harriers and red-tailed and rough-legged hawks.

Downy western grebe hatchlings are everywhere in early summer, riding on the backs of handsome ruby-eyed parents, hanging on even during their parents' dives for food. They share the marshes with offspring of dozens of other water birds including more than 60,000 ducklings and goslings that hatch here in a good year. Altogether more than 275 bird species have been counted here, some in huge numbers, of which at least 180 species nest on refuge lands.

But it is the tremendous fall waterfowl concentrations on the Lower Klamath and Tule Lake units that have attracted world renown, filling the entire sky when they come through in October and November, funneling southward from breeding grounds as far away as Siberia.

Sometimes 150,000 snow geese can be seen in a single glance. There can be 80 percent of the world population of their smaller cousins, Ross' geese, plus Canadas, white-fronted, even an occasional emperor goose, and more than 20 duck species. It is an awesome and unforgettable sight and a delight to photographers when the birds fly up en masse in the late-day sun against a backdrop of snowy Mount Shasta.

Spring concentrations, usually in early March, are only a little less overwhelming— but tundra swans, up to 10,000, may be even more impressive then.

Significant nesting groups are here, too: white pelicans, their northernmost colonies producing up to 1,500 young; double-crested cormorants, great blue herons, white-faced ibis, California and ring-billed gulls, Caspian and Forster's terns, and sometimes hundreds of floating nests of golden-tufted eared grebes.

Breeding avocets, coots, and black-necked stilts can be seen by the hundreds— as, in fact, can almost all the wildlife except some that congregate in breeding colonies where they are protected from disturbance. Even these can be viewed readily feeding on the marsh and water areas in early morning and late afternoon.

Interesting small birds come, too—bright hermit warblers, common summer nesters; Townsend's solitaires, nesting and common in fall; tricolored blackbirds, fox sparrows, coveys of mountain quail, and a myriad of others.

Mule deer graze beside the marsh in Lower Klamath and in uplands on the west of Tule Lake where pronghorns are occasionally seen. Yellow-bellied marmots sun themselves on boulders and rock piles.

Coyotes go mousing in the fields, bounding up and down to pounce on small victims, pausing barely long enough to eat them "the way you and I eat peanuts," a staffer observed.

Best places to see the greatest numbers and variety are tour roads on the Tule Lake and Lower Klamath units. Upper Klamath and Tule Lake Refuges also offer canoe trails. The Clear Lake unit, providing habitat for pronghorn antelopes and nest sites for pelicans, is unstaffed with only limited areas open to visitors. Upper Klamath is almost entirely marsh and water with a fine canoe trail where water birds, including red-necked grebes, can be seen. Boats are available for rental, and camping also, at a nearby Forest Service concession. (All canoe trails can be restricted during nesting season.)

The Bear Valley unit protects a major winter eagle roost. They can be seen easily flying in and out from Highway 97 near Worden, Oregon, especially at dawn in January and February. Klamath Marsh is 38,277 acres of habitat for water birds and sandhill cranes; visitor facilities are largely in the planning stage.

The headquarters Visitor Center has information on what is available on the various units and how best to see everything, with displays on history and wildlife of the area and a short audiovisual program on the significance of the Klamath Basin Refuges.

Impressive as are the bird concentrations here, they were even greater a generation ago—up to 6 million or more in the 1950s. Why the decline? Other than the reduced availability of wetlands due to drainage and drought, no one is quite sure. But the change points up the critical significance of refuges such as these, without which such populations would have no place to go for their continued existence.

How to get there: From Tulelake take Highway 139, then west five miles on East-West Road, then one-eighth mile south via Hill Road to Klamath Basin Refuge headquarters. There get maps, data, and directions for all refuge units.

Open: Daylight hours. Visitor Center 8–4:30 weekdays, 8–4 weekends (closed Christmas, New Year's).

Best times to visit: March-May and mid-September to mid-December, but much to see all year—eagles mid-December to February.

What to see: Huge concentrations of migrating and nesting waterfowl as well as grebes, pelicans, waders, shorebirds, raptors, coyotes, mule deer, bald eagles in winter, many others.

What to do: Auto-tour routes on Lower Klamath and Tule Lake, other roads of varying quality for driving, hiking (some closed in wet weather). Public roads also afford viewing. Photography (blinds available by reservation). Canoe trails. Fishing in Upper Klamath and Klamath Marsh. Group tours and presentations can be arranged. Various limited hunting seasons from September to mid-January on parts of refuge (waterfowl mornings to 1 p.m.).

Where to stay: Motels—Tulelake, California; also Merrill, Oregon, and Klamath Falls, Oregon, 25 miles north. Campgrounds—in Tulelake; also Lava Beds National Monument, adjacent to Tule Lake unit on south.

Weather: Winter travel can be difficult, extremely changeable; frost possible most months.

Points of interest nearby: Lava Beds National Monument (see Campgrounds); Miller Island State Wildlife Management Area, 25 miles northwest; Medicine Lake

Highlands of Modoc National Forest, 25 miles south (one of the world's largest shield volcanoes); Crater Lake National Park, 75 miles northwest; Klamath Tour Loop, 120-mile auto tour of interesting natural and historic places in area; Winema National Forest has sections of Pacific Crest Hiking Trail from Canada to the Sierras. Annual Eagle Conference with raptor-related presentations and activities, mid-February in Klamath Falls.

For more information: Klamath Basin National Wildlife Refuges, Route 1, Box 74, Tulelake, California 96134. Phone: (916) 667–2231.

Alturas
MODOC

MODOC (California)

Modoc is a high oasis filled with attractive habitat for ducks and other waterbird species on the edge of the great basin desert in northeastern California— almost 200 small islands scattered over more than two dozen lakes and ponds. Around them is typical great basin sagebrush upland where pronghorn antelopes sometimes appear by the hundreds in migration treks.

Sandhill cranes perform courtship dances and nest. White pelicans are on hand in good numbers in summer along with snowy egrets and great blue herons.

Late spring to early fall are the best times to come. Ducks and geese migrate through, peaking in fall at up to 20,000 ducks and 15,000 geese—mostly Canadas with some snows and white-fronteds—and come again in smaller groups in spring. Many of the Canadas and 11 species of ducks stay to nest, courting in bright breeding plumage in May and later leading downy broods in ponds along the entrance road. Dusky coots are there, too, with startlingly bright-hued offspring, along with eared, western, and pied-billed grebes and killdeer doing their "broken-wing" act to distract attention from their nests and young.

Shorebirds can appear in large numbers in spring when sometimes hundreds of snipe, Wilson's phalaropes, avocets, and black-necked stilts are around the ponds and meadows, and many stay to nest. White-faced ibis and black-crowned night herons usually nest in the center of Teal Pond.

Upland birding is best around headquarters or by permission in certain closed areas (ask the office). Short-eared owls and red-tailed hawks are common all year.

Mule deer are common year-round; coyotes, badgers and minks are, too, but are wary and hard to spot. Not so Belding's ground squirrels, which are everywhere, especially along the dike road, scurrying at high speed only to brake to a sudden stop and assume their upright "picket-fence" pose.

Antelopes can be unpredictable but most often appear in November and March; when they come, 500 may cross over a corner of the refuge in two or three days, apparently oblivious to their surroundings and easy to view.

Winter is the least agreeable time (though snow and freezing weather can occur in any month here), but a dozen or so bald eagles often make Modoc their winter headquarters. Sometimes several can be seen in a single tree near the office. Some areas may be closed to public use during fall hunting season.

How to get there: Modoc is three miles south of Alturas, California. Go south from Alturas on Route 395, east on County Road 56 and south on County Road 115, following signs.

For more information: Contact the Refuge Manager, Modoc National Wildlife Refuge, P.O. Box 1610, Alturas, California 96101. Phone: (916) 233-3572.

SACRAMENTO (California)

Swirling flights of wintering and migrating waterfowl fill the air with their calling and gabbling in late fall, peaking in late November and December when up to two million birds are at Sacramento and its valley subrefuges.

This is one of the most important wintering areas in the Pacific Flyway for ducks and geese that nested and first took to the air around the prairie potholes and as far north as Wrangel Island, Siberia—the snow geese flying night and day often at speeds of 50 mph to get here.

Over half of the pintail ducks in North America can be among the million and more waterfowl here at least part of the time from October through February in the 24,000 acres of fields and ponds in the northern Central Valley of California, bordered by the Sierra Nevada Mountains on the east and the coastal range on the west.

Notable among the half-million and more geese are the endangered Aleutian Canada geese, the rare Tule white-fronted geese (about 6,000), Pacific white-fronted geese, cackling Canada geese, and Ross' geese, distinguished from their cousins, the more numerous snow geese, by absence of the "grinning patch" alongside the bill.

Thousands of shorebirds may be here as well, though on a different schedule. Great numbers of dowitchers, also western sandpipers, greater yellowlegs, killdeer, and long-billed curlews are here in February and March when water levels are ideal for their kind of mudflat foraging.

Sacramento is listed as one of the outstanding photographic opportunities among national wildlife refuges for good reason. The sight of hundreds of thousands of waterfowl feeding in the shallow mirrorlike marsh or rising and swirling in the air like leaves in the wind, taking flight against the background of the coastal range or a red sunset, is unforgettable. Blinds are available (reserve ahead) but they are not necessary for stunning panoramas like these, best seen just after sunrise or silhouetted at sunset, or when a raptor's appearance starts up thousands of resting and preening birds at midday.

Dowitchers are here all year and nest. So do Virginia rails, gallinules, great blue and black-crowned night herons, and snowy, cattle, and great egrets and white-faced ibis. The most common ducks are pintails, mallards, green-winged teal, northern shovelers, American wigeon, and ruddy ducks.

Black-shouldered kites perch in the larger willows and cottonwoods and a few nest in them. A visitor in winter or spring almost certainly will see one of these lovely white-plumaged raptors hovering over an upland field, or at any time of year get a thrilling close-up view (through binoculars) of a harrier or kestrel swooping down and carrying off a meal.

Yellow-billed magpies, resident only in the California valleys, are easily seen here. Nuttall's woodpeckers nest in wooded areas, and cliff swallows construct mud colonies around bridges. Many other small birds migrate during breeding—some only six miles, however, to the westward coastal range.

European wigeon are spotted almost every year. Endangered peregrine falcons zoom through. A few bald eagles are usually around when the waterfowl are. Striking white pelicans are around all year (but do not nest). Brilliant-hued ring-necked pheasants commonly stroll along brushy areas.

Black-tailed deer graze upland fields and marsh margins. Jackrabbits are omnipresent. Other mammals are here but less visible—skunks, muskrats, ground squirrels, raccoons, a few ringtail cats (which sometimes use wood duck houses for dens), and 12 species of bats.

Yellow and blue wildflowers carpet vernal pools when they begin to dry up in April.

How to get there: From Sacramento take I-5 north to Norman Road Exit, follow refuge signs east on Norman Road then north on 99-W.

Open: Daylight hours. Office/Visitor Center 7:30–4 weekdays, also weekends October through February.

Best times to visit: October through February (peak mid-November to mid-December).

What to see: Tremendous waterfowl concentrations, large numbers of shorebirds.

What to do: Self-guided auto and walking tours; photography (photoblinds available, reserve ahead).

Where to stay: Motels—several in Willows. Campgrounds—Sacramento River State Recreation Area, 25 miles south; Woodson Bridge State Park, 45 miles north.

Weather: Summer temperatures commonly 100-plus. Winter rains rarely can close auto-tour routes.

Points of interest nearby: Mendocino National Forest, 20 miles west; Gray Lodge State Wildlife Area, 40 miles west; Clear Lake, fishing and recreation area, 60 miles southwest; Shasta Lake, fishing and recreation area, 75 miles north.

For more information: Sacramento National Wildlife Refuge, Route 1, Box 311, Willows, California 95988. Phone: (916) 934–2801

Also administered as part of Sacramento NWR Complex are:

Butte Sink NWR—733 acres, closed to public use by refuge deed to provide waterfowl sanctuary.

Colusa NWR—4,040 acres of ponds and uplands with similar wildlife and three-mile auto-tour route, located three miles southwest of Colusa on Highway 20.

Delevan NWR—5,633 acres near Maxwell managed largely for waterfowl resting and feeding. No visitor facilities but a small section is open to fishing February 1–October 1.

Sutter NWR—2,591 acres south of Sutter, used for resting and feeding by large waterfowl numbers—no visitor facilities and usually floods at least part of every winter, but the area can be viewed from the Oswald county road that bisects it.

Sacramento River NWR—a refuge in the process of land acquisition, eventually planned to provide a greenway corridor of riparian habitat along 100 miles of the Sacramento River. Public use has been in the planning stage.

SALTON SEA (California)

Tens of thousands of shorebirds visit Salton Sea in April, turning the mudflats to living carpets of birds, rising like waves when they relocate to different feeding spots—probably the highest numbers and diversity of any inland area in the West. Sometimes there are 36,000 western sandpipers, 10,000 whimbrels, 6,000 avocets—just for example.

All but a few of Salton Sea's 46,991 acres are under the sea itself, but the margins afford a vantage point for some of the most spectacular birding anywhere, not only in spring (when Salton Sea has been noted as a significant wetland on the Western Hemisphere shorebird route) but throughout the year.

Great concentrations of waterfowl and wading birds as well are present in season—probably the most significant numbers of those that migrate along the Colorado River and the inner Coastal Flyway—190,000 ducks, both wintering and migrant, and thousands of snow and Canada geese and occasionally brant.

And there is an abundance of others. Passerines go through, too—western tanagers, lazuli buntings, black-headed and blue grosbeaks, Bullock's orioles, warbling vireos, and yellow and Wilson's warblers, among many others; the brushy areas around headquarters are as good a locale as any on the refuge for these.

In winter, during the annual Audubon Christmas Bird Count, Salton Sea often reports highest counts in the nation for such species as rough-winged and bank swallows, Scott's orioles, orange-crowned and yellow-rumped warblers (3,747 in one year), redstarts, burrowing owls, mountain plovers (1,100 in one field of this rare species), long-billed dowitchers, long-billed curlews, marsh wrens (120,000), and ruddy ducks (17,050). Eared grebe concentrations approach 1.5 million during January-February migration, when they use Salton Sea as a staging site.

The bird list is an impressive 378 species and still counting.

Late spring and summer storms off Baja Peninsula can blow in blue-footed and brown boobies, fulvous whistling ducks, roseate spoonbills, frigate birds, and pomarine and parasitic jaegers.

Summer is blistering—temperatures 100-plus for six months running—but the birds don't mind. Black-necked stilts nest on every water's edge. Up to 100 wood storks arrive in late June and hang about till fall. Yellow-footed gulls and nonbreeding brown pelicans are here. Hundreds of great blue herons and great and snowy egrets nest. So do the snowy plover, gull-billed tern, black skimmer, endangered Yuma clapper rail, Forster's tern—and among land birds, black and Say's phoebes and Abert's towhees, the latter all around the picnic area.

In fall snow geese arrive and some 30,000 stay the winter, moving in great white flocks to and from feeding and resting spots, along with sandhill cranes, Canada geese, white-faced ibis, and 20 or so duck species—pintails, shovelers, wigeon, canvasbacks, and also scoters.

Part of the attraction is the sea itself—375 square miles with a 115-mile shoreline, the largest inland body of water west of the Rockies, formed when the mighty Colorado burst its man-made channels in 1905 and rampaged for two years. At 228 feet below sea level it is one of the lowest spots in the United States, also one of the hottest and driest (rainfall can be less than an inch a year).

The lake is supported now mostly by runoff from irrigated farmlands, water of dubious quality, carrying agricultural chemicals and having a high saline content—30 percent saltier than seawater—with an interesting side effect. Barnacles introduced unintentionally by seaplanes during World War II have thrived and are relished as food by ruddy ducks. But water quality requires continuous monitoring.

Coyotes, raccoons, and cottontail rabbits are the most common mammals. Kit foxes, bobcats and badgers are here too but not in large numbers.

Trails are limited due to lack of land area. The best way to see the refuge is to take the interpretive hiking trail to Rock Hill, climbing the hill for a beautiful overview to the Superstition Mountains to the southwest and the Chocolate Mountains on the northeast.

But birds don't respect refuge boundaries and several other places should be visited, too (see below).

How to get there: From San Diego take Route 8 east to El Centro, Route 86 north to Brawley, Route 111 north to Sinclair Road, then left six miles to refuge.

Open: Daylight hours. Office 7–3:30 weekdays.

Best times to visit: September-October and January through April (a fall hunting program keeps parts off-limits to afford quiet sanctuary).

What to see: Great variety and sometimes spectacular numbers of waterfowl, shorebirds, songbirds, plus occasional odd visitors from Mexico. Occasional endangered Yuma clapper rails and Aleutian Canada geese.

What to do: Observation platform; picnicking; bird-watching—to cover entire area, take refuge Rock Hill trail; then stop by Morton Bay, Alamo River Delta, and Red Hill Marina, all marked as one goes east from the refuge on Sinclair Road, north on Garst Road and follow it to Red Hill. Photography can be good.

Where to stay: Motels—in Brawley. Campgrounds—at Salton Sea State Recreation Area, 25 miles north; Red Hill County Boat Landing, two miles northwest; Finney-Ramer State Waterfowl Area, 16 miles southeast.

Weather: Summer blisteringly hot (see text).

Points of interest nearby: All campgrounds (above) are good for birding. See also *What to Do* (above). Joshua Tree National Monument, 80 miles north.

For more information: Salton Sea National Wildlife Refuge, P.O. Box 120, Calipatria, California 92233. Phone: (619) 348-5278.

Coachella Valley NWR at Thousand Palms, administered by Salton Sea, was established for a fascinating little creature, the Coachella Valley fringe-toed lizard, endangered because so much of its habitat has been lost to development. It adapts by being literally as comfortable in sand as a fish is in water—able to race across the blistering desert and when threatened with predation or excessive heat, to dive headlong into the sand and disappear. So fragile is its small remaining habitat that the refuge itself is off-limits—but go to the Visitor Center next door to the Coachella Valley Preserve, administered jointly with the California Fish and Game, The Nature Conservancy and others, and learn about (and possibly see) not only one of the lizards but wonderful stands of native palms on a desert oasis, plus good birding on a self-guided trail.

SAN FRANCISCO BAY (California)

Two endangered species coexist precariously in one salt marsh at San Francisco Bay Refuge—California clapper rails, tawny-breasted water birds with clattering calls, that can swim as well as tread the reeds; and the salt-marsh harvest mouse, one of few mammals in the world able to drink saltwater.

Both are visible when high tides force them to the top of the marsh vegetation. Their small numbers contrast with the tremendous concentrations of many of the other wildlife species on this 18,000-plus acres of the country's first urban refuge, which is still being expanded and developed.

Some 70 percent of all the shorebirds in the Pacific Flyway winter or stop here, along with large numbers of waterfowl and wading birds, shorebirds peaking around one million in spring and fall migration and up to 700,000 waterfowl and 30,000 wading birds.

Delicate and beautiful avocets and black-necked stilts are here by the thousands all year, nesting and delighting photographers as they probe for food on and close by the shore. Marbled godwits, willets, western and least sandpipers, short- and long-billed dowitchers do not usually nest but are gone and back so quickly from family chores farther north that their presence on the fertile mudflats is noted at all seasons.

Swift peregrine falcons keep an eye on the wintering shorebirds, sometimes swooping down to pick up a quick meal as visitors watch.

Snowy and great egrets and great blue and black-crowned night herons are common to abundant all year (one small island has a large nesting colony of them), along with pintail ducks, mallards, and, seasonally, gadwalls, scaup, shovelers, cinnamon teal, and canvasbacks.

Black-shouldered kites, those consummate beauties of the raptor clan, hover in hunting flights and nest in the drought-resistant coyote bush, seldom more than 10 feet off the ground. Forster's terns have broods, sometimes 1,700 in a colony, in isolated and protected shore locations, along with Caspian terns—500 or so, rare snowy plovers, and endangered California least terns. Both brown and white pelicans are here seasonally in good numbers.

Harbor seals hunt and produce families as they historically have along the tidal sloughs, hauling out to rest on mudflats at low tide, pups sometimes seen as early as April from the fishing pier.

More than 30 miles of trails are marked out for hikers and cyclists through the narrow 25-mile shoreline of this refuge, which has more land below water than above it. It is a large part of what bay wetland remains and is here mostly as the result of efforts by various citizens' groups, especially the South San Francisco Baylands Refuge Committee, which exerted pressure when rapid development threatened to overtake all. Renamed the Citizens Committee to Complete the Refuge, it has been responsible for adding even more ecologically important land.

Now, though surrounded by fairly dense development, with San Francisco only a 45-minute drive away, it retains a feeling of remoteness (often the result of a haze that obscures distances), and the approachable birds seem to feel it—as do the 15,000 schoolchildren who come with their teachers every year (this refuge has the largest public use program of any in the country).

How to get there: From San Francisco take Route 101 south to Route 84, which is the Dumbarton Bridge. Cross the bridge and exit the freeway, following Thornton Avenue .5 mile south. To get to the Environmental Education Center continue south to Route 237, then follow Taylor Road northeast to the Center.

Open: Daylight hours. Visitor Center 10–5 daily. Office 8–5 weekdays. Education Center 9–4 weekdays.

Best times to visit: September through April offers most wildlife diversity.

What to see: Shore- and wading birds, waterfowl, black-shouldered kites, harbor seals.

What to do: Driving and walking routes; observation platforms; photography; fishing from piers for stripers, sturgeon, sharks, others.

Where to stay: Motels—numerous in San Francisco and nearby. Campgrounds—closest are Sunol Regional Wilderness, at Fremont, and Del Valle Regional Park, near Livermore.

Points of interest nearby: Golden Gate National Recreation Area, including Muir Woods National Monument, 14 miles north of San Francisco; Coyote Hills Regional Park, just north of refuge; Cargill Salt Company, solar salt production, adjacent to refuge.

For more information: San Francisco Bay National Wildlife Refuge, P.O. Box 524, Newark, California 94560. Phone: (510) 792–0222.

Other refuges administered by San Francisco Bay:

Antioch Dunes—first refuge established for an endangered insect and plants, the Lange's metalmark butterfly and the beautiful yellow Contra Costa wallflower and Antioch Dunes evening primrose. Public use limited to a few conducted tours through the year—ask at office.

Castle Rock—a 14-acre island offshore from Crescent City, stopover for the entire population of endangered Aleutian Canada geese, also important seabird colony with murres and four species of marine mammals, including threatened Steller's sea lions. No public access.

Ellicott Slough—119 acres with no public access, set aside to preserve habitat for the endangered Santa Cruz long-toed salamander.

Farallon—a group of small islands 26 miles west of San Francisco forming the largest continental seabird colony south of Alaska. More than 200,000 birds summer here, including breeding Cassin's auklets, murres, oystercatchers, puffins, and others, along with 7,000 seals and sea lions. It is closely protected and patrolled with no public access. Several bay area groups sponsor annual observation boat trips offshore.

Humboldt Bay—established for the black brant, of which almost the entire western population of some 200,000 stops by here to feed on ellgrass (its only food) during migration. Other waterfowl and shorebirds occur here in good numbers. Several hundred harbor seals haul out here and have their pups in midwinter adjacent to the refuge. Trails and other visitor facilities are planned; for recent word on this, contact Humboldt Bay National Wildlife Refuge, Route 1, Box 76, Loleta, California 95551. Phone: (707) 733–5406.

Marin Islands—two small islands off San Rafael with substantial nesting colonies of herons and egrets. A new refuge with no visitor access, but tours are possible in the future.

Salinas River—a 518-acre coastal wetland northeast of Monterey, with the endangered Smith's blue butterfly, brown pelican and breeding grounds for the rare snowy plover. Open but with extremely limited facilities.

San Pablo Bay—11,697 acres of marsh and open water north of Oakland established primarily as rest and feeding area for canvasback ducks. More than half the Pacific Coast population can winter here, with rafts of 5,000 a common sight; also good shorebird populations as well as clapper rails and the harvest mouse. Open daylight hours but extremely limited visitor facilities; it's a 2.5-mile walk to Lower Tubbs Island from parking area 10 miles west of Vallejo on Highway 37.

SAN LUIS
★
•Fresno

SAN LUIS REFUGE COMPLEX (California)

Waterfowl and shorebirds flock together in spectacular numbers here along with stately sandhill cranes, bald eagles, and a wonderful variety of species in a natural reserve covering more than 100,000 acres.

The sights of these masses of birds on the water or taking wing, their calls filling the air, against a sparkling marsh amid gently rolling grasslands can be breathtaking, the wilderness atmosphere so total there is no sound not generated by nature itself.

Up to a million migrant and wintering ducks and geese can be here—mallards, green-winged teal, pintails, ring-necked and shoveler ducks, and snow, Ross', white-fronted, and Canada geese, including up to 3,500 of the threatened Aleutian strain. Sometimes Ross' geese—half the world population—are on Merced Refuge, along with cackling Canadas and up to 15,000 sandhill cranes, the largest wintering population in California, taking to the air in great bugling groups.

Shorebirds and others can be equally remarkable—in a good year up to 100,000 long-billed dowitchers, 250,000 western and least sandpipers, 75,000 dunlins, 70,000 black-necked stilts, and 12,000 long-billed curlews, as well as 20,000 marsh wrens, up to 200 burrowing owls, 500 kestrels, and one million blackbirds, including the Brewer's, yellow-headed, red-winged, and tricolored.

Among the raptors, 150 beautiful black-shouldered kites sometimes adorn a single clump of trees—with other birds of prey equally notable. A trip around the auto-tour route at dusk on San Luis may pass 50 or 60 perched along five miles of fence posts.

This is one of the few places in California where threatened Swainson's hawks are readily seen and photographed from March to September. Harriers and red-tailed hawks, and merlins in warm months, commonly soar and hunt over fields and marshes. Bald eagles come when the waterfowl are here, and swift peregrine and prairie falcons are seen then on a daily basis. Great horned and barn owls are abundant.

Look for yellow-billed magpies along the Salt Slough on San Luis. California quail are common on San Luis and pheasants on all units; Belding's savannah sparrows (threatened) at Merced; and black phoebes, white-crowned sparrows, ash-throated flycatchers, mockingbirds, and western meadowlarks are on all, as are great blue herons and snowy and great egrets.

Coyotes hunt the marsh edges at Kesterson and San Luis, and California ground squirrels and cottontails are everywhere.

A small herd of Tule elk—smallest of North American elk but still imposing (adult males can weigh 700 pounds with antlers four feet across) is on San Luis. Once they darkened the Central Valley, according to old accounts, before market hunting brought them close to extinction. They were saved partly through the efforts of an early cattle baron, Henry Miller, an immigrant butcher who took the name because it appeared on his ticket west and ended up owning much of the land between here and Oregon.

Miller paid hunters to bring elk and release them alive on his property. Now there are almost 3,000 in herds around the state. Their nucleus herd browses inside a 750-acre protected area on San Luis where they "bugle" during the rutting (mating) season and occasionally charge visitors who get too close to the enclosure.

Pairs of the endangered San Joaquin kit fox and also the giant garter snake are here in small but stable numbers.

The complex is made up of San Luis, Merced, and Kesterson refuges plus the new San Joaquin River refuge, planned as 10,000 acres in the San Joaquin River floodplain—36 miles of riparian habitat sheltering nesting ducks, greater sandhill cranes, Aleutian Canada geese, white pelicans, Swainson's hawks, and one of the largest populations of threatened tricolored blackbirds in California, among others; plus the Grassland Wildlife Management Area, a collection of easements on privately owned seasonal wetlands and grasslands covering more than 40,000 acres. Now officially included in the Western Hemisphere Shorebird Reserve Network, it offers fantastic birding.

Kesterson is 12,000-plus acres where a visitor must walk to see things—but it's worth it. Herons and egrets nest. The vernal pools are spectacular—these are seasonal wetland pools that evaporate slowly March through May with multicolored wildflower communities adapted to their cycle, as well as California tiger salamanders, and preceding the flowers a bloom of invertebrate life that can be impressive in itself—bright red quarter-sized tadpole shrimp, for example. Most vernal pools have been lost to agriculture; probably most of the largest and best left are on Kesterson.

(Kesterson received considerable publicity when selenium contamination from surrounding farmlands caused death and deformities among nesting waterfowl. The 1,200 acres of evaporation ponds that caused the problems have been filled in and are being monitored but no further reproduction problems have been seen.)

These refuges and management areas represent 40 percent of the wetlands remaining in California's Central Valley (largely seasonal wetlands, often dry in the summer and less interesting then, though still with significant raptor and diverse songbird populations). While similar, each has significant distinctions setting it apart from the others, so if at all possible one should plan to visit all of them (except for the San Joaquin River, which has no visitor use as yet). For the Grasslands, see directions below; tours are led seasonally. For information call the Grassland Water District at (209) 826–5188.

How to get there: From Los Banos: to San Luis—go eight miles north on Mercey Springs Road/Highway 165 to Wolfsen Road, turn right there 2.5 miles to entrance. To Merced—go east 18 miles on Highway 152 to Highway 59, left there seven miles to Sandy Mush Road, left there eight miles to refuge entrance. To Kesterson—go north on Mercey Springs Road/Highway 165 to Highway 140, left there seven miles to refuge entrance. To Grasslands—go 3.5 miles north on Mercey Springs Road/Highway 165, left on Santa Fe Grade Road to Highway 140; these 11 miles go through the heart of the wetlands area (snow geese and shorebirds concentrate here in midwinter).

Open: Half hour before sunrise to the half hour after sunset. Office 8–4:30 weekdays.

What to see: Waterfowl; shorebirds; raptors including bald eagles and Swainson's hawks; songbirds; Tule elk.

What to do: Auto-tour routes (except on Kesterson); observation tower; photograph (pit blinds can be reserved except in hunting season); fishing for catfish, striped bass, green sunfish (handicapped access site at San Luis). Hunting permitted on parts of Kesterson, San Luis and Merced in state waterfowl season on Wednesdays and weekends mid-October to early January.

Where to stay: Motels—in Los Banos, also Santa Nella (northwest of Los Banos on

I-5). Campgrounds—near Los Banos, also San Luis State Recreation Area, 20 miles southwest.

Weather: Summers hot, dry; winters mild, sometimes rainy with periods of dense "Tule fog" (especially at Merced).

Points of interest nearby: The Santa Fe Grade Road north of Los Banos, surround by wetlands and marsh vegetation, excellent birding—and the refuge is 2.5–3 hours from the Pacific Ocean, Kings Canyon and Yosemite National Parks, Monterey, and San Francisco.

For more information: San Luis National Wildlife Refuge Complex, P.O. Box 2176, Los Banos, California 93635. Phone: (209) 826–3508.

TIJUANA SLOUGH
(California)

San Diego

TIJUANA SLOUGH

One of the last and best remaining estuarine habitats in southern California in this 1,056-acre refuge shelters a long and wonderful list of birds (over 350 species and still counting), including several endangered and threatened species that can be seen readily here.

It is part of the Tijuana River National Estuarine Research Reserve with a Visitor Center administered jointly with the state parks department for the National Estuarine Reserve. Trails go into varied habitats supported on this relatively small refuge— beach, mudflats, estuary, lagoons, riparian, and some remnant coastal upland sage scrub.

Tijuana Slough was established primarily for several endangered and threatened species:

The light-footed clapper rail has lost almost all its habitat except here and on two other small refuges administered by Tijuana Slough: Sweetwater and Seal Beach. Best way to see it here is to visit during monthly winter high tides and scan the marsh from Sea Coast Drive, the northwest refuge boundary.

The California least tern also nests at these three refuges. At Tijuana it nests behind dunes parallel to the beach and can be seen from the beach (visitors restricted from entering the fragile dunes).

California brown pelicans—common to abundant in late summer and fall; see from the beach near the Tijuana River mouth.

Least Bell's vireo—nests in relatively inaccessible riparian areas, hard to see (ask at office).

Belding's savannah sparrow—breeds in summer in pickleweed, easy to see (ask at office).

Salt marsh bird's beak—an endangered plant related to the snapdragon, hard to see (ask at office).

Hundreds of shorebirds forage at the river's mouth, a real birding hot spot from late summer through early spring. They include marbled godwits, snowy plovers, willets, and western sandpipers, best seen from the Interpretive Trail.

The best time for a wide variety of birds is during fall migration—September through November—and the best place is from trails through the varied habitats.

To get to the refuge office/Visitor Center from San Diego, take I-5 south to the Coronado Avenue exit, west on Coronado to Fourth Street, left there to Caspian Way, right there to traffic circle, left there into parking lot. Hours 8–4 weekdays (plans for possible weekend openings). For another good birding place, go straight on Hollister Avenue from Coronado I-5 exit to Sunset, then right to the river and bird around Myers Ranch County Park. At the end of Sunset is the refuge east boundary, good for songbirds and raptors.

For more information: Tijuana Slough National Wildlife Refuge, P.O. Box 335, 301 Caspian Way, Imperial Beach, California 91933. Phone: (619) 575–1290.

Also administered by Tijuana Slough:

Sweetwater Marsh—315 acres of endangered species habitat surrounding the wonderful Visitor Center, operated by the city of Chula Vista. This tiny bit, essentially all that is left of the once-great salt marshes around San Diego Bay, was created out of a court-ordered settlement of a lawsuit over the planned development of a flood-control channel, hotel, and highway-widening project. For that reason it is cherished and visitation limited to established trails, overlooks, and conducted field trips from which the endangered least tern, Belding's savannah sparrow, light-footed clapper rail, and others might be seen. The Visitor Center includes among many other interesting exhibits a shark and stingray petting pool, a burrowing owl aviary, and an especially well-stocked bookstore. To get there take Chula Vista E Street exit off I-5 and go to west end of E Street where shuttle bus runs from parking lot Tuesday through Sunday 10–5.

Seal Beach—911 acres near Long Beach superimposed on a U.S. Navy weapons station, established to preserve wetland complex. Closed to public access.

Hawaiian and Pacific
Islands

The Hawaiian Islands in the mid-Pacific Ocean, nearly 2,400 miles from the nearest continental landmass, are among the most beautiful and idyllic on the face of the earth. High volcanic mountains and lush green valleys are surrounded by green crystalline waters, with fine weather all year, ranging from an average 74 degrees in February to 80 in September, varying but little from day to night.

Fourteen national wildlife refuges are located in Hawaii and other Pacific islands. All those on the populated Hawaiian Islands protect endangered birds; Northwestern Hawaiian Islands and Central and South Pacific Refuges support endangered species and large nesting seabird colonies.

On the remote and mostly unpopulated "out" islands are some of the largest seabird colonies in the world—up to 10 million albatrosses, frigatebirds, shearwaters, boobies, sooty and fairy terns, and petrels. There are also four endemic species of land birds—the Nihoa finch and millerbird and the Laysan finch and duck—and vital habitat for the endangered monk seal, a marine mammal unique to the Hawaiian Islands.

Ninety percent of Pacific green sea turtles nest on one of these remote atolls.

When Captain Cook first visited Hawaii in 1778, there were about 75 species of birds here that were found nowhere else in the world. Of these, 20 have become extinct and more than half the rest are threatened or endangered. So many exotics—both plant and animal—have been introduced that on the populated islands one generally must go to places over 1,500 feet in elevation, preferably on forested land, to see native plants and birds. Most of those visible at lower elevations have been introduced.

The limited amount of available land is at such a premium that refuges sometimes must make do with what is left in the more populous centers. On Oahu, for example, one Pearl Harbor unit is 36.6 acres adjacent to a landfill. The unit contains a small but precious bit of wetland, where the endangered Hawaiian stilt finds sanctuary.

Kilauea Point on the island of Kauai is probably the most interesting refuge open to the public. Albatrosses sail along eye-to-eye with visitors and nest behind headquarters. Red-footed boobies and wedge-tailed shearwaters pair off. Red-tailed and white-tailed tropicbirds court in graceful flights, long tails streaming, and there are green sea turtles, dolphins, and sometimes whales.

Naturalist visitors also may enjoy the beautiful state parks where there are trails and camping; national parks where volcanic activity is evident; and dozens of hiking trails throughout the islands. There is excellent material available on these at bookstores and park and refuge offices, including the information-packed *Atlas of Hawaii*, by the University of Hawaii, which also produces a booklet on Hawaiian National Parks; a bird booklet by the Hawaiian Audubon Society; and a booklet that describes the hiking trails. Other information is available from the State Department of Land and National Resources, 1151 Punchbowl Street, Honolulu, Hawaii 96813. Several good booklets have been published by the state and U.S. Interior departments on Hawaii's endangered birds, plants, and wildlife.

There are camping areas, lovely drives, and pleasant natural areas within a short distance of almost any place on these islands, especially as one gets away from the large airports and population centers. Air shuttles commute regularly among the various islands, and some have stops away from the main airports.

The refuges on the main islands, other than those on Kauai, are not generally intended for public access; they harbor endangered species, are not very large, and public access would disturb the creatures the refuges are there to protect. Refuge lands are gradually being added, however, and existing refuges developed, so the traveler should check for recent information with the Hawaiian and Pacific Islands National Wildlife Refuge Complex, 300 Ala Moana Boulevard, Room 5302, P.O. Box 50167, Honolulu, Hawaii 96850. Phone: (808) 541-1201.

HAWAII

Hawaii

HAWAII
1 HAKALAU FOREST
2 KAUAI REFUGE COMPLEX
3 PEARL HARBOR & JAMES C. CAMPBELL

HAKALAU FOREST ★
Hilo

HAKALAU FOREST (Hawaii)

Dense tangles of rainforest and tropical birds and plants to be seen nowhere else populate Hakalau, a name appropriately meaning "many perches."

Tiny endangered orange akepas and little yellow akiapola'aus flit about a virgin forest canopy of koa trees believed to be 300–500 years old, with trunks six feet through. And the native ohia trees flower all year, attracting insects and therefore both insectivorous and nectar-sipping birds.

Native forest birds are abundant—brilliant red iiwis, dark crimson apapanes, yellow-green amakihis—birds that have been largely eliminated from the rest of the Hawaiian Islands by development and introduction of exotic species.

The canopy is atwitter with them (though they are often so high it is easier to hear than to see them). Endangered Hawaii creepers cling to tree trunks, and endangered 'Ios, or Hawaiian hawks, prospect from lower branches. Endangered pueos (short-eared owls) hunt for small prey in open areas. Fallen logs can be gardens in themselves where dozens of ferns and other tropical plants, many of these rare also, sprout in decayed vegetation.

This is not an easy place to see. Even the drier highlands have 100-plus inches of rain a year—up to 300 inches as the terrain descends. The whole refuge is so wet even in the dry season (June to September) that refuge staff wear rubber boots all the time. It is almost two hours by 4-wheel-drive vehicle from any hotel or gas station.

Until recently it was open only by special permit but as of early 1992, the Maulua tract is open the last weekend of every month to hikers and birders. However, it is still necessary to reserve if possible three weeks ahead. This is for safety: the refuge needs to know how many enter so they can be sure all who enter come out.

This is real wilderness. The road enters the refuge at 6600 feet, then descends to 5,200 feet. The lower reaches of the refuge (down to 2,500 feet) are densely forested and have no roads or trails. Parts are unexplored and all but impenetrable. Take a compass if venturing off-road, and wear raingear.

But it is a wonderful place, without which many of the hundreds of rare plants and birds here would almost certainly become extinct.

To get there from Hilo (where one can reserve 4-wheel drives) turn north off Saddle Road onto Mauna Kea Summit Road; go two miles, turn right onto Keanakolu (dirt) Road; go 15.5 miles along east flank of Mauna Kea to refuge sign and gate to Maulua tract. Hilo has hotels and Mauna Kea State Park at Pohakaloa, extremely rustic cabins. See Volcanoes National Park while you're here (65 miles south).

For further information: Hakalau Forest National Wildlife Refuge, 154 Waianuenue Avenue, Room 219, Hilo, Hawaii 96720. Phone: (808) 969–9909 (office open 8–4 weekdays).

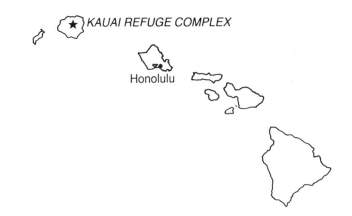

KAUAI REFUGE COMPLEX

Honolulu

KAUAI REFUGE COMPLEX (Hawaii)

Laysan albatrosses face into oceanic trade winds and sail on seven-foot wingspreads eye-to-eye with visitors at spectacular Kilauea Point Refuge, located along an extinct volcanic rim on one of the most beautiful islands in the world.

Red-tailed tropicbirds fly in graceful aerial courtship dances, always in counterclockwise circles, long tail feathers streaming behind. Graceful white-tailed tropicbirds also nest. Red-footed boobies pair off, sometimes 1,600 nests covering the hillside. Albatrosses raise families in grassy areas behind refuge headquarters—one of the few places this impressive bird can be seen on land.

Wedge-tailed shearwaters dig nest burrows on the refuge slopes. (There are 1,000 nests between Kilauea Point headquarters and the historic lighthouse.) Many are easily seen, and the moaning calls of the birds can be heard everywhere as they incubate and later brood their young.

Magnificent frigatebirds soar overhead, often swooping to steal the catch of other seabirds. Nene geese, once nearly extinct, are here year-round.

Visitors can look over into crystalline green waters and see spinner dolphins, endangered green sea turtles, endangered monk seals and humpback whales. One whale gave birth just below the trail, observed by visitors.

The wildlife here, much of it easily observed, and the dramatic scenery, steep cliffs rising from the sea, are like no other refuge in the United States, and the island of Kauai, waterfalls dropping into limpid coves, mountains rising from the sea, is one of the most beautiful in the world. (The movie *South Pacific* was filmed here.)

585

Points of interest nearby: Na Pali State Park—trails, isolated beaches, beautiful views; Anini County Park, great snorkeling at Hawaii's largest reef; Waimea Canyon—about 80 miles, stunning, called the Grand Canyon of the Pacific.

For more information: Kauai National Wildlife Refuge Complex, P.O. Box 87, Kilauea, Kauai, Hawaii 96754. Phone: (808) 828–1413.

Also part of the Kauai Complex are:

Hanalei NWR—917 acres of river bottom maintained for the Hawaiian stilt, coot, moorhen, and duck, all endangered; no access to the refuge proper but visitors can see these and other birds from a county road that transects the refuge—and the enchanting view from the refuge overlook is probably one of the most photographed in Hawaii. It is also possible to rent a kayak and go through the refuge along the Hanalei River (but not land).

To view Hanalei continue on the Kuhio Highway from the lighthouse five miles to Princeville and past it a mile, staying on the main road. There's a good chance to see Hawaiian waterbirds year-round and other migratory shorebirds, including golden plovers, September to March by continuing on the main road past a covered bridge, turning left on a county road that dead-ends shortly afterward (the turnaround can be muddy).

Huleia—Another river valley refuge for endangered water birds but covered with dense jungle and mangrove swamp so less visible. A beautiful overlook surveys mountains, bluffs, and historic Menehune fish pond. Kayaks can be rented in Nawiliwili Harbor to paddle up the Huleia River, which flanks the refuge (but don't land here, either). To get there follow road signs from Lihue toward Nawiliwili Harbor and then to the fish pond overlook.

PACIFIC/REMOTE ISLANDS COMPLEX (Hawaii)

Some of the largest concentrations of seabirds anywhere inhabit these tiny, remote, mostly unpopulated island refuges that span more than 12,000 square miles in the Pacific Ocean in both northern and southern hemispheres.

They are crowded together in noisy, sometimes quarrelsome congregations that can cover every available space, and it is hard to see how the birds can sort themselves out and parents find their own.

More than 10 million frigatebirds, sooty terns, albatrosses, shearwaters, boobies, tropicbirds, sooty and fairy terns, and petrels find homes on these little mid-ocean dots of land. Some come down only to nest and then leave again for a lifetime spent almost entirely on the wing (albatrosses don't return to nest until they are seven years old).

The islands are vital habitat also for endangered Hawaiian monk seals, nesting grounds for green sea turtles, and home for literally millions of marine species.

Oldest of these as a refuge is *Hawaiian Islands NWR*, an island chain a thousand miles long encompassing only 1,769 acres of land but almost 300,000 acres of reefs and water, designated in 1909 by President Theodore Roosevelt. Before then visitors had slaughtered birds for their decorative feathers and introduced competitive or predatory creatures such as rabbits and rats with devastating effect. They still are recovering.

There are remnants of prehistoric occupation by early Polynesians, and fascinating geologic forms. Tremendous underwater volcanic peaks rise in sheer cliffs without beaches; there are coral-encrusted collapsed cones in the atolls, and low sandy beaches surrounded by submerged coral. The Nihoa millerbird and finch and the Laysan teal and finch are found nowhere else in the world but in this group, as are unique plants such as the Nihoa palm.

Other refuges are Baker Island, Howland Island, Jarvis Island, and Johnston, Midway, and Rose atolls. Howland was the destination of Amelia Earhart when she disappeared in 1937. Rose Atoll in American Samoa (15 degrees below the Equator) is one of the smallest atolls in the world, less than 20 acres protected by reefs, nesting area for green sea turtles and 15 seabird and shorebird species as well as giant clams.

One of the most abundant birds found on the remote refuges is the sooty tern, believed to fly for two to three years without touching down either on land or water until it returns to its nesting colony. Up to one million sooties can be present on Laysan. One of the loveliest birds found here is the white or fairy tern, which lays a single egg on a bare branch or rock with no nest construction whatever. Somehow both egg and young manage to stay in place and survive.

The black-footed albatross is abundant on several of the islands, as is the Laysan albatross; and present at various times are black and brown noddies, wedge-tailed and Christmas shearwaters, red-tailed tropicbirds, several species of boobies, petrels, and many others.

As notable as the tremendous size of these assemblages is their life patterns. The albatross relies on an eight-foot wingspread to balance so delicately on air currents that it can glide for miles at sea without seeming to move more than a few feathers, and its remarkable homing ability is such that it can return 3,000 miles over unmarked seas in 10 days. Along with shearwaters and petrels, albatrosses have tubular nostrils thorugh which they excrete salt, making it possible to drink seawater safely.

Tiny swift petrels ride on air cushions inches above ocean swells and burrow deep nests in the ground. There are gray-backed terns, whose eggs can have pink yolks; streamer-tailed tropicbirds, said to be able to fly backwards; and frigate or man-o'-war birds, earning their nickname from a piratical habit of stealing other birds' fish.

Birds that nest in Alaska's far north stop here for the winter—golden plovers, bristle-thighed curlews, wandering tattlers.

Access to most of these remote places is difficult, often dangerous, to boatmen as well as to the sensitive natural inhabitants. All are closed to public access. Special use permits may be approved for researchers and photojournalists. But except for rare calls by special permit and by refuge staff itself, most of the refuges are seldom visited except by their avian inhabitants.

For further information: Pacific/Remote Islands National Wildlife Refuge Complex, 300 Ala Moana Blvd., Honolulu, Hawaii 96813.

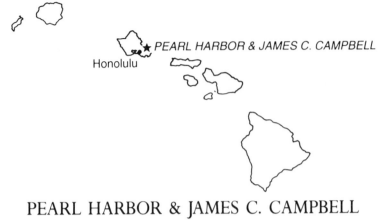

PEARL HARBOR & JAMES C. CAMPBELL
(Hawaii)

Two small but significant refuges on Oahu—61-acre Pearl Harbor and 143-acre James C. Campbell—were established specifically for protection of the endangered Hawaiian coot, Hawaiian gallinule or moorhen, Hawaiian duck or koloa, and black-necked stilt. Migrants that use the refuges include Pacific golden plovers, ruddy turnstones, wandering tattlers, and sanderlings. Other species such as the cattle egret, black-crowned night heron, barred dove, cattle egret, and spotted munia also are here.

The two Pearl Harbor units on the south shore inside Pearl Harbor naval base protect large nesting stilt groups. Neither has public facilities but one, containing a 36.6-acre wetland next to a landfill, can be viewed from behind a fence built to protect the birds.

The James C. Campbell units on the northeastern shore are used mainly by the coots and stilts, moorhens and koloas. It is open to educational study groups by reservation between August 15 and February 15.

Administered with these is 45-acre Kakahaia Refuge on Molokai, also established to protect the endangered stilt and coot. It is closed but a small section next to the ocean is leased to the county as a picnic area; from here visitors can see some of the birds.

Related places of interest for Oahu visitors include excellent snorkling and viewing in Hanauma Bay; a state marine sanctuary with dazzling tropical fish; and several birding locales described in the booklets "Hawaii's Birds," by the Hawaii Audubon Society, and "Hawaii's Endangered Waterbirds."

For further information: U.S. Fish and Wildlife Service, P.O. Box 340, Haleiwa, Hawaii 96712. Phone: (808) 637–6330.

Alaska

A laska comes from the Aleut Eskimo word meaning "great land," a name given it when few if any persons could more than imagine its greatness. But they imagined correctly. To see a small part of it even today—a glimpse of a herd of caribou crowding one another with spreading yard-wide antlers; a cliffside literally covered with tens of thousands of seabird nests overhanging the sea; the scream of a bald eagle high in the air over a streambed where hundreds of thousands of salmon are struggling upstream; the vastness of miles and miles of Arctic tundra awash with multihued wildflowers in the spring, blanketed with scarlet and gold moss and lichen in the fall; mountains and rivers, some of the highest and longest in the world, that have been wild and undisturbed since their cataclysmic creation by natural forces— is to sense something of the greatness of the whole.

The tundra is one of the most fragile environments on earth. A lichen may take a century to regrow after being grazed by caribou. Battle scars still mar the Alaska landscape a half century after World War II.

Moose, reindeer, Arctic foxes, and polar bears make their home here; also great Kodiak bears and at least representative numbers of some of the wild populations that have largely disappeared from the southern United States—lynx, wolverines, martens, and timber wolves. There are also mountain goats and sheep, and many others. Whales, seals, and walruses swim offshore, and upstream five species of North Pacific salmon spawn.

Some of the great seabird colonies of the world are here—millions of puffins, murres, fulmars, cormorants—as well as shorebirds and passerines and waterfowl that come here to nest in the short northern summer and then return to spend the fall and winter over the entire United States, and in fact the whole hemisphere. Some fly 20,000 miles round-trip. This ecologically fragile land is the nursery on

which waterfowl and other bird populations of much of this part of the world depend
for their survival.

Alaska is by far our largest state—more than twice the size of Texas. From its
eastern end to the western tip of the Aleutian archipelago, it stretches almost over
a map of the contiguous United States. It has a glacier the size of Rhode Island. It
encompasses four time zones. Its weather can be warm and sunny in summer—
Anchorage and the Kenai Peninsula often have conditions not unlike the midwestern
United States—but near the sea it can be shrouded much of the time in fog, and
above the Arctic Coast there are always ice floes. Winters are long and cold with
deeply subzero temperatures and wind chills down to minus 126 degrees. Daylight,
which lasts around the clock in midsummer, disappears entirely, leaving only the
aurora borealis to light up the darkness in fantastic flickering hues of rose, green,
and gold.

Refuges are represented in almost every significant natural section of Alaska, from
65-acre St. Lazaria Island, a vital home for oceanic birds, to the 19.5 million-acre
Arctic National Wildlife Refuge with its great Porcupine River caribou herds. The
Aleutian Islands with their sea otters and other marine mammals stretch over a
thousand miles along that southwestern archipelago; *Izembek* is at the head of that
chain, where the entire world population of black brant can be seen during fall
migration. *Kenai* is located on the Kenai Peninsula, where moose and many other
wild creatures makes their homes in a huge de facto wilderness just two hours'
drive from Anchorage. *Kodiak* encompasses most of Kodiak Island off the Alaskan
Peninsula, home of the great Kodiak brown bear. *Yukon Delta* Refuge faces the Bering
Sea and is one of the world's great nesting colonies of waterfowl, shorebirds, and
songbirds; and there is 3.3 million-acre *Nunivak Island,* where shaggy musk-oxen live.

The large refuges need to be large. While Alaskan wildlife populations of some
species are abundant, the state could not be described as teeming with wildlife in
the usual sense. The climate, short growing season, and general ecological conditions
are too harsh for that. An animal in this northern area requires a larger territory
to survive than the same species in a more hospitable clime. So while wildlife occur
in good numbers, the population is spread over a wide area. One does not simply
set foot on one of these refuges and automatically find great herds and flocks of
wild creatures presenting themselves. As at any refuge, wildlife observation requires
time and patience—perhaps even a bit more here.

Many refuges are not easy to see because of weather conditions and relative
inaccessibility. Kenai, on the Alaska highway system with numerous hiking trails,
canoe routes, and campsites, is fairly easy to visit. *Tetlin* also has road access.

For the others it can be quite a different story. Plan on coming between May and
October—the rest of the year is too harsh for all but the hardiest. Even then it is
not always simple. On most there are few if any roads, few if any places to stay
close by. Access to some is not possible at all—as in the case of rocky nesting islands
surrounded by treacherous waters. To many refuges, access is by hiking or charter

airplane only. This can be costly and "bush" pilots are not invariably reliable—
sometimes because the conditions in which they are flying are not reliable. Fog and
rain especially near the sea can stop flying for weeks at a time.

Nature observation and hiking are among the most rewarding activities. Backpacking can be one of the best (though not the only) ways of doing this. Camping
is permitted in most places, although on most refuges a visitor needs to be aware
of native inholdings where inhabitants subsist on the land as in past centuries and
where trespassers are not always welcome (take a map and compass). A wonderful
trip on some refuges is rafting down the slowly meandering rivers, stopping to camp
on sandbars along the way and hike out around the area. Bring your own equipment,
or arrange for it with an outfitter.

Pack out what you pack in—do not bury garbage or debris. Leave a travel plan
with someone you will notify on your return. Do not disturb cabins or food caches
unless in emergency—someone else may be depending on those supplies.

Fishing can be some of the best in the world for salmon, trout, grayling, sheefish—
"tarpon of the north"—and others. (But don't compete with brown bears during
the salmon runs. They don't take kindly to this. And release all you do not plan to
consume immediately. Be aware, too, that "hook and release" is frowned on as
disrespectful misuse of the resource by many local Eskimo cultures.)

Photography can be marvelous with the long hours of daylight, especially for the
almost indescribable grandeur of Alaskan scenery (though coastal areas can be misty
much of the time). Little Arctic ground squirrels, unused to human contact, can be
confiding. But success in wildlife photography, here as elsewhere, goes to the patient.

Much of Alaska is a water-dominated area where ceaseless battle is waged between
higher animals, including humans, and insects. It is impossible to take too much
insect repellent.

Cross-country skiing and snowshoeing are possible for those not frozen out by
Thanksgiving. A transcendent experience in March is to go out on the snow by
dogsled and watch a whole hemisphere of night sky illuminated with constantly
moving multihued northern lights.

On any trip, plan as far in advance as possible and consult with refuge staff, who
can give valuable advice on everything from bear avoidance to how to equip a survival
kit.

All this should be said so that one will not go to an Alaskan refuge unprepared.
The visitor who is willing and able to take nature on its own terms, expecting no
more special convenience for his comfort than is offered the wild inhabitants, will
find this one of the most glorious places on earth (especially in summer and when
the sun is shining).

There are many places of related interest for one planning a trip to Alaska, prime
among them being Denali National Park, with hiking, camping, backpacking, breathtaking scenery, wildlife—everything, and excellent guidebooks for seeing it all. Two
magnificent national forests, the Chugach and Tongass, occupy large parts of southeast

and south-central Alaska. The state parks are among the best in the nation. A clearinghouse for information on all public lands in the state is the Alaska Public Lands Information Center, 605 West Fourth Avenue, Anchorage, Alaska 99501. Phone: (907) 271–2737.

There also are ferry trips to various places, including spectacular Glacier Bay and the Inside Passage up from Seattle. There are raft trips, side trips to the Pribilof Islands and many, many others.

About all of this there is abundant informational material available (though it should be spelled out more clearly that Alaskan tourist costs generally are quite high). The Alaska Geographic Society has a series of beautiful booklets on various sections of the state—Cook Inlet, Admiralty Island, and others. Probably the best and most comprehensive is the fact-filled "Milepost," printed annually by the same publishers, and available at most bookstores. It covers almost every possible subject related to Alaska.

Again, the visitor should contact in advance either the Alaskan regional refuge office in Anchorage, or any of the refuges included therein. Refuge staff members can be extremely helpful in suggesting how to plan a trip best suited to individual wishes and capabilities. The regional refuge office is: U.S. Fish and Wildlife Service, 1011 East Tudor Road, Anchorage, Alaska 99503. Phone (907) 786–3487.

More seabirds nest on *Alaska Maritime* refuges than breed in all the rest of North America—40 million on some 3,000 headlands, islands, islets, spires, and rocks. There are also both sea and land mammals—tens of thousands of sea lions, seals, walruses, and sea otters, and on headlands and islands caribou, huge brown bears, Dall sheep, reindeer, furry musk-oxen, Sitka black-tailed deer, and wolves.

The refuge is divided into five units.

The *Aleutian Islands* Unit, a chain of volcanic islands more than 1,000 miles long stretching almost to Siberia, was set aside originally to save the sea otter. It accomplished this and provided sanctuary for many others, too—10 million seabirds in huge nesting groups, eagles, sea lions, caribou, brown bears, reindeer, and others. Birds scarce elsewhere are here in numbers to stagger the imagination. Scenery is spectacular.

The *Bering Sea* Unit includes far-flung islands and headlands between the Aleutians and the Bering Strait, most famous of which are the Pribilofs, largest bird colony in North America with up to three million murres, puffins, and kittiwakes.

The *Chukchi Sea* Unit includes 200,000 acres mostly north of the Arctic Circle, ranging from low barrier islands to high, rocky spires in the western Brooks Range, with a half-million nesting murres and kittiwakes, as well as walruses, polar bears, caribou, grizzly bears, musk-oxen, moose, and Dall sheep.

The *Gulf of Alaska* Unit includes precipitous island seabird colonies.

The *Alaska Peninsula* Unit is 715,000 acres on a small headland and over 800 islands and islets, nesting and resting places for seabirds, and colonies of northern sea lions.

Alaska Peninsula/Becharof Refuge includes the spectacular upper half of the Alaskan peninsula, a scenic and wildlife wonder, more than 3.5 million acres, much of which looks as if no one had ever set foot on it. It has 2,500 to 3,000 brown bears—one of the world's largest concentrations of those huge beasts, gathering around spawning salmon swimming upstream from the world's most valuable and pristine fishery, Bristol Bay.

Eagles are here, northern hawk-owls—a great array of interesting waterfowl and land and seabirds, also caribou, moose, wolves and wolverines, seals, and sea otters.

Becharof Lake is the second-largest lake in Alaska, with islands on which bears are said to den.

The *Arctic* National Wildlife Refuge is the largest refuge in the United States and one of the largest in the world—19.5 million acres, with caribou, grizzly bears, lynx, eagles, wolves, and great flocks of migratory birds that come from the southern 48 states and at least three other continents to breed in the isolation of its north slope tundra.

Winters here have no daylight and summers have no darkness. There are ice floes even in summer, some of the most imposing mountains on the continent, and blankets of wildflowers. A refuge leaflet suggests best times to see wildlife are "from evening until noon the next day."

Innoko is 6,000 square miles of black spruce muskeg, 20,000 lakes, wet meadows, horsetail marsh, and spruce- and birch-covered hills in west-central Alaska where there are timber wolves, moose, black and grizzly bears, and sometimes a quarter-million waterfowl.

The entire world population of Pacific black brant fills the sky over *Izembek* Lagoon in the fall, attracted by the world's largest eelgrass beds there. Virtually all the world's emperor geese come through, as do tens of thousands of other waterfowl and shorebirds. Alaskan brown bears roam widely.

The Arctic Circle passes through the center of *Kanuti*'s 1.4 million interior acres where almost 150 bird species come to nest during the sunlit six months—white-fronted geese, sandhill cranes, Pacific and common loons, tundra and trumpeter swans, golden plovers, and many others. Both black and grizzly bears are here.

In microcosm at *Kenai* are almost every kind of geologic feature and wildlife habitat to be found anywhere in Alaska, and most of its wild creatures, too. Moose browse in willow thickets. Mountain goats skip over peaks. Wolves and coyotes mingle their calls with loons'. Bald eagles fish. This is one of Alaska's most accessible refuges.

Kodiak belongs to the huge Kodiak brown bears that live there, preying on the salmon that fight their way up the streams to spawn from June to October. Sometimes dozens of the huge half-ton or more males may gather along a few miles of streambed. Eagles prey on the fish, too.

Rafting down the meandering rivers of the interior *Koyukuk/Nowitna* refuge complex one might see almost any of the wildlife common to either one: moose, beavers, otters, bears, eagles overhead, even an occasional wolf.

Waterfowl come from five continents to nest on *Selawik's* nutrient-rich wetlands. Black and Alaskan brown bears are here, too, Arctic and red foxes, and moose with six-foot antler spreads. Some 400,000 caribou migrate across the refuge twice a year.

Tetlin is a 700,000-acre pristine river valley holding a diverse ecosystem where black and grizzly bears flourish with timber wolves, caribou, and beavers. Bald and golden eagles, tundra and trumpeter swans, and dozens of waterfowl, shorebirds, and passerine species nest. It is one of two refuges (with Kenai) readily accessible by road.

Huge bull walruses can cover the beaches at Cape Pierce on 4.2 million-acre *Togiak* refuge in southwestern Alaska. Steller's sea lions claim Cape Newenham. Togiak is a breeding and resting area for waterfowl and shorebirds from Russia, Japan, Mexico, South America, New Zealand, and the South Pacific as well as the lower United States.

Millions of waterfowl, shorebirds, and passerines fly every year from six continents to nest and raise young on *Yukon Delta,* which encloses 26 million acres—about the size of Indiana. Some of them fly nonstop over open sea from Australia and islands throughout the South Pacific.

Within *Yukon Flats* Refuge the Yukon River breaks free of canyon walls to spread unconfined for 200 miles in a vast floodplain. These lowland areas carry one of the highest waterfowl nesting densities in North America. By fall millions of birds— pintails, scaup, oldsquaw, and many others—will be staging for the postbreeding return trip to three continents.

Following are birds of special interest found commonly or abundantly at Alaskan Refuges.

Birds common or abundant at seasons indicated:

S: SPRING   s: SUMMER   F: FALL   W: WINTER

Arctic Loon: Arctic s, Kenai Ss, Tetlin Ss
Red-necked Grebe: Kenai sF
Black-footed Albatross: Kodiak SsF
Northern Fulmar: Kodiak SsFW
Sooty Shearwater: Kodiak SsF
Short-tailed Shearwater: Kodiak SsF
Fork-tailed Storm Petrel: Kodiak SsFW
Pelagic Cormorant: Aleutian Islands SsFW, Kodiak SsFW
Red-faced Cormorant: Kodiak SsF

Emperor Goose: Aleutian Islands FW, Izembek SFW, Kodiak SW
Barrow's Goldeneye: Kenai SsF, Kodiak SFW
King Eider: Kodiak SW
Steller's Eider: Izembek SWF, Kodiak SW
Harlequin Duck: Aleutian Islands SFW, Kodiak SsFW
Northern Goshawk: Kenai SsFW, Kodiak SsFW
Bald Eagle: Aleutian Islands SsFW, Izembek SFW, Kenai SsF, Kodiak SsFW, Tetlin
  SsF
Merlin: Arctic s
Spruce Grouse: Kenai SsFW, Tetlin SsF
Willow Ptarmigan: Izembek SsFW, Kenai SsFW, Kodiak SsFW
Rock Ptarmigan: Aleutian Islands SsFW, Kodiak SsFW
White-tailed Ptarmigan: Kenai SsFW
Sandhill Crane: Kenai SF, Tetlin S
Black Oystercatcher: Kodiak SsFW
Wandering Tattler: Arctic s, Kodiak Ss
Black Turnstone: Kodiak Ss
Surfbird: Kodiak S
Rock Sandpiper: Aleutian Islands FW, Izembek SsFW, Kodiak SFW
Red-necked (Northern) Phalarope: Arctic s, Izembek SF, Kenai Ss, Kodiak SsF
Red Phalarope: Arctic s, Izembek SF
Parasitic Jaeger: Aleutian Islands SF, Arctic s
Pomarine Jaeger: Aleutian Islands SF, Arctic s
Long-tailed Jaeger: Arctic s
Mew Gull: Arctic s, Kenai SsF, Kodiak SsFW, Tetlin Ss
Black-legged Kittiwake: Kodiak SsF
Aleutian Tern: Aleutian Islands s
Common Murre: Kodiak SsFW
Pigeon Guillemot: Aleutian Islands SsFW, Kodiak SsFW
Marbled Murrelet: Kodiak SsFW
Ancient Murrelet: Aleutian Islands s
Crested Auklet: Kodiak FW
Tufted Puffin: Kodiak SsF
Horned Puffin: Kodiak SsF
Snowy Owl: Arctic SsFW
Gray Jay: Kenai SsFW, Tetlin SsFW
Boreal Chickadee: Arctic SsFW, Kenai SsF, Tetlin SsFW
American Dipper: Arctic s, Kodiak SsFW
Wheatear: Arctic s
Arctic Warbler: Arctic s
Yellow Wagtail: Arctic s
Bohemian Waxwing: Kenai SsF

Golden-crowned Sparrow: Kenai Ss, Kodiak SsF
Lapland Longspur: Kenai S, Kodiak SsF, Tetlin S
Snow Bunting: Aleutian Islands SsFW, Izembek SFW, Kodiak SsF, Tetlin S
Rosy Finch: Aleutian Islands, SsFW, Izembek SFW
Hoary Redpoll: Arctic SsF, Tetlin SW
Pine Grosbeak: Kodiak SsF

    (*Note*: Many Alaska refuges are still developing complete bird lists; interested birders should consult texts on individual refuges, particularly the Pribilof unit of Alaska Maritime.)

ALASKA

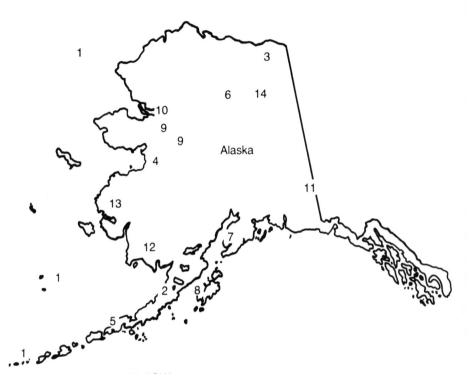

ALASKA
1 ALASKA MARITIME
2 ALASKA PENINSULA / BECHAROF
3 ARCTIC
4 INNOKO
5 IZEMBEK
6 KANUTI
7 KENAI
8 KODIAK
9 KOYUKUK / NOWITNA
10 SELAWIK
11 TETLIN
12 TOGIAK
13 YUKON DELTA
14 YUKON FLATS

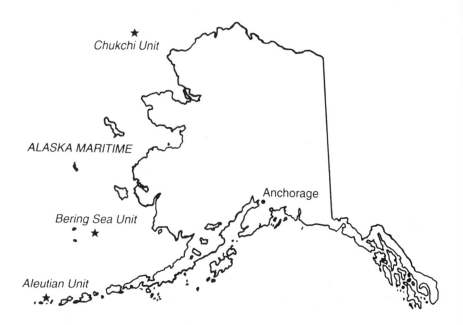

Chukchi Unit

ALASKA MARITIME

Anchorage

Bering Sea Unit

Aleutian Unit

ALASKA MARITIME (Alaska)

Forty million seabirds nest on 3,000 headlands, islands, islets, spires and rocks in the Alaska Maritime National Wildlife Refuges—more than breed in all the rest of North America.

Superimposed on a map of the lower United States, the southeasternmost island of this huge refuge complex would be in Savannah, Georgia, the northernmost would be on the Canadian border, and the westernmost on the California coast. More than half of its 4.5 million acres is in wilderness.

Seabirds gathering in great colonies use specialized nesting sites in every conceivable place—rock ledges, crevices, on boulder rubble, pinnacles, in burrows—adaptations that allow as many birds as possible to group together successfully with each using the least possible amount of space.

There are in addition both sea and land mammals—tens of thousands of sea lions, seals, walrus, and sea otters, and on headlands and islands caribou, brown bears, Dall sheep, reindeer, musk-oxen, Sitka black-tailed deer, and wolves.

The refuge complex is divided into five units.

The *Aleutian Islands* Unit is a chain of volcanic islands more than 1,000 miles long stretching almost to Siberia. On its Pacific side is the Aleutian Trench, a nutrient-rich undersea structure 50 to 100 miles wide and over 25,000 feet deep.

Originally set aside chiefly to bring back the persecuted sea otter from near-extinction, it not only accomplished this but provided sanctuary for many other creatures as well. Ten million seabirds crowd into huge nesting groups, and there are bald eagles, sea lions, caribou, brown bears, reindeer, and others.

The 200-odd islands in the archipelago cover 2.7 million acres, most of which are included in the refuge. Outside contact was first made with the Aleutians in the mid-1700s by Russian explorers who quickly noticed the rich, luxuriant fur of the sea otter, then present in the many tens of thousands. The Russians had a hunting quota, but after the United States acquired Alaska, unrestricted hunting greatly reduced both the otters and the native Aleuts, who were pressed into the traders' service. In 1911 hunting was halted, but by 1913, when the refuge was established, the sea otters' survival seemed all but impossible.

But they have come back. The population is now estimated at well over 60,000. These beautiful, intelligent marine mammals have the world's most valuable fur and interesting habits of floating on their backs while nuzzling their young and cracking open shellfish food with rocks, sometimes anchoring themselves and their young with a ribbon of kelp while taking a nap, shading their eyes with a paw.

Birds scarce elsewhere are here in numbers to stagger the imagination: fulmars, storm-petrels, cormorants, kittiwakes, murres, auklets and puffins in vast colonies along the steep ledges, on beaches, in caves and burrows. The largest known fulmar colony in the world, a million birds, is on Chagulak Island. The world's largest auklet (crested and least) colony is on Kiska. Alaska's largest tufted puffin colony, 100,000 birds, is on tiny Kaligagan. Most of the world's fork-tailed storm petrels are on this refuge complex. And there are hundreds of nesting bald eagles and peregrine falcons along with some gyrfalcons and snowy owls. The Aleutian Canada goose, almost wiped out by introduced Arctic foxes in the Aleutians and islands south of the Alaska Peninsula, is now gradually being restored. There are great numbers of songbirds—multitudes of Lapland longspurs, rosy finches, winter wrens, snow buntings—and rock ptarmigans that nest in summer and change into white plumage to plunge into the snowbanks for winter cover.

Bird life is active throughout the year. Harlequin ducks, Steller's and king eiders, oldsquaws, and most of the world's emperor geese spend the winter. Thousands of shorebirds touch down during migration; and with the proximity of Siberia there are Asiatic species seldom if ever seen elsewhere in the United States—whooper swans, Mongolian plovers, Steller's eagles, long-toed stints, falcated teals, spotted redshanks, smews, and among smaller birds the bramblings, Oriental cuckoos, Siberian rubythroats, Asiatic rose finches, and reed buntings.

Ancient murrelets stage mass migrations of young, tumbling down from burrow nests to the sea when only a few days old. Parakeet and whiskered auklets all raise numbers of offspring, as do red-faced cormorants and many others.

Sea lion colonies are common, as are harbor seals, and walruses occasionally haul out on Amak Island in winter. Fur seals migrate through and so do several species of whales and porpoises.

Introduced reindeer live on Atka. Unimak Island has brown bears, caribou, wolves, wolverines, and numbers of smaller mammals. Three species of salmon spawn. Orchids and lady's slippers, pink Siberian spring beauties, and Kamchatkan rhododendron bloom.

Much of this wildlife abundance as well as the spectacular scenery against which it exists—including still-active volcanoes that spew smoke and steam about the landscape—are seen by few but the wild inhabitants (perhaps one reason why they thrive). This is because most of the islands are difficult to get to, hard to get around when one is there, and sometimes difficult to get out of. In recent years Reeve Aleutian Airlines has scheduled flights to Cold Bay, Adak, Attu, Umnak, and Shemya, but most airfields are in military zones and military clearance is required to go there.

Trips to Attu, westernmost link in the Aleutian chain and a must for birders who wish to pick up the most possible species including stray Asian types, are most often arranged in late May–early June through Attours, 2027 Partridge Lane, Highland Park, Illinois 60035, telephone (312) 831–0207. (Attu, site of the only World War II battle on U.S. soil, is also a National Historic Landmark.)

Weather is mostly in the tolerable range—usually 60 in summer, down to 10 in winter—but the area is subject to violent storms and dense fog that can last for weeks. Clear sunny days are rare. Also, beyond Cold Bay most places have no place to stay (though camping may be permitted).

But all these arrangements must be cleared well in advance. For anyone prepared to be entirely self-sufficient in a wild situation, these can be fascinating places. Further information can be obtained from the Adak office of the Aleutian Islands National Wildlife Refuge Unit, Box 5251 NAS Adak, FPO Seattle, Washington 98791. Phone: (907) 592–2406.

The *Bering Sea* Unit includes far-flung islands and headlands between the Aleutian Islands and the Bering Strait. Topography varies from small, sandy islands like the Sand Islands off the Yukon Delta to large volcanic islands like St. Matthew in the Pribilofs. Some of the most serious potential threats to the seabirds and marine mammals in the islands and headlands of this unit are related to oil development in the outer continental shelf. Oil spills can cause destruction of the birds and their food chain, and increased activities associated with exploration and development may adversely affect marine mammals.

The largest bird colony in North America—up to three million murres, puffins, and red- and black-legged kittiwakes (largest nesting colony of the latter in the world)—is on the Pribilof Islands. These nesting colonies are on the island's layered volcanic cliffs, edged by rocky beaches. There is also a colony of 800,000 northern fur seals on national fisheries' land there. Visits to the Pribilofs are most easily arranged in a package tour through Reeve Aleutian Airlines out of Anchorage.

The *Chukchi Sea* unit includes some 200,000 acres mostly north of the Arctic

Circle ranging from low, sandy barrier islands in the Arctic Ocean to high, rocky spires in the western Brooks Range. Nearly half a million kittiwakes and murres breed on cliffs at Cape Lisburne and Cape Thompson. Hundreds of walruses haul out annually at Cape Lisburne when the sea ice recedes well offshore. In winter polar bears are found there. Thousands of caribou congregate near Cape Lisburne after summer calving, and grizzly bears, musk-oxen, woverines, moose, and Dall sheep are also found there. Camping is permitted but access is difficult.

The *Gulf of Alaska* Unit extends from Alaska's south-central coast near Kodiak Island, eastward to southeast Alaska and includes Tuxedni, St. Lazaria, Hazy, and Forrester islands. Topography is often precipitous, with seabirds using cliffs, talus slopes, burrows, boulder rubble, and rock crevices to breed and nest. Seabird colonies on St. Lazaria, 15 miles from Sitka, and the Chiswell Islands, 35 miles from Seward, are easily seen from pleasure or charter boats.

The *Alaska Peninsula* unit is 715,000 acres on a small headland and over 800 islands, sea stacks, columns, islets, and rocks on which cormorants, auklets, murres, and others are found off the south side of the Alaska Peninsula. There are no tours to view these areas and most are extremely difficult to reach.

Because of recent threatened status for northern sea lions, access to many of their colonies may be off-limits.

For further information on any of these units: Alaska Maritime National Wildlife Refuges, 2355 Kachemak Bay Drive, Homer, Alaska 99603. Phone (907) 235–6546.

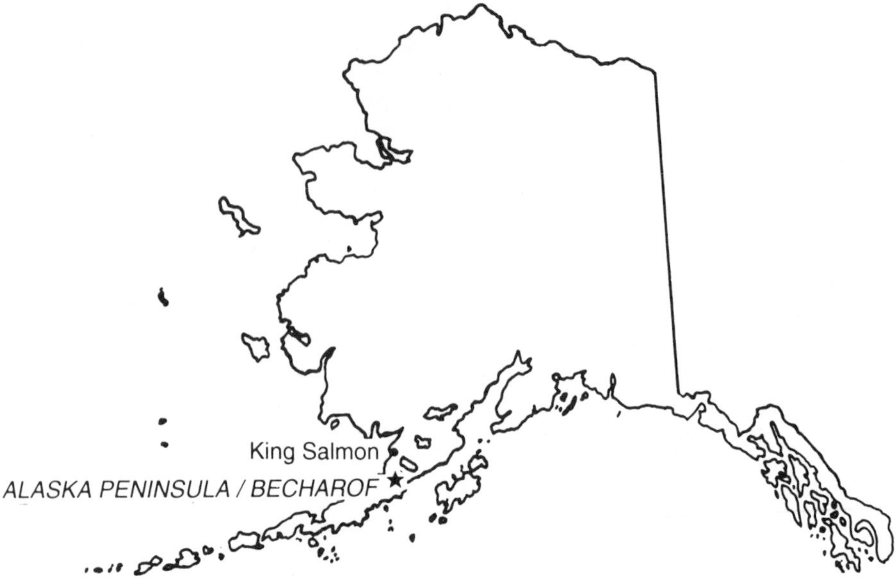

King Salmon

ALASKA PENINSULA / BECHAROF

ALASKA PENINSULA/BECHAROF (Alaska)

This spectacular upper half of the Alaskan peninsula is a scenic and wildlife wonder, more than 3.5 million acres much of which appears as if men had never set foot on it. The world as far as the eye can see is filled with tundra, mountains, and still-smouldering volcanoes—part of the "Ring of Fire" that rims the Pacific Ocean.

Alaskan brown bears are here in great numbers—probably 2,500 to 3,000 of them—one of the world's largest concentrations of this creature, which can weigh over 1,000 pounds and may stand nine feet tall. They congregate around salmon from the world's most valuable and pristine fishery—Bristol Bay—fighting their way up clear streams fed by snowmelt and rainfall to spawn.

Hundreds of eagles pair off and raise families. Willow and rock ptarmigans nest; so do northern hawk-owls and boreal owls, gyrfalcons, redpolls, yellow and Wilson's warblers, golden-crowned sparrows, black turnstones, black oystercatchers, and wandering tattlers. On cliffs and offshore islands are peregrine falcons, tufted and horned puffins, red-faced and pelagic cormorants, pigeon guillemots, and murres.

Hundreds of thousands of other water birds, many of which nest to the north on Yukon Delta and winter to the south on Izembek Lagoon, come through in spring and fall—emperor, white-fronted and Canada geese, and others. It is a major staging area for bar-tailed godwits.

A herd of about 15,000 caribou are constantly on the move, calving, grazing, and trotting into the wind to escape attacks by white-socks flies and other voracious insects. One radio-collared individual traveled 120 miles in four days.

Moose feed along the streams in winter and move into brushy willow uplands in summer. And there are wolverines, wolves, river otters, red foxes, and beavers. Fishing can be outstanding for rainbow trout, Arctic char, northern pike, and grayling, as well as for five species of salmon—king, coho, red, pink, and dog.

Seals, sea lions, and sea otters inhabit the offshore waters and haul up on beaches and ledges, and gray whales migrate through.

The vistas are magnificent, climbing from coastal lowlands on the Bristol Bay side to steep glaciated mountains and volcanoes that form the spine of the refuge, plunging to a Pacific coastline that is heavily fjorded, with steep cliffs, sea stacks, and sandy and cobble beaches.

Castle Cape Fjords' contrasting light and dark layers are a famous guidemark to shipping. Mount Veniaminof, which erupted in 1983, is the world's largest cone volcano, a National Natural Landmark with a massive base 30 miles in diameter and a summit crater 20 miles around. Mount Paulik volcano is the most prominent mountain on Becharof Refuge. Caribou have been observed using the ice-covered approaches to the peak to escape insects in August. Mt. Chiginagak's 6,000-foot peak dominates the Ugashik Unit of the Alaska Peninsula Refuge. Its rugged, glacier-covered slopes hid a World War II crash site for 42 years until discovered in 1987 by a refuge biologist looking for radio-collared bears. Gas rocks on the south shore of Becharof Lake display continually seeping volcanic gasses. A short distance away, the geologically active Ukinrek Maars exhibits the scars of a violent 1977 eruption.

Becharof Lake is the second largest lake in Alaska, with islands on which bears are said to den. Its tributaries contribute over four million salmon annually to the Bristol Bay fishery.

Like most Alaska refuges, this is not easy to see. The interior is roadless, requiring chartered air travel. Terrain is rough, requiring sturdy hiking gear and fit physical condition. Weather is unpredictable, requiring warm water-repellent clothing (not down, which becomes soaked). A chartered plane can leave a camper stranded for days until skies clear (so extra provisions should be taken). June to September offers optimum conditions.

But the sights and experiences here are well worth the careful preparations. Refuge staff—also refuge literature—are helpful in advising where to see what and when, and in advising what preparations are necessary. The King Salmon Visitor Center, operated jointly by the Bristol Bay Borough, the National Park Service, and the U.S. Fish and Wildlife Service, is located in the terminal building at the King Salmon Airport.

Some remarkable wildlife sightings are available right in the town of King Salmon, where refuge headquarters is located—especially late March to early May when waterfowl are staging. There can be thousands of tundra swans, white-fronted geese, pintails, mallards, mergansers, and others, including Eurasian wigeon on the Naknek River. Townspeople say the swans' constant calling keeps them from sleeping at night. Eagles are around town all year, and after spring ice breakup, beluga whales pursue smelt up the river at each high tide.

Daily flights are scheduled from Anchorage to King Salmon where there are inns and air taxis for charter to remote spots. All these should be reserved well ahead. Visitors here might wish also to see Katmai National Park and Preserve, which adjoins but requires chartered air to reach Brooks Lodge, usually booked months ahead.

For further information: Refuge Manager, Alaska Peninsula/Becharof National Wildlife Refuge Complex, P.O. Box 277, King Salmon, Alaska 99613 (hours 8–4:30 weekdays). Phone (907) 246-3339.

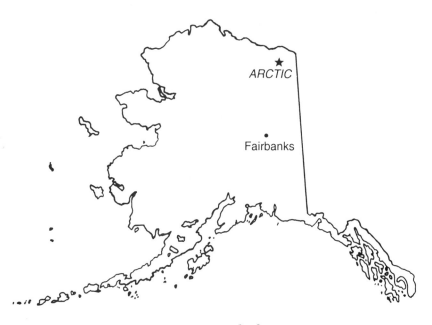

ARCTIC (Alaska)

This prize of the national wildlife refuge system is the largest refuge in the United States and one of the largest in the world—19.5 million acres—seeming to human eyes almost limitless.

Bounded by the Arctic Ocean on the north and Canada on the east, its plains, mountains, marshes, and lakes harbor caribou, grizzly bears, lynx, eagles, Dall sheep, wolves, and great flocks of migratory birds that come from the lower 48 states and at least three other continents to breed in the isolation of the tundra on its north slope.

There are ice floes along its northern shores even in summer, some of the most imposing mountains on the continent, and blankets of wildflowers in spring and summer—Arctic poppies, lupines, and rhododendrons together with scarlet bearberries and orange and gold lichens and mosses that explode with color in the fall.

Arctic foxes, polar bears, seals, martens, wolverines, and musk-oxen are here, along with nesting ptarmigans, peregrine and gyrfalcons, snowy owls, merlins, rough-legged hawks, Pacific, yellow-billed and red-throated loons, golden plovers, harlequin ducks, and many others. Most of the birds present on the refuge are nesters.

Its winters have no daylight and temperatures can fall to 50 below; its summers, in the 35–75 degree range, have no darkness. The sun does not set between May

10 and August 2, and a refuge leaflet suggests that the best way to see wildlife is to hike around "from evening until noon the next day."

It is so close to the North Pole that compass readings must be adjusted to 36 degrees to compensate for the magnetic declination.

The spectacular Brooks Range runs from east to west, dividing the refuge into north- and south-draining slopes. Towering snowclad peaks drop off on the south slope into spruce forests. On the north slope rounded hills covered with deep cushiony moss give way to the treeless Arctic plain.

It is underlain 2,000 feet deep with permafrost. This, along with the cool summer temperature, helps prevent moisture loss so that the ground is soft and spongy under the low, lush vegetation, despite annual precipitation of only four to eight inches, similar to that of the Southwest U.S. desert.

Ten major rivers drain into the Arctic Ocean after passing through this vast lacework of streams, deltas, and lagoons, a tremendous undisturbed feeding ground for millions of migratory birds before they go south for the winter.

It is one of the most scenically magnificent wildlife and wilderness areas in North America as well as one of the most fragile—which is why environmentalists fight to prevent oil exploration: the sight of these vast lands and waters, for aeons unaltered except by the natural cataclysms that created them, is an unforgettable experience.

It is a trip to be undertaken only with careful planning. There are no auto-tour routes or interpretive hiking trails. There are hazardous streams, mountains, weather, animals. On the other hand, anyone in resonable health willing to make the effort to become properly equipped and learn what's out there can experience the Arctic Refuge safely.

Camping is permitted anywhere. So is hiking. Some visitors hike across the range for several weeks supported by what they can carry in a backpack, but that is not necessary. It is possible to fly from Fairbanks or Deadhorse to Fort Yukon or Barter Island, for example, then charter a plane to a river where one can put up a tent and stay several days or a week exploring (air charters are $300–$1,000 per person depending on destination). River float trips can be taken either individually or with outfitters.

Refuge staff can be helpful, but start well in advance and first send for and study the excellent refuge booklets on all aspects of planning a trip.

Possible sights and experiences can only be suggested.

Anyone on the north slope in early summer will see some of the estimated 200,000 caribou. Females calve on the coastal plain and the herd then migrates more than 1,000 miles to wintering grounds, presenting a rolling sea of antlers (both males and females grow them) audible as well with clicking hooves and anklebones. (Visitors who negotiate steep rocky inclines covered with ease by these impressive animals say they understand why their bones click.)

Fossils are found in many places on the refuge and are especially visible in the streambeds—most of the refuge was once under the sea. Moose frequent willow thickets around rivers and small lakes. Dall sheep leap delicately along mountain slopes. Smaller mammals such as weasels and Arctic ground squirrels seem as curious about visitors as they about them. Wolves and bears can be anyplace, but prime areas for them and other wildlife are the lovely Sheenjek and Ignek Valleys.

Birds are everywhere—longspurs, wheatears, and gray-crowned rosy finches in alpine tundra; wagtails, hoary redpolls, and Arctic warblers in riparian thickets. But probably the most important bird habitat is the strip of marsh and coastal lagoons along the northern coastal plain. Thousands of shorebirds and others nest there. Later a half-million oldsquaws stage along with similar numbers of eiders and many thousands of snow geese, pintails, wigeons, buffleheads, and shorebirds that require these quiet places to rest and feed before the long migration south to wintering grounds over much of the lower 48 states.

Finally it should be said that the Arctic, although it has a huge variety, is not teaming with wildlife in the usual sense. The environment is too harsh. Wildlife is scattered across this huge area, for every living thing scrapes a precarious existence requiring a large territory in order to survive.

Nowhere is the Arctic effect better seen than in the vegetation of the north slope, most of which hugs the ground in a lovely mosaic. This is one reason geologic forms appear so spectacular: no tall trees soften their spare outlines. Willow trees that grow to 20 feet elsewhere are only a few inches high here; small shrubs may be a century old.

For further information: Arctic National Wildlife Refuge, Room 266 Federal Building, 101 Twelfth Avenue, Box 20, Fairbanks, Alaska 99701. Phone: (907) 456–0250 (office open 8–4:30 weekdays).

INNOKO (Alaska)

Without experiencing it one can hardly imagine the vastness of these 6,000 square miles (3.85 million acres) of black spruce muskeg, 20,000 lakes, wet meadows, horsetail marsh, and spruce and birch-covered hills in west-central Alaska inhabited by timber wolves, moose, black and grizzly bears, and at peak times a quarter-million waterfowl.

The solitude is almost indescribable—but it is not quiet.

"You can't go anyplace without a yellowlegs swearing at you," said the refuge manager. Wolves howl at night. Moose grunt in rutting season. Eagles scream—20 pairs nest on the refuge, along with ospreys, kestrels, great gray and northern hawk owls, and in the woods, spruce and ruffed grouse and three-toed and black-backed woodpeckers.

About 20 percent of the refuge provides wetland nesting habitat for waterfowl—pintails, green-winged teal, wigeon, shovelers, scaup, goldeneyes, black and surf scoters, Canada and white-fronted geese, along with Arctic and red-throated loons, red-necked grebes, and others.

By early July a boater might come around a river bend and run into a flock of 4,000 to 5,000 flightless (moulting) white-fronted and Canada geese.

Beavers are busy in every waterway—thousands of them.

Sounds travel. You hear the high bugling of a flock of sandhill cranes but they're too far away, you discover, to walk to.

Among the smaller birds in various habitats are redpolls, Bohemian waxwings, Swainson's and varied thrush, boreal chickadees, ruby-crowned kinglets, and Arctic, orange-crowned, Wilson's, and blackpoll warblers.

You can run into anything, including lynx, black bears, huge grizzly bears, red foxes, wolverines, martens, weasels, and some of the smaller creatures they prey on. Or nothing, at least for a long time—for while large numbers of creatures inhabit this place, the harsh northern climate is such that they must spread over large territories to survive, especially those (unlike the breeding waterfowl) that stay all year. Even the caribou that winter here must stay on the move to find new grazing grounds.

It is a hard place to visit—no auto-tour routes, no interpretive hiking trails. Many places a visitor might go have not been visited other than by native people in its 10,000-year human history, except possibly by a few gold rush miners, traders, or trappers who left little trace. But to those who are willing to go to the trouble, that is what makes it an unforgettable experience. As one put it, when you leave everything of civilization behind out there you begin after a few days "to feel cleansed."

It is not only difficult to see even a part of this refuge, but costly. The best way would be to charter a float plane for a week out of Anchorage and fly over the refuge, find a likely spot, and put down and set up camp. Then every day fly around to a different place, set down, and hike around and look. (After a week of this, you realize it might take years to really see it all).

Float trips are also possible, arranged out of McGrath.

Before planning any trip consult as far in advance as possible with refuge staff, not only on arrangements but where and when best to see special things (like waterfowl), and get advice on everything from bear avoidance to what to take in your emergency kit. Tell them when you're leaving and plan your return. But take extra food and don't set too definite a schedule. Weather changes can always keep you out there longer than you've planned.

For further information: Innoko National Wildlife Refuge, Box 69, McGrath, Alaska 99627. Phone: (907) 524–3251.

IZEMBEK (Alaska)

The entire world population of Pacific black brant fills the sky in a great dark cloud over Izembek Lagoon in the fall, their cries shutting out all other sounds. Landing on the water they gabble noisily while feeding on the eelgrass, an aquatic plant that resembles an eel and is the main food of this attractive small dark goose that breeds mostly above the Arctic Circle and winters as far south as the Mexican west coast.

The presence of the world's largest eelgrass beds and the brants' dependence on them were the main reason for establishment of this 321,000-acre refuge of marshes, lagoons, low heath vegetation, and soaringly beautiful and rugged volcanic peaks at the lower end of the Alaska Peninsula. But many others come to the feast.

Virtually all of the world's emperor goose population comes through, along with 60,000 or so Taverner's Canada geese, sometimes 100,000 dabbling ducks—pintails, teal, mallards—bound for the lower 48 states, and great flocks of rock sandpipers, ruddy turnstones, semipalmated plovers, and least and western sandpipers.

Alaskan brown bears, called the world's largest land carnivore, roam widely, along with barren ground caribou, wolves, wolverines, weasels, tundra hares, river otters, and red foxes, and in nearby waters sea otters and sea lions, with several thousand harbor seals that bask on exposed sandspits.

Most waterfowl arrive here mid-April to mid-May but fall concentrations also can be truly awesome, starting with arrival of the first brant in late August on the first cool north wind. Others follow on each succeeding north wind until thousands are flying back and forth, calling in an almost incessant din, finally departing, often almost all in one night in late October or early November, leaving the wetlands to hardier ones that stay all winter, sometimes in huge numbers—waves of handsome oldsquaws, harlequin ducks, white-winged and black scoters, and Steller's, common, and king eiders.

Rock and willow ptarmigan nest, the latter sometimes filling lowland thickets. Gyrfalcons, peregrines, and bald eagles all breed here, too, as do semipalmated plovers, rock sandpipers, rosy finches, golden-crowned sparrows, Lapland longspurs, and snow buntings, and on near-shore islands, Arctic and Aleutian terns and glaucous-winged and mew gulls.

Red, silver, pink, and chum salmon crowd the spawning streams, along with a few king salmon at the edge of their range. They attract sometimes a hundred or more eagles as well as the huge brown bears, followed warily by wolverines, minks, otters, and glaucous-winged gulls.

The scenery is magnificent when not obscured by cloudy wet weather—jagged Aghileen Pinnacles, Mount Dutton, Frosty Peak, and sometimes-steaming Pavlof Volcano descending to broad treeless valleys that can be covered with beautiful wildflowers (marred in places by debris from World War II).

But fog and clouds can dominate, especially November through May, and winds can seem incessant, though temperatures are equable—seldom below zero in winter or over 65 in summer.

To get there one can fly by commercial airline to Cold Bay, which has limited hotel-boardinghouse accommodations. A state ferry visits monthly May through October. From there one can hike and camp out, or be flown out by charter, or drive if a car can be rented, as is only sometimes possible—rental cars are few and high-priced. Try to arrange ahead for a 4-wheel drive vehicle. The refuge has 45 miles of roads of which a 2-wheel drive can manage about half.

An observation building overlooks Izembek Lagoon, 11 miles out on Grant Point, and wildlife can usually be seen along the road.

For further information: Izembek National Wildlife Refuge, P.O. Box 127, Cold Bay, Alaska 99571 (hours 8–5 weekdays). Phone: (907) 532–2445.

Also administered by Izembek:

Unimak Island (Alaska Maritime NWR)—First and largest island in the windswept fogbound Aleutian chain, Unimak is almost one million acres of snow-topped peaks, active volcanoes, moving glaciers, and vast tundra covered with lakes and streams supporting caribou, brown bears, wolves, foxes, bald eagles, peregrine falcons, tundra swans, sea lions, and harbor seals. Large waterfowl concentrations stop in migration—brant, emperor, and Taverner's Canada geese, eiders, scoters, and others. Pelagic cormorants, kittiwakes, and murres nest on cliffs, and several million short-tailed shearwaters have been sighted in Unimak Pass. There are no visitor facilities and no roads, but a determined person can fly to the village of False Pass via commercial airline, hike from there and camp out, or be flown out by charter aircraft (landings are allowed only on lakes and below mean high tide on beaches).

Pavlof Unit, *Alaska Peninsula NWR*—Including state and native corporation lands interspersed with refuge, this is more than 1.5 million acres along the Pacific side of the Alaskan Peninsula from Port Moller to the tip. Most is upland and rugged mountains but the few wetlands support nesting tundra swans and other water birds. Brown bears are here, as well as caribou, wolves, wolverines, red foxes, and seasonally emperor geese and large numbers of seabirds. Access is best by chartered aircraft from Cold Bay or King Salmon.

KANUTI (Alaska)

The Arctic Circle marks the line where 24-hour summer daylight begins. It passes through the center of this 1.4 million-acre interior Alaska refuge that is home during this sunlit six months to almost 150 species of birds—in winter to a handful of ravens and other hardy types.

Spring marks the beginning of the annual life cycle of hundreds of thousands of birds that seek these isolated wetlands to raise families, including white-fronted geese that summer here every year. There are also tens of thousands of individuals of other water-oriented species—sandhill cranes, loons (Pacific and common), grebes (horned and red-necked), tundra and trumpeter swans, and almost two dozen species of ducks.

Scattered flocks of pintails show up when the ice breaks up in mid-May and quickly pair off, as do shovelers, wigeon, mallards, green-winged teal, Barrow's and common goldeneyes, buffleheads, oldsquaws, and white-winged and surf scoters. This northern habitat is particularly valuable to them because pothole and other nesting areas in the lower 48 states have been disappearing due to drought and agricultural drainage.

Shorebirds come thousands of miles to take advantage of this habitat—whimbrels, golden plovers, semipalmated plovers, yellowlegs, red-necked phalaropes, and others.

Kanuti is a mosaic of placid streams, wetlands, and muskeg, hundreds of lakes of every size and shape, boreal forests, black spruce and shrubs, birch and poplars alongside broad meadows. Most of it lies in a basin formed by the Koyukuk and Kanuti rivers, with the great Brooks Range to the north and the Ray Mountains to the south.

It is one of four Alaskan refuges encompassed by a solar basin (the others are Nowitna, Innoko, and Koyukuk)—characterized by encircling hills, light winds, low rainfall, severe winters, and short warm summers when the sun circles without setting.

Dramatic summer electric storms often set fires, which are allowed to burn themselves out or be extinguished by rain unless they threaten historical sites (of which there are a number dating to prehistoric times) or villages occupied by native populations. Hardly any of the refuge is untouched by fire—but most often these blazes result in greater ecological diversity and benefit to wildlife.

Black and grizzly bears are here—black bears in wooded areas, grizzlies in more open areas—and there are about 10 wolf packs. Moose browse among willows and in marshy places. Beavers are omnipresent, slapping their tails vigorously on the water at sight of a visitor, usually carrying woody material to refurbish lodges or resupply food caches.

In wooded sections are martens, quick, alert small mammals of which it was said by naturalist Henry Collins more than a quarter-century ago "few of us will ever see alive in the wild this owner of one of the world's choicest furs. Trapping has increased the marten's wariness and confined it to sanctuaries and the remote wilderness." Here is this remote wilderness it survives in comfortable numbers.

Another beautiful fur-bearer, the lynx—the only one of our cats with black-tipped bobbed tail—is adapted to all habitats—forest, swamp, desert, mountain—its population cyclical with that of its chief prey animal, the showshoe hare.

Wolverines are here, otters, minks, and muskrats, along with a great array of small prey-base mammals such as voles and lemmings.

Peregrine falcons nest, as do northern harriers and rough-legged hawks, and boreal and northern hawk owls. Willow ptarmigans change garb, brown feathers for nesting, white for hiding in snowbanks in winter.

Robins and varied thrushes nest along with horned larks, four species of swallows, six kinds of flycatchers, Lapland longspurs, eight kinds of sparrows, snow buntings, hoary and common redpolls, and eight kinds of warblers, including the Arctic, orange-crowned, Townsend's, and blackpoll.

A field station and Visitor Center are shared with Gates of the Arctic National Park at Bettles, a village on the north side of the refuge, where lodging is available. Otherwise the best way to see all this is by float trip or camping out, or perhaps both, from late June through August. Charter planes and outfitters are available from both Anchorage and Fairbanks, where the refuge headquarters is located.

Any trip should be planned as far ahead as possible, in consultation with refuge staff on the various alternatives available (including variable water levels for float trips).

The summer window of opportunity is mid-June through August. Winter can be a numbing 70 below, not counting wind chill. But if you can stand the cold, the collisions in the sky between solar and terrestrial atoms can cause spectacular displays of rose, green, gold, and multicolored northern lights. A good way to see them is to go out by dogsled in March and watch the whole sky, a 360-degree hemisphere, filled with this splendor.

For more information: Kanuti National Wildlife Refuge, Room 112, Federal Courthouse Building, 101 Twelfth Avenue, Box 11, Fairbanks, Alaska 99701. Phone: (907) 456–0329.

KENAI (Alaska)

Here at Kenai in microcosm are almost every kind of geologic feature and wildlife habitat to be found over the whole of Alaska and most of its wild creatures as well.

Huge-antlered moose nibble greenery in willow bogs and thickets. Dall sheep and mountain goats skip over high peaks. Wolves' and coyotes' calls mingle at night (wolves howl longer and more mournfully, coyotes yip). Lynx are here, as are foxes, black and brown bears, wolverines, otters, and more than 160 species of birds on this 1.97 million acres of heathland, muskeg, rolling hills, meadows, and spruce-birch-aspen forests in south-central Alaska. There are more than 1,200 lakes ranging in size from small potholes to 74,000-acre Tustumena, all drained by more than a thousand miles of rivers and streams in which five species of salmon spawn.

Common and Pacific loons call from many ponds. Willow, rock, and white-tailed ptarmigans shed brown plumage for white in winter, the better to hide when plunging into snowbanks. Spruce grouse forage on spruce buds and pick up grit along roads. Goshawks, largest and fiercest of accipiters, hunt year-round.

Bald eagles swoop down on fish along river corridors. Stately trumpeter swans nest in remote areas but later feed over many of the refuge lakes.

There are 1.35 million acres of designated wilderness—69 percent of the refuge—where one can go and see no other human for days. There are more than 100 miles of paved and graveled road, another 100 miles of hiking trails, 140 miles of canoe routes, 13 campgrounds, and hundreds of fishing lakes and streams that have been mapped and charted for visitors.

Trails are mapped by length, elevation, and difficulty; lakes and streams for size, depth, and fish available (15 species, including Arctic char, grayling, Dolly Varden, rainbow trout, and salmon (a world-record 97.4-pound king salmon was caught in the Kenai River); camping spots for their various facilities. Canoe trails cover much of the north part of the refuge and information includes what may be seen, terrain that may be encountered, and length of time each probably will require. Canoes can be rented in the area.

In winter there are cross-country skiing and snowshoeing—some roads are kept open all year.

The Kenai mountain area covers about a third of the refuge and rises from near sea level to over 6,000 feet. Here are mountains interspersed with large lakes and capped by the extensive Harding Ice Field—a plateau of ice that heads extensive glaciers leading down the valleys of the refuge.

All this is within two hours' drive, 110 miles south, of Anchorage, on Sterling Highway, which bisects the refuge.

Kenai became a refuge largely at the urging of local people and conservation groups to ensure habitat preservation for the wide-ranging moose. Now several thousand of these great beasts, largest deer in the world, are here, standing up to seven and a half feet at the shoulder, weighing up to 1,700 pounds and with antlers that can spread six feet or more. They graze along graveled roads or even along the state highway, bulls appearing clumsy with their high muscled shoulders and lower hindquarters (which enable them to negotiate snowdrifts handily) but in motion they are the exemplar of light-footed grace, trotting along at the speed of a fast horse.

Coyotes are sighted in early and late day (which in northern summers can mean almost until midnight). A dense black bear population forages on berries. Beavers are in many streams and ponds, and minks hunt along the water's edges. Caribou were exterminated early in the century but reintroduced, and now three small herds are doing well here.

Alaskan brown bears are lured to salmon-spawning streams in summer when these great fish challenge rapids and waterfalls, attempting and sometimes succeeding in covering a rise of perhaps 30 feet within 200 feet of swift-running waters. Some fall back to rest in a quiet eddy only to try again and perhaps succeed, or, spent, to die, in one of the most dramatic and moving sights in nature.

Mountain goats and Dall sheep dwell on high mountain outcrops and sometimes are seen where the Russian and Kenai rivers join along the Sterling Highway just off the refuge. Stop and scan the mountainsides for small white moving dots resembling patches of snow. Once spotted they can be observed easily as they leap about the steep inclines, often with their lambs after early June.

A dozen kinds of waterfowl nest, including harlequin ducks, Barrow's goldeneyes, pintails, green-winged teal; also horned and red-necked grebes, northern phalaropes, Arctic terns, glaucous-winged and mew gulls, yellowlegs, and some wandering tattlers. Ravens, magpies, redpolls, boreal chickadees, and mischievous gray jays are always about, the latter pilfering from any insecurely fastened picnic basket.

Less common but of special interest to birders are rosy finches and black-backed and northern three-toed woodpeckers. Great horned owls are frequently seen or heard; less so are great gray, boreal, saw-whet, and hawk owls. Pine grosbeaks, golden-crowned sparrows, varied thrushes, and Bohemian waxwings are common nesters.

Summer wildflowers are beautiful—poppies, lupines, shooting stars, and acres of fireweed at low elevations, with miniature varieties on alpine terrain.

Wildlife observers should take the 19-mile loop road through the 42,000-acre Skilak Wildlife Recreation Area (turn left on Skilak Lake Road on entering refuge from the east and follow signs) for some of the best wildlife-viewing and scenic vistas on the refuge.

Try to plan trips at times other than summer holiday weekends or the first week of moose season. But even then one can find in this most accessible of all Alaskan refuges places that seem—and are—utter wilderness, especially backpacking in the southern part of the refuge. Snowy 6,000-foot peaks are reflected in mirrorlike lakes, rippled only by the passage of beavers or a moose. The only sounds are the calling of birds and rustling of leaves, and each vista seems more splendid than the last.

How to get there: From Anchorage go south on Seward Highway (Highway 1) to Sterling Highway, turn right (west) and continue to refuge. For Visitor Center continue on through Soldotna, cross Kenai River bridge, turn left at light onto Funny River Road, then right immediately onto Ski Hill Road and follow signs.

Open: 24 hours. Headquarters/Visitor Center 8–4:30 weekdays, 10–6 weekends, closed winter holidays.

What to see: Whole spectrum of Alaskan wildlife including moose, eagles, waterfowl, others.

What to do: More than 100 miles paved and gravel roads, hiking trails, photography (light is often misty), canoeing, fishing, cross-country skiing, snowshoeing. Fishing outfitters in Anchorage and locally, camping/rafting/horse pack trip outfitters in Kenai, Soldatna. Air taxis available locally.

Best times to visit: Spring through fall.

Where to stay: Motels—in Soldotna, Kenai. Campgrounds—13 on refuge, also Chugach National Forest, state parks in area.

Weather: Summers pleasant, winters cold but no worse than upper midwest.

What to take and wear: Sturdy footgear, raingear for drizzles. Dress in layers with sweaters—70 degrees is a heat wave here.

Points of interest nearby: Kenai Fjords National Park with Exit Glacier (walk on it); Portage Glacier, Visitor Center at Chugach National Forest; historic Russian church; boat trips out of Seward and Homer visit bird colonies, sea lions, otters, whales, glaciers, icebergs, beautiful scenery. Good caribou-viewing at Kenai River flats, west of refuge.

For more information: Kenai National Wildlife Refuge, P.O. Box 2139, Soldotna, Alaska 99669. Phone: (907) 262–7021.

KODIAK (Alaska)

Kodiak belongs to the bears, the eagles, and the salmon, and the first two flourish largely because of the abundance of the last. When any of six species of Pacific salmon (pink, sockeye, coho, king, chum, and steelhead) are spawning there may be hundreds of eagles and huge Kodiak brown bears, largest land carnivores on earth, congregated to gather up some of the great fish fighting their way up the fast streams and rivers.

The salmon return in waves of hundreds of thousands to this ruggedly beautiful island off the coast of southwest Alaska from June to October, leaping against rapids so strong it seems unlikely that even their great exertions can propel them to egg-laying grounds in lakes upstream where they themselves began life.

Many die before achieving this; others as soon as they have spawned. Waiting for them are the eagles—more than 200 pairs nest here—and the great bears for which this almost 2,500-square-mile refuge, more than two-thirds of Kodiak Island, was set aside in 1941.

Sometimes several dozen of the 2,700 bears on the refuge—densest population in the world—may be gathered along a few miles of streambed, males standing nine feet tall and weighing 1,400 pounds.

Other mammals have been transplanted here—reindeer, Sitka black-tailed deer, snowshoe hare, mountain goats, and beavers, all now with viable populations. Otters and weasels sometimes den under refuge cabins. Foxes are common and many are the handsome silver and cross varieties.

Whales, porpoises, sea otters, seals, and Steller's sea lions are in the estuaries.

Birds are wonderful, too—more than 200 on the refuge list: land, oceanic, and occasional Asiatic species. Spring brings yellowlegs, black-bellied and golden plovers, and tens of thousands of seabirds to the shores and to nearby islands and cliffs— sooty and short-tailed shearwaters, pelagic and red-faced cormorants, black-legged kittiwakes, murres, pigeon guillemots, and horned and tufted puffins.

Common nesters—some of them year-round residents—include goshawks, tundra swans, willow and rock ptarmigans, black oystercatchers, surfbirds, glaucous-winged gulls, marbled murrelets, Lapland longspurs, snow buntings, and redpolls.

Hardier species nest farther north, many of them in Yukon Delta National Wildlife Refuge, and come back to winter here—well over a million birds including handsome oldsquaws, Steller's eiders, white-winged and surf scoters, and emperor geese and others.

Eagles are always in view and with young ones reach a total population well over 1,000 in fall.

Wildflowers can be stunning—orchids, irises, fields of fireweed, shooting stars, Indian paintbrush, and thousands of fruiting plants such as salmonberries, blueberries, and elderberries, all nourished by the mild moist climate. Temperatures seldom fall to zero in winter and only rarely rise to 80 in summer; average annual precipitation is 60 inches, giving rise to the nickname "Alaska's Emerald Isle," and said to be as green as anyplace on earth.

Scenery is magnificent—4,000-foot mountains, their valleys blanketed with low tundra vegetation, dense stands of alders and willows, and hundreds of lakes within 800 miles of convoluted shoreline indented by dramatic fjordlike inlets (often obscured by rain and fog).

Another refuge unit on the northwest corner of nearby Afognak Island has dense stands of virgin Sitka spruce forest and Roosevelt elk.

Kodiak has cabins available near interesting wildlife-viewing locations that must be reserved well ahead. They have no facilities other than shelter. There is also a bear-viewing program during the summer salmon run on O'Malley River, in which visitors are taken (for a fee) to spend four days near the site. Participants are chosen in March by lottery among applicants (write the refuge).

To get to Kodiak, fly from Anchorage or take a ferry from Seward or Homer. The headquarters/Visitor Center is on the road from the airport to the town of Kodiak where there are motels, rental cars, charter planes, and boats for hire to look at seabird colonies in the bay, all best reserved ahead. There is also camping in nearby Fort Abercrombie State Park, and several remote lodges (ask Chamber of Commerce).

It is also possible to see wildlife from a system of public roads around Kodiak.

Information on this is furnished by the Alaska Natural History Association, available through the refuge.

But one must charter-fly into cabins and other interior refuge areas—there are no roads. Take good-quality rain gear and hip boots. Hiking can be difficult, with little level ground, much of it covered with shoulder-high, damp vegetation. There are native-American inholdings, and land access fees may apply for use of these areas. A map of inholdings is available at refuge headquarters and visitors should verify ownership status prior to their visit; boundaries typically are not posted. Be prepared to be self-sufficient in a wet, wild, wonderful place—for Kodiak is that, most of it probably unchanged since the Russian explorer Vitus Bering discovered Alaska in 1741 (and sailed right by Kodiak, not seeing it in the fog).

Before planning a trip consult with refuge headquarters: Kodiak National Wildlife Refuge, 1390 Buskin River Road, Kodiak, Alaska 99615 (8–4:30 weekdays). Phone: (907) 487–2600.

KOYUKUK/NOWITNA COMPLEX (Alaska)

Rafting slowly down the meandering rivers of this interior Alaskan refuge complex one might see almost any of the wildlife common on these refuges: moose, beavers, otters, brown or black bears, eagles soaring overhead, even an occasional wolf.

This is probably the best way to see 3.5 million-acre Koyukuk or 1.5 million-acre Nowitna since there are no wildlife drives, or developed hiking trails. The rivers are travel ways for man and wildlife alike.

Moose nibble at river's edge or sometimes stand neck-deep in the water to escape the hordes of mosquitoes. Populations of these great beasts are as dense on Koyukuk as anywhere in Alaska, 10 per square mile in prime areas.

Owls such as great horned, great gray, boreal, and the northern hawk owl roost in white spruce trees near the riverbank. Because it may be light for all 24 hours in the northern summer, their hunting takes place in twilight hours. Arctic terns, which flew halfway around the earth to get here, vigorously defend nests on river sandbars.

Large numbers of black bears forage on blueberries and highbush cranberries; they also sometimes wade or swim in the rivers to seek respite from the fearsome insects. Omnivores, they also feed on moose calves. Wolves hunt riverbanks. There are also red foxes, martens, lynx, snowshoe hares, and smaller creatures, which are prey for the larger ones. Tiny northern red-backed voles are probably the singlemost abundant mammal on Nowitna—of immense ecological importance. Their combined weight is believed to exceed that of all the large mammals.

Majestic trumpeter swans, largest waterfowl in the world, rare elsewhere, nest here along with one-third of the world's interior white-fronted geese and ducks of more than a dozen species.

Smaller birds are around, too—robins, gray-cheeked thrushes, Wilson's and yellow warblers, northern shrikes.

Wildflowers can be beautiful—carpets of bluebells, wild irises, monkshood, fireweed, wild roses.

A float trip on the nationally designated wild Nowitna River to its confluence with the Yukon could take a week, starting through a 20-mile canyon heavily forested with black and white spruce, some of them 80 feet tall, then opening out into a broad scenic valley spread with lakes, streams, and marshes.

The Koyukuk trip is quite a different matter. It could take all summer to float the 400 miles along the Koyukuk River if you started on the south fork at the Haul Road for the Alaska pipeline—but an interesting, beautiful and shorter version could go from Huslia to the Yukon. White sandbars make good campsites in many places. Across from the confluence of the Koyukuk and Yukon is the border of Kaiyuh Flats, also known as the Upper Innoko unit.

Alaskan brown bears might be along more open stretches and river banks, foraging on all sorts of food, including drying salmon on fish racks. Swift peregrine falcons might zoom by overhead—since a few nest in this vicinity.

About 100 miles below Huslia get out and climb a hill and you might see in the distance the 16,000-acre Nagahabara Sand Dunes, 200 feet high, active sand dunes formed 10,000 years ago by windblown deposits during the Pleistocene period.

Sandhill cranes nest and with common, red-throated, and Pacific loons contribute to the wilderness sounds with wild, high-pitched cries that can be heard for miles.

Koyukuk and Nowitna are two of four Alaskan refuges lying in major river valleys—land forms characterized by wide flats with low bordering forested hills. Light winds, low rainfall, severe winters, and short warm summers are typical here where the summer sun circles without setting.

There are several ways to arrange trips here, costly if they involve charter planes at $200 per hour. Consult refuge staff in Galena (reachable by commercial airlines and with food and lodging) for latest information. Be prepared for a wilderness trip that is memorable but possibly arduous, requiring careful preparation. You must be self-sufficient, relying on your own camping equipment, food, and emergency first-aid kit.

Or if you don't mind cold weather consider coming in winter to look at the Western Arctic caribou herd, which can come in huge numbers then. It's a natural spectacle that few persons ever see because these animals are in a remote area where temperatures reach 80 below. In the Arctic midwinter, sometimes they are in near-total darkness.

One way is to hire a local "musher" and go out by dogsled to see them along with the northern lights, never more spectacular than here, with scarlet, purple, gold, and green flashing about the night sky in a display that once seen can never be forgotten.

For more information: Koyukuk/Nowitna National Wildlife Refuge Complex, Box 287, Galena, Alaska 99741. Phone: (907) 656–1231.

Kotzebue

SELAWIK

SELAWIK (Alaska)

Selawik straddles the Arctic Circle near where 10,000 years ago animals—including humans—and plants migrated across a now-submerged Bering land bridge between North America and Siberia.

Asian birds still appear here to the great interest of birders, and there are other wildlife species, too, especially waterfowl that come from five continents (North and South America, Africa, Asia, and Australia) to nest on nutrient-rich wetlands that all but cover this 2.1 million acre refuge with 21,000 lakes in northwestern Alaska (the rest is tundra and birch, willow, and taiga spruce forest).

There are spectacular mammals as well—black and Alaskan brown bears, about 2,000 moose with up to six-foot antler spreads, wolves, beavers, otters, wolverines, Arctic and red foxes, occasional musk-oxen—and some 400,000 caribou from the Western Arctic herd that migrate across the refuge twice a year on a latticework of trails.

Those who have seen this migration find it hard to describe the scene adequately: the earth can seem to be all moving animals, bull caribou in fall carrying four-foot-long antlers and snorting as they move to attract the attention of females still followed by their calves of the year.

The entire group is so graceful they seem almost to float over the ground, soundless except for the males' snorting and the clicking of their ankle bones. They seem to be ambling slowly along but even at an apparently slow pace they go faster than most men can run. They tear off bits of lichen as they go that—so fragile is this tundra environment—may not regrow for 30 to 100 years. But the caribou keep moving, so no forage spot is destroyed for future grazing.

The refuge produces 60,000 ducklings a year, pintails, mallards, scaup, wigeon, green-winged teal, scoters, and oldsquaw, and thousands of white-fronted and Canada geese. By fall the population of graceful tundra swans is some 7,000, with similar numbers of stately sandhill cranes, and over the whole refuge hundreds of thousands of shorebirds and passerines—yellowlegs, golden plovers, whimbrels, red knots, yellow wagtails, and northern wheatears, along with snow buntings, rosy finches, and warblers.

Fisheries include sheefish, "tarpon of the north," which swim up the Selawik River to spawn and can weigh up to 60 pounds; also northern pike, burbot, Arctic char, grayling, and in the Kobuk River delta, chum salmon.

In the northeast corner of the refuge a 35-square-mile active sand dune (reachable by float plane in summer) offers excellent hiking with splendid mountain views.

Hot springs at two locations at the headwaters of the Selawik River stay open all winter (though temperatures on this refuge can drop to 60 below, with the wind chill 126 degrees below zero). They were the center of historic trading routes. There are cabins and a bathhouse, used mainly by native residents—sometimes by tribal doctors for healing sessions. (The refuge has some 2,000 native residents who live in village inholdings on subsistence use of refuge resources.)

There are archeological sites dating back to the land bridge.

Selawik is reachable by boat, aircraft, snowmobile, cross-country skiing, and dogsled. Refuge headquarters in Kotzebue, where there is a modern hotel, is reachable by commercial air several times daily from Anchorage. Several native villages are reachable by commuter or charter air, from which one can go out by boat.

Probably the best way is to bring or arrange with an outfitter for boat, camping equipment, and food, and go for a float trip of a week or 10 days on the nationally designated wild Selawik River. It is slow-flowing and almost any of the refuge wildlife might appear. The window of opportunity is from June after ice has broken up and water is high (but fierce insects are out) to early October, when water is beginning to freeze over again. Some persons like August-September best—it's cool, temperatures 20–50, sometimes drizzly, but few insects. Bull moose are beginning to grunt and bellow, stars are beginning to appear, and fall colors—gold-to-orange birches, scarlet bearberry, and others—are beautiful.

Best way to see caribou is to fly in late August–early September to Ambler (which has a lodge) and fly or boat from there to National Park Service land to watch them swimming south across the Kobuk River—an amazing congregation, great herds of cows and calves swimming together, the bulls with flowing snowy white manes. (But it is also possible to take snowmobile, dog team, or ski-equipped aircraft and go out to see them heading northward in March and April.)

Plan any trip as far ahead as possible, and get advice from refuge staff on how to see what, when, and how (you'll need hip boots, compass, and warm water-repellent clothing).

For more information: Selawik National Wildlife Refuge, P.O. Box 270, Kotzebue, Alaska 99752. Phone: (907) 442–3799.

Tok
•
TETLIN ★

TETLIN (Alaska)

The visitor approaching Tetlin from the Alaska-Canada Highway beholds in one wondrous glance all its vast pristine river valley spread before him—700,000 acres of spruce forests, muskeg, hundreds of lakes, and two rushing glacier-fed rivers. Along the southern refuge boundary the Nutzotin Mountains rise to 9,000 feet and beyond them the Wrangells, their 14,000-foot peaks snowclad all year.

In this huge expanse is a diverse ecosystem complete and unaltered by human activity, where black and grizzly bears flourish with timber wolves, caribou, and beavers. Dall sheep skip about the mountains. Moose forage in willow thickets.

On the water and in the air are bald and golden eagles, tundra and trumpeter swans, dozen of species of ducks and geese, and many shorebirds and passerines—132 bird species nest. Tetlin was set aside as a refuge to protect one of the highest nesting densities in Alaska of waterfowl—also of ospreys—on the Northway Tetlin flats at the headwaters of the Tanana River.

Tetlin is one of two Alaska refuges readily accessible to the visitor by road (the other is Kenai), and much of the wildlife can be seen from a series of pull-offs along 100 miles of the Al-Can (know locally as Alaska Highway), which adjoins the northern refuge boundary. A well-equiped Visitor Center is located close to the eastern end;

headquarters is at Tok, 25 miles northwest of the refuge. There is more good wildlife-viewing from two campgrounds, a hiking trail, and an observation platform.

Some 200,000 sandhill cranes come in spring and fall, their high bugling calls filling the air as they move to and from their breeding grounds. Hawks migrate through in May—goshawks, sharpshins, gyrfalcons—and some stay to nest.

Lesser yellowlegs are everywhere piping their "tew-tew" calls and exploring the water's edges. On the lakes are Pacific loons, trumpeter swans, horned grebes, white-winged scoters, and an assortment of dabblers—mallards, shovelers, wigeon, and green-winged teal.

Spruce grouse forage around forest edges. Blackpoll, Wilson's, and yellow-rumped warblers and common and hoary redpolls scout nest sites in the varied forest habitat. Lapland longspurs and Savannah sparrows flit about open areas.

Swainson's thrushes throw out heart-stopping melodies. Usually dusk singers, they sometimes continue all night long in this northern summer where there is no darkness—a mixed blessing to light-sleeping campers. Gray jays pilfer crumbs from picnickers.

Best time to come is June to August, when all the birds are here, and different wildflowers burst into bloom every week—lavender pasqueflowers, northern ane-mones, drooping pink globes of bog rosemary, Arctic lupines, Jacob's ladder, and in wet areas, northern lady's slipper orchids and hooded ladies' tresses. By mid-August alpine and bog blueberries appear. After mid-October and until mid-April the refuge is locked into winter (where the record low is 72 below in January, and snow can occur anytime).

How to get there: From Fairbanks drive south on Richardson Highway to Delta Junction; from there take Alaska Highway southeast to Tok (total 205 miles). Headquarters is in Tok, Mp (milepost) 1314; refuge is southeast on Alaska Highway.

Open: 24 hours. Office 8–5 weekdays. Visitor Center 7 a.m.–7 p.m. Memorial Day–Labor Day.

Best times to visit: June to August.

What to see: Diversity of wildlife—waterfowl, raptors, passerines, shorebirds, plus mammals; also beautiful scenery and wildflowers.

What to do: Wildlife observation from highway and highway pull-offs, also from campgrounds, hiking trail, observation platform. Planes can be chartered in Tok for overview of refuge, also for camping in the interior. River-rafting, canoeing. Note: considerable land within the refuge, especially along the high-way, is held privately and boundaries should be respected.

Where to stay: Numerous motels, campgrounds, RV parks in Tok. Primitive camping anywhere on refuge (air taxis can be arranged in Tok).

Weather: June-July can have daytime temperatures over 80, nightly lows to 40 degrees, with rapid changes possible. Snow can occur in August.

What to take and wear: Sturdy waterproof footgear; maps and compass for interior hiking.

Points of interest nearby: Alaska Public Lands Information Center, Tok; Kluane National Park, just across border in Yukon Territory; Wrangell St. Elias National Park/ Preserve just south of the Tetlin refuge; Yukon-Charley Rivers National Preserve, 160 miles north; Fortymile Wild and Scenic River, north of Tok on the Taylor Highway; Denali National Park, 300 miles west.

For more information: Tetlin National Wildlife Refuge, P. O. Box 779, Tok, Alaska 99780. Phone: (907) 883–5312.

TOGIAK (Alaska)

Huge bull walruses with tusks two feet long haul out to cover the beaches and fill the air with their grunting and groaning, "tusking" one another when crowded by their neighbors at Cape Pierce on this vast 4.2 million acre refuge in the southwestern corner of Alaska.

Steller's sea lions claim Cape Newenham, the next promontory westward. Landward of them both is one of the largest mainland seabird colonies in Alaska—up to 1.5 million horned and tufted puffins, black-legged kittiwakes, common murres, parakeet auklets, pelagic cormorants and others, mostly perched precariously on seaside cliffs.

Back of the coastline are salt lagoons and bays which are critical resting, feeding and staging areas for migratory waterfowl. In spring and fall over half the world's population of Pacific black brant are there.

Togiak is a breeding and resting area for waterfowl and shore-birds returning from wintering areas in Russia, Japan, Mexico, South America, New Zealand and the South Pacific as well as the United States—tundra swans, emperor, white-fronted and Canada geese, king, spectacled and Steller's eiders, harlequin ducks, pintails, scaup, goldeneyes, and others.

Shorebirds cover the wetlands in summer—surfbirds, red knots, wandering tattlers, dowitchers, Hudsonian and bar-tailed godwits, and eight kinds of sandpipers.

The fishery resources are stupendous. More than one million salmon return every year to swim up more than 1,500 miles of rivers and streams on the refuge until the smaller tributaries turn red with their spawning colors and seem to hold more fish than water. The Kanektok is the highest-rated river in the country by fishermen for rainbow trout, Arctic char and grayling, as well as for five species of salmon—king, silver, pink, chum and sockeye. (Some areas have "no-bait" catch-and release rules).

The Ahklun Mountains cover 80 percent of the refuge; below them, the tundra comes alive in spring with a carpet of rosy bloom followed by fruiting blueberries, salmonberries and others. A plot two feet across can hold 40 species of tiny blooming and fruit-bearing plants.

Great brown and black bears and bald eagles gather to feed on the spawning salmon and smelt runs. Moose browse along brushy waterways. Caribou, once exterminated but reintroduced, are increasing. And there are wolverines, red and arctic foxes, hoary marmots, beavers, minks, and in smaller numbers, wolves and lynx feeding on tundra voles, arctic shrews and other small prey.

Six species of whales ply offshore waters—gray, sei, minke, beluga, goosebeak, and orca.

Sandhill cranes nest on the Nushagak Peninsula, peregrine falcons along coastal ledges and river corridors.

Rufous hummingbirds appear when the tundra blooms, along with robins, fox and golden-crowned sparrows, Lapland longspurs and snow buntings; and hunting over them, golden eagles, gyrfalcons, harriers, rough-legged hawks and boreal, short-eared and northern hawk-owls (which cannot wait for night in summers of 24-hour daylight).

These wildlife congregations are accustomed to isolation, but the refuge is planning ways to permit observation that will not disturb them—such as a possible viewing area for the walruses and seabird colonies along the coast.

Equipment can be rented in Dillingham for fishing, camping, air-taxi and river-rafting trips, with guide services if desired. Dillingham also has two hotels—but all these should be arranged months ahead, if possible. Visitors might also wish to plan a trip to nearby Wood Tikchik State Park—1.5 million acres of glacial mountains, black spruce forests, mirrorlike lakes, salmon, moose, bears and other wildlife and incredible scenery. The state also has a walrus-viewing area on Round Island.

Prospective visitors should be warned: this is a beautiful but harsh part of the world. Lakes can be covered with ice from October to April, and weather is subject to sudden and violent change. Travelers should always carry a survival kit. Any trip should be planned carefully and as far ahead as possible, with advice from refuge staff and their excellent brochures.

For further information: Togiak National Wildlife Refuge, P.O. Box 270, Dillingham, Alaska 99576 (hours 8–5 weekdays). Phone: (907)842-1063.

YUKON DELTA (Alaska)

The road ends at Anchorage; beyond that it is necessary to fly—but that is what most of the residents of this remote and wind-swept refuge of tidal marsh and tundra do best.

Yukon Delta, 400 miles west of Anchorage facing the Bering Sea, is one of the largest refuges in North America, enclosing 26 million acres—about the size of Indiana—including nearly 5.4 million acres in native inholdings where Eskimos continue traditional life-styles.

It is also one of the wildest and most isolated, with almost incredible numbers of nesting birds—millions of waterfowl, shorebirds, and passerines. They fly here every year from six continents, almost every part of the Western Hemisphere and beyond—South America, Southeast Asia, Africa, New Zealand, and Antarctica as well as most of the lower United States. Here they raise their young, hurrying to finish the task in the short northern summertime to return again in some of the longest and most arduous migration journeys known.

Golden plovers, bar-tailed godwits, and rare bristle-thighed curlews fly to islands throughout the South Pacific and some to Australia, sometimes 2,000 miles or more nonstop over open seas.

Whimbrels, black-bellied plovers, dowitchers, surfbirds, black turnstones, dunlin and rock, least and western sandpipers move along the Pacific Coast, while solitary, pectoral, and semipalmated sandpipers go inland, and then winter in Central and South America as far south as Cape Horn and Tierra del Fuego.

Mew gulls migrate to the lower U.S. west coast; Bonaparte's to both west and east coasts and Sabine's to Cape Horn and as far as Antarctica. Arctic terns may travel 22,000 miles round-trip between breeding and wintering grounds, the longest migration trip of any living thing.

Oldsquaws move to the Bering Sea where they mingle with sea ducks from Russia. Greater scaup divide and about half move down the Pacific Flyway, the other half southeasterly across Canada to the Great Lakes and eventually to the Atlantic coast. White-fronted geese fly 2,500 miles to the interior California valleys.

The refuge provides nesting area for 80 percent of the world's emperor geese and most of the tundra swans of both the Pacific and Atlantic Flyways. It is the major nesting grounds for spectacled eider in North America, for more than half the continental population of black brant, and virtually all cackling and Pacific white-fronted geese, and the most important breeding area in the range of the lesser sandhill crane. It is the major nesting area for several North American shorebirds, including black turnstones, dunlins, western and rock sandpipers, and bar-tailed godwits.

Probably no other area of similar size is so critical to so many species of water birds. It can be an almost unbelievable sight—this vast coastal tundra covered with literally uncounted tens of thousands of lakes, ponds, and streams. It is nearly one-third underwater, and most of the rest is less than 10 feet above sea level—all of it filled with calling and flying birds from the time of ice breakup in June until the end of the short northern summer (some birds are already starting to flock for a 3,000-mile southern migration in early July).

Small birds can be everywhere, too—redpolls, snow buntings, Lapland longspurs, Savannah, tree, and fox sparrows, gray-cheeked thrushes, and such Asian visitors as Arctic warblers, northern wheatears, and yellow wagtails. And there are long-tailed and parasitic jaegers, red and red-necked phalaropes, Pacific and red-throated loons. Nesting raptors include golden eagles, rough-legged hawks, and gyrfalcons. Altogether there are 145 breeding bird species.

All these varied types can breed because even in this limited elevation there is diverse habitat: heath tundra with mosses, lichens, and dwarf prostrate shrubs; grasslands; both fresh and salt marshes and bogs; and small willow and alder thickets where willow ptarmigans find winter food and cover.

Millions of salmon of five Alaskan species are here as well, swimming up the Yukon and Kuskokwim rivers to spawn every year—king (or chinook), coho, sockeye, chum, and pink. There are huge numbers also of many other fish species—whitefish, northern pike, burbot, Pacific herring, grayling, Dolly Varden, and many others.

Beluga whales and occasional walruses come up the rivers in early spring. Mountains on the eastern side of the refuge rise to 2,000 feet, and here and in appropriate coastal habitat are represented almost all of Alaska's land mammals: black and brown bears, moose, caribou, red and Arctic foxes, wolves, wolverines, tundra hares, numerous minks and muskrats, and some otters.

But the birds own this refuge—though visiting them is no easy matter, nor necessarily always desirable. Disturbance to this fragile area as to any nesting locale, even one so large, is never beneficial. Before planning a trip check as far in advance as possible with refuge headquarters in Bethel, reachable by commercial airline from Anchorage (there are no roads). There it is possible to charter a flight over the refuge, or arrange to be put down for a week's camping and be picked up later, or ride with a regularly scheduled mail plane to an Eskimo village, where guides may be available. One can sometimes find a boatman who will take visitors out. There are motels in Bethel, and restricted tent camping is permitted.

Best time to come for birds is June, tapering off through mid-August, though it can be good through September. Be warned: weather can be rainy and overcast with high winds much of the time. Try to set aside 10 days for a better chance to catch good weather and allow for delays in case there's not. Hip boots are appropriate almost everywhere, warm clothing year-round—and one cannot bring too much insect repellent. No-see-ums (biting midges) are EVERYWHERE in August—they can turn a cup of tea black. (Don't rule out February-March for magnificent scenery and often brighter, if colder, weather).

The main home of Alaskan musk-oxen today is a 1.1-million-acre tract of Yukon Delta refuge on *Nunivak* Island 20 miles west of the Alaska coast in the Bering Sea. These great shaggy beasts once roamed over much of Asia and North America, moving south with the glaciers at one time as far as Iowa and New York—but by 1920, when the species became protected, they were almost gone, the result of indiscriminate slaughter. Thirty-one were brought from Greenland in 1935 and have done so well they have reached what is regarded as carrying capacity of this island, about 500, so small groups have been taken to reinstate them elsewhere in their former range.

These odd, bulky animals, standing almost four feet high at the shoulder, are covered with long, shaggy black fur almost to their feet. Called by Eskimos "Oomingmak," the bearded ones, they became known for their stolid herd defense against an enemy in which the entire group stands its ground with massive horns facing outward while one male dashes out to threaten an aggressor. This worked well against wolves but not against rifles.

Nunivak is one of the few places where a sizable herd can be seen in the wild— and they are not easily seen even here, for although they are relatively unwary, 500 animals can space themselves fairly widely over an island of this size. Also, Nunivak is a de facto wilderness, inhabited almost solely by Eskimos and wild animals for the past 2,000 years, so there are no roads to travel about easily.

Best way to see them would be to fly to Mekoryuk, Nunivak's only village, by scheduled airline, and there hike out or arrange to be taken out to see them either by boat in summer (a somewhat hazardous trip) or in winter by snowmobile. The latter is regarded as safer and generally preferable, especially in February and March, which have up to 12 hours' daylight, many bright sunshiny days, and temperatures not too bad by Alaskan standards. Restricted tent camping is permitted. Otherwise one must arrange with a local family to stay in their home.

With these caveats Nunivak is a fascinating island, with a large reindeer herd and on its precipitous western cliffs some of the largest nesting seabird colonies in the world for kittiwakes, murres, pelagic cormorants, horned and tufted puffins, parakeet and crested auklets, and pigeon guillemots. There are also songbirds, including occasional Asian drop-ins and the rare McKay's bunting, a winter visitor that nests only on Bering Sea islands.

To visit either Nunivak or the mainland Yukon Delta, plan as far ahead as possible and consult with refuge staff on what you wish to see and when, and how to do it.

For more information: Yukon Delta National Wildlife Refuge, P.O. Box 346, Bethel, Alaska 99559. Phone: (907) 543–3151.

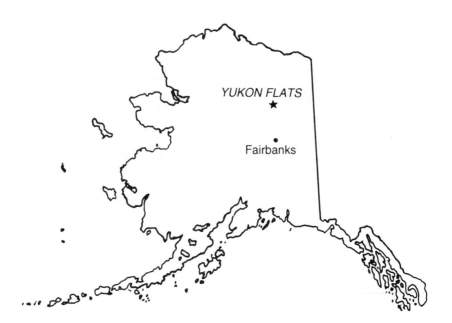

YUKON FLATS
★

Fairbanks

YUKON FLATS (Alaska)

Urgent calls and whirring wings of a million or more waterfowl fill the crisp air every spring over this 8.63-million-acre refuge, larger than the state of Vermont.

They are returning to raise families on some 40,000 lakes and ponds and hundreds of miles of braided and meandering rivers and streams. Here the Yukon River, which reaches its northernmost point within the refuge, breaks free from canyon walls and spreads unconfined in a vast flood plain for 200 miles.

Trumpeter swans are here, and 11,000 or so majestic sandhill cranes, whose bugling cries can be heard for miles, all of them at their most vocal as they proclaim breeding territories.

By fall millions of birds will be staging for the return trip to three continents— North and South America and Asia. The lowland areas of this refuge have one of the highest nesting densities of waterfowl in North America—over 90 ducks per square mile. This vast wetland is seen as increasingly important as pothole breeding habitat in Canada and the lower 48 becomes less available, gradually disappearing due to drought and agricultural drainage.

Northern pintails are among the most numerous dabbling duck nesters—65,000; among the divers, 125,000 scaup; other common waterfowl include American wigeon, mallards, canvasbacks, northern shovelers, scoters, oldsquaws and Canada and white-fronted geese.

Sixteen thousand loons also take advantage of these lush breeding grounds, and at least 100,000 horned and red-necked grebes. Flocks of hundreds of red-necked phalaropes fly overhead with high twittering calls, and there are thousands of Arctic terns, spotted and solitary sandpipers, yellowlegs, and other shorebirds.

About half of the Yukon Flats refuge is within the Yukon River floodplain. The rest is divided between gently rolling uplands forested with white spruce, birch, and aspen and mountains dominated by alpine tundra vegetation. Black bears forage on bearberries, blueberries, cranberries, crowberries, and soapberries in forested river bottoms and lowlands. Grizzly bears are more common in open and mountainous areas.

Moose roam around willows and marshes throughout the refuge, which also provides occasional winter habitat for two major caribou herds. One of the densest populations in Alaska of beautiful long-furred lynx is in the Black River drainage in the southeastern section. Twenty percent of the refuge is mountains, and here in the rugged White Mountains Dall sheep make their homes.

Peregrine falcons nest on rock ledges. So do golden eagles and red-tailed hawks. All range through the refuge preying on abundant small mammals—northern red-backed voles, lemmings, and others—which also must watch out for an array of owls, including the large great gray, boreal, short-eared, northern hawk, and snowy that hunt during the 24 hours of summer daylight, along with northern harriers, rough-legged hawks, northern goshawks, gyrfalcons, and other raptors that find homes here. Three-toed woodpeckers live in wooded areas.

Chinook, coho, and chum salmon from the Bering Sea swim up the Yukon to spawn in the freshwater streams where they first saw life, in the longest salmon run in the United States; some travel nearly 2,000 miles into Canada.

Best way to see all this de facto wilderness is to camp or go on a float trip, or perhaps both. Ten major rivers cross the refuge, including a portion of the designated wild and scenic Beaver Creek. One float trip on the Yukon can be started and ended from road points; others involve use of charter aircraft that can cost $200 or more an hour. Charters and outfitters are located in Fairbanks.

Five rural villages located within the refuge are serviced by commercial air. Fort Yukon has limited accommodations. Some have guides—but all this should be arranged well ahead. Primitive camping is permitted anywhere on the refuge but check with refuge headquarters for land status information to avoid trespass on large blocks of privately owned land.

Trips should be planned as far in advance as possible, best from mid-May to mid-September (fall colors are beautiful) in consultation with refuge staff. (Winters can be bitterly cold, with temperatures to 70 below. The ice booms, trees crack, and in the clear air the faintest sound carries for miles.)

For more information: Yukon Flats National Wildlife Refuge, Room 110, Box 14, Federal Building, 101 Twelfth Ave., Fairbanks, Alaska 99701. Phone: (907) 456–0440.

Refuges of the Future

A number of new refuges in the planning, acquisition or early development stages include:

Archie Carr NWR (Florida)—Twenty miles of beach with the second largest concentration of nesting loggerhead turtles in the world, largest in the western hemisphere—more than 10,000 annually.

Balcones Canyonlands (Texas)—41,000 acres of juniper-oak hill country protecting the endangered black-capped vireo and golden-cheeked warbler.

Crane Meadows (Minnesota)—remnant sand prairie, oak savanna and wet meadow/bog, important breeding ground for greater sandhill cranes, with abundant deer, also migratory waterfowl and bald eagle use.

Hamden Slough (Minnesota)—Nesting prairie chickens, also breeding and migratory habitat for 15 waterfowl and shorebird species.

Kealia Pond (Hawaii)—Wetland providing essential habitat for two endangered Hawaiian water birds, the Hawaiian stilt and Hawaiian coot.

Lake Wales (Florida)—7,000 acres of scrub habitat now rare in central Florida will significantly enhance recovery of 13 endemic plant species listed as rare or endangered, plus associated animal species.

Wallkill River (New Jersey)—Eventual planned 7,500 acres, with deer, black bears, wood ducks, great blue herons, habitat for increasingly rare black ducks, other migratory waterfowl, raptors, marsh and water birds.

Regional
Acknowledgments

NORTHEAST AND MID-ATLANTIC

For contributing to this section special thanks are due to: Jason Barker; David L. Beall; Barry Brady; Gregory Breese; Glenn A. Carowan, Jr.; Lloyd A. Culp, Jr.; Paul D. Daly; John L. Fillio; David J. Frisque; Thomas Goettel; Andrea M. Graham; Steve Haydock; Grady E. Hocutt; Janet Kennedy; William Koch; Jim Kurth; Anthony Leger; J. Frederick Milton; Edward S. Moses; Thomas Mountain; Douglas M. Mullen; Richard F. Nugent; George F. O'Shea; Harold C. Olsen; Charles Pelizza; John D. Schroer; Sherman W. Stairs; Richard Steinbach; Tom Stewart; Mark Sweeny; Don V. Tiller; L. Theresa Villanueva; Jerry L. Wilson; Kelly Wolcott; Kathleen Zeamer; Robert A. Zelley.

SOUTHEAST

Thanks to: Glen W. Bond, Jr.; James (Donny) Browning; Frank Bryce; Jim Burkhart; Mike Canada; Karen S. Cartlidge; Kelly Davis; Larry R. Ditto; George R. Garris; Patrick D. Hagan; Rae S. Hagen; William H. Hegge; Albert R. Hight; Deborah G. Holle; Jerry Holloman; Jim C. Johnson; David Kitts; Larry Klimek; Todd Logan; Patricia E. Metz; Burkett S. Neely, Jr.; James Oland; Don R. Perkuchin; Leon I. Rhodes; Elton (Jim) Savery; Ronnie L. Shell; Ronald C. Snider; Bonnie Strawser; John T. Taylor; Stephen R. Vehrs; Joe D. White; Dorn Whitmore; Patricia E. Young.

GREAT LAKES

Thanks to: Betsy Beneke; Charles Blair; Richard Frietsche; Jay Hamernick; James Heinecke; Leland E. Herzberger; Joseph Kotok; Thomas J. Larson; James Lennartson; John Lindell; Glen Miller; Thomas S. Sanford; John Schomaker; Robert Stratton, Jr.; Michael Tansy; Gerald Updike; Norrel F. Wallace; Darold Walls.

MID-SOUTH

Thanks to: Douglas J. Baumgartner; Robert J. Bridges; Bobby W. Brown; Jerome T. Carroll; George Chandler; Steven R. Emmons; Lee R. Fulton; Paul Gideon; Vicki C. Grafe; Dale Guthrie; Andrew Hammond; Glenn Harris; Joe Hardy; Marvin T. Hurdle; Gary Juenger; Donald J. Kosin; Marvin L. Nichols; Charlotte Parker; Martin D. Perry; Howard E. Poitevint; Thomas F. Prusa; Carrell L. Ryan; Eric Sipco; Harry T. Stone; Donald E. Temple; Jimmie L. Tisdale; John R. Walther; Tim Wilkins; Paul M. Yakupzack.

NORTH-CENTRAL

Thanks to: David Aplin; Ronald L. Bell; Richard M. Birger; Gerald L. Clawson; Robert M. Ellis; Peter Finley; George E. Gage; Fred G. Giese; Richard Gilbert; John Guthrie; David Hilley; Robert Howard; Royce R. Huber; Dean F. Knauer; Steve Knode; John Koerner; Rolf H. Kraft; Steven Kresl; Jerry Kuykendal; George W. Peyton; David G. Potter; Karen A. Smith; Milton Suthers; Paul Van Ningen; William Wilson; David Wiseman.

SOUTHWEST

Thanks to: Johnny H. Beall; Ronald G. Bisbee; Jon Brock; Ken Butts; Domenick Ciccone; Donald Clapp; Kevin S. Cobble; Jerry D. French; J. Brent Giezentanner; James R. Good; Milton K. Haderlie; Berlin A. Heck; Rodney F. Krey; Stephen Labuda, Jr.; LeMoyne B. Marlatt; Wesley V. Martin; Arnold W. Nidecker; Philip W. Norton; Ron Price; Dennis E. Prichard; Joe B. Rodriguez, Jr.; Robert W. Schumacher; Wayne A. Shifflett; James S. Smith; David A. Stanbrough; Ronald S. Sullivan; Steven P. Thompson; James M. Williams; Gregory A. Wolf.

MOUNTAINS

Thanks to: Margaret M. Anderson; Ronald M. Anglin; Steve Berlinger; Mike Bryant; Martha K. Collins; Mike Fisher; John R. Foster; Jerre L. Gamble; Daniel Gomez; Mike Hedrick; Don Hultman; Francis T. Maiss; Jon M. Malcolm; James McCollum; Gary Montoya; Larry D. Napier; Hugh Null; Eugene C. Patten; Daniel L. Pennington; Jack L. Richardson; Kevin Ryan; Gene A. Sipe; Richard Sjostrom; Alan K. Trout; Bruce Zeller.

WEST COAST

Thanks to: Tom Alexander; E. Clark Bloom; Forrest Cameron; Thomas J. Charmley; Richard A. Coleman; Elizabeth Couch; Nancy Curry; Jim Dougan; David E. Goeke; Willard B. Hesselbart; James A. Hidy; Randy Hill; Roger D. Johnson; Gary W. Kramer; Morris C. LeFever; Anne Marocchini; Ron Ryno; Palmer C. Sekora; Kenneth Voget; Marc M. Weitzel; Bruce Wiseman; Gary R. Zahm.

HAWAIIAN AND PACIFIC ISLANDS

Thanks to: Jerry F. Leinecke; Ken McDermond; Craig Rowland; Kathleen Viernes; Richard Voss; Richard C. Wass.

ALASKA

Thanks to: Aaron Archibeque; Jay Bellinger; Steve Breeser; Daniel Doshier; Tom Early; Glenn Elison; Phillip J. Feiger; Ronald E. Hood; Ted Huer; John L. Martin; Ron Perry; Mike Rearden; Dave Stearns; Fred Zeillemaker.

Index